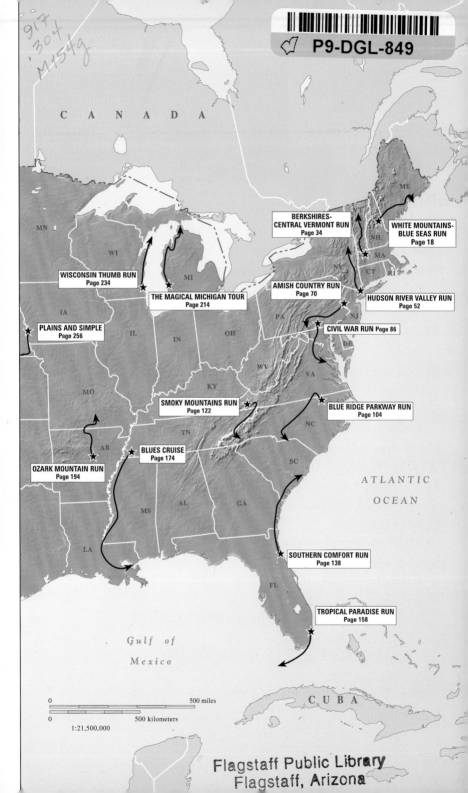

917
304
M154g

P9-DGL-849

C A N A D A

MN

WI

MI

WISCONSIN THUMB RUN
Page 234

THE MAGICAL MICHIGAN TOUR
Page 214

IA

IL

IN

OH

PLAINS AND SIMPLE
Page 256

MO

**BERKSHIRES-
CENTRAL VERMONT RUN**
Page 34

ME

NH

**WHITE MOUNTAINS-
BLUE SEAS RUN**
Page 18

NY

MA
CT RI

AMISH COUNTRY RUN
Page 70

NJ

PA

HUDSON RIVER VALLEY RUN
Page 52

CIVIL WAR RUN Page 86

DE

WV

VA

KY

SMOKY MOUNTAINS RUN
Page 122

BLUE RIDGE PARKWAY RUN
Page 104

TN

NC

AR

BLUES CRUISE
Page 174

OZARK MOUNTAIN RUN
Page 194

SC

MS

AL

GA

ATLANTIC

OCEAN

LA

SOUTHERN COMFORT RUN
Page 138

FL

TROPICAL PARADISE RUN
Page 158

Gulf of

Mexico

0   500 miles
0   500 kilometers
1:21,500,000

CUBA

Contents

Preface
to the Fourth Edition

A lot has changed since the first edition of *Great American Motorcycle Tours*.

The biggest change has been the sweep of digital technology. Today a handful of digital devices can turn your motorcycle into a traveling office. Stay connected and you can detour around every spring shower and map each mile of a coast-to-coast ride without taking a single wrong turn.

That's not always a good thing.

Some of my favorite memories came when the ride would throw me a curve. I'd have a heightened sense of awareness when I was hopelessly lost and wondering when and where I'd find my way. Of course I always would and *that* became the story I'd share. And there were times when the weather would turn and I'd stuff old newspapers under my sweatshirt to stay warm or hide under a bridge to avoid unexpected rain and lightning. Had I relied on GPS mapping and online weather tracking, none of these things would have happened. It would have been adventure-lite.

When I ride for research, I'm connected. When I ride for pleasure, my desire is to cut myself off. As my friend, Harley-Davidson's Amanda Lee, suggests, there are times when you have to *get off the laptop and get on the blacktop.* So I'll offer this: If your ride doesn't require that you create an article, novel, or book report, I hope you'll consider getting back to basics. Carry the iPhone as a luxury, not as a tool to negate spontaneity and dictate directions. It's far more exciting when you don't take the ride, but when you *let the ride take you.*

Finally, a note about this edition. It's been completely revised and updated. Literally *thousands* of phone numbers, addresses, hours, prices, and historical facts have been added or brought up to date to give you the information you need for your motorcycle tours. Twenty-two chapters have been revisited and in many cases re-traveled; three new runs—Michigan, Kansas/Nebraska, and Texas—introduced me to three new regions that I guarantee will please any rider. It's well-researched, easy to read, and reflects years of intense riding and fine-tuning. I'm certain that when it comes to trip planning, it's the best investment a rider can make. I hope you find it useful as you embark on your own voyage of discovery. Now it's time to get off the laptop...

...and get on the blacktop.

Why I Ride

by Peter Fonda

A motorcycle is the only way to see America. If you ride, you already understand how the feelings of freedom and nature are enhanced. When traveling by car or plane these feelings are missing. Gone.

Which is why I ride.

When I travel by motorcycle, I feel the wind and see the endless skies and stop when I want and where I want, fetching my rod from the saddlebag and fly-fishing for an hour or two. Hours don't matter, really, because on the road I develop a more natural use of time and never feel as if I have to be anywhere.

Which is why I ride.

I have a friend who joins me each year on a long run from Los Angeles to Montana. On this ride, we have only two rules: We will ride only back roads (a lengthy process when exiting L.A.), and we have no fixed destination on Day One—only the desire to return to the open road. Within a few hours we've extricated ourselves from the city and its traffic and are cruising north on 395, threading the needle between the Inyo Mountains and the Sierra Nevada. A motorcycle may be just a vehicle, but it is also the instrument we use to experience life, to explore, to discover new people and places, and to affirm our friendship.

Which is why I ride.

Gary McKechnie has written the first national motorcycle touring guide, and I trust it will lead you to moments like these. It's fun to read and filled with pertinent information for riders, and the 25 tours he describes can rescue you from the interstate highways and deliver you into the heart of America. He's traveled the country and found back roads and general stores, national parks and small-town diners, cowboy saloons and British pubs. He leads you to roads laced with the smell of pine trees and bordered by rushing streams, where you can park your bike, fetch your rod out of your saddlebag, and spend a few hours fly-fishing.

Which is why I ride.

Read this book, and you will too.

With immeasurable love and gratitude, this book
is dedicated to my mom,
Lois Ann Mercier McKechnie, who gave
everything and deserved more;
and to my wife, Nancy Howell McKechnie,
my loving travel companion on the road
and in my life.

Introduction

No single defining moment marks the Big Bang in the universe of motorcycle touring, but one good candidate may have been the day billionaire publisher Malcolm Forbes settled into the saddle of his own Harley-Davidson. That's the day the image of bikers transformed from Marlon Brando into Marlin Perkins.

Other factors played a supporting role: Baby boomers' incomes afforded them small luxuries, and soon they added motorcycles to their toy collections. Harley-Davidson, after years of decline, turned into one of the business success stories of the 20th century, embodying the strengths of American enterprise.

Those of us who had ridden for years watched all of this with fascination. We were already on the road, riding Yamahas, Suzukis, BMWs, Kawasakis, and Hondas. A few free spirits straddled Triumphs, Ducatis, and Moto Guzzis. We had long recognized that travel and motorcycling combined two passions that offered similar benefits: adventure, freedom, and the thrill of exploration.

My great-granddad John Philip McKechnie (born in 1877) grew up to ride a motorcycle, which I find fascinating. Equally impressive was finding pictures of his son Ian C. McKechnie (my granddad) riding his new Harley across the New Mexico desert in the 1920s. Later, in the 1950s, Ian's son John (my dad) rode an AJS 500 while he was in the army.

Genetic coding was in full swing, and I started riding when I was 14, teaching myself how on my brother Craig's 1972 Yamaha 250. I had to teach myself because Craig didn't know that I knew where his motorcycle key was hidden (the top left drawer of his desk). Riding around my neighborhood while he was out with friends, I soon grew tired of this bike and wanted something larger and faster. There was only one way to get it. Displaying diligence and a strong work ethic, Craig was finally able to afford a Honda 360. I found the key and started riding that.

Years later, I finally bought my own

Pack It Up

A few pairs of jeans, a jacket, boots, rain gear, sunglasses, and gloves are naturals to pack for your ride, but what about a video camera? As a person who likes to chronicle my tours, I carry what others may call luxuries, but I call them tools of the trade.

- Digital camera: The cost of a decent digital camera has dropped, and so has the price of memory cards. Some higher end models shoot decent video as well.
- Video camera: They're vulnerable to water and weather, but if you'd like to create a movie presentation of your trip, a decent digital video camera can capture those images.
- Digital recorder: I do some of my best and most productive thinking as I ride, capturing my thoughts through a small recorder looped around my neck.
- iPhone: Or BlackBerry or similar PDA…Let's face it—it'd be nice to be disconnected when we ride, but most of us have the urge—or need—to touch base via email or text. They're also a good safety feature and with mobile access to the Web, you can check weather, road closures, hours, and rates in advance.
- Binoculars: A small pair can enhance images, especially when you're riding through a national park or across a desert.
- Journal: They're easy to start, but hard to sustain. If you can keep up the writing, you'll have a great record of what could be the ride of your life.
- Travelers checks: Not an original idea, just a smart one.
- ATM/credit card: Along with travelers checks, it's easy money.
- A copy of *Great American Motorcycle Tours.*
- As always, for reasons completely unrelated to motorcycling, a life-size cutout of Tina Louise.

Even if there's no reason to do it, the allure of a covered bridge will always tempt you to cross it.

Ready? Set? Go.

Unless you rent a bike that's already been checked out and readied for a ride, you'll have to prepare for your epic journey yourself. Ray Towells, a dedicated rider and motorcycle entrepreneur, has ridden enough to offer practical advice on packing and pre-ride preparations. Ray's British, so read this with an accent.

Pre-Ride

Have your mechanic check your bike and make sure it's ready for the road. Don't ask for a comprehensive tune-up; just have him check the brake linings, pads, tires, oil, fuses, and spares.

Let someone know how long you'll be away and leave a rough itinerary. If you're planning a three-day trip, and it's been five days since you called, your friend will know something's wrong.

Clothing

Dress for the climate. If you wear full leathers in Florida in summer, you're an idiot. Try to find a leather jacket with a removable lining or sleeves that zip off. Beyond that, you won't need much—a few pairs of jeans, shorts, and T-shirts. When riding in a cold climate, bring thermal underwear. The average biker doesn't want to dress up, but casual shoes, polo shirts, and khaki pants can pass in a nice restaurant.

Safety and Practicalities

For supplies, I always carry a cell phone, water container, foam earplugs to protect against noise, and a small flashlight. In remote areas, I pack a small first-aid kit with bandages, aspirin, sunscreen, water purification tablets, and I also carry a roll of reflective tape. If you lose power to your lights, the tape will be a godsend.

When people see a $20,000 touring bike, they get ideas. Carry a Kryptonite lock. Bring an extra set of keys for your bike and hide them. Use heavy-duty tape to stick them under your saddle, for instance, or inside your headlight or spotlight.

If you break down and have to leave your bike, try to hide it off the road and cover it; this is where a dark bike cover will come in handy.

Tool Kit

Bring a standard tool kit that includes, at a minimum, vise grips or pliers; Allen wrenches, hex wrenches, and an adjustable wrench; a small screwdriver kit with multiple heads; small, medium, and large hose clamps; a roll of speed tape or electrical tape; standard wire; and two or three feet of electrical wire and a few connectors. You should also carry a puncture repair kit for your tires.

Tight Muscles: Work It On Out Now

After a few hundred miles in the saddle, my muscles have a tendency to get tight and screw up the next day's ride. Exercise physiologist Richard Cotton explains that muscles can get stiff when confined to sedentary positions. Day after day of riding without stretching reduces the length of your muscles, which limits your range of motion and, if you move suddenly, can cause injury. Cotton recommends starting and ending the day with easy stretching exercises. The entire series should take no longer than five minutes and can significantly improve the quality of your ride.

Pre- and Post-ride

Chest: On some bike configurations, your shoulders are rolled forward and your chest muscles tighten up. To stretch your chest, place your palms flat against a door or a tree and twist your upper body.

Neck: After fighting the wind and the weight of your helmet, stretch your neck muscles by placing two fingers on your chin and pushing it toward your chest while raising up the back of your head. Next, look over your left, then right, shoulder for 10 seconds on each side.

Upper back: Before and after the ride, do a few trunk twists—keeping your legs slightly spread and hips square to the front while turning your shoulders from side to side.

Lower back: Few bike seats are designed to protect your lower back, so when you dismount, put your fist against your lower back, stretch backward, and raise your chest toward the sky. Don't let your legs bow, since the arching comes from the hips.

Triceps: Stretch your triceps by putting your palm between your shoulders

1976 RD 250, and later still a 1982 Suzuki 650. By then I was old enough to hit the road. I took short trips and, when my other brother, Kevin, bought a BMW R65, I expanded my range, skimming up the Atlantic Coast with him, turning left across Canada, and then heading down along the Mississippi. So began an undying fascination with travel by motorcycle.

Others have come to share this fascination, as supported by figures compiled by the Motorcycle Industry Council. With few exceptions, the sale of new motorcycles has increased every year since 1992. Almost 40 million Americans ride motorcycles, scooters, or ATVs (all-terrain vehicles). About a hundred motorcycle touring/rental businesses operate in the United States alone, and in the last few years, an increasing number of motorcycle-geared television programs have hit the air. Motorcycling has become mainstream.

Even with all these factors out there, what sparked my own voyage of discovery was the realization that one element was missing.

with your elbow pointing up. Pull your elbow behind your head for 10–30 seconds. Do this for both arms.

Quadriceps: To loosen up the top of your thighs, stand next to your bike and grip the handlebar with one hand. Take the opposite leg and pull it backward from the ankle, bringing your heel up to your butt. Do this for 10 seconds with each leg.

Hamstrings: To stretch the back of your legs, stand and cross one leg in front of the other. Bend forward from your hips until you feel a comfortable stretch. Reverse positions and repeat to stretch your other leg.

Calves: Find a solid object (wall, tree, etc.), and then lean over and push against it while pressing into the ground to alternately stretch each leg behind you.

Back and Butt: While lying on your back, put both hands below one knee and pull that knee toward the opposite shoulder. Do this for several seconds, alternating legs. Follow up by putting both arms behind your knees and drawing both legs toward your chest.

While Riding

Lower Back: Most riders tend to ride with their shoulders down and back arched forward. To counteract the stress of this position, occasionally arch backward and roll your pelvis forward to create a curve in your lower back. Riding with an S curve as opposed to a C curve prevents lower back stiffness.

Legs: Stretch each leg over the foot pegs or swing them back and forth against the pressure of the wind.

Overall: Vibrations can cause numbness in your hands, feet, and butt. At each gas stop take a few minutes to get the blood flowing and the muscles moving. Shake your hands and feet, stretch your fingers, do arm circles forward and backward, and take a short walk.

Travel guides had been written about tours of baseball fields and historic Native American sites. You could buy a specialized travel guide if you were disabled or traveled with pets. There were books on how to pack your clothes and where you could take your kids. But there wasn't a single national touring guide for motorcycle travelers.

Sure, there were articles in motorcycle magazines, but they tended to discuss bike mechanics, not the experience of the ride. In the few books that did detailed tours, the theme invariably turned to the author's coming of age and the remarkable

discovery that America isn't such a bad place after all.

Personally, I never worry about gear ratios when I'm riding through Amish Country, and it didn't take a midlife crisis to convince me that the United States is the greatest nation in history. That's why I believed this book needed to be written. But I knew that even after investing a solid year and a half in on-the-road research and dealing with countless physical, logistical, and financial challenges, I'd be sharing my findings with independent spirits who were reluctant to follow

Relaxing by a river is sometimes as enjoyable as riding a nice stretch of road. If your schedule's always going, do yourself a favor. Stop. Just stop.

and hit the road on a motorcycle, things were different. I was free to travel where and when I wanted. Released from the confines of airplanes and climate-controlled automobiles, I developed a sense of discovery and learned that everything worked out all right, even when things went wrong. For every flat tire, broken chain, or wrong turn, I was rewarded with an unexpected kindness from a stranger or a detour leading to a better road.

I also found that, after a few days in the saddle, everything waiting back home seemed trivial, routine. I relished the feeling of adventure, of living in the moment. For me, these events came at unexpected times. When you meet a real live prospector in a Western town or hang out with a Maine clam-digger to talk about his life, well, you'll understand the power of these moments, too.

SELECTING THE BEST TOURS IN AMERICA

Since freedom is the foundation of this book, you're sure to wonder how I selected the runs and roads included. How can I say with certainty that these tours represent the best rides and roads in America? I couldn't in 2000, and I still can't now. There are states I haven't covered at all and because of limited space, thousands of back roads and blue highways have been left out.

someone else's road map. I pressed on because I also knew that there were millions of miles of roads to travel, and some riders might waste months trying to find which were the best and why. I knew that valuable two-week, two-wheeled vacations could be squandered on boring roads leading to ordinary places. Sure, there are no special roads for motorcycles, just as there are no special roads for RVs. But as a rider, you know what you're looking for. You want to ride on back roads where you shed routine and adopt a lifestyle in which every minute is an adventure.

When I had a desk job, I followed the same route to work day after day. Slowly, this habit seeped into my travels: If an interesting road suddenly came into view, I'd pass it by to remain true to my self-inflicted schedule. I rarely strayed from the chosen path.

After I finally escaped from my cubicle

When selecting the original tours and adding new ones, I relied on the advice of riders, motorcycle rental companies, and personal bias for routes that would expose you to places offering a combination of culture, history, and scenery. I also tried to be equitable in representing different regions of America, so you'll get a good overview of our nation and, I hope, find at least one tour that's relatively accessible. In some cases, starting and ending points are conveniently close to neighboring tours that you can string together.

In short, I have tried to produce a guide to essential information that you can access more quickly than by surfing the Internet—and one that won't weigh you down when you're on the road. Lodging options, nightspots, and restaurants are included in each chapter. Variety is the benchmark here, with recommendations for activities based on the tempo and tone of the area. Depending on the town, I'll just as soon point you toward a greasy spoon and an ordinary motel as a casual restaurant and a unique inn. As for on-the-road repairs, you'll need to attend to those on your own. Comprehensive warranties and roadside assistance should keep you out of trouble. Plus, there are other books—your owner's manual, for instance—that offer useful and in-depth repair information.

Be open to another aspect of riding: realizing that these tours offer spiritual pleasures, as well as physical ones. The roads will speak to you often, whether you're on your bike or in a town. In Lenox, Massachusetts, you may experience this feeling while listening to the Boston Symphony Orchestra at Tanglewood, or in Lone Pine, California, when you sit down at a diner and watch the sun set over the mountains.

If nothing else, please remember this: *Use this book as a guide, not the gospel.* If I neglected to mention the general store where you buy Moon Pies in South Carolina, go find it and buy one. If you know a branch road I missed, then take it. It was physically and logistically impossible to find every scenic overlook and list every biker-friendly business along these routes, so add your own routes and make your own discoveries. I'd love it if you find things I didn't.

I did my best writing about the highlights of these runs, but I'm sure I missed something along the way. If you have any suggestions for material to include in future editions of this book, or if you'd like to suggest one of your favorite rides, email me at planetelvis@yahoo.com and I'll post it on my site, www.motorcycle america.com.

There you have it.

Now open the garage, saddle up, and go meet your country.

Advice from a Road Scholar

The more you ride, the more you learn. A few decades on the road and several thousand miles in the saddle have given me some insights that may improve the quality of your own ride.

Even if you're in a hurry to reach Point B, try not to leave Point A after mid-afternoon. Chances are you'll be racing the sun and you'll miss the moments you're riding for. If you leave in the morning, you'll have a full day to make unscheduled stops and discover points of interest.

Don't run a marathon. While you could ride 600 miles a day, 200 miles max is easy and allows for unexpected discoveries.

If you get off-schedule, don't worry. The purpose of touring isn't to reach as many places as possible, it is to experience as many sensations and places as you can. Don't kill yourself with a self-inflicted plan.

Reward yourself. Every so often, stop at a place you don't think looks very interesting at first. Take a break and meditate.

Watch what's going on around you. A conversation with a general store clerk, a swim in a pond, or the sight of glistening pebbles in a riverbed can be just as pleasing as a good stretch of road.

In general, the best times I've found for riding are May and September. Nowhere is it too hot or too cold, kids are still in or headed back to school, and few places are charging peak season prices.

Have a contingency plan in case your day gets rained out. Write postcards; see a museum or a movie; read, rest, or go to the library; talk to locals. If a day gets screwed up by weather, roll with it.

Carry a few sealable plastic bags. Somehow rain can find wallets and you might want to stow that and any small electronics inside.

If you use a magnetic tank bag, don't toss your wallet in it. The powerful magnets that can withstand 90-mile-an-hour winds can also demagnetize ATM and credit cards in a flash.

It can be maddening when a truck

ahead of you slows you down to its pace. If you pass, often the truck speeds up, and then you've got to worry about a tailgater. Instead, just pull over for a few minutes and take a break. It'll give the truck time to move on and allow you to return to scenic roads unobstructed by Yosemite Sam mud flaps.

It gets mighty cold—especially out West—when the sun goes down. Even if you don't think you'll need it, bring along long underwear.

If you can't avoid the small animal in front of you, grit your teeth and go for it. It's not worth laying down your bike to save a squirrel.

And remember that loose gravel, wet leaves, and oil slicks don't care how long you've been riding. Don't get so swept up in the ride that you neglect safety.

I hate paying banks three bucks to get my money from their ATMs. So I look for a drugstore (CVS, Walgreens, etc.), where I use my debit card for gum or candy or batteries and get cash back. Not only do I avoid a fee, I get something I want.

When I arrive in a town, before I check into a hotel or start walking around, I stop at the local chamber of commerce or visitors center and get maps and advice on hours, admission fees, and what's worth seeing. The staff know what's shakin', and they'll always have current information on back roads.

Don't forget alternative newspapers (usually free) and the Friday edition of most daily newspapers that include listings and reviews of local restaurants, concerts, and special events.

Ask nicely, and some local libraries may allow you to use their computers for free Internet access. Get online to check out upcoming towns, attractions, and seasonal operating hours, and to print out discount coupons if offered.

If you have to ride in peak tourist season, do your best to get up early and wander around the town. Minus the presence of other tourists, it reveals a more natural sense of the community.

A word about the lodging prices listed throughout this book: They are listed for peak seasons, but will vary by day and by month. If they seem to skew high, check their off-season rates and ask for a discount—AAA, AARP, AMA. To secure even better rates, visit websites like www.hotels.com or www.priceline. com. You can deduct approximately 10–15 percent if you're a solo traveler, and even more if you can travel in an off- or shoulder season. The same with admission prices—those are for adults and you can ask for a senior discount if you qualify.

If you plan to visit more than one national park, spring for the $80 America the Beautiful Pass (only $10 for ages 62 and older). It's good for admission to any national park for one year.

It's nice to wear full leathers and clothes that reflect the hard riding you've done, but use common sense and courtesy and dress appropriately when at certain restaurants.

Yes, the boots do make you look like Fonzie, but if you plan on joining any walking tours or beating your feet around a town, you'll appreciate the comfort of a pair of walking shoes.

Take wrong turns. Get lost. Make discoveries.

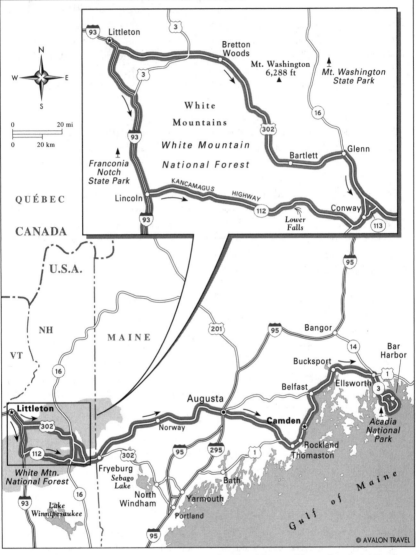

White Mountains–Blue Seas Run

Route: Littleton to Camden via Mount Washington, Kancamagus Highway, Fryeburg, Yarmouth, Waldoboro, Thomaston

Distance: Approximately 280 miles

First Leg: Littleton, New Hampshire to Camden, Maine (210 miles)

Optional Second Leg: Camden to Bar Harbor, Maine (72 miles)

Helmet Laws: No helmets are required in New Hampshire or Maine.

White Mountains—Blue Seas Run

Littleton, New Hampshire to Bar Harbor, Maine

From the mountains to the oceans white with foam, this run is relatively short, but with distinct changes in landscape and culture it actually feels quite large. Individually, the two legs described here offer experiences that are not breathtaking, but still enjoyable; a nice balance of mountain rides, coastal runs, and an opportunity to get off your bike and head out to sea. Note that many stores and restaurants—especially in Maine—close from mid-October to Memorial Day.

Also consider alternate routes and side trips that will add some horsepower to your ride—particularly down some of Maine's peninsulas. While I've included some options here, you're ever so welcome to add your own.

When you hit those rare long stretches of road, you'll have time to think. I thought about New Hampshire's license plates; the ones stamped with the state motto, Live Free or Die. It's appropriate, considering New Hampshire has no helmet law, no state sales tax, and no state income tax.

It's quite ironic, however, when you consider who's stamping out those tags.

LITTLETON PRIMER

At first glance, Littleton, New Hampshire, looks like a blue-collar town that never experienced a recession. A Main Street program has kept up the town's appearance, and the lack of a mall (amen!) brings many of its roughly 6,000 citizens downtown throughout the day. Equidistant from both Boston and Montreal (160 miles in either direction), Littleton is nestled in the Connecticut River Valley and sits at the doorstep of two great roads that sweep into the 780,000-acre White Mountain National Forest. This location alone makes it worth the ride.

Historically, Littleton has tended to stay in the shadows. Named after the region's surveyor, Colonel Moses Little, the town made its first contribution to American history during the Revolutionary era when unusually straight tree trunks around town were recycled as masts for sailing

19

ships. If you happen to be building a sail-ing ship, strap one of those mothers onto your handlebars and bolt.

About a century later, prior to the Civil War, Littleton was an essential stop on the Underground Railroad. If you're invited into some of the town's older homes, check out the basements where runaway slaves were shielded until they could continue their trek to Canada. At the turn of the 20th century, two companies—one man-ufacturing stereoscopic view cards and the other, gloves—did their part to keep the town in the black. Aside from those high-lights, things stayed pretty quiet until an author ranked Littleton among his hun-dred favorite small towns and retirees and families started taking a second look at the place.

Now it's your turn.

ON THE ROAD: LITTLETON

When you arrive, you'll do so on Route 302 (Main Street) which barrels through the center of town, a fact that makes this unappealing for a leisurely cruise. Instead, take advantage of the cheap curbside parking—just drop a dime in the slot and you'll own that section of pavement for the next hour. Since Littleton isn't an upscale village, but a working town that happens to attract a handful of tourists, these bar-gain rates extend from parking meters into the restaurants, inns, and hotels. What's more, the town's independent merchants don't put on a show for your cash; they seem genuine and friendly.

Logistically, Littleton is a perfect start-ing point for a ride, since it's the largest town on the western end of Route 302 and also close to the Kancamagus Highway (112). Visually, the town seems locked in the 1950s. When night falls, you can just listen to the Ammonoosuc River flowing past, order a burger, fries, and a chocolate frappe at a Main Street diner, and then walk across the street to catch the evening picture show. Simple pleasures in a pleas-ant town.

PULL IT OVER: LITTLETON HIGHLIGHTS
Attractions and Adventures

The Littleton Conservation Commission tends three trails that showcase different aspects of the outdoors, from bird-watch-ing to geological history to scenic over-looks. A free trail guide is available at the Chamber of Commerce, and a self-guided walking tour takes you past a dozen his-torically significant buildings.

I can't promise a Smithsonian-sized ex-perience at the **Littleton Area Historical Society** (1 Cottage St., 603/444-6435), since it's open only on Wednesdays. Built in 1905, the old opera house/fire station was renovated in 2001. If you're moti-vated—seriously motivated—the local society members will show you a Victo-rian melodeon and artifacts from the local glove company, and they will share the story of the Kilburn Brothers, who kicked off the DVD of their day—the stereo-graphic view card.

Shopping

You could travel all over the nation to verify it, but it might be simpler just to believe **Chutters** (43 Main St., 603/444-5787, www.chutters.com) when it claims to be one of three general stores in Amer-ica that still sells penny candy from a jar. That's 1,000 pieces of candy for a fin. Double that if you've got a sawbuck. It also features New Hampshire–made prod-ucts and boasts the world's longest candy counter—and it's mighty long.

Blue-Plate Specials

While many cities offer an endless chain

Why Do Them Leaves Look Funny?

If you don't mind battling motor homes for the road, arrive during fall foliage when "leaf peepers" descend on New England like locusts on Kansas corn. They're here to watch the leaves change from a uniform green to an autumnal palette of oranges, reds, and yellows. Why do leaves change color? They don't, Gomer.

Here's the skinny: About two weeks before they "turn," a cell layer forms at the base of each leaf that prevents moisture from entering. The chlorophyll, which makes the leaf green, isn't able to renew itself, so the leaf's true color can be seen. Depending on exposure to the sun, elevation, and the chemical makeup of the tree, different colors appear. Sugar maple leaves are primarily red and orange, white ash turns yellow and purple, and the pin cherry's purple-green leaves turn yellow. Most color changes start at higher elevations and work their way down the mountains and hills.

of chain restaurants, Littleton is pleased to promote home-cooked comfort foods. **Topic of the Town** (30 Main St., 603/444-6721) offers another all-day breakfast, along with daily specials and turkey dinners, jumbo sirloin, Greek salads, chicken, ribs, and lovely frappes—all served in a generic diner setting. Perfect.

Drop by the **Littleton Diner** (145 Main St., 603/444-3994, www.littletondiner.com) for New England–style home-cooked food and a tasty reminder that not every restaurant needs million-dollar ad campaigns. Here since 1930, the diner serves breakfast anytime (try the pancakes), a roast turkey dinner, soups, salads, and sundaes, all amidst the satisfying clatter of diner flatware. The place is open daily for breakfast, lunch, and dinner, a testament to its tagline: There's Always Something Cooking.

Watering Holes

You'll find scant options for nightlife in Littleton, but, as a local observed, "This is New England, and that's how people like it." There's a tavern adjoining the **Italian Oasis Restaurant** (106 Main St., 603/444-6995) inside Parker Marketplace. The Oasis also has a microbrewery and serves mixed drinks.

Since there's not much shaking after dark, if a good flick is playing at **Jax Jr. Cinemas** (32 Main St., 603/444-5907), you'll want to stop in and relive the days when you hung out at the Saturday matinee. Quirky fact: This theater's claim to fame is that it premiered the 1930s Bette Davis movie *The Great Lie*. Locals are still abuzz.

Shut-Eye

There are campgrounds, cabins, and cottages listed on the chamber website. For more options on motels and campgrounds, call the Chamber of Commerce (603/444-6561, www.littletonareachamber.com).

Motels and Motor Courts

No unwanted surprises at **Eastgate Motor Inn** (335 Cottage St., Exit 41 at I-93, 603/444-3971, www.eastgatemotorinn.com).

This family-owned operation offers nicer-than-average rooms (some with a fridge) and above-average service, and it is usually booked by tourists who like a clean room, pool, free breakfast, and cash in their pocket. If you'd rather save your money for the road, consider this standard motel, with rates from around $74.

Inn-dependence

Thayer's Inn (136 Main St., 603/444-6469 or 800/634-8179, www.thayersinn. com) would seem perfectly at home in Mayberry. It opened in 1843 as a stage-coach stop, and some traditions continue. A few rooms still have shared baths, but all are clean and comfortable, with rates from around $70. This is a great place to stay if you're on a budget and even if you're not. President Grant gave a speech from the front balcony, but ask for a room in back—a lot of traffic rolls down Route 302. A continental breakfast is included in the rate.

Chain Drive

These chain hotels are in town, or within 10 miles of the city center:
Best Western
For more information, including phone numbers and websites, see page 439.

ON THE ROAD: LITTLETON TO CAMDEN

Get ready for a most excellent ride. This run offers three options: You can either take Route 302 across the White Mountains; you can drop south to reach Highway 112 (the famed Kancamagus); or make a day trip of both roads before doubling back the following day to reach Maine. If you can take only one road, take Highway 112.

The ride starts slowly. As you roll out of Littleton on Route 302 east, you'll pass

the old Kilburn Brothers Stereoscopic View Factory. It's an apartment building now, but if you have any of these cards in your attic, now you'll know where they came from.

I once vowed to ride interstates only to pick up time (or, patriotic as I am, to serve the national interest). I make an exception for I-93 because this stretch rivals any back road you'll find. Follow it south toward the town of Lincoln where a detour at Exit 38 leads to the **Frost Place** (Ridge Rd., Franconia, 603/823-5510, www.frostplace. org, $5 donation), once the home of poet Robert Frost, who read his poem "The Gift Outright" at JFK's inauguration. Frost Place displays first editions of his books, photos, memorabilia, and a poet-in-residence who hosts readings in the old barn. Credit the harsh New Hampshire winters for a summers-only schedule: Memorial Day through Columbus Day.

Back on I-93, subtle hints such as towering mountains, plummeting roads, and a reduction to two lanes tell you you're entering Franconia Notch and dazzling eight-mile-long **Franconia Notch State Park** (603/823-8800, www.nhstateparks. com). Stuffed between the highest peaks of the Franconia and Kinsman ranges, this section of earth offers abundant places to explore. Pull off at the first exit (34C), and choose from swimming, camping, fishing, picnicking, and hiking around Echo Lake. Back on I-93, you'll jump on and off the road as you work your way south, taking the next exit (34B) to see the **New England Ski Museum** (603/823-7177, www. skimuseum.org, free). The base for the aerial tram here doubles as an information center for details on camping, hiking, and access to Profile Lake, and passage to the 4,200-foot peak of Cannon Mountain.

The next exit (34A) is near an 800-foot gorge called **The Flume** (www.visitnh.

gov/flume). If you can, make time for roughing it. Franconia Notch is a stunning park, and it's worth the layover to breathe fresh air and experience nature. There are no hotels in the park, but **Lafayette Campground** (603/823-9513, www.reserveamerica.com), with 97 tent sites, showers, and a store, places you at "Notch Central." Prior to May 3, 2003, this is where you could have looked up to see the "Old Man of the Mountain" (Nathaniel Hawthorne's Great Stone Face). Popularized in 1805, the natural granite profile disintegrated overnight in the fog and darkness and left a void for locals. Still, this section delivers The Basin that, like Keith Richards, is a 25,000-year-old glacial pothole.

Afterward, the going gets tricky, but stay on I-93 and watch for Exit 33 to get you onto Route 3 and into North Woodstock for a flirt with the past at **Clark's Trading Post** (603/745-8913, www.clarkstrading-post.com). It may seem corny, but this is a throwback to the days when you took road trips with your folks. Clark's has been at it for more than 75 years with trained bears, steam trains, and old-fashioned gadgets that tourists (circa 1962) love. Admission is $17. After Clark's, turn left onto a well-named connector road called "Connector Road," and at the next T, turn left to access Highway 112, the western tip of the Kancamagus Highway (known as "the Kanc").

Since the Kanc has no gas stations, stores, or hamburger clowns on its 34-mile stretch to Conway, the town of Lincoln has thoughtfully added a dense concentration of the type of urban congestion you're trying to escape. Race past these and soon you'll be in the midst of mind-boggling alpine scenery and rideable roads. Goose it and get into the rhythm of the road, but be prepared to brake when you reach some

20 mph hairpin turns and scenic viewing areas such as the Hancock Overlook.

Soon you'll learn that the road switches more frequently than Little Richard. You may head east, northwest, southeast, and then northeast to go east again. With the Kanc's multiple turns and seven-degree grades, you'll be hugging the centerline and shifting like a maniac.

After you cross Kancamagus Pass at 2,855 feet, you'll swoop down the mountain like a falcon, snatching great views to your left and following the road that now skirts the Swift River. To backtrack to Littleton and enjoy another winding and wild ride through forests and scenic overlooks, watch for Bear Notch Road that intersects the loop created by Highway 112 and Route 302, tosses in a tangle of roads, and at Route 302 can boomerang you back west.

Continuing east on the Kanc, you'll pass the **Rocky Gorge Scenic Area,** which leads to a wooden footbridge. Just over a mile later, you'll be at the Lower Falls, a great spot for a dip in the Swift River. Picnic spots, campgrounds, and riverfront rest areas mark the eastern edge of the highway, and with little fanfare, you'll reach the end of the road at Highway 113. The majority of traffic heads north to reach the outlet town of North Conway—but there's urban ugliness in this direction, my friend. Instead, start heading for the Maine coast via Route 302.

As state lines go, the entrance to Maine is minimalist—just a stark sign reading "Maine." My image of the state had been a frozen tundra where housewives carve blubber from dead seals. However, at first glance, you could put this road in Vermont or the Adirondacks. In earlier rides I headed towards the coast believing that I'd find wonderful oceanfront roads, but that turned out not to be so. That said, there's a nest of two-lane roads that reach into the preserved Maine wilderness. This is one of the best regions to do what motorcyclists love to do, and that's just to guide your ride across the state slowly towards the coast, grabbing any inland road that tempts you. If you're not ready to go off-script, get out your calculator since there are a number of numbers to follow over the next 135 miles.

A few miles over the border is Fryeburg where CR 5 takes you up towards Lovell. This is where you can split to the right on CR 93 east (aka Sweden Road) for about 10 miles before the road T's and you head north at CR 37 in South Waterford. The name is apt since there is water here—Bear Pond, Keoka Lake, McWain Pond—that you skirt around before CR 37 wraps up in East Waterford and CR 118. Take CR 118 east for about 15 miles towards the small towns of Norway and South Paris and by the time you roll into Norway, you'll be on CR 117, which is the only number you'll need to remember for about 25 miles. Now you have time to just skim down this slow and easy remote road all the way to the town of Leeds on the shores of Androscoggin Lake. It's a large lake, but not large enough to warrant a ferry here, so you have the undeniable pleasure to ride around its shores; first by taking CR 106 three miles up its west shore to the town of North Leeds, then completing the arc via county roads 219 and then 133 towards Winthrop and, finally, taking U.S. 202 east to Augusta.

While I try to avoid larger towns, I didn't mind going through Augusta because I knew it would take me to my ultimate goal, and that was getting onto CR 17. Its alias, Rockland Road, reveals that this path will take you on a slow descent all the way down to the coast—and it does it in style.

I was traveling in September, about a month before the peak of fall foliage, but already the beauty of nature was supernatural. For mile after mile there were ponds and small lakes and gentle rises and peaceful falls. There were nice fields and easy curves and a weirdly pristine natural landscape that looked as if a grounds crew had been tending to it for months. After listening to folks from Maine brag about their state, this seemed to reflect the essence of their pride. By the time I reached CR 90 at West Rockport, I realized I could have brought the ride to a quicker conclusion by jogging east to reach Rockport and Camden. Instead, I was into the ride so I continued south on 17 into Rockland which is accented by a beautiful harbor and decked out with an old-fashioned active downtown. Rockland includes some great diners and plenty of evidence that the town takes pride in presenting the **Maine Lobster Festival** (207/596-0376 or 800/562-2529, www.mainelobsterfestival.com) each August.

If there's time, hang around Rockland. When it's time to head out, it's only a few miles via U.S. 1 north to reach beautiful Camden. Of course, if you're still ready to roll, you can just turn south on U.S. 1 and about 1,900 miles later, you'll reach the end of the road in Key West, Florida.

I think Camden makes more sense.

ALTERNATE ROUTE: ROUTE 302

Although the Kancamagus Highway is an obvious choice, following Route 302 out of Littleton is a close second. After passing through the center of town, turn left at the Eastgate Motor Inn. It's an inauspicious beginning, but soon the road turns mighty pretty.

Route 302 leads to Fosters Crossroads, where you'll start a southeast descent toward Bretton Woods and the famous **Mount Washington Inn** (603/278-1000 or 800/314-1752, www.mountwashingtonresort.com), which sits majestically off to your left. If you can't spot the white frame palace and its red roof, follow the sightline of tourists who have it pinned down with cameras and binoculars. Staying at the grand hotel can be an expensive option, but looking is free. The inn boasts fantastic views of the White Mountains bordered by the Presidential Range, as well as all the amenities that make this a resort: horseback riding, tennis, entertainment, and an 18-hole Donald Ross course. Add to this the 900-foot white-railed veranda and broad porte-cochère, and you know you're riding into the lap of luxury. If the inn is full, it books the Bretton Woods Motor Inn and Townhomes at Bretton Woods as well.

On your left in Bretton Woods, you'll see the ingenious **Mount Washington Cog Railway** (603/278-5404 or 800/922-8825, www.thecog.com), which takes passengers to the chilly peak of Mount Washington. At 6,288 feet, Mount Washington is the highest point in the Northeast—called Agiocochook by Native Americans and believed to be the home of the Great Spirit. Settlers Abel Crawford and his son Ethan carved out the first footpath to its summit in 1819. That footpath is still in use. If you're fascinated by all things mechanical, you'll be impressed by how this railroad can ascend a 37-degree grade. The three-hour tour isn't cheap—$59 for adults. Then again, this *is* the highest peak in New England... then again, it is $59. Then again, the train *is* called Old Peppersass.…

Farther on, you'll ride past Saco Lake and enter dazzling Crawford Notch, as the road slices into the folds of the mountains and begins to loosely follow the Saco River toward Bartlett. For the next six miles, you'll encounter the unspoiled rugged beauty of the Presidential Range. **Crawford Notch State Park** (603/374-2272, www.nhstateparks.org) offers picnic areas, hiking, waterfalls, and a visitors center. After an exhilarating run through the notch, you'll reach Glen and the junction of Route 16, which leads north to the **Mount Washington Auto Road** (603/466-3988, www.mountwashingtonautoroad.com). Although it's several miles north in Gorham, riding up Mount Washington is worth the detour if it's worth $14 to tackle eight miles of 12-degree grades and wind speeds clocked at 231 mph (back in 1934). If so, put your visor down and chain yourself to your seat. Open only from mid-May to late October, the road provides killer views of the White Mountains, Presidential Range, and beyond. If you haven't been blown off the mountain, double back to Route 302 and head for the coast.

CAMDEN PRIMER

Tourism bureaus tend to go overboard promoting their town or state. Camden is different. It actually delivers on its promise of beauty. This harbor town is where the mountains (Appalachians) meet the sea (Atlantic), and the confluence makes a dramatic setting.

Although Camden is approximately the same size as Littleton, the village is far more active. Robert Ripley once estimated that if all Chinese citizens marched four abreast, they could walk around the world and the march would never end. That's about true for traffic here during Camden's peak season. Of course, that's on a nice day with warm weather. Fog and gray rains wash in and out frequently and can turn a great ride into a desolate and depressingly wet mess.

Laconia Motorcycle Week

A year after 400 riders spent a few days at Weirs Beach, New Hampshire, the first sanctioned "Gypsy Tour" was held in Laconia in 1917. Popular with America's few thousand riders, the Gypsy Tour developed a following through the 1920s and 1930s. In 1938, motorcycle hill-climber Fritzie Baer and his partners (the Red Hat Brigade) started a 30-year effort to keep the rally at full steam. But during the 1960s, the hill climbs and road races were cancelled as the rally fell out of favor with local police.

Things came to a head a week before the 1965 rally when a state law was passed giving police authority to arrest riders who loitered in groups of three or more. That was bound to spark trouble, and it did. At the "Riot of Laconia," motorcyclists battled police and the National Guard which helped diminish Motorcycle Week into Motorcycle Weekend. In 1975, camping along Highway 106 was outlawed and the rally continued to lose steam and attendance dropped to a new low of 25,000. But as the Sturgis and Daytona rallies grew in size and popularity, locals took a fresh look at Laconia. In 1991, Motorcycle Week was back, the term "Gypsy Tour" came back the following year, and the hill climbs returned to Gunstock the year after that.

Today, hundreds of thousands of motorcyclists arrive for nine days of motorcycle events, including races, hill climbs, touring, parades, vintage bikes, swap meets, demo rides, and the blessing of the motorcycles. The rally (603/366-2000, www.laconiamcweek.com) is held annually in mid-June.

As in most New England towns worth visiting, the central district is best seen on foot. Adjacent to the marina, you'll find a large parking lot with motorcycle-reserved spaces. From there, you can set off to eat seafood, browse bookshops, check out local crafts, eat seafood, cruise on a schooner, and eat seafood.

Summertime, obviously, is peak tourist season, with a very affluent group setting up shop and tourists arriving for the windjammer cruises that set sail from the harbor. Big, fat money rolls in from banking families, cruise line owners, and personalities like John Travolta, Kirstie Alley, and Martha Stewart, who arrive to buy large properties and even entire islands. But after they've left and the tourists are gone, the locals get back to work.

So here it is. It's not a wild town, but if you appreciate nature, you won't find a better base for day trips to search out Maine's best roads and natural attractions.

ON THE ROAD: CAMDEN

To see the best of Camden, you'll need at least two very full days. Reserve part of the first sunny day for a ride to Mount Battie. Leaving town on U.S. 1 North, you'll enjoy nice elevation changes for about two miles before reaching **Camden Hills State Park** (207/236-3109). Fork over $4.50, and you can ascend the 1.6-mile road in a steady, steep climb and reach the 790-foot summit of Mount Battie a few minutes later. Although the ride is short, you'll remember the view for a thousand years. From a stone tower lookout, you'll see the ocean meeting the mountains a few miles distant. The effect is spiritual. The sun shines so brightly on the water that the ocean looks like an endless white desert. Small islands break off from the mainland; roofs sprout through the tops of fir trees; small coves shelter schooners; and the wakes of clipper ships look like wisps of cotton. On a clear day, as your eyes follow the coast northeast to Bar Harbor's Cadillac Mountain (more than 40 miles away), it seems as if you can see forever.

PULL IT OVER: CAMDEN HIGHLIGHTS
Attractions and Adventures

In Camden satisfaction comes from seeing the world by your bike and someone else's boat. A fleet of schooners takes two-hour cruises around Penobscot Bay that put you among coastal mountains, seals, eagles, porpoises, and lobster boats. As you check out different charters, ask if you'll be able to help raise the sails, take the wheel, or simply kick back with a beer or wine. Costs are usually about $30. Options include the 65-foot windjammer *Appledore* (Camden Town Landing, Sharp's Wharf, 207/236-8353, www.appledore2.com) and schooner *Lazy Jack II* (Camden Town Landing, 207/230-0602, www.schooner-lazyjack.com), a 13-passenger 1947 Bahamian charter boat restored and brought to Camden in 1987. The schooner *Surprise* (Camden Town Landing, 207/236-4687, www.camdenmainesailing.com) is a 44-foot, 1918 classic on which Captain Jack serves cookies and fruit and spins yarns. Schooner *Olad* (Camden Town Landing, Sharp's Wharf, 207/236-2323, www.maineschooners.com) offers a 57-foot windjammer that departs every hour with 21–40 passengers.

Want to stay at sea overnight or longer? Check out the deluxe **Maine Windjammer Cruises** (Camden Town Landing, 207/236-2938 or 800/736-7981, www.mainewindjammercruises.com) for weekend, four-day, and week-long cruises departing Monday and Friday. Promoted as America's oldest windjammer, the *Lewis R. French* (Camden Town Landing, 800/469-4635, www.schoonerfrench.com) offers three- to six-day cruises for up to 22 nonsmoking crewmembers.

For fishing trips, contact **Georges River Outfitters** (1384 Atlantic Hwy., Warren, 207/273-3818, www.sportsmensgifts.com). Native Maineiac Jeff Bellmore is a United States Coast Guard captain and master Maine guide who hosts customized fresh- and saltwater excursions and limits boats to two passengers for one-on-one (or -two) advice. Freshwater catches include salmon, bass, trout, and perch; ocean runs are for stripers, bluefish, and mackerel. If you've got a few hundred bucks, then Georges River Outfitters has a captain, boat, and guide for you.

Maine's great outdoors has inspired generations of artists. Several miles east of Camden, **The Farnsworth Art Museum** (16 Museum St., Rockland, 207/596-6457, www.farnsworthmuseum.org) displays one of the larger collections of works by the Wyeths of Maine, recognized as the first family of American art. Additional works reflect all eras, from colonial to American impressionism to the present, with 8,000 items on display. Admission is $12.

You may want to make tracks to see the collection at the impressive **Owls Head Transportation Museum** (Rte. 73, Owls Head, 207/594-4418, www.ohtm.org). Located a few miles south and west of Camden, the mechanical menagerie here includes a 1937 Mercedes 540K, a World War I Fokker tri-plane, a Stanley Steamer, a 1963 prototype Mustang, a 1938 Indian Junior Scout, and a crazy contraption called the Scripps—Booth Bi-Autogo (a two-wheeled automobile/motorcycle that features Detroit's first V-8 engine). The displays are dazzling—and fun. Summer events include an antique motorcycle show featuring more than 200 vintage bikes.

If you're inspired to further explore the wilderness, a few hours from Camden are two businesses that are worth a side trip. **Northern Outdoors** (207/663-4466 or 800/765-7238, www.northernoutdoors. com) and **New England Outdoor Center** (207/723-5438 or 800/766-7238, www. neoc.com) coordinate adventures for all things Maine. They can help arrange rafting, fishing, climbing, canoeing, kayaking, whitewater rafting, hunting, and fishing excursions.

Blue-Plate Specials

Cappy's (1 Main St., 207/236-2254, www.cappyschowder.com) is the place for bikers, sailors, locals, and anyone who likes good food and good service. You'll find real clam chowder, crab skins, and shrimp—and those are just the appetizers. Come here at night, and the lively bar talk will surely include conversation about boats, bikes, and microbrews such as Old Thumper, Goat Island Light, and Blue Fin Stout. Microbrew tastings are held in Cappy's crow's nest from 4 to 6 P.M.

Besides Mount Battie, the best view in town is of the harbor. Sit on the deck at the **Waterfront Restaurant** (40 Bayview St., 207/236-3747, www.waterfrontcamden. com), and the harbor is yours—along with lobster, steak, and an oyster bar. The full bar is open until the customers go home.

Watering Holes

You'd think that a seaport town would have a host of pubs where sailors could drink and compare parrots, but most grog is served in civilized restaurants here. If you're looking for a place to drink, in addition to Cappy's bar, you can head down the alley and hang out at **Gilbert's Public House** (Bayview Landing, 207/236-4320) for cold brews and live bands.

Shut-Eye
Motels and Motor Courts

Camden still has some old-fashioned motels. Consider the **Towne Motel** (68 Elm St., 207/236-3377 or 800/656-4999, www.camdenmotel.com). In the heart of town (and the closest motel to the harbor), it has 18 rooms that start at $109 in peak season and drop considerably in shoulder seasons. A light continental breakfast is included. North of town is the classic **Birchwood Motel** (Belfast Rd., 207/236-4204, www.birchwoodmotel.com), where summer rates for the 15 oceanview rooms range between $89 and $109. You'll love its clean, old-school look.

Inn-dependence

The Belmont Inn (6 Belmont Ave., 207/236-8053 or 800/238-8053, www.the-belmontinn.com) is two blocks off U.S. 1 and offers 10 times the solitude you might expect. Wraparound porches, a great sitting room, breakfasts on the porch, and 99 windows give this private house a serious breath of fresh, outdoor air. The large rooms have a distinctly homey feel, and high season rates start at around $200. If the day's ride has worn you out and you can afford the privilege, this is quite a nice option.

Chain Drive

These chain hotels are in town, or within 10 miles of the city center:

Best Western, Hampton Inn

For more information, including phone numbers and websites, see page 439.

CAMDEN TO BAR HARBOR

After hanging around Camden long enough to get your soul recharged, it's time to hit the road, Jack. The sad fact is that even though you're heading up one of the most striking coastlines in America, you won't see much of it unless you're offshore on a lobster boat. If you sift through the rubble, the mundane views reveal a few jewels, such as the bridge at Verona, but mostly you'll see traffic clogging the main artery to Mount Desert Island, part of Acadia National Park. Stick with U.S. 1 until Ellsworth, where you can take Route 3 south into what the locals call "Bah Haabah."

At Hulls Cove, look for the **Visitors Center** (207/288-3338, www.nps.gov/acad). Rangers at the center offer volumes of material, from the *Beaver Log* newspaper to information on ranger-led programs, weather, tides, fishing, and camping. A free film narrated by Jack Perkins (of *A&E Biography* fame) tells the story of how "Rusticators" from elite circles in Philadelphia, Boston, and New York popularized the island. Money from the likes of Pulitzer,

Ford, Vanderbilt, and J. P. Morgan financed mansions patronizingly called "cottages."

For motorcycle travelers, the most relevant information pertains to the 27-mile Park Loop Road, which follows the island's coast and then knifes its way through the center of the park. You could race it in an hour, but allow three for abundant photo ops. If you have a sound system, spring for an Acadia audio tour; if not, a cheaper paperback booklet should suffice. Either will fill you in on the island's history and natural beauty. A few highlights:

It was John D. Rockefeller who advanced the design of 45 miles of carriage roads, created with the stipulation that no motor cars would be allowed (he never mentioned motorcycles). In any event, this was a summer haven for rich folks and they all felt so privileged to have this hideaway that, in 1919, they agreed to donate well over 30,000 acres of mountains, lakes, and sea to the government. Not only was it an incredibly nice gesture, it made Acadia the first national park east of the Mississippi.

Everything was going swell until 1947

At Home in Maine

Maine's residents are called "Mainers" or "Maineiacs." If you're not from here, friend, you're "from away."

Like the rest of America, Maine is threatened by the "national village." The Maine accent ("Ayuh, the clomms ah hahmless") is in danger of turning into a Midwestern drone as kids pick up vanilla speech patterns from the tube. The other assault comes from rich outsiders, who made their stash and now want to buy a piece of charming Maine. After they arrive, instead of appreciating the state for what it is, they try to re-create what they left behind, sometimes posting "No Trespassing" signs on beaches where natives had walked for years. According to one Maineiac, "It pisses us off." The bright side, he adds, is that folks "from away" usually last only four or five years before leaving "'coz they can't take the weather, anyway."

Ayuh.

when what became known as the Great Forest Fire swept over most of the island and burned more than 17,000 acres to cinders. Also lost in the conflagration were the mansions of "Millionaire's Row." Good heavens, Lovey...charcoal!

In peak season, a $20 fee ($10 during the shoulder seasons) grants you access to the Park Loop Road, and you'll immediately appreciate the efforts of the people who gave us the gift of Acadia. In addition to the main road, branches lead off to less trafficked sections of the park, although nearly every road leads to great cliff corners, dips, and rises. Scenic ocean views are frequent, and if you time it right you'll arrive when the normally silent Thunder Hole booms with the full fury of the sea. If there's fog, the landscape becomes an impressionist painting. If you're riding on a clear day, the peak of Cadillac Mountain (1,532 feet) may afford a matching view of Camden's Mount Battie—and exposure to the first rays of sunlight to fall on the United States.

When you've looped the park and had your fill of beauty, you can roll into downtown Bar Harbor where tourist central is comprised of a village green and mismatched buildings that house bookstores, drugstores, and the ever-present gift shops. Considering you've ridden this far, it's all worth checking out.

PULL IT OVER: BAR HARBOR HIGHLIGHTS
Attractions and Adventures

Like Camden, Bar Harbor's season runs from about mid-May to late October—weather willing. The best attractions here are the outdoor activities, which is why deep-sea fishing charters, windjammer cruises, island cruises, lighthouse cruises, and kayak rentals abound. The town pier is the best place to pick up brochures and make your selection.

Want to get out of the saddle and up a mountain? You can learn the ropes at **Atlantic Climbing School** (26 Cottage St., 207/288-2521, www.climbacadia.com), with beginner to advanced programs that take you to Acadia for instruction on spectacular cliffs bordered by the sea. Prices run $70–250, depending on the sort of climbing you'll be doing and the number of people in the class. If you've got time, get a piece of the rock. Reservations are required.

If you prefer getting away from the crowds and captains, charter a boat. Ask what's included—fuel can be expensive. **Mansell Boat Rentals** (135 Shore Rd., Manset, 207/244-5625, www.mansellboatrentals.com) rents a variety of boats, from sailboats to Boston Whalers. Experience is necessary, a deposit is required, and you'll have access to some of the finest sea and shores in the nation.

Coastal Kayaking Tours (48 Cottage St., 207/288-9605 or 800/526-8615, www.acadiafun.com), Maine's oldest sea kayak outfitter, has more than 100 sea kayaks, 20 trainers, guides, and tours that can last from a few hours to a few days. You'll get a hearty upper-body workout and the opportunity to watch sea life from sea level.

Having done a similar tour on Cape Cod, I can vouch for the amazing sights that appear on a whale-watching charter. Offered from late May to late October, **Bar Harbor Whale Watch Co.** (207/288-2386 or 888/942-5474, www.whalesrus.com) will take you out on trips that last around three hours. You'd think that spotting a whale would be a rarity, but generally the pilot can track them down from the telltale spout and then maneuver the boat so close that you can actually see the huge humpback, finback, and minke whales drifting just below the surface. Be sure to wear your leathers, since it can get cold on the boat. They also offer lobster fishing, seal watching, and sunset cruises.

It sounds kind of odd, but you may appreciate the collection at the **Wendell Gilley Museum of Bird Carving** (corner of Main and Herrick Sts., Southwest Harbor, 207/244-7555, www.wendellgilleymuseum.org). It's slightly out of the way in Southwest Harbor, but worth it if you need a fantastically detailed bird carving for your office. Gilley, a late native son, earned a national following, and you'll see why when you examine the intricately carved songbirds, shorebirds, eagles, and other birds of prey. Incredible. The museum shop sells bird carvings, carving tools, and field guides for nature lovers. Hours vary, so call ahead.

Shopping

If you're a devotee of America's million-plus microbreweries, you'll be happy to find the **Atlantic Brewing Company** (15 Knox Rd., 207/288-2337, www.atlanticbrewing.com) in rural Bar Harbor. Stock up on Bar Harbor Real Ale, a nut brown ale with a round, malty body. Other brews include Blueberry Ale, Ginger Wheat, and the cleverly named Coal Porter. Choice two is the **Bar Harbor Brewing Company** (8 Mount Desert St., 207/288-4592, www.barharborbrewing.com), which has received first-place finishes in world beer championships with brews like Thunder Hole Ale and Cadillac Mountain Stout. Both offer free tours.

After a hard ride, it's time for the great indoors and a good cigar. In the summertime, **Joe's Smoke Shop** (119 Main St., 207/288-2886) has enough cigars to fill a walk-in humidor. Plus, there's an intimate bar where you can enjoy a martini or a glass of wine, brandy, port, or scotch.

Blue-Plate Specials

How many diners can back up a "Get in Here and Eat!" sign with great food? Since 1969, **Bar Harbor Route 66 Restaurant** (21 Cottage St., 207/288-3708, www.bhroute66.com), a funky, collectibles-filled diner, has served roadhouse specialties like chicken pot pies and hot turkey dinners, as well as fish and pasta. It's open for lunch and dinner, with happy hour from 5 until "66 minutes past" (6:06 P.M.).

The Thirsty Whale Tavern (40 Cottage St., 207/288-9335, www.thistywhaletavern.com) offers fine spirits, sandwiches, and beer in a basic bar—uh, tavern—setting. You'll find chicken, burgers, haddock, clams, and a dozen beers, including some microbrews, on tap.

Galyn's Galley Restaurant (17 Main St., 207/288-9706, www.galynsbarharbor.com) was constructed inside an 1890s boarding house, so you can check in and check out fresh lobster, scallops, fish, and the specialty prime rib. Upstairs, the intimate lounge features an antique mahogany bar. If you don't drink alcohol, just order one of the homemade, super sweet desserts, chased with a shot of insulin.

Shut-Eye

If you have to stay over, Bar Harbor has more than 3,000 hotel rooms. Check www.barharborinfo.com for listings. If the weather's right, camping is another option. Campsites within Acadia National Park need to be reserved well in advance. Call the National Parks Reservations service at 800/365-2267, or go to www.recreation.gov.

Chain Drive

These chain hotels are in town, or within 10 miles of the city center:
Best Western, Days Inn, Fairfield Inn, Holiday Inn, Quality Inn
For more information, including phone numbers and websites, see page 439.

Resources for Riders

White Mountains–Blue Seas Run

Maine Travel Information
Maine Campground Owners Association—207/782-5874, www.campmaine.com
Maine Office of Tourism—888/624-6345, www.visitmaine.com
Maine Road Conditions—866/282-7578, www.511maine.gov

New Hampshire Travel Information
New Hampshire Fish and Game Department—603/271-3421,
   www.wildlife.state.nh.us
New Hampshire Office of Travel and Tourism—603/271-2343 or
   800/386-4664, www.visitnh.gov
New Hampshire Road Conditions—866/282-7579, www.511nh.com
New Hampshire State Parks—603/271-3556, www.nhparks.state.nh.us

Local and Regional Information
Acadia National Park Information—207/288-3338, www.nps.gov/acad
Bar Harbor Chamber of Commerce—207/288-5103 or 800/288-5103,
   www.barharborinfo.com
Camden Chamber of Commerce—207/236-4404 or 800/223-5459,
   www.camdenme.org
Littleton Chamber of Commerce—603/444-6561,
   www.littletonareachamber.com or www.golittleton.com
Mount Washington Valley Chamber of Commerce—603/356-5701 or
   800/367-3364, www.mtwashingtonvalley.org
White Mountain National Forest—603/528-8721, www.fs.fed.us/r9/white

Maine Motorcycle Shops
Big Moose Harley-Davidson/Buell—375 Riverside St., Portland, 207/797-6061
   or 800/427-5393, www.bigmooseharley.com
North Country Harley-Davidson—3099 N. Belfast Ave., Augusta, 207/622-7994
   or 800/934-1653, www.northcountryhd.com
Reid's Cycle—1300 Atlantic Hwy., Northport, 207/338-6068,
   www.reidscycle.com

New Hampshire Motorcycle Shops
Laconia Harley-Davidson—239 Daniel Webster Hwy. (Rte. 3), Meredith,
   603/279-4526, www.laconiaharley.com
Littleton Harley-Davidson/Buell—Rte. 116, Bethlehem, 603/444-1300,
   www.littletonharley.com
Littleton Motorsports—515 Union St., Littleton, 603/444-5003,
   www.littletonmotorsports.com
Manchester Harley-Davidson/Buell—115 John E. Devine Dr., Manchester,
   603/622-2461 or 800/292-5393, www.manchesterhd.com
White Mountain Harley-Davidson—1275 White Mountain Hwy., North
   Conway, 603/356-7775

Berkshires–Central Vermont Run

Lenox, Massachusetts to Stowe, Vermont

If you live west of the Mississippi or south of the Mason-Dixon line, reaching your region's best roads can take hours. This is where New England is different. The dense concentration of rivers, hillocks, and mountains compresses a nation's worth of ideal motorcycling roads into a relatively small area. Of course, it's not just the roads that make this trip one of the best in America. This tour fulfills the criteria for a perfect run: culture, history, and scenery.

In Lenox, you'll find culture in abundance at novelist Edith Wharton's home, The Mount, in summer stock theaters, and at Tanglewood (the summer venue of the Boston Symphony Orchestra). A short ride away is Stockbridge, Norman Rockwell's final hometown. From the heart of the Berkshires, fantastic road leads to Vermont and historic Plymouth Notch, the preserved village and birthplace of the reticent yet surprisingly eloquent Calvin Coolidge. Neighboring Woodstock is the quintessential New England village and your final destination, Stowe, is as

enjoyable in mild weather as it is when skiers arrive in winter.

LENOX PRIMER

In the latter half of the 1800s, this tranquil farming region was "discovered" by famous and wealthy residents of Boston and New York. First, Nathaniel Hawthorne wrote *The House of Seven Gables* and *Tanglewood Tales* while living near Lenox, and then Samuel Gray Ward, the Boston banker who later helped finance the purchase of Alaska, built a summer home near Hawthorne's cottage. Through Hawthorne's words and Ward's wealthy friends, Lenox became *the* place to establish summer homes that were, in fact, gigantic mansions their owners sloughed off as "cottages." In Lenox, actors, authors, bankers, and industrialists like Andrew Carnegie added flash to the Gilded Age.

Around the turn of the 20th century, a federal income tax overturned the fortunes of many of these families, and the mansions were later sold with many being

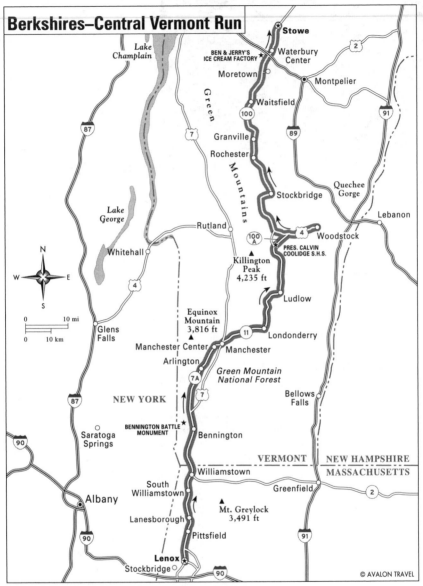

Berkshires–Central Vermont Run

Route: Lenox to Stowe via Williamstown, Arlington, Manchester Village, Plymouth Notch, Woodstock, Rochester, Waitsfield

Distance: Approximately 210 miles

First Leg: Lenox, Massachusetts to Woodstock, Vermont (122 miles)

Second Leg: Woodstock to Stowe, Vermont (88 miles)

Helmet Laws: Massachusetts and Vermont require helmets.

converted into the schools, hotels, and resorts you'll see today. Although it lost a few millionaires, Lenox found new life through music. In 1937, locals enlisted the Boston Symphony Orchestra to make Tanglewood—an estate between Lenox and Stockbridge—its summer home. Today, Tanglewood hosts one of the world's leading music festivals and has made this town the summertime cultural capital of the Northeast.

If you travel here in the peak season of July and August, be warned that prices—especially for dining and lodging—rise dramatically. Then again, the upscale attitude hasn't sidelined local favorites like breakfast diners and working-class bars.

Take it all in, then in the evening when the streets are quiet and the moon is rising over the Berkshire hills, walk through the Lenox streets. The evening mist, historic buildings, and peaceful silence will transport you back 200 years.

ON THE ROAD: LENOX

The core of Lenox is small. Small, I tell ya, just two blocks wide and about four blocks long. You could goose it and clear town in less than ten seconds. But that's not what Lenox is about. And since parking is free, rest your bike. The longer you stay, the more you save.

Take your time and see the primary street (Church Street); walk along Main Street (Route 7A); and drop down back alleys to discover less trafficked antique shops, art galleries, and coffee bars. Stop by the circa 1815 Berkshire County Courthouse, which now houses the Lenox Library.

Since Lenox proper doesn't offer a wealth of roads, think about investing a half day on an extremely casual and educational short loop to neighboring Stockbridge. Even during peak tourist season,

the back roads are lightly traveled and immensely fun.

In the heart of town, the Paterson memorial obelisk marks the intersection of Route 7A and Route 183 South. Head down Route 183 and you've entered a canopy road that runs past a lake called the Stockbridge Bowl, which you can reach by turning left down Hawthorne Street. When you reach it, you'll discover that this glacial lake is reserved for the residents of Stockbridge (if you're discreet I doubt you'll get carded). This is a perfect place to swim, blessed with an amazing vista of the surrounding Berkshires.

Back on Route 183, Tanglewood will soon appear on your left. Since concerts don't begin until dusk, keep riding straight for several more tree-lined miles until you cross Route 102 to reach the Norman Rockwell Museum on your left. Farther down Route 183 on your right is Chesterwood, the equally fascinating home and studio of sculptor Daniel Chester French—best known for his masterpiece, the Lincoln sculpture within the Lincoln Memorial. His studio is still cluttered with several Lincoln studies and other striking pieces.

Return to Route 102 East, and you'll enter the village of Stockbridge, where you can stop for a drink at the Lion's Den inside the famous **Red Lion Inn** (Main St., corner of Rtes. 7 and 102, 413/298-5545, www.redlioninn.com), which has been serving travelers since 1773. Naturally, there are a few gift shops and restaurants in town—although none of special note. When you're ready to ride back to Lenox, return to Route 7 North (turn left at the fire station) and watch for Berkshire Cottages Blantyre and Cranwell on your right, quite visible examples of the magnitude of the wealth that once resided in these hills.

Just ahead, Route 7A splits off to the

left. Follow that and soon you'll find you've completed a soothing circle tour. Now you're back home in Lenox.

PULL IT OVER: LENOX HIGHLIGHTS
Attractions and Adventures

During July and August, the Boston Symphony Orchestra gets the hell out of Beantown and heads to **Tanglewood** (West St./Rte. 183, 413/637-5165 or 617/637-5165, www.bso.org). The site of the world's leading music festival, Tanglewood has been drawing crowds since 1937 and is a must-see if you're here in season. Guest conductors, including Andre Prévin and John Williams, have taken the lead beneath The Shed, and non-BSO summer nights feature such artists as YoYo Ma, Garrison Keillor, and James Taylor. Before you go, pack a blanket and swing by **Loeb's Food Town** (42 Main St., 413/637-0270), a great little downtown grocery where you can pick up a baked chicken, beer, wine, and everything else for your evening under the stars. Lawn tickets are reasonably priced, which makes this perhaps the best outdoor concert venue in America—and the best musical picnic you'll ever enjoy.

Edith Wharton, one of America's most celebrated authors, foreshadowed this book's success by winning the 1921 Pulitzer Prize for *The Age of Innocence.* You'd be surprised just how contemporary her works remain. Wharton's restored estate, **The Mount** (2 Plunkett St., Rtes. 7 and 7A, 413/551-5111, www.edithwharton.org, tours $16), was built in 1902 based on the classical precepts of her book *The Decoration of Houses.* Tours are conducted daily May through October and present a great way to experience the Berkshires as Wharton might have. A biography lecture series takes place on Mondays and readings from her books are presented on the verandah on Wednesdays.

Highbrow bikers look forward to **Shakespeare & Company** (70 Kemble St., 413/637-1197, www.shakespeare.org), which is near The Mount and stages plays by Shakespeare as well as Berkshire playwrights in three theaters year-round.

A quiet and natural destination to ride your bike, not to mention a peaceful place to get centered in the morning, **Berkshire Wildlife Sanctuaries** (472 W. Mountain Rd., 413/637-0320, $4) is just a few miles from town. In season the trails are open dawn–dusk daily. Part of the larger 1,500-acre Pleasant Valley Sanctuary, the Berkshire section offers several miles of walking trails and abundant wildlife.

Norman Rockwell was the Charles Kuralt of canvas, capturing an America that existed only in our minds. While the somewhat stark **Norman Rockwell Museum** (Rte. 183, Stockbridge, 413/298-4100, www.nrm.org, $15, add $5 for an audio tour) doesn't exactly capture his sincerity, it does display the world's largest collection of his original art, with nearly 500 works. The collection includes the original *Four Freedoms,* an inspiring series on American ideals that alone makes this museum well worth the ride. Outside the museum, you'll find Rockwell's former studio. It was moved here and now appears as it did when he worked on his pivotal work, *The Golden Rule.* Before you leave, one must-have souvenir is his autobiography which reveals that this seemingly easygoing man had a rambling life filled with a passion for excellence. Just right for reading on the road, you can pick up a copy here. The museum and store are open 10 A.M.–5 P.M. daily.

You may not know the name Daniel Chester French, but I guarantee that you know the work of this American sculptor.

A few blocks from the Rockwell Museum is **Chesterwood** (4 Williamsville Rd., Stockbridge, 413/298-3579, www.chesterwood.org, $10), a 122-acre Italian-style villa where he created masterpieces like the monumental Lincoln sculpture that's part of the Lincoln Memorial (1922) and Concord's Minute Man (1875). After viewing his home and seeing some 500-plus works in the well-stocked studio, stroll the grounds and you'll likely sense the power of the natural surroundings that inspired these works of Americana. Chesterwood is open 10 A.M.–5 P.M. daily.

Herman Melville lived in **Arrowhead** (780 Holmes Rd., Pittsfield, 413/442-1793, www.mobydick.org, $12) from 1850 to 1863, writing books such as *Moby-Dick.* After the world traveler and gifted writer found it difficult to raise a family on modest royalties, he packed it up for a desk job in New York City where he worked for the last 19 years of his life as a customs inspector. Arrowhead is loaded with many of Melville's personal artifacts, and if you like his books, then it's worth the detour. The home is open 9:30 A.M.–5 P.M. Memorial Day–Columbus Day, with tours on the hour.

Blue-Plate Specials

On my last visit to Lenox, I noticed that three of my affordable favorites—a pizza place, a breakfast joint, and a downhome café—had folded. For those sort of places, you'll have to travel down to Great Barrington or up towards Pittsfield. But there is a cost-conscious option in Lenox: **The Scoop** (26 Housatonic St., 413/637-9192, www.scooplenox.com) promotes its ice creams and sorbets, but they also serve diner-style breakfasts all day, and at lunch and dinner the menu showcases burgers, wraps, and classic sandwiches.

A few miles north of Lenox en route to Pittsfield on Route 7, the **Dakota** (1035 South St., 413/499-7900, www.steakseafood.com/dak), has been serving big food in a big Pacific Northwest setting since the 1960s. The featured items include fresh salmon, prime rib, lobster, and hand-cut steaks. Expect to wait for a table. Expect the meal to last for days.

Watering Holes

Want to look like a local? Pull up a barstool at the **Olde Heritage Tavern** (912 Housatonic St., 413/637-0884). It offers all the ingredients of a neighborhood bar: Foosball, darts, jukeboxes, local characters, pub grub (burgers, wings, pizzas, liquor, and pitchers of Newcastle Brown Ale and others). Not just a bar—this is a New England tavern. Last call is 12:30 A.M.

Shut-Eye

Lenox has dozens of inns and a healthy number of independent motels. In high season, many inns and hotels require minimum stays on weekends, and prices rise accordingly, so check in advance. Three lodging services can help you: For countywide reservations contact the **Berkshire Visitors Bureau** (888/256-7480 or 413/743-4500, www.berkshires.org); you can also check the **Chamber of Commerce**'s (www.lenox.org/lodging) listing of local digs; or, if you prefer to stay south of town in Lee, Lenoxdale, Stockbridge, or Great Barrington, the **Berkshire Lodging Association** (413/528-4006, www.berkshirelodging.com) offers a list of inns, hotels, and motels.

Inn-dependence

Even with 31 rooms and suites at three neighboring houses, the woods surrounding the **Cornell Inn** (203 Main St., 413/637-0562 or 800/637-0562, www.cornellinn.com, $80–110 high season) provide an intimate and comfortable setting. There's a pond and patio area to enjoy when the weather's right. The service is friendly and the homey room styles range from Colonial to Victorian.

Dig deep if you'd like to stay at **Garden Gables Inn** (135 Main St., 413/637-0193 or 888/243-0193, www.lenoxinn.com, $190 and up on weekends in high season). Although it's on the main drag, the setting is secluded and peaceful with five acres providing a buffer from the tourists. A swimming pool and comfortable rooms make this a safe and relaxing choice.

Chain Drive

These chain hotels are in town, or within 10 miles of the city center:

Best Western, Comfort Inn, Econo Lodge, Hampton Inn, Holiday Inn Howard Johnson, Knights Inn, Quality Inn, Ramada, Rodeway, Super 8, Travelodge

For more information, including phone numbers and websites, see page 439.

ON THE ROAD: LENOX TO WOODSTOCK

When you leave Lenox, Route 7A merges with Route 7 on the road to Pittsfield. While tense traffic is the price you'll pay to reach the Berkshire County seat, you'll be duly rewarded when you take a one-block detour to the nondescript **King Kone** (133 Fenn St., 413/496-9485), at the corner of Fenn and 1st Streets in Pittsfield. Just $1.70 buys either a small, medium, or large cone at this old-fashioned ice cream shack. Go for the large. It doesn't cost any more, it's nearly a foot tall and, damn, it's a pretty sight.

After navigating the traffic of Pittsfield, head north on Route 7. Two miles past Lanesborough you can detour right onto North Main Street and ride an additional nine switchback-rich miles to reach

the summit of Mount Greylock. At 3,491 feet, it's the state's highest peak and where a 100-foot-tall war memorial offers a view of five states. If you have neither the time nor the inclination to scale the summit, just keep rolling on Route 7.

By the time you reach New Ashford you're all set for several miles of great elevations and terrific plunges that surround the Brodie Mountain ski area. Farther up the road at Routes 7 and 43, watch for the **Store at Five Corners** (413/458-3176, www.5-corners.com). A general-store anomaly, during its history it's been a tavern, a mustering point for mounted militia, a stagecoach stop, a gas station, a tea room, and a social center. Today, basic staples (thread, detergent, tape) rest beside gourmet groceries, and the market has become an attraction unto itself. No pork rinds in sight, but if you're looking for fine wines, garlic parsley pasta, and other imported fare, you'll find plenty to peruse.

Just a few hundred yards past the Store at Five Corners is the most visually appetizing sight you've seen in a while. Scan the horizon to your right, and the valley looks like a Dalí painting as it melts into low hills a mile away. In fall, the view will prepare you for upcoming scenes of old men in overalls selling pumpkins by the roadside, cornstalks stacked like teepees, and dogs sleeping on the porches of cozy homes. Sunflowers sag under their own weight, and flower gardens speckle yards. The smell of fresh air mingles with the spicy aroma of trees, sweet corn, and smoking chimneys.

Soon you are in Williamstown, a tranquil village built around Williams College (c. 1793). If you're ahead of schedule, take a break downtown where the antiques are pricey and the merchandise is probably available elsewhere. Still, the town is cool, and the **Sterling and Francine Clark Art**

Institute (225 South St., 413/458-9545, www.clarkart.edu, free November–May, $12.50 in summer) is well worth a visit. Even if your walls are hung with paint-by-number masterpieces, you can relive college art appreciation class here, viewing works by artists of the caliber of Sargent, Remington, and Degas. It's open daily except Monday until July 1, then seven days a week through summer.

You know life is good when Route 7 continues north, its steep grades dropping you into the thick of purple and yellow and green hills. The hues reveal that you are entering Vermont, the name derived from the French words *vert* (green) and *mont* (mountain). Within a few miles, you'll notice that something's missing: There are no billboards in Vermont. None. Natural beauty is the state's best advertising. *Trés magnifique.*

Compensating for the lack of billboards, however, are maple syrup sellers. Maple syrup is sold from front porches. Maple syrup is sold from car trunks, at diners, in gas stations, schools, prisons, basements, attics, duck blinds, churches, tollbooths, and bomb shelters. I'd guess that the tidal wave of Vermont maple syrup packaged in jars, jugs, bottles, and canisters will remain long after our sun has flickered out.

As you approach Bennington, you'll certainly notice the 306-foot-tall Bennington Battle Monument. You can see it from 50 miles away, but if you'd like to see it up close, turn left on Main Street (Highway 9) when you hit the center of town. Follow Main Street a short distance to Monument Avenue, where you'll turn right, then right again, taking you to the monument.

When you roll into the north end of Bennington, watch the road signs and veer onto parallel Route 7A. Now you can relax again as you begin your voyage through Vermont. As you approach the village of Arlington, you sense there are no worries here—just mountains to watch and a quiet back road that's coaxing you along. The riding here is sublime and you may never want to stop, but I suggest that you do since you're fast approaching **Snow's Arlington Dairy Bar** (3176 VT Route 7A, 802/375-2546). A favorite with riders, Snow's has been on the ground since 1962, serving hot dogs, chilidogs, fries, and shakes. Pull over, grab a picnic table, and enjoy the surrounding woods. If you carry an AARP card, time your ride for Tuesday's Senior Day and get 10 percent off.

Nine miles later you'll reach Manchester Village, but not without passing hills colored with countless shades of green and bordered by the flowing Batten Kill River. Given the time and desire, you can park your bike and explore the woods and river with full-service **BattenKill Canoe Ltd.** (802/362-2800 or 800/421-5268, www.battenkill.com). It leads tours or turns you loose on the crystal clear, trout-rich waterway that flows beside lonely country lanes and quiet meadows and into deep woods. Although Manchester is a small town, there are other detours to make. To experience 5.2 miles of steep grades and sharp curves, take a scenic ride to the summit of 3,848-foot **Mount Equinox** (802/362-1114, www.equinoxmountain.com, $10), the highest peak in the Taconic Range. The toll road leads to a restaurant, walking trails, and picnic sites, but the Carthusian monastery is off-limits to travelers. Tell 'em you wanna be a monk, and maybe they'll let you in.

Hildene (1005 Hildene Rd., 802/362-1788, www.hildene.org, $12.50), the 24-room Georgian revival mansion once owned by Robert Todd Lincoln (Abe's kid), is on your right off Route 7A. Later home to Lincoln's few descendants, the

Cool Calvin

Calvin Coolidge never did say much, but when he did, you could rest assured he knew what he was talking about. Here's one of Coolidge's comments that's become a favorite inspirational quote:

Nothing in the world can take the place of persistence. Talent will not; nothing is more common than unsuccessful men with talent. Genius will not; unrewarded genius is almost a proverb. Education will not; the world is full of educated derelicts. Persistence and Determination alone are omnipotent. The slogan "Press On" has solved and always will solve the problems of the human race.

house features original furnishings and family effects, as well as formal gardens.

A few miles farther north, the merchants of Manchester Center (est. 1761) tricked out their outlet stores so that wealthy shoppers would think they were getting a good deal. Although outlets no longer mean savings, just try saying that to anyone leaving Polo, Bass, Izod, Calvin Klein, Nautica, Big Dog, or Godiva, and expect to be jerked off your bike and beaten with a sack of size 34 Jordache jeans. Aside from this, with its river, side streets, and non-outlet stores and restaurants, Manchester is well worth a break.

When you leave Manchester, turn right at the roundabout and say *au revoir* to Route 7A and howdy do to Route 11. You've cleared the orgy of outlets and dodged swarms of shoppers, and once again it's just you and the positive strokes that come with traveling by motorcycle. Your bike is scaling the hills northeast of town, and as you enter the Green Mountain National Forest, a scenic pull-off provides a glorious aerial view of Manchester. Since you won't be traveling here in winter, the rising and falling road will give you a chance to practice 1200-cc ski jumps. On any hill, just tap it into neutral, stand on your foot pegs, and stretch forward as you

feel the smooth fall, soft dip at the base, and the slow rise. Feels just like the real thing.

At Londonderry, Route 11 stops, zigs to the left, then introduces you to State Road 100. That's *the* most *righteous* State Road 100. Never before in the history of motorcycling has one road done so much for so many. SR 100 cleaves a path through the center of the Green Mountains and plunges you into the heart of Vermont, where apple trees and general stores and Holstein cows create a new, yet strangely familiar, landscape.

Running toward Ludlow, a riverside ride takes you through wide-open spaces to the junction with Route 155, where you'll veer right to continue on SR 100. In the weeks leading to fall foliage, apple trees are brilliant red, and scattered colors change from dark green to bright red to greenish yellow.

Although Ludlow seems to have seen better days, the Okemo Mountain Ski Resort here offers nice elevations, just as upcoming Tyson provides a pleasing ride beside Echo Lake, which I'm sure is perfectly suitable for swimming when it heats up for a few hours each year. This brings up a point: Sunny, pleasant Vermont can become *Night on Bald Mountain*

A simple headstone for a simple man: Calvin Coolidge rests directly across from the small village where he was raised, and where he was sworn into the presidency by his father, a justice of the peace.

in moments. Stow some warm clothes or carry a butane torch in your saddlebags to stave off frostbite.

This is where SR 100 gets interesting. Very. As you near Killington, you'll realize that the ground was laid out by God and the road was probably designed by an engineer who rode an Indian Chief. You'll experience great twists, exhilarating turns, frequent rises, and thrilling drops. The ride gets even more exciting when you turn right to SR 100A.

On the run, you'll see tarpaper shacks with cords of firewood so massive you'd be hard-pressed to tell where the kindling ends and the homes begin. Mountains towering along the roadside are straight from *Land of the Giants*. Don't spare the horsepower as you ride northeast toward Plymouth Notch and the **President Calvin Coolidge State Historic Site** (3780

Rte. 100A, Plymouth, 802/672-3773, www.historicvermont.org/coolidge, $7.50), a turn-of-the-20th-century village preserved in honor of its famous son.

If you doubt that just about anyone can become president, witness this. Coolidge was born on the Fourth of July, 1872 in a sleepy village tucked in the folds of sleepy hills. Even if you don't know a thing about our 30th president, I guarantee you'll spend more time here after you read his observations about government and the United States and learn that he was the last president to write his own speeches. As you tour the village, you may even buy some cheese from the small factory that Calvin's son John operated until he passed away in May 2000. Afterward, take a few minutes at the cemetery across the street. The Coolidge family fronts the road, with Calvin's headstone deservedly marked with the presidential seal.

The SR 100A adventure continues to the junction of Route 4, where you'll turn right for the final 10-mile trip to Woodstock. This winding, level road follows the flow of the Ottauquechee River. Be careful: The curving river can hypnotize, and there's no guardrail. Keep your eyes on the road, and soon you'll be in Woodstock—a most interesting town.

WOODSTOCK PRIMER

If ever a town was sent from Central Casting, it's Woodstock. Everything is here: the church steeple, village green, lazy river, covered bridge, American flags. This is Currier & Ives country.

Woodstock was chartered in 1761 and settled in 1768. The colonial homes, many of which are still standing, were built well and inexpensively using abundant natural materials. Early Woodstock was like a commune, in which bartering replaced cash purchases. Small businesses, including hatters, silversmiths, printers, cabinetmakers, tanners, and jewelers, took up residence in town, while on the outskirts, lumber and sawmills, cider presses, brick kilns, and iron-casting furnaces came into operation.

Self-sufficiency, ingenuity, and humanity are hallmarks of Woodstock's history. Slaves here were freed a century before the Civil War; the earliest Morgan horses were stabled here (as were Jersey cows and Merino sheep); and when farming and industry dropped into the background, America's first ski town was installed here in 1934 and helped make Woodstock a center for tourism. And it still is.

ON THE ROAD: WOODSTOCK

Woodstock is a perfect stop for motorcycle travelers because the roads are right; the beauty is omnipresent; the streets are clinically clean; and great restaurants and neighborhood bars let you kick back after a day on the road.

Only minor flaws exist in this dream state. Woodstock is notorious for its speed traps and some locals grumble that merchants cater too much to wealthy tourists. But more prominent is the fact that Route 4, the road you came in on, is also the primary truck route. Every few minutes, distant rumblings and the squeal of jake brakes announce the arrival of a semi. If you can block out the truck traffic, take solace in simple touches, such as a picture of Calvin Coolidge in a storefront window.

As in Lenox, the town center is best seen on foot, and you'll find plenty of metered parking (and a convenient information booth) at the village square. If the booth is closed, the Woodstock Town Crier on Elm Street is a blackboard on which locals list such newsworthy events as raffles, chicken dinners, hayrides, and garden club meetings. Even the local movie venue—the

© NANCY HOWELL

Gorgeous gorge: A view from the top of the Ottauquechee Bridge east of Woodstock. It's almost 170 feet to the bottom.

town hall—is a throwback to the 1920s. Even more information is available at the Welcome Center on Mechanic Street, where you can pick up maps of the surrounding area and enjoy what's known as the cleanest bathroom facilities around.

Outstanding shops include the **Village Butcher** (18 Elm St., 802/457-2756), with its few hundred types of wine, cheese, and meat. Here since 1886, **FH Gillingham & Sons** (16 Elm St., 802/457-2100, www. gillinghams.com) remains an old-time general store, selling everything from fresh milk in bottles to hardware, wine, and microbrews. If you're inspired by the scenery and want to learn more about the state, drop by **Pleasant Street Books** (48 Pleasant St., 802/457-4050, www.pleasantstbooks.com), which has two floors filled with more than 10,000 old volumes—from Civil War to travel to Vermonticana. Among them are rare books, first editions, and complete sets.

I'm not sure why, but I think that small towns like this are better viewed after dark. Take some time and walk around after the sun goes down. Though the shops may be closed, you'll have a chance to distance yourself from tourists, pause by the bridge, and watch the Ottauquechee River roll past. Come morning, for a short ride you can join the caravan of bikers on the six-mile run east to **Quechee Gorge.** This is a popular spot for motorcycle travelers and I think that maybe the draw is the 1960s tourist shop that's weighted down with Quechee Gorge spoons, Indian moccasins made in Taiwan, and cedar altars sporting plastic Jesuses. Despite the lack of quality gifts, there's no shortage of tourists ready to buy a geegaw for the breakfast nook in Idaho.

In reality people are here because of the sight of a 168-foot vertical drop below Vermont's oldest steel span bridge. Don't bungee jump—a safer route is the half-mile trail that leads down to the Ottauquechee River. Walking down isn't too bad—smokers do it. Hikers do it, bikers do it, and so do little children. But all are far less enthusiastic about hiking up.

At the bottom, take a break and recline on one of the thousands of wide river rocks. The dry riverbed is a good place to think, as evidenced by all the people writing, sketching, and painting. When you want to ride the road again, farther up Route 4 is the **Quechee Gorge Village,** an old-fashioned shopping plaza that features an antiques center, country store, hypercool diner, and candle shop. When you're done, tie down your plastic Jesus with a bungee and return to Woodstock.

PULL IT OVER: WOODSTOCK HIGHLIGHTS
Attractions and Adventures
Thankfully, most things worth doing are done outdoors in this pristine countryside. Even though some may seem like grade-school field trips, these excursions are intriguing.

You may scoff that a farm would be of interest, but you haven't yet been to **Billings Farm** (Rte. 12 and River Rd., 802/457-2355, www.billingsfarm.com, $11). This pastoral parcel of land was created to educate the public about the value of responsible agriculture and land stewardship (the passions of lawyer, railroad entrepreneur, and philanthropist Frederick Billings and his wealthy grandson-in-law, Laurance S. Rockefeller). The circa 1871 working farm is a living museum, with guides hosting demonstrations of how they did it in the old days—from rug-hooking to butter-churning to wooden-tool-making. The guides toss out useful data as well: "Count the number of fogs in August, and you can match the number of snows in the winter." Surprisingly fascinating. It's open 10 A.M.–5 P.M. daily May–October, until 3:30 P.M. November–February.

Across the street, the **Marsh-Billings-Rockefeller National Historic Park** (Rte. 12, 802/457-3368, www.nps.gov/mabi, $8, open daily 10 A.M.–5 P.M. June–mid-October), Vermont's first national park, was donated to the United States in 1992 by Frederick Billings's granddaughter, Mary French Rockefeller, and her husband, the late Laurance S. Rockefeller. The park interprets conservation history using the 1870 forest established by Billings as a case study. I highly recommend a guided tour of the family mansion and gardens.

Out toward the Quechee Gorge, the **Simon Pearce Gallery** (1760 Quechee Main St./Rte. 4, Quechee, 802/295-2711, www.simonpearce.com) is open 10 A.M.–9 P.M. daily. While the name suggests a colonial-era factory, this is actually part of a larger chain of glass galleries started by an Irish immigrant in 1981. The timeline doesn't diminish the quality of the work, however. After watching the artists whip a glass out of molten sand, you'll want to raise a glass to their skills. Quality glassware, as well as off-kilter factory seconds, is sold in the gift shop. If your house has settled at a slant, spring for the seconds.

Back in town, locals avoid the megamall googolplex and gather to enjoy movies in a refined setting at the **Town Hall Theatre** (802/457-2620) on the village green. Where else could you watch *Perils of Pauline* in Dolby?

Blue-Plate Specials

Here since 1955, **Wasp's Snack Bar** (57 Pleasant St., 802/457-3334) has diner stools at the counter and eggs, bacon, pancakes, hash browns, and coffee cooking and brewing behind it. You'll have to look for this local hangout, since the signage is minimal. No dinners here, but lunch offers anything the cook can make, plus homemade specials and soups. Nothing fancy, but it's just right.

Homemade "rich super premium" ice cream (served in the basement) is the foundation—as it should be—for **Mountain Creamery** (33 Central St., 802/457-1715). Upstairs, you can eat country breakfasts until 11:30 A.M. and big sandwiches noon–6:30 P.M. If you like your road food sweet, load up on pies, cakes, muffins, cookies, and brownies.

West of the village, on Route 4, is the **White Cottage Snack Bar** (462 Woodstock Rd., 802/457-3455), a *Happy Days*–era roadside diner that draws in tourists and riders who just want a messy hamburger, sloppy chili dog, and a full line of soda fountain treats. Also west of the village, about seven miles away in Bridgewater, is the **Long Trail Brewing Company** (junction of Rtes. 4 and 100A, Bridgewater

Corners, 802/672-5011, www.longtrail.com). Their visitor center is modeled after Munich's Hofbrau Haus and they serve six varieties of microbrews and great pub food, and feature an outdoor deck on the Ottauquechee River. This is a good place to grab lunch and a fresh beer. Watch your speed in Bridgewater—cops patrol it carefully.

Watering Holes

Since 1976, **Bentley's** (3 Elm St., 802/457-3232, www.bentleysrestaurant.com) has been Woodstock's neighborhood bar and, to be fair, restaurant. A few couches, a 1920s style long bar, and creaky wooden floors give this place after-hours appeal. Great lunches and dinners are served, but the microbrews, wines, and casual setting make this spot equally enjoyable for an evening conversation and a good drink—although it often gets wicked busy.

Shut-Eye

Motels and Motor Courts

The large and clean **Shire Motel** (46 Pleasant St., 802/457-2211, www.shiremotel.com, from $98 in summer) has been here since 1963. Situated in the heart of town, it has 42 rooms with all size beds.

A few miles west of town, **Pond Ridge Motel** (506 Rte. 4 W., 802/457-1667, www.pondridgemotel.com, $79–119 high season) offers 13 decent rooms with doubles or queens. If you're staying for a long period of time, consider one of the four rooms with kitchenettes.

Inn-dependence

The **Woodstocker B&B** (61 River St./Rte. 4, 802/457-3896, www.woodstockervt.com, from $110–250) seems like home, with fresh-baked cookies and breads laid out each afternoon. Board games, a whirlpool tub, and killer breakfasts with oven-puffed pancakes add to the effect. This is a great location within walking distance of the village and it has spacious rooms with queen or two double beds—although sounds can carry.

Smack dab on the village green, the largest and most upscale hotel in town, **Woodstock Inn** (14 The Green, 802/457-1100 or 800/448-7900, www.woodstockinn.com, $275 and up in summer), also includes Richardson's Tavern, a restaurant, and premium rooms overlooking a putting green. With 144 rooms, this inn is a popular spot for tourists with deep pockets, and its location and amenities may coax you to join them (if they'll offer an 80 percent discount).

Chain Drive

These chain hotels are in town, or within 10 miles of the city center:

Comfort Inn, Econo Lodge, Hampton Inn, Holiday Inn, Super 8

For more information, including phone numbers and websites, see page 439.

ON THE ROAD: WOODSTOCK TO STOWE

The moment you get home and put your bike in the garage, write a letter to the Vermont highway commissioner and say thanks for the additional 90 miles of SR 100 beyond Woodstock. At the intersection of Routes 4 and 100A South at Bridgewater Corners, you'll find a service station and general store. If you arrived by car, you'd get gas and snacks and leave. But on a bike, you'll want the experience to last. I sat on the porch, read the local bulletin board, watched people buy maple syrup, and enjoyed the reprieve from my routine. You'll have these experiences on the road, too—and often. Take advantage of them.

Routes 100 and 4 are the same for about six miles, and you'll ride north on SR 100 when Route 4 fades away. The road is slow and curving; the idea of a straightaway is foreign in Vermont, which I credit to Vermont's 1964 sale of surplus straightaways to Kansas.

As you swing into satisfying turns, you'll question whether this ride is actually the shortest route between Points A and B. It's not—and that's good. SR 100 rolls through gorgeous farmland, fields, and forest. It rides beside rivers and mountains. And it introduces you to the protectors of the free enterprise system: individuals who live miles from the shadow of a mall and make their living as independent merchants. In the yards of unpainted frame houses and log cabins, signs advertise bread, carved flutes, honey, antiques, artwork, and, of course, maple syrup. This short stretch slowly reveals the diversity of the nation and confirms that this motorcycle tour is a great American adventure.

You'll have little time to contemplate the sensations you feel, because roughly five miles past the split of Routes 4 and 100, you're in the thick of it. South of Pittsfield, you'll see yellow warning signs with the twisting black line that herald a series of quick turns that'll shift your bike beneath you like a hopped-up pendulum. Working the throttle, clutch, and brake in a symphony of shifting makes for a magical experience.

The bucolic nature of Vermont is on display. The roads weave randomly through this countryside, where the rusted edge of tin roofs sag lazily and crumbling mortar flakes off red chimneys. You'll see broken barns and unpainted covered bridges spanning rivers strewn with boulders. The road leads to tight turns and cramped quarters, changes in elevation compensating for monochromatic greenness. Cornfields and farmland don't offer much visual appeal, but if you're not a local, it's strangely satisfying to watch Vermont farmers turn the earth, work the combines, and roll tractors weighted beneath bales of hay.

Depending on its mood and the lay of land, the wide White River will surface on your left or right. With no guardrails to keep you out of the drink, keep one eye on the road and one on the river. The flowing road leads to a small village, the town of Rochester, where it's worth applying the brakes and taking a break. This commercial district is only about two blocks long, but it has everything a motorcyclist needs: a gas station, small market, and the **Rochester Cafe and Country Store** (SR 100, 802/767-4302), which features an old-fashioned soda fountain where you can order breakfast and hot and cold sandwiches.

The ride north from Rochester passes ordinary towns and villages every few miles, but the highlights you'll remember are the long stretches of emptiness. On the sloping roads south of Granville, gravity sucks you into a vortex of trees, leaves, and wild grass until you're completely enveloped by the environment. The Granville Gulf Reservation promises "six miles of natural beauty to be preserved forever." And it delivers. The force of nature is strong here: As you coast downhill, a stream on your right goes uphill. A great waterfall is on your left and it offers a splendid place to stop for a picture and a frigid spray of Vermont water.

The region changes from rural to upper class near Waitsfield. Between here and Morefield is the grandly titled "1800 to 1850 Mad River Valley Rural Historic District." Along with the nice homes and a sense of wilderness, the smell of pine mingles with the scent of stables.

This journey now comes to a close. When you reach SR 100B, Stowe is just 18 miles away. That's 18 more miles of mountains, smooth roads, Vermont farmlands,

and Waterbury—home of Ben & Jerry's, the ice cream capital of the world.

Life is good.

STOWE PRIMER

The village of Stowe lies about six miles southeast of the ski area, and the road north (Route 108) merits a visit as much as the village. Compared to Lenox and Woodstock, there's not much ground to cover here, but motorcycle travelers like going off on a tear along Routes 100 and 108, which intersect at the center of the village.

As far as background, the town was chartered in 1763 and named after descendants of England's Lord Stowe. As far as legend, most people recognize Stowe as a ski resort, although there's actually more of a summer theme in place. When Stowe began a gradual transformation into a resort destination more than a century ago, the main activities were shopping in the village, swimming in swimming holes, and riding up the mountain road to the peak of Mount Mansfield—at 4,393 feet, Vermont's highest point.

That's pretty much what happens today.

ON THE ROAD: STOWE

You've already ridden some of Vermont's best roads on the way up, but if you can't get enough of mountain riding then head north on Route 108 and ride up to Smuggler's Notch. Not only is this a most excellent road for motorcyclists, it was also a favorite route for independent Vermonters who smuggled goods from the United States to Canada during the 1807 Embargo Act. The road proved just as popular for transporting escaped slaves in the 1800s and bootleg liquor during Prohibition. This narrow, isolated road still threads the needle between Mount Mansfield and

Sterling Peak, carved through rock formations created about 400 million years ago. At the summit, you may be able to make out outcroppings like Elephant's Head, Singing Bird, and Smuggler's Face.

You may even run across some lost bootleggers.

PULL IT OVER: STOWE HIGHLIGHTS
Attractions and Adventures

Most of the town's attractions involve natural pursuits. At the **Fly Rod Shop** (2703 Waterbury Rd., 802/253-7346, www. flyrodshop.com), Bob Shannon and staff offer a complete selection of equipment, including locally tied flies and rod and wader rentals. Between May and October, guides can take you to the best fishing spots in the area. But do you have room in your saddlebags for a 20-pound king salmon? Well, do you—punk?

At **Catamount Fishing Adventures** (Barrows Rd., 802/253-8500, www.catamountfishing.com), Willy Dietrich offers four- to eight-hour fly-fishing or spin-fishing excursions in backwoods Vermont. The eight-hour trip includes a free lunch. Trips are based on your level of expertise, so if you normally fish with a shotgun, you're a beginner. Choose from canoe, float tube, small motorboat, or side stream tours in pursuit of trout, bass, and northern pike.

After hugging the road for days at a time, here's a chance to soar like an eagle. Glider rides at **Stowe Soaring** (Morrisville-Stowe State Airport Rte. 100, Morrisville, 802/888-7845 or 800/898-7845, www.stowesoaring.com) range from $99 for 10 minutes to $199 for 40 minutes, with $40/10-minute increments in between. If you've never soared, when the rope pops off the sailplane you'll at first be startled by the lack of engine noise (none, since there isn't an engine) and then thrilled that the experience feels as freeing as riding your motorcycle. From as much as a mile high, look for the Adirondacks to the west, Jay Peak to the north, Mount Washington to the east, and nothing but air below.

Several hundred years before roads were paved for you and for your bike, Native Americans were cruising the area in their canoes. With rivers and lakes laced across the Green Mountains, you can do the same in a rented kayak or canoe, gliding through farms and forested countryside on the wide and winding Lamoille and Winooski rivers. Three canoe and kayak outfitters are based in Stowe: **AJ's Ski & Sports** (350 Mountain Rd., 802/253-4593 or 800/226-6257, www.ajssports. com); **Umiak Outfitters** (849 S. Main St, 802/253-2317, www.umiak.com); and **Pinnacle Ski & Sports** (3391 Mountain Rd., 802/253-7222, www.pinnacleskisports. com). Since you can't transport a canoe yourself, find where the boats are already in the water. Kayaks rent for about $40 and canoes for about $45 for a full day, with discounts available if you book in advance. Be sure to ask about guided and self-guided river tours.

One of the most popular attractions in the area is located several miles south of Stowe on SR 100 and about a mile north of I-89. It's **Ben & Jerry's** (1281 Waterbury-Stowe Rd., 802/882-1240 or 866/258-6877, www.benjerry.com) and it's pretty interesting. Backed by $5 business diplomas from a correspondence course and a collective life savings of $8,000, in 1978 Ben Cohen and Jerry Greenfield found an abandoned gas station in Burlington and opened an ice-cream parlor. Not only did they vow to use only fresh Vermont ingredients in their ice cream, they also pledged 7.5

percent of pretax profits to employee-led philanthropy. This is the way a business should be run—and the way ice cream should taste. Take the half-hour first-come, first-served tour for $3 and then score some free ice cream hauled up straight from the production line. Beats touring a fertilizer factory.

To walk off the ice cream, when you get back to Stowe put on your walking shoes and set out for a trip past mountains, woods, and farms. The **Stowe Recreation Path** is a 5.5-mile greenway that stretches from Main Street along the West Branch River and Mountain Road to the covered bridge at Brook Road. If you go the distance, keep in mind it'll be another 5.5 miles back. Footnote: The path was named by *Travel + Leisure* as one of the "19 Great Walks of the World."

Blue-Plate Specials

There are absolutely no fast food joints in Stowe, so get ready for some real food. The gathering spot for locals, **McCarthy's** (454 Mountain Rd., 802/253-8626), serves one of the best breakfasts in town. Stick around and chow down on homemade breads, soups, and pie at lunch. The food is cheap and healthy.

At dinnertime, look for **Cactus Cafe** (2160 Mountain Rd./Rte. 108, 802/253-7770, www.cactuscafestowe.com), known as much for its tequilas and 16-ounce handmade margaritas as for its food. Along with Mexican standards (enchiladas, fajitas, quesadillas), are ranch camp ribs and sirloin steaks. If you can't get enough of the great outdoors (who can?), dine in the perennial garden.

If you've got a hankering for wild boar, venison, or pheasant, park it at **Mr. Pickwick's** (433 Mountain Rd., 802/253-7064, www.englandinn.com). It's open daily for lunch and dinner and serves more than

150 varieties of ale, including fresh wheat beer and lambic ales from Belgium. Have a designated rider in your group? Then try one of each. Gotta cigar? Complement it with your choice from the selection of vintage ports, rare cognacs, and single malt scotches.

Watering Holes

In the center of town, **The Whip Bar and Grill** (18 Main St., 802/253-7301, www.greenmountaininn.com) is downstairs at the Green Mountain Inn. Sure, it's a hotel bar, but it feels more like a pub, with its high-back chairs and English riding club design. They serve meals here, and enhance them with great brews.

Gracie's (18 Edson Hill Rd., 802/253-8741) became so popular in a basement bar downtown, that it moved into a much larger location on Edson Road. The new location features a patio, bar, and a menu of burgers, nachos, seafood, and steaks.

At the **Backyard Tavern** (395 Mountain Rd., 802/253-9204) you'll find a basic bar menu with cheeseburgers and chicken fingers, a pool table, a great jukebox, pinball, and $3 draft pints daily.

Try the **Sunset Grille & Tap Room** (140 Cottage Club Rd., 802/253-9281). There's a restaurant here also, but in the Tap Room you can dine on wings, bar pizzas, burgers, and BBQ while watching sports shown on a variety of TVs. Occasionally, the place hosts a cookout on the patio, and pickup horseshoe and volleyball games shape up out back. When you're bored with that, check out the huge domestic beer selection.

Shut-Eye

In the village, **Stowe's Visitor Information Center** (51 Main St., 802/253-7321 or 800/247-8693, www.gostowe.com) also assists travelers with lodging, and there are

40-plus independent inns, hotels, and motels, which offer more than 1,700 rooms. **Stowe Country Homes** (541 South Main St., 802/253-8132, www.stowecountryhomes.com) represents more than a dozen rental cabins, farms, and resorts. If you're traveling with a large group and need a base, check 'em out.

Motels and Motor Courts

After a long day, the **Stowe Inn** (123 Mountain Rd., 802/253-4030 or 800/546-4030, www.stoweinn.com) can make your night. The staff is friendly, the rooms are warm and comforting, and the living room and lounge are designed for a relaxing post-ride conversation. A standard room goes for $99 mid-week and $119 weekends in summer, and the complimentary continental breakfast puts everything over the top.

About 2.5 miles north of the village is the clean and basic **Stowe Motel** (2043 Mountain Rd., 802/253-7629 or 800/829-7629, www.stowemotel.com, $88 and up off-season, $110 and up high season). Sixty rooms and efficiencies are spread between three properties, with king and queen beds at each. Rooms include a continental breakfast.

Inn-dependence

Right in the heart of town, the **Green Mountain Inn** (18 Main St., 802/253-7301 or 800/253-7302, www.greenmountaininn.com, $159 and up high season) is a renovated 1833 home-turned-inn.

It features 81 antiques-filled rooms, 15 suites, 4 efficiencies, and 5 townhomes. The central location and amenities, including a health club, heated outdoor pool, canopy beds, fireplaces, and whirlpool tubs, are just right after the ride. So is the pub. There's a two-night minimum on summer and fall weekends.

After Julie Andrews and Christopher Plummer escaped from the Nazis—no, wait…that was the movie—anyway, after the Von Trapp family left Austria, they wound up in its American counterpart, Stowe, and opened the **Trapp Family Lodge** (Rte. 108—up two miles from town, left at the white church, then two more miles, 802/253-8511 or 800/826-7000, www.trappfamily.com, $245 and up high season). The lodge has sustained itself in large part on the strength of the family's story. Included on the 2,500 acres are 96 rooms in the main lodge with spectacular mountain views, nightly entertainment, a fitness center, three pools, tennis courts, and hiking trails. On Sundays in the summer, there are concerts in the Trapp Family Lodge Concert Meadow, a natural amphitheater. The dining room, lounge, and tearoom feature a European theme.

Chain Drive

These chain hotels are in town, or within 10 miles of the city center:

Clarion

For more information, including phone numbers and websites, see page 439.

Resources for Riders

Berkshires–Central Vermont Run

Massachusetts Travel Information
Massachusetts Road Conditions—617/374-1234
Massachusetts State Park Campgrounds Reservations—877/422-6762,
    www.reserveamerica.com
Massachusetts Department of Travel & Tourism—617/973-8500 or
    800/227-6277, www.massvacation.com

Vermont Travel Information
Vermont Attractions Association—802/229-4581, www.vtattractions.org
Vermont Campground Association—www.campvermont.com
Vermont Chamber of Commerce—802/223-3443, www.vtchamber.com
Vermont Department of Forests, Parks, and Recreation—802/241-3655 or
    888/409-7579, www.vtstateparks.com
Vermont Department of Tourism—802/828-3237 or 800/837-6668,
    www.travel-vermont.com
Vermont Fall Foliage Hotline—802/828-3239 or 800/837-6668,
    www.vermontfallfoliage.com
Vermont Fish and Wildlife—802/241-3700, www.vtfishandwildlife.com
Vermont Hospitality Council—www.visitvt.com
Vermont Road Conditions—http://511.vermont.gov

Local and Regional Information
Berkshires Visitors Bureau—413/743-4500, www.berkshires.org
Lenox Chamber of Commerce—413/637-3646, www.lenox.org
Stowe Chamber of Commerce—802/253-7321 or 877/467-8693,
    www.gostowe.com
Woodstock Chamber of Commerce—802/457-3555 or 888/496-6378,
    www.woodstockvt.com

Massachusetts Motorcycle Shops
North's Service—675 Lenox Rd., Lenox, 413/499-3266 or 866/499-3266,
    www.northsservice.com
Ronnie's Cycle Sales & Service—150 Howland Ave., Adams, 413/743-0715;
    and 501 Wahconah St., Pittsfield, 413/443-0638, www.ronnies.com
RPM's Cycle Sales & Service—326 Merrill Rd., Pittsfield, 413/443-5659

Vermont (and nearby New Hampshire) Motorcycle Shops
Granite State Harley-Davidson—351 Miracle Mile, Lebanon, NH,
    603/448-4664, www.granitestateharley.com
Lebanon Motor Sports—63 Evans Dr., Lebanon, NH, 603/448-9434,
    www.lebanonmotorsports.com
Ronnie's Cycle Sales & Service—2601 West Rd., Rte. 9, Bennington,
    802/447-4606, www.ronnies.com

Hudson River Valley Run

Tarrytown, New York to Saratoga Springs, New York

If you've avoided touring New York State because friends convinced you there was nothing here but the traffic of New York City, tune them out, tap your bike into gear, twist the throttle, and head up the Hudson River.

Twenty-five miles north of NYC are the neighboring communities of Tarrytown and Sleepy Hollow, a perfect base from which to begin a tour of the Hudson River Valley. Though close to the capital of capitalism, it's worlds away in texture and feel. You might think you took a wrong turn in Bavaria, but this is indeed America—an America that began more than 150 years before the nation existed. The villages and the following 180 miles will introduce you to a world of distinctive literature, art, history, and cuisine. They will also offer great river roads, hills, scenic vistas, pubs, and diners and lead you into the outstanding Adirondacks.

TARRYTOWN PRIMER

Although Tarrytown looks like an active modern suburb, the sense of history here is omnipresent. In the early 1600s, this area was home to a tribe of the Mohegan family, the Weckquaesgeek. They lived, fished, hunted, and traded along the Pocantico River relatively undisturbed until 1609 when Henry Hudson sailed up the river searching for the northwest passage to India. When he got home he had a technician adjust his GPS system.

Settlers began arriving soon after. The Dutch named the area Slaeperig Haven (Sleepy Harbor) for its sheltered anchorage. Other Dutch settlers arrived, and by 1685, Frederick Philipse owned nearly half of what is now Westchester County. In the 1730s, members of the Livingston family began building riverfront estates, such as Clermont, Wilderstein, and Montgomery Place, all of which are open for tours.

Fast forward to the American Revolution. British soldier/spy John André was captured here, and the papers he was carrying revealed Benedict Arnold's traitorous plan to surrender West Point. A half century later, in 1820, Rip Van Winkle's

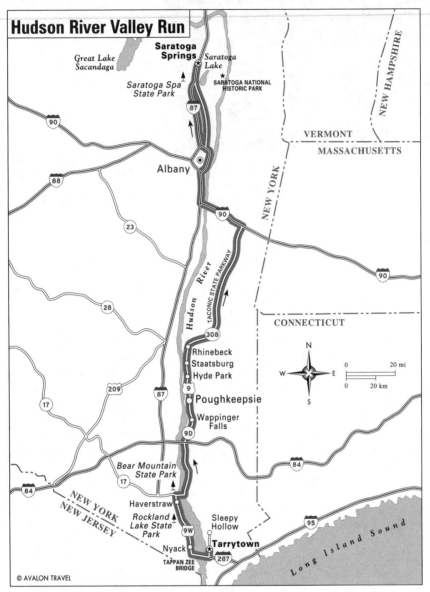

Hudson River Valley Run

Route: Tarrytown to Saratoga Springs via Nyack, Bear Mountain State Park, Hyde Park, Staatsburg, Rhinebeck, Taconic State Parkway

Distance: Approximately 180 miles

First Leg: Tarrytown to Hyde Park (88 miles)

Second Leg: Hyde Park to Saratoga Springs (92 miles)

Helmet Laws: New York requires helmets.

© AVALON TRAVEL

creator, Washington Irving, drew further attention to the region with the publication of *The Legend of Sleepy Hollow.*

The tranquil area continued to grow. The second half of the 1800s saw freight arrive and depart by river and rail. Factories were built, followed by estates built by the people who built the factories. With the likes of Jay Gould, William Dodge, and John D. and William Rockefeller taking up summer residence, Tarrytown became a destination for the wealthy until the Great Depression, when new income taxes forced many of the *nouveau poore* to give up their estates.

In the mid-1950s, the Tappan Zee Bridge and New York State Thruway were built, opening up the town for commuters. City workers began driving up from NYC and driving up real estate prices. Today, Tarrytown still displays a distinct degree of affluence. So look sharp.

ON THE ROAD: TARRYTOWN

When you arrive in Tarrytown, give yourself a moment to adjust to your surroundings. Couples walk past carrying bags of fresh produce; neighbors stop and pass the time outside antique shops; and merchants thank God they're not working in a mall. You may think you've entered Pleasantville, but you're cruising through one of the oldest villages in America.

Tarrytown's main drag isn't really Main Street but Route 9, the road of choice for buses, trucks, teens, tourists, seniors, and soccer moms hauling vanloads of ball-kicking kids. With all of this traffic buzzing around, it's best to just park your bike and explore on foot. There are several antiques shops and galleries here and if you follow the scents emanating from bakeries, gourmet shops, ethnic restaurants, and coffee bars, you'll eventually arrive in the heart of downtown, which encompasses about six square blocks.

Since Tarrytown is primarily a residential area, amusing diversions are few, but give yourself at least a few hours to roam the streets. The **Sleepy Hollow Tarrytown Chamber of Commerce** (54 Main St., 914/631-1705, www.sleepyhollowchamber.com) is a smart first stop. Located in a narrow building next to the fire station on Main Street, this is where you can score information from the rack of brochures. If something sparks your interest, track it down. If there's little for you here, just consider this the perfect starting line for an extraordinarily full ride.

PULL IT OVER: TARRYTOWN HIGHLIGHTS
Attractions and Adventures

Sometimes, there's a whole lotta shakin' going on at the **Music Hall** (13 Main St., 914/631-3390, www.tarrytownmusichall.org). Built in 1885, this hall is one of the oldest in Westchester County and has hosted over a century of performances by artists like Bruce Springsteen, Chuck Mangione, Tito Puente, Dave Brubeck, Tony Bennett, Judy Collins, Dizzy Gillespie, Lionel Hampton, Lyle Lovett, Wynton Marsalis, Tom Paxton, and Leon Redbone. Folk and classical concerts are performed here as well, and the acoustics are alleged to rival those of Carnegie Hall. If there's a show in town, listen up.

For music of a different sort, head to the banks of the Pocantico River in **Rockefeller State Park Preserve** (Route 117, 1 mile east of Route 9, 914/631-1470, www.friendsrock.org). Washington Irving described it as "one of the quietest places in the whole wide world. A small brook glides through it, with just murmur enough to lull one to repose." If you stow a rod and reel, brown trout are here for catch-and-release fly-fishing, and you can find bass in Swan Lake. Non-resident day licenses (about ten bucks) can be purchased at the park office or Sleepy Hollow Village Hall.

A few miles north of town, you can ride your bike onto an estate to see how the other 0.0001 percent lives. When John D. Rockefeller got tired of living in a dumpy fixer-upper, he had Johnny Jr. build **Kykuit** (pronounced KI-cut, Route 9, entrance at Philipsburg Manor, 914/631-9491, www.hudsonvalley.org), which means "high place." The neoclassical country mansion and gardens, which overlook the Hudson, were completed in 1913 and served as home to four generations of Rockefellers, including Nelson A., who added 20th-century sculptures to the estate's gardens. Vintage carriages and cars (such as a 1918 Crane Simplex) are on display in the Coach Barn, and there's a café on site. It may not be something you've planned to do on a motorcycle tour, but this is a magnificent American estate. Reservations are suggested, with different styles of tours requiring different fees, from $23. Kykuit is open daily except Tuesdays May–October.

When you're in Tarrytown, remember that right next door is Sleepy Hollow. For a road story you'll tell later, retrace the route Ichabod Crane used to flee from the Headless Horseman in *The Legend of Sleepy Hollow*. To duplicate Ichabod's flight, take Route 9 from Patriot's Park (along the old Albany Post Road) to the Sleepy Hollow Bridge under the shadow of the Old Dutch Church. Watch your head.

Shopping

Get within 25 feet of fragrant **Tarrytown Gourmet** (45 Broadway, 914/366-6800) and your schnoz will go into olfactory overdrive. Provisions include fresh pears, mangoes, sweet red plums, olive oil, hot pepper oil, cookies, gourmet pizzas, olives, salami, imported cheeses, candies and cakes, iced drinks, teas, and coffees. Here's a place to get fat and happy and pack up a picnic for the road ahead.

Blue-Plate Specials

Since 1985, **Santa Fe Restaurant** (5 Main St., 914/332-4452, www.santaferestaurant. com) has succeeded by serving Mexican and Southwestern cuisine in the heart of Dutch country. Go figure. Home-cooked without flavor enhancers, all dishes can be spiced to your satisfaction and tolerance for pain. The comfortable neighborhood feel is matched by a full range of Mexican beers and more than 30 premium tequilas. *¡Muy bueno!* The restaurant is open daily for lunch and dinner.

The type of restaurant you look for on a ride, **Horsefeathers** (94 N. Broadway, 914/631-6606) has a pub-style atmosphere with home-style comfort foods like meatloaf, burgers, and mashed potatoes, along with soups, pasta, steaks, and chicken. The big draw is the extensive collection of beers—more than 100 micros—from across the country and around the world. Homey and comfortable, Horsefeathers is open daily for lunch and dinner.

Sunset Cove (238 Green St. at Washington Irving Boat Club, 914/366-7889, www.sunsetcove.net) may have the nicest view on the Hudson. The menu features soups, salads, and sandwiches at lunch, primarily seafood at dinner. The real appeal is the outdoor dining on the river itself—enjoy BBQ and the tiki bar. Pull up a chair on the patio and peer beneath the Tappan Zee Bridge for a view of the New York City skyline 25 miles away. A definite stop for riders.

Shut-Eye

There are few inns in Tarrytown, so if you need to stay the night, you'll probably wind up at one of the chains below—the less expensive options are across the Hudson in Nyack.

Chain Drive

These chain hotels are in town, or within 10 miles of the city center:

Best Western, Comfort Inn, Courtyard by Marriott, Days Inn, Hampton Inn, Hilton, Holiday Inn, Hyatt, La Quinta, Ramada, Residence Inn, Sheraton, Super 8

For more information, including phone numbers and websites, see page 439.

ON THE ROAD: TARRYTOWN TO HYDE PARK

Like John Lennon, New York has a fascination with the number 9. Within a few miles of Tarrytown, you'll discover Route 9, Route 9A, Route 9W, Route 9G, and Route 9D. Right now, head to Route 9W by going west over the Tappan Zee Bridge (aka I-287/I-87/New York State Thruway) into Rockland County, and let the joy begin.

As you roll over the Tappan Zee Bridge, the mighty Hudson River floods past 150 feet below. The setting captured on canvas by 19th-century Hudson River School artists will no longer seem embellished as you begin your ride through a landscape that rivals the magnitude of a Greek epic poem. When you peer downriver to the hazy outline of New York City, you'll picture—if not Odysseus and his crew—then Hudson's ship, the *Half Moon,* under full sail.

A few miles past the bridge, Route 9W branches north off I-287 and heads into the hills. You can decide to ride Route 9 north along the river road past the towns of Nyack and Haverstraw, but a local rider turned me on to a better alternative: By staying on I-287/I-87 and following it northwest, you'll soon be riding along the southern edge of **Harriman State Park**

West Point

I was never in the military, but my mom took me to Marineland once. If you're interested in military history, **West Point** (Route 218, 845/938-2638, www. usma.edu) is worth the six-mile detour north from Bear Mountain State Park. Washington garrisoned his troops here during the Revolutionary War, and in 1802, President Jefferson signed the act of Congress creating the U.S. Military Academy. And that's not all: Lee, Grant, Patton, Eisenhower, and Schwarzkopf all learned to march here.

Since September 11, 2001, it's been more difficult, but not impossible, to gain access to West Point. You can travel onto the post if there's a specific event such as a chapel service, football game, or an event at the performance arts center. Even easier, you can sign up for a tour. Two tours—one an hour, the other two—depart from the Visitors Center and will take you by the Main Cadet Chapel, Trophy Point, and the Parade Field with the longer tour adding the Old Cadet Chapel and West Point Cemetery. To schedule a tour, call 845/446-4724 or visit www.westpointtours.com. If you don't have time for a tour, the Visitors Center, which features a 30-minute movie, is open 9 A.M.– 4:45 P.M., and the West Point Museum is right next door.

(845/786-2701). Stay on the road until you reach Route 17 in Sloatsburg and keep an eye out on your right for the entrance to picturesque Seven Lakes Drive. This is a cool, serene, lonely ride through the woods, which reveals, yes, seven lakes—Sebago, Tiorati, Stahahe, Askoti, Cohasset, Kanawaukee, and Skannatati.

This is when you derive the pure pleasure of motorcycling. Feel the fresh air on your skin and in your lungs and listen to the hum of the bike as you ride for miles through the forest and approach a new paradise: **Bear Mountain State Park** (845/786-2701, www.friendsofpalisades.org), a must-see for a high-altitude ride and stunning views of the valley. For motorcycle travelers, the real appeal of the park is ascending Bear Mountain. Passage to the peak comes when you slip off of Seven Lakes Drive and onto Perkins Memorial Drive, a road that introduces another memorable motorcycling moment. Be warned: If you suffer from vertigo, dropsy, or the shakes, don't take this ride since the road twists like your drunken uncle at a wedding reception. While the speed limit is a sensible 25 mph, you could push it to 26 since small boulders have been thoughtfully placed along the road's edge to keep you from going over it. If you take it between summer and the fall foliage season, it is nearly empty and the forest is moist and cool. The downside: On the ride up, sheer drops fall off to your left, and branches and wet leaves can send you skidding. Still, the road is worth the price of admission (free) since you'll be treated to a kaleidoscope of majestic vistas. The beautiful valleys stretched out like long, verdant branches must have been touched by the finger of God. This is America.

When you reach the peak, derive pleasure from the solitude and serenity. An abundance of table-size boulders makes it easy to spread out a picnic, and if you travel off-season or just after a holiday weekend, chances are only a few random travelers will join you.

When it's time to descend, place your bike in neutral and coast; the silence is satisfying. Though it may be slightly dangerous to pull over, do so if there's no traffic behind you—the view of the Hudson River and Bear Mountain Bridge will stay with you forever. The rest of the ride will find you "in the zone" as you begin swinging into corners, diving into short stretches of canopy roads, and cowering beneath boulders looming over the road until you return to Bear Mountain Circle at the confluence of three highways. Right now you're at the circa 1915 Bear Mountain Inn which is worth a stop, if for no other reason than to score a great souvenir picture—its rock and wood construction recalls a Yosemite lodge. Picnic tables, a pool, and Hessian Lake are adjacent to the inn, and there are trails where you can take a walk and think about the ride so far.

From the entrance/exit here, you've come full circle to Route 9W North, which you'll follow toward the Bear Mountain Bridge. Like crossing the Tappan Zee from Tarrytown, crossing east to Route 9D reminds you why you're on a bike. If your timing is right, you may even ride over the speeding Montrealer, the train that slips up the Hudson on the riverside rail between NYC and Canada.

Now you're in Putnam County and on Route 9D (aka the Hudson Greenway Trail) which is a beautiful mountain road that hugs the base of the hills. Passing Phillipstown, the Hudson darts in and out of view nearly as often as the white picket fences, evergreens, and estate homes. The road sticks with the Hudson as you drive north, passing small general stores hawking beer and sandwiches and also a castle on a hill. You may be tempted to speed, but force yourself to relax. You can hurry at work, but when you're traveling...please take your time.

The twists and turns continue into Wappinger Falls, where you'll reach a bridge in the center of town. If you turn left and continue to follow Route 9D, the road is scenic, though not as fast, and eventually leads to your first major commercial center: Poughkeepsie. You, being on a journey of discovery, are not going to settle for this or settle down here. After hooking up with Route 9, keep heading north to your first overnight: Hyde Park.

HYDE PARK PRIMER

Just as fans of Mark Twain trek to Hannibal and worshippers of Donny Osmond pilgrimage to Utah, students of history head to Hyde Park. Along with World War II veterans and Depression-era children who grew up on relief packages, baby boomers, scholars, and foreign tourists whose countries were saved by Franklin Delano Roosevelt arrive to pay their respects to the 32nd president, whose home and gravesite are located here.

Most of us have heard of Hyde Park, so it's a bonus that it turns out to be a perfect place to rest your bike, stay the night, enjoy a decent meal, and get an education. In 1705, New York provincial governor Edward Hyde presented this parcel of land to his secretary, Peter Fuconnier. Hyde's munificence earned him a namesake estate and, later, a namesake town, established in 1821. Mills sprang up on Hudson River tributaries, and, by the turn of the 20th century, Roosevelts, Vanderbilts, and other wealthy families began settling in.

ON THE ROAD: HYDE PARK

Sorry, there is no true commercial district within Hyde Park—and that's one of its assets. The town rests along a straightaway highlighted with a handful of attractions, so take it for what it is: a quiet and historically significant stop between Tarrytown and Saratoga Springs.

PULL IT OVER:
HYDE PARK HIGHLIGHTS
Attractions and Adventures

If FDR had never achieved national prominence, you may never have heard of Hyde Park. But he did, and today the **FDR National Historic Site** (4079 Albany Post Rd./Rte. 9, 845/229-9115 for headquarters or 800/337-8474, www.nps.gov/hofr) is a shrine for those who want to see how this pastoral countryside helped shape an extraordinary man. With the exception of 13 years in Washington and a few more in Albany, FDR spent his entire life here. This is also his resting place; he and Eleanor are buried in a rose garden adjacent to the house. Unless you arrive with the NPS America the Beautiful Pass, admission is $14 for the house and museum tour, $7 for the FDR museum alone.

The tour starts in the visitors center where, if you're not familiar with the arc of his life, a 22-minute film, *A Rendezvous With History,* will prepare you for what's to come. His home, once known as Springwood, is filled with original books, china, paintings, furniture, and an old kitchen chair modified slightly by FDR himself—with the addition of wheels, it became his favorite wheelchair. In the **FDR Presidential Library and Museum** (the first presidential museum ever built), the desk demands special attention. It's just as it was on the day he died in April 1945. Motorcyclists may get a kick out of the 1938 Ford Phaeton shown in the basement. It's equipped with manual controls for the disabled president. After hours spent roaming the estate, however, I found the most

Art of the Valley

If you experience a sense of déjà vu along the Hudson, you may have seen it before…During the 1800s, popular imagination considered the Hudson to be the American Rhine, and its imposing country estates surely rivaled those of the German river or the chateaux of the French Loire district. Frederick Church and fellow artists captured this prevailing sentiment in an art movement called the Hudson River School. Images of the trees and lakes, waterfalls and rivers of the Hudson and Catskill Mountains were adorned with Grecian temples and sweeping panoramas. As you ride through the valley, the essence of those images will reappear time and again—minus the Grecian temples.

intriguing and touching displays were the letters and gifts the president received from average Americans expressing gratitude for the relief programs that put them back to work. The site is open 9 A.M.–5 P.M. daily.

You can't think of Franklin without thinking of his wife Eleanor, the woman he referred to as his "legs and eyes" since she was ready and able to go where he couldn't—from coal mines to the front lines—and report back on issues of importance. Still, FDR and his mother froze Eleanor out of their world and the tacit agreement was that Eleanor would reside a few miles away at Val-Kill (Stone Cottage). Established as a furniture factory to provide work to local artisans, Val-Kill served as Eleanor's retreat from 1926 until 1945. After FDR died, it became her primary residence and a gathering place for world leaders, including Churchill, JFK, Krushchev, Nehru, and Marshall Tito (who left the Jackson Five to lead Yugoslavia). **Val-Kill** (Rte. 9G, 800/337-8474, www.nps.gov/elro, $8) now serves as the Eleanor Roosevelt National Historic Site. It's open 9 A.M.–5 P.M. daily in summer, 9 A.M.–5 P.M. Thursday–Monday off-season.

Nobody muttered, "there goes the neighborhood" when the Vanderbilts moved to town. **Vanderbilt Mansion** (Rte. 9, 845/229-7770, www.nps.gov/vama, $8) reflects that family's obsession with building homes large enough to drain the kids' inheritance. This Beaux-Arts mansion was the home of Louise and publicity-shy Frederick, who, like myself, was recognized primarily for being a splendid yachtsman, a gentleman farmer, and an "unassuming philanthropist." Louise died in 1926 and Freddy in 1938, and Louise's niece inherited the property a year before she told her neighbor (FDR) that she was donating it to the nation. As you leave the grounds, on your left is an overlook with a tremendous view of the mighty Hudson. The home is open 9 A.M.–5 P.M. daily, December–April.

In Hyde Park, the CIA isn't educating double naught spies. Here, the CIA is the **Culinary Institute of America** (845/471-6608, www.ciachef.edu). Down the road on Route 9, it is the only residential college in the world devoted entirely to culinary education. Founded in 1946 in New Haven, Connecticut, the school moved into this turn-of-the-20th-century former Jesuit seminary in 1972. Today, college-age apprentice chefs, servers, and maître d's at the 150-acre campus are—surprisingly—studying alongside doctors, lawyers, and stockbrokers who dropped out of their careers to do something fun. You may see the campus when you drop in to eat, although one-hour tours (845/451-1588, $5) conducted by students are available 10 A.M. and/or 4 P.M. on Mondays, Wednesdays, and Thursdays.

If your alter-ego is an angler and you want to catch your own meal, the river, streams, ponds, and creeks here are well-stocked with rainbow, brook, and brown trout, as well as bluegills, sunfish, bullhead, rock bass, and small and large striper. For guide services, check out **Hudson Valley Angler** (Red Hook, 845/758-9203, www.hudsonvalleyangler.com).

Blue-Plate Specials

If this is a once-in-a-lifetime ride, consider a once-in-a-lifetime dining experience. The aforementioned **Culinary Institute of America** (Rte. 9, 845/471-6608 for reservations, www.ciachef.edu) features four student-staffed restaurants and a bakery that open to the public. If you travel with appropriate dress in your saddlebags, take a break from the roadside diners and enjoy a classic meal at the American Bounty (regional and seasonal), St. Andrew's Cafe (casual contemporary à la carte), Escoffier (French cuisine), or Caterina de Medici (fine Italian). Prices are slightly lower than they will be when your CIA chef begins working for a five-star restaurant a few weeks hence. The restaurants are closed the first three weeks of July, December 20–January 5, and some holidays.

The retro 1930s American diner decor is right on target at **Eveready Diner** (Rte. 9, 845/229-8100, www.theevereadydiner. com), and so is the menu for motorcycle travelers. Pull up here and order from a menu featuring soups, burgers, and daily specials (the beef stew is great on a cold day). The diner is open 24 hours Friday and Saturday, 5 A.M.–1 A.M. weekdays.

An inspiring American tale is revealed at **Coppola's** (Rte. 9, 845/229-9113), where an immigrant family arrived in 1954, grew dissatisfied as dishwashers, and opened their first local restaurant in 1961. Now there are three restaurants run by the family's second generation. This is traditional Italian cuisine, with extraordinary veal parmigiana, penne à la gorgonzola, and seafood specials served indoors or on the deck.

Watering Holes

In 1933 as he signed the bill ending Prohibition, FDR was quoted as saying, "I think this would be a good time for a beer." Six decades later, some locals at the **Hyde Park Brewing Company** (4076 Albany Post Rd., 845/229-8277, www.hydeparkbrewing.com) took up the cause in this microbrewery across from Roosevelt's birthplace. One of Hyde Park's rare nightspots to boast a full bar and live music, the pub serves six beers (including Rough Rider Red Lager and Von Schtupp's Black Lager)—all brewed right here. The pub is open daily.

Sports fans and Irishmen hang out 'til the wee hours at **Darby O'Gill's** (3969 Albany Post Rd., 845/229-6662). It's open daily, or maybe I should say nightly, since closing time isn't until 4 A.M. Along with beer and mixed drink specials, there are massive high-def televisions.

Shut-Eye

The choices of lodging in Hyde Park range from motels to...motels. Contact the Chamber for a complete list, or to find larger inns and chains, backtrack to Poughkeepsie.

Motels and Motor Courts

The same family that runs Coppola's restaurant also runs the **Village Square Country Inn** (4167 Albany Post Rd., 229/7141, www.coppolas.net, $70 and up), which has 22 rooms, an outdoor pool, and provides a continental breakfast. Otherwise, the **Roosevelt Inn** (4360 Albany Post Rd., 845/229-2443, www.roosevelt-innofhydepark.com, $70–135) is a good, old-fashioned American motel. Try one of 25 clean rooms, some with king beds and some with fridges. Get off to a good start at the retro coffee shop, serving breakfast 7–11 A.M. The **Quality Inn** (4142 Albany Post Rd., 845/229-0088, $60 and up) is clean and cheap. Along with its 61 basic economy rooms, it tosses in a continental breakfast, cable TV, and a clerk on duty 'round the clock.

Inn-dependence

If you have an urge to splurge, stay at the **Belvedere Mansion** (10 Old Rte. 9, Staatsburg, 845/889-8000, www.belvederemansion.com, $225 and up), where the hillside setting at this spa-turned-inn offers a great view of the Hudson. The first floor of the main house is a restaurant (as well as a handy pub) and the upstairs features six rooms adorned with 18th-century French antiques and trompe l'oeil cloud-painted ceilings. Riders who share my budget may opt to bunk down in the converted stable, which is now a row of reasonably priced rooms ($95 and up) featuring queen beds, private baths, and a patio. The gravel driveway is a nuisance for kickstands, but if you're riding solo, a single concrete slab will hold your bike.

Chain Drive

These chain hotels are in town, or within 10 miles of the city center:
Econo Lodge, Quality Inn, Rodeway

For more information, including phone numbers and websites, see page 439.

ON THE ROAD: HYDE PARK TO SARATOGA SPRINGS

Leaving Hyde Park, the two-lane road begins with some slow curves accented by stands of pines. The village itself—just a few stores and shops—can be bypassed to embark on the next leg of your journey. Although there are no identifiable signs, from here to Germantown in neighboring Columbia County, you'll be riding through the Mid-Hudson Valley, a 32-square-mile area recognized by the Department of the Interior as a National Historic Landmark District.

Miles north, you'll cruise through the village of Rhinebeck, which—midway between Albany and New York—was a logical stop for commercial river and road traffic. At the corner of Route 9 and East Market Street (Rte. 308) is the intersection of the old King's Highway and Sepasco Indian Trail. On your left is the circa 1766 **Beekman Arms** (845/876-7077, www.beekmandelamaterinn.com) which boasts that it's the oldest inn in America. Although you'll find a few hundred other "oldest inns" around the country, "The Beek" gets points for hosting George Washington, Benjamin Harrison, and FDR—who wrapped up each gubernatorial and presidential campaign with a front-porch speech. In 1775, this was the Bogardus Tavern, a bar that stayed open while the Fourth Regiment of the Continental Army drilled on its front lawn before the war. If you're tired enough to stop, but not tired enough to stay the night, kick back with an ale in the warm, rich setting of the Colonial Tap Room.

If your schedule allows, take Route 9 north, detour onto Stone Church

Road, and head to the **Old Rhinebeck Aerodrome** (9 Norton Rd., Red Hook, 914/752-3200, www.oldrhinebeck.org), an antique aircraft museum that displays World War I and Lindbergh-era aircraft such as a 1917 Fokker DR-1 tri-plane, a 1915 Newport 11, and a 1918 Curtiss-Jenny, along with old cars and vintage motorcycles including several Indians, a 1913 Excelsior, 1909 Merkel Light, and a 1916 Royal Enfield with sidecar. At 2 P.M. mid-June–October Saturdays and Sundays, it also presents a flying circus reminiscent of the Great Waldo Pepper. If you're ready to get off the bike, drop $65 bucks and climb into a 1929 open cockpit biplane for a 15-minute barnstorming ride. The aerodrome is open 10 A.M.–5 P.M. daily mid-May–late October. Admission costs $10 Monday–Friday, $20 for the weekend air show.

If there's time to spare, Routes 9G and 9J roughly follow the Hudson all the way to Albany. If time is tight, turn right onto East Market Street (Rte. 308) just past the Beekman Arms and motor past splendid examples of Italianate revival homes and Victorian architecture. If you've spent the morning in Hyde Park, it may be afternoon as you head east—so as the sun settles over the Hudson, you'll feel the warmth on your back and smell the scent of the forest as you cruise down the road. Long shadows fall before your bike, and Little Wappinger Creek occasionally skims into view. In the early fall, acres of harvested cornfields accent the landscape, and the country ride becomes distinguished by its even, level serenity. Six miles after you turn onto Route 308 in a lazy loop toward Rock City, the road becomes Route 199.

The pleasure of cruising through four more miles of farmland will adjust your attitude and prepare you to ride one of the most beautiful roads in America. The Taconic State Parkway (TSP) cautions it is for "passenger cars only," but the sign is obviously the work of some corrupt anti-motorcycle administration. Rest assured that motorcycles are allowed.

Even if you forsake river views, the road is faster and less congested than Route 9. The result is that you'll enjoy a ride that acknowledges that life may be short, but it can be big.

The road is so pristine that the sweeps and dips and gentle drops affirm your existence. The cool air and sweet smell of your surroundings are only part of the adventure. You'll drop close to a hundred feet in less than a mile; you'll encounter stunning views and roadside wildflowers, black ash, slippery elm, arrowwood. Scenic overlooks punctuate the parkway. Look for one in Columbia County where the historic Livingston Manor stood, once the focal point of a 160,000-acre estate along the Hudson River.

Just as you pass over Routes 2 and 7, past the signs for Ancram and Taghkanic, the view will not only knock your socks off, but your boots may fly, too. On a clear day, at least 50 miles of rolling hills unfold to the horizon and possibly to the next galaxy. The view is yours. Use it.

Mea culpa: If I didn't have to take you on the following roads, I wouldn't. The TSP connects with I-90 and, to make time through Albany, you'll be shoved onto I-87. The switch from pastoral scenes to six lanes of fast, tense traffic will change your karma in an instant. The antidote is clearing Albany and finding Route 9 once again. While it's not as picturesque as its counterpart further south, it does clear up near a neat little town called Round Lake (which is worth a quick look) and will calm you down until you reach my favorite American city, Saratoga Springs.

SARATOGA SPRINGS PRIMER

For a long stretch, many towns across the nation inexplicably opted to clear out their historic districts and place their bets on strip malls. In Saratoga Springs, they decided to put more than a thousand buildings on the National Register of Historic Places. The result is—if this makes sense—the town is so real it looks fake.

Broadway, the town's main boulevard, is an artifact that gains the most attention. When Gideon Putnam laid out the 120-foot wide thoroughfare in the early 1800s, he did it to ensure that a team of four horses could make a U-turn. The wide avenue and broad sidewalk make this the most enjoyable street in the nation for walking, riding, or enjoying a libation at a neighborhood bar. Farther up Route 9, you can ease away the kinks of the ride by dropping into a mineral bath at 2,200-acre **Saratoga Spa State Park** (S. Broadway, 518/584-2535, www.saratogaspastatepark.org).

The baths are still here because, in the early 1900s, this was the place to "take the waters." Now it's the place to kick back after a day on the road. Salty waters from ancient seas are trapped beneath limestone layers and sealed by a solid layer of shale. Because the Saratoga Fault zigzags beneath the town, it releases water made bubbly by carbon dioxide gas. Local Iroquois Indians knew well before the 1700s that minerals entering the water also added to the spring's therapeutic value.

Although Saratoga had earned its historical stripes in the Revolution ("Gentleman Johnny" Burgoyne surrendered his Crown Forces nearby on October 10, 1777), it was during the Civil War that John Morrissey, a street fighter who had been indicted twice for burglary, once for assault, and once more for assault with intent to kill, channeled his destructive energies into a horse-racing track. His gamble worked, and by the turn of the 20th century, the Saratoga Race Track complemented his Saratoga casinos.

Although reform politicians later closed the track, it quickly reopened through a loophole and its fortunes rose and fell until well after World War II when the New York Racing Association formed. That's when the focus of the track changed from mere gambling to the love of horse racing. Today with the track drawing summer visitors and the spas providing warm relief year-round, Saratoga is still in the running.

ON THE ROAD: SARATOGA SPRINGS

One of the fringe benefits of a good motorcycle tour is rolling into a town that would make a perfect vignette in a Mark Twain novel or Charles Kuralt feature. Saratoga Springs is one of those places. Even when the ponies aren't racing on America's oldest track, Saratoga is a must-see.

Within blocks of Broadway, you'll find side streets dotted with cool shops. In Congress Park there are wide lawns and a sculpture by Daniel Chester French (of Lincoln Memorial fame). Around town are slices of Americana that will make you wonder if you've wandered onto the set of *It's a Wonderful Life.*

Sometimes I wonder. Each time I ride here I get the sense that this town is strangely like Bedford Falls. When you pass the stunning Adirondack Trust at Broadway and Lake, you expect to peer in at Mr. Potter counting George Bailey's bankroll. As you walk or ride the avenue, the preserved architecture, liveliness of the street, and pleasant look on townspeople's faces as they actually shop along the main street is emotionally powerful and thoroughly satisfying.

Two streets in particular are worth exploring by bike. Head toward Skidmore College on North Broadway and you'll view grand homes reflecting architecture from the Greek Revival, Arts and Crafts, and postmodern periods. The second is Union Avenue, a broad boulevard bordered by palatial homes accented with gazebos, Gothic gables, gingerbread trim, and stained-glass windows.

For any tour—on foot or on your bike—swing by the Visitors Center in **Drink Hall** (297 Broadway) and pick up maps and a fact-filled brochure titled "Strolling Through Saratoga Springs" which suggests five walking tours that will acquaint you with the very best of what this town has to offer.

PULL IT OVER: SARATOGA HIGHLIGHTS
Attractions and Adventures

Where else can you sit back and bet on thoroughbreds shaking the ground from just 10 feet away? And all for three bucks! Don't pass up a visit to the **Saratoga Race Course** (Union Ave., 518/584-6200 in July and August or 718/641-4700 off-season, www.nyra.com/saratoga). The "sport of kings" is held at America's oldest racetrack, and the sense of tradition here is omnipresent. From the swells in the box seats to the two-bit bettors clenching their tickets trackside, this spectacle guarantees a good time. The racing season lasts slightly more than 30 days in July and August, so if you insist on competing with van-driving tourists during peak season, be sure to reserve one morning for "Breakfast at the Track," and stick around for the famed Travers Stakes in August. The track is closed Tuesdays.

After a hard day's ride—hell, even after an easy day's ride—**Congress Park** on Broadway is therapeutic. The turn-of-the-20th-century setting is enhanced by the Canfield Casino, once a favorite hangout of larger-than-life Diamond Jim Brady. Numerous quiet spots beckon you to stretch out on the lawn and enjoy nature. Settle back and listen to the groundskeepers manicure the grounds and watch geese overhead slicing their way south. You'll find another peaceful place by the Daniel Chester French statue erected in memory of Spencer Trask, a man, says the inscription, whose "one object in life was to do right and observe his fellow man. He gave himself abundantly to hasten the coming of a new and better day." Not a bad legacy, Spence.

After the racetrack, Congress Park, and Broadway's shops and pubs, take time to explore **Saratoga Spa State Park** (S. Broadway, 518/584-2535). Within its 2,000-plus acres are 18- and 9-hole golf courses (518/584-2008), the Gideon Putnam Resort & Spa (24 Gideon Putnam Rd., 518/584-3000 or 800/732-1560), a performing arts center (518/587-3330), and the circa 1930s Roosevelt Baths & Spa (37–39 Roosevelt Dr., 518/226-4790). Just a mile south of town, this is a perfect short run. Riding south down Broadway, take a right and enter the Avenue of the Pines, a picturesque road that leads to the Gideon Putnam Resort. Later, ride the Loop Road past Geyser Creek into the heart of the park.

In addition to watching the ponies, another popular outdoor activity is hanging out at Saratoga Lake, just four miles from the city center. Ride Route 9 South (Union Ave.) to Route 9P South and head over the bridge. The eight-mile-long lake is great for sailing, rowing, bass fishing, and waterskiing and several small restaurants have sport decks where you can pull over to enjoy a sandwich and a beer while looking out over the lake. To get out on the

Americade Motorcycle Rally

A late arrival to the rally circuit, the first "Cade" hit the road in May 1983. Originally called "Aspencade" after a New Mexico rally that celebrated the changing colors of the aspen, "Aspencade East" was hosted by veteran motorcyclist Bill Dutcher at the resort community of Lake George, New York, and attracted more than 2,000 attendees. To distance itself from typical rallies, this event stressed that it was "not the place for shows of speed, hostile attitudes, or illegally loud pipes."

In 1986, the name was changed to reflect the multi-brand, national-sized rally it had become. **Americade** (518/798-7888, www.tourexpo.com) is now the world's largest touring-focused event. Some of this is thanks to the Tour Expo tradeshow that's a big part of the event, as are mini-tours, self-guided tours, seminars, social events, and field events. Perhaps its greatest advantage is its location. Americade takes place at the southern gateway to the 6.1 million acre Adirondack Park, a preserve which is larger than Yellowstone, Glacier, Smokey Mountain, Yosemite, and Olympic National Parks *combined*. Ride slowly and take pleasure in its 2,800 lakes and ponds, 30,000 miles of rivers and streams, and 43 mountains with elevations over 4,000 feet.

water, you can rent a fishing or pontoon boat at the **Saratoga Boatworks** (549 Union Ave./Rte. 9P, 518/584-2628, www.saratogaboatworks.com), while **Point Breeze Marina** (1459 Rte. 9P, 518/587-3397, www.pointbreezemarina.com), Saratoga's largest marina, rents pontoons, speedboats, fishing boats, and canoes. You can find gear, bait, and tackle at shops near the marinas.

Saratoga National Historical Park (648 Rte. 32, Stillwater, 518/664-9821, www.nps.gov/sara, $3) is a must-see. Before the battles of Saratoga on September 19 and October 7, 1777, few colonists felt certain that their ragtag army and militias could forge America into an independent country. But after General John Burgoyne surrendered his 6,000 British soldiers to General Horatio Gates on October 17, the American Revolution had reached a turning point and it was only a matter of time before Gates's colleague Washington would drive things home. The dioramas, exhibits, films, and 10-mile battlefield tour road are emotional reminders of America's quest to be free. The park is open 9 A.M.–5 P.M. daily, April–mid-November.

Civil War buffs may be familiar with the name Mount McGregor. To provide for his family, a dying Ulysses S. Grant lived here while completing his memoirs. The catch is that had Grant not died here, the **Ulysses S. Grant Cottage** (518/587-8277, www.grantcottage.org, $4) would have been torn down to make room for the adjacent prison. Ignore the shouts of the cons and enjoy the steep ride to the peak. Take Route 9 North left onto Corinth Mountain Road, and then take a quick right and follow signs to Grant Cottage. Hours are iffy and it's only open in the summer. Call in advance.

If you're thrilled by thoroughbreds like Man o' War, Secretariat, and Seabiscuit, then it's a given that you should head to the **National Museum of Racing and Hall of Fame** (Union Ave. across from Saratoga Race Course, 518/584-0400, www.racingmuseum.org, $7). Open daily, the museum's films, special exhibits, equine art, and miniature wax figurines of jockeys (at least I *thought* they were miniatures) tell the story of horse racing. Kick in an extra three bucks for the Oklahoma Track Tour, an early morning behind-the-scenes tour of stables, the backstretch, and the area where grooms prepare horses for the race. Pony up an extra five bucks and experience the thrill of seeing what it's like to ride a racehorse. Sitting astride a mechanical horse and watching visuals gathered by a "jockey-cam," you go through three races: a warm-up, out of the training gate, and then into a real race to see and feel the perspective, adrenaline, and sensation of the real thing.

Sure, it seems cheesy riding a trolley after getting off your bike, but the information shared by the drivers/historians of **Trolley Tours** (518/584-3255) will spike your learning curve. And for only a $1.50! Trolleys run 10 A.M.–8:30 P.M. Tuesday–Sunday July–Labor Day, departing from the visitors center and various stops along Broadway.

At some point you may wind up at the **Saratoga Performing Arts Center** (Saratoga Spa State Park, S. Broadway, 518/587-3330, www.spac.org) for an outdoor concert by artists like James Taylor, Bruce Springsteen, and the Dave Matthews Band (as well as the Philadelphia Orchestra and New York City Ballet). Then, finally, reward yourself with a taste of indulgence. What takes place at the **Roosevelt Baths & Spa** (37–39 Roosevelt Dr., Saratoga Spa State Park, 518/226-4790) may sound like punishment for Cool Hand Luke, but Lordy! does it feel good after a ride. In this old-fashioned spa, you can get wrapped up in hot sheets, have someone squeeze the tightness out of your muscles, then plunge into steamy, sweat-inducing water…paradise. Prices range from $25 for a mineral bath to $85 for a one-hour massage. Hours vary by season; call in advance. Note: If the Roosevelt's closed and you gotta have someone rub you the right way, call on the affordable **Crystal Spa** (120 S. Broadway, 518/584-2556, www.thecrystalspa.net) which is open year-round.

Shopping

Normally I wouldn't recommend a souvenir store, but Saratoga Springs is such an incredible town it's worth a memento or two. One place to find some great horse and racing prints is at **Impressions of Saratoga** (368 Broadway, 518/587-0666, www.impressionssaratoga.com), and there are some fantastic new, used, and vintage guitars and smaller instruments for making music on the road over at **Saratoga Guitar** (438 Broadway, 518/581-1604, www.saratogaguitar.com). If Elvis could ride his Honda 350 and carry a guitar in *Roustabout,* you have the right to do the same.

On a long tour, one of the greatest pleasures is escaping routine and digging into a good book. You'll find a ton of them within a vacated bank vault at **Lyrical Ballad Bookstore** (7 Phila St., 518/584-8779). One of the finest used and rare bookstores I've seen, it's brimming with 100,000 editions, which means there are more topics here than in a year's worth of Oprah. The bookstore is open 10 A.M.–6 P.M. Monday–Saturday, 11 A.M.–6 P.M. Sunday.

Gotta jones for a stogie? **Smokin' Sam's Cigar Shop** (5 Caroline St., 518/587-6450) is open until midnight in season.

You don't have to travel to Palm Beach to watch pony boys whacking the ball; they've been doing it around here since 1898. If you're here between July and Labor Day, cruise over to **Saratoga Polo** (518/584-8108, www.saratogapolo.com, $25) to watch the world's top polo players get a "chukker" going. Granted, it's ritzy, but the action's fast and furious—even more so when I rode my bike on the field.

Blue-Plate Specials

Compton's Restaurant (457 Broadway, 518/584-9632) opens daily for breakfast (served all day) and lunch. This diner isn't old-fashioned, it's just really old. You wanted an early start? Breakfast begins at 4 A.M. on weekdays and 3 A.M. on weekends. Inhale two eggs, home fries, toast, and coffee, plus ham, bacon, sausage, or hash—all for about five bucks.

Traditional Southern food is hard to find even in the South these days, but **Hattie's** (45 Phila St., 518/584-4790, www.hattiesrestaurant.com) has been serving Louisiana cuisine like fried chicken, ribs, catfish, pork chops, and homemade desserts since 1938. If you can't tour south of the Mason-Dixon, grab a table here. In season, Hattie's is open seven days a week for breakfast, lunch, and dinner, and off-season for dinner Wednesday–Sunday. Enjoy the full bar and outdoor revelry on the patio in the summer.

The **Saratoga Diner** (153 S. Broadway, 518/584-4044) has been known to locals and diners since 1948. The lunch specials include soup, an entree (pork chops, stuffed peppers, turkey), and dessert. They're open 6 A.M.–midnight and 24 hours on the weekends.

Watering Holes

Opened in 1970, **Saratoga Tin & Lint Company** (2 Caroline St., 518/587-5897) is Saratoga's quintessential neighborhood bar. In a basement setting complete with low ceilings, Tin & Lint features creature comforts like wooden benches and one of the best jukeboxes on the road. If you need more convincing, keep in mind that Soupy Sales—*the* Soupy Sales—downed a brew or two here once. You can buy pints of ale for $3 and pitchers for $7 until 4 A.M. daily.

The Parting Glass (40–42 Lake Ave., 518/583-1916, www.partingglasspub. com) is an Irish pub serving affordable pub-style food, all of which can be washed down by your choice of 100 bottled beers or 36 beers on tap. The pub features live Irish and American folk music, darts, and shuffleboard. For a more tranquil evening, **Gaffney's** (16 Caroline St., 518/587-7359, www.gaffneysrestaurant.com) is primarily a restaurant, although one that offers lots of locals as well as knowledgeable travelers a quiet place to listen to a variety of music (rock, jazz, blues) with a cold beer or a bottle of wine.

Shut-Eye

Numerous independent motel/spas line Broadway, the majority of them clean and tidy. Motels are great when traveling by bike; just park right out front. If you arrive in racing season, ouch! You'd better win a lot of cash: Rates can more than double and some places may expect three-night minimums.

Motels and Motor Courts

Smack dab in the middle of everything is the plain Jane **Saratoga Downtowner Motel** (413 Broadway, 518/584-6160 or 888/480-6160, www.saratogadowntowner. com, $89 and up off-season, $239 and up race season). It has 42 AAA rooms, continental breakfast, and—get this—an indoor pool beneath a retractable roof that opens in the summer. The **Springs Motel** (189 Broadway, 518/584-6336, www.springsmotel.com, $95 off-season, $195 race season) is near the racetrack and the state park. It has 28 spacious and clean rooms.

Inn-dependence

In its early days as a resort town, Saratoga Springs created some notable inns and hotels. One of the finest is the **Adelphi Hotel** (365 Broadway, 518/587-4688, www.adelphihotel.com, $130 and up shoulder season, $255 and up race season), not only because of its grandeur, but because of the subtle anachronisms captured in the blend of 1920s art deco style and tropical casualness. The 34 rooms boast high ceilings, private baths, and a far-from-generic decor. The day gets off to a perfect start with breakfast on the verandah and wraps up in one of the coolest lobby bars you'll find. This is the premier spot to relax and relive the 1920s, whether you're passed out under the palms or sampling a cocktail, beer, or daiquiri in the faux-painted bar.

Kathleen and Noel Smith are two of the friendliest people running one of the nicest inns in Saratoga. **Saratoga Arms** (495 Broadway, 518/584-1775, www.saratogaarms.com, $195 and up off-season, $350 and up race season) offers large, comfortable rooms right on Broadway and within walking distance of the action.

For a more natural and cost-effective setting, stay at the **Saratoga B&B** (434 Church St./Rte. 9N, 518/584-0920, $109–239, www.saratogabnb.com) and adjacent **Saratoga Motel** (440 Church St., 518/584-0920, www.saratogabandb.com, $79–149). Both sit on five wooded acres a few miles up Route 9N and are popular with riders for the motel setting and lower rates.

Chain Drive

These chain hotels are in town, or within 10 miles of the city center: **Best Western, Comfort Inn, Courtyard by Marriott, Hampton Inn, Hilton, Holiday Inn, Residence Inn, Sheraton** For more information, including phone numbers and websites, see page 439.

SIDE TRIP: ADIRONDACKS

Just because this ride ends at Saratoga Springs, it doesn't mean yours has to. Just north of Saratoga, **Americade** (www.tourexpo.com), the world's largest tour rally, attracts hordes of riders to the Lake George area in early June.

Even off-season, you can enjoy a nice run up to Lake George via dependable Route 9. The road sweeps through slow curves and a few forgettable towns, campgrounds, and past random log cabins. The forest is tranquil and peaceful, and smooth back roads lead to the Adirondacks, Vermont, and Great Lake Sacandaga. Some say that I-87 North to Canada is one of the most scenic roads in the United States.

Lake George itself has a veneer as a tacky tourist town littered with T-shirt shops and mini-golf. Motels abound in Lake George and tourist cabins dot Route 9N. If you have time and a full tank, take a ride around Lake George—it's a magnificent lakeshore run.

Resources for Riders

Hudson River Valley Run

New York Travel Information

New York Camping Reservations—800/456-2267, www.reserveamerica.com
New York State Parks—www.nysparks.com
New York State Thruway Road Conditions—800/847-8929 or
    www.nysthruway.gov
New York State Travel and Tourism—800/225-5697, www.iloveny.com

Local and Regional Information

Adirondack Bed & Breakfast Association—www.adirondackbb.com
Dutchess County Tourism—845/463-4000 or 800/445-3131,
    www.dutchesstourism.com
Hudson River Valley Information—800/232-4782, www.hudsonvalley.org
Hyde Park Chamber of Commerce—845/229-8612, www.hydeparkchamber.org
Saratoga County Chamber of Commerce—518/584-3255 or 800/526-8970,
    www.saratoga.org
Sleepy Hollow Tarrytown Chamber of Commerce—914/631-1705,
    www.sleepyhollowchamber.com

New York Motorcycle Shops

Albany Honda—390 New Karner Rd., Albany, 518/452-1003
Brunswick Harley-Davidson/Buell—68 Weibel Ave., Saratoga Springs,
    518/279-1145, www.brunswickharley.com
Dutchess Recreational Vehicles—737 Freedom Plains Rd. Poughkeepsie,
    845/454-2810, www.dutchessrec.com
Ed's Service Motorcycles—600 Violet Ave., Hyde Park, 845/454-6210,
    www.eds-service.com
Haverstraw Motorsports—64–66 Rte. 9W, Haverstraw, 845/429-0141,
    www.haverstrawmotorsports.com
Prestige Harley-Davidson—205 Rte. 9W, Congers, 845/268-6651 or
    866/668-7292, www.prestigeharleydavidson.com
Rockwell Cycles—1005 Rte. 9W, Fort Montgomery, 845/446-3834,
    www.rockwellcycles.com
Spitzies Harley-Davidson—1970 Central Ave., Albany, 518/456-7433 or
    888/210-8481, www.spitzies.com
Woodstock Harley-Davidson—949 Rte. 28, Kingston, 845/338-2800,
    www.woodstockharley.com
Zack's V-Twin Cycles—799 Violet Ave., Hyde Park, 845/229-1177,
    www.zacksvtwin.com

Amish Country Run

New Hope, Pennsylvania to Intercourse, Pennsylvania

This is a journey that will take you into the past, from the colonial accents an hour north of Philadelphia to a Revolutionary War landmark and then into the heart of 19th-century farmland. Along the way, you'll ride beside the historic Delaware River and also be presented with unlimited views of Pennsylvania's most pristine farmland. Some of America's finest back roads and friendliest people are found in this region.

NEW HOPE PRIMER

Few towns, I think, are so at ease with themselves as is New Hope. It seems to saunter through history content to take on whatever the era expects.

Of course it's had plenty of practice.

From its roots in the American Revolution, it reached new peaks in the 1930s when some of the nation's best playwrights introduced shows here. By the 1980s it had evolved into a yuppie-friendly village and since has continued to change with subtle shifts. When you arrive you'll probably view New Hope through the prism of your age. Young riders may see it as a nouveau/ retro Haight-Ashbury; couples may see it as a place to bring the kids; and older motorcycle travelers will find a charming shopping village.

New Hope is all of this, but it is also something greater. It is a historic community that predates Philadelphia. It was at Coryell's Ferry where George Washington prepared for his fabled crossing of the river before making the real voyage a few miles south. A century later, the town became the birthplace of the New Hope School of Artists, whose members left Philadelphia to gain inspiration from the summer countryside and later fostered the Pennsylvania impressionist movement. It is an actors' community—as a young man, Robert Redford honed his skills here at the Bucks County Playhouse. It is a walking town where a short bridge spans the adjacent Delaware River and heads straight into downtown Lambertville, New Jersey.

Perfectly positioned about an hour south

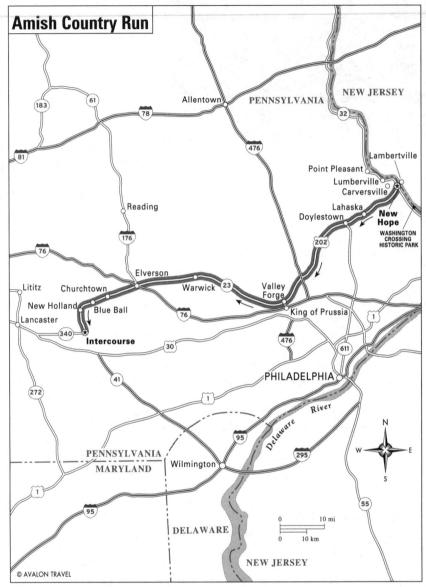

Amish Country Run

Route: New Hope to Intercourse via Lahaska, Doylestown, Valley Forge

Distance: Approximately 110 miles

First Leg: New Hope to Intercourse (110 miles)

Helmet Laws: Pennsylvania does not require helmets (conditions apply).

of New York City and about an hour north of Philadelphia, New Hope is most of all a popular Point B for motorcycle travelers enjoying weekend runs from across New York, New Jersey, and Pennsylvania.

ON THE ROAD: NEW HOPE

You'll be floored by what you'll discover beyond the boundaries of New Hope; but before you head out, take some time and hang around town. If you've been here before, you'll notice that the once-exclusive veneer which had been created by New Hope's high-class galleries, cafés, and upscale boutiques has now given way to a more middle-class collection of independent cigar shops, bars, and variety shops that sell an abundance of quirky collectibles.

To find your feet, drop by the **visitors center** (1 W. Mechanic St., 215/862-5030), where you'll find maps, brochures, and guides that will introduce you to an impressive number of nearby attractions and sites. After taking a good look at the village—which is easily worth the investment of a half day or more—dodge the tourists and take off on Route 32 North (aka River Rd.) for a short, slow, and seductive ride beside the beautiful Delaware River.

Within a few miles, the trimmed hedges and manicured lawns of the town give way to some sharp curves, narrow roads, and a tunnel of green. Fresh fields and fat stone walls rise and fall with the earth as the road follows the lead of those walls, pushing you up and around tight corners and then face to face with a flood of spectacular scenery.

Since it's so easy to get into the groove of the road, it's hard to believe that this landscape is only a few miles from the downtown tourist scene. By the time you reach the junction of Routes 32 and 263 a

few miles later, you're well into the country and within view of **Dilly's Corner** (Rtes. 32 and 263, 215/862-5333, open seasonally Tues.–Sun.), a nostalgic diner where it seems everyone in Pennsylvania converges to load up on hamburgers, cheeseburgers, shakes, and sundaes.

Back on Route 32 North, you'll approach Lumberville and a wonderful stretch of woods that soon opens up to reveal the wide Delaware River on your right. Depending on the season, you may encounter a flotilla of people drifting lazily downriver in slick black innertubes.

This is a peaceful ride, and when you pass sections where landscaped lawns and untouched grasses grow side by side, there's a real satisfaction knowing that no one's screwed this up yet. Keep your eyes open because, coming up on your left in Lumberville, the Old Carversville Road rises steeply. When you get on this hard-packed back road, it puts you in the thick of the woods, where small cabins and homes are hidden well below a thicket of tall trees and snaking limbs. The road is narrow and the woods are quiet and, after several miles, you'll reach one small bridge and then another and then you arrive in the heart of Carversville.

Compared to the solitude of the forest road, it seems like there's a lot of action here even though downtown's only about the size of an average backyard. Aside from the landmark inn across the street, most activity is taking place at the **Carversville General Store** (215/297-5353). Well-stocked with groceries, drinks, and a small diner, it does double duty as the town post office and theater. How so? On the last Monday of each summer month, they project them "moving picture shows" onto the side of the building.

After retracing your route back through the forest road toward Lumberville, turn

Not all soldiers made it across the Delaware on Christmas night, 1776. Some young patriots ended up here—in a cemetery upriver of Washington Crossing.

left to follow Route 32 North again. When you pass the village of Devil's Half Acre, the stunning views and weaving road unleash you into some Le Mans–style driving that'll sweep you into small bumps and quick ascents. The best part of the ride is finding that along this one road in the Delaware Valley, there's very little commercialism, so for now it's just the road and you.

Several miles on is Point Pleasant, home of **Bucks County River Country** (215/297-5000, www.rivercountry.net), the point of origin for the armada of inner tube passengers you passed downriver. For me, places like this make a tour great. There's a village store here and if you have time and a bathing suit, rent a tube, raft, canoe, or kayak and take the day off; just cruise down the Delaware, drifting at a lazy 1.5 mph in cool water. There are no rapids, so just relax and enjoy the soothing, peaceful experience.

From here, you can continue your

northward trek toward Upper Black Eddy and Lake Nockamixon, or dash east along the Delaware into Frenchtown, New Jersey, or take virtually any road in any direction for a longer ride, or turn back and head home to New Hope.

That's the beauty of New Hope and its surroundings. No matter where you ride, you'll be satisfied.

PULL IT OVER: NEW HOPE HIGHLIGHTS
Attractions and Adventures

Seven remarkably cool, must-ride miles south of New Hope is the site of a turning point in American history: **Washington Crossing Historic Park** (1112 River Rd./Rte. 32, Washington Crossing, 215/493-4076, www.ushistory.org/washingtoncrossing). On a slushy and sleeting Christmas 1776, George Washington massed part of the Continental Army and took a gamble on the future of America—which turned out to be a much bigger

The Crux of the Crossing

There's a strong chance that America wouldn't exist today had it not been for the actions of Washington and his men on Christmas 1776. No one knew if they would make it. Knowing that his men needed inspiration, a few days before their mission to cross the Delaware and attack the Hessians, Washington had Thomas Paine's *The American Crisis* read aloud to his troops. Did it help? Consider this opening paragraph and then consider how you would have felt.

These are the times that try men's souls: The summer soldier and the sunshine patriot will, in this crisis, shrink from the service of their country; but he that stands it now, deserves the love and thanks of man and woman. Tyranny, like hell, is not easily conquered; yet we have this consolation with us, that the harder the conflict, the more glorious the triumph. What we obtain too cheap, we esteem too lightly: it is dearness only that gives every thing its value.

gamble than he expected. Of the three divisions scheduled to cross the river that night, only Washington and his men managed the nearly impossible feat. What's more, they marched nearly ten miles, many barefoot, through the snow to reach Trenton in time to attack and defeat 900 Hessian mercenaries and capture enough food and supplies to sustain themselves through the brutal winter of 1777.

If you only know Washington from the dollar bill, get to know the real man by watching the introductory video and visiting the historic buildings and boathouse stacked with replicas of the workhouse Durham boats. Here's another tip: On the return trip to New Hope, stop and pay your respects to his spirit and those of the young soldiers buried near the river at a Revolutionary War cemetery a few miles on. It's about halfway between Washington Crossing and New Hope on Route 32 (about five miles northwest of the park's visitors center).

The phrase "iron horse" originally referred to locomotives but, over generations,

was attached to motorcycles. You can experience the original incarnation at the **New Hope & Ivyland Railroad** (32 W. Bridge St., 215/862-2332, www.newhoperailroad.com, from $17). They have four steam locomotives and Number 40 is a 1925 full-gauge model that pulls passenger cars through the hills and valleys of Bucks County. If that gets your motor going, give serious thought to upgrading to the rare "locomotive cab ride," since this is one of few steam railroads that allows passengers to ride up front with the engineers. Trips depart several times daily in season.

Perhaps the most casual cruising experience anywhere would be with the **New Hope Canal Boat Company** (149 S. Main St., 215/862-0758, www.canalboats.com, about $10). The Delaware Canal flows sixty miles between Easton and Bristol, and from New Hope a mule team will pull your barge along for several miles along the canal to show you a different side of New Hope. If you're traveling in a group, call ahead to reserve a private barge for a canal party—and stock up on a cooler full of beer.

Visit Washington Crossing and your image of Washington will change from an old man on a dollar bill to a man of mythic heroism.

Right in the heart of town, **Bucks County Playhouse** (70 South Main St., 215/862-2041 or 215/862-2046, www.buckscountyplayhouse.com), is the state theater of Pennsylvania. Far enough from Broadway to try out plays and close enough to take them to NYC if they were any good, this has been a launching pad for great playwrights like George S. Kaufman and Moss Hart. Hopeful actors Robert Redford, Grace Kelly, Dick Van Dyke, Tyne Daly, and Liza Minnelli caught the stage right here. Tickets for main stage shows are around $25.

In addition to floating down the Delaware in an inner tube, you can head to **Coryell's Ferry** (22 S. Main St., 215/862-2050) for a 45-minute cruise on the river, picking up intelligence about the history of the area and what happened the night Washington made his crossing. It's still in the same location where John Wells—the town's founder and first ferryboat

operator—began his business in 1718 and where, in 1776, patriot John Coryell provided service to Washington's troops and to America by keeping the Redcoats stranded on the opposite bank.

Shopping
There are several stores in the heart of town that feature leather in various configurations. The one you really want to see was created by Joe "NY Joe" Wynne, a motorcycle enthusiast and former co-manager of NYC H-D. **After the Ride** (115 S. Main St., 609/862-0172, www.aftertheride.com) features moto-clothing, jewelry, and high-end leathers, some of it even custom tailored. Who wears their hypercool "pyrate" fashions? Keith Richards, Ozzy Osborne, Laurence Fishburne, Will Smith, and Aerosmith, for starts. **Fred Eisen Leather Design** (129 S. Main St, 215/862-5988, www.fredeisenleather.com) sells Indian-style clothing, as well as belts and saddlebags with a Western theme. A few doors down, **Sterling Leather** (97 S. Main St., 215/862-9669, www.sterlingleather.com) sells a similar line of hats, moccasins, boots, and accessories. At **Living Arts Tattoo** (12 W. Mechanic St., 215/862-3816) you can pick up an indelible souvenir, from a tiny first tattoo to an elaborate custom piece.

Aging baby boomers trying to retrieve the junk they threw away can buy it back at **Love Saves the Day** (1 S. Main St., 215/862-1399), which is crammed with Beatles memorabilia, lunch boxes, '60s TV merchandise, old Playboys, vintage clothing, black velvet Springsteen, and rare Star Wars items which, I guess, are all a far site more valuable than the contents of a Bernie Madoff portfolio.

If you'd like to stash a few books in your saddlebags, head to **Farley's Bookshop** (44 S. Main St., 215/862-2452, farleysbookshop.com) and load up on literature. The store is filled with rooms stacked with shelves loaded with an uncommonly huge amount of new books and magazines.

Across the river at the former OTC Cracker Factory, **River Horse Brewing** (80 Lambert Ln., Lambertville, 609/397-7776, www.riverhorse.com) brews a half-dozen kinds of beer at any one time. Order 'em all and enjoy a six-pack. It's open noon–5 P.M., so you can walk through the brewery, buy gifts in the store, and get samples in the sampling room.

Blue-Plate Specials

Over the Delaware River at **Sneddon's Luncheonette** (47 Bridge St., 609/397-3053, Lambertville), the sound of dishes slapping and silverware clanging go right along with the old-fashioned wood paneling and heart-shaped wireback chairs. The home-cooked breakfasts and lunches, mostly soups and sandwiches, will take you back home (provided your home was a diner).

There are numerous fine dining restaurants around New Hope, but one of my favorites is **Wildflowers Garden Restaurant** (8 W. Mechanic St., 215/862-2241, www.wildflowersnewhope.com). It stands out for having good food that doesn't cost a fortune (around $10 for lunch and $15 for dinner). Although the outdoor patio may be crowded, the riverside setting is the perfect place to relax and experience New Hope. Entrees feature such diverse fare as Yankee pot roast and extremely tasty Thai food. I highly recommend it.

Watering Holes

Evenings are as enjoyable as days in New Hope, and being in a walking town means you can park your bike and bar-hop your way across the river into New Jersey. Start in New Hope at the crowded and cool **Fran's Pub** (116 S. Main St., 215/862-5539), which entertains with a pool table, jukebox, pizzas, burgers, sandwiches, widescreen TV, and a cooler filled with beers. Look around and notice that tattoos are as abundant as brands of brew. Enjoy happy hour (4:30–6:30 P.M.) on the nice outdoor patio, a great place for people-watching.

Every night at **John and Peter's** (96 S. Main St., 215/862-5981, www.johnandpeters.com) is like a talent show audition. Since 1972, folks have packed this low-key joint to be treated to shows by such performers as Leon Redbone, George Thorogood, Norah Jones, and Martin Mull—and nearly 50,000 other acts. It's got a neat patio and a cool atmosphere and if it's Monday and you're talented, drunk, or both, take part in open mic night. Smoking is allowed.

Up and down Main Street, you'll find other sidewalk cafés, open-air bars, and places heralded as "martini bars" and "libation lounges." One noteworthy spot is **Havana's** (105 S. Main St., 215/862-9897, www.havananewhope.com). On a typical night, it's packed with revelers enjoying the expansive, laid-back, Key West patio–style setting and full liquor bar. Here since 1978, Havana's has the good sense to feature blues, rockabilly, R&B, and funk acts.

Shut-Eye

With its only motel going out of business, and large chain hotels changing names, the best chance to find a room is in a bed-and-breakfast. They are plentiful in New Hope and in neighboring communities like Lambertville and Lumberville. The good news is that competition between the inns raised the level of service and comfort; the not-so-good news is that prices rose as well. There are far too many to list, so for a complete and current listing check www.newhopechamber.com (215/862-9990) and follow the link to Lodging.

Inn-dependence

A small property in a nice setting, **Porches** (20 Fishers Alley, 215/862-3277, www.porchesnewhope.com, $95 and up weekdays) is an 1880s cottage-style home in the heart of town, with the nicer and more private rooms in annex buildings on the property. The pace is informal, and most of the 1920s-decor rooms overlook the Delaware Canal Towpath. After a full country breakfast of fruit, bacon, sausage, pancakes, and fresh bread, you can waddle off to start your day.

Also in town are two notable historic inns: **Wedgwood Inn** and its sibling **Aaron Burr House Inn** (80 and 111 W. Bridge St., 215/862-2570, www.wedgwoodinn.com and www.aaronburrhouse.com, $95–125). Both are traditional with 20 individually decorated rooms to choose from, some with tubs, fireplaces, king beds, and bay windows. The screened flagstone patio is a relaxing setting. In addition to a full breakfast, owner Carl serves complimentary hot and cold drinks and other refreshments in the afternoon, and in the evening chocolates and a nip of his secret-recipe almond liqueur.

The setting for the **1740 House** (3690 River Rd., Lumberville, 215/297-5661, www.1740house.com, $150 and up) is perfect, albeit pricey for a moto-tour. It's a little way out of town; the advantage is being on a beautiful site overlooking the Delaware and having a riverside pool to relax in when you've finished your ride. Each of the 23 rooms is decorated in Early American style, and each has a balcony and a river view.

Chain Drive

These chain hotels are in town, or within 10 miles of the city center:

Courtyard by Marriott, Hampton Inn
For more information, including phone numbers and websites, see page 439.

ON THE ROAD: NEW HOPE TO INTERCOURSE

If I were in an episode of *The Twilight Zone*—the kind where somebody's stuck someplace forever—I would hope Rod Serling would send me riding endlessly across the Pennsylvania countryside. This desire starts in the rides around New Hope and continues upon leaving New Hope on Route 202 towards Lahaska. On the way out of town, you'll pass a complex called **Peddler's Village** (215/794-4000, www.peddlersvillage.com) and while it looks like a tourist trap, the 70 stores and nearly a dozen restaurants that spread across a shopping village are not too bad. Plus, it's not so far from New Hope that you couldn't frequent one of their pubs and

The spirit of George Washington and the determination of his men are celebrated in the magnificent Washington Arch of Valley Forge.

taverns and, provided you're sober, ride back to town.

Stay on Route 202 and you'll ride into Doylestown, a picture-perfect town that's small enough for a manageable and brief stop. Downtown is particularly clean and nice, with a movie theater, bookstore, and various independent merchants. One of the prime attractions here is the interesting **James A. Michener Art Museum** (138 S. Pine St., 215/340-9800, www.michenermuseum.com), named for Doylestown native, famed author, and philanthropist James Michener. Located in a refurbished 1880s prison, it showcases rotating exhibits as well as Michener and his works, and other Bucks County residents including Pearl S. Buck, Oscar Hammerstein II, Moss Hart, George S. Kaufman, Dorothy Parker, and S. J. Perelman.

When you follow Route 202 out of Doylestown, you'll be riding toward King of Prussia and I'm afraid the road will fizzle out for a long stretch. A less taxing alternative is riding in an arc well north of King of Prussia to explore roads that link small towns like Lansdale, North Wales, Gwynedd, and Skippack. There are too many turns to list here, but eventually, you'll take Valley Forge Road to descend toward the front door of this spectacular historical gem.

Though never the site of a battle, as in Washington Crossing this is where America's pursuit of liberty hung in the balance. By surviving the harsh winter of 1777–1778 and the loss of 2,000 men to the elements, Washington's troops proved they were tough enough to see the Revolution through to its conclusion. That's why you should stop at the **Valley Forge National Historical Park** (610/783-1077, www.nps.gov/vafo). You probably won't visit in winter, but you may still feel chills when you think about what happened in this place.

Take off on a superb 10-mile loop tour around the 3,500-acre site, knowing that when morale dropped, Washington offered $12 to the soldiers who constructed the first log cabin built to his specs. It worked. The men created new shelters and, with the arrival of a Prussian officer named Friedrich Wilhelm Ludolf Gerhard Augustin von Steuben (aka Baron von Steuben), they also developed a new sense of discipline and esprit de corps. Along the ride are replicas of these cabins as well as monuments that dot the roadside. It doesn't cost anything to see the museum and film at the visitors center, and in May 2009 they re-opened the home that served as headquarters for Washington and his staff (making it the Pentagon of its day). Take advantage of the museum and historical movies, and pay tribute to the people who endured the winter to help create a nation.

Within miles, as you begin the ride west from Valley Forge, you'll see that the road gets significantly and magnificently nicer as Route 23 forms a slow arc through the low hills. The road is absolutely perfect with scenery that is vibrant and energizing, cool and warm. In regions like the French Creek Watershed District, there are a series of nice hills and dips with expansive farmlands spreading off to the horizons north and south. Over and over again come wonderful small towns like Warwick, Elverson, Churchtown, and Blue Ball, where the extraordinarily fertile orchards, groves, and fields are visible reminders of why you ride. Your own free-riding spirit is matched by that of home-crafters who have posted signs to sell handmade cedar chests, quilts, and root beer.

In the town of New Holland, New Holland Road leads to the south en route to Route 340. You know you're entering the heart of Amish Country because the sweet smell of fields of produce gives way to the odiferous aroma of Amish farms and horse-drawn buggies. But the scents are worth the price of admission because they signify that, once you turn west on Route 340, you'll soon be enjoying Intercourse.

INTERCOURSE PRIMER

It was one of the most amazing sights of my journey. As I rode into Intercourse and raised my visor, the blunt chill of the evening air hit my face. I scanned the road, and a motion drew my attention to the ridge of a hill. An Amish farmer stood tall on the back of a mule-driven wagon and the hay was stacked high behind him. Silhouetted against the setting sun, he was a vision from 1820. I was in Intercourse and in the past.

This place was originally called Cross Key, but the name was changed because of (select one): A) the intersecting roads, B) the entrance to a horse racing track, or C) the "intercourse," or social interaction

and support that's symbolic of the village. The residents can't agree either. Although Lancaster gets the tourists, Intercourse is the hub of the Amish people. Surrounded by farmlands, Intercourse is a museum without walls—although the walls are closing in. A few miles in any direction are modern buildings and businesses that must surely tempt young farmers.

While New Hope's Bucks County thrives on culture and diversity, the strengths of Lancaster County are dining and simplicity. There's not much shakin' at night; but during the day, there are fantastic country roads to ride and the most satisfying roadside restaurants you'll ever find.

ON THE ROAD: INTERCOURSE

When you hit the road in Intercourse don't expect to be treated like Harrison Ford in *Witness*. No, the Amish aren't going to ask you to strap on a tool belt and help raise a barn and they probably won't welcome

No tractors or combines in Amish Country. Just manual labor and pristine farmland.

© NANCY HOWELL

The Amish Way of Life

No stress, no worries. The joy of being a kid is evident on the faces of Amish children gathered at a local pond.

Despite their identification as the Pennsylvania Dutch, Amish ancestors hailed from Germany, not Holland. They left Deutschland (get it?) to seek religious freedom. Today's Lancaster County "Old Order Amish" stress humility, family, community, and separation from the world. All Old Order members drive buggies, not cars. Their homes do not have electricity, and their children are educated as far as the eighth grade in one-room schoolhouses.

As for personal appearance, Amish women seldom cut their hair, and they wear a black prayer covering if they're single and a white one if they're married. Men wear dark suits, straight-cut coats with lapels, suspenders, solid-colored shirts, and black or straw broad-brimmed hats. It's not a costume, but an expression of their faith. It's also worth noting that they don't avoid change entirely. They just take longer to consider a new product before deciding to accept or reject it. So, don't discount an Amish data encryption service.

I spoke with a Mennonite resident of Intercourse who explained the Amish policy of giving young men free rein to leave the church and community, known as "rumspringa." He told me, "It's like this way: You're getting taught from a young age what's right and what's wrong. So, when you're 18, you're an adult and you're supposed to know what's right and what's wrong, and then when you learn temptations, you're on your own. If you do wrong, then you're dealing with the law."

But Amish youth must deal with more than mere legal pressures. If an Amish youth forsakes his lessons and upbringing, giving in to the same temptations as his "English" peers, he's considered an outcast from the church and the community and cannot return.

you into their homes, either. But if you're respectful and keep your camera out of sight, you won't be viewed as one of the rude "English" either.

Aside from hanging around the general stores in town, maybe the best way to understand and appreciate the community is to pick up one of the widely distributed maps of Amish Country. Quite detailed and easy to follow, it reveals dozens of roads that intersect the farms here and as long as you remain within the rough rectangle they form, you can ride for many miles and many hours without seeing a trace of progress.

One route leaves Intercourse on Route 340 East, passing Spring Garden and White Horse and turning left onto Churchtown Road before Compass. So far, the ride reveals nothing out of the ordinary, but when you turn left (north), you'll notice there are no phone or electrical lines running to the homes. Their absence makes the landscape as pure and authentic as any place you'll find.

Follow the road all the way to Route 23, then turn left to head west. You're on the periphery of the Amish farms, returning past small towns like New Holland and Bareville. Near Leola, turn left (south) on Route 772 and the road will put you in the thick of the farms. The ride is quiet and calm, interrupted occasionally by a horse-drawn carriage or hay wagon rolling down the lane. You won't tire of the sight, but be very careful riding at night, since these dark carriages can be hard to see.

Speaking of night riding, you may want to try it at least once. I did, and what I took to be a massive region of nothing turned out to be a busy farming area—but I couldn't tell until I saw that I was riding just yards away from massive farmhouses. Nearly hidden in the dark, they were lit only by candles and lanterns.

Sharp 90-degree curves dividing the farms keep you alert, as will the crop of Amish children who gather near the road to stare at you and your bike when you ride past. Route 772 takes a sharp right at Hess Road, where you turn and continue on Route 772 to a scenic road called Scenic Road (really). Now do yourself a favor and get lost. With U.S. 30 to the south and Route 23 to the north, you may pass the Amish equivalent of a commercial district: buggies lined up at repair shops, tobacco drying in barns, and carpenters crafting simple furniture with even simpler tools.

While any day's great for a ride here, head out on a Sunday morning and you'll see hundreds of Amish worshippers walking and rolling down country roads to church, a service that's usually held in the home of a fellow parishioner. It's an unusual sight because, of nearly any other place in America, these may be the most "country" country roads you can ride. Each road will tempt you, and if you want to go off on a tear, have at it. Get lost. Explore. And enjoy your ride into the past.

PULL IT OVER: INTERCOURSE HIGHLIGHTS
Attractions and Adventures

There's really not a lot going on in Intercourse, so you may as well not do anything at the **Kitchen Kettle Village** (Rte. 340, 717/768-8261 or 800/732-3538, www.kitchenkettle.com). Actually, this is a popular little shopping village so there's a chance you may find a new pair of handcrafted leather boots, score some fresh-off-the-lathe furniture, or listen to some folk musicians. If your bike is wired for sound, this is where you can pick up an in-depth audio tour of Amish country. The village is open 9 A.M.–5 P.M. daily.

It's an expensive diversion (prices float close to $200), but the **United States Hot**

Air Balloon Team (141 Hopewell Rd., Elverson, 610/469-0782 or 800/763-5987, www.ushotairballoon.com) takes daily flights over the Amish farmland. Be sure before you commit—baskets can hold up to eight people so your vision of a private excursion is possible, but not likely. They have two launch sites, one in St. Peters and one in Lancaster. You can help prepare the balloon for flight, and then settle in for a long drift over the rolling countryside, followed by snacks and a champagne toast. You'll have to leave your bike on the ground.

Compared to Intercourse, Lancaster's a metropolis (which is why I steer clear), but there's something worth seeing here on Tuesday, Friday, and Saturday mornings. The historic **Central Market** (717/291-4723), in the heart of Lancaster at Penn Square, has been at this location since the 1730s and is America's oldest publicly owned, continuously operated farmers market. It may take a few hours to figure out how to strap a dozen bags of farm-fresh produce, pastries, syrups, salmon cakes, quarts of milk, flowers, crab cakes, baked goods, chow-chows, and relishes onto your bike, but it'll be worth it. Back toward town on pleasing Route 340, the **Bird in Hand Farmers Market** (2710 Old Philadelphia Pike/Rte. 340, 717/393-9674, www.birdinhandfarmersmarket.com) is smaller but equally popular. A load of Amish farmers sell here as well, and when you look into their doleful eyes, I doubt you can escape without buying some homemade products, whether it's pickles, fudge, nuts, jellies, or jellied pickle nut fudge. Really, really good stuff.

In the heart of Intercourse, **W. L. Zimmerman and Sons** (3601 Old Philadelphia Pike/Rte. 340, 717/768-8291) is where the Amish and English shop for dry goods and groceries. Opened in 1909, the store caters to its base by offering an amazing inventory of products last seen in a 1939 A&P catalogue. Although a larger store has opened next door, in this old store you'll be shopping shoulder to shoulder with taciturn young Amish men and their equally stoic wives.

Blue-Plate Specials

Although Amish country is shy on tattoo parlors and tanning salons, there's no shortage of great restaurants, the kind you crave when you're on the road or have just raised a barn. In some cases, you'll share a large table with other travelers.

Slightly smaller than Beijing, the **Plain & Fancy Farm** (3121 Old Philadelphia Pike/Rte. 340, Bird-in-Hand, 717/768-4400, www.plainandfancyfarm.com) serves food nearly as large. This ranks among my five favorite road food pit stops, and the busloads of diners here would concur. Lunch and dinner are served at huge picnic tables inside the barnlike building, where you'll eat as much roast beef, sausage, chicken, mashed potatoes, bow-tie noodles, vegetables, and ice cream as your big ol' belly can hold. And how many places do you know serve shoofly pie?

The Smucker family does well producing filling country foods, the kind you'll find at **Bird-in-Hand Family Restaurant** (2760 Old Philadelphia Pike/Rte. 340, Bird-in-Hand, 717/768-1550, www.bird-in-hand.com). The menu features ham, pork and sauerkraut, lima beans, roast turkey, new potatoes, and the like. Most items are made from scratch (such as the homemade soups), with some ingredients and dishes delivered by Amish farmers. And aside from Plain & Fancy Farm, how many places do you know serve shoofly pie?

Stoltzfus Farm Restaurant (Rte. 772 E., 717/768-8156, www.stoltzfusfarm-restaurant.com), serves big food, such as homemade sausage, chicken, hamloaf, chow-chow, applesauce, apple butter, sweet potatoes, and corn, plus desserts like cherry crumb, apple crumb, and fresh shoofly pie. And how many places do you know serve shoofly pie? Yes, three is the correct answer. Open for lunch and dinner daily except Sunday, closed December–March.

In a little truck stop in 1929, Anna Miller cooked up chicken and waffles for travelers. Today, **Miller's Smorgasbord** (Rte. 30 one mile east of Rte. 896, 717/687-6621) serves lunch and dinner daily, plus breakfast every day in season. Mix and match omelettes, pancakes, French toast, homemade breads, soups, baked apples, roast turkey, baked ham, fried chicken, fish, shrimp, sautéed mushrooms, mashed potatoes, baked cabbage, chicken pot pie, cakes, and pies that'll kick off your very own sumo wrestler training program.

Shut-Eye

Thanks to its relative closeness to Lancaster, there are countless lodging choices. But ask anyone, and they'll tell you it's better in Intercourse.

Inn-dependence

I would rank the **Amish Country Inns & Spa** (3542 Old Philadelphia Pike, 717/768-2626 or 800/664-0949, www.amishcountryinns.com, $149 and up) as one of America's best inns. Elmer Thomas restored this 1909 Victorian home, and his staff practices courtesy as art. The rooms befit a five-star hotel, the breakfasts are superb, and the top-floor suite is great for couples. Rates start at $149 and reach as high as (yipes!) $379 for the largest suite. Out back, Elmer created themed cottages, which feature large rooms, microwaves, desks, fireplaces, generous baths, whirlpool

tubs, fridges, wet bars, and Amish furnishings built specially for the rooms. Suffice it to say this is absolutely first-rate for riders who can splurge. Elmer's son runs the other recommended option in the heart of town: the **Best Western Intercourse Village Inn** (Rtes. 340 and 772, 717/768-3636 or 800/717-6202, $109–139). A standard hotel, it nonetheless stays true to Elmer's vision of cleanliness and friendliness. An on-site restaurant serves home-cooked breakfast, lunch, and dinner. There are laundry facilities here, too.

Chain Drive

These chain hotels are in town, or within 10 miles of the city center: **Best Western, Comfort Inn, Days Inn, Econo Lodge, Fairfield Inn, Hampton Inn, Holiday Inn, Howard Johnson, Knights Inn, Motel 6, Quality Inn, Ramada, Red Carpet Inn, Rodeway, Scottish Inns, Sleep Inn, Super 8, Travelodge**

© NANCY HOWELL

Fill 'er up! A barn-size ad for dairy fresh milk in Amish Country.

For more information, including phone numbers and websites, see page 439.

SIDE TRIP: LITITZ

One of the peak moments in motorcycle touring is when you discover a new town that hasn't been harmed by homogenization. From the northwest corner of the previous ride (on Route 772), it's only a short ride to Lititz (north of Lancaster) where almost nothing has happened and which sports that look favored by Norman Rockwell. Ride Route 772 north into this small town, and you'll arrive in a busy little shopping district with a Main Street and a shaded park centered around a stream and natural spring and all of the essentials to qualify as a neat town. There's the historic **General Sutter Inn** (14 E. Main St., 717/626-2115, www.generalsutterinn.com, $70–130), which features the 1764 Restaurant and 16 spacious rooms. It's tempting to stay the night. Around the corner, **Glassmyer's Restaurant** (23 N. Broad St., 717/626-2345), serves diner meals topped off by creations like egg creams and phosphates from the old-fashioned soda fountain.

But the highlight of Lititz is the aphrodisiacal aroma wafting from the **Wilbur Chocolate Factory** (48 N. Broad St., 717/626-3249, www.wilburbuds.com). Chances are you've never heard of or received a box of Wilbur Chocolates, but that shouldn't stop you from sniffing your way around the Candy Americana Museum, which details the history of cocoa, the life cycle of a candy bar, and Wilbur's "Wheel of Fortune" candy horoscope. A gift shop features T-shirts, ordinary candy, and a gift pack containing five 10-pound chocolate bars—yes, *50 pounds* of chocolate bargain-priced at $179. Overhead, the ceiling rumbles beneath the weight of Wilbur gears and belts cranking out another batch of chocolates.

Provided you don't fall into a diabetic coma, spend some time bumming around downtown and then take your time riding back on the country roads of your choice. On the boomerang return, you'll pass Mennonite children skimming through the hills on simple scooters, farmers selling fresh produce, flowers, homemade bread, and root beer. You may even pass the random harness maker who can turn his expertise at creating harnesses into making custom saddlebags for your own iron horse.

Resources for Riders

Amish Country Run

Pennsylvania Travel Information
Pennsylvania Road Conditions—866/976-8747, www.paturnpike.com
Pennsylvania State Parks—888/727-2757, www.dcnr.state.pa.us
Pennsylvania Tourism and Lodging Information—717/232-8880,
    www.patourism.org
Pennsylvania Visitor Information—800/847-4872, www.visitpa.com

Local and Regional Information
Bucks County Visitors Bureau—215/639-0300 or 800/836-2825, www.bccvb.org
Harrisburg (Intercourse) Weather—814/231-2408
Lambertville (NJ) Chamber of Commerce—609/397-0055, www.lambertville.org
Lancaster County (Intercourse) Information—717/299-8901 or 800/723-8824,
    www.padutchcountry.com
New Hope Chamber of Commerce—215/862-9990, www.newhope-pa.com
New Hope Visitors Center—215/862-5030, www.newhopevisitorscenter.org

Pennsylvania Motorcycle Shops
Action Motorsports—1881 Whiteford Rd., York, 717/757-2688,
    www.actionmotorsportsyork.com
B&B Yamaha—343 Champ Blvd., Mannheim, 717/898-5764,
    www.bblancasterpa.com
Classic Harley-Davidson—983 James Dr., Leesport, 610/916-7777,
    www.classicharley.com
Don's Kawasaki—20 E. Market St., Hallam (York), 717/755-6002,
    www.donskawasaki.com
Lancaster Harley-Davidson—308 Beaver Valley Pike, Willow Street,
    717/464-2703, www.lancasterhd.com
Laugermans Harley-Davidson—100 Arsenal Rd., York, 717/854-3214,
    www.laugerman.com
Ray's Yamaha Polaris Victory—5560 Perkiomen, Reading, 610/582-2700,
    www.raysyamahapolarisvictory.com
Sport Cycle Suzuki—309 Hafer Dr., Leesport, 610/916-5000,
    www.sportcyclesuzuki.com

Civil War Run

Gettysburg, Pennsylvania to Fredericksburg, Virginia

As you ease into this Pennsylvania ride, you may sense that the state is a microcosm of American history. From the Declaration of Independence to the Exposition of 1876, from Amish farmland to the fields of Gettysburg, it seems that everything we're about is all contained right here.

This will be a poignant trip through the killing fields of Pennsylvania, then across a mood-changing Maryland state park, past Civil War highlights, and into two historic Virginia walking towns. The route may not reveal all there is to know about the Civil War, but along the way you'll gain an appreciation for the countryside and your country.

GETTYSBURG PRIMER

In July 1863, Confederate soldiers were headed for Harrisburg, intent on capturing the city. But when an advance team ran across Union troops, the encounter sparked the flash point of the Battle of Gettysburg. Within three days, the Civil War reached its turning point as Robert E. Lee's 75,000

men and George G. Meade's 97,000 soldiers faced off. At the height of the battle, more than 172,000 men and 634 cannons were spread out over 25 square miles. When the final shot was fired, 51,000 casualties bloodied the fields.

Although the war continued for two more years, the Battle of Gettysburg broke the spirit and strength of the Confederacy. Months after the battle, the dedication of the Soldiers National Cemetery at Gettysburg gave President Lincoln the opportunity to praise the sacrifice of the soldiers and state what he felt were essential truths about our experiment with democracy.

To be sure, this has evolved into a tourist town with more than two million people arriving each year to tour the battlefields, and a million more arriving to see the town itself. While roughly a century and a half of progress has added modern touches to the town, the hallowed grounds of the battlefields have been well preserved to honor the sacrifices and bravery of men on both sides of the conflict.

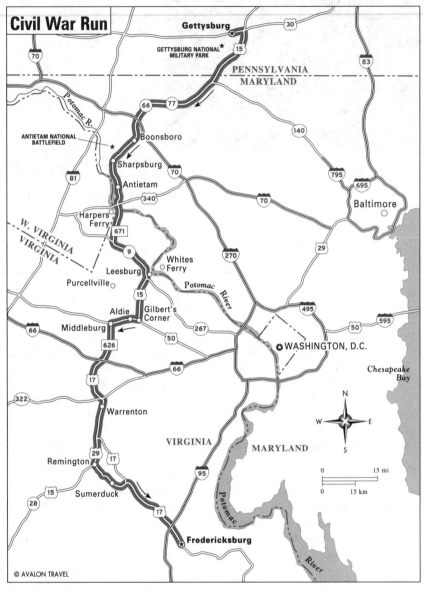

Civil War Run

Gettysburg
30
15
★ GETTYSBURG NATIONAL MILITARY PARK
70
83
PENNSYLVANIA
MARYLAND
Potomac R.
66
77
140
ANTIETAM NATIONAL BATTLEFIELD
Boonsboro
★
Sharpsburg
795
81
70
Antietam
695
340
70
Baltimore
Harpers Ferry
671
W. VIRGINIA
VIRGINIA
9
270
Whites Ferry
Leesburg
29
Purcellville
Potomac River
15
Aldie
Gilbert's Corner
495
50
595
Middleburg
626
267
66
50
★ **WASHINGTON, D.C.**
66
Chesapeake Bay
17
322
N
W E
S
Warrenton
VIRGINIA
MARYLAND
29
17
0   15 mi
Remington
95
0   15 km
15
Sumerduck
28
Potomac
17
Fredericksburg
River
© AVALON TRAVEL

Route: Gettysburg to Fredericksburg via Catoctin Mountain Park, Antietam, Harpers Ferry, Leesburg

Distance: Approximately 170 miles

First Leg: Gettysburg, Pennsylvania to Leesburg, Viriginia (92 miles)

Second Leg: Leesburg to Fredericksburg, Virginia (80 miles)

Helmet Laws: Pennsylvania does not require helmets for riders over 21; Maryland, Virginia, and West Virginia require helmets.

ON THE ROAD: GETTYSBURG

Gettysburg's legend in American history is so large, it's surprising to find that the actual places of note are confined within a relatively small area. At its core Gettysburg is still a small town and as you walk through the historic district, try to picture it circa 1863 when only small farms were found in the outlying countryside. Use your imagination to visualize the community then and try to picture the people living in peace when all hell broke loose.

The town square is bisected by U.S. 15 Business Route, the main north–south road through town, and by east–west U.S. 30. This is the perfect base for your tour since you'll experience the richness of history both here and at the battlefield visitor center, about a mile south.

But first, bordering the town square are two sites worth a stop. On the southeast side of the square, the **David Wills House** (8 Lincoln Sq., 717/334-2599, www.davidwillshouse.org), is the home of the young lawyer who extended the invitation

Honest Abe gives an honest reaction to *Great American Motorcycle Tours:* He loves it.

to Lincoln to make "a few appropriate remarks." After arriving, Lincoln stayed in the second-floor room and worked on his speech the night before the dedication of the cemetery. Completely restored, for $6.50 you can visit the entire home as well as Lincoln's room and see related exhibits and mementoes. For an interesting photo, outside the home is a life-size statue of Lincoln talking to a statue that looks like Perry Como. Stand in front of Perry and pose with the president.

Across the street, the **Gettysburg Hotel** (1 Lincoln Sq., 717/337-2000, www.hotelgettysburg.com) has welcomed its share of presidents as well, primarily Eisenhower and his staff, who stayed here when the summer White House came to town.

After walking the square, ride south down U.S. 15 Business Route turning onto Route 97 to reach the new in 2008 $100 million battlefield visitor center. Obviously, you'll want to ride the battlefield, but do this only after taking a guided tour since it's important to know where you are to understand what you are seeing. After a tour you'll know more about places such as Little Round Top and the site of Pickett's Charge. From the summit of Little Round Top, you overlook the "Valley of Death" bordered by Devil's Den, a haven for Southern sharpshooters. Then there's one of the saddest places in America: the infamous "Wheatfield," where 6,000 Union and Confederate soldiers were killed, wounded, or captured during just four hours of bloody fighting.

After your guided tour, head to the **The Gettysburg National Military Park Visitor Center** (1195 Baltimore Pike, 717/334-1124, www.nps.gov/gett), where park rangers will fill in the blanks. They'll tell you about the 3,500 soldiers killed here and buried in the cemetery, nearly 1,000 of their identities known only to

A monument of General Gouverneur K. Warren keeps watch over the Valley of Death at Little Round Top in Gettysburg.

God. You'll hear about the battle and its terrible aftermath—the burial of the dead, bodies being eaten by hogs, and looters whose punishment was burying dead horses. But what you'll want to hear most is the story of Lincoln's visit and the Gettysburg Address.

You may have read Lincoln's speech, but only after you've seen Gettysburg will you understand its importance. It was Lincoln's "I Have a Dream" speech as he re-affirmed the pursuit of democracy and, in less than two minutes and 300 words, addressed the nation's past, present, and future. After the speech was back in his pocket, "the United States are" became "the United States is" with Lincoln laying out how the war could save the nation envisioned by the authors of the Constitution.

From Little Round Top to the site of Pickett's Charge, this is a spiritual ride. Ride later in the day or very early in the morning when the tourist crowds thin.

That's when you can take your time to really see the roads and retrace the trails forged by soldiers of both sides, and you cannot help but be moved by the experience.

PULL IT OVER:
GETTYSBURG HIGHLIGHTS
Attractions and Adventures

The **Gettysburg National Military Park Visitor Center** (1195 Baltimore Pike, 717/334-1124, www.nps.gov/gett) is ground zero for your Gettysburg experience. To see what needs to be seen in the cemetery, travel with a tour guide. Each day during the summer there are about 20 free ranger-led tours and, not surprisingly, the best and most enlightening information comes straight from these men and women whose love of history is palpable. A separate fee (about $10) will get you into the introductory film "A New Birth of Freedom," the cyclorama painting of the battle, and the museum which exhibits muskets, bayonets, artillery fuse plugs, swords, field glasses, flags, the drum of a drummer boy, and pictures of very old veterans from Gettysburg's 75th anniversary in 1938.

If you really want to know more details of the Battle of Gettysburg, invest in a private, licensed guide from **Gettysburg National Military Park Guided Tours,** which can be arranged at the visitors center. You'll have to be serious about this since you'll need to rent a car to transport the guide who will take you on a personalized two-hour tour based on your interests. Great for real Civil War buffs, it's $70 for 7–15 people.

The option that seems to be the most popular with most people is the **Gettysburg Tour Center** (778 Baltimore St., 717/334-6296 or 800/447-8788, www.gettysburgbattlefieldtours.com) which

Gettysburg Battle Facts

It was a horrifying three days (or four, when you consider people were still being killed on July 4), and the scope of it still resonates nearly a century and a half later. The community survives on history, which is why facts like these are important to know:

Well over a century later, John Burns —the "Citizen Hero of Gettysburg"— stands ready with his rifle.

© NANCY HOWELL

- Nearly seven million bullets were fired at Gettysburg by more than 160,000 soldiers. How many were Union, and how many Confederates? One park guide doesn't care. "They were *all* American soldiers," he explained.

- The oldest fighter was John Burns, the "Citizen Hero of Gettysburg." At 72, this veteran of the War of 1812 heard the commotion, got dressed in his blue swallowtail coat and top hat, grabbed his rifle, and started fighting alongside the fabled Iron Brigade on McPherson's Ridge. He was hit three times—the first bullet hit his belt buckle, the second his arm, and the third his ankle, which knocked him to the ground. Burying his ammo, he got up, limped towards home, and when confronted, he lied to Confederate soldiers that he was simply a farmer caught in the crossfire. They let him pass and he lived until 1872.

- In 1938, at the 75th anniversary of the battle, a 94-year-old veteran was asked if he was enjoying his stay in Gettysburg. "A lot more than I did 75 years ago," he said.

- In a letter home, one soldier wrote to his wife, "Soldiering is 99 percent boredom, and one percent sheer terror."

- At Gettysburg, more than 32,000 men were wounded, and 8,000 died. About 94 percent were killed by bullets, less than 1 percent by bayonet.

- Of the 1,328 monuments at Gettysburg, the best may be the Peace Memorial—the only one not dedicated to war. After the 50th anniversary of the battle in 1913, soldiers from the north and south pooled their own money and raised additional funds to create the monument built, not coincidentally, of Alabama limestone and Maine granite. The inscription, "Peace Eternal in a Nation United," says it all.

offers a fairly affordable way to get some good background information and a lay-out of the area. The $24.95 history lesson takes place aboard an open-air double-decker bus you would normally make fun of, but the schedule is punctual and the information factual (although little of it is presented with a great deal of creativity or enthusiasm). Still, it stops at historic sites such as Pickett's Charge and Bloody Run so you can take mental notes and return later to explore on your own. The depar-ture point can vary based on the time of year, so call ahead.

Aside from a motorcycle, one of the coolest ways to see the Gettysburg battle-field is in a 1930s Yellowstone Park bus. **Historic Battlefield Bus Tours** (55 Stein-wehr Ave., 717/334-8000, www.historic-tourcompany.com) offers 2.5-hour tours for about $20. The restored open-top clas-sics are visually appealing and with only 17 passengers you'll get more attention.

If your bike is equipped with audio, you may want to skip the bus tour and trade $17.95 for a two-hour narrative CD tour of the battle's history that you can pick up at the **American Civil War Museum** (297 Steinwehr Ave., 717/334-6245, www.get-tysburgmuseum.com). The narrative takes you through the battle's three days, telling you when to turn and where to look. The park itself offers a more affordable option: a free 90-minute podcast you can download and play as you take a walking tour. Check into that at **www.civilwartraveler.com.**

It's hard to believe World War II's most illustrious general could be overshadowed, but when Dwight Eisenhower bought a home in Gettysburg in 1950, he was destined to take a back seat to the battle. He used his farm here (the only home he ever owned) as a weekend retreat and temporary White House. Today, it is the **Eisenhower National Historic Site** (1195 Baltimore Pike, 717/338-9114, www.nps. gov/eise). If you grew up liking Ike, you'll like the tour ($7.50), which is available from the National Park Service Visitor Center. Access to the Eisenhower Farm is by shuttle bus only, so give your bike a rest in the center's parking lot. The displays are rich in personal items, such as Ike's World War II jacket and helmet.

Shopping

If your den looks suspiciously like a Civil War museum, then Gettysburg is where you'll want to stock up on items for the new wing. There are several impressive collectibles and antiquarian shops, includ-ing **The Union Drummer Boy** (13 Bal-timore St., 717/334-2350, www.uniondb. com), which carries more memorabilia than a soldier carried in 1863: authentic muskets, carbines, artillery, revolvers, uni-forms, swords, letters, leather goods, relics, artillery shells, flags, documents, bullets embedded in wood, and artifacts aplenty.

Blue-Plate Specials

The Lincoln Diner (32 Carlisle St., 717/334-3900) is just right for motorcycle travelers. An authentic 24-hour diner, it serves such staples as fried clams, fried oysters, breaded veal, and the obligatory cholesterol-rich breakfasts. Watch your diet at home, but this place may tempt you to pull an Elvis and pig out on a hot fudge banana royale.

Don't miss **Dunlap's** (90 Buford Ave., 717/334-4816, www.dunlapsrestaurant. com). It's been here forever, thanks to a menu that features ham, turkey, beef cooked and sliced on-site, fried chicken, real mashed potatoes, sandwiches, stuffed flounder, steaks, and big breakfasts. Dun-lap's tops it off with cheap prices.

General Pickett's (571 Steinwehr Ave., 717/334-7580) is not a chain but a genuine honest-to-goodness buffet. Made-from-scratch soups, fresh-baked breads, a salad bar, and down-home entrées are all wrapped up with homemade pies and cakes. On the corner of the square, the **Plaza Restaurant** (28 Baltimore St., 717/334-1999, www.gettysburgplaza.com) also includes a lounge that's larger than the dining room. The specialty is Greek food (heroes, kebabs, souvlaki), but you can also go for steaks, crab legs, and home-made soups. Credit the lounge for keeping the joint jumpin' until 2:30 A.M.

Watering Holes

On the town square, **The Pub & Restaurant** (20–22 Lincoln Sq., 717/334-7100) gives you options: Head to the restaurant for a traditional entrée (chicken, steak, pasta, etc.) or buy a brew at the hammered copper-top bar. Popular with college students who like the $2 pitchers, the full bar also serves ales, domestic brews, and other spirits. If the weather's right, grab a sidewalk table and enjoy the evening and a cool one.

Also in the heart of downtown, the **Flying Bull Saloon** (28 Carlisle St., 717/334-6202), may be the best biker-style bar in town. Low-key and dark, it sets the stage with a pool table, darts, and a small stage for local bands. In addition to bar food, there are drink specials like Thursday's pitchers of Pabst for two bucks. Ah...college days.

As the name implies, the **Spring House Tavern** (89 Steinwehr Ave., 717/334-2100, www.dobbinhouse.com) is more like a colonial pub. In the basement of the Dobbin House, tavern waitresses wear colonial costumes, and candles light the room. Although it doubles as a family restaurant, the full bar, a handful of tap beers, and its unique setting make this place worth seeing.

Sharpshooters (900 Chambersburg Rd., 717/334-4332, www.sharpshootersgrille.

com) is a bar at the Inn at Herr Ridge. During the battle of Gettysburg, the home and outbuildings served as a Confederate hospital, but time and capitalism have turned it into a faithfully restored pre–Civil War tavern. Saloonkeepers serve beer straight from the ice into your sweaty hands. While the lounge is small and comfortable, a large deck can get you outdoors to enjoy the cool summer nights. In addition to bar food, entertainment varies from darts, foosball, and video games to a first for me: a black-light poolroom.

Shut-Eye

Numerous independent hotels are located near the battlefield, each offering similar rooms but different amenities—some feature a pool or whirlpool tub. In the heart of town, **Gettysburg Hotel** (1 Lincoln Sq., 717/337-2000 or 800/528-1234, www.hotelgettysburg.com, $99–153) is a full-service Best Western. This 1797 landmark has covered parking, a restaurant, and a few suites with fireplaces and whirlpool tubs. Their pub, McClellan's Tavern, is a popular watering hole.

Inn-dependence

For descriptions of and reservations for the majority of area inns, check **Inns of Gettysburg** (www.gettysburgbedandbreakfast.com).

Ride down the street to the **Farnsworth House Inn** (401 Baltimore St., 717/334-8838, www.farnsworthhouseinn.com, $145 and up), if you don't mind a gravel drive and the fact that a Confederate sharpshooter made this his post. The Victorian home has a sunroom and country garden breakfasts. It also offers a restaurant with dishes like country ham, peanut soup, meat casserole, and pumpkin fritters. Rumor has it some of the rooms are haunted, but the rates are the same with or without ghosts. Note: The

100 bullet holes in the house may make it slightly drafty in winter.

Traveling in a group? Looking for a place in the historic district? Consider **James Gettys Hotel** (27 Chambersburg St., 717/337-1334 or 888/900-5275, www. jamesgettyshotel.com, $145 and up). An inn in the 1830s, it served as a hostel and apartment house before being restored as an 11-room inn. Riders appreciate amenities including complimentary continental breakfasts and rooms and suites that sleep up to four. Suites include a kitchenette with microwave, refrigerator, coffeemakers, and two-burner stove.

A first-class option is the **Brickhouse Inn** (452 Baltimore St., 717/338-9337 or 800/864-3464, www.brickhouseinn.com, $109 and up). Equidistant between downtown and the visitor center, this place is a bargain when you consider the courtesy and service that culminates with an extraordinary breakfast served on the backyard patio. First-rate.

Chain Drive

These chain hotels are in town, or within 10 miles of the city center:

Best Western, Comfort Inn, Days Inn, Econo Lodge, Hampton Inn, Holiday Inn, Quality Inn, Red Carpet Inn, Sleep Inn, Super 8, Travelodge

For more information, including phone numbers and websites, see page 439.

SIDE TRIP: YORK HARLEY-DAVIDSON TOUR

Next to the Harley headquarters in Milwaukee, York (roughly 30 miles east of Gettysburg) is the site of most interest to riders. At more than 230 acres and with more than 1.5 million square feet under its roof, **Harley-Davidson's Final Assembly Plant** is the largest H-D facility, where more than 3,200 employees crank

out 700 bikes a day. This tour is infinitely more interesting than a similar tour near the company headquarters.

Offered weekdays only (with Saturday tours added in summer) the one-hour factory tour begins as a guide takes you to the shop floor to view the parts manufacturing process and the final motorcycle assembly lines. It's absolutely cool to see strips of sheet metal stamped, pressed, and bent into fenders and fuel tanks. You'll follow the entire process and see how the component pieces are meshed with engines to create Softails, police bikes, cruisers, and special-order bikes. You can test-sit the newest models and spend as much time as you like in the renovated museum, which focuses on the history, people, process, and product in the York factory. Tours are offered on a first-come first-served basis, arrive early. Tours depart between 9 A.M.–2 P.M., with the tour center and gift shop open 8 A.M.–4 P.M. Call 717/848-1177 or 877/883-1450 for tour times and availability. Reservations are required for groups of 10 or more, call 717/852-6590. The York Visitor Center (at the plant) can be reached at 717/852-6006. On the tour, you'll need to wear close-toed shoes and leave your camera behind—so don't get any ideas about starting your own motorcycle corporation. The plant is off U.S. 30 at 1425 Eden Road, one mile east of I-83.

ON THE ROAD: GETTYSBURG TO LEESBURG

Even though it'll be a short run to Leesburg, don't plan on leaving late since the roads ahead are beautiful and peaceful and you'll be racing the sun if you decide to stop in Catoctin, Antietam, or Harper's Ferry. Try to give yourself a full day to enjoy the country.

U.S. 15 Business Route South, the level two-lane road leaving Gettysburg, passes statuary and monuments that suggest that the entire town is a cemetery. Just past the town limits, **Rider's Edge** (2490 Emmitsburg Rd., 717/334-2518) is a convenient stop for last-minute gear. About six miles later, you'll approach the Mason-Dixon line as you hook up with U.S. 15 South, which turns into a larger highway, albeit narrower than an interstate. Although this is no back road, it provides surprisingly nice vistas of farmland and continues over the Maryland state line before Route 77 West veers off to the right and positions you for one of the great rides.

Your disappointment over leaving U.S. 15 dissipates the moment you enter Maryland's **Catoctin Mountain Park.** Among America's top roads, this is one that you can ride like an animal. This two-lane exclamation point is a thrill-a-minute road that rolls past valleys, twists, lakes, sharp curves, deer, and rivers. Past Pryor's Orchards (purveyor of jelly, honey, nuts, and apples), you'll spot a great river and a setting as intriguing as Sherwood Forest. Glance up and the mountain peaks reveal themselves well above the forest. Look ahead and the road is a grab bag of mild curves and sharp edges, like an abridged version of New Hampshire's Kank. There are side roads leading deeper into the park, so if you have time to spare, get lost and you may stumble across a waterfall or wind up at the gates of Camp David. When you return to Route 77 where the sun dapples through the branches above, the road is intersected by the legendary Appalachian Trail. This marks the point where a steep descent weaves down the hill.

Too soon, you're out of the woods. Instead of continuing into the traffic of Hagerstown, turn left on Route 66 and drop south toward the town of Sharpsburg and the Antietam battlefield. The road is marked by apple orchards and hand-painted signs announcing bales of straw for sale, and a few miles down there's a general store in Mount Aetna where you can pull over for a soda pop. By the time you reach the junction at I-70, you'll be content to blow past it because you're sure there are far better roads ahead. There are. Ahead the asphalt is as fluid as a river, leading to farmland vistas and bucolic countryside, bumps and small hills, and sweeping turns that throw you into great straightaways.

At Boonsboro, the roads T's at Alternate U.S. 40 and you take a funky fork south and ride several blocks to get on Route 34 West. Soon you'll be on the Sharpsburg Pike, and although the route switches direction often, you'll pass villages and avoid cities and have a blast all the way to Sharpsburg. When you hit the intersection at Route 65, turn right and ride about two miles to the **Antietam National Battlefield** (301/432-5124, www.nps.gov/anti, $4). Sadly, even more than the events of September 11, 2001, this site marks the bloodiest day in American history. When Lee made his first invasion to take the war into the North, he brought 40,000 troops. General George B. McClellan led more than 80,000 Union soldiers. When they met on September 17, 1862—a year before the Battle of Gettysburg—more than 23,000 men were left dead, wounded, or missing. To learn more, watch a film in the visitor center's theater: There's an introductory film shown daily on the hour or a one-hour documentary about the battle shown daily at noon. The loop road will lead you on a self-guided tour that's just over eight miles with 11 stops along the way, or, for a fee, tour guides who know much more than a brochure can be retained through www.antietambattlefieldguides.com.

Next, prepare yourself for a weirdly wild ride. From Route 65, return to Route 34 and turn right, where a block later, Mechanic Street is on your left. Turn here. Soon this will become Harpers Ferry Road and soon it will become a road you love. Almost immediately, there are oddly angled cornfields creating nice dips, and sharp curves and slow curves wrapping around stone walls and cornstalks. This blacktop roller coaster hauls you up a hill, slings you one way at the peak, and then drops and lifts you up again before slinging you the other way.

White churches and cemeteries mark the road, and new sights flash past: bales of hay, the stone bridges, the one-lane bridge that's perfect for a photo, the river, and the valley that gives you a sense of cosmic proportion since it all seems nearly void of life, save for a few homes that pockmark the woods. Somewhere along the way, there's a very tricky and very important fork near a blip of a community called Samples Manor; although, you can turn left or right here and end up in the same place. I swung to the right to stay on Harpers Ferry Road and continued south toward Pleasantville, riding through miles of desolate primeval forest where the lack of civilization convinced me that I had ridden off the face of the earth. Just about the time you'd be tempted to shoot up a signal flare, you'll spy the Potomac peeking through the narrow woods to your right. You'll merge onto Sandyhook Road in a ramshackle riverside town that looks like coal-mining country—without the coal. File away a mental image, roll under a bridge, make a buttonhook turn to reach that same bridge (U.S. 340), and cross into Virginia.

Follow U.S. 340 West for a minute or two and you'll be in West Virginia and at the visitor center of **Harpers Ferry National Historical Park** (304/535-6029, www.nps.gov/hafe, $6). A must-see stop, this is where radical abolitionist John Brown, hoping to jump-start a slave rebellion, rounded up 18 slaves and attacked the U.S. Army arsenal in October 1859. Didn't happen. However, the Civil War *did* happen—and because of its placement where the Shenandoah and Potomac rivers meet, during the Civil War this town (like Liz Taylor) changed hands eight times. There is not a single museum here. Instead, there are *25* museums in a park that spans three states: West Virginia, Virginia, and Maryland. You'll see a restored town, hiking trails, guided tours, interpretive tours, and living history programs. While the park is open all year, most programs are held in the spring and summer.

From Harpers Ferry, double back on U.S. 340 so you can eye the ruggedly handsome Shenandoah River. Ahead, Route 671 is the continuation of Harpers Ferry Road where you turn right at the well-stocked service station. You'll gather that Virginia must have gotten a good price on scenery, because there's far more of it here than in Addis Ababa. Later, you may see evidence of the state's wildflower program, which blankets highway medians with flowers, such as black-eyed Susans, daffodils, goldenrod, and ox-eye daisies.

Route 671 is a fast two-lane road, with pretty valleys and canopy roads that are in direct contrast to the sharp twists, weaves, ascents, and descents you'll be making. Although McMansions threaten what was once unspoiled scenery, the road's all right and lasts about eight miles until you reach Route 9 (aka Charles Town Pike). Turn left at a little country store and head towards Leesburg on Route 9, taking a well-deserved break to see great stone walls stretched across fields, farmhouses dotting the tops of low hills, and cornfields everywhere. If it's dusk and the conditions are right, you may have the pleasure of watching a great gray fog rolling in over the hills.

Shortly, Route 9 merges with Route 7. It's been a great ride, and now it's time to head east and rest up in Leesburg.

LEESBURG PRIMER

Anyone who's heard of the Civil War has heard the oft-repeated phrase describing it as "brother against brother." To see how true that is, this reality was embodied in the area surrounding Leesburg.

After John Brown's raid on Harpers Ferry in 1859, folks in Loudoun County feared a slave insurrection. And even though this was never the site of a major battle or even a significant skirmish, in May 1861 Leesburg voted 400–22 to secede from the Union. Just a few miles away, the Germans and Quakers of Waterford voted 220–31 to remain with, *and fight for,* the preservation of the United States. Thus, the area spawned Virginia's only organized Union force: the Loudoun Rangers, led by Quaker Sam Meade, who scouted, patrolled, and skirmished with Confederate forces in the area.

These conflicts are no longer apparent as today's lifestyle reflects a more genteel history. And though this may not be the most historical town you'll stay in, it's worth an overnight on your way south.

ON THE ROAD: LEESBURG

Leesburg is just right for a bike ride. Downtown, which is at the intersection of Market Street (Rte. 7) and King Street (U.S. 15), is a manageable size; there's plenty of parking for bikes, and the diners, nightclubs, and riders from assorted clubs are visible reminders that you're in the right place.

If your interests lean towards obtaining a quick and painless history lesson, for

just three bucks head inside the **Loudoun Museum** (16 Loudoun St., 703/777-7427, www.loudounmuseum.org). A smart first stop, you can always count on the short video that explains the history of Loudoun county and the Battle of Ball's Bluff, a small but important skirmish that represents the first and largest conflict fought in Leesburg. Between May and October, there are historical walking tours ($10) available by reservation if you have the desire to learn even more about Leesburg's participation in the Civil War or, as the locals call it, "the War of Northern Aggression." All in all, it's a nice museum that also includes slices of colonial history and information on local farmer John Binns who, in 1804, wrote a "Treatise on Practical Farming." This introduction to modern farming techniques (some of which are still in use) drew praise from the king of gentleman farmers, Thomas Jefferson.

The remainder of downtown is like a smaller Charleston; the houses have been

Cruising across the Potomac with *White's Ferry*: a short trip that creates a lot of memories.

preserved well, although their scale is not as impressive. Cluttered antiques shops abound. If shopping's not your thing, take U.S. 15 a mile north to Battlefield Parkway and see Ball's Bluff Battlefield and then attend to a plan more important than investing in your 401(k). Think about shoving some grub in a saddlebag and then ride up U.S. 15 to White's Ferry Road where you turn east and follow a narrow path to the water. Scratch around for four bucks (seven bucks round-trip) and board *White's Ferry* (24801 White's Ferry Rd., 301/349-5200) for a short and enjoyable ferry ride over the wide and tranquil Potomac River. When you reach Maryland a few minutes later, park it and enjoy a picnic—an inexpensive pleasure that feels like a million bucks.

PULL IT OVER: LEESBURG HIGHLIGHTS
Attractions and Adventures

What happened at **Ball's Bluff Battlefield** (Battlefield Pkwy., 703/779-9372) marks a significant day in Civil War history. In 1861, Union troops were convinced it wouldn't be long before they'd whip the Rebels into submission. But after 1,700 Union soldiers crossed the Potomac and came face to face with an equally determined 1,700 Confederate troops defending Leesburg, they changed their minds. When the smoke cleared, there were 155 Rebel casualties—which was a pittance compared to the Union's 900-plus casualties representing men who were shot, drowned, wounded, and captured. Even worse, bodies of the drowned men floated downstream to bring the reality of the war to the front door of Washington, D.C. The stinging defeat had some benefits: A committee was formed to investigate Union defeats and corruption and to tighten up the war effort. There's a park

and cemetery here, as well as a mile-long hiking loop with interpretive signs that help you follow the battle. On weekends between May and October, free tours are given.

At Butts/BTI Whitewater (10985 Harpers Ferry Rd., Purcellville, 540/668-9007 or 800/836-9911, www.btiwhitewater.com), they rent two sizes of inner tubes ($19–30), with the option of renting a companion cooler that floats in its own inner tube. Genius! Leave your bike behind, because Butts will bus you up the Shenandoah River, tell you where to get off in Maryland, and then let you drift for two hours and over three rapids before meeting you back in Ol' Virginny for the bus ride home.

Loudoun County, the area surrounding Leesburg, is a rider's paradise. There are dozens of back roads and scenic byways lined with stone-stacked fences, horse farms, vineyards, and towns and villages steeped in history. If it looks like wine country, you're right. You can pick up a map of the Loudoun Wine Trail and the county's vineyards and attractions from the **Loudoun County (Leesburg) Visitors Center** (112-G South St. SE, 703/771-2617 or 800/752-6118, www.visitloudoun.org). There's evidence of this at **Leesburg Vintner** (29 S. King St., 703/777-3322, www.leesburgvintner.com), which has been recognized as Virginia's wine retailer of the year. You'll find barrels of wine (cleverly packaged in bottles), as well as gourmet picnic foods like cheese, crackers, peanuts and other Virginia products.

Blue-Plate Specials

Leesburg Restaurant (9 S. King St., 703/777-3292) serves breakfast, lunch, and dinner daily. In the morning, an equal number of riders and locals appear to frequent this place, a down-home restaurant since 1865. I think this is where Grant threw his victory party.

The perfectly named **Mighty Midget Kitchen** (202 Harrison St. SE #A, 703/779-7880) was crafted out of the fuselage of a World War II–era B-29 bomber. A downtown Leesburg institution since 1947, it serves something called a "hamburger doner" (a German-style hamburger), as well as hot dogs, fries, and soda pop. There's indoor and outdoor patio seating as well as beer and wine served in a *beirgarten* setting.

For a nicer meal, there's none nicer than at the **Tuscarora Mill** (203 Harrison St., 703/771.9300, www.tuskies.com), which, oddly enough, is built within the shell of an old 1899 mill. Coincidence? It's not something I do often, but splurging on something other than diner food can be a nice reward, and entrées like smoked chicken pasta, sesame roasted Atlantic salmon, and a strip steak, plus a nice lounge, can be the perfect conclusion to a long day's ride.

Watering Holes

Although Leesburg seems to have an upscale veneer, it's not above supporting a biker bar in the heart of town. The **Downtown Saloon** (7 N. King St., 703/669-3090) has been around since 1965 perhaps because there are no additives—just a love of motorcycling and the three Ps: peanuts, pinups, and pool. Come here to enjoy bar food, live bands, and a comfortable setting where you can kick back and map out the next leg. As you enjoy your brew, look at the county courthouse through the window and consider the sign that reads "Better off here than across the street."

The Kings Court Tavern (2C Loudoun St. SW, 703/777-7747) is less biker than Brit. A pub theme runs throughout, with private booths, a long bar, TVs, and liquor.

Downstairs at **Ball's Bluff** (2D Loudoun St. SW, 703/777-7757), the underground pub features a well-stocked bar, darts, occasional live music, and traditional food, such as wings, sandwiches, and salads.

Shut-Eye
Inn-dependence

The **Loudoun County B&B Guild** (www.loudounbandb.com) represents many inns throughout the county, as does the county itself—www.visitloudoun.org. One close to downtown is the **Norris House Inn** (108 Loudoun St. SW, 703/777-1806 or 800/644-1806, www.norrishouse.com, $125 and up). This inn features a parlor, a library, a sunroom, and a rambling verandah overlooking the gardens. Antiques accent guest rooms, some of which have fireplaces. The downside: Parking's in a garage a few blocks away.

Chain Drive

These chain hotels are in town, or within 10 miles of the city center:

Best Western, Hampton Inn, Holiday Inn, Ramada

For more information, including phone numbers and websites, see page 439.

ON THE ROAD: LEESBURG TO FREDERICKSBURG

Unlike Wild West desert straightaways where you can strap your handlebars in place and take a nap, roads in Virginia demand your attention. That's the good part. The downside is that the ride to reach Fredericksburg is enjoyable, but it isn't flawless. This is the route I chose because it was largely the most direct and easy to follow, but don't hesitate exploring the nest of back roads on your own.

Leave Leesburg on U.S. 15, the same road that leads out of Gettysburg. It's not impressive at first, just an ordinary road with an ordinary job. But about a dozen miles later at Gilbert's Corner, turn right and ride on U.S. 50 west toward Aldie, followed by Middleburg. If you follow U.S. 50 for another 3,000 miles, you'd reach Sacramento, California. There are beautiful horse farms here, and if you owned an Arabian instead of a bike, you'd probably move in. The passion for all things equestrian is omnipresent in this area and the people shopping in the upscale uptown district of Middleburg are clearly devoted to horses—you can see it in their faces.

When you leave Middleburg behind, turning left to take County Road 626 (aka Halfway Road) south, nothing is sudden. The road reads like a book, revealing a little at a time until the whole story is right in front of you, and here the subject is open Virginia land. When you reach the Plains (which ain't too fancy), look for a service station and then some smooth country riding—nice shallow dips, split-rail fences, sweeping curves, weeping willows, and rustic homes.

Take Route 245, a nice road that crosses beneath I-66, turns into U.S. 17, and then veers off to your left on U.S. 15/29 to bypass Warrenton. Eventually you'll ride into small towns like Remington and ride out seconds later looking for Route 651 toward Sumerduck, a remote road that mixes things up with some tight twists, graceful curves, inclines, and one-lane bridges. From here, the roads are country, and you get the strong feeling you're entering the South. You are. Within a few miles, you've switched channels from *Masterpiece Theatre* to *Hee-Haw*. It's hard to believe this change in cultures happens less than an hour's drive from the nation's capital.

When Route 651 rejoins U.S. 17, turn right and follow it to Fredericksburg, one of the nicest towns you'll have the pleasure to meet.

FREDERICKSBURG PRIMER

Why was Fredericksburg so vital to Civil War soldiers? Open a map, put your finger on this city, and you'll be pointing midway between the Confederate capital of Richmond and the Union capital of Washington, D.C. With that and the high banks of the Rappahannock River providing a natural defensive barrier, as well as a rail corridor capable of keeping both armies supplied, the desire to hold the town led to four separate battles fought in and around the city.

How bad did it get? Consider that Fredericksburg changed hands 10 times during the war and left more than 100,000 casualties with 85,000 men wounded and 15,000 men killed. Add it up and that's more casualties than in the three previous wars (the Mexican–American War, the War of 1812, and the Revolutionary War) *combined*. Needless to say, Fredericksburg was considered the bloodiest landscape in America.

Fortunately, since the Civil War the town has never been reduced to that level of horror. Today, a good vibe runs throughout Fredericksburg where the residents are friendly and the pace is slow, and it all goes a long way in making this one of your most rewarding stops. Along with a sense of history, folks have a sense of humor, so certain tours are far more enjoyable than any I've seen elsewhere. Add to this a walkable downtown district filled with restaurants, art, and antiques-filled shops and you've arrived at the perfect base to reach other Civil War sites, such as Spotsylvania to the east or the Stonewall Jackson Shrine to the south.

ON THE ROAD: FREDERICKSBURG

Of all the historical towns I've visited, I'd say Fredericksburg does the best job of making history interesting and entertaining without turning it into a Disney cartoon caricature.

To get started, park your bike, put on some walking shoes, and do the town. At a good clip you can see it all in a day, although I'd wager you may want to stick around a little longer. For about eight blocks, both sides of Caroline Street provide numerous diversions from cheap antiques to a cool diner to historic homes.

Swing by the **Fredericksburg Visitor Center** (706 Caroline St., 540/373-1776) to buy tickets for everything historical in town, such as the Hugh Mercer Apothecary Shop, the Rising Sun Tavern, Mary Washington House, and Fredericksburg/Spotsylvania National Military Park. These tours are a must while you're here, and buying a Day Pass will save you 40 percent over the price of individual tickets. The center also has great maps for walking tours that highlight different eras of the town's history. If you'd rather save the shoe leather, **Trolley Tours of Fredericksburg** (706 Caroline St., 540/898-0737, www.fredericksburgtrolley.com) departs for a tour of historic homes,

attractions, and the famous Sunken Road. In addition to seeing Federal, Confederate, and the nation's oldest Masonic cemeteries, it's a smart way to get a lay of the land and know where to return to on your bike.

On foot, just head north on Caroline Street and allow time to drop into shops along the way. At the corner of Caroline and Amelia Streets, step into the **Hugh Mercer Apothecary Shop** (1020 Caroline St. 540/375-3362, open daily, $5). Running the shop while the good doctor is out, docents dressed as colonial-era wenches demonstrate the "modern medicines" the doc uses to treat patients. The kick is that they never break character, even while discussing the medicinal value of leeches, herbs, amputations, mustard plasters, and a "good puking." With the right person playing the role, this is one of the most fun tours you'll find. If you're a doctor, you'll have plenty to talk to your peers about. If you're a lawyer, you'll find plenty of times to think *malpractice.*

About three blocks north at the **Rising**

Confederate soldier Richard Kirkland, moved by the anguished cries of the enemy at Fredericksburg, scaled a protective wall to aid the dying. When soldiers held their fire, he became known as "The Angel of Marye's Heights." This sculpture was created by Felix George Weihs De Weldon in 1965.

Sun Tavern (1304 Caroline St., 540/371-1494), the format is the same and just as entertaining. Anywhere else, this would be a brief walk through an old building. Not here. The Rising Sun Tavern was built in 1760 by Charles Washington, the younger brother of George Washington, and, quite likely, the Billy Carter of Colonial America. You can learn a lot here—for example, tavern decks had only 51 cards. You had to pay one shilling, sixpence for the 52nd card. Otherwise, you were not "dealing with a full deck."

After checking out the remaining historical sites, hop on your bike and ride to the **Fredericksburg Battlefield** (1013 Lafayette Blvd., 540/373-6122, www.nps.gov/frsp). Although the museum is much smaller than the one at Gettysburg, the introductory video does a good job of explaining the battles that happened here. When you exit out the back door, a self-guided tour starts at the Sunken Road, which feels like one of the saddest places in America. In December 1862, Confederate soldiers sheltered behind a high stone wall above the road were able to cut down Union troops like lambs at the slaughter.

It must have been a brutal scene, but a monument a little farther down may restore a bit of your faith in humanity. The monument is dedicated to Richard Kirkland, a 19-year-old Confederate soldier who couldn't bear to hear the dying cries of the enemy. He jumped the wall and ran to the aid of the suffering men, giving them water from his canteen. How'd he survive the crossfire? Both Confederate and Union soldiers held their fire while he was on his mission of mercy.

There you go. Another bit of history and heroism thanks to the man known as "The Angel of Marye's Heights." From here it's time to wrap up your tour with a nice dinner and a quiet evening at your inn.

PULL IT OVER: FREDERICKSBURG HIGHLIGHTS
Attractions and Adventures

Collectively, the **Fredericksburg/Spotsylvania National Military Park** maintains nearly 6,000 acres of land and admission to all local battlefields as well as the Stonewall Jackson shrine is free. Both the **Fredericksburg Battlefield Visitor Center** (1013 Lafayette Blvd., 540/373-6122, www.nps.gov/frsp) and **Chancellorsville Battlefield Visitor Center** (Rte. 3 W., 540/786-2880) help interpret the four battlefields: Fredericksburg, Chancellorsville, The Wilderness, and Spotsylvania Courthouse.

More history is found at the **Fredericksburg Area Museum** (907 Princess Anne St., 540/371-3037, www.famcc.org, $7), housed in two buildings. The museum contains an assortment of Civil War weapons in an old 1860 Town Hall/Market House that survived Civil War battles. Within a Beaux-Arts building, there's an interesting collection from Fredericksburg's own history.

It turns out that the Father of our Country also had a Brother-in-Law of our Country, and that was Colonel Fielding Lewis who married George's sister, Betty. She and Fielding lived at **Kenmore Plantation & Gardens** (1201 Washington Ave., 540/373-3381, www.kenmore.org) which Washington himself surveyed when the land was part of a 1,300-acre plantation. Guides claim that an award given for the home's plasterwork ranks this among one of the most beautiful houses in America (a bit of an overstatement since the honor was given in the 1930s). Worth it if you're a fan of Washington's (or presidential sisters), the tour can drag so it's an $8 crapshoot.

If you left your dulcimer at home, one of the neatest shops in Fredericksburg is **Picker's Supply** (902 Caroline St., 540/371-4669 or 800/830-4669, www. pickerssupply.com). Even if you don't play, you will be tempted to pick up a banjo, mandolin, or fiddle for the road. If you do jam, check out the vintage guitars.

Blue-Plate Specials

The reason why you may be drawn to **Goolrick's** (901 Caroline St., 540/373-3411) is that it's the oldest continuously operating soda fountain in America. Open daily for breakfast, lunch, and dinner, Goolrick's features an abridged menu of sandwiches, soups, homemade macaroni and potato salad, and fresh-squeezed lemonade. A great old-fashioned flashback, it's a neat place to order up a thick milkshake and imagine you're still in high school.

Here since 1960, **Anne's Grill** (1609 Princess Anne St., 540/373-9621) is a testament to simple meals and superior service. Big home cooking, breakfast all day, burgers, steaks, seafood at lunch and dinner, sassy waitresses, and lots of locals. Anne's Grill is closed on Wednesdays and 2–4:30 P.M. daily.

Anne's counterpart is down the street at the **2400 Diner** (2400 Princess Anne St., 540/373-9049). For more than half a century, it, too, has been serving good dishes done right. There's a little bit of everything here, from subs and chicken to steaks and fish—ah, the pleasure of road food. The diner's open 7 A.M.–9 P.M. Monday–Saturday, and until 3 P.M. Sunday.

Watering Holes

When you visit **J. Brian's Tap Room** (200 Hanover St., 540/373-0738, www. jbrianstaproom.com), you may be drinking shoulder to shoulder with D.C. politicians. Photos show that this place attracts a mix of conservative and liberal imbibers.

Why not? It's a cool place with 20 beers on tap, including Woodchuck Cider and Bass Ale. Happy hour lasts 4–7 P.M., and the Wurlitzer jukebox is authentic. Oh, yeah—George Washington once owned this place.

Shut-Eye

Fredericksburg has several inns, but if you prefer the modern conveniences of a TV, large bed, and private bath, you may do better at a chain hotel. Call the visitors center for current listings.

Motels and Motor Courts

The **Inn at Olde Silk Mill** (1707 Princess Anne St., 540/371-5666, www.innattheoldesilkmill.com, $89–159) was once an old motel, but has been upgraded, with rooms and suites accented with Civil War antiques. A complimentary continental breakfast is included.

Inn-dependence

The **Richard Johnston Inn** (711 Caroline St., 540/899-7606 or 877/557-0770, www. therichardjohnstoninn.com, $105 and up weekdays, $135 and up weekends) features seven rooms and two suites, some of them uncommonly large, many filled with antiques and reproductions, and all with a private bath. Built in the late 1700s, the inn has a great spot in the heart of downtown, with generous parking and a full breakfast.

Chain Drive

These chain hotels are in town, or within 10 miles of the city center:

Best Western, Comfort Inn, Econo Lodge, Hampton Inn, Hilton, Holiday Inn, Howard Johnson, Motel 6, Quality Inn, Ramada, Residence Inn, Sleep Inn, Super 8, Travelodge

For more information, including phone numbers and websites, see page 439.

Resources for Riders

Civil War Run

Maryland Travel Information
Maryland Tourism—866/639-3526, www.visitmaryland.org

Pennsylvania Travel Information
Pennsylvania Road Conditions—866/976-8747, www.paturnpike.com
Pennsylvania State Parks—888/727-2757, www.dcnr.state.pa.us
Pennsylvania Tourism and Lodging Information—717/232-8880,
    www.patourism.org
Pennsylvania Visitor Information—800/847-4872, www.visitpa.com

Virginia Travel Information
Virginia Camping—800/933-7275, www.dcr.state.va.us
Virginia Civil War Trails—888/248-4592, www.civilwartrails.org
Virginia Highway Helpline—800/367-7623
Virginia Tourism—800/847-4882, www.virginia.org

Local and Regional Information
Fredericksburg Visitor Center—540/373-1776 or 800/678-4748, www.visitfred.com
Gettysburg Convention and Visitors Bureau—717/339-0767 or 800/337-5015,
    www.gettysburgcvb.org
Loudoun County (Leesburg) Visitors Center—703/771-2617 or 800/752-6118,
    www.visitloudoun.org

Pennsylvania Motorcycle Shops

Action Motorsports—1881 Whiteford Rd., York, 717/757-2688,
www.actionmotorsportsyork.com

Battlefield Harley-Davidson/Buell—21 Cavalry Field Rd., Gettysburg,
717/337-9005 or 877/595-9005, www.battlefieldharley-davidson.com

Don's Kawasaki—20 E. Market St., Hallam (York), 717/755-6002,
www.donskawasaki.com

Hanover Powersports—717/632-8801, 1754 Carlisle Pike, Hanover,
www.hanovercycles.com

Laugermans Harley-Davidson—100 Arsenal Rd., York, 717/854-3214,
www.laugerman.com

Motosports—2117 Baltimore Pike (Rte. 94 S), Hanover, 717/632-7093,
www.motosportsinc.com

Riders Edge Yamaha—2490 Emmitsburg Rd., Gettysburg, 717/334-2518,
www.ridersedgeyamaha.com

Virginia Motorcycle Shops

Battlefield Motorcycles—1103 Lafayette Blvd., Fredericksburg, 540/371-7433

Extreme Powersports—10725 Courthouse Rd., Fredericksburg, 540/891-4009,
www.extremepowersport.com

Fredericksburg Motorsports—430 Kings Hwy., Fredericksburg, 540/899-9100
or 888/899-9129, www.youroneforfun.com

Loudoun Motorsports—212 Catoctin Circle SE, Leesburg, 703/777-1652,
www.loudounmotorsports.com

Morton's BMW—5099A Jefferson Davis Hwy., Fredericksburg, 540/891-9844,
www.mortonsbmw.com

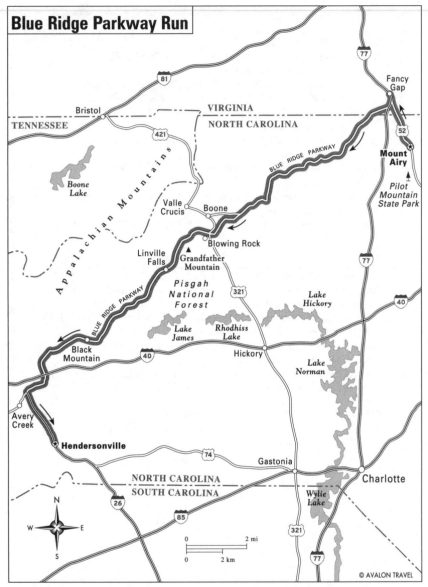

Blue Ridge Parkway Run

Route: Mount Airy to Hendersonville via Blowing Rock, Valle Crucis, Little Switzerland

Distance: Approximately 190 miles

First Leg: Mount Airy to Blowing Rock (100 miles)

Second Leg: Blowing Rock to Hendersonville (90 miles)

Helmet Laws: North Carolina requires helmets.

Blue Ridge Parkway Run

Mount Airy, North Carolina to Hendersonville, North Carolina

Without resorting to hyperbole I'd say the Blue Ridge Parkway (BRP) is the most beautiful road ever built and it is one reason why you own a motorcycle. This 469-mile-long, toll-free dream starts in Front Royal, Virginia, and winds its way through the Appalachians before slithering to a close in Cherokee, North Carolina.

After making this run, FDR shot up on my shortlist of favorite presidents. Why? In order to put Americans back to work he's the one who got this road-building project going in September 1935. The masterstroke was the decision not to allow commercial vehicles on the road. Because you don't need to worry about semis or delivery vans here, you're given free rein to soak in the very best America has to offer. To be fair, sometimes sections of the BRP can be washed out by floods or mudslides or maybe a heavy fog can drift in and reduce visibility to just a few feet which makes riding extremely dangerous. But when it's right, it is *just* right.

Of course, it's not just the road that makes this ride worth it. The welcoming Southern vibe is as smooth as molasses.

MOUNT AIRY PRIMER

There's little you need to know about Mount Airy except this: Andy Griffith was born here, and so was the Happiest Girl in the Whole USA (aka Donna Fargo). Oh yeah, Chang and Eng Bunker, the original Siamese twins, lived here, but they pale in comparison to Andy Taylor and Barney Fife.

As a member of *The Andy Griffith Show* Rerun Watchers' Club and a fan of the Blue Ridge Parkway, it's a given that I'd think this is a great place to kick off a magnificent ride. Add to that the fact that the Mount Airy residents I met can be nothing but friendly and there's even more reason to come here and sit a spell.

But again, without Andy, this would be just another Southern town. But he is why people travel here. Griffith grew up on Haymore Street, and the small-town boy certainly made good. If you're familiar with *The Andy Griffith Show,* you'll recognize the influences that made it to television. There's Floyd's barbershop, the diner, and all the elements of a sleepy North Carolina town.

It's worth noting that Griffith always tried to define the line between the reality of his childhood and the fictional world he inhabited professionally, but that's never stopped townspeople from trying to turn their town into Mayberry. The Surry County Arts Council publishes the *Mayberry Confidential,* which includes breaking news on Aunt Bee's bake sale and the Little Miss Mayberry pageant. It hosts Mayberry Days and the word "Mayberry" precedes a chamber's worth of businesses—including Mayberry Auto Sales, Motor Lodge, Mall, Alarm Company, Cab Company, Candle Shop, Consignments, Embroidery, Flea Market, and a few dozen others including Septic Pumping Service.

You'll find it all an intriguing blend of fantasy and reality, and you should just enjoy it. Grab a bite at the diner, get a trim at Floyd's, and head to Wally's Service Station for a tour in a squad car.

And say Hey to Gomer.

ON THE ROAD: MOUNT AIRY

For such a small town, there's a surprising amount to experience here. Not thrilling, not magnificent, just...American. A visit downtown and a ride to Pilot Mountain should fill up a day, and by nightfall you'll have acquired a lifetime of memories. One word of caution before arriving: many downtown businesses are closed on Sunday.

Ride your bike to Main Street and start with a North Carolina breakfast at **Leon's Burger Express** (407 N. Main St., 336/789-0849), an old-fashioned diner stuck in the 1950s. Coca-Cola wallpaper,

red vinyl seats with silver tacking on back, a pie display—it's all here, plus coffee and friendly service.

Walk back to the **Visitors Center** (200 N. Main St., 336/786-6116 or 800/948-0949, www.visitmayberry. com) where there's a short video on Andy's contributions to Mount Airy and a staff that can help you with trip planning, lodging, a squad car tour, or dining recommendations.

Around now, **Floyd's City Barber Shop** (336/786-2346) should be open, so backtrack past Leon's and drop in to meet Russell Hiatt. Like a Penny Lane barber, he takes a picture of everyone who stops in. With more than 50,000 photographs on his wall, Hiatt claims he has the world's most important wall since Berlin.

Also downtown you'll pass Opie's Candy Store, the Mayberry Soda Fountain, and Mayberry on Main, but you may be more interested in knowing that you're in the heart of a motorcycle-friendly town. Before you go, check out www.visitmayberry.com/rallymayberry.aspx where they've detailed nearly a dozen tours in the region. Here's one that's short and sweet:

Saddle up and get on U.S. 52 South for a quick 15-mile ride to Pilot Mountain which you'll soon see on the horizon. The highway gives you some great curves before it leads to the exit at **Pilot Mountain State Park** (1792 Pilot Knob Park Rd., Pinnacle, 336/325-2355, www. ncparks.gov). Admission to the park, open 8 A.M.–8 P.M. daily, is free.

On the steep ascent to the peak, you may pass bicyclists that are screaming down the mountain road like hornets. Lean back and the road to the top unfolds before you. As you near the final turn, the view is tremendous. From 1,400 feet above the upper Piedmont Plateau you can see U.S. 52 darting through the forests toward

Mount Airy and glimpse Winston-Salem through the haze on the far horizon.

After rolling back down to Mount Airy, there's another stop for gearheads, Gomers, and Goobers: **Wally's Service Station** (625 S. Main St., 336/786-6066, www.wallysserviceatmayberry.com). The station was built in 1937 and went through several owners until super-fan Wes Collins restored it as a gift shop and recreation of Gomer's service station. The owners don't mind you hanging around, sipping on an RC Cola and eating a Moon Pie. You can even leave your bike behind and take a guided tour in a vintage replica of Mayberry's squad car created from '62–'64 Ford Galaxies. Call 336/789-6743 or visit www.tourmayberry.com for reservations. For hardcore fans, right next door the owners even built an exact replica of the Mayberry courthouse, featuring jail cells one and two.

You've just about done it. You could go see the world's largest granite quarry or wait for evening to eat some more. Or, would you believe it? At the old-fashioned **Cinema Theatre** (142 Main St., 336/786-2222), movies cost just a few bucks. Or maybe by now you've done what you haven't done in ages: You've relaxed and realized that you don't have to do anything except watch the flicker of fireflies and listen to the silence.

Welcome to Mayberry.

PULL IT OVER: MOUNT AIRY HIGHLIGHTS
Attractions and Adventures

In September 2004 during the town's annual Mayberry Days, Andy Griffith made one of his few trips home to attend the unveiling of TV Land's bronze statue of Andy and Opie walking to the ol' fishin' hole. It stands in front of the **Andy Griffith Playhouse** (218 Rockford St., 336/786-7998),

which is also home to the world's largest collection of Andy Griffith memorabilia. Stop in and see Griffith-related television scripts, records, yearbooks, and even wrappers of "Andy Griffith Whole Hog Sausage."

For a fact, *The Andy Griffith Show* contributed to the revival of bluegrass music (remember the Darling Family?), and that music's still being picked, plucked, and sung at an open jam session at the Andy Griffith Playhouse each Thursday, as well as the Voice of the Blue Ridge which is presented on the third Saturday of each month. On Saturday mornings, head downtown to the Cinema Theatre and sit in on a classic: WPAQ-AM has been broadcasting bluegrass musicians live every weekend since 1948.

For something more refined, check out the area's local wineries. Mount Airy is located within the 1.4 million square mile **Yadkin Valley Wine Region** (www.yadkinwines.com) which is home to a few dozen wineries. Check the website for a list and directions that can create a great country ride.

Blue-Plate Specials

You can't come to Mount Airy without eating at **Snappy Lunch** (125 N. Main St., 336/786-4931). Oprah has eaten here. So did Hal Smith (Otis) and Aneta Corsaut (Helen Crump). Breakfast is fine, but lunch is mandatory. The pork chop sandwich is fat, greasy, and stacked with coleslaw and other ingredients researchers are still trying to figure out. Damn, it's good. Owner Charles Dowell, one of the nicest restaurateurs in the South, has been cooking here since the 1950s.

Another local favorite for locals and riders is **Goober's 52** (458 N. Andy Griffith Pkwy., 336/786-1845, www.goobers52.com), which is a party in itself.

Wild, colorful, and eclectic, their menu features twists on sandwiches (NYC Reubens, N'awlins po'boys, Philly cheesesteak) as well as salads, pastas, BBQ ribs, and rubbed steaks. There's a full bar with beer and mixed drinks, a fire pit, occasional live music, and merchandise from salad dressings to tie-dyed shirts. Don't miss it.

Barney's Cafe (206 N. Main St., 336/786-8305) serves breakfast all day and at lunch adds their signature Barney Burger, as well as the daily five dollar "meat and two sides" special which could mean meatloaf, chicken and dumplings, country steak, spaghetti, or the cook's choice. It's open until 6:30 P.M.

Pandowdy's Restaurant (243 N. Main St., 336/786-1993) is the rare downtown eatery open in the evening, but more than that keeps this place packed every night. Credit the Southern hospitality of the waitresses and dishes that outperform even four-star restaurants; the filet mignon is one of the most tender and satisfying I've ever eaten. Pandowdy's does lunch and dinner Wednesday–Saturday.

Watering Holes

Riders have found sanctuaries in town including **Kickers Bar and Grill** (2767 Park Dr., 336/374-5110, www.kickersbar.com) which is one of the best biker friendly bars in the state. In addition to friendly servers and cold beers, they host rallies and sports competitions and feature pool tables, pinball, foosball, karaoke, live bands, cookouts, and an outdoor patio. This may be the only bar where you can get married, with services conducted by the accommodating Reverend Red. The bar is open daily until 11 P.M., weekends until 2 A.M. Also try **B-52's Bar & Grill** (972 N. Andy Griffith Pkwy., 336/719-2411) where they rotate their drink specials that you can savor at their outdoor tiki bar. Back down the Parkway, **Goober's 52** (458 N. Andy Griffith Pkwy., 336/786-1845 www.goobers52.com) is really a restaurant, but at the bar and on the patios, the joint's always jumpin'.

Shut-Eye
Motels and Motor Courts
The **Mayberry Motor Inn** (501 N. Andy Griffith Pkwy, 336/786-4109, www.mayberrymotorinn.com, $60 and up) is an old-fashioned motor lodge with standard rooms and a pool. The exception is Aunt Bee's Room, which the owner decorated with twin beds, a vanity, and other memorabilia she bought from the Raleigh estate sale of Frances Bavier, America's Aunt Bee. You can't sleep in this room, but the others are open.

Inn-dependence
If you named your kid Opie, chances are you're destined to stay at the **Andy Griffith Home Place** (711 Haymore St., $175 year-round), the small home where Andy grew up. It accommodates up to four people, which is great if you're riding with a group. Andy's place is now run by the **Hampton Inn** (2029 Rockford St., 336/789-5999, $99 and up) which is nice and clean. Rates buy you local calls, access to a swimming pool, and a good night's sleep in a king or queen bed. The Hampton Inn is close enough to the attractions for convenience, but far enough away for a quiet night's sleep.

An inn may better reflect the feeling of Mayberry, plus you'll have a chance to talk to locals. Named one of the top 10 bed-and-breakfasts in the nation, the **Sobotta Manor** (347 W. Pine St., 336/786-2777, www.sobottamanor.com) is a Tudor Revival mansion built in 1932 that's been restored as an elegant and comfortable inn with 10 foot ceilings, black walnut walls, and a gentlemen's parlor. Considering its reputation, rates seem reasonable—$139–159. Consider several other grand old homes, including **Maxwell House** (618 N. Main St., 877/786-2174 or 877/786-2174, $125 and up); the **Thompson House** (702 E. Pine St., 336/719-0711, www.bbonline.com/nc/thompsonhouse, $120 and up) which has a nice porch with rockers; and **Thomas House** (739 N. Main St., 336/789-1766, www.thomashousebb.com, $90 and up).

Chain Drive

These chain hotels are in town, or within 10 miles of the city center:
Best Western, Hampton Inn, Holiday Inn, Knights Inn, Quality Inn
For more information, including phone numbers and websites, see page 439.

ON THE ROAD: MOUNT AIRY TO BLOWING ROCK

Before leaving Mount Airy on U.S. 52 North, consider stocking up on some sandwiches, fried chicken, soft drinks, and other portable food. Even though restaurants are plentiful off the parkway, you'll have more fun dining alfresco.

The five-mile ride to Fancy Gap, Virginia, takes you to the Blue Ridge Parkway and along the way you'll pass signs of the rural South: a drive-in, some flea markets, and wrestling fliers tacked to telephone poles. There's another subtle change here as the air starts to smell oddly fresh, naturally scented by the grass and flowers of the surrounding mountains and valleys.

Gradually the hodgepodge patchwork of businesses and houses gives ways to trees and valleys as you approach the parkway. Now the mountains rush to greet you and soon you and your bike will be rocking

back and forth as you tuck into corners at 45 mph. From the opposite lane, fellow motorcycle travelers should be coming around the corners as if they're flying off an assembly line.

Just after the Mountain Top Restaurant, enter the BRP, turn left, and the road is yours from mile marker 200 all the way south to mile marker 392. If you travel off-season, it is mind-blowing to realize that out of 300 million Americans, you're one of a chosen few fortunate enough to be on this road. That satisfaction grows as you ride the overpass above the interstate and pity the motorists who have no idea what they're missing.

It doesn't take long to realize the BRP represents "the Golden Age of Road Building." To your left, you'll spy Pilot Mountain, an acropolis 20 miles distant. Because views like this come fast and frequent here, every few miles scenic overlooks have been added for your convenience. But it doesn't take an overlook to persuade you to stop. Often cars and bikes have pulled over and barefoot drivers and riders who've kicked off their boots have settled into the soft grass to enjoy picnics, naps, and nature.

Even though you may have felt the wind and sun on your face before, for many reasons it seems more satisfying on the Parkway. Flip up your visor, flood your lungs with fresh air, and enjoy a road that's completely free of commercial traffic, businesses, and billboards. The only things here to command your attention are the dogwoods and evergreens, the meadows, glades, and the stone bridges.

As you ride, you'll recognize that this may be the only road in the country where the speed limit is just right. At 45 mph, it's the perfect speed for experiencing everything and seeing everything, like High Piny Spur, elevation 2,805 feet, where the grand vista is an endless field of varying textures and colors.

The road continues, smooth and flowing. Although there are nice straights for relaxation, it is never boring, never threatening. The Blue Ridge Parkway is noticeably absent of restrictions, and there are no speed traps, no signs telling you the road is air-patrolled. It simply trusts you to do the right thing. And if you want to take a break, exits such as Alder Gap (3,047 feet) and Sheets Gap (3,342 feet) allow you to get on and off the parkway with ease.

After more than 50 miles the BRP keeps giving you greenery and great curves. Just before mile marker 259, the **Northwest Trading Post** sells crafts and marks the arrival of more tremendous views at lookouts at The Lump, Benge Gap, and Calloway Gap.

As you roll to a close you'll look back at what was actually a brief ride, but one that you'll likely repeat again—if not on your bike, often in your memory as you sit at your desk and recall one of the finest roads in the nation. For now, you have only to enjoy the last few miles until you pass mile marker 291 and start looking for the exit at U.S 221/321 into Blowing Rock.

BLOWING ROCK PRIMER

Funny how some towns get started. During the Civil War, Southern soldiers started packing up their families and sending them into the safety of these hills. After Appomattox, some soldiers joined their families here and Blowing Rock grew bit by bit until the population hovered around 100.

The number was sufficient for incorporation, although not nearly enough to spoil the solitude and scenery of the Blue Ridge. Soon seasonal residents started heading for the mountains to escape the South's summer heat and when they did, a resort town formed, complete with boardinghouses, inns, shops, and restaurants.

Today, the commercial district is limited to a handful of stores, so you can park your bike and walk the town in a few hours. But there's more to Blowing Rock. You haven't really seen the town until you've entered its forests, climbed its hills, and ridden its sublime mountain roads. So don't rush it.

ON THE ROAD: BLOWING ROCK

Downtown Blowing Rock isn't that large, but it is a perfect base for exploring the larger-than-life mountains that surround it. Part of that means heading to a small hill town called Valle Crucis.

From the center of Blowing Rock, ride northwest on U.S. 221 just a few miles to reach Shulls Mill Road, which leads right onto the Blue Ridge Parkway. Another quick right takes you to the **Moses Cone Manor House.** It's worth a short stop. Aside from the mansion itself, the textile magnate's Flat Top Manor comes groovin' up slowly with mountain crafts such as dulcimers, quilts, and "snake" sticks, as well as a full library of books on the Blue Ridge. Take a breather and relax on the verandah that overlooks a small mountain lake and 3,600 acres of riding, hiking, and horseback riding trails.

When you get back on the parkway, head north and just past mile marker 292 exit at U.S. 221/321 and continue north toward Boone. The city's about six more miles on and along the way you'll see signs coaxing you to hop off your bike and hop on the touristy Tweetsie Railroad, an old-fashioned amusement park and home of two authentic steam locomotives. Before you reach downtown, watch for Highway 105 where you'll hang a left and follow the winding road about two miles into the North Carolina countryside. At the corner of Broadstone Road just turn right and stay on Broadstone as you head for the hills.

At first, the slapdash homes and shaky riverfront cabins will lead to the unshakeable belief that you're leaving civilization behind. If you can, ignore the numerous entrances into "exclusive mountain developments" that have scarred the area, just enjoy the tight turns that whip you into Valle Crucis. At first, you'll pass an annex, but keep riding until you see an old Esso sign and red gas pump that tells you that you've arrived at the original circa 1883 **Mast General Store** (Highway 194, 828/963-6511, www.mastgeneralstore.com).

For me, arriving here created one of those unforgettable motorcycle moments since this mercantile has been here since bills were paid in produce, roots, herbs, and chickens. Stepping inside, I was in an old general store which doubles as a post office (mailboxes rent for a few bucks a year), and I heard the creaking wooden floors, saw the 1913 pot-bellied stove, and looked at the mountain men who still sit around and chew Mail Pouch tobacco and talk about what mountain men talk about.

But the Mast General Store peddles wares for outsiders as well.

Need a hoe handle? It's here. A Union suit? Check upstairs. It also sells birdhouses, cinnamon brooms, musical spoons, marbles—cat's eye and rainbow shooters—cider mix, rocking chairs, and leather jackets. It was a perfect place to grab a five-cent cup of coffee, sit a spell on the back porch, and watch the fat bumblebees hover around the flowers.

When you're ready to leave the past behind, return to Highway 105 and head south to Linville where you can hook up to U.S. 221 North, also known as Blowing Rock Highway. Although there's nearly 20 miles to go to reach Blowing Rock, consider one more stop. Along the way you'll spy the entrance to **Grandfather Mountain** (828/733-2013 or 800/468-7325, www.grandfather.com, $15) which, at close to 6,000 feet, is the highest peak in the Blue Ridge Mountains. The area is also a wildlife habitat for black bears, white-tailed deer, mountain lions, and bald eagles, while the road itself introduces a new type of wild life: an 18 degree

The Essence of the South

In addition to a love of America, native North Carolinian Charles Kuralt had a way with words—especially when he was describing aspects of his home state. In a newspaper article from 1987, displayed at the Mast General Store, he refers to a visit here to explain the beauty of the American South.

Where should I send you to know the soul of the South? I think I'll send you to the Mast General Store...

You cannot get to know either the store or the people in it if you are in a hurry to reach the bright lights. In its essence, the South is rural, slow, and charming, cluttered and eclectic, rich in old tales, old artifacts, and human friendship. The South cannot be hurried through. Vacationers who take the interstate from New York to Miami miss the South completely...

grade to the peak! This seems like the most challenging stretch in the state since turns are so tight and inclines so steep that you'll swear you've reached the top several times, but the road keeps rising. This is why hinged vehicles have to unhitch and leave their trailers at the gate. Even on the last leg up, the corners continue for miles until you reach the top where you find the Mile-High Swinging Bridge, an anxiety-inducing 228-foot-long steel cable suspension bridge hanging eight stories above a chasm. Although it's securely tethered to the ground, when the wind kicks in, it can get pretty spooky.

By the way, the winds *can* kick in. When gusts of wind rock the bridge (record speed: 196.5 knots) and whistle through the protective fencing, those brave enough to cross gain access to an extraordinary view of the Blue Ridge Mountains, views that'll last for years. See it for yourself.

The road down is as fascinating as the ride up, and heading back to Blowing Rock via U.S. 221 is a mental massage (although the optional Blue Ridge Parkway north is equally incredible). Streams and snaking roads form a graceful combination to follow and along the way you'll pass the rural **Blue Moon Station** (6371 U.S. 221 S., 828/295-6100), a circa 1881 general store where you can stock up on jams, jellies, fishing and hiking supplies, apple butter, peach cider, local honey, crafts, pottery, Moon Pies, and vintage Southern libations: Nehi, Dr. Pepper, and RC Colas...in the bottle.

An Appalachian *beaujolais nouveau*.

PULL IT OVER: BLOWING ROCK HIGHLIGHTS
Attractions and Adventures
If you wonder how the town got its name, head over to the **Blowing Rock** (U.S. 321, 828/295-7111, www.theblowingrock.com,

$6). This is North Carolina's oldest attraction and the place where you can buy the stuff you bought when you were a kid, including genuine rubber tomahawks, cowboy hats, and a book of dirty mountain sayings ("He really crapped in the oatmeal" is a good'un.) Skeptical at first, I quickly found that this really is a windy place where powerful gusts of mountain air rush flying up from the valley floor. If you forgot your blow dryer, stop here.

Whitewater rafting expeditions are the specialty of **High Mountain Expeditions** (Main St. and U.S. 221, Blowing Rock, 828/898-9786 or 800/262-9036, www.highmountainexpeditions.com). They'll set you up for a wet and wild afternoon and all you need is some cash, a swimsuit or shorts, a T-shirt, and tennis shoes. You'll be loaded in a van for a 45-minute mile ride to Wilson's Creek or the Watauga or Nolichucky rivers. After navigating the rapids through gorges and descents, you'll be driven back to Blowing Rock. They also offer caving and overnight excursions. For gear you'd need for hiking, camping, rock climbing, or backpacking, check **Footslogger's** (921 Main St., 828/295-4453, www.footsloggers.com).

Blue-Plate Specials
Hankering for a plate of liver mush? You'll find it at **Knights on Main** (870 Main St., 828/295-3869, www.knightsonmainrestaurant.com), plus potatoes, grits, baked apples, breads, and cereals—and that's just breakfast. In business since 1949, this is a busy roadside joint, where the staff hustles but you never feel rushed. This is the best place to get your morning started or ratchet down at night.

Speckled Trout Cafe (corner of Main St. and U.S. 221, 828/295-9819, www.speckledtroutcafe.com) features standard appetizers and entrées with an emphasis on fresh trout, seafood, and an oyster bar. Off-season, tables are easy to come by; in peak season, you could starve to death before you get a seat. The fresh rainbow trout is raised in the mountains, and then prepared pan-fried, broiled, or baked. It's open for breakfast, lunch, and dinner.

Swing by the **Blowing Rock Grille** (349 Sunset Dr., 828/295-9474), where owner-rider Larry Imeson welcomes fellow riders. Boasting of a dozen homemade soups and pastries, he adds salads and sandwiches to the mix served inside or on the patio. The diverse clientele varies from riders to suits to sun worshippers to celebs. Since 1977 **Woodlands** (8304 Valley Blvd., 828/295-3651, www.woodlandsbbq.com) has been serving up great barbecue beef, pork, chicken, and ribs with a side of live music as locals play each evening. It's a busy local favorite that features a popular lounge.

Shut-Eye
Motels and Motor Courts
One of the coolest places I can recommend is the **Mountainaire Inn and Log Cabins** (827 N. Main St., 828/295-7991, www.mountainaireinn.com) which features wonderful cabins that sleep up to six people and are dressed out for comfort. Depending on the season (high season is July–October), prices range from $125 up to $295. Some cabins have hot tubs, fireplaces, and cathedral ceilings, and all have a large front porch where you can sit in a rocker and watch your bike. They also offer smaller motel rooms at a smaller price. Go for a cabin if you can.

Inn-dependence
Crippen's Country Inn (239 Sunset Dr., 828/295-3487 or 877/295-3487, www.crippens.com, $129 and up high season) offers a parlor, spacious rooms, and a great location only a few feet from the village.

The fine dining restaurant gets lots of attention as well.

Chain Drive
These chain hotels are in town, or within 10 miles of the city center: **Best Western, Fairfield Inn, Holiday Inn, La Quinta, Red Carpet Inn, Scottish Inns, Sleep Inn, Super 8**
For more information, including phone numbers and websites, see page 439.

ON THE ROAD: BLOWING ROCK TO HENDERSONVILLE
After you leave Blowing Rock, it'll take less than five seconds to ease back into the feel of the Blue Ridge Parkway. It starts right away with sweeping, slow descents and corners.

A few miles south, one of the first secrets to reveal itself is Price Lake which appears on your left and is a perfect place to stage a photo of you on your mount. Take a glance over the side and you'll see a small waterfall. If you have time, a few miles further south at mile marker 297, the Julian Price Memorial Park has boat rentals, fishing, and camping.

From here, the Parkway offers so much, but asks so little. All you have to do is ride slow and smooth and soak in the overlooks that are beyond belief, especially at mile marker 302. Yet this isn't the only incredible sight you'll see on the ride. Only a mile later, look ahead and you'll spot the Linn Cove Viaduct, an incredible 1,243-foot segmental bridge that snakes around the slopes of Grandfather Mountain and rivals the Bixby Creek Bridge of the Pacific Coast Highway. Until you reach the information center just over the viaduct, I'll let you know that in 1983 this was the last section of the BRP to be completed. As you ride it, you and your bike seem to float off of the mountain on a road suspended above the landscape. My gut instinct was to just skip the Parkway and spend the day riding back and forth across the bridge.

So far you haven't even reached the exit for Grandfather Mountain and you've already had a full day's worth of inspiring views. But there's more. For the next 48 miles you'll be riding through a section of the Pisgah National Forest as the road takes some slow dives and leads to immaculate ascensions.

When you reach mile marker 312, you'll see a stone tunnel ahead but you can take the exit at the Pineola Gap to stop at **Christa's Country Corner** (Hwy. 181, 828/733-3353). Although Christa named the store after herself, she accepts that more customers remember Moses, the fat Labrador who was the store's mascot for years. The place brims with all the items you'd expect a general store to stock: homemade preserves (featuring Moses's picture), Dr. Enuff soda (I'd never heard of it either), cans of snuff, udder balm, and Moon Pies (which taste great slathered in udder balm).

Getting back on the parkway is like hooking up with an old friend. You're back to hugging curves and riding at angles even Pythagoras couldn't calculate. There are some rollercoaster drops and fantastic views and about 30 miles of the best riding in America. Granite columns rise on your left, valleys and mountains on your right. You'll crane your neck to see it all, but if you want a longer look, just stop. Slow down to take advantage of winding roads that validate every reason you concocted to convince your spouse you really *needed* a bike.

You're riding past apple orchards now, then the North Carolina Minerals Museum at mile marker 321, and then Spruce Pine, a small town six miles off the parkway. Stop if you like, or keep riding and

you'll reach towns like Little Switzerland, which features a café/bookstore and a town the size of a high-school gym.

I chose to keep riding because the hills kept appearing and I wanted to pump the throttle and rocket over them. Accustomed to seeing traffic and billboards and people, it was a constant thrill to ride this amazing example of roadwork and notice relatively scant development in the valleys below. Things would get even better.

Starting near mile marker 342, the curves became more frequent and the tunnels more numerous and my exclamations of "Oh, my God!" more urgent. After a brief stop at the Licklog Ridge, for nearly 40 miles I sliced through a valley as the road rating changed from PG to R. The world was zooming towards me through my fairing and it was a little disappointing to sense that I was getting close to the end of the run. I could have made a stop at the free **Folk Art Center** (mile marker 382, 828/298-7928, www.southernhighlandguild.org), where crafters and country artisans showcase quilts, hand-carved woodwork, and other stuff that doesn't come off an assembly line. Instead, I rode on and grabbed the exit at I-26 for the cleanest and most direct route to Hendersonville—the hub of all things good.

HENDERSONVILLE PRIMER

Although Hendersonville takes a back seat to Asheville in popularity, I'm not sure why. It has everything a city should have—minus the congestion. Here, the chain businesses and box stores are relegated to the outskirts of town, the downtown still attracts locals as well as tourists, and it sits right in the middle of everything worth seeing.

Hendersonville began as an escape for Floridians who faced yellow fever at the turn of the 20th century, and still remains a favorite of Floridians who bring their kids to summer camp or to escape the heat. Not a bad idea, since brisk mountain breezes keep humidity low and summertime temperatures hover in the comfortable low 80s. What's more, the nearby Blue Ridge Mountains block severe weather patterns at Asheville, so folks under Hendersonville's thermal blanket savor a mild climate year-round. The unique weather and geological patterns also affect the foliage, creating a deluge of dogwood, azalea, and apple blossoms in spring and fall.

ON THE ROAD: HENDERSONVILLE

Like Broadway Avenue in Saratoga Springs, Hendersonville's Main Street is a wide avenue designed so a team of four horses could make a U-turn. The street is still touched by small-town nostalgia. Along it, you'll find diagonal parking, independent merchants, and a branch of the original Mast Store that you saw near Blowing Rock. You can get caught up in shopping (antiques emporiums, art galleries, a music store, wine cellar, herb shop, Irish pub, beer brewing store), but you'll have just as much fun on the road.

Consider where you are: 3 miles to the Flat Rock Playhouse and Carl Sandburg home, 15 miles to the Blue Ridge Parkway, 17 miles to Chimney Rock, 18 miles to Pisgah National Forest, 19 miles to the Biltmore Estate, and less than 20 miles to the towns of Saluda, Tryon, Bat Cave, and Brevard. You're at the center of a wheel, with spokes leading to all of these great places.

A great loop picks up most of these places on a full day's ride. Leave Hendersonville on U.S. 64 West toward Brevard, but when U.S. 64 turns left, stay straight on U.S. 276 into a section of **Pisgah National Forest** (1001 Pisgah Hwy.,

828/877-3350, www.cs.unca.edu/nfsnc). Straight and narrow at first, the surroundings then become a canvas of wonderful woodlands, accented with waterfalls and roadside streams.

At the visitors center on your right, pick up information on horseback riding, hiking trails, camping facilities, and fishing streams. Four miles down the road, there's a great photo opportunity at Looking Glass Falls. After you pull over for a picture, you can climb down the steps for a closer look—but if you get much closer to the rocks you'll be pummeled into submission by the powerful falls. Ride another two miles and you'll reach Sliding Rock, where it's highly recommended that you should stop your bike, put on your trunks, and experience the forest's most exhilarating natural attraction. Slipping and sliding down the flat boulders offers the same sensation as skimming down a 60-foot icicle.

The road is just as exciting, like a luge competition as U.S. 276 continues its asphalt rush for eight more fun miles until you once again reach the Blue Ridge Parkway for a mighty great ride north. Enjoy traveling with your old friend for several spectacular miles until you reach Alternate U.S. 74 by Asheville and turn right. Ahead is a strange mix of twists and turns to contend with before reaching Bat Cave where the road slips into U.S. 64. You won't see Adam West or Burt Ward here since Bat Cave is just a short stretch of gift shops and restaurants with dining decks overlooking mountain streams, but it's got a great name. A few miles on, U.S. 64 leads to **Chimney Rock Park** (828/625-9281 or 800/277-9611, www.chimneyrock-park.com), site of a 1,200-foot-tall, 500 million-year-old rock tower that features hiking trails, catwalks from rock to rock, and a commanding view of the Hickory Nut Gorge. When the skies are clear or the

Red, White, and Bluegrass

If you opt to ride to (or reside in) Asheville, "along about sundown" on Saturdays between July 4 and Labor Day, **Shindig on the Green** (828/258-6107) takes place in a park in the heart of town. The free fest attracts big circle mountain dancers, cloggers, ballad singers, storytellers, bluegrass musicians, and old-time string bands who gather to play downhome red-hot-and-blue music. If you play, grab a guitar and join a pickup band.

forests are ablaze with color, it's worth the $14 to experience this vision. The town here borders on tacky, but it is home to **Heavenly Hoggs** (374 U.S. 64, 828/625-8070, www.heavenlyhoggs.com), an unexpected find that features antique bikes, parts, and apparel. Call for hours.

Stay on U.S. 64 and you'll reach the beautiful lakefront curves of Lake Lure which eventually takes you across a small bridge and to the entrance of Highway 9 South, a quiet country road that puts you in the middle of a long stretch of forests. While riding Highway 9 South you'll come across the junction for Route 108 that you can follow south for several miles into the town of Tryon, a community centered around equestrian events. Leave Tryon by U.S. 176 north (another great country road), and get ready to experience a mighty odd town.

Miles of great country road ahead, Saluda is the site of the steepest railroad grade in America, but it's better known for Coon Dog Day, a Fourth of July festival that brings families out of the hills to show off their hunting dogs, crown a new Coon Dog Queen, and listen to toe-tappin' mountain music. Downtown's rather small, but you can walk among the shops including **J. C. Thompson's Grocery Market and Grill** and the **M. A. Pace** general store.

From Saluda, stay on U.S. 176 and

the ride returns to its familiar temperament, twisting and turning, diving and soaring as it takes you into the village of Flat Rock. This highly cultured area is home of the **Flat Rock Playhouse** (2661 Greenville Hwy., 828/693-0403, www.flatrockplayhouse.org), which is also North Carolina's state theater. Absent any coon dogs, Flat Rock gets by with the Carl Sandburg home.

"The People's Poet" lived here at **Connemara** (828/693-4178, www.nps.gov/carl, $5), which is still just the way he left it. His guitar rests by his recliner, and the house is cluttered with original books, notes, awards, and walking canes, as if he'd just stepped out to feed the goats on his family farm. Even if you're not familiar with his poems and biographies of Abraham Lincoln, the chance to walk through some pleasing North Carolina countryside is well worth the price of admission.

It's been a full day. If you met the challenge of skimming down frigid Sliding Rock, dig the icicles out of your underwear and ride U.S. 176 the last few miles back to Hendersonville.

PULL IT OVER: HENDERSONVILLE HIGHLIGHTS
Attractions and Adventures

It's hard to improve upon nature, but

they've done it at **Pisgah National Forest** (1001 Pisgah Hwy., 828/877-3350 for the ranger station or 877/444-6777 for reservations), with campgrounds, nature trials, horseback riding, swimming, fishing, and picnic sites. At the ranger station, don't miss the "Cradle of Forestry in America" display describing George Vanderbilt's work with Dr. Carl Alwin Schenck to prevent clear-cutting and encourage area settlers to practice a new science called Forestry.

It may be slightly far from your base (about an hour from Hendersonville), but **French Broad Rafting Expeditions** (828/649-0486 or 800/570-7238, www.frenchbroadrafting.com) offers some great whitewater runs along the French Broad River. If you can push thoughts of *Deliverance* out of your head, take a five-mile raft trip over Class I–III rapids for around $45, or indulge in a full-day excursion that travels nine miles and rides over Class I–IV rapids, and includes lunch for about $70.

These great outdoors can be matched by only one example of the great indoors: **Biltmore Estate** (Hwy. 25, Asheville, 800/543-2961, www.biltmore.com). Well beyond description, Biltmore was created by George Vanderbilt in 1895, with America's largest home taking 6 years, 11 million bricks, and 1,000 workers to build. His humble abode encompasses 250 rooms, 65 fireplaces, 43 bathrooms, 34 bedrooms, and 3 kitchens, all of which covers more than four acres of floor space. A tour can be an expensive proposition (about $55, a few bucks less if you purchase tickets online) and it'll cost an extra $10 for an audio tour that provides a detailed history of the estate (although a free pamphlet lets you pick up the history of the main rooms). Either way, you cannot help but be impressed by the mansion's magnitude, where even the stables seem

as large as a subdivision. You may assume this'll be just a home tour, but add to this the unique craftsmanship, painted ceilings, unusual furnishings, family history, and a chance to score some free wine from a tapped barrel in the winery and it's all far beyond anything you can imagine.

Hendersonville is the county seat and to showcase the area's history, they restored the courthouse on Main Street and added an intriguing little museum on the first floor. It'll take about 30 minutes to see the displays on the Birth of a Nation, primarily of settlers and soldiers and Indians who lived in the area—from Cherokees to Tories to patriots to Civil War soldiers and troops from World War I to today. Good displays, good information, and it's free.

Shopping

Here since 1924, the **Curb Market** (221 N. Church St., 828/692-8012, www.curbmarket.com) is the place to stock up on great North Carolina goods like blueberry jam, pickled squash, relishes, jellies, chowchow, moonshine syrup and cakes in a jar, and walking sticks. Every item is locally grown, homemade, or handcrafted by Henderson County residents. You've got to love a place where the inventory didn't roll off an assembly line. Call ahead for shopping days.

Much of Hendersonville's appeal is finding that its downtown Main Street is still active and filled with people frequenting independent stores. I won't single out one store since there are plenty to find: jewelry stores, thrift shops, art galleries, clothing stores, and even a music store. A pleasant reminder of pre-mall America.

Blue-Plate Specials

Mike's on Main (310 N. Main St., 828/698-1616) is a century-old soda fountain and drug store that seems to be frozen somewhere between the 1920s and 1950s. It's preserved its embossed tin ceiling along with a collection of straw dispensers, milkshake mixers, pie carousels, and hand-dipped ice cream. Remember grabbing a hamburger and shake after school? Kids still do it today. Mike's is open for breakfast and lunch.

Renee Ellender was raised down in Louisiana and incorporates her mother's recipes from Bayou Terrebonne to whip up a mess of gumbo, jambalaya, red beans and rice, po' boys, and other south Louisiana dishes down a flight of stairs at **Cypress Cellar** (321C N. Main St., 828/698-1005). A full bar helps wash some of that there cayenne pepper down, Antoine. Stop here for lunch or dinner.

Similar to Mike's soda fountain is a spectacular place called **Harry's Grill and Piggy's Ice Cream** (102 Duncan Hill Road, 828/692-1995). Harry's is a small restaurant with a kind of 1930s service station–diner feel, where they serve large portions of comfort foods and sandwiches at low prices. Through an archway, Piggy's is the popular ice cream parlor–soda fountain. You can't miss the complex, it's surrounded by overwhelming displays of 1950s era roadside advertising art. It's all good.

Watering Holes

Hendersonville doesn't seem like a partying town, but there are sure some great bars and pubs and wine cellars downtown. **Hannah Flanagan's Pub** (300 N. Main St., 828/696-1665, www.theoriginalhannahflanagans.com) is a friendly place within stumbling distance of your room and it features 100 beers including Harp, Guinness, and Pabst on tap, a full liquor bar, Irish specialties, and live entertainment. The **Black Rose Public House** (222 N. Main St., 828/698-2622), is a restaurant during the day (shepherd's pie,

corned beef), but after 9 P.M. it's 21 and up and an inviting place where you can buy a pint for five bucks and pretend you're in Manchester. The **Corner Pocket** (245 N. King St., 828-692-7665, www.thecornerpocket.com) has a game room, domestic and imported draft and bottled beer, a full liquor bar, and, most importantly, seven regulation pool tables. Although it's an exclusive members-only club, membership is a reasonable five dollars a year.

Shut-Eye

I-26 rolls past a few miles outside of town, so Hendersonville has its share of chain hotels and several large inns.

Motels and Motor Courts

Cottages are always a great find, although some require a minimum stay of three nights during peak season. But that's not a bad thing, considering the per-night rate drops for three nights and drops even more for weekly rentals—and you get added time to use H-Ville as your mountain base. Check with the visitors bureau for a full list, but down the road in a nice country setting is the large and impressive **Cottages of Flat Rock** (1511 Greenville Hwy., 828/693-8805, www.thecottagesofflatrock.com, $75–125).

Inn-dependence

The **Waverly Inn** (783 N. Main St., 828/693-9193 or 800/537-8195, www.waverlyinn.com, $189 and up) is just a few blocks from downtown. The owners will kindly put your bike under cover, feed you a breakfast the size of Montana, and lure you to the five o'clock social hour to enjoy free drinks and mingle with fellow guests on the verandah. Room rates vary greatly depending on the season, but all are country comfortable. Innkeepers John and Diane Sheiry are as nice as can be—and John can tell you about great back roads even moonshiners don't know about. Right next door, the 16-room **Claddagh Inn** (755 N. Main St., 828/693-6737 or 866/770-2999, www. claddaghinn.com, $95–175) is similar in size and style to the Waverly. The rooms are more sparingly decorated, although they do serve a full breakfast. Away from town, **The Lodge on Lake Lure** (361 Charlotte Dr., Lake Lure, 828/625-2789 or 800/733-2785, www.lodgeonlakelure.com, $160–289) recalls a day in the Adirondacks. This former state troopers' retreat has been transformed into an idyllic escape overlooking Lake Lure and Bald Mountain. Vaulted ceilings, hand-hewn beams, evening lake cruises, and a hearty mountain-gourmet breakfast await you. Good as gold.

Chain Drive

These chain hotels are in town, or within 10 miles of the city center: **Best Western, Comfort Inn, Days Inn, Econo Lodge, Hampton Inn, Holiday Inn, Quality Inn, Ramada, Red Roof Inn**

For more information, including phone numbers and websites, see page 439.

Resources for Riders

Blue Ridge Parkway Run

North Carolina Travel Information
North Carolina Bed & Breakfasts—800/849-5392, www.ncbbi.org
North Carolina Historic Sites—919/733-7862, www.nchistoricsites.org
North Carolina National Forests—828/257-4200, www.cs.unca.edu/nfsnc
North Carolina Parks and Recreation—919/733-4181, www.ncsparks.net
North Carolina Travel and Tourism—919/733-8372 or 800/847-4862,
   www.visitnc.com

Local and Regional Information
Blowing Rock Chamber of Commerce—828/295-4636 or 877/750-4636,
   www.blowingrock.com
Blue Ridge Parkway Information—828/271-4779, www.nps.gov/blri
Hendersonville Information Center—828/693-9708 or 800/828-4244,
   www.historichendersonville.org
Mount Airy Chamber of Commerce—336/786-6116 or 800/948-0949,
   www.visitmayberry.com

North Carolina Motorcycle Shops
Action Cycle Sports—2349 Old Hwy. 421, Boone, 828/262-1558,
   www.actioncyclesports.com
Boone Action Cycle—8483 Hwy. 421 N., Vilas, 828/297-7400,
   www.booneactioncycle.com
Dal-Kawa Cycle Center—112 Kanuga Rd., Hendersonville, 828/692-7519 or
   800/692-7519, www.dalkawa.com
Forsyth Motosports—5599 University Pkwy., Winston-Salem, 336/767-2020,
   www.forsythmoto.com
Harper Cycle and Marine—1108 Spartanburg Hwy., Hendersonville,
   828/692-1124, www.harpercycle.com
Mount Airy Suzuki—1995 Rockford St., Mount Airy, 336/786-5343,
   www.mtairysuzuki.com
Parkway Harley-Davidson—20 Patton Cove Rd., Swannanoa, 828/298-1683,
   www.parkwayharley.com
Schroader's Honda—220 Mitchell Dr., Hendersonville, 828/693-4101,
   www.schroaders.com
Worth Honda-Kawasaki—600 W. Pine St., Mount Airy, 336/786-5111

Smoky Mountains Run

Jonesborough, Tennessee to Waynesville, North Carolina

An impressive ride starts in a yarn-spinning country town that should have been the capital of what could have been a state, then rolls through high-terrain twists and a most incredible park at the epicenter of hundreds of miles of motorcycle-perfect roads. In the end, you'll reach a most satisfyingly fine mountain town.

JONESBOROUGH PRIMER

It's picturesque and certainly different from most of America's homogenized communities, but just think if things had *really* gone Jonesborough's way. Back in 1769, folks began thinking that the tail section of what's now western North Carolina would actually be better off if it were a free state separated from what's now the northeastern edge of Tennessee. With that, they embarked on the "first free state" project to create a 14th state called Franklin. In the middle of it all would be the burgeoning capital of Jonesborough.

Things came together in 1784, when the North Carolina government agreed to let the region go and save itself the burden of taxing and providing for the region. That's when the folks of Franklin realized that now *they* would have to deal with taxes, infrastructure, defense, and advancing their quest for statehood. By 1789, the plan fell apart, Vermont became the 14th state, and North Carolina legislator Willie Jones never did see his namesake hamlet grow up to be a state capital like Pierre, Montpelier, or Frankfort. Instead, the town sat back and waited. Eventually, its location made it the gathering place for yarn spinners and tellers of tall-tales until it became the permanent site of the International Storytelling Center and an annual storytelling festival. All in all, it's pure Americana in a well-presented village; a small but interesting location that kicks off an extraordinary ride.

ON THE ROAD: JONESBOROUGH

Throughout this book you'll notice that sometimes I suggest heading out of town

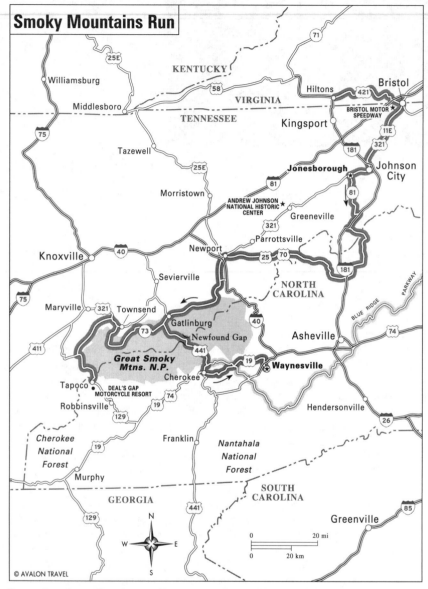

Smoky Mountains Run

Route: Jonesborough to Waynesville via Greeneville, Newport, Gatlinburg, Cherokee

Distance: Approximately 300 miles

First Leg: Jonesborough to Gatlinburg, Tennessee (125 miles)

Second Leg: Gatlinburg, Tennessee to Waynesville, North Carolina (75 miles)

Optional: Great Smoky Mountains National Park Loop (100 miles)

Helmet Laws: Tennessee and North Carolina require helmets.

for a country ride while in others I lean toward hanging out in the historic district. That's what you should do here. Although Bristol—the birthplace of country music and site of a great NASCAR track—is only about 30 minutes up the road, you should be able to wring a full day out of Main Street's stores and the tales spun at the International Storytelling Center.

If you rode in from Johnson City on Highway 11E and entered the town via Boone Street, you've already passed the visitors center which houses a small art museum, clean restrooms, and a staff as helpful as the wealth of paperwork it provides. Stock up here on guides to downtown and storytelling events, and base your day around getting into the slow-paced pleasures of the South. Main Street is a few blocks over, where the focal point of the commercial center is the 1913 Washington County Courthouse. Sitting in silence, it keeps an eye on things...the rusted tin roofs, the chipped mortar on historic brick buildings, and the curious travelers who found they could ditch the highway to discover a cool little town.

After you park and start to explore, you'll notice a small creek running through town, passing small houses with gingerbread trim and a row of churches whose three steeples form a perfect line down the street. You can take your time since there are no parking meters to watch—although signs suggest a two-hour limit. I'm not sure how tightly parking's enforced since other transgressions may be overlooked. I learned this from a genuinely helpful woman who, noticing my enthusiasm for the people and the culture of the area, confided, "Come back t'morrah and I'll bring you some moonshine. I know people what have steels..."

What a country. What a town.

PULL IT OVER:
JONESBOROUGH HIGHLIGHTS
Attractions and Adventures

While the center of the town's commerce is the shops of Main Street, the center of Jonesborough culture is a complex that includes a 200-year-old country inn, a 14,000-square-foot education building, and a surrounding three-acre park. This is the **International Storytelling Center** (116 W. Main St., 423/753-2171 or 800/952-8392, www.storytellingcenter. com), the only facility on earth devoted exclusively to the power of storytelling.

If you grew up hooked on movies and television, you'll be impressed that even minus lights, lasers, or music, the simple art of speaking can keep you entertained. Visiting storytellers make special appearances, and if you're inspired to learn the craft yourself you can pick up books and audios on how to spin a yarn. To hear

Taking it easy and mapping out the road ahead in charming Jonesborough: The slow-paced small town could have been the capital of a region that could have been a state.

fledgling storytellers weave their tales, call for a schedule. Also, on Tuesday evenings at 7:30 P.M., you can watch the action unfold at a pickup session at a neat little eatery called the **Cranberry Thistle** (103 E. Main St., 423/753-0900).

Shopping

Too many stores that sell glass objects push a heapin' helpin' of crappy crystal unicorns and clowns, but the **Jonesborough Art Glass Gallery** (101 E. Main St., 423/753-5401) has some pretty impressive pieces of glass as art—whether it's a glass globe, vase, or neon piece. Check out the oversized metal butterfly chair that, unlike its 1960s counterpart, actually looks like a butterfly.

One of the better antiques and collectibles marts I've seen is the cleverly named **Jonesborough Antique Mart** (115 E. Main St., 423/753-8301, www.jonesboroughantique.com). It features two levels of Southern folk art and memorabilia that you'd expect to see either at a 1930s service station or in Jed Clampett's cabin. Another plus is the wealth of *Andy Griffith Show* souvenirs, books, trading cards, shirts, and license tags—and lord knows the world needs more Andy stuff.

Then there's the **Celtic Cupboard** (121 E. Main St., 423/913-2889), which isn't strictly Irish (it sells kilts), but authentic enough that if you want a nice Claddagh ring, harp music CDs, biscuits (aka cookies), or Irish books, this is the place to find them. Gotta love the T-shirt featuring the inspiring Irish blessing 'Po'g mo tho'in' (translation: kiss my ass).

Blue-Plate Specials

I was surprised that none of the several restaurants along Main Street served the kind of big food I love in the South. On Main Street, the food's fancy or spare, but here are a few to choose from: **Cranberry Thistle** (103 E. Main St., 423/753-0900) is a deli café where the locals hang out for breakfast, lunch, and dinner, all homemade and delicious. Greens, beans, and catfish are on the menu. There are different size tables and mismatched chairs and a small stage for open mic storytellers and musicians. Kind of like a hillbilly Greenwich Village.

Bistro 105 (105 W. Main St., 423/788-0244) is a smart-looking, casual eatery that's open for lunch and dinner and serves homemade salads, pasta, sandwiches, and entrées like Thai stuffed chicken, veal chops, and cedar plank salmon. The **Main Street Café** (117 W. Main St., 423/753-2460) is another simple restaurant open for breakfast and lunch and serves fresh sandwiches, salads, homemade soups, and locally-brewed beer. Back near the entrance to town, **The Pizza Parlor** (416 E. Jackson Blvd./Hwy. 11E, 423/753-8862) is a small, family-run place that features a basic lineup of pizzas, spaghetti, and subs. Nothing fancy at all, but hot food at a good price. And yes, that's really its name.

Watering Holes

Washington isn't exactly a dry county—but it's close. Here it's "liquor by the drink," which means you can at least grab a beer or wine at a Jonesborough restaurant. But since finding a good place to grab a cold brew is tough, you may want to check out the offerings in Johnson City, about 10 miles north. Riders have discovered **Kemosabe's Road House** (2926 Boones Creek Rd., 423/282-3830), just off I-181. It's an old barn converted into a bar, with live blues and classic rock, pool tables, beer, wine, and mixed drinks.

Shut-Eye
Inn-dependence
Right in the heart of town is the **Eureka**

Inn (127 W. Main St., 877/734-6100, www.eurekajonesborough.com, $109–129). The 1797 building has been brought up to speed with voice mail, data ports, soundproof insulation, private baths, and cable—all balanced by period antiques in each of its 14 rooms. A continental breakfast is included. If you really, really like old stuff, the **Hawley House B&B** (114 E. Woodrow Ave., 423/753-8869 or 800/753-8869, www.hawleyhouse.com, $105–150) is the oldest building in Tennessee's oldest town. Don't expect a Westin; this is an 18th-century log structure, restored with antiques and folk art. The rooms, each with a private bath, overlook a meadow or the village.

Chain Drive
Most chain hotels are 10 miles north of Jonesborough in Johnson City:
Best Western, Comfort Inn, Days Inn, Doubletree, Econo Lodge, Hampton Inn, Holiday Inn, Quality Inn, Ramada, Red Roof Inn, Sleep Inn, Super 8
For more information, including phone numbers and websites, see page 439.

SIDE TRIP: BRISTOL, VIRGINIA

Only about 30 miles north of Jonesborough on Highway 11E is the town of Bristol. You need to see it and there are a few reasons why.

When roots music took root, the nation was reminded of the contributions of the incredible Carter Family of Maces Springs, Virginia. Their story started when fruit tree salesman Alvin Pleasant (A. P.) Carter roamed through the hills of the Clinch Mountains and hollows of Poor Valley and heard songs that mountain families had passed down through generations. The songs haunted him, so when he got home, A. P. transcribed the music and lyrics as best he could recall. In August 1927, A. P. spied a newspaper ad seeking musicians to audition for a Columbia Records representative who was traveling to nearby Bristol. So, with his wife Sara on autoharp and her 18-year-old cousin Maybelle on guitar, the Carter Family played their folk tunes in a warehouse-turned-recording-studio. Within minutes, the three had created the foundation of country music, with songs like "Wildwood Flower," "Will the Circle Be Unbroken," and "Worried Man Blues."

The legendary Bristol Sessions also produced Jimmie Rodgers (the Singing Brakeman), but that's not the only reason why you should visit Bristol. The town is also unique because its Main Street straddles the state line—the south side's in Tennessee, and the north side's in Virginia, and each side has some cool stores. Ride here because Hamburger Hamlet is where Hank Williams ate his last meal before dying in the backseat of a car on New Year's Day, 1953. Ride here because on Mondays, Tuesdays, and Thursdays you can head to a plaza on Main Street for free concerts by local bluegrass musicians. Make the ride because racers at the **Bristol Motor Speedway** (151 Speedway Blvd./ Hwy. 11E, 423/989-6900, www.bristol-motorspeedway.com) are tearing around the short track—"The Fastest Half-Mile in the World"—and amateurs in cars and on bikes are ripping up the drag strip on "Street Fight" nights.

It's a cool town, and the locals are more than helpful, especially the folks at the **Bristol Chamber** (423/989-4850, www.bristolchamber.org), who'll guide you every step of the way.

One last tip: The absolute best thing to do if you're ready for a great ride and great music is to take the supremely fantastic U.S. Highway 58/421 West to Hiltons to see the old Carter Family homestead.

On the short and magnificent 30-minute ride from Bristol, the landscape looks suspiciously similar to Switzerland, and it'll excite you. If you time your ride for a Saturday, members of A. P. and Sara's family host a live 7:30 P.M. show at the **Carter Family Fold** (Route 614/A. P. Carter Hwy., 276/386-6054, www.carterfamilyfold.org). Since 1976, groups like the Corn Lickers, Zephyr Lightning Bolts, Slate Mountain Ramblers, and even Johnny Cash and June Carter have performed in an old barn adjacent to A. P.'s general store, playing traditional folk and bluegrass music the way the Carters did—right in the heart of the Clinch Mountains. Cost: $7. Memories: Priceless.

ON THE ROAD: JONESBOROUGH TO GATLINBURG

On my last visit to Jonesborough, I reviewed my previous road trip and wondered if there was a better route to Gatlinburg. There was, and this is it.

On Main Street, head southeast and the road becomes scenic Route 81 as it takes you in the direction of Erwin. Within a few short miles the town fades away and you're in the countryside where you'll slip into an easy two-lane country road bordered by pastures and cattle and horses and spreading hills. It's an extremely gentle road where the dips and rises and slow little spins guide you along creeks and past old weatherbeaten barns. Although remote, it is not desolate, and at points you'll pass over and ride beside the Nolichucky River. After about 15 miles you'll reach I-26.

I try to avoid interstates, but it's only about six miles southwest on I-26 to reach the exit where you and your bike are about to join up with wonderful U.S. 19W which is ready to deliver some terrific backwoods

riding. I've tackled some monumental roads in Switzerland, and this reminded me of that thrill—and the challenge. Almost immediately the winding two-lane snaked up into the hills and got eerie in a way since there didn't seem to be any towns or any people.

Think of riding your motorcycle *up* a ski trail and you'll have a good idea of what this is like. The road weaves and climbs constantly and you'll have to pay close attention to navigate the turns, although an occasional straightaway appears and you can goose it. And there are unusual sights like a waterfall that bursts from a cliff, abandoned cabins that have collapsed on themselves, empty general stores whose windows are dusted over, and dirt roads that flare off into the woods.

You're riding in the Pisgah National Forest, which is worth a book by itself, and for mile after mile the black road leaps up and down or wraps itself around the hills. You can toss your ab-crunch machine after this—your torso's getting a workout just leaning into all the curves.

When you reach Sioux, the land opens up and as you continue towards Ramseytown, you may recognize that all along the road there are often strands of headlights approaching from the opposite lane, likely these are local riders who wring the most out of these mountains every day. Eventually U.S. 19W comes to a T where there's a gas station and a general store, and you turn right to head southwest on a road that presents a lot of curves but no serious switchbacks. What it does have are nice vistas of valleys and rivers and reminders that you're in the Deep South—the roads here have names like Possumtrot, Lickskillet, and Snake Bite Holler. This easy and quirky vibe continues until you hook up again with I-26 (which had taken an alternate route to reach this point).

The Nature of the Smokies

Atop the Newfound Gap on the border of North Carolina and Tennessee, there are several displays that reveal a bit about the park. One that caught my attention highlighted naturalist Harvey Broome's observations about nature... which also happens to mirror the reasons why we ride.

Man has created some lovely dwellings—some soul stirring literature. He has done much to alleviate physical pain. But he has not created a substitute for a sunset, a grove of pines, the music of the winds, the dank smell of the deep forest, or the shy beauty of the wildflower.

A quick jog south on I-26 will take you to Route 213 at Mars Hill that will once again lead you west across North Carolina en route to Tennessee. After riding in the wide open, Route 213 will seem pretty dense at first but it clears out after Petersburg. The road actually becomes a North Carolina scenic byway before it reaches the junction of U.S. 25/70 West, where you turn right and the great views return in abundance. There are signs advertising whitewater rafting and the road clears and returns to easy Carolina cruising where it's not too tame nor too wild. You can goose it when you want, but be cautious enough to anticipate moments when curves appear or the sight of the **Hot Springs Campground** (315 Bridge St., 828/622-7676, www.nchotsprings.com) tempts you to rest for a bit on the banks of the French Broad River. A popular site for riders as well as hikers coming off the Appalachian Trail, Hot Springs Campground has campsites and cabins, and the actual mineral hot springs are a short walk away.

A few miles ahead is the town of Hot Springs. With a block or two of cafés, sports bars, and rafting outfitters wrapped up by beautiful roads and countryside, it's become a popular base for weekend riders.

In fact, a fleet of motorcycles outside the combination inn, restaurant, and tavern called **Iron Horse Station** (24 South Andrew Ave., 866/402-9377, www.theironhorsestation.com) makes it look like the entire town's a bike dealership. Of course, U.S. 25/70—also known as the Dixie Highway—rolls out of town as well, becoming a slow and meandering two-lane where you'll have nothing to distract you except scenery. Just after the Tennessee state line in Del Rio, you'll reach another rest stop for riders, the **Rock House Saloon** (4848 U.S. 25/70, 423/623-9494) and another few minutes ahead, just past the junction of Highway 107, even more riders are pulling over at the **Shack Market Deli** (3125 U.S. 25/70, 423/623-7067), and doing what they love best: hanging out at picnic tables and enjoying nature.

From here, the road continues to improve. After testing you with some hard twists, you get to run through the open countryside with the road regularly whipping up and over the French Broad River. Enjoy it while you can because too soon the road reaches Newport, which seems too large and too empty to compete with the road you've just taken. At the junction of U.S. 321 head south where, aside from a Cracker Barrel just past I-40, there's not much of interest, so you keep heading toward Cosby. You are back into the wide-open spaces again, in sight of the Smoky Mountains and 1950s-era signs that still pitch folksy souvenirs, cabins for rent, and cheap tourist attractions. The other advantage is the distinct California feel that arrives in the greenery of the approaching mountains, and the Yosemite-like sweeps and turns in the valleys. At the small, community-run **Smoky Mountain Visitors Center** you can stop to pick up some Gatlinburg brochures and coupons and see a display of a still and jars of moonshine. After that, U.S. 321 takes a sharp right—and so should you.

The road rides along the periphery of the northwest corner of Great Smoky Mountains National Park, and it reveals just a hint of what you'll see in the next few days. It's private, narrow, calming, and a pleasure to ride—but when the road turns to a four-lane, it's a sign that you're getting close to the center of Gatlinburg, just in time to rest your bike and yourself.

GATLINBURG PRIMER

Fudge shops, old-time photo parlors, and wax museums didn't create Gatlinburg. They're here because the Smoky Mountains are here, and the part that has been preserved is part of the most visited national park in America. Why not? There are more varieties of trees here than in the entire European continent. There are animals found here that are found no place else on earth. The elevations range from a modest 840 feet to an impressive 6,643 feet along the Appalachian Mountains chain that runs clear up to Canada. In this one park are ecosystems that include wetlands, grassy balds, spruce forests, cove hardwoods, and the largest remaining old growth forest east of the Mississippi.

That's why it's hard to believe that, not so long ago, it was getting razed all to hell. But in the mid-1920s, some folks realized clear-cutting and logging were destroying what God had created and started a drive to protect the region. With support from a variety of sources, they managed to raise enough money and public interest to buy about 800 square miles of forest and save it. Soon families that lived well out of the way of civilization were picked up and moved out, taking with them their few possessions, folk tales, and mountain music. Moving in during the Great Depression were some 4,300 men working for the CCC (Civilian Conservation Corps), who arrived to build roads, bridges, cabins, and campgrounds; stock rivers with fish; fight fires; and practice trades. By 1940, Franklin D. Roosevelt arrived to dedicate what would become America's most visited national park.

Most visited—but lightly funded. Be sure you see it before it's razed all to hell.

ON THE ROAD: GATLINBURG

In a few days when you leave town en route to Waynesville, you'll ride across the Smokies on U.S. 441 and see spectacular sites along the way—but now you have to choose between seeing even more spectacular roads or playing hooky by playing tourist in town. Either way is fine, and some tourist choices are detailed here. For now, however, consider that there are more than 270 miles of roads in the park and that should be enough to convince you to plan a perfect day trip starting and ending in Gatlinburg, after riding down one of the most popular motorcycling roads in America.

From the center of town, head east on U.S. 441 into **Great Smoky Mountains National Park** (865/436-1200, www.nps.gov/grsm). A pullout by the welcome sign makes a great backdrop for you and your bike, and the **Sugarlands Visitors Center** (865/436-1291), about a mile ahead, is a definite first stop. You'll see a wonderfully written and produced film about the history and nature of the park, as well as a topographical map that gives you, in miniature, a sense of what you're about to encounter. Free road maps, a park newspaper, and information on camping, fishing, waterfalls, horseback riding, and informative ranger-led tours are all available. How informative? On a walk in the woods, a ranger warned us not to go off the trail, noting that "as long as you can see your feet, you can also see a snake." Considering rattlers and copperheads were here before me, I kept an eye on my feet.

The park straddles the Tennessee–North Carolina border and sits diagonally on that line, so directions may not mean much. Just leave the visitors center and turn right on Little River Road (Hwy. 73) toward Cades Cove, a good half-hour away. En route, you'll ride immediately into cool forests that slide along the riverbanks with the rough texture of the rock and wide sweep of clear water leading you down the road.

After miles of this slow, steady, and magical run, you'll reach an intersection where Highway 73 forks right towards Townsend. Skip it for now, and instead head straight on Laurel Creek Road into Cades Cove, the valley where the settlers lived before they were resettled. If you time your ride for off-season or early in the morning, you'll enjoy a peaceful one-way tour, stopping at the preserved primitive churches and cabins and overlooks along the way. Be warned that in peak season, the single-lane road is packed like an L.A. freeway, and your patience will cool as your bike overheats. But if you can see it in its natural, vehicle-free state, you'll witness

Wreckage left on the road by reckless riders decorates the famous (or infamous) "Tree of Shame" at the Deal's Gap Motorcycle Resort.

a pristine paradise with numerous sites that will tempt you to rest awhile.

After Cades Cove, double back to Highway 73, hang a left, and follow it to U.S. 321. A few miles ahead on your left is the Foothills Parkway, which is mostly overlooked by motorists, although motorcyclists have discovered that it's another superb road. It either whirs along the Little Tennessee River or rides atop the spine of a mountain chain for 18 miles before it dumps you out at Calderwood Lake. From here, turn left onto U.S. 129, and you'll be riding toward your rendezvous with destiny.

You've now reached what some folks call the **"Tail of the Dragon"** (www.tailofthe-dragon.com), the start—or finish—of the legendary motorcycling road that offers, for your pleasure and amusement, 318 curves in 11 miles. I was so focused on not dying, I lost count after 293. If you suffer from a heart condition, bad back, or are

Wide-open Cades Cove was home to rural families for generations. When the land was purchased for a national park, they moved out and complete emptiness moved in. On a day when there are few travelers, the loop ride is calming.

pregnant, do not ride this attraction. Otherwise, gird your loins, check your shocks, and head for the hills. Chances are you'll ride slowly and sensibly, distracted only by the multiple curves that block your path and the constant drone of a nearby sewing machine factory. This whirring noise is actually the whining, high-pitched, two-stroke scream of sports bikes racing to complete the entire 11 miles in as little as—believe it or not—*10 minutes.*

About 1.5 miles over the North Carolina border, at the junction of U.S. 129 and Route 28, the ride slithers to a close in Tapoco at the **Deal's Gap Motorcycle Resort** (17548 Tapoco Rd., Tapoco, 828/498-2231 or 800/889-5550, www. dealsgap.com). At the general store/hostel here (rooms start at about $60), every rider in the Southeast congregates, picking up snacks, food, and drinks and sharing tales of their rides. On the other side of the parking lot is the fabled "Tree of Shame"

where bits of scrap metal salvaged off wrecked bikes hang as a caution for others and a backhanded tribute to riders stupid enough to speed.

After reaching Deal's Gap, only the time of day will determine which way you'll ride to return to Gatlinburg. If you have time, you may head off on Route 143 West and see the scenic Cherohala Skyway, or go full bore and make the complete circle tour to return via U.S. 441. Otherwise, you can look forward to turning around and revisiting the same roads you rode on the way up. Not a bad deal, Deal's Gap.

PULL IT OVER: GATLINBURG HIGHLIGHTS
Attractions and Adventures

There seems to be more activities in and around Gatlinburg than there are in the entire state of Tennessee. Most are along downtown's main strip (which is an attraction in itself) and brochures and discounts for most activities flood racks in nearly every shop and restaurant. My approach was like grazing at a buffet: I looked over the selections and picked the few that interested me most.

Whitewater rafting is huge here, and if you haven't done this before you've probably seen photos suggesting that it's a 10-mile stretch of exploding bursts of water. In reality, for the most part the huge, swirling rapids appear only after drifting through a long stretch of placid, calm flats. Even so, the brief adrenaline shots will provide a thrill you won't soon forget.

About 40 minutes from town via a different leg of the scenic Foothills Parkway **Rafting in the Smokies** (865/436-5008 or 800/776-7238, www.raftinginthesmok-ies.com) has an armada of rafts and guides who navigate the Nantahala, Ocoee, Big Pigeon, and Lower Pigeon rivers—each of which offers different degrees of difficulty. Here, and at other operations like **Rolling River Thunder Company** (800/408-7238, www.rollingthunderriverco.com), **Wild-water Ltd.** (800/451-9972, www.wild-waterrrafting.com), and the **Nantahala Outdoor Center** (888/590-9268, www.noc.com), rates hover around $40 for a three-hour excursion, although some offer coupons in their brochures or online.

On the outskirts of Gatlinburg is the crowded city of Pigeon Forge, which brings to mind a trailer park with amusement rides. Its popularity is in no small measure due to Dolly Parton, the hometown gal who grew up, left, and came back to buy a failing amusement park and rename it **Dollywood** (865/428-9488 or 800/365-5996, www.dollywood.com). Today the park is the state's top tourist attraction, and so impressed was I with Parton's business acumen that I completely forgot her other, more prominent attributes. The entire park is simple and satisfying, with an old-fashioned feel created by flume rides, thrill rides, a general store, the world's largest bald eagle rookery, a chapel that's actually used for Sunday services, and specialty shops like the "craft preservation schools" where artisans pass along their talents by teaching skills such as woodcarving, blacksmithing, and soap-making.

Shopping

The core of downtown is like nothing else you've seen. While it looks like it goes on forever, the main commercial stretch is only a half-mile (double that if you shop both sides of the street). It just seems long because every inch of U.S. 441 is occupied by a gift shop, fudge shop, store, attraction, restaurant, motel—or a combination of all six. Fortunately, three waterways (Roaring Fork, Baskins Creek, and the Little Pigeon River) intersect the town and help calm things down. Aside from two downtown bike shops—**Sevier County Custom Choppers** (450 Parkway, 865/430-8000) and **Smoky Mountain Harley-Davidson** (530 Parkway, 865/430-1602) which sells accessories—there are too many stores to recommend just a handful. So park your bike and wander up one side of the street and down the other and find whatever flops your mop. If you want to save your shoe leather and expand your range, the town operates a trolley that runs five routes around the city and it costs only 50 cents per ride or just two bucks for an all-day pass.

Blue-Plate Specials

There are a billion chain restaurants in Gatlinburg and Pigeon Forge, but since you already know the items on their menus, you'll need to know what the independents serve: *Meat.* A place that loves motorcyclists is **The Alamo Steakhouse** (705 East Parkway, 865/436-9998, www.alamosteakhouse.com) which can be a little pricey, but compensates by providing great service, a nice setting, and steaks consistently voted the best year after year. **Bennett's** (714 River Rd., 865/436-2400, www.bennetts-bbq.com) is a huge, rustic restaurant with wood everywhere and readers' choice awards for best ribs, beef, pork, and chicken. Pig out at the endless soup and salad bar; drink up at the saloon. **Howard's Restaurant** (976 Parkway, 865/436-3600, www.howards-gatlinburg.com) has been in town since 1946. In addition to its nice creekside setting, Howard's serves items like Southern-fried catfish, trout, a 20-ounce T-bone for two, a 16-ounce signature steak, and gourmet burgers. For basic food and a beer, the **Smoky Mountain Brewery & Restaurant** (1004 Parkway, 865/436-4200) is designed like a lodge and has a far-flung menu of wood-roasted steaks, pizzas, fresh breads, burgers, and handcrafted beers.

© NANCY HOWELL

The view of U.S. 441 far surpasses the view from any desk. Getting lost in these woods is one of the best riding experiences in America.

Watering Holes

Gatlinburg's a tourist town, so chances are you'll find a bar and brew waiting at most restaurants along U.S. 441. Popular with riders is **Hogg's and Honey's** (745 Parkway, 865/436-8515, www.hoggsandhoneys.net), that's "a sports bar by day, a party place by night." The cool balcony is a great place to sit, sip a brew, order some wings, and watch the crowd below.

Shut-Eye

Nearly every type of lodging ever created is available in Gatlinburg. There are log cabins, Swiss chalets, motels, hotels, inns, and condos. It's safe to reserve a night at one of the chain hotels listed here (I really enjoy the Best Western Twin Islands—where a river flows outside the balconies). If you're traveling in a group and have designs on a chalet or private home to use as a base while you explore the mountains, the best bet is to visit the Chamber of Commerce website (www.gatlinburg.com) for a comprehensive listing of prices, amenities, and locations. If you're based in the center of town, you can park your bike and walk.

Chain Drive

These chain hotels are in town, or within 10 miles of the city center:
Best Western, Clarion, Comfort Inn, Days Inn, Econo Lodge, Fairfield Inn, Hampton Inn, Hilton, Holiday Inn, Howard Johnson, Quality Inn, Ramada, Red Roof Inn, Rodeway, Scottish Inns, Sleep Inn, Super 8, Travelodge
For more information, including phone numbers and websites, see page 439.

ON THE ROAD: GATLINBURG TO WAYNESVILLE

Odds are you already dipped into the park the day before, but today's the day you get to make the 40-mile run up and over the peaks and into North Carolina. There are pullouts and scenic vistas and spur roads and points of interest along the way, so don't anticipate clearing the park quickly. Give yourself (at the very least) half a day to fully appreciate the ride east.

Some advice before you head out: First, find a gas station far from the park entrance since the two last-chance stations will seriously gouge you without shame. Also, stop at any market and buy provisions for a picnic. You'll know why soon.

Miles past the park entrance sign and the Sugarlands Visitors Center, which you may have seen the day before, the Smoky Mountains will welcome you. I know the term "the woods primeval" is thrown out a lot, but I can't help but throw it back in. From the road, you'll see quiet walkways laced into the woods, coaxing you to stop your ride and replace biking boots with hiking boots. The trails are threaded into the forests beside rocks painted with a sheen of algae and glistening water.

Like the trails, the road is not dangerous or demanding. It is perfectly designed to give you the opportunity to park your bike, appreciate nature, take some pictures, and return to the flow of the forest. The woods and water features are right, and the 35 mph limit slows you down so you can gaze over the valleys and find steep ravines cut into the hills. Along the roadside and throughout the park are flame azaleas, rhododendrons, mountain laurels, fire pinks, trout lilies, yellow trillium, and 1,600 other types of flowers. There are also trees, many trees—sweetgum, poplar, dogwood, sycamore, pines, and paw paws. Less than 10 miles into the park, the **Chimney Top Picnic Area** opens up on the right. With plenty of parking and picnic tables right beside a roaring river, this is a well-known spot where people— mostly locals—are throwing cookouts and

lazing back and enjoying the sensation of the river, trees, and fresh air. Remember that picnic lunch you packed? Now's the time to unpack it. Lose the schedule and take a break.

When you're done and back on the road, you'll see that there are no sheer drops and few switchback curves. Although the road lacks danger, it makes up for it with an abundance of slow curves and magnificent vistas. Keep in mind this is the most visited park in the U.S., so the key to fully enjoying all of it is knowing when to travel here. If you can ride in a shoulder season when the roads are relatively empty, it's like renting Disneyland for a private party.

You'll soon get the hint you're rising in elevation, because your ears will pop and you'll notice 500-foot drops appearing off the side of the road. Near mile marker 14, you're at 4,837 feet; and when you get sidetracked at the pullout, you'll see that the road you rode seconds earlier is now more than 300 feet below. About five miles ahead, you've ridden to 5,046 feet and you're on the peak of Newfound Gap on the border of Tennessee and North Carolina. Buses and cars and vans are parked here, their passengers swarming the sidewalks and lookout point and pointing out thread-thin roads hundreds of feet below. One odd fact is that the Appalachian Trail cuts through the parking lot, and there's a slight chance that some hikers may stumble into view. Northbound hikers are just 205 miles into their six-month, 2,178-mile walk. You can take a quick walk onto the Trail and it doesn't take long to lose yourself in the woods. How through-hikers leave here to face another 1,973 miles to Mount Katahdin, Maine, is beyond me. Maybe they should take a motorcycle.

If you travel between late spring and early fall, the extraordinary sights of the gap will actually pale in comparison to what you'll see around the corner at **Clingman's Dome.** The road may close off-season, but if it's open when you arrive, within seven miles the side road to reach it will rise to a peak elevation of 6,634 feet and deliver views that are farther, wider, and more impressive than what you've already experienced. From here, a half-mile trail will take you to the actual summit, and the chance to rest your bike and relax with the views is a Zen moment.

Coasting off the mountaintop, the landscape ahead looks as if a sheet has been laid over the earth, with the folds and interlocking fingers of the ground looking quite graceful. Dropping into North Carolina won't take much effort. At some points you can just tap it into neutral and for mile after mile all you'll hear is the steady spin of your tires on pavement. Releasing the throttle and letting gravity do the work, I felt that roads rarely get any better for bikes. Like water flowing down a stream, I'd splash against a curve, wash into the next corner, and drift through the woods. It seemed endless. As the bike coasted, I went out for a cup of coffee, read a magazine, came back to the bike, and it was still coasting. Few things can lift your spirits like this.

The park ends near the town of Cherokee, and there's the option of staying here if you choose. A better choice, I'd argue, is tacking to the left off U.S. 441 and onto the Blue Ridge Parkway for another 26 miles to a far nicer stop in Waynesville. The only things that may stop you are if the BRP is closed, if it's getting dark, or if there's fog settling in. The first one will guarantee you can't ride it, and the second two are extremely hazardous and should convince you to bypass it. If you can go, you'll be on one of the best and most scenic roads in America, riding at an easy 45 mph to reach U.S. 74 East that leads to one of the nicest towns in western North Carolina.

WAYNESVILLE PRIMER

While growing up, I was aware of fictional towns like Beaver Cleaver's Mayfield and Encyclopedia Brown's Idaville and I always thought I'd want to live in places like that. Now I can just move to Waynesville. It's in the mountains, there's a fantastic and thriving downtown, there are lakes nearby, and wonderful roads lead to wide-open countryside. All of this started with Colonel Robert Love, a Revolutionary War veteran who donated land for the courthouse, jail, and public square. So, why aren't you visiting Loveville? The town's name was a tribute to his commanding officer, General "Mad" Anthony Wayne.

There's something about war and Waynesville that makes them go together. At the end of the Civil War, the last shots east of the Mississippi were fired about 25 miles away at Sulphur Springs, but lacking a satellite dish, no one knew the war had ended nearly a month earlier. After peace broke out, Waynesville residents took up agriculture for about a century, shifted to industry after World War II, and in the mid-1990s, merged their town with neighboring Hazelwood to become a tourist destination based on a great climate, improved cultural environment, and the blessings of the Blue Ridge and Smoky Mountains.

ON THE ROAD: WAYNESVILLE

You've already ridden some of the nation's best roads just to get here, and if it was too late the previous day to ride the Blue Ridge Parkway, head west on U.S. 19/276 through Maggie Valley, and you'll find an entrance that'll lead back onto the parkway. A different option is working your way over toward Hendersonville to sample another section of the Blue Ridge Parkway run.

That's the appeal of Waynesville: having complete access to the great mountain and forest roads that surround you. Pisgah National Forest is just to the north and the east; Nantahala National Forest is to the south; and the Smoky Mountains are to the west. So after you walk around downtown, head out of town to the motorcycle museum and ask the locals to point you toward any of a dozen great rides in the area.

All of this will make even more sense if you arrive on a Sunday, when most of the places are closed, the proprietors are locked up in church, and all you can do is ride.

PULL IT OVER: WAYNESVILLE HIGHLIGHTS
Attractions and Adventures

One of the coolest attractions in these parts is about five minutes from Waynesville in Maggie Valley. It's the **Wheels Through Time Museum** (62 Vintage Ln., Maggie Valley, 828/926-6266, www.wheelsthroughtime.com, $12), a 38,000 square foot showcase of classic motorcycles and automobiles. Unfortunately, the economy has affected its schedule and it may or may not be open when you arrive, so call in advance. If the stars line up, you'll discover that motorcycle enthusiast Dale Walksler translated his passion for bikes into this significantly impressive collection.

The museum features more than 250 rare, running condition antique bikes—30 of them pre-1916—as well as some mouth-watering motorcycle memorabilia. There are commercial, police, and military bikes, hill-climbing bikes, racing bikes, Evel Knievel's jump bike, "one-offs," and a display that bridges early motorcycle technology to the advent of the H-D Knucklehead (which Walksler believes is the grandfather

of the modern motorcycle). Automobiles get a fair shake, with 1930s classics represented by a 1929 Duesenberg, a 1915 Locomobile, a 1932 Clobes, and Steve McQueen's Cadillacs and Packards.

Shopping

The large spaces that served as department stores in the past are now Waynesville's galleries, boutiques, and sporting goods shops. Merchants have done a great job of bringing their town back, and roaming around downtown should take the better part of half a day, with a return visit for dinner that evening. While you're browsing, drop in at **Osundu Books** (184 Main St., 828/456-8062, www.osondubooksellers.com) and check out some of their books on local history, trails, and volumes by and about people in the area.

One of the best stores in town is the **Mast General Store** (63 Main St., 828/452-2101, www.maststore.com). An annex of the original in Valle Crucis, this one found a home in a 1930s mercantile which still has the old cabinetry, oiled floors, a mezzanine, and barrels filled with old-fashioned candies. If you need anything—and I mean *anything,* from jams, frying pans, hats, and tents to dulcimers, dusters, gee-haw whimmydiddles, or an idiot stick, you'll find it all here.

Blue-Plate Specials

I've had the good fortune to dine in a lot of places, and my good fortune improved when I found the restaurants in Waynesville. Give some of these a try. **Nick and Nate's** (111 Main St., 828/452-0027) offers a lunch buffet as well as hand-tossed pizzas and handcrafted on-tap micros like Sweetwater Georgia Brown and Alley Cat Gaelic Ale.

Everyone knows about **Whitman's Bakery** (18 Main St., 828/456-8271). It's been packed every day since 1945, with customers sidling up to the counter to order sandwiches and pastries to go, while folks with more time order the same to eat in the neat little dining area. Lunch is served from 11 A.M. to 4 P.M., so time it right to hit the bakery and sandwich shop to order huge hamburgers, hot dogs, tuna melts, hoagies, stacked sandwiches, and daily specials. The bakery's 100 different breads are absent of pre-mixes and preservatives.

Bogart's Restaurant (303 S. Main St., 828/452-1313, www.bogartswaynesville.com) is a popular spot noted for its burgers, soups, and affordable flame-grilled steaks. Daily specials at lunch and dinner will also save you some cash for the road. Good food, great price.

Watering Holes

As in Jonesborough, there's not a lot shakin' after dark, and most folks determined to find active nightlife ride out of town and into Maggie Valley where coveted liquor licenses mean places stay open past 9 P.M. If you're smart enough not to drink and ride, stay close to your base and drop in at **O'Malleys on Main** (172 N. Main St., 828/246-0898). It's half pub/half restaurant, with warm and inviting booths where you can order simple but filling fare such as Reubens, shepherd's pie, fish and chips, BLT wraps, barbecue, and chowders. It's open 'til 2 A.M., so you've got plenty of time to quaff a beer or imported ale, order from the full liquor bar, toss darts, or shoot a game of pool.

Shut-Eye
Motels and Motor Courts

Down the street from the shopping village is the extremely clean and biker-friendly **Oak Park Inn** (196 Main St., 828/456-5328, www.oakparkinn-waynesville.com, $59–90). The owners take great care of the old-school motel, and its 37 units are standard, although 5 come with a kitchenette. This makes for a good base for exploring the surrounding country.

Chain Drive

These chain hotels are in town, or within 10 miles of the city center:
Best Western, Days Inn, Super 8
For more information, including phone numbers and websites, see page 439.

Resources for Riders

Smoky Mountains Run

Tennessee Travel Information
Tennessee B&B Innkeepers—931/924-3869, www.tennessee-inns.com
Tennessee Department of Tourism—615/741-2159 or 800/462-8366,
    www.tnvacation.com
Tennessee Road Conditions—877/244-0065, www.tn511.com
Tennessee State Parks—888/867-2757, www.tnstateparks.com

North Carolina Travel Information
North Carolina Bed & Breakfasts—800/849-5392, www.ncbbi.org
North Carolina Historic Sites—919/733-7862, www.nchistoricsites.org
North Carolina National Forests—828/257-4200, www.cs.unca.edu/nfsnc
North Carolina Parks and Recreation—919/733-4181, www.ncsparks.net
North Carolina Travel and Tourism—919/733-8372 or 800/847-4862,
    www.visitnc.com

Local and Regional Information
Gatlinburg Chamber of Commerce—865/436-4178 or 800/588-1817,
    www.gatlinburg.com
Great Smoky Mountains National Park—865/436-1200, www.nps.gov/grsm
Haywood County Chamber (Waynesville)—828/456-3021,
    www.haywood-nc.com
Historic Jonesborough Visitors Center—423/753-1010,
    www.historicjonesborough.com
Sugarlands Visitors Center—865/436-1291

Tennessee Motorcycle Shops
Honda of Greeneville—808 Tusculum Blvd., Greeneville, 423/639-2671,
    www.greenevillehonda.com
Jim's Motorcycle Sales of Johnson City—1209 W. Market St., Johnson City,
    423/926-5561, www.jimsmotorcyclesales.com
Sevier County Custom Choppers—450 Parkway, Gatlinburg, 865/430-8000
Smith Brothers Harley-Davidson—3518 Bristol Hwy., Johnson City,
    423/283-0422, www.smithbrosharley.com
Smoky Mountain Harley-Davidson—105 Waldens Main St., Pigeon Forge,
    865/774-3445
Volunteer Cycles—103 South Blvd., Sevierville, 865/774-7170 or 877/774-7170,
    www.volunteercycles.com

North Carolina Motorcycle Shops
Ghost Town Harley-Davidson—82 Locust Dr., Waynesville, 828/454-0066,
    www.ghosttownharley.com
Steve's Cycle Center—3302 Dellwood Rd., Waynesville, 828/926-0127
Waynesville Cycle Center—18999 Great Smoky Mountain Expy., Waynesville,
    828/452-5831, www.waynesvillecycle.com

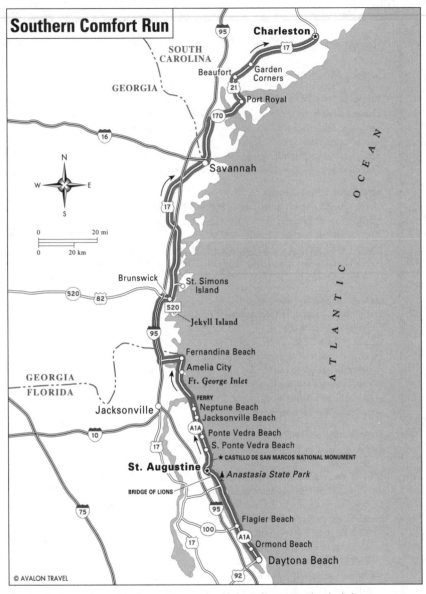

Southern Comfort Run

Route: St. Augustine to Charleston via Amelia Island, Jekyll Island, St. Simons Island, Savannah, Beaufort

Distance: Approximately 250 miles

First Leg: St. Augustine, Florida to Savannah, Georgia (150 miles)

Second Leg: Savannah, Georgia to Charleston, South Carolina (100 miles)

Helmet Laws: In Florida, helmets are optional if you are over 21 and carry a minimum of $10,000 in medical insurance. South Carolina does not require helmets if you're over 21. Georgia requires helmets.

© AVALON TRAVEL

Southern Comfort Run

St. Augustine, Florida to Charleston, South Carolina

This run worships the Holy Trinity of the Lower Atlantic's historic walking towns, and gives riders the chance to savor the seaside from a historic Spanish colony down to the heart of Daytona, then boomerang back to Georgia's barrier islands and magnolia-scented, mint julep–sipping, well-preserved antebellum towns all the way to Charleston.

ST. AUGUSTINE PRIMER

After seeing several dozen "oldest cities," I'd say St. Augustine has earned bragging rights to the title. Even though Spanish explorer Ponce de Leon never actually landed in St. Augustine, and it was 20th-century entrepreneurs who created the Fountain of Youth legend, there are *still* a few dozen reasons to see St. Augustine. When Don Pedro Menendez de Aviles arrived on August 28, 1565, the Feast Day of St. Augustine, he established the first permanent European settlement in North America. With his arrival, he brought European traditions, customs, laws, weights

and measures, and city designs to a new continent.

Before settling in, though, Menendez first had to defeat a French fleet, which he did with the assistance of a well-timed hurricane. After that, top on his list was making peace with the native Timucua Indians who were here to greet him. At these early summit meetings the Timucua were probably thinking, "These Spaniards seem like such nice people.... "

During the next 150 years, English corsairs and freelance pirates continued to attack and sack the town until the Spanish installed a home security system. In 1672, they started building the Castillo de San Marcos: A squat, sturdy fort that to this day overlooks Matanzas Bay and the entry into the Atlantic. Over time, a flurry of treaties and trades passed the town from Spain to England, then back to Spain, and finally to the United States in the 19th century. The Timucua weren't consulted about any of this.

Traces from these eras remain, but most

of what you see in town took shape during the 1880s. As part of his plan to build railroads and resorts along Florida's east coast, Henry M. Flagler created the magnificent Ponce de Leon Hotel, a short 24-hour rail journey from New York.

What the Spaniards and Flagler fostered is still present today: the homes, the Castillo de San Marcos, city gates, grand hotels, and cemeteries. This is one of the rare towns that knew better than to raze more than 400 years of history in favor of a new parking garage. The result: St. Augustine has character and style.

The town boasts great brewpubs, Key West–style bars, horse-drawn carriages, 42 miles of beaches, a first-class marina, fishing charters, hidden alleys and courtyards, and excellent riding weather. And the rest is history.

ON THE ROAD: ST. AUGUSTINE

Few other places in Florida rival St. Augustine as a walking town, but it's also a riding town. Take half a day or longer for a coastal run south to Daytona Beach. Even if it's not Bike Week (roughly the last week of February through the first week of March) or Biketoberfest (first week of October), there's still enough shakin' to keep you entertained.

Remember these directions: Cross the beautiful Bridge of Lions and head south.

Bike Week

The spectacle that became Bike Week began in Daytona on January 24, 1937. After the running of the first race across three miles of road and beach, it was Ed Kretz who won the prize—but the long-distance winner was Bike Week itself.

Although the races were scrubbed in 1942 to save resources for the war effort, fans continued to arrive on the shore to hold an impromptu party called Bike Week. By 1947 when the beach-road races resumed, the party was going at full throttle thanks in large part to ex-GIs astride surplus military motorcycles. Although attendance rose as decades passed, locals became increasingly more leery of bikers and by the late 1980s, fed-up city officials and businesses stepped in. The chaotic drunken bacchanal was reorganized into a supervised drunken bacchanal.

Now **Bike Week** (800/854-1234, www.officialbikeweek.com) is a cultural phenomenon that attracts nearly 500,000 riders from around the world. Usually held from the last week of February through the first week of March, festivities revolve around bikes, races, concerts, T-shirts, games, T-shirts, drinking, swap meets, T-shirts, drinking, and contests with some more T-shirts thrown in for good measure.

Seeing a blank space on the fall calendar, October's Biketoberfest premiered in 1992. Although smaller and less threatening than its bigger older brother, Biketoberfest attracts an estimated 175,000 bikers who are eager to enjoy a final pre-winter party.

© NANCY HOWELL

Local legend suggests Juan Ponce de Leon discovered Florida when he landed in St. Augustine. Although it's a myth, the man received a statue in the historic district.

That's it. That's all you have to do. Stay on Highway A1A when it veers to the left, and, with the Atlantic Ocean to the east, it's a straight seaside shot down the coast and one of the easiest rides you'll ever make.

At an altitude of six feet above sea level, two-lane Highway A1A takes you along Anastasia Island and 50-odd miles of sandy white beachfront. Appearing in rapid succession is the county fishing pier, beach ramps, motels, and oyster bars. Other than that, the coast is clear.

This is a far gentler ride than the Pacific Coast Highway because instead of being a few hundred feet above the ocean, you're right beside it, with the Matanzas River creeping along on your right. After passing Highway 206, look to your right for **Fort Matanzas National Monument** (904/471-0116, www.nps.gov/foma, free). A short ferry ride takes you to the fort that

was built in 1740 for the Spaniards' southern defense of St. Augustine.

The road remains the same, always pleasing and with little growth to screw up the view. You'll ride through **Marineland** (9600 Oceanshore Blvd., 904/471-1111, www.marineland.net), opened as the world's first "oceanarium" in 1938. After suffering after the arrival of the interstates and Disney, the tourist attraction reopened as an educational facility in 2006, a place where guests can interact with dolphins. From here, 15 miles of calm riding take you to Flagler Beach, where the **Pier Restaurant** (215 S. Hwy. A1A, 386/439-3891), at the junction of Highway 100, is the best place on the coast to rest your bike and enjoy an ocean view with breakfast, lunch, or dinner.

There's little else to note but a world of great riding to savor as you ride south. Enjoy it now because 20-odd miles later after you pass Ormond Beach, you'll enter wide lanes of tourist traffic at Daytona Beach. Stick with it; just past the Ocean Center (a large convention facility) is Main Street. Although the mood is suspiciously quiet when bikers aren't in town, take time to poke around here and the Boardwalk—they're both kinda dirty, but you'd kick yourself if you didn't stop.

Of the several bars on Main Street, there's one you have to see. Remember how incredible it was to drink your first beer? Well, friend, you can relive yesteryear with a visit to the **Boot Hill Saloon** (310 Main St., 386/258-9506, www.boothillsaloon. com). If you've fantasized about the bar's decor, you won't be disappointed. There are pool tables and a ceiling cloaked with bras left behind by female patrons, as well as Polaroid pictures taken of same patrons. It's open 'til 3 A.M. daily. As you ride the street, keep an eye open for other Main Street landmarks, including Froggy's,

Down the Line

Whether you're headed to Bike Week in Daytona or to New England for Laconia or Americade, Amtrak's Auto Train can provide you with a 900-mile shortcut. In addition to cars, the Auto Train carries bikes on its overnight run between Lorton, Virginia (outside Washington, D.C.) and Sanford, Florida (outside Orlando). The Auto Train departs daily at 4:30 P.M. (from either location) and arrives around 9 A.M. the following morning. Provided your vehicle has at least four inches of ground clearance, a 15 x 8 palette can hold up to four bikes, although no trike bikes or sidecars are allowed. Just ride up a four-foot ramp and into a tire-wide groove, and your bike is firmly confined by canvas straps.

Not only will you save a few days and the cost of a hotel room, but the meals on board are served in style (on china and tablecloths); the lounge is open late; and the huge seats can substitute for a bed—although sleepers are available. Rates in coach and first class vary by season and direction. For current rates and reservations, contact **Auto Train** (800/872-7245, www.amtrak.com).

Dirty Harry's, Full Moon Saloon, Bank and Blues, and The Wreck.

The Atlantic Ocean and Boardwalk lie a few blocks east. Changing facilities gives you the opportunity to swim, tan, or chill. Although the Boardwalk is pretty grungy, its bars and adjacent pier keep tourists and, sadly, runaway kids, coming.

Next, head a few blocks south of Main Street to U.S. 92 (aka International Speedway Boulevard). Turn right and follow it for several miles, and when you spot the massive racetrack, pull over at **Daytona 500 Experience** (386/681-6800, www.daytona500experience.com). Open 10 A.M.–6 P.M. daily, this is the attraction part of the track, and, despite its slant toward cars and not bikes, it's still pretty damn cool. Admission is $24, and the track features interactive displays—after a demonstration by a pit crew, you're challenged to test your skills at cleaning windshields and changing tires. One of the racing movies shown on the 55-foot screen puts you in the driver's seat. Acceleration Alley costs $5 and is a motion simulator ride that puts you behind the wheel for six minutes as you drive the track at virtual speeds of up to 200 mph. If that's not enough to satisfy your motorcycling soul, invest in the pricey but powerful Richard Petty Riding Experience (www.1800bepetty.com, $135). Although you don't get to drive unless you've already driven another Petty car at a smaller track, you do ride shotgun in a souped-up heap of metal that hits 170 mph on the Super Stretch. I did this and discovered myself shouting several new and, as far as I know, completely original streams of profanity. There are no side windows, just netting, a helmet, three laps, and comp admission to Daytona USA (you're saving $24). Definitely call ahead for scheduled driving days.

After you wipe that smile off your face, work your way back toward Highway A1A, stopping along Beach Street or Ridgewood

Avenue, home to several motorcycle dealers and customizers. When you ride back into St. Augustine and cross the Bridge of Lions once again, you'll get the best view of the city. From the crest of the bridge, you can see yachts moored in the harbor, the bayfront promenade, the plaza, and the fort to your right.

Now all you have to do is park your bike, find a quiet restaurant, or sit by the bayside and find what Ponce de Leon never discovered: eternal youth.

PULL IT OVER: ST. AUGUSTINE HIGHLIGHTS
Attractions and Adventures

Flagler College (74 King St., 904/829-6481) was built in 1883 as an extraordinarily luxurious resort known as the Ponce de Leon Hotel. Today, it is a four-year school for some lucky punks. They lead tours here, and if you like history and architecture, you'll find fantastic photo ops around campus.

On the north end of the island, **Anastasia State Recreation Area** (1340-A S. Hwy., A1A 904/461-2000, $4) offers picnic areas, a nature trail that crosses above fragile sand dunes, canoes, sailboarding rentals and instruction, four miles of beachfront, and 139 tent and trailer campsites (800/326-3521 www.reserveamerica.com). The park is open 8 A.M.–sundown daily.

The guys at **Camachee Island Charters** (105 Yacht Club Dr., 904/825-1971, www.camacheeislandsportfishing.com) can arrange charters on 30-plus boats from 20 to 48 feet. Charters typically head out about 50 miles (yowzah!) to reach the Gulf Stream, where you'll troll or fish with live bait for marlin, sailfish, dolphin, wahoo, kingfish, tuna, amberjack, and anything else swimming under your boat. This outfit also arranges night, river, and shark-fishing excursions, as well as tournament charters.

Conch House Sportfishing (57 Comares Ave., 904/829-8646 or 888/463-4742, www.conchhousesportfishing.com) also offers private charters for half- and full-day runs; tackle and bait are provided. Seriously consider this place since the Conch House doubles as an active watering hole, especially on weekends when everyone heads here for outdoor entertainment, drinking, and water sports.

After several rounds of pillaging in the 100 years following the city's founding, in 1672 the Spanish decided to protect themselves and began construction of the **Castillo de San Marcos** (Bayfront, 904/829-6506, www.nps.gov/casa, $6). The fort had a dual purpose: to guard the first permanent European settlement in the continental United States and to protect the sea route for Spanish treasure ships returning home. Although never taken by military force, the fortress was ceded to the British—and then back again to the Spanish—before becoming a possession of the United States in 1821. History still echoes in these walls. Wander around the fort and take a ranger-led tour if possible. There are bastions to climb, cannons to sight, and darkened rooms that once housed prisoners and soldiers. A must-see, the fort is open 8:45 A.M.–4:45 P.M. daily.

Not content to let history create an authentic attraction, some hustler rewrote history in the 1930s by claiming a sulfurous spring here was the Fountain of Youth sought by Ponce de Leon. Suckers have been swallowing that line ever since, and if you don't mind joining their company, the **Fountain of Youth** (11 Magnolia Ave., 904/829-3168 or 800/356-8222, www.fountainofyouthflorida.com, $8) awaits. What was on the site was an Indian village as evidenced by the excavated burial grounds of Timucua Indians. When you're here, it's fascinating to consider what America looked like when the Spanish arrived. There were no roads, no cities, no Pilgrims…just Native Americans and a continent that stretched unexplored to the Pacific. Open 9 A.M.–5 P.M. daily.

While no single store stands out along **St. George Street,** this pedestrian boulevard in the heart of the historic district is where most everyone goes. An eclectic collection of shops dot the mall, along with a few bars and restaurants. It's also the gathering site for several historic tours.

Blue-Plate Specials

At **Scarlett O'Hara's** (70 Hypolita St., 904/824-6535, www.scarlettoharas. net), the menu is basic—a little of everything—but even a hamburger or red beans and rice seems extra good when eaten on the front porch here. The service is good, prices are fair, and the patio bar is a nice, shady hideout. Scarlett's serves lunch and dinner.

Across the Bridge of Lions, the independent **Gypsy Cab Company** (828 Anastasia Blvd., 904/824-8244, www.gypsycab.com) does everything right, serving lunch and dinner on weekends and just dinner on weekdays. Parking's tight and there may be a wait, but it's worth it. The menu of fish, steak, veal, and chicken dishes changes almost daily and is always good. After trying the Cajun shrimp, call and thank me.

Watering Holes

Tradewinds Lounge (124 Charlotte St., 904/829-9336, www.tradewindslounge. com) defies the trend of trendy bars; this is the real deal. Here since 1964, this watering hole for locals also attracts a cross-section of tourists, students, dropouts, and beach bums. Weekdays, happy hour runs 5–8 P.M., with live music playing from

then until closing. Tradewinds has it all: a full bar, margaritas, rum punch, and, of course, beer. All it's missing is grog.

O. C. White's (118 Avenida Menendez, 904/824-0808, www.ocwhites.com) is a restaurant, too, but the patio areas out front are just across from the yacht marina, so it's a great place to have a beer and enjoy the outdoors. Not wild, but perfect for talking and looking.

Yet another restaurant, **A1A Aleworks** (1 King St., 904/829-2977, www.A1Aaleworks.com) is a great place to grab an inexpensive lunch or dinner, and it's usually crowded with a lot of young locals. As the name implies, it's also a great place to grab a cold one (choose from seven micros, as well as domestics) or a drink from the full bar. Upstairs, the balcony seems borrowed from Bourbon Street. Have a drink and watch the yachts sailing in on the bay.

Shut-Eye

St. Augustine has dozens of inns, chain hotels, and moderately priced independent motels—but sometimes that's not enough. Make reservations well in advance, and note that weekday rates are lower than those listed here.

Motels and Motor Courts

The **Monterey Inn** (16 Avenida Menendez, 904/824-4482, www.themontereyinn.com, $59–150) has a great bayside location and clean rooms that overlook yachts at anchor, sailboats skimming past the harbor, horse-drawn carriages, and the fabled Bridge of Lions. Fifty-nine units have double, queen, or king beds, cable TV, and phones; there's also plenty of parking, a swimming pool, and AAA discounts on rooms.

The **Bayfront Inn** (138 Avenida Menendez, 904/824-1681 or 800/558-3455, www.bayfrontinn.com, $99 and up) is a clean, standard hotel with a nice view and a good location (two blocks from the Bridge of Lions). The hotel features a regular array of amenities, including a swimming pool, whirlpool, cable TV, and telephone.

Leaving the city behind, a five-minute ride north on Highway A1A takes you to the beach and a selection of smaller and older motels. The 29-room **Ocean Sands Motor Inn** (3465 Coastal Hwy./N. A1A, 904/824-1112 or 800/609-0888, www.oceansandsinn.com, $79 and up) has a good location and good rates. Rooms come complete with private patios, cable TV, coffeemakers, refrigerators, and microwaves. Bring your own food, and you may never leave.

Inn-dependence

The **Casablanca Inn** (24 Avenida Menendez, 904/829-0928 or 800/826-2626, www.casablancainn.com, $169 and up high season) features 20 guestrooms (15 with hot tubs) and, therefore, more camaraderie among guests who take advantage of the bayfront verandah, off-street parking, and complimentary breakfast. A sister property, the Secret Garden Inn, has three secluded courtyard suites complete with tiled baths, balconies, queen beds, and kitchenettes. Opened in 1888, the **Casa Monica Hotel** (95 Cordova St., 904/827-1888 or 800/648-1888, www.casamonica.com, $180–249) was vacant by 1932 and became the St. Johns County Courthouse from 1968 to 1997. Hotelier Richard Kessler restored this landmark in the heart of downtown, and once again the Moorish Revival accents of the original are clearly visible throughout, from its 137 rooms and suites (including three-story suites in the towers) to its themed dining room, swimming pool, cafés, and shops. Expect elegance, class, and fun.

Chain Drive

These chain hotels are in town, or within 10 miles of the city center:
Best Western, Comfort Inn, Days Inn, Econo Lodge, Fairfield Inn, Hampton Inn, Hilton, Holiday Inn, Knights Inn, La Quinta, Quality Inn, Ramada, Red Carpet Inn, Rodeway, Scottish Inns, Sleep Inn, Super 8, Travelodge
For more information, including phone numbers and websites, see page 439.

ON THE ROAD: ST. AUGUSTINE TO SAVANNAH

As you head north out of St. Augustine on San Marco Avenue, you'll pass the St. Augustine School for the Deaf and Blind, where young Ray Charles studied. Take a right at May Street, and, after scaling a steep bridge (look to your right for another fantastic view of the old city), you'll arrive in Vilano Beach which features a few motels and restaurants. Far more appealing is the sight of the Atlantic Ocean.

The road is a combination of country lane and beach road, two lanes of low-key riding right beside the water. A fringe benefit is found in the frequent series of pullouts and steps that lead down to the beach. When the waves and the weather are right, you'll be hard-pressed to stay on your bike.

By the time you reach South Ponte Vedra Beach, the waves will be hidden by towering walls of vegetation, but if you look closely you'll see narrow gaps in the brush. If suggested barriers like these don't deter you, prop your bike up on the sandy shoulder and sneak through the vegetation to find a secluded stretch of beach that's close to its natural state.

Within miles, this run comes to a close. Between Daytona and here, you'll have ridden a good 90 miles of Florida's best uninterrupted shoreline. When you reach

Ponte Vedra, Jacksonville Beach, and Neptune Beach, though, your view is blocked by dense commercial growth. Still, taking Highway A1A is better than riding through Jacksonville, a city where riding offers all the charm of a stomach virus.

After a sharp left after Neptune Beach, Highway A1A weaves up toward the Mayport Naval Station and past a creepy fishing village to reach the **St. Johns River Ferry** (904/241-9969, www.stjohnsriver-ferry.com, $3). As if you needed another reason to justify why you ride, sometimes motorcycles are waved to the front of the line. The crossing doesn't take long, but the ferry leaves only once every 30 minutes.

You'll be dropped off at Fort George Island, and within 15 miles, you'll be on a nice pine-rich road through Little Talbot Island State Park before it enters the southern end of Amelia Island, the only place in America that has been ruled under eight flags. Fernandina Beach, on the north end, is the only town on the island and this solitude has made the entire package popular with honeymooners, families, and retirees. You may be tempted to spend an evening here. There are tidy bed-and-breakfasts, large inns, magnificent resorts, and a downtown district with bookstores, restaurants, and unusual stores. Despite this, I'd have preferred this place when moral watchdogs dubbed it a "festering fleshpot," because of its reputation as a hotbed for pirates, brothels, and bawdy ladies.

Highway A1A is called South Fletcher Avenue along this strip of coast; from here, turn left at Atlantic Avenue. Stay straight, and after the road becomes Centre Street, you'll see one of the oldest bars in Florida—the **Palace Saloon** (117 Centre St., 904/491-3332). This most impressive watering hole in the heart of town is half grog shop and half historical museum where the barkeeps have been priming the pumps and delivering frosty mugs of beer to sailors, locals, shrimpers, and travelers since 1903.

Having bypassed Jacksonville, you have to head west on Highway A1A to reach I-95 North, where you can make up some time. Within a few miles, you'll be in Georgia. At Exit 6, take U.S. 17 toward the towns of Brunswick, Jekyll Island, and St. Simons Island, all of which are concentrated at the end of the road. **Jekyll Island** (912/635-3636, www.jekyllisland.com) is accessible via Highway 520, which runs straight into the heart of the resort town. Although you've ridden fewer than 40 miles, you've entered the real South, where the pace is molasses slow. In the 1880s, millionaires like Goodyear, Gould, Pulitzer, Rockefeller, and Morgan paid $125,000 for the island to use it as a hunting preserve and family retreat. Today, the getaway is a state park and worth a brief detour.

Return to U.S. 17 and work your way through Brunswick and past St. Simons Island. From here north, U.S. 17 (aka the Coastal Highway) won't actually take you near the coast, but it will keep you off of I-95 for a slow, meandering rural ride for about 85 miles. When this country ride comes to a close you'll have reached Savannah, one of the finest cities in the South.

SAVANNAH PRIMER

If you judged by recent events alone, the most important moments in Savannah's history would be the release of the film *Forrest Gump* and John Berendt's extraordinary book about a local murder case, *Midnight in the Garden of Good and Evil.* More important than these two events, however, were the actions of James Edward Oglethorpe and General William T. Sherman.

I'll start with Oglethorpe. In February 1733, he led 114 settlers to a high bluff on the Savannah River to create a new colony settled by poor people, soldiers, and foreign Protestants. Although the colony failed when Parliament cut off all funds in 1751, Oglethorpe's planned city of lush squares bordered by beautiful homes survived under the leadership of royal governor James Wright. Today those preserved squares put Savannah in a class by itself.

Then there was Sherman. In late 1864, after Sherman had torched Atlanta, he and his men marched to the sea—and Savannah. Savannahians did a quick head count and compared their 10,000 retreating soldiers against Sherman's 70,000 advancing soldiers and, displaying a remarkable degree of common sense, decided to surrender. Sherman gave the city of Savannah to President Lincoln as a Christmas present, an act that surely endeared him to the locals...

About as much as when his soldiers tossed aside tombstones in the Colonial Park Cemetery so they'd have room to pitch their tents.

ON THE ROAD: SAVANNAH

If you've never been to the real South, Savannah is a great place to start. In spring (when everyone else is here), the dogwoods and azaleas are in bloom, and the Spanish moss clutches at gnarled oak branches. Inside the ordinary brownstones surrounding the squares, elegance and a sense of tradition reveal themselves in the velvet drapes, cut crystal chandeliers, and oil portraits of long-gone ancestors. Savannah *is* the South.

Just as Daytona Beach worked you up, Savannah will settle you down. Start by circling the fabled squares between Bay Street and Forsyth Park. You are riding within the nation's largest historic district—more than two miles square. It didn't always look like this. Between 1945 and 1950, some idiots demolished more than 950 homes to make room for parking lots. That's when some women got wise and bought a single $22,000 house and jump-started the city's dormant preservation movement. You'll pick up this piece of intelligence at the **Savannah Visitors Information Center** (301 Martin Luther King Jr. Blvd., 912/944-0455, www.savannahvisit.com).

The visitors center, a restored train station, is the best place to start learning about what you just saw on your ride since there's a small museum here and the center is the departure point for nearly a million tours. The bus tours outperform the actual tours inside historic houses, since many docents will just point at objects and mumble, "This is a mirror from 1794. This is a table from 1812. This DVD player is from 1799..." Back on board, the driver's narrative should fill in the blanks for you young whippersnappers.

Make mental notes, and with leads provided by the tour guide you'll discover a lot of places to visit on your own during the day. For some reason, I prefer seeing this town after dark when the streets are less crowded and the squares more attractive. Obviously you'd want to wander where there's plenty of foot traffic. Get a map and walk over to Monterey Square to see the Mercer House. Forsyth Park, with its glistening fountain and ancient oaks, is a perfect romantic setting if you want to fling some woo.

There's a notable concentration of nightlife a few blocks from the river at the **City Market,** where there may be DJs, live bands, and dancing in the square—but no square dancing. Also check out **Vinnie Van Go-Go's** (317 W. Bryan St., 912/233-6394, www.vinnievangogo.com) for New

York–style pizza. A few blocks away, down by the riverside, you may want to park your bike atop Bay Street, since the decline to reach River Street quickly drops 42 feet. That's not too precipitous a plunge, but the millions of bumpy, rounded paving boulders—once used as ballast on slave ships—make parking and riding tough. As you walk this nine-block stretch of shops, restaurants, bars, and tourist traps, it's hard to conceive that this was once a row of cotton warehouses. Along the way, you may notice a cavernous void amidst the rows of shops. At this site, human misery reached its peak as newly arrived slaves were sold to the highest bidder.

If the squares slow you down during the day, you may just want to get on your bike and ride about 18 miles east of Savannah on U.S. 80 to **Tybee Island** (800/868-2322, www.tybeevisit.com). It's a nice ride out, past very low and wide salt marshes, with very little to interrupt your view. On Tybee, the **Crab Shack** (40 Estill Hammock, 912/786-9857, www.thecrabshack.com) is "where the elite eat in their bare feet." The Buffett-inspired waterfront restaurant was created during a "bar raising" in the early 1980s, and it thrives on beer, live gators, seafood, and music.

Hang out here or ride back to Savannah, where you can check into a hotel, find an inn, or follow Sherman's lead and kick over a few tombstones and pitch a tent in the cemetery.

PULL IT OVER: SAVANNAH HIGHLIGHTS
Attractions and Adventures

Full descriptions of most tours—ghosts, historical, *Midnight* book tours—are available at the **Savannah Visitors Information Center** (301 Martin Luther King Jr. Blvd., 912/944-0455, www.savannahvisit.com). My luck has been consistently good

with **Gray Line Tours** (912/234-8687 or 800/426-2318, www.oglethorpetours.com, $15–29). Like other outfits, they offer a narrated tour through Savannah's historical homes and haunts, and theirs are usually chock full of historical goodness.

Blue-Plate Specials

If you come to Savannah and don't eat at **Mrs. Wilkes' Dining Room** (107 W. Jones St., 912/232-5997, www.mrswilkes.com), I'll personally track you down and take you there myself. This is the best food in Savannah and may be the best food in the South (although the Lady & Sons—next listing—would argue). Between 11 A.M. and 2 P.M., for about $16 (cash only) it serves everything you need to get fat and happy: huge platters of fried chicken, beef stew, okra, sweet potatoes, cornbread, tea, and banana pudding, all carted to a communal table where you dine with a dozen other visitors. The result is good conversation and great food. Be ready to wait; the line can stretch out the door and down the block. The restaurant is open for lunch on weekdays only.

The Lady & Sons (102 W. Congress St., 912/233-2600, www.theladyandsons.com) followed in the footsteps of Mrs. Wilkes, serving lunch ($14) and dinner ($18) in a similar buffet style (on weekends as well), but without the communal seating. Locals and travelers contend that this surpasses the quality of Wilkes, and it may. You should definitely try both while you're here. Expect good hearty Southern dishes, with an emphasis on fried chicken and cheese biscuits. One item, hoecakes, led to the popular "Our hoes are complimentary" T-shirts.

Since 1903, locals have been heading to **Clary's Cafe** (404 Abercorn St., 912/233-0402, www.claryscafesavannah.com) for down-home cooking and occasional ethnic dishes. Ever since "The Book" *(Midnight in the Garden of Good and Evil)* came out, tourists have been poking around here, too—this is where Luther, the nut everyone thought was going to poison the town water supply, ate. With the drugstore gone, this is just a restaurant now, and since the food's trailing behind the legend, it may be best for breakfast.

Watering Holes

You wouldn't expect it, but Savannah has a large Irish population (faith and begorrah, Cleetus), so pubs are popular. **Six Pence Pub** (245 Bull St., 912/233-3156) features standard pub grub, but it has an atmosphere that'd be just as good even if it served nothing but beer. Live entertainment varies from Irish folk to rock to blues.

On any given night at **Kevin Barry's Irish Pub** (117 W. River St., 912/233-9626, www.kevinbarrys.com), you may find U.S. Marines sharing the bar with businessmen smoking big cigars. Beer is sold by the pint, with an emphasis on the Half and Half (Guinness/Harp). When Irish music plays (nightly starting at 8:30 P.M.) there's a $2 cover to get into the music room.

Churchill's Pub (13–17 West Bay St., 912/232-8501, www.thebritishpub.com) may be the most authentic pub in Savannah. To complement a full range of draught ales, try the Bubble & Squeak, roast beef and Yorkshire pudding, bangers and mash, and shepherd's pie. This is a great place to kick back and enjoy pool, darts, drinks, a fireplace, 21 beers and ales on tap, and a rooftop terrace.

A restaurant sits upstairs at the 18th-century mansion known as the **Olde Pink House** (23 Abercorn St., 912/232-4286), but a buried treasure lies below: **Planter's Tavern**, a low-key basement piano bar with twin fireplaces and easy listening pianists playing jazz and old Johnny Mercer tunes. The setting, the bar, and the comfortable couches make it one of the most pleasingly civilized nightspots in Savannah.

Shut-Eye

Savannah features dozens of chain hotels and a greater number of inns. Book well in advance, because rooms go fast.

Inn-dependence

Right on the banks of the riverfront district, the **Olde Harbour Inn** (508 E. Factors Walk, 912/234-4100 or 800/553-6533, www.oldeharbourinn.com, from $179) entered this world in 1892 as a warehouse. It may cost a bit, but the experience of waking up with a view of the Savannah River (and the ease of walking straight to the shops, restaurants, and bars of the district) may be worth the price.

Hidden jewel **Joan's on Jones** (17 W. Jones St., 912/234-3863 or 888/989-9806, www.joanonjones.com, $160–185) is an 1893 Victorian townhouse tucked into a nice residential area. Rooms with exposed brick walls and a suite within a walled courtyard garden, which sleeps up to five, offer a real sense of privacy. It's all a half-block from Mrs. Wilkes' Dining Room. A true Southern atmosphere, a real Savannah experience.

The generic name of the **Bed & Breakfast Inn** (117 W. Gordon St., 912/238-0518 or 888/238-0518, www.savannahbnb.com, $129–159) suggests a no-frills approach to inn-keeping. Surprisingly, the rooms are spacious, the full breakfast hearty, and the location convenient (only a block from Forsyth Park).

Chain Drive

These chain hotels are in town, or within 10 miles of the city center:

Best Western, Comfort Inn, Courtyard by Marriott, Doubletree, Econo Lodge, Fairfield Inn, Hampton Inn, Hilton, Holiday Inn, Hyatt, La Quinta, Quality Inn, Ramada, Red Roof Inn, Residence Inn, Sleep Inn, Super 8

For more information, including phone numbers and websites, see page 439.

ON THE ROAD: SAVANNAH TO CHARLESTON

It's a short ride from Savannah to South Carolina. All you have to do is find U.S. 17, ride north across the Hugh Talmadge Memorial Bridge, and boom—you're there. Now you're in the lowcountry where the road is as flat as a sheet of paper. U.S. 17 shoots past marshland for several miles before retreating into the woods with a right turn onto Alternate Route 170.

Right away you'll see signs of the Deep South: hand-lettered posters for bush hoggers, pine forests, and the El Cheapo general store and gas station. But the enjoyment is hard to sustain because just as you start into a nice run, subdivisions and trailers begin popping up. After passing a trace amount of commercialism, you'll settle back into the South Carolina countryside as you follow Route 170 northeast toward the town of Beaufort.

Now the savannahs open up and a few curves appear, along with the requisite Baptist church and adjoining cemetery. Although you're less than a half hour from Savannah, it's compelling to think of the people who have lived and died in this remote region believing that the outside world couldn't penetrate their lifestyle. In this marshland, you soon cross the long, low Broad River Bridge. This spot is scenic in an Everglades sort of way. Just after the bridge, turn right on Route 802 toward Port Royal. There's plenty of nothing to see at first, but then you'll begin to follow the waterfront toward downtown **Beaufort** (800/638-3525, www.beaufortsc.org), which just happens to be South Carolina's second-oldest township. While old antebellum homes and the waterfront provide great photo ops, obvious points of interest are hard to find.

Oddly, the setting looks more southern the farther north you ride. From Route 802, take Route 280 to reach U.S. 21 north; you'll find these roads by looking for the greatest concentration of mobile homes and video stores in North America. At the end of U.S. 21 you have the option of turning right onto two-lane U.S. 17 which is known here as the Charleston Highway. Do this and you'll ride by scenes from the past, gas stations from the 1930s; wisteria vines; peaches, tomatoes, and plums sold out of trucks on the roadside; and men in overalls straight out of a Margaret Bourke-White photograph.

A local rider suggested a better roundabout route which involves turning *left* onto U.S. 17 which leads, just a short distance later onto SR 21, also known as Old Sheldon Church Road. Heading northeast, you'll be riding towards Yemassee, a favorite destination for riders. A few miles up the road on your right you'll see the Old Sheldon Church itself—or what's left of it. Originally burned during the American Revolution, it was either torched again by Sherman's troops or stripped after the Civil War by folks needing building materials. Either way, the ruins create an eerily cool site.

Continuing on SR 21, you'll reach Yemassee and the Hendersonville Highway (U.S. 21) which heads northeast to pass Hendersonville and reach Walterboro, along the way presenting some curvy country roads and rice plantations for variety. The town of Walterboro is the top of the arc, bringing you to SR 64—also known as the Charleston Highway—that'll lead you on a slow and steady 50-mile path to Charleston, the hometown of Rhett Butler.

CHARLESTON PRIMER

Grab a history book and study Charleston. This city is English, Spanish, African, Caribbean, Union, Confederate, old, and young.

Like residents of St. Augustine and Savannah, Charlestonians recognize the irreplaceable value of history, and their town has changed little, at least in the historic district. Despite being bruised by bombings, fires, pirates, earthquakes, hurricanes, tornadoes, and war, Charleston seems content with itself and its history.

Even if you know little about the South, you've likely heard about Charleston's fabled "bluebloods," the native Charlestonians who still talk about the Civil War ("the Woh-ah") as if the damned Yankees still controlled Fort Sumter. Yet it is their determination to preserve this epoch that makes this town one of America's top travel destinations.

Although the bluebloods would draw my red blood for saying so, they have General Sherman to thank for this. After he gave Savannah a reprieve, he also bypassed Charleston. Some say this was because Sherman had a soft spot for the city since serving at Fort Moultrie in the 1840s.

Come to think of it, speculating as to why Charleston remains the way it is, is irrelevant. It's here. Enjoy it.

ON THE ROAD: CHARLESTON

It may go against a biker's independent spirit to rely on a tour guide for the skinny on a town, but that may be your best bet for understanding Charleston's layered history. The city was shaped by events during the American Revolution, the Civil War, and the Jazz Age (remember the Charleston?), and by Hurricane Hugo, which nearly ripped the place to shreds in 1989.

If you decide to make like the masses and hop on a tour, you'll be fine. They're all right. Most depart from the excellently detailed **Charleston Visitors Center** (375 Meeting St., 843/853-8000 or 800/774-0006). I had good luck with **Gray Line Tours** (843/722-4444 or 800/423-0444, www.graylineofcharleston.com). For a generic, Ma and Pa Kettle–style bus tour, the 90-minute ride was surprisingly informative and an easy way to get an overview of the city. The $20 tour passes the standard points of interest for all Charleston tours—such as historic churches, Fort Moultrie, Old Citadel, Battery waterfront, Rainbow Row—but the guides are well read and make it more exciting than your preconceived notions would lead you to believe.

Consider following up this low-pressure tour with another more detailed one. I can't say enough good things about **The Story of Charleston** (843/723-1670, www.tourcharleston.com), which demonstrates the difference between studying with a student and learning from a professor. The walking tour ($18) goes well beyond dates and architecture to illuminate Charleston's religious, sociological, and cultural history, filling in enough blanks to make you dangerous. This company also hosts other walking tours: the Pirates of Charleston and the Ghosts of Charleston.

Other necessary tours beckon (Fort Sumter, USS *Yorktown*), but the evening is just as important here. As you've guessed, historic Charleston is a great walking town, and every point can be reached on foot within minutes.

The center of activity takes place along Market Street, which would need little alteration to be a Civil War scene. Women weaving intricate baskets sit near the edges of the marketplace and horse-drawn carriages clop past.

From here, walk a few blocks south. At Vendue Range, turn left and walk past the fountain to the pier where large porch swings invite you to take a load off. From the end of the pier, you can see Fort Sumter—it looks like a black birthday cake with a flagpole candle. Beyond it lies the Atlantic Ocean.

Having learned the city's layout, walk a few more blocks south to the Battery, which is far more pleasant at dusk. The cannons, mortars, statues, and oak trees all spell "photo op," and the site provides a relaxing place to view the harbor.

Returning toward the nightlife of Market and Meeting streets, get lost as you did in Savannah and St. Augustine. Each "single home" has something different to reveal, from the old carriage stepping stones to the second-floor chandelier-lit "salons" that are cooler and more suitably adorned than any floor below or above. Watch for the barbed iron installed on houses when fears of a slave insurrection spread across the city.

After the sun sets, wander the streets until you find a place to settle back, and then give silent thanks to General Sherman for taking the left fork to Columbia.

PULL IT OVER: CHARLESTON HIGHLIGHTS
Attractions and Adventures

You know where the Civil War was fought, but Charleston is where it all started. What began here led to 600,000 casualties in four years. South Carolina had seceded, yet Union forces occupied Fort Sumter at the entrance of Charleston Harbor. The Confederates wanted them out; the Yankees refused; and on April 12, 1861, the Rebels fired from Fort Johnson, sparking a

33-hour bombardment that resulted in the surrender of Fort Sumter. Of course, the Union wanted its fort back and starting in July 1863, the Siege of Fort Sumter commenced as the Union began dropping an estimated seven million pounds of shells weighing 30–440 pounds on top of the men defending Fort Sumter. It took 587 days before the Confederates called it quits on February 17th, 1865. The National Park Service maintains the fort, and park rangers are here to answer your questions. **Fort Sumter Tours** (843/722-2628, www.spiritlinecruises.com) depart from Aquarium Wharf or Patriot's Point. The tour, which costs $16, lasts just over two hours.

Although a few things have changed since 1842 (like the admission of women), tradition holds true at **The Citadel** (171 Moultrie Ave., 843/953-5000 or 843/953-6779 for groups, www.citadel.edu). The best part about a visit here is watching the Dress Parade by the South Carolina Corps of Cadets, which usually takes place Friday afternoons during the school year at 3:45 P.M. You don't need a ticket; just show up early. Call ahead if you'd like to arrange a guided tour. Otherwise, you're on your own.

It's hard to see everything at the **Charleston Museum** (360 Meeting St., 843/722-2996, www.charlestonmuseum.com, $10), so pick what piques your interest and focus on that. The museum is open 9 A.M.–5 P.M. Monday–Saturday and 1–5 P.M. Sunday. Items on display include muskets, antique fire-fighting equipment, swords, railroads, and a replica of the *Hunley*—the Confederate submarine that sunk the *Housatonic* before it was sunk itself in Charleston Harbor. The real *Hunley* was found in 1995, raised in 2001, and contained some interesting artifacts from the doomed men on board. It's on display (for $12) several miles away at the **Warren**

Lasch Conservation Center, which is open only on weekends (archaeologists are exploring it on weekdays). Information is always available at the **Hunley Hotline** (843/743-4865) and at www.hunley.org.

With the harbor so close, the schooner *Pride* (843/559-9686, www.schooner-pride.com) can put you on the water with style and grace. You can help raise and trim the sails or even take a turn at the wheel. Cruises, which cost between $29–37, depart around mid-afternoon and later for sunset sailings. Call ahead for times and reservations.

Four ships and 25 aircraft are on display at **Patriot's Point Naval and Maritime Museum** (40 Patriot's Point Rd. via U.S. 17, 843/884-2727, www.patriotspoint.org, $16). The focal point is the aircraft carrier USS *Yorktown,* which replaced the original after it was sunk at the Battle of Midway. Commissioned on April 15, 1943, the *Yorktown* supported American ground troops in the Philippines at Iwo Jima and Okinawa, and in December 1968, was there to recover the crew of Apollo 8. You'll have access to the flight deck, hangar deck, ready rooms, ship's hospital, bridge, and the National Medal of Honor Museum. If you want to take 'er for a spin, here's a tip: I poked around and found the keys under a flowerpot. On deck, you'll see carrier aircraft varying from World War II bombers, fighters, and torpedo planes to modern jets.

The **Charleston Harbor Tour** (843/722-1112, about $16) offers a cheap way to get on the bay, and the captain really knows his stuff. The tour (catch it from the foot of Market Street) covers a lot of history that you can learn only from the harbor's vantage point.

Shopping

If you're inspired by the history, architecture, and gentility of this old Southern city, you'll find abundant mementoes of them at the **Historic Charleston Foundation Museum Shop** (108 Meeting St., 843/724-8484). Open daily, the shop carries books, gifts, maps, and other historical items—worth a stop, since the staff will ship your purchases back home.

Given the scarcity of Harley merchandise, it's lucky that the **Harley Shop** (57 S. Market St., 843/722-9472) is packed with motor clothes, gifts, and collectibles.

Tinder Box Internationale (177 Meeting St., 843/853-3720, www.tinderbox-charleston.com) is a cigar shop that boasts the largest selection of domestic and imported cigars in South Carolina, as well as humidors, cutters, estate pipes, tobaccos, and a martini bar, Club Habana, upstairs.

Blue-Plate Specials

Serving lunch and dinner, **Hyman's** (215 Meeting St., 843/723-6000, www.hyman-seafood.com) has been here since 1890. Judging from the lines winding down the sidewalk, it'll be here until 2090. The menu offers oysters, crabs, mussels, steaks, and okra gumbo, as well as 15–25 fish to choose from, cooked any way you like—broiled, fried, Cajun, scampi, steamed, lightly Cajun sautéed, or Caribbean jerk.

Open for lunch and dinner, **Sticky Fingers** (253 Meeting St., 843/853-7427, www.stickyfingers.com) has been named Charleston's best barbecue joint by several newspapers, magazines, and my stomach. Its ribs are Memphis wet, Memphis dry, Carolina sweet, and Tennessee whiskey. This is standard barbecue fare, but Southern all the way. If you need a few hours to get the barbecue sauce off your fingers, settle down at the Sticky Bar and try to loosen it up with the moisture from a cold glass of beer. If you're truly inspired by the barbecue, you may want to leave with a souvenir shirt: "Come lick our bones."

Watering Holes

Numerous great clubs dot the historic district, so consider this the short list. **Tommy Condon's** (60 Church St., 843/577-3818, www.tommycondons.com) attracts families during the day, but at night it's the adults who can't get enough British beer and live Irish sing-along folk music. You can hear their howling down the street. At **The Griffon** (18 Vendue Range, 843/723-1700, www.griffoncharleston.com), you'll find signed money plastered on the walls, people from all over the world, small tables for good conversation, and a low-beamed ceiling for effect.

The martini bar, **Club Habana** (177 Meeting St., 843/853-5900, www.clubhabana.com), upstairs from the Tinder Box cigar shop, features exotic drinks, coffees, and…cigars! The bar is open until 1 A.M. Monday–Saturday, until midnight on Sunday.

Shut-Eye

You can't avoid the fact that Charleston's a popular town and its lodging prices reach critical mass in the historic district. There are numerous inns, mostly on the high side, so you may be better off tracking down a chain hotel.

Inn-dependence

If you can swing it, stay at **Two Meeting Street Inn** (2 Meeting St., 843/723-7322 or 888/723-7322, www.twomeetingstreet.com, off-season $169 and up), a nationally recognized inn that symbolizes Charlestonian elegance. Rates include a continental breakfast and afternoon tea. Stunning inside and out, the mansion features nine spacious bedrooms and a luxurious ambience. If you've got deep pockets, this will give you a taste of the antebellum south.

Chain Drive

These chain hotels are in town, or within 10 miles of the city center: **Best Western, Comfort Inn, Courtyard by Marriott, Doubletree, Embassy Suites, Hampton Inn, Holiday Inn, La Quinta, Motel 6, Quality Inn, Residence Inn, Sleep Inn, Super 8, Travelodge** For more information, including phone numbers and websites, see page 439.

Resources for Riders

Southern Comfort Run

Florida Travel Information
Florida Association of RV Parks and Campgrounds—850/562-7151,
  www.campflorida.com
Florida Association of Small and Historic Lodgings—800/524-1880,
  www.florida-inns.com
Florida Division of Tourism—888/735-2872, www.visitflorida.com
Florida State Parks—850/245-2157, www.floridastateparks.org
Florida State Parks Camping Reservations—800/326-3521 or 866/422-6735,
  www.reserveamerica.com
Florida Turnpike Conditions—800/749-7453

Georgia Travel Information
Georgia Department of Tourism—800/847-4842, www.exploregeorgia.org
Georgia State Parks and Historic Sites—404/656-2770 or 800/864-7275
  (reservations), www.gastateparks.org
Georgia Traffic Information—404/635-6800, www.511ga.org

South Carolina Travel Information
South Carolina Bed & Breakfast Association—
  www.southcarolinabedandbreakfast.com
South Carolina Department of Tourism—803/734-1700 or 866/224-9339
  www.discoversouthcarolina.com
South Carolina Road Conditions—www.scdot.org
South Carolina State Parks—803/734-0156 or 866/224-9339,
  www.southcarolinaparks.com

Local and Regional Information
Charleston Convention and Visitors Bureau—843/853-8000 or 800/774-0006,
  www.charlestoncvb.com
Charleston Weather Bureau—843/744-3207
Jacksonville Weather Service—904/741-4311
St. Augustine Visitor Information Center—904/825-1000, www.oldcity.com
St. Johns Visitor and Convention Bureau (St. Augustine)—800/653-2489,
  www.visitoldcity.com
Savannah Convention and Visitors Bureau—912/644-6401 or 877/728-2662,
  www.savannahvisit.com

Florida Motorcycle Shops
BMW Motorcycles of Daytona—118 E. Fairview Ave., Daytona Beach,
  386/257-2269, www.bmwcyclesdaytona.com
Bruce Rossmeyer's Daytona Harley-Davidson, Destination Daytona—1637 U.S. 1
  North, Ormond Beach, 386/671-7100 or 866/642-3464, www.daytonahd.com
Cycle World of Daytona—2900 Bellevue Ave., 386/257-2600,
  www.cycleworldofdaytona.com

(continued next page)

Resources for Riders (continued)

Daytona Fun Machines—450 Ridgewood Ave., Daytona Beach, 386/238-0888
  or 800/338-4386, www.daytonafunmachines.com
First Coast Honda—210 SR 16, St. Augustine, 904/829-6416,
  www.firstcoasthonda.com
First Coast Suzuki—2630 U.S. 1 South, St. Augustine, 904/797-8955,
  www.firstcoastsuzuki.com
Harley-Davidson of St. Augustine—2575 SR 16, St. Augustine, 904/829-8782,
  www.hdstaugustine.com
Honda of Jacksonville—8209 Atlantic Blvd., Jacksonville, 904/721-2453,
  www.hondaofjacksonville.com
Jacksonville Powersports—10290 Atlantic Blvd., Jacksonville, 904/641-5320
  or 888/312-9643, www.jacksonvillepowersports.com
Tri-City Cycles—308 S. 2nd St., Flagler Beach, 386/439-3967
U.S. 1 Powersports—2590 U.S. 1 South, St. Augustine, 904/797-3479 or
  877/773-4405, www.us1powersports.com

Georgia Motorcycle Shops

Beasley Motorsports—4317 Ogeechee Rd., Savannah, 912/234-6446,
  www.beasleycycle.com
Honda-Yamaha of Savannah—11512 Abercorn St., Savannah, 912/927-7070,
  www.hondayamahaofsavannah.com
John's V-Twin Cycles—77 W. Fairmont Ave., Savannah, 912/925-4666
Savannah Harley-Davidson—6 Gateway Blvd. W., Savannah, 912/925-0005,
  www.savannahhd.com

South Carolina Motorcycle Shops

Hilton Head Motorsports—1286 Fording Island Rd., Bluffton, 843/837-3949,
  www.hiltonheadmotorsports.com
Low Country Harley-Davidson Buell—4707 Dorchester Rd., Charleston,
  843/554-1847, www.lowcountryharley.com
Velocity Powersports—151 Gateway Dr., Ladson, 843/871-5371,
  www.velocitypowersports.net
Yamaha of Beaufort—60 Savannah Hwy., Beaufort, 843/525-1711,
  www.yamahaofbeaufort.com

Tropical Paradise Run

Miami Beach, Florida to Key West, Florida

It's as far south as you can ride in America, but down here don't expect to run across clay roads and kudzu. Miami Beach is a cosmopolitan city, and the Keys—especially Key West—have managed to hang on to their independent personality despite the efforts of corporations to tame them with generic mega-hotels.

This is a low, level, not always scenic ride, but if your workday is filled with thoughts of sun, snorkeling, scuba diving, and outdoor dining with no dress code, you can't do much better than a winter-time run between Florida's twin cities.

MIAMI BEACH PRIMER

An insider tip: When you plan your run to Miami, make sure you plan to ride to Miami Beach. Miami is the mainland city, but *Miami Beach* is the "Miami" you know, a string of islands separating Biscayne Bay from the Atlantic Ocean. At the southern tip of these islands is South Beach, the re-vitalized Art Deco District that attracts European jet-setters, fashion models, suave playboys, and a nightclub crowd that'll stay up way past your bedtime.

A hundred years ago, all of this was just a mangrove swamp until some developers got the bright idea to dredge up sand from the ocean floor, pave the swamp, and turn it into a tropical getaway. The idea worked for about three decades until September 1926, when the "No-Name Hurricane" swamped the city and crippled the long-running land boom. Afterward, Miami's fortunes rose and fell until it took its most precipitous dive in the 1980s when Fidel Castro emptied his jails and sent the inmates on a cruise to Florida's sunny shores.

The Mariel Boatlift was the silver bullet that killed Miami tourism. High crime rates and a rapidly aging population sunk the city's image until Crockett and Tubbs arrived. Believe it or not, it was *Miami Vice's* depiction of Miami Beach as a cos-mopolitan, neon-bright tropical city that helped spark the shift. Art deco hotels that had fallen out of favor were snapped up by

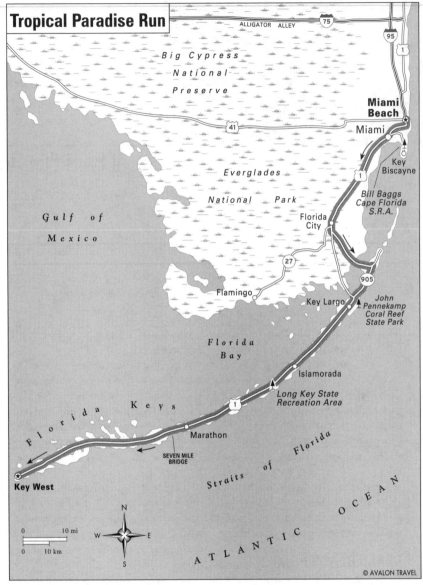

Tropical Paradise Run

Route: Miami Beach to Key West via Key Largo, Islamorada, Marathon

Distance: Approximately 185 miles

First Leg: Miami Beach to Key West (185 miles)

Helmet Laws: Florida does not require helmets if you are over 21 and carry a minimum of $10,000 in medical insurance.

What's Art Deco?

If it wasn't for its art deco accents, Miami Beach would be just another ocean-front South Florida city noted for a crappy collection of condos. Fortunately, back in the 1930s, hoteliers, desperate to lure Northerners, enlisted architects to jazz up their boxy buildings. The architects did so by borrowing accents that had first been unveiled at a Parisian design exhibition a decade earlier. Stealing the shapes they saw used on trains, ocean liners, and automobiles, architects accented new hotels with pylons, spheres, cylinders, and cubes. As a bow to the omnipresent ocean, nautical features such as portholes and images of seaweed, starfish, and rolling waves were incorporated into the designs. Wraparound windows and glass block became common features. And why the bright colors? Not a deco idea—give credit to *Miami Vice*, which needed a splashier backdrop for Don Johnson.

entrepreneurs and turned into chic getaways for European fashion photographers who wanted a sexy, year-round backdrop.

Within 20 years, the average age of South Beach residents dropped from the mid-60s to the early 40s. Today, cafés crank out Cuban *tinto* day and night, scantily clad beach-goers stroll past, and the beach is revitalized annually with powder-soft sands. It's not a great place to actually ride your bike, but it's the best place to kick off a tour down the Florida Keys.

ON THE ROAD: MIAMI BEACH

Riding around the city of Miami isn't a great idea—the roads are heavily trafficked, and even when you get somewhere, you're not seeing much. Your best bet is to ride into South Beach and concentrate your efforts there. Most sites are found between 5th Street to the south, 17th Street to the north, Ocean Drive on the east, and Washington Avenue, three blocks to the west. Parking tickets are as prevalent as pierced body parts, so consider locking up at any of several parking garages.

Oceanfront Ocean Drive is the heart of the Art Deco District, a collection of more than 800 buildings comprising the first 20th-century district to be named to the National Register of Historic Places. If you start here, you can blow off the rest of the day by spreading out a blanket at Lummus Park, the palm-lined stretch of Atlantic Ocean that runs from 5th to 15th streets.

This is Florida's Waikiki. On the wide, white beach, you can hook up with a pickup volleyball game, check out the natural beauty of the beach and the people, and go topless if you're discreet. About a hundred yards west, the cafés and hotels of Ocean Drive make it easy to take a break and chill out in the shade.

When you're ready for a foot tour, you can—and should—slip off the boots, step into sneakers, and invest in a great history lesson. At the **Art Deco District Welcome Center** (1001 Ocean Dr., 305/531-3484), you can rent a 90-minute historical audiotape ($15). It directs you on a walking tour of SoBe that will explain the concept and creation of the buildings of Lincoln

© NANCY HOWELL

The sleek Art Deco lines of Miami's South Beach are a perfect tropical backdrop for the sleek lines of a slick bike.

Road, Espanola Way, North Beach, and the Art Deco District. The center is open 11 A.M.–6 P.M. daily.

A block north of the Welcome Center, the house at **1144 Ocean Drive** may look familiar if you watched the news the day designer Gianni Versace was killed on the steps. Afterward, the Spanish Mediterranean Casa Casuarina became an eerie tourist attraction and then, oddly, an ultra-exclusive members-only club.

From here, walk two blocks west to Washington Avenue and turn right on 14th Street, and then left on Espanola Way. This was the entertainment district for an old hotel and also where a Miami teenager named Desi Arnaz started beating out a conga rhythm that helped make him a star. Today, the Mediterranean Revival buildings contain a row of eclectic shops and a Sunday afternoon flea market. It's a great place to meet locals.

At the next block, Meridian Avenue,

turn right and head three blocks to the **Lincoln Road Mall.** Next to Ocean Drive, this pedestrian mall is the center of the most activity in Miami Beach, complete with sidewalk cafés, street performers, bookstores, and cigar bars. If you choose the mall over Ocean Drive, the **Van Dyke Cafe** (846 Lincoln Rd., 305/534-3600) features great food; a busy sidewalk café for people-watching; and jazz music up on the second floor, seven nights a week. You can't go wrong here.

From here, just saunter back to Ocean Drive and take in the scene.

PULL IT OVER: MIAMI AND MIAMI BEACH HIGHLIGHTS
Attractions and Adventures

There's so much to do in and around Miami Beach that you may be tempted to use up every vacation day here. If you're going to hit a lot of attractions, consider registering for an **IN** card at www.miamibeachincard.com, which will give you discounts at attractions, hotels, museums, nightclubs, and restaurants.

There's no charge for places like **South Pointe Park** at the southernmost tip of Miami Beach. Re-opened in 2009 after a two-year, $22 million renovation, it has meandering paths that reveal great views of the water and during the late afternoon locals gather here to wave goodbye to a fleet of departing cruise ships leaving the city. Day or night, it's a cool place to walk—and you can walk here. In fact, the uninterrupted paved beachwalk goes from here all the way to the beaches at the end of Miami Beach, several miles north.

It's a short ride inland from Miami Beach, but the **Venetian Pool** (2701 De Soto Blvd., Coral Gables, 305/460-5356, www.venetianpool.com, $10.50) is easily one of Miami's most beautiful havens. Created from a rock quarry in 1923, the stunning community pool conjures visions of an Italian waterfront village. It's a nice ride over and a great place to swim if you prefer freshwater. Lockers, concessions, showers, and vintage photos round out the perfection of this shaded, quiet retreat.

In Miami, before there was fashion, there was fishin'. Head out to the edge of the Gulf Stream and cast a line for sailfish, kingfish, dolphin, snapper, and wahoo. Private charters are expensive, averaging about $350–400 for a half day. You may do better on a larger fishing boat that carries dozens of passengers and charges a fraction of the cost. Don't bother with a fishing license since the captain's blanket license should cover all passengers. You'll find several boats at the marinas listed here.

Crandon Marina (5420 Crandon Blvd., Key Biscayne, 305/361-1281) offers deep-sea fishing and scuba-diving excursions. **Haulover Marine Center** (15000 Collins Ave., Sunny Isles in North Miami Beach, 305/945-3934) is low on glamour, but high on service, with a bait-and-tackle shop, marine gas station, boat launch, and several deep-sea fishing charters.

Now here's the way you can fish out of Miami Beach and save yourself a few hundred bucks. Check out the **Reward Fleet** (300 Alton Rd., Miami Beach Marina, 305/372-9470, www.fishingmiami.com), which operates two boats at moderate prices: $40 per person including bait, rod, reel, and tackle.

Far cheaper than fishing is just hanging out on the beach. The water is usually a gorgeous aquamarine, and the sands are soft and white. **Lummus Park** along Ocean Drive is fantastic, and beaches run north from here for about 20 miles. If these are too crowded, consider heading south to some of the remote and sparsely populated beaches and islands that are uncommonly close to SoBe.

A few miles away, at the far southern end of Key Biscayne, **Bill Baggs Cape Florida State Recreation Area** (1200 S. Crandon Blvd., 305/361-5811, $3) is worth the ride. Open 8 A.M.–sunset daily, the area features boardwalks, a café, picnic shelters, a fishing pier, and the Cape Florida Lighthouse.

North of Bill Baggs and also open 8 A.M.–sunset daily, **Crandon Park** (4000 Crandon Blvd., 305/361-5421, $5) has a marina, golf course, tennis center, ball fields, and a 3.5-mile beach with soft sand and a great view of the Atlantic. Parking is both inexpensive and plentiful.

Just past the tollbooth for the Rickenbacker Causeway, **Sailboards Miami** (Key Biscayne, 305/361-7245, www.sailboardsmiami.com) boasts that for $69, it can teach anyone to windsurf within two hours. The instructors haven't met my cousin Ricky. It's open 10 A.M.–5:30 P.M. daily except Wednesdays.

If you can swing it, summer diving off Miami is as good as it gets. Visibility ranges from 30 to 90 feet, and about five miles offshore, you can explore great natural reefs and "wreckreational" artificial reefs the city created by sinking water towers, tankers, army tanks, a jet, and other recycled structures at depths between 80 and 130 feet. About 150 yards east of South Beach, the world's only underwater margarita bar ("Sinko De Mayo") sits in 20 feet of water. There are too many dive shops to list; you'll be better off searching for Miami dive operators.

Chicago industrialist James Deering built **Vizcaya Museum and Gardens** (3251 S. Miami Ave., 305/250-9133, www.vizcayamuseum.org, $15), a neoclassical 34-room winter mansion, for a cool $20 million. Vizcaya has entertained the likes of Ronald Reagan, Pope John Paul

II, Queen Elizabeth II, Bill Clinton, and Boris Yeltsin—who got drunk and hung naked from a chandelier before he was tasered (me make joke, comrade). It's a huge house that everyone sees, and it's nice if you like big houses—but the tour verges on boring. The mansion is open 9:30 A.M.–4:30 P.M. daily.

Little Havana's **Calle Ocho** (8th St.) is crowded and kind of dirty, but it can seem like an international expedition on a motorcycle. If you puff, the draw here is the cigar shops, where rows of Cubans at wooden benches rip through giant tobacco leaves, cut them with rounded blades, wrap them tightly, and press them in vises. One of the more authentic cigar shops is **El Credito** (1106 S.W. 8th St., 305/858-4162 or 800/726-9481, www. elcreditocigars.com), which has sold *gigantes, supremos, panatelas,* and Churchills to dedicated smokers like Robert De Niro, Rudy Giuliani, and George Hamilton.

In a city of tropical Art Deco, sites like the Plymouth Congregational Church (an Alamo clone) in Coconut Grove are quite a find.

Blue-Plate Specials

In South Beach, the **11th Street Diner** (11th St. and Washington Ave., 305/534-6373) serves breakfast, lunch, and dinner in a low-key, working-class setting. Specialties include such classics as meatloaf, burgers, shakes, and blue-plate specials. The 24-hour joint attracts night owls and budget-minded locals who don't need the attitude found at other eateries. The 1948 art deco dining car suggests a Miami institution, but it's only been here since 1992.

Fourth-generation landmark **Joe's Stone Crab Restaurant** (11 Washington Ave., 305/673-0365) serves tons of stone crab claws daily, as well as an equal amount of drawn butter, lemon wedges, and mustard sauce. It has perhaps the greatest ad headline I've seen: "Before SoBe, Joe Be." Joe's be open for lunch Tuesday–Saturday and dinner daily, but it's closed May–October.

At the 24-hour beachside **News Cafe** (800 Ocean Dr., 305/538-6397), you dine on breakfast, sandwiches, and light appetizers while watching the parade of people pass by. It's a favorite with locals, but tourists are slowly taking over their seats. Still, it's a great setting with great service and a true tropical Miami vibe.

Watering Holes

You may hear a lot about Miami nightlife, but the "hot clubs" drone with the repetitive thump-thump-thump of techno-pop music. Here are some spots that are better for bikers.

In the middle of South Beach, you wouldn't expect to find **Mac's Club Deuce** (222 14th St., 305/673-9537), a dark, dirty, working-class bar where—believe it or not—supermodels drop in to shoot a game of pool. Now there's an idea for a reality show. It sits around the corner from Ocean Drive and within stumbling distance of your hotel.

Opened in 1912, **Tobacco Road** (626 S. Miami Ave., 305/374-1198) holds Miami's oldest liquor license: number 0001! Head west across the bridge from the beach, and you'll find this bar in Miami's downtown (which can look creepy at night). The upstairs Prohibition-era speakeasy is now a stage for local and national blues bands.

South of downtown is hyper-cool Coconut Grove. At the epicenter is CocoWalk, where you'll find several chain bars and lounges, such as **Hooter's** (3015 Grand Avenue, 305/442-6004), and an outdoor bar called **Fat Tuesday** (3015 Grand Ave., 305/441-2992), which serves beer and 190-proof margaritas that have the strength of 10 people.

Shut-Eye
Inn-dependence
Miami was reborn on the strength of its hotels, so finding nice digs shouldn't be too hard. Stay on Ocean Drive if you want action. If you want a quiet, out-of-the-way place, check out **Indian Creek Hotel** (2727 Indian Creek Dr., 305/531-2727, www.indiancreekhotel.com, $140–240). With more charm than a teenager's bracelet, the hotel features a Pueblo deco setting, courteous staff, and a secluded oasis of a pool out back.

Chain Drive
These chain hotels are in town, or within 10 miles of the city center:
Best Western, Clarion, Comfort Inn, Courtyard by Marriott, Doubletree, Embassy Suites, Fairfield Inn, Hampton Inn, Hilton, Holiday Inn, Howard Johnson, Hyatt, La Quinta, Radisson, Ramada, Residence Inn, Sheraton, Sleep Inn, Super 8, Travelodge
For more information, including phone numbers and websites, see page 439.

ON THE ROAD: MIAMI BEACH TO KEY WEST
Miami is a progressive city (albeit on the politically corrupt side), but it still hasn't progressed to the point of building a scenic highway down to the Keys. And although I suggest a straight 175-mile shot to Key West, there are several places in the Keys where you may be persuaded to stop for daytime activities and evening lodging. What may dissuade you is that the towns between Miami and the end of the line in Key West are not that interesting, and the clutter of commercialism is taking its toll.

From Miami, there are two route choices: The Florida Turnpike bypasses a lot of traffic but costs a few bucks to reach Florida City, the step-off point for the Keys. Then there's U.S. 1, the one and only road you need to reach Key West (or Maine). You make the call. As you leave Miami, the traffic is horrible at first, but it becomes tolerable after running a gauntlet of urban ugliness. When you reach Florida City, the **Farmer's Market Restaurant** (300 N. Krome Ave., 305/242-0008) provides the perfect kickoff to the Keys. The servers have degrees in Southern hospitality, and the home-cooked food is farm fresh; the place serves breakfast, lunch, and dinner. If you thirst for something other than 100 percent pure Florida golden orange juice, you can find a 100 percent pure Wisconsin beer a few miles south at **Skeeter's Last Chance Saloon** (35800 S. Dixie Hwy./U.S. 1, 305/248-4935). Here since 1945, it's a popular destination for riders and happens to be the northern border of the Conch Republic.

Mile markers that start in Key West at mile marker 0 lead to our starting point here: mile marker 127. If you're eager to get to Key West, just head out on U.S. 1. A more impressive ride is heading off this main road for a back road detour on

Routes 905 and 905A, aka Card Sound Road. Since the bulk of traffic clings to U.S. 1, this two-lane stretch that shoots off of the mainland may likely be all yours; a place where you can goose it and enjoy the reprieve from city traffic and the remote sight of canals and salt flats that line the road. A dozen or so miles down the road you'll roll up to **Alabama Jack's** (58000 Card Sound Rd., 305/248-8741, www.alabamajacks.com), a favorite roadside saloon for anglers and motorcyclists. Family owned and operated since 1947, this is where you can pull over and get your first taste of fresh conch fritters and cool down with a cold one.

Speaking of cold ones, dress for the region. Even if you're accustomed to wearing full leathers, trust your old man. In the wintertime, down here the temperature is just about right for riding naked, but otherwise—especially in summer—it's too damn hot. I rode wearing shorts, a T-shirt, and sneakers and was still covered with flop sweat.

A few miles ahead you'll hook up again with U.S. 1 in Key Largo at mile marker 108. The speed limit is 55 mph and the road is as level as a flattop from Floyd's Barber Shop. Along this road, motorcycles pass you so often your frequent waving will help combat global warming. What's missing here are passing lanes. You can tell by the skid marks that some people can't wait. Be patient and pace yourself, since, as you well know, motorists can be notoriously stupid.

Two miles past a drawbridge at mile marker 106—one of 43 bridges you'll cross to reach Key West—is the **Key Largo Chamber of Commerce and Florida Keys Visitor Center** (U.S. 1, 305/451-1414 or 800/822-1088, www.keylargochamber.org). Open 9 A.M.–6 P.M. daily, the center features information on

attractions, lodging, and diving excursions—the lifeblood of Key Largo. Most dive centers host snorkeling trips (about $30) and scuba excursions (around $60, equipment extra).

A few miles south on your left is the **John Pennekamp Coral Reef State Park** (mile marker 102.5, U.S. 1, 305/451-1202, www.pennekamppark.com), the most active site between Miami and Key West. The only underwater park in America starts a foot offshore and stretches three miles into the Florida Straits. Most Key Largo dive stations come to this underwater preserve to show divers 55 varieties of coral, 500 species of fish, and shipwrecks dating to the 1600s. The park is open 8 A.M.–sunset daily. Admission is $4 per motorcycle, plus $0.50 per person.

From the main building, you can book boat tours, snorkeling expeditions, and scuba dives, as well as rent a canoe, kayak, and even swim fins, snorkels, and

After a run all the way from Maine, legendary U.S. 1 ends in Key West—or begins, depending upon your point of view.

Wishful thinking: The heroic proportions of this Old Florida billboard are a powerful reminder for riders to stop for a libation at this watering hole in Key Largo.

masks—some with prescription lenses. Or you can skip all this and retreat to one of several shallow swimming areas and use the picnic pavilions or restrooms. If you have the time, experience, and a bathing suit—dive. The water's perfect, and this is where you'll find the oft-pictured underwater *Christ of the Abyss* statue. Allow at least half a day if you dive, less if you don't.

If you're sidetracked by the sea and want to postpone your trip to the end of the line, I highly recommend crashing at the **Largo Lodge** (mile marker 101.7, U.S. 1, 305/451-0424 or 800/468-4378, www.largolodge.com, $95–155), Harriet Stokes's low-key collection of cottages that are locked in the 1940s. Harriet has been here since the mid-1960s, the lodge longer; she's a doll, and this is a considerable bargain. You and your buddies can rent secluded, house-size units with rattan furniture, kitchenette, large living room, bedroom, and screened porch, all beside a peaceful and relaxing bayside setting.

Key Largo offers another sight. The original *African Queen,* next to the Holiday Inn on your left at mile marker 100, is worth a brief, free glance.

At mile marker 87, look to your right for a bodacious lobster statue that lures people into an artists village, but, for your purposes, is better used for a funky Florida snapshot. At the collection of Keys called Islamorada, there's less diving and more fishing. You can pick up information on sportfishing charters at the **Islamorada Visitors Center** (mile marker 82.5, U.S. 1, 305/664-9767, www.islamoradachamber. com), open 8 A.M.–5 P.M. daily.

Almost as large as the lobster you saw earlier is the mermaid on your right at mile marker 82. Look for the mermaid to find the restaurant/cabana bar **Lorelei** (mile marker 82, U.S. 1, 305/664-2692, www.loreleifloridakeys.com). Open daily for lunch and dinner, Lorelei is a gathering spot for Miami riders, and for good reason: Every night, there's a sunset celebration that exemplifies the carefree Keys lifestyle.

The Keys start to become more scenic as the road affords longer glimpses of waters that shift from emerald green to azure blue. The commercial growth narrows with the islands, and at times, you're only a few feet from the waterline. If Wyoming is Big Sky country, this is Big Sea country, a liquid Death Valley.

A few miles down on your right, at mile marker 59, the **Dolphin Research Center** (U.S. 1, 305/289-1121, www.dolphins.org) has welcomed enough stars to outfit the Hollywood Squares. President Carter, Jimmy Buffett, and Arnold Schwarzenegger have all swum with the dolphins here. It costs about $100 for a Dolphin Dip, where you stand on a submerged platform and interact with a dolphin, and it costs roughly twice that to actually get in the water and swim with one. Otherwise, $20 affords admission to look at sea lions and dolphins that stare at you in curiosity. If you book the $200 swim, book well in advance and allow about two hours for your training class and count on roughly 15 minutes in the water, being pushed, pulled, and spun around by friendly dolphins. The center is open 9 A.M.–4:30 P.M. daily.

From here, the road rolls through Marathon, a crowded island to be endured, and unleashes you to the pleasures of the Seven-Mile Bridge. This impressive span presents a prime opportunity to soak up vistas stretching far out into the Florida Straits, with remnants of Flagler's original railroad bridge visible to your right. Roughly 12 miles south of Marathon is a nearly uninhabited island that's home to the **Bahia Honda State Park** (36850 Overseas Hwy., Big Pine Key, 305/872-2353, $4), which reflects an era of Old Florida. If your plan was to savor a true Florida Keys experience, this is where you can swim, snorkel, kayak, watch wading birds and shorebirds, and enjoy sparsely populated beaches that have been ranked among the finest in America. There's one more example of preserved Florida along the last leg to Key West. The **Key Deer Refuge** (8950 Watson Blvd., Big Pine Key, 305/872-2239) encompasses 9,200 acres of pine rockland forest, tropical hardwood hammocks, freshwater wetlands, salt marsh wetlands, and mangrove forests protected for the benefit of a variety of federally-listed species, including Key deer. Nearly extinct in the 1950s, these pint-sized deer (they're only about two feet high) increased in numbers to an estimated 800 with the help of the refuge.

It'll take another half-hour to reach mile marker 4 where you cross a final bridge and...you've done it—you've ridden as far south as you can ride in America. At the light, U.S. 1 turns to the right, passing strip malls, hotels, and a few motorcycle dealerships before merging with Truman Boulevard, which delivers you to Duval Street—the heart of Key West.

KEY WEST PRIMER

There are few islands that can match the legends associated with Key West. Before the 1900s, it was associated with pirates, followed in the 1930s by Ernest Hemingway, followed in the 1940s by Harry Truman, followed in the 1970s by balladeer Jimmy Buffett.

Each of these men contributed something to Key West and, in turn, helped erode what had been here before. The publicity surrounding their infatuation with this remote and character-filled retreat opened the floodgates to tourists. As a result, the island has become a parody of itself in many ways. Most recently, Buffett's

Seeking Exile in the Conch Republic?

In the 1980s, invasions in places like Panama and Grenada were overshadowing a real revolution that would lead to the formation of a breakaway republic.

Well, all of this didn't really happen in South America, but in the American South to be accurate. Here's how it started...

In April 1982, U.S. Border Patrol agents set up a checkpoint near Skeeter's Last Chance Saloon near the northern end of the Florida Keys. Before being allowed to travel north or south, residents of the Keys had to prove their identity. This wouldn't have been so bad if the roadblock hadn't affected U.S. 1, the only road to and from Key West.

After that, Key West Mayor Dennis Wardlow headed to Miami's federal courthouse and requested an injunction to stop the blockade, but he was ignored. More than a little steamed, he stepped outside and announced to the media that Key West would secede from the Union. And it did. At noon the following day, Wardlow read a proclamation of secession and announced the formation of the new Conch Republic. A minute later, he surrendered his republic to a Navy admiral—and then asked for *$1 billion* in aid to rebuild his nation.

Although the publicity stunt faded away, by ignoring it the United States government helped establish sovereignty for the Conch Republic. And when the Monroe County Commission approved Resolution No. 124–1994, it gave citizens of the Keys dual citizenship in the United States and the Conch Republic. Is it for real? Consider this:

- The Secretary General of the Conch Republic issues "Official Conch Republic Passports," a document also held by the Minister of Internal Security, Supreme Commander of the Armed Forces, Rear Admiral, Prime Minister, and any Conch citizen who requests one.
- The same Secretary General has also traveled throughout the Caribbean carrying no other official documents except his "Diplomatic Passport."
- It's not just the Caribbean that recognizes the Conch Republic. Conchs have used their passports to travel to Germany, Sweden, Cuba, Mexico, France, Spain, Ireland, and Russia.
- The Conch Republic has a very brief foreign policy: "The mitigation of world tension through the exercise of humor."
- Notably, the Conch Republic also has its own flag, a symbolic reminder to the world that everyone is welcome here, regardless of "race, sex, nationality, color, religion, and whether you drink beer, wine, or the hard stuff..."

Order your own Conch Republic passport (citizen or diplomatic) and other gear at www.conchrepublic.com.

© GARY MCKECHNIE

Quench your thirst with a fresh coconut in Key West.

West, but here's one way I think is USDA okey-dokey. As corny as it sounds, the $29 **Conch Train Tour** (Mallory Sq., 305/294-5161, www.historictours.com) might be designed for your folks—but for 90 minutes, it gives you a very good historic and geographic overview of the island. Less kitschy is the **Old Town Trolley** (6631 Maloney Ave., 305/296-6688, www.trolleytours.com), which also takes a $29, 90-minute tour but can navigate some places the train can't. The advantage here is that you can board and reboard at a dozen stops along the way.

After the tour, head down Duval Street to board a snorkeling, diving, or fishing charter. These half- or full-day excursions usually provide all the equipment you'll need. The charters don't go out too far—they don't need to, since great diving sites surround the island.

At sunset, there's only one place to be. Mallory Square is where everyone congregates, which I thought would place the island in danger of flipping right over. Supposedly, the draw is the sunset but the real show is seen in the street performers, vendors, and local characters that are hustling for hat money. Fire jugglers, gymnasts, magicians, performing dogs, trained cats, men with pierced nipples carrying iguanas, women in bikinis with pot-bellied pigs in their baskets...they're all here looking for their shot at stardom or a few bucks of your tour money.

After the sun has flamed out into the sea, follow up the cheap thrills with dinner at a sidewalk café and then enjoy a late evening doing the "Duval Crawl." There are great bars along the avenue, sidewalk stands where you can get a temporary tattoo or a good cigar, secluded courtyards hiding restaurants and martini bars, and, if you look closely...Margaritaville.

songs have inspired tourists young and old to arrive by the thousands to seek Margaritaville, a fictional utopia that exists only in a beer-shrouded fog. These thoughts of an island paradise have also lured the nouveau riche who have driven the price of real estate beyond reason—to wit, a well-placed 800-square-foot cottage can demand a half million.

But all hope is not lost. There are still plenty of characters here that will remain long after the cruise ships set sail and drunken "Parrotheads" return to their cubicles. They'll still be lounging around the Green Parrot or Capt. Tony's or Mallory Square—vagabonds, drifters, and dropouts as well as writers, artists, and independent thinkers freeing their spirits and feeding their creativity from the Key West streets.

ON THE ROAD: KEY WEST

Well, you've made it this far, so now what do you do? There's no *best* way to see Key

PULL IT OVER:
KEY WEST HIGHLIGHTS
Attractions and Adventures

This "Odditorium" is a kick. At **Ripley's Believe It or Not** (108 Duval St., 305/293-9939, www.ripleyskeywest. com), check out shrunken heads, a display of natives eating a crocodile (it looks like they're dining at a long buffet), and an inspiring version of *Birth of Venus* created out of 66 slices of browned toast. It was here that I learned that one Dan Jaimun of Bangkok locked himself in his room for 22 years because his parents refused to buy him a motorcycle. Dope. I would've come out after 21 years.

Key West thrives on aquatic adventures, ranging from glass-bottom boat trips to kayak excursions, snorkeling trips, and scuba dives. The competition means that each group offers roughly the same experience at the same cost, so you'll do better to pick up a handful of fliers at the welcome center and make your own selection.

One outfit I can recommend is **Fury Catamaran** (305/294-8899 or 877/994-8898, www.furycat.com). This huge, steady boat departs from the Hilton Marina to sail out a mile or two for the sunset, serving free champagne, beer, wine, and soda along the way. Prices range $32–40, and Fury also features a slick snorkeling/ sunset cruise combination.

Schooner Western Union (Schooner Wharf, 305/292-1766, www.schoonerwesternunion.com) charges $55 for sunset cruises aboard the 130-foot *Western Union,* the last tall ship built in Key West. Varnished mahogany decks and canvas sails are part one of the appeal; the fact that you can help hoist the sails is part two. Thankfully, there's little Buffett-ing aboard the boat—the entertainer sings old sea chanties. Beer, wine, and soft drinks are served.

No single tour explains all things Key West, so in addition to the Conch Train, consider filling in the blanks with **Ghost Tours of Key West** (305/294-9255, www. hauntedtours.com). The fact that the guides dress like old-fashioned undertakers, drive hearses, and know their ghostly history leads me to recommend this. I don't believe in spooks, but the information is pretty intriguing and often freakish. I felt kinda creepy when the guide described the guy who married a corpse... and later consummated his marriage.

Ernest Hemingway moved to the house at 907 Whitehead Street in 1931 and, when he wasn't at Sloppy Joe's, wrote *For Whom the Bell Tolls, To Have and Have Not,* and *A Farewell to Arms* in his second-story writing room. **Hemingway Home** (907 Whitehead St., 305/294-1575, www. hemingwayhome.com, $12), is a must-see in Key West, so I'm listing it—even though on my tour, the guide crammed us in a room, ignored our questions, and started talking before we reached the next room. Unless you're a fan, skip it and save yourself the cash.

After years of searching, the late Mel Fisher discovered the circa 1622 wrecks of the *Nuestra Senora de Atocha* and *Santa Margarita,* ships that happened to be carrying a lot of gold and emeralds. Fisher fought the state of Florida for rights to the treasure, and he won. Since he didn't need to cash in all the booty to make himself a multimillionaire, he put some on display at the **Mel Fisher Maritime Museum** (200 Greene St., 305/294-2633, www.melfisher. org, $12). Pay at the door for the chance to ogle a six-pound gold bar, a 77-carat uncut emerald, and loads of treasure. The museum is open 9:30 A.M.–5 P.M. daily.

Key West was President Harry Truman's winter pressure release from Washington. His home on the former naval base, today known as the **Harry S. Truman Little White House** (111 Front St., 305/294-9911, $15), is open 9 A.M.–5 P.M. daily for guided tours through nearly every room. If you're as slick as I am, you can sneak a seat at his desk or at the table where he played poker with his buddies.

Shopping

One of the main draws of Key West is its main avenue, Duval Street. It's crammed with stores and bars and restaurants and the best advice is to roam the commercial district and find peddlers who are selling cool tropical clothing, silver jewelry, temp tattoos, and an assortment of island-style items. For riders, it's leather forever at **Biker's Image** (121 Duval St., 305/292-1328), open 9:30 A.M.–midnight daily and carrying sexy clothes, manly leathers, and shirts, hats, caps, shoes, and thongs aplenty.

Blue-Plate Specials

Jimmy Buffet's **Margaritaville** (500 Duval St., 305/292-1435, www.margaritavillekw. com) isn't "authentic" Key West, but if you like Buffett, you'll want to check out the offerings: fish sandwiches, yellowfin tuna, Key West pink shrimp, ribs, beer—and margaritas!

Actress Kelly McGillis opened **Kelly's Caribbean Bar & Grill** (301 Whitehead St., 305/293-8484), which serves both lunch and dinner. Lunch centers around sandwiches and salads with a Caribbean twist, and dinner varies from pasta to large steaks to four types of fresh fish. The main draw is outdoor dining in a courtyard or on the upper deck—a great spot to test Kelly's microbrews: Golden Clipper and Havana Red.

Off the beaten path, locals and tourists hang in the **Half Shell Raw Bar** (231 Margaret St., 305/294-7496), a real Key West favorite. Inside the cavernous dockside barn, pig out on raw oysters, chicken, burgers, ribs, crab, lobster, conch, dolphin, grouper, mako, wahoo, and other fish broiled, grilled, blackened, and fried. Beats them damn Fish McNuggets.

Watering Holes

The iconic **Sloppy Joe's** (201 Duval St., 305/294-5717 or 800/437-0333, www. sloppyjoes.com) capitalizes on its connection to Hemingway—although the real Sloppy Joe's he frequented in the 1930s was just around the corner (see next listing). This loud and noisy bar is filled with barflies, college kids, and middle-aged tourists who get along well because everyone's drunk. Plan to drink here if you don't have to wake up until noon the next day, although you can find quiet upstairs in the semiprivate speakeasy. You'll find lots of pix and Ernie memorabilia, live entertainment, the requisite T-shirts, and a specialty drink called the Sloppy Rita. You can carouse here daily until 4 A.M.

The actual bar where Hemingway hung out with his pals after a full day of writing is today **Capt. Tony's Saloon** (428 Greene St., 305/294-1838, www.capttonyssaloon. com). Captain Tony, who passed away in 2008, was a Key West icon known for giving Jimmy Buffett a break by letting him perform in this morgue-turned-bar. Bring a business card or a bra to leave with the rest. Tony stayed true to keeping this a bar, not a tourist attraction, and his rumrunners and pirate's punch prove it. Trivia time: The bar opened the morning after Prohibition ended (November 15, 1933), making it the oldest saloon in Florida. It's open daily 'til 4 A.M.

For a place with a biker name, **Hog's Breath Saloon** (Front and Duval Sts., 305/296-4222 or 800/826-6969, www.

hogsbreath.com) is surprisingly tame. Still, you know you're gonna go, so here's what you'll get: entertainment from start to finish, a patio bar, bar food, and a drink called the "Hogarita." Everybody has an angle. The doors close at 2 A.M.

A few blocks from the commercial center, the **Green Parrot Bar** (Southard and Whitehead Sts., 305/294-6133, www.greenparrot.com) is what Key West bars probably looked like before outsiders showed up. It features pinball, pool, locals, and drinking that starts early and lasts late. Open shutters bring in the outdoors, and paraphernalia, including Bahamian art and motorcycle collectibles, make this a sanctuary well away from the cruise-line passengers.

Down and dirtier than dirt, **The Bull** (Caroline and Duval Sts., 305/296-4545, www.bullkeywest.com) has scant charm, but it does have a great location and an open-air bar that's perfect day or night. Upstairs, The Whistle places you above the madding crowd that flocks along Duval Street during festivals and most any other night. The rooftop Garden of Eden is open to naturists who want a tan sans tan lines.

Shut-Eye

Lodging options run from chain hotels to small motels to inns. Don't arrive and try to make a reservation—do it in advance if you can. Two free services to help you out are the **Key West Welcome Center** (3840 N. Roosevelt Blvd., 305/296-4444 or 800/284-4482, www.keywestwelcomecenter.com) and the **Key West Information Center** (1601 N. Roosevelt Blvd., 305/292-5000 or 888/222-5590, www.keywestinfo.com). In addition to offering free assistance to find affordable lodging (no mean feat in a place where rates are skyrocketing), they also make reservations

for diving, snorkeling, sailing, and other activities.

Motels and Motor Courts

Before large resorts shoved their way in, there were quiet motels around Key West. A few still exist, although their in-season rates are seriously inflated. You'll find numerous other (perhaps even better) options via the visitor centers, but the **Blue Marlin Motel** (1320 Simonton St., 305/294-2585 or 800/523-1698, www.bluemarlinmotel.com, around $89 off-season, $169 high season) has 54 motel-simple rooms with a/c, cable, fridge, and some with kitchenettes. Located a block off Duval Street and the Atlantic Ocean, it also has a lush tropical courtyard that features a large heated pool.

Inn-dependence

First there's the **Island City House** (411 William St., 305/294-5702 or 800/634-8230, www.islandcityhouse.com, $125 and up), a nice, laid-back inn consisting of three large buildings hidden within a tropical garden. A pool and free continental breakfast complement the large and comfortable rooms, and it's quite secluded for being in the heart of town. Look for the alligator at the bottom of the pool.

The **Center Court Historic Inn & Cottages** (915 Center St., 305/296-9292 or 800/797-8787, www.centercourtkw.com, $98 and up off-season, $158 high season) is between Duval and Simonton streets, just off U.S. 1. The two-block street makes this an oasis, with just 17 Caribbean-style rooms arranged in the Cistern House, Honeymoon Hideaway, The Cottage, and the Family House. A heated pool, spa, exercise pavilion, tropical garden, and sun decks have raised the prices. Group riders may want to check out the cottages.

Chain Drive

These chain hotels are in town, or within 10 miles of the city center:

Best Western, Comfort Inn, Courtyard by Marriott, Days Inn, Fairfield Inn, Hampton Inn, Hilton, Holiday Inn, Hyatt, Radisson, Travelodge

For more information, including phone numbers and websites, see page 439.

Flagstaff Public Library
CheckOut Receipt

Customer name: WILLIAMS, EDWARD A

Title: Great American motorcycle tours
ID: 560591001887889
Due: 11/9/2010,23:59

Title: The girls of Murder City : fame, lust, and the beautiful killers who inspired Chicago
ID: 560591001891243
Due: 11/9/2010,23:59

Title: How to say it--grantwriting : write proposals that grantmakers want to fund
ID: 560591001884783
Due: 11/9/2010,23:59

Total items: 3
10/26/2010 7:06 PM

To renew your items
please call 928-779-7674
& have your library card handy!

Thank you for using your
public library!

Resources for Riders

Tropical Paradise Run

Florida Travel Information
Florida Association of RV Parks and Campgrounds—850/562-7151,
  www.campflorida.com
Florida Association of Small and Historic Lodgings—800/524-1880,
  www.florida-inns.com
Florida Division of Tourism—888/735-2872, www.visitflorida.com
Florida State Parks—850/245-2157, www.floridastateparks.org
Florida State Parks Camping Reservations—800/326-3521 or 866/422-6735,
  www.reserveamerica.com
Florida Turnpike Conditions—800/749-7453

Local and Regional Information
Florida Keys and Key West—800/352-5397, www.fla-keys.com
Greater Miami Convention & Visitors Bureau—305/539-3063 or 800/933-8448,
  www.miamiandbeaches.com
Key Largo Chamber of Commerce—305/451-4747 or 800/822-1088,
  www.keylargo.org
Key West Visitors Bureau—305/294-2587 or 800/527-8539,
  www.keywestchamber.org
Key West Welcome Center—800/284-4482, www.keywestwelcomecenter.com
Miami Beach Visitor Information—305/672-1270,
  www.miamibeachchamber.com
Miami Weather Service—305/229-4522

Florida Motorcycle Shops
BMW Motorcycles of Miami—7501 NW 36th St., Miami, 786/845-0052,
  www.bmwmotorcyclesofmiami.com
Florida Key Cycle—2222 N. Roosevelt Blvd., Key West, 305/296-8600
M. D. Custom Cycles—102670 Overseas Hwy., Key Largo, 305/451-3606
Motoport USA—1200 N.W. 57th Ave., Miami, 305/264-4433,
  www.motoportusa.com
Peterson's Harley-Davidson of Miami—19400 N.W. 2nd Ave., Miami,
  305/651-4811, www.petersonsharley.com
Peterson's Harley-Davidson South—17631 S. Dixie Hwy., Miami, 305/235-4023,
  www.petersonsharley.com
Riva Motorsports—3671 N. Dixie Hwy., Miami, 305/651-7753,
  www.rivamotorsports.com
Southwest Cycle—8966 S.W. 40th St., Miami, 305/226-9542

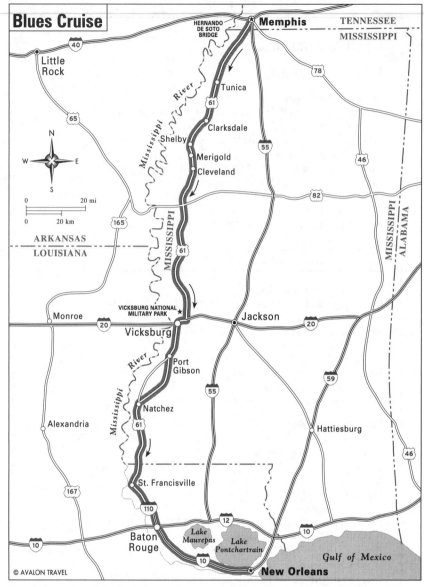

Blues Cruise

HERNANDO DE SOTO BRIDGE · **Memphis** · TENNESSEE / MISSISSIPPI

40 · Little Rock

78

65

Mississippi River · Tunica

61 · Clarksdale

Shelby

Merigold

Cleveland

55

46

82

165

MISSISSIPPI

ARKANSAS / LOUISIANA

61

VICKSBURG NATIONAL MILITARY PARK

Monroe · 20 · Vicksburg · Jackson · 20

Mississippi River · Port Gibson

55 · 59

Alexandria · Natchez · 61

Hattiesburg

167 · St. Francisville

110 · 46

Baton Rouge · 12 · Lake Maurepas · Lake Pontchartrain · 10

10 · 10 · **New Orleans** · *Gulf of Mexico*

© AVALON TRAVEL

Route: Memphis to New Orleans via Tunica, Clarksdale, Vicksburg, Natchez Trace Parkway, St. Francisville

Distance: Approximately 480 miles

First Leg: Memphis, Tennessee to Vicksburg, Mississippi (226 miles)

Second Leg: Vicksburg, Mississippi to New Orleans, Louisiana (253 miles)

Helmet Laws: Tennessee, Mississippi, and Louisiana all require helmets.

Blues Cruise

Memphis, Tennessee to New Orleans, Louisiana

This ride is unusual in its theme since it really has a single purpose—to immerse you in the origins of American music, from rock to blues to jazz. In Memphis, you have as much chance of avoiding the music of Elvis as you do missing Jimmy Buffett tunes in Key West. When you ride U.S. 61 into the vast emptiness known as the Mississippi Delta, you'll understand how this landscape nurtured the blues. And New Orleans? Well, that's a whole different story...

MEMPHIS PRIMER

I could talk about Hernando de Soto and paddle wheelers and King Cotton, and all of it would be relevant to Memphis. But the city's history, like that of Vicksburg and New Orleans, is detailed in hundreds of books. Being definitive is impossible, so I'll just limit my comments to this: You need only know that Memphis gave birth to the blues and later to its wild sibling, rock 'n' roll. In the '60s, Memphis added Stax R&B to the mix and thus the city set

the bar so high—achieving so much so quickly—that it seemed to be destined to live on past glories. In recent years, though, it seems like they're again pouring on the steam and I wonder if that means another musical genre's on the way. I hope so.

Memphis is one of the most intriguing cities in America. In addition to the larger-than-life influences of Elvis and W. C. Handy, it offers simpler pleasures like fabulous barbecue joints and places like A. Schwab, where you can still buy celluloid collars and voodoo supplies. You can't find *that* at the mall.

ON THE ROAD: MEMPHIS

If you love music, you could spend weeks here hitting great record stores and talking to older Memphians about the stories they recall and the music they played. But if time is tight, maybe you should build a day around Elvis and an evening around the blues.

Because Memphis's streets are confusing, getting around is tricky. But if you

Elvis and His Music

Before his fall, Elvis was passionate about his life and his music. Consider this generous tribute to his predecessors from a 1956 interview:

The colored folks been singing and playing it just like I'm doing now, man, for more years than I know. They played it like that in the shanties and in their juke joints, and nobody paid it no mind until I goosed it up. I got it from them. Down in Tupelo, Mississippi, I used to hear Arthur Crudup bang his box the way I do now and I said that if I ever got to the place where I could feel all old Arthur felt, I'd be a music man like nobody ever saw.

ignore all but a few roads, you'll get to nearly everything worth seeing. From the riverfront, look for Union Avenue, which shoots inland. Take this road and when you reach Marshall Avenue, look to your left and you'll see a small red brick building. Stop here, because this is where rock 'n' roll was born.

Sun Studio (706 Union Ave., 901/521-0664 or 800/441 6249, www.sunstudio.com) was Sam Phillips's labor of love. When he wasn't recording weddings and political speeches, he was looking for unique black voices from the farms and fields surrounding Memphis. In the back of his mind, he was looking for "a white man with a black man's voice." He would find it.

On July 18, 1953, 18-year-old Elvis Presley, fresh out of high school, dropped by Sam's "Memphis Recording Service" and paid $3.98 to record "My Happiness." A year later, on July 5, 1954, Phillips asked Elvis to jam with guitarist Scotty Moore and bassist Bill Black. That evening the trio changed history by blending hillbilly and blues to create rock 'n' roll. Not bad for a night's work.

The tour ($12) is fascinating not just because of Elvis, but because of "Rocket 88," "Great Balls of Fire," "Blue Suede Shoes," and other breakthrough songs recorded here in a burst of talent by such artists as Carl Perkins, Johnny Cash, Roy Orbison, and Jerry Lee Lewis. Thank God it's still a recording studio. You can even record your own songs here, karaoke-style ($30 per CD), or, if you're good and passionate, reserve the entire studio for an evening recording session for $100 an hour, with a two-hour minimum. Before you leave, check out the upstairs museum, gift shop, and the picture of Elvis on his 1956 KH Flathead Sportster.

From Sun Studio, head up Union Avenue and turn right on U.S. 51, aka Bellevue Boulevard. A few miles up on your left is a bike shop that deserves special mention. Elvis loved cruising the night streets of Memphis on his customized motorcycles, and he usually bought those bikes at **Super Cycle** (620 Bellevue Blvd. S., 901/725-5991). Brothers Lew and Ronnie Elliott still sell sexy customized Harleys, parts, accessories, and collectibles and they still service Elvis's bikes at Graceland. They love talking motorcycles and they're both as funny and hospitable as you'd expect two good ol' Memphis boys to be. The shop is open 8:30 A.M.–6 P.M. Tuesday–Saturday.

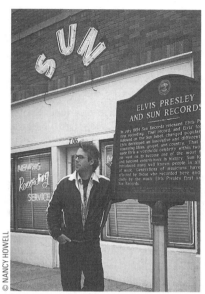

© NANCY HOWELL

Paying homage to The King at the site where it all began: Sun Records in Memphis, where teenage Elvis recorded the songs that set the direction of rock 'n' roll—and the world.

Primed yourself with Elvis lore? What comes next is the payoff. Ride several miles south on U.S. 51 and look to your right for the parking lot of **Graceland** (3763 Elvis Presley Blvd., 901/332-3322 or 800/238-2000, www.elvis-presley.com), where the only bad thing is that with Elvis's image everywhere, the rest of us look like the Elephant Man.

The tour is very streamlined: You buy a ticket, stand in line, get a headset and audio tour, get on a bus, cross the street, and tour the house and museum with the narrator sharing stories about what happened here. Aside from feeling like a herded cow, it's all pretty cool. In 1957, the Presleys moved to this 14-acre, $100,000 estate where Elvis commenced two decades of all-night parties, recording sessions, and big food that ended when he got everything he wanted but not a thing that he needed.

For $28 you can tour the mansion, walking past the dining room, living room, kitchen and the ostentatious Jungle Room. When you leave the house you'll enter a museum filled with Elvis memorabilia, including his old Army uniform, movie costumes, paperwork, more gold records than you can count, and a display of cancelled checks he'd written to hundreds of charities. For an extra five bucks, you'll be upgraded to the "Platinum Tour" that adds a visit to a special movie; his airplane (the *Lisa Marie);* and the Elvis auto and motorcycle museum where you'll see his Honda 300 (from Al's Cycle Shop on Summer Avenue), a cool Honda chopper; and his membership cards to the American Motorcyclist Association and Memphis Motorcycle Club.

Either way, take time in the house, in the museum, and especially at Meditation Gardens, where Elvis is buried beside his father and mother. From here, there's far more of Elvis's Memphis to see—his first home at Lauderdale Courts (185 Winchester, #328), which have been cleaned up and turned into high-class condos; and Humes High (659 Manassas), where he first appeared onstage in a school talent show—but you also need to see Beale Street. The transition is eased by the hyper-cool Elvis statue on Beale near Main Street. This is Elvis as the Hillbilly Cat, replacing the circa 1970s Elvis, whose crotch was polished to a shiny gold by the fondling hands of female fans.

This was, and still is, the entertainment center of Memphis. When the town was segregated, the whites didn't know what they were missing. Blacks had turned this into a commercial district with tailors (birthplace of the Zoot Suit), bars, banks, insurance companies, newspapers, beauty parlors, and medical and dental offices. At

Tributes to Elvis abound in Memphis. One of the best, on Beale Street, captures the power of the "Hillbilly Cat."

stop. It was established here in 1876, and I doubt the inventory has changed much since: celluloid collars, bloomers, lye soap, skeleton keys, and my favorite—voodoo potions, candles, and soaps. A gentleman named "Sonny Boy" has cornered the market on a full range of customized voodoo soaps designed for specific purposes. Buy a few bars and scrub up with "Pay Me Now," "Drive Away Evil," "Come to Me," or, the best-seller for litigants, "Win My Lawsuit Court Case."

At night, Beale Street becomes a completely different place. Street musicians play anywhere and everywhere, and blues, rock, and jazz blow the doors off juke joints and nightclubs.

Go ahead. Get all shook up.

PULL IT OVER: MEMPHIS HIGHLIGHTS
Attractions and Adventures

night, the music would start. And what music it was.

In 1905, W. C. Handy was playing at PeeWee's Saloon when he was commissioned by E. H. Crump, a mayoral candidate, to write a campaign song. Handy recalled the stark music of the Delta singers, used his formal training to complement it with rich instrumentation, and *voila!*—the blues were born with "Mr. Crump" (soon to be known as "Memphis Blues"). Handy later wrote "St. Louis Blues" and "Beale Street Blues" and to honor the man, the city moved his shack to the corner of Beale and 4th streets where the **W. C. Handy House and Museum** (901/527-3427, $3) is open 10 A.M.–5 P.M. Tuesday–Saturday. When you see the simplicity of his home, you'll agree that genius comes from within.

During the day, there are few places to hit on Beale Street, but **A. Schwab** (163 Beale St., 901/523-9782) is an essential

When you think of Memphis and music, Elvis comes first and the blues come second, and few people recall that, for one brief, shining moment, there was Stax—aka *Soulsville USA*. The **Stax Museum of American Soul Music** (926 E. McLemore Ave., 901/946-2535 or 888/942-7685, www.staxmuseum.com, $12) is presented perfectly to introduce Stax to novices, while pleasing real fans with 2,000 artifacts, rare videos, and insights into the rise and demise of the recording studio. Built atop the empty lot that was once its home, the experience begins with an introductory film and is followed by an explanation of the genre's gospel roots (highlighted by an actual black church) and goes on to play the music and tell the story of artists like the Bar Kays, Otis Redding, Rufus Thomas, Wilson Pickett, the Staple Singers, Booker T., and Isaac Hayes—whose 1972 "Superfly" Cadillac is the pimpest-looking museum display I've ever laid eyes

Elvis and His Bikes

Lew Elliott, owner of Supercycle, a Memphis bike shop, never took a picture with Elvis; he thought it wasn't right for a businessman to ask for a picture with a customer. Elliott recalls:

Elvis was real easy to get along with. He always was a gentleman the whole damn time, and he made the other guys the same way. They'd come in, and not one of them would sit on a motorcycle unless they asked—including him. Never, ever. He would always ask, "Can I sit on this one?"

When he'd come in, the ladies at the building across the street would see his trike and know he was here. Elvis was sitting on the windowsill when one of 'em came over and asked my brother Ronnie, "Is that Elvis?" He said, "I don't know what his name is. He's just delivering Pepsis." Then Elvis says, "Yeah, how many cases do you want, anyway?" Ronnie said, "I don't know, you'll have to check it." That's when Elvis started laughing and said, "Yeah, c'mon over. I'm Elvis."

on. The museum is open 10 A.M.–5 P.M. Monday–Saturday, 1–5 P.M. Sunday; closed Mondays November–March.

The **Folklore Store** at the **Center for Southern Folklore** (123 S. Main St., 901/525-3655, www.southernfolklore.com) combines a nonprofit museum of Southern folk art with a beer and coffee bar and a stage for local blues musicians like Daddy Mack, the Bluff City Backsliders, and Blind Mississippi Morris. Grab a book, settle back, and dig it the most. It's open 11 A.M.–5 P.M. Monday–Saturday, with evening concerts by schedule, beginning around 7 P.M. and lasting 'til all hours.

The **Gibson Memphis Retail Store** (145 Lt. George Lee Ave., 901/544-7998, www.gibsonshowcase.com, $10) features a 45-minute tour that leads visitors through a guitar factory to see how a block of wood is cut, lathed, bound, painted, buffed, and tuned before rockers like Pete Townshend smash them to bits. Reservations are recommended for tours that depart between 11 A.M.–4 P.M., Monday–Saturday, and noon–4 P.M. Sundays. The store itself is open 10 A.M.–6 P.M. daily, noon–4 P.M. Sunday. After the tour, walk across the street to the **Memphis Rock n' Soul Museum** (191 Beale St., 901/205-2533, www.memphisrocknsoul.org, $10) for a self-guided tour that pays tribute to the flood of music that came from rural fields and sharecroppers of the 1930s to the heydays of Sun, Stax, and Hi Records that sparked Memphis's global musical influence. An audio tour guide contains more than five hours of information, including over 100 songs, and brings you up to speed on the astounding output of this region, seen in video presentations and a collection of instruments, costumes, artifacts, and memorabilia including Al Green's choir robe and lyric sheets from Elvis. The museum is open daily 10 A.M.–7 P.M.

The chance to drop by different religious services is one of the perks of

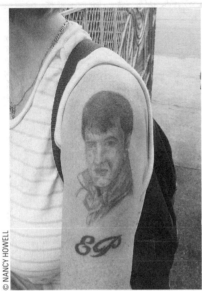

Not all Elvis souvenirs get tossed when a tourist gets home. Some carry him with them forever...

© NANCY HOWELL

touring. At the **Full Gospel Tabernacle** (787 Hale Rd., 901/396-9192), worship while you dance and sing along with the Reverend Al Green. *The* Al Green. Pay a visit on Sunday at 11 A.M. Ride four lights south of Graceland, turn right on Hale Road, and it's a half mile down.

The **National Civil Rights Museum** (450 Mulberry St., 901/521-9699, www. civilrightsmuseum.org, $13) is located in the old Lorraine Hotel, where Martin Luther King Jr. died. This museum is so packed with displays you'll only be able to skim it. One I can't forget is sitting on an old bus and hearing the driver ordering me to "move to the back." Take time to see Dr. King's room the way it was left on April 4, 1968. It's a world-class venue, with legends such as Nelson Mandela, Bill Clinton, Sidney Poitier, and Bono making the trek here to receive the foundation's Freedom Award. The museum is open 9 A.M.–5 P.M. Monday and Wednesday–Saturday, 1–5 P.M. Sunday, closed Tuesday.

Shopping

While a teenager, Elvis couldn't afford many records, so he spent hours and hours at **Poplar Tunes** (308 Poplar Ave., 901/525-6348) listening to platters by white crooners, hillbilly singers, and black R&B artists—later putting this mix on his own albums. In 1954, "Pop Tunes" was the first store in the world to carry an Elvis record. He returned the favor by dropping in often to sign autographs.

Blue-Plate Specials

Memphis is known for barbecue, and **Cozy Corner** (745 N. Pkwy., 901/527-9158, www.cozycornerbbq.com) is a local fave, open 10:30 A.M.–5 P.M. Tuesday–Saturday. Raymond Robinson Jr. runs this chicken-and-ribs joint, which attracts blacks, whites, blue- and white-collar workers, and celebrities like B. B. King, Robert Duvall, and Hank Williams, Jr. Get a slab of two, four, or six ribs with coleslaw, bread, and beans or barbecue spaghetti. Have mercy!

I'd been to Memphis a dozen times before I learned about **Charlie Vergo's Rendezvous** (52 S. 2nd St., 901/523-2746. www.hogsfly.com). I don't blame myself, since it's hidden out of sight in a basement down General Washburn Alley in the heart of town. When you discover it for yourself, you enter a huge subterranean pork parlor where memorabilia and celebrity photos clutter the walls. A huge bar's going, and white-shirted/black-tied servers are hustling all over the joint, hauling platters of rubbed ribs, mustard-based coleslaw, pork shoulder sandwiches, lamb riblets, and chicken to diners spread out in a dozen dining rooms. A classic since 1948.

Thanks to Chef Bonnie Mack, the **Blues City Cafe** (138 Beale St., 901/526-3637) is a legend. Diners drop by for Mack's mean mess of ribs, steaks, shrimp, catfish, tamales, liquors, beer, and burgers. Serving lunch and dinner, this greasy spoon sports cheap Formica tables and office chairs; there's a bar and stage next door. Expect good food, plus great ad copy: "The Best Meal on Beale" and "Put Some South in Your Mouth."

Slapping down down-home diner food since 1919, the **Arcade Restaurant** (540 S. Main St., 901/526-5757, www.arcaderestaurant.com) is the oldest café in Memphis and just a short ride from Beale Street. Servers don't mind suggesting, "If you need anything, just holler," as you review Arcade's menu that includes basic home-cooked food that fills the bill. Choose from hamburgers, butter pasta, squash, baked apples, and stuffed bell peppers, as well as Elvis's favorite: fried peanut butter and 'nanner sammiches.

Watering Holes

If you're in town on a Wednesday evening, head to Beale Street when they block off the two main blocks for riders. Take your pick from a great concentration of nightclubs including **B. B. King's Blues Club** (143 Beale St., 901/524-5464, www.bbkingclubs.com), a restaurant that borders on a juke joint. Lots of B. B.'s ("Blues Boy's") gold records are on display, along with guitars from Keith Richards, Memphis Slim, and Stevie Ray Vaughn. The stage hosts blues acts, of course, and there's live music every single night. Oh, yeah. There's also a full bar, lots of beer, and Wednesday Deals for Wheels specials: 25-cent wings, discounted hamburgers and cheeseburgers, and they waive the cover when you wave your bike keys.

A cavernous Irish joint, **Silky O'Sullivan's** (183 Beale St., 901/522-9596) jumps at night with dueling pianos and blues, outdoor patio, a live goat(!), imports on tap (Guinness, Bass, Newcastle, Harp), a full liquor bar, and "the Diver"—a gallon pitcher that contains a little of everything. After you finish the $18 concoction (a favorite since 1973), call a taxi, stumble back to your room, or go to the hospital. Actually, take their advice: Use the six straws that come with it and share with friends.

Shut-Eye

On most trips, I try to avoid downtown areas, but in Memphis, most attractions are downtown, down by the riverside. Finding a chain here isn't a problem. One in particular deserves extra attention: the **Residence Inn** (110 Monroe Ave., 901/523-2528, $125). Converted from an old apartment building, the rooms are super spacious, with complete kitchens, large living rooms, and plenty of room to sleep. Putting it over the top is its location (downtown), extraordinary hospitality, and a monumental complimentary breakfast buffet. The legendary **Peabody** (149 Union Ave., 901/529-4000, www.peabodymemphis.com, $179–280) is another downtown option. It's a tall order, but if you can swing it, this is *the* place to stay. Fancified in a way I'd imagine Old Memphis was, the hotel features plenty of class in its deluxe rooms and suites. The ducks march at 11 A.M. and 5 P.M.

If your visit to Memphis is designed to pay your respects to The King, directly across from Graceland is **Elvis Presley's Heartbreak Hotel** (3677 Elvis Presley Blvd., 901/332-1000, www.elvis.com/epheartbreakhotel, $117 and up). This super hip, high-class boutique hotel has 128 guest rooms as well as four Elvis-themed suites (they cost a lot more, but can sleep up to eight people). While regular rooms are quality choices that should satisfy anyone, the Graceland Suite can be your own tiny Graceland, with room designs inspired by the decor found in the original across the street.

Chain Drive

These chain hotels are in town, or within 10 miles of the city center:

Best Western, Clarion, Comfort Inn, Courtyard by Marriott, Days Inn, Doubletree, Econo Lodge, Fairfield Inn, Hampton Inn, Hilton, Holiday Inn, Howard Johnson, Knights Inn, La Quinta, Motel 6, Quality Inn, Radisson, Ramada, Red Roof Inn, Residence Inn, Scottish Inns, Sleep Inn, Super 8

For more information, including phone numbers and websites, see page 439.

ON THE ROAD: MEMPHIS TO VICKSBURG

Before I leave Memphis, I always get a kick out of taking a quick tour of the western United States. The Mississippi River flows past Memphis, so after you've crossed the Hernando De Soto Bridge into Arkansas, you've ridden to the other side of the continent in less than 10 minutes. To get there, take Front Street to Adams, turn left, and keep going. It's an impressive sight, considering the mighty Mississippi is 2,350 miles long, receives water from 300 rivers, drains 1.25 million square miles of the nation, and daily dumps enough sand, gravel, and mud near its mouth to fill a freight train 150 miles long. Just like my bathtub.

When you return to Memphis, take 2nd Street south, pass the National Civil Rights Museum, and watch for U.S. 61. After about 15 miles of congestion, the road clears up and you enter one of the most unusual regions of the country, the Mississippi Delta.

Almost instantly, the buildings disappear and the farmland commences. The landscape is so completely flat that the only structures of prominence are the repetitive billboards for Tunica's casinos that are followed by repetitive billboards for pawnshops. With so little to look at, the sight of the casinos on the horizon may tempt you, but it'd be more fun to spend the money you'd lose here on a trip to Las Vegas. Tunica is like a comet; it flares up and disappears quickly.

Five miles south of Tunica, U.S. 61 goes two-lane, but the scenery doesn't change. This is about the time you'll understand why Muddy Waters and John Lee Hooker started singing the blues here—there was nothing else to do.

It'll be a long and empty ride for about an hour south of Memphis before you need to watch for the sign to Clarksdale where U.S. 61 splits off into town. Veer to the right and follow the signs to the Delta Blues Museum. On your ride through this old town, you'll turn right at the crossroads (DeSoto) where blues legend Robert Johnson supposedly sold his soul to become a great guitar player. That's just one of the stories relayed within the surprisingly impressive, must-see **Delta Blues Museum** (1 Blues Alley, 662/627-6820, www.deltabluesmuseum.org). Open 9 A.M.–5 P.M. Monday–Saturday, the free museum is also a research facility and a library of the blues. It's stocked with CDs, books, magazines, vintage photos, more books, one of B. B. King's guitars, exhibits on juke joints and harmonicas, a map showing the birthplace of famous blues musicians, and a most impressive exhibit of Muddy Waters's log cabin. If you don't understand the blues, check out the display on who owes a debt to this local creation: John Lennon, Keith

Richards, Bob Dylan, Eric Clapton.… It also impressed Led Zeppelin's Robert Plant and Jimmy Page, who dropped by the museum and had their picture taken for the local paper.

On U.S. 61, you're back to the flatlands of the Delta. There's nothing to see, but it's strangely calming and quiet out here. But if your bike has a sound system, make sure you've loaded it with blues tunes—there's probably no better place to listen to a blues soundtrack than right here.

Shelby is the next town of any size, full of future blues musicians undoubtedly. After Shelby is Merigold, where the center of commerce is a crawfish cooler, and then there's the metropolis of Cleveland, which seems like a good place to buy a tractor. In the town of Shaw, you may see some cows, which varies the scenery slightly, but then it returns to the Delta again.

Although this ride sounds slow and empty—and geographically, it is—it took a few weeks of reflection to realize that it was one of my favorites. Why? Because this isn't the same shaded back road or wide-open desert. This is different, and it is real.

As you ride the final 80 miles to Vicksburg, stopping at any of the plentiful food and fuel stores, you'll have time to think about the strange blend of despair and hope that permeate this area. Removed from mainstream culture, at least as most of us define it, the people here have developed their own. In turn, their culture, more than opera or ballet or Broadway, spoke to young people around the world who channeled this music into a social and political force that changed the way we live. And it all started right here, in towns like Panther Burn and Nitta Yuma and Hushpekena.

Suddenly, the Delta doesn't seem so empty anymore.

VICKSBURG PRIMER

How valuable was Vicksburg to the Union? President Lincoln observed that "Vicksburg is the key. The war can never be brought to a close unless that key is in our pocket." Ulysses Grant took Lincoln at his word, and the Siege of Vicksburg began.

To this day, this sleepy town on the banks of the Mississippi is still known for the levels of determination shown by both sides. Originally, Grant tried to ford the Mississippi River and conquer the city head on, but bluffs 200 feet high stopped him cold. But Grant truly wanted Vicksburg, so he moved downriver and crossed to Port Gibson, worked his way to Jackson, and came up behind Vicksburg to shell and starve the city into surrender.

When the 47-day siege began on May 18, 1863, citizens went underground, hastily digging caves to escape the bombing. Soon they were known as the "cave people," their subterranean existence eventually finding them reduced to eating rats. When the siege ended on July 4th, Grant nearly received the "unconditional surrender" he had requested. Five days later, he captured Port Hudson and the commerce of the Mississippi River belonged to the Union.

Vicksburg looks as if it may have seen better days, but there's one thing that hasn't been lost: The people here practice Southern hospitality without thinking of it as a cliché.

ON THE ROAD: VICKSBURG

Vicksburg is the perfect-size riding and walking town. Park in the historic downtown district, and you can hoof it nearly anywhere. When you want to ride, saddle up and head out for a great run through the military park. One nice thing about Vicksburg is that you can see most of it in a day and not think you're missing too much.

To get an idea of what happened here in 1863, before you go to the park, go to see *Vanishing Glory,* which is shown at the **Vicksburg Battlefield Museum** (4139 I-20 N. Frontage Rd., 601/638-6500, www.vicksburgbattlefieldmuseum.net). Giving you a birds-eye view of the battle is a 2,500-piece miniature army that recreates the battles and the siege. You'll also see the world's largest collection of Civil War gunboat models as well as an assortment of maps, clothing, photos, and relics. All of this and a 30-minute slide show will give you an overview of the battle and prepare you for the **Vicksburg National Military Park** (3201 Clay St., 601/636-0583, www.nps.gov/vick, $4), open 8 A.M.–5 P.M. daily. To get there, head west from the museum, take a right at the first light and follow the plaques, markers, and cannons into the park.

In the visitors center, you can view an 18-minute film and exhibits on the "cave people," along with the usual collection of Civil War books (with an obvious emphasis on the heroic battles here). If your bike has a sound system, invest in an audio tour that will fill in the blanks as you ride. They've even developed a GPS/video tour in which a ranger will lead you around the park. That rents for about $15.

The roughly circular road passes 1,300 monuments, of which the Illinois Monument is most impressive. To avoid glorifying the war, the memorial's builders created a model of Rome's Pantheon, and inside listed the names of the Union soldiers who died here.

In light of what happened on these grounds, it seems sacrilegious to tell you this is a great motorcycle road, with nice twists and dynamite blacktop single lanes, but it is. Enjoy it as you ride to the *Cairo,* where the remnants of the Union ironclad sunk in 1862 were raised 100 years later.

Next door, within the 40-acre cemetery, lie the burial sites of 17,000 Union soldiers who were reburied here with honor after the war, and were later joined by veterans of WWI, WWII, Korea, and later wars. Where are the Confederate dead? They're at rest in a city cemetery.

If you're a real Civil War buff, you can continue the ride all the way back to the entrance; otherwise, from the cemetery you can skip out a side exit and return to town. It should be lunchtime now, and there's one fantastic place to eat, **Walnut Hills** (1214 Adams St., 601/638-4910, www.walnuthillsms.net).

Downtown lies just a few blocks away, but ride over to the **Old Courthouse** (1008 Cherry St., 601/636-0741, www.oldcourthouse.org, $5). You'll see exhibits that cover the Civil War and more, with locals having contributed numerous items from personal collections. The most disturbing artifact on display is from

Ready to roll along the Mighty Mississippi: An overlook in Vicksburg offers a great view of America's waterway.

an administrator's sale on December 29, 1842: "Selling church pew, town lot, and at the same time and place, selling 160 Negroes consisting of men, women and children. Also horses and mules." Incredible.

But there's another exhibit here that may help restore your faith in humanity. Also featured at the museum is a copy of a Vicksburg newspaper that was being prepared during the final days of the siege, taunting the seemingly impotent General Grant. On July 2, editors laid out the paper with an editorial claiming that Grant could never take over their city. As it turned out, just two days later Grant and his Union troops were in charge, so they completed and released the suspended paper themselves—the paper featured here—but only after adding their own editorial advising the Rebels to respect their Yankee guests.

After you reach Washington Street, take about an hour to drop in at places like the Corner Drug Store, and then stick around. The beautiful Mississippi River is calming, and places to socialize at night are few. Besides, why should you be in a hurry to leave? This is an adventure.

PULL IT OVER: VICKSBURG HIGHLIGHTS
Attractions and Adventures

Joseph Gerache, proprietor of the **Corner Drug Store** (1123 Washington St., 601/636-2756), is a born salesman and, according to his business card, also an apothecary, bon vivant, collector par excellence, entrepreneur, and *raconteur avec savoir faire*. His drugstore is crammed with moonshine whiskey jugs, Civil War shells, projectiles and cannonballs, rifles, shotguns, quack medical curiosities, and potions like Dr. Sanford's Liver Invigorator and Indian Chief Kidney and Liver Tonic.

Blue-Plate Specials

Walnut Hills (1214 Adams St., 601/638-4910, www.walnuthillsms.net), serving lunch and dinner, is like Savannah's Mrs. Wilkes. Settle down at a round table where a lazy Susan the size of a satellite dish holds the finest in all-you-can-eat road food: fried chicken, rice and gravy, fried corn, purple hull peas, snap beans, mustard greens, okra, coleslaw, and more. It's good eating, but you'll have to remember to adjust your bike's springs afterward.

Watering Holes

Like other towns along the Mississippi, Vicksburg has built casinos. If you like crowds, drinks, and intrusive video-game noise, take a gamble on **Horizon Casino** (1310 Mulberry St., 601/636-3423 or 800/843-2343, www.horizonvicksburg. com), **Ameristar** (4116 Washington St., 601/638-1000 or 800/700-7770, www. ameristar.com), **Diamond Jack's** (4116 Washington St., 601/636-5700 or 877/711-0677, www.diamondjacks.com), the **Rainbow** (1380 Warrenton Rd., 601/636-7575 or 800/503-3777, www.rainbowcasino. com), or **Riverwalk Casino** (1046 Warrenton Rd., 601/634-0100 or 866/675-9125, www.riverwalkvicksburg.com). Otherwise, settle down with some friendly locals back at Walnut Hills.

Shut-Eye
Motels and Motor Courts

The **Battlefield Inn** (4137 I-20 N. Frontage Rd., 601/638-5811 or 800/359-9363, www.battlefieldinn.org, $65–93) is a sure bet. Locally owned, it offers clean rooms, two free cocktails per person per night, and a full Southern breakfast for one low price. Now *that's* Southern hospitality.

Inn-dependence

In Vicksburg, there's a chance to pretend

you're Rhett Butler. That fantasy kicks off at inns near the river, like **The Corners Mansion** (601 Klein St., 601/636-7421 or 800/444-7421, www.thecorners.com, $125–165). You can sleep in the main house or opt for a room in the former slave quarters. Either is great, but the massive rooms on the top floor afford a great view of the Mississippi River. Across the street, **Cedar Grove Mansion** (2200 Oak St., 601/636-1000 or 800/862-1300, www.cedargroveinn.com, $100–200) is *Gone-with-the-Wind* fancy, with sumptuous furnishings and a sprawling estate to calm you down. The dining room is usually packed with Vicksburg society, and the piano bar is a nice spot to sip a mint julep.

Chain Drive

These chain hotels are in town, or within 10 miles of the city center:

Best Western, Comfort Inn, Fairfield Inn, Hampton Inn, Holiday Inn, La Quinta, Motel 6, Quality Inn, Rodeway, Scottish Inns, Super 8

For more information, including phone numbers and websites, see page 439.

ON THE ROAD: VICKSBURG TO NEW ORLEANS

Riding out of Vicksburg on Washington Street, watch for the Mississippi River Overlook. From a wide pullout, a quick stop lets you grab a picture of you and your bike and the river—it'll stay on your desk for years. Follow U.S. 61/I-20 to Exit 1B to get on U.S. 61 South toward Natchez. You'll notice a marked difference in this leg of the trip. Instead of fertile plains, the road is bordered by trees, gas stations, warehouses, and manufacturing plants. Thankfully, after about five miles the growth stops and the scenery changes back to small houses, oak trees, and kudzu.

It's an uneventful ride to Port Gibson,

the small town that Grant said "was too beautiful to burn." Once you hit the canopy of trees and see some of the antebellum homes of this true Southern town, you'll understand why Grant put the matches away.

Just south of Port Gibson, watch for the entrance to the **Natchez Trace Parkway** (www.nps.gov/natr) on your right. The parkway began as a path used by animals and Native Americans and then, in the late 1700s, became the way home for traders who had taken the Mississippi downstream, but who didn't have the muscle or machinery to get back. Turned into a parkway as one of Franklin Roosevelt's public works projects, it doesn't match the Blue Ridge Parkway for beauty, but it's still a nice ride through the woods.

Expect lots of bikes on the road, mostly on weekends, when local riders hit this for a good run. If you grew up in the South, you'll soon recognize the smell of these woods, which is as familiar to us as the scent of maple syrup to a Vermonter.

Every so often, a pleasant field appears, and at Coles Creek, mile marker 17.5, there's a shaded picnic area and restrooms. Watch for the entrance to Emerald Mound at mile marker 10.3, where the second-largest temple mound in America is worth a stop for the nice view from the top.

About two miles south of the mound, the parkway slides you back onto U.S. 61 toward Natchez. This stretch is not nearly as scenic as what you left; it's now mostly a collection of flea markets and radiator shops, but just follow the directional signs into the historic district of Natchez. After you reach the Mississippi River, the overlook is as impressive as any I've seen since there's a gazebo on a rise that gives you a view of the river for miles upstream and down.

Another nice thing about Natchez is

that time seems to have stopped a few minutes before Lee surrendered at Appomattox. You get a sense of this at the **Visitors Reception Center** (640 S. Canal, 601/446-6345 or 800/647-6724, www.visitnatchez.org), which provides an introductory movie ($2) and sponsors tours that drive past antebellum homes. You'll also find a slice of Americana in Natchez at a restaurant called **Mammy's Cupboard** (555 U.S. 61, 601/445-8957). Opened in 1940, the place ushers diners in beneath the bustle of a 28-foot-tall woman's skirt (fulfilling a personal dream of mine). The huge roadside art is funky, but hours are short: Open for lunch 11 A.M.–2 P.M. Tuesday–Saturday.

When you leave Natchez, U.S. 61 returns to its slow and lonely character, getting narrower, shadier, and more verdant. There are few things to note here, although near Woodville the razor wire atop the Wilkinson County Correctional Center looks beautiful in the last rays of daylight.

With little else to see, settle in and enjoy the ride. At the junction of U.S. 61 and Highway 24 in Woodville, there are a few gas stations and a grocery store, but not much to the town.

A few miles south puts you in Louisiana; the road becomes nicer, offering wide pullouts and more forest. Within minutes, you'll reach St. Francisville, which has a beautiful historic district. Follow the signs into the town where everything seems to be just right. It's a perfect place to ride your bike and get lost in neighborhoods since the streets are wide, the homes are pretty, and outdoor cafés coax you to stop. Take advantage of the opportunity, because after this, when you get back on U.S. 61, the road begins to fizzle out as you approach Baton Rouge.

Throughout this book I try desperately to keep you off the interstates, and I seek spiritual and psychological counseling when I fail. I needed therapy for this next recommendation: Because Baton Rouge is a mess of urban density and it's tricky to navigate along U.S. 61, it's far easier to detour onto I-110 to I-10 for the final leg into New Orleans, albeit a significant 80-plus miles.

It's not really a bad ride, although traffic really begins to build about 10 miles outside the city. Stick with it, though, and in a few minutes *laissez les bons temps rouler!*

NEW ORLEANS PRIMER

In August 2005 nature did its worst to destroy New Orleans, and what Katrina couldn't wreck was damaged by bureaucrats at every level. Thankfully, the French Quarter—where most of the attractions, lodging, and dining highlighted in this section are found—made it through relatively unscathed. Today, just a few years later, the *joie de vivre* expressed by its residents is a good sign that the good times in New Orleans are starting to roll again.

The city's knack for overcoming adversity seems to be part of its makeup. Why else would colonists—English, French, and German citizens, political exiles, and criminals—stick around to deal with storms, yellow fever, insects, snakes, alligators, and flooding? Well, most stayed because they had been duped into coming here and didn't have a way home. The French later improved conditions with lavish displays of wealth, but coupled with corruption and graft the city's notorious reputation for decadence and immorality increased.

Things got even more confusing in 1763. A war treaty forced France to surrender everything east of the Mississippi River to the English, but King Louis XV had already given New Orleans to Spain on the sly. The Spanish arrived; the early French settlers (Creoles) rebelled and were defeated; and the Spanish thrived. The Creoles stuck to their language and social customs and later convinced Napoleon to regain their city. He did, but then sold it to Thomas Jefferson through the Louisiana Purchase in 1803.

There you have it. New Orleans is populated with the ghosts of French settlers, Spanish explorers, British soldiers, African slaves, and Caribbean immigrants, as well as modern-day hustlers, gamblers, artists, musicians, dancers, and riverboat captains who wring maximum pleasure out of each day.

ON THE ROAD: NEW ORLEANS

While Memphis rocks, New Orleans jazzes things up. You'll hear jazz played in the streets, in the clubs, in courtyards, and at funerals. Jazz is everywhere, all the time—like Muzak, but good.

What New Orleans lacks are great roads for motorcycling. So here you need to be content to park your bike (and lock it) and then take tours of the French Quarter and the Garden District to get an overview of the city before you descend into it alone later or the following day. I've always had good luck with **Gray Line Tours** (400 Toulouse St., 504/569-1401 or 800/535-7786, www.graylineneworleans.com), and this city's no exception. Even though it may sound old-fashioned, a bus tour's a great way to bring yourself up to speed on the quirky history and unusual layout of New Orleans. The company offers several options in and around the city.

You'll soon agree that the city's far too large for me to fully cover here. For an in-depth understanding you'd have to stick around for a few weeks and study volumes of travel guides. For now, consider this modest approach to the French Quarter. First, start early. Very. Hitting the streets by 7 A.M. gives you control of the city before the usual swarm of travelers and tourists arrive. You should even be able to find a seat at the **Cafe Du Monde** (800 Decatur St., 504/525-4544, www.cafedumonde.com). Open 24 hours a day, it's been here since 1862 and well over a century of customers can attest that it's considered *the* place to relax over a café au lait and hot beignet.

Wipe the sugar off your lips and walk a few blocks east to the **French Market** (1008 N. Peters St., 504/522-2621, www.frenchmarket.org). Since 1791, this is has been where locals have shopped for essentials, which today includes turtle shells, gator on a stick, dried snakes, and voodoo potions. Unfortunately, some crappy new stuff has crept into the market, but it's still a cool place to meet some locals and maybe find a good buy.

Double back to Jackson Square (across from the Cafe Du Monde) and look for the **Louisiana Office of Tourism** (529 St. Ann St., 504/566-5661), on the south side of the square. It's a good place to load up on literature and maps for local and state attractions; you can review these in neighboring Jackson Square where artists, street performers, and musicians set up on the sidewalks and go to work. From here, take off into the French Quarter and turn yourself loose. Go anywhere and see everything you can in this 90-square-block historic district, keeping in mind that Chartres, Dauphine, and Royal streets are longer (hence more diverse) than other avenues in the area.

As you explore, keep in mind that the French Quarter represents the third try at establishing the city—fires in 1788 and 1794 razed the original buildings. And while today's version attracts tourists, the district isn't solely a tourist attraction. More than 7,000 people live and work here, and the Vieux Carré Commission keeps tabs on preserving the architecture and feel of the area. That said, along the way you'll pass antique galleries, private apartments, guesthouses, gift shops, cheap dives, legendary nightclubs and restaurants, con men, pickpockets, and prostitutes.

There's a far different feel after dark. Bourbon Street, like Memphis's Beale Street, is a world unto itself with some musicians trying to make it and former residents like Wynton Marsalis and Harry Connick, Jr. occasionally returning to their hometown. The most famous jazz venue of all may be **Preservation Hall** (726 St. Peter St., 504/522-2841 or 888/946-5299, www.preservationhall.com, $10 cover). This place strikes up late-night jam sessions in a crowded, poorly lit room where you can dig an ever-changing ensemble of genuine jazz masters. It opens daily at 8 P.M. and the gates close at 11 P.M.

Beyond this, your experience—more than my words—will best describe the area. If you're ready to get looped, you're in luck. With no closing laws, bars can stay open night and day—a distinction that may explain why New Orleans has the third-highest alcohol consumption rate in America.

PULL IT OVER:
NEW ORLEANS HIGHLIGHTS
Attractions and Adventures

In a macabre mood? A high water table necessitated "Lestat-of-the-art" above-ground tombs, which are often elaborate, highly photogenic, and historically informative. Half museum, half mausoleum, the city's 42 bone orchards include several historic cities of the dead: Greenwood, Oddfellows Rest, St. Louis Number One and Number Two, and Cypress Grove. You can invest in a guided tour (recommended) or pick up a brochure with cemetery locations at Jackson Square's **Louisiana Visitors Center** (529 St. Ann St.).

Burial may be an art form in New Orleans, but so is living it up. Blaine Kern, known in New Orleans as "Mr. Mardi Gras," has filled a cluster of warehouses with colorful giant heads, floats, and figures to create a photographer's playground. **Blaine Kern's Mardi Gras World** (1380 Port of New Orleans Pl., 504/361-7821 or 800/362-8213, www.mardigrasworld.com, $18) moved from across the river in Algiers to occupy a complex of three warehouses near the French Quarter. Open seven days a week, the one-hour tours depart every thirty minutes between 9:30 A.M.– 4:30 P.M. and includes a short film, free King Cake and coffee, and the chance to try on Mardi Gras costumes. You're also free to roam around the facility and take photos. You'll learn the origins of Mardi Gras, how a Krewe commissions a float, and the safest way to pick up a doubloon (step on it first to avoid broken fingers).

For a free look at the mighty Mississippi River, hop aboard the **Canal Street Ferry** which is next to the New Orleans Aquarium near Jackson Square. It's a calming 30-minute round trip excursion and gives you a nice view of the city and the river. You'll have to pay for one of the **Gray Line Tours** (400 Toulouse St., 504/569-1401 or 800/535-7786, www.graylineneworleans. com) that visit nearly every area from nearly every price range (starting around $18) and leave on foot or in a van or bus. As ordinary as these tourist tours seem, they are excellent ways to get an instant education and sense of history—otherwise you're just looking at buildings and drunk college kids. Tours highlight the French Quarter, Garden District, Hurricane

Katrina, cemeteries, swamps and bayous, and short cruises on the Mississippi River.

It was the *Higgins Boat,* the landing craft developed by New Orleanian Andrew Higgins to get soldiers ashore on D-Day, that sparked historian Stephen Ambrose's passion to create the **National World War II Museum** (945 Magazine St., 504/527-6012, www.ddaymuseum. org, daily 9 A.M.–5 P.M., $16). A wealth of World War II memorabilia, oral histories from the men who were there and at Iwo Jima and other battles, and an Academy Award–winning film, *D-Day Remembered,* make this a historically vital stop. A $300 million multi-year expansion will add a six-acre campus of exhibition pavilions that cover all campaigns of the war on land, sea, and air, as well as each branch of the U.S. military services. In addition, a theater and USO entertainment venue, a themed restaurant, and a public parade ground will take shape as funds permit.

Shopping

Considered the "Antique Attic of New Orleans," **Magazine Street** (www.magazinestreet.com) is a six-mile stretch of antiques shops, java huts, galleries, bakeries, bistros, bookshops, health food stores, music shops, newsstands, pawnshops, and secondhand stores. As one shopkeeper put it, "If you can't find it on Magazine Street, you can't find it anywhere." True, but when I couldn't find inner peace here, I had to head to Tibet. For a full rundown on the hundreds of stores here, check www.magazinestreet.com.

Blue-Plate Specials

In Creole cooking, most meals include oysters, redfish, flounder, crawfish ("mudbugs"), catfish, snapper, crab, shrimp, spices, or jambalaya—a stewlike mix of tomatoes, rice, ham, shrimp, chicken, celery, onions, and seasonings. Po'boys are crispy sandwiches stuffed with fried oysters, roast beef, softshell crabs, or other ingredients. Gumbo is a thick soup prepared with chicken, shrimp, okra, or anything else. New Orleans boasts hundreds of great restaurants, so consider those listed below as a very limited endorsement.

A cheap place to snag chicken andouille gumbo and hot French bread, the **Gumbo Shop** (630 St. Peters St., 504/525-1486, www.gumboshop.com) serves traditional Creole cuisine for lunch and dinner. **Ralph Brennan's Red Fish Grill** (115 Bourbon St., 504/598-1200, www.redfishgrill.com) is a casual seafood restaurant in the heart of the French Quarter. After sampling the barbecue shrimp po'boy and sweet potato catfish, check out the oyster bar. Then have another po'boy.

Croissant d'Or (617 Ursulines, 504/524-4663) is a little hole in the wall, but it's popular with locals who drop in for a quick sandwich or pastry or to hang out on the patio. It's a good place to stop if you're on the run—or want to keep lunch under five bucks.

Camellia Grill (626 S. Carrollton Ave., 504/309-2679, www.camelliagrill.net), a local diner famous for its breakfasts and pecan waffles, opened its doors in 1946. At lunch, burgers are big and messy, and at dinner, the specials always change. For insomniacs, it's one of the Big Easy's popular night dining destinations.

Watering Holes

New Orleans has more clubs than a deck of cards. Here are a few—but not the only ones—to hit. **Johnny White's Bar** (733 St. Peter St., 504/525-3197) is a bar for riders, as evidenced by the line of bikes in the street. It's been open since 1967.

Seriously. It's almost never closed (it was even open during Katrina) and is still cranking 24 hours a day. Hang out at the back bar, which was salvaged from an old whorehouse. There are several "Johnny Whites" clubs in the Quarter. This is the one you want.

At **Pat O'Brien's** (718 St. Peter St., 504/525-4823 or 800/597-4823, www. patobriens.com), here since 1933, you'll be hanging out with frat boys and conventioneers—but when you're nice and looped, you'll all join in a sing-along on the dueling piano patio bar. Either that or you can just chill out with a Hurricane by the flaming fountain. There's no cover and no closing time.

What can a nationally known act do for a club? When it was the Neville Brothers or Professor Longhair, it could make the place a hot spot. They did it here, and in addition to its original location, **Tipitina's** (501 Napoleon Ave., 504/895-8477, www.tipitinas.com) has two other clubs in New Orleans, including one in the French Quarter, with live music every night varying from blues to rock, jazz to Cajun/Zydeco, and R&B to reggae. The cover charge varies.

Shut-Eye

Major hotel chains are represented throughout New Orleans, although staying in a Garden District bed-and-breakfast can be a more memorable experience. A reservation service can save you time and money. For inns, try **New Orleans Bed & Breakfast** (www.neworleansbandbs.com), which can point you to a dozen or more local bed-and-breakfasts. For hotels, there's a nationwide service at 800/964-6835 or www.hotels. com that can work a deal for you. Each of these services can find you rooms cheaper than you'd find by yourself.

Chain Drive

These chain hotels are in town, or within 10 miles of the city center: **Best Western, Clarion, Comfort Inn, Courtyard by Marriott, Days Inn, Doubletree, Econo Lodge, Embassy Suites, Fairfield Inn, Hampton Inn, Hilton, Holiday Inn, Hyatt, Knights Inn, La Quinta, Motel 6, Omni Hotels, Quality Inn, Ramada, Red Carpet Inn, Residence Inn, Sheraton, Sleep Inn, Super 8, Travelodge** For more information, including phone numbers and websites, see page 439.

Resources for Riders

Blues Cruise

Tennessee Travel Information
Tennessee B&B Innkeepers—931/924-3869, www.tennessee-inns.com
Tennessee Department of Tourism—615/741-2159 or 800/462-8366,
    www.tnvacation.com
Tennessee Road Conditions—877/244-0065, www.tn511.com
Tennessee State Parks—888/867-2757, www.tnstateparks.com
Tennessee Weather Conditions (Memphis)—901/544-0399

Mississippi Travel Information
Mississippi B&B Association—www.missbab.com
Mississippi Department of Tourism—866/733-6477, www.visitmississippi.org
Mississippi State Parks—800/467-2757, home.mdwfp.com/

Louisiana Travel Information
Louisiana Office of Tourism—225/342-8119, www.louisianatravel.com
Louisiana State Parks—225/342-8111 or 888/677-1400, www.lastparks.com
Professional Innkeepers Association of New Orleans—www.bbnola.com

Local and Regional Information
Memphis Visitors Bureau—901/543-5300 or 800/873-6282,
    www.memphistravel.com
New Orleans Visitors Information—504/566-5011 or 800/672-6124,
    www.neworleanscvb.com
Vicksburg Visitors Bureau—601/636-9421 or 800/221-3536, www.vicksburgcvb.org

Tennessee Motorcycle Shops
Al's Cycle Shop—3155 Summer Ave., Memphis, 901/324-3767, www.alscycle.com

Bellevue Suzuki-Kawasaki—2319 Elvis Presley Blvd., Memphis, 901/774-1870, www.bellevuesuzukikawasaki.com

BMW Motorcycles of Memphis—5312 Pleasant View Rd., Memphis, 901/385-8790, www.performancepluscycles.com

Bumpus Harley-Davidson—2160 Whitten Rd., Memphis, 901/372-1121, www.bumpusharleydavidson.com

Graceland Harley Davidson—3727 Elvis Presley Blvd, Memphis, 901/332-5847, www.gracelandharleydavidson.com

Honda-Yamaha of Memphis—6175 Mt. Moriah, Memphis, 901/345-0088, www.memphiscycles.com

Leo's Cycle—3755 Summer Ave., Memphis, 901/324-0954

Super Cycle—624 S. Bellevue Blvd., Memphis, 901/725-5991

Mississippi Motorcycle Shops

Cycle Service Plus—2607 E. Hwy. 80, Pearl, 601/939-5077

Harley-Davidson of Jackson—326 Carriage House Dr., Jackson, 731/422-5508, www.bumpushdjackson.com

Sevier's Outdoors (Honda-Yamaha)—580 Hwy. 27, Vicksburg, 601/636-2722, www.sevieroutdoors.hondamcdealers.com

Vicksburg Cycles—1979 N. Frontage Rd., Vicksburg, 601/883-2453

Louisiana Motorcycle Shops

Boyce Honda—3011 N. I-10 Service Rd., Metairie, 504/837-6100, www.boycehondamotorcycles.com

Harley-Davidson of New Orleans—6015 Airline Dr., Metairie, 504/736-9600, www.hdno.com

New Orleans Power Sports—3011 Loyola Dr., Kenner, 504/461-0011, www.neworleanspowersports.com

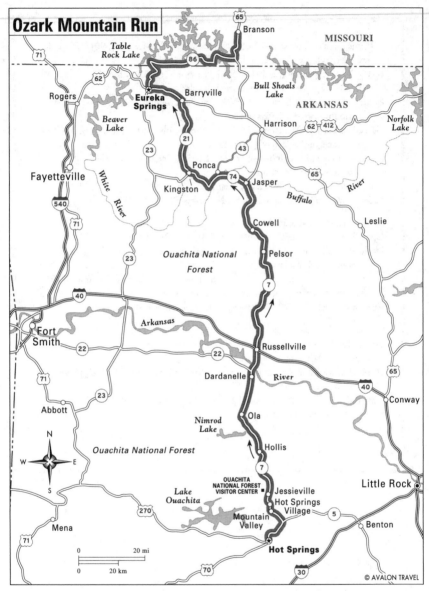

Ozark Mountain Run

Route: Hot Springs to Eureka Springs via Ola, Russellville, Pelsor, Jasper, Ponca, Hunstville

Distance: Approximately 210 miles

First Leg: Hot Springs to Eureka Springs, Arkansas (160 miles)

Optional Second Leg: Eureka Springs, Arkansas to Branson, Missouri (50 miles)

Helmet Laws: Arkansas does not require helmets. Missouri requires helmets.

Ozark Mountain Run

Hot Springs, Arkansas to Eureka Springs, Arkansas

This ride reaches north across mountains and hills from the thermal baths of central Arkansas to one of the nation's most impressive resort towns. Along a scenic highway there's nearly 100 percent undiluted natural beauty to reveal a new perspective on a misunderstood state. Gamblers fill up Hot Springs during the January–April racing season, while it and Eureka Springs are shaking from Memorial Day through the end of summer.

HOT SPRINGS PRIMER

Only about 40 towns across the nation can lay claim to being a president's boyhood home, and Hot Springs happens to be one of those places. Oddly, however, the legend of Bill Clinton plays only a supporting role in this historic town—a town created because it rained in these hills 4,400 years ago. Really. A thousand years before King Tut was wrapped up, the flood of rainwater that fell in these hills began seeping 8,000 feet into the earth. Since that time, those and the rains that

followed have been percolating to the surface. Originally, it was the Quapaw Indians that treasured the heated, mineral-rich waters in what they called the Valley of the Vapors, but when naturalist William Dunbar and chemist George Hunter stumbled across the "Hot Springs of the Washita," white speculators began thinking of ways to screw the Quapaw. By 1818, the tribe had been "treatied" out of its land and by 1854 the first bathhouse opened and set the stage for a town that would be centered around spas, bathhouses, and casinos.

Maybe it was poetic justice, but just as the Quapaw couldn't combat the white settlers, the settlers' descendants couldn't combat a tribe of moral crusaders who, by the mid-1960s, had preached the town's illegal but accepted casinos out of business. That and a simultaneous crackdown on prostitution pretty much scuttled the city's economy, and the town languished for a few decades until the National Park Service acquired and began to restore the old bathhouses in the 1980s. That's when

Water, Water Everywhere

Wherever I go, I find it fascinating that when I reach a place known for a *thing,* whether it's sunflower seeds or burlap sacks, some locals seem to know every speck of knowledge about that thing. In Hot Springs, that thing is water. The man at Mountain Valley imparted some of his wisdom to me, telling me how the water here percolates up through rock formations to carry with it 47 parts per million (ppm) of calcium, 130 ppm of bicarbonate, 4.9 ppm of magnesium, 4 ppm of sodium, 1 ppm of potassium, and an alkaline (CaCo3) level of 190. He said there are trace amounts of enriched and purified silica and a radon level of 43.3 picocuries per liter. At its deepest point, the water's boiling at 3,200 degrees but cools down to a relatively tepid 143 degrees at the surface. He *knows* this. It was like talking to Rain Man.

To see the end result of all of this, there are 47 "hot springs" in town. For a free sample, park at the thermal water station at Hill-Wheatley Plaza on Central Avenue near the NPS Administration Building (two other "jug fountains" are on Reserve Street and on Bathhouse Row). Use a thermos if you have one, otherwise buy an empty jug at the shop across the street and tap into the fountain that splashes out 4,400-year-old water that tastes morning fresh.

residents looked around and realized that their historic hometown should, and could, be revived.

That's what they did, and that's why you're here.

ON THE ROAD: HOT SPRINGS

What impresses me most about Hot Springs is that much of the town is a national park—and I'm not talking about a sprawling woodlands on the outskirts of town. If you walk down one side of Central Avenue past the historic bathhouses, you're in the Hot Springs National Park. Cross the street to visit a gift shop or check into a historic hotel, and you've entered the *town* of Hot Springs. It's weird and very pleasing. Every town should have its own national park.

But Bill Clinton, bathhouses, and history alone don't make a great town. You also need the surrounding lakes,

the wooded roads laced through the Ouachita Mountains of Central Arkansas, the extraordinarily nice people, and horse racing at Oaklawn Park which runs at full gallop from the end of January through April. The heart of the old city is easy to navigate, and new growth is relegated to the outskirts, so riding or walking is a pleasure.

While it's tempting to take off and get lost on some back roads, there's enough to see in town and on the ride north that you can park your bike and get some satisfaction as a street walker in the historic district. The first part of really seeing the town is soaking in the architecture on **Central Avenue.** It all looks like a movie set and reflects an unusual montage of styles, from Gilded Age hotels to Miami art deco apartments to Grecian temples, built to please a cross-section of resort guests (which must have included ancient

© NANCY HOWELL

Hot Springs is suspiciously absent of tributes to the hometown boy who made good—save for this photo-realistic woodcarving prominently displayed on Central Avenue. It's either Clinton or a young Buddy Hackett.

Greeks). The focal point of it all is the stunning lineup of eight bathhouses.

A century ago, these were opulent retreats where guests would take the waters, plunge into hot tubs, work out in then-state-of-the-art gymnasiums, and relax in sun-filled solariums. To see how your ancestors vacationed, visit the restored and ornate **Fordyce Bathhouse** (369 Central Ave., 501/624-2701, www.nps.gov/hosp), where a museum turns back the clock 100 years through films, archival photos, exercise equipment, chiropody and mechano-therapy rooms, a gymnasium, and immaculately restored tile baths. Among the historic displays is an antiquated sign that cautions "Do Not Urinate in Vapors"—which provided me with a new moral code.

Between Fordyce and the neighboring Maurice Bathhouse, a set of stairs leads up to a half-mile-long promenade that runs parallel to Central Avenue. Impressive

when it was built in the 1880s, it is still impressive today. Spa guests once came here to stroll and show off their direct-from-St.-Louis peacock finery; today the walkway elevates you above the town for some great photo ops of Central Avenue and historic downtown.

After the promenade, mount up for a steep ride to Mountaintop View Road. The shaded incline begins near the historic Arlington Hotel and rises like a vertical go-kart track to the peak of Hot Springs Mountain at 1,256 feet. Along the way, there are several pullouts and overlooks for souvenir photos, with the **Hot Springs Mountain Tower** (501/623-6035) an extra boost to provide up to 70 miles of aerial reconnaissance.

Back at the base of the mountain, you have free rein to tour the shops of downtown, tear off on a country run, lay down some cash on an Oaklawn thoroughbred, or peel off your boots and soak your feet in the steaming hot mineral waters of the main spring. But please...do not urinate in vapors.

PULL IT OVER: HOT SPRINGS HIGHLIGHTS
Attractions and Adventures

Even though President Clinton chose Little Rock (an hour east) as the location for his presidential library, I was surprised there was hardly any historical reference to him in his own hometown. One site that makes a feeble effort is his childhood home at **1011 Park Avenue** (which is the northern end of Central), just a small white house on a hill where Clinton lived from 1954 to 1961. Only a wooden marker notes that a famous American lived here once. You'll see it on your ride north.

To experience what kept the Quapaw here for so long, soak yourself at the **Buckstaff Baths** (509 Central Ave., 501/623-2308, www.buckstaffbaths.com). Here since 1912, this is the oldest operating bathhouse in America. You can kick back and sweat it out with thermal mineral baths, hot packs, steam cabinets, Swedish massages, or an oddly soothing sitz bath. A second option is **Quapaw Baths and Spa** (413 Central Ave., 501/609-9822, www.quapawbaths.com), which has been fully restored to its former glory. There are thermal baths, massages, facials, reflexology, hot stone massage, aromatherapy, and couples massages.

Some of Hot Springs's first tourists were gangsters who recognized that this out of the way resort destination featured a racetrack, brothels, and casinos. Considered neutral territory, mobsters would put away their differences and relax together until they were refreshed and rested and ready to go home and kill each other. You'll get the story of Capone, Luciano, Siegel and other goodfellas at **The Gangster Museum of America** (113 Central Ave., 501/318-1717, www.tgmoa.com).

A few miles from the historic district is Hot Springs's other leading attraction, **Oaklawn Park** (2705 Central Ave., 800/625-5296, www.oaklawn.com), which has been the center of thoroughbred racing since 1904. In season, bettors swarm the town to make some easy money while also establishing Hot Springs's first peak season. The rest of the year, you can bet on simulcast races across the nation and drop into a gaming room for electronic blackjack, poker, and other games.

At the opposite end of the adrenaline spectrum is **Garvan Woodland Gardens** (500 Arkridge Rd., 501/262-9300 or 800/366-4664, www.garvangardens.org, $8.75), about four miles out of town. It may not sound exciting, but think of it as a dumping ground for the workday stress you're forced to carry. Park your bike and walk amidst 210 acres of quiet trails intersected by bridges, pavilions, lakes, bird sanctuaries, and waterfalls.

After race season, summertime marks the second wave of tourism, when a lot of people head for the water. On Lake Hamilton, you can take a narrated paddleboat cruise aboard the **Belle of Hot Springs** (5200 Central Ave., 501/525-4438, www.belleriverboat.com, $16), but more unusual is a **National Park Duck Tour** (418 Central Ave, 501/321-2911, www.rideaduck.com), a 75-minute historic tour aboard an amphibious vehicle. Leaving from the center of town, you drive over to the shores of Lake Hamilton—then down the boat launch ramp and smack dab into the water.

Fifteen miles from town, 40,000-acre Lake Ouachita lends its name to **Lake Ouachita State Park** (5451 Mountain Pine Rd., Mountain Pine, 501/767-9366). Created by the Blakely Mountain Dam, the lake was named one of the cleanest in America and it's a favored destination for locals who come here to swim, ski, dive, boat, and fish. Along nearly *700 miles* of shoreline, you'll find campgrounds and cabins, picnic areas, walking trails, swimming areas, and a marina with boat rentals, bait, and supplies. From Hot Springs, head three miles west on U.S. 270, then 12 miles north on Route 227.

Shopping

The premier bottler in Hot Springs's history is **Mountain Valley Water** (150 Central Ave., 501/623-6671 or 800/643-1501, www.mountainvalleyspring.com). It's been here since 1871 and maintains a store that's partially a museum, with postcards, old signs and bottles, and a historical review of how Mountain Valley franchisers ran the Starbucks of their day. In the lobby, a painting of Spanish explorer Hernando De Soto shows him receiving a jug of healing waters from the friendly natives

in the spring of 1542; but since he died that June, I doubt the waters were really that healing. Eisenhower had better luck. After his heart attack, doctors told him to drink Mountain Valley water and he was kicking around more than a decade later. To understand the appeal of bottled water, stop by and "quaff the elixir."

Nearly every town has a leather shop, and here it's the **National Park Outfitters** (364 Central Ave., 501/624-5207) which carries biker stuff like vests, jackets, gloves, headgear, saddlebags, hats, and sunglasses. **Cheyenne Trading** (412 Central Ave., 501/321-0267) also carries buckskin boots and Native American souvenirs and feathers.

If you're lured into the woods or onto the lakes, you can find all the gear you need at **Trader Bill's Outdoor Sports** (1530 Albert Pike, 501/623-8403, www.traderbills.com). Along with the state's largest selection of fishing tackle, it also carries beer, ice, live bait, and hunting supplies.

© NANCY HOWELL

President Clinton's favorite Hot Springs BBQ joint: McClard's. Cheap eats in an old-fashioned diner setting.

Blue-Plate Specials

Bill Clinton's favorite Hot Springs diner is **McClard's Bar-B-Q** (505 Albert Pike Ave., 501/623-9665, www.mcclards. com). When you arrive at this small cinder-block building, you'll be "honey"ed and "sugar"ed to bits. Sit in a booth at a scuffed Formica table and compete with a full house of locals shoveling in pulled pork and ribs and chicken and cole slaw and iced tea. I prefer a different style of barbecue, but if you're here, why not give it a try? And forget that Clinton's diet led to a quadruple bypass.

There's a bigger variety of home cooking at **Granny's Kitchen** (362 Central Ave., 501/623-1177), with the matronly proprietor fixing up comfort foods like meat loaf, liver and onions, and pork chops, each for about eight bucks. Breakfast includes a typical lineup of eggs, sausage, hash browns, oatmeal, and cinnamon rolls.

The town's best breakfast may be at the **Colonial Pancake and Waffle House** (111 Central Ave., 501/624-9273). It's been here since 1962 and looks exactly like the places where you ate when you were still ordering off the kids' menu. It features thick china, small booths and tables, and a range of buttermilk, buckwheat, and blueberry pancakes, as well as waffles served plain, malted, pecan, buckwheat, buckwheat pecan, and the senior-favorite oat bran. Don't forget eggs, hash browns, prunes, and sliced bananas and milk.

A quick "bodacious burger" or "classy dog" can be found at **Bubbalu's** (408 Central Ave. 501/321-0101).

Watering Holes

If you're not grabbing a drink at the track, choose from a few saloons within walking distance at the heart of the historic district. Try **Magnolia's** (510 Central Ave., 501/624-5500), which serves up live music, drink specials, and a full American menu. When the rallies roll into town, riders roll over to **Lucky's** (711 Central Ave., 501/622-2570), a basic bar where everyone can grab some pizza and a cold one.

Shut-Eye

Does a rider sleep in the woods? At **Lake Ouachita State Park** (5451 Mountain Pine Rd., 800/264-2441 for cabin reservations), you can rent two- and three-bedroom cabins with fireplaces, as well as A-frame cabins that sleep up to six people. All are fully equipped, and some are lakefront. The park also has 112 campsites.

Inn-dependence

A towering testament to the original glory days of Hot Springs, the **Arlington Hotel** (239 Central Ave., 501/623-7771 or 800/643-1502, www.arlingtonhotel. com, $89 and up) has the best location of any hotel in town (across from the main spring and national park). The old-fashioned lobby, grand dining room, spa, and uncommonly spacious and homelike guestrooms will put you at ease. Rates begin easy, but watch out—they can peak sharply. Historic footnote: Room 443 is the Al Capone Suite, the crook's favorite hideout when he was in town.

Chain Drive

These chain hotels are in town, or within 10 miles of the city center: **Best Western, Clarion, Comfort Inn, Days Inn, Econo Lodge, Embassy Suites, Hampton Inn, Holiday Inn, Howard Johnson, Knights Inn, Quality Inn, Rodeway, Super 8, Travelodge** For more information, including phone numbers and websites, see page 439.

You never know what you'll find on the road. In Hot Springs, it's this magnificent bull.

© NANCY HOWELL

ON THE ROAD: HOT SPRINGS TO EUREKA SPRINGS

I have to confess that my pre-ride vision of Arkansas was an image of stereotypical rednecks, hillbillies, and bad haircuts. I've learned how wrong I was. Arkansas—at least the northwest sector that houses Highway 7—contains the perfect mix of friendly folks, great roads, historic towns, and unbelievable terrain. This ride through the hills of Arkansas will set you firmly on the foursquare path to righteous riding.

As you ride north on Central Avenue, aside from a few neat old motor courts that are now dilapidated, the junk side of town is brief. Just past Bill Clinton's boyhood home, the road drops and curves and the fun begins. You'll need to watch when Highway 7 makes a sharp left near a gas station a few miles out of town. Soon you'll be riding through Mountain Valley, home of the water empire; and about a dozen miles later you're in a new community

called Hot Springs Village which marks the point where the scenery becomes more beautiful. Part of the beauty lies in places like **Coleman's Rock Shop** (5837 Hwy. 7, Jessieville, 501/984-5328) which accents the route with hard-to-pass-up displays of fire red, glacier green, and brilliant cobalt-colored chunks of glass.

On your left in Jessieville is the **Ouachita National Forest Visitor Information Center** (501/984-5313), which is well worth a stop to pick up brochures on the road, flora, and fauna you'll soon see. This is the entrance point of the Scenic 7 Byway, and you'll know this because the air is slightly spicy, the pines are more tightly packed, and a massive sign announces "Entering Scenic 7 Byway." Some things you should know about the woods: You're entering a 1.8 million-acre forest that stretches from the center of Arkansas to southeast Oklahoma; it was created in 1907 by Teddy Roosevelt, which makes it the oldest national forest in the South; and the French spelling was created from the Indian word "washita," which means "good hunting grounds." Now you may proceed.

Instantly, the road becomes sublime. There are slow drops and casual S-curves and streams like Bear Creek and the LaFavre River that create a slow and peaceful introduction to the woodlands. Fifteen miles later, with its single gas pump, the Hollis Country Store assures you that you're entering the country.

The hills ahead aren't terrifyingly tall—they're just the right size for a cheap thrill. It gets even better. About five miles past Nimrod Lake you'll climb great hills and from the ridgeline the views open up above sunken valleys and the porous landscape below is sprinkled with mirror-like lakes. As if in a balloon, you're drifting along the road and watching the land far below. A few miles later and, hello!, you're in Ola, where the twisting road leads to a neat little town. Since a glitch in the ride is just ahead, this may be a good place to take a break.

Between Ola and the upcoming towns of Dardanelle and Russellville, there's not a lot of scenery, and soon city traffic will drive you nuts. Stick with it, and once you've passed over I-40 you'll be back in the pines and see a good sign: "Caution: Steep Curves and Sharp Drops for Next 63 Miles." Get ready for the fall.

There are big drops ahead, and as civilization recedes in your mirrors, dirt roads fly off into the woods. In the Piney Creeks Wildlife Area of the Ozark National Forest, the roads become narrower and higher and about the time your ears pop, you're at Moccasin Gap. Ahead, about seven miles south of the town of Pelsor, there's a perfectly placed rest stop and overlook for photos. Although, reducing about 500 square miles of the majestic Ozarks into a 4x6-inch image won't even begin to do them justice.

From here the road returns to a mix of turns and sweeps and pastures and clearings, jumping up over hills then falling down the other side into more banked corners. Past the town of Cowell and approaching Jasper, the scenery switches to broken-down shacks and cottages that are attractive in the sense that they reveal another aspect of America. The road begins to ascend again to reach the **Hog Heaven Scenic Overlook,** and they're right, it is scenic and wonderful. Considering all the power-lifting your bike's been doing, it's about to let you down on a precipitous road that clings tenaciously to the side of the mountain. You'll fall nearly four miles to reach the highly recommended **Cliff House Restaurant** (Hwy. 7, 870/446-2292, www.cliffhouseinnar.com). I've eaten at a lot of diners, and this is one of the finest. They serve some of the best home cooking in the South and top it off with an incredible widescreen view of the valley and mountains. If you'd like to save the rest of the ride until daybreak, there's a just-as-clean motel ($65 and up) on the ground floor. Call ahead for reservations.

After lunch at the Cliff House, give the gas a break and let a seven-degree drop shoot you down the hill for the last three miles into the town of Jasper, where there are several shops and restaurants around the town square. Just outside Jasper, turn off Scenic 7 Byway and turn into Highway 74 West. There's nothing demanding or dangerous right away, but the keen, steep road slices into a place called Low Gap, which has a general store, a cemetery, and the nearly hidden entrance to the **Buffalo National River** (870/449-4311, www. nps.gov/buff), the oldest national river in America. If you have the guts to ride to it, a pockmarked gravel road leads down to the river at the Steel Creek entrance to your right. You'll know you've found it when you see towering limestone buttes more akin to the Dakotas.

Just slightly north of Highway 74 on Highway 43 is Ponca, worth a brief detour since it leads into a gorge. If your schedule allows an overnight, or if you just want to get some gas and snacks, an outfitter and lodge here, **Buffalo Outdoor Center** (800/221-5514, www.buffaloriver.com), can lead you to or arrange trail rides, floating trips, and hot air balloon rides in this beautiful backcountry. What kept me on the road was the feeling that things were going to get a whole lot better. And they did.

Back on Highway 74 came the highlight of the ride: great straights where I was able to pump up the speed, followed by extremely steep drops and similarly steep ascents. More than that, though, were changes in landscapes that—and I loved this—changed from a North Carolina feel at Ponca to scenes of Vermont countryside and pastures at the Elk Refuge, followed by glimpses of central California's grasslands and then traces of a Wyoming prairie. Incredibly, there were four or five ecosystems and landscapes to savor within 10 miles. It was absolutely stunning, and I wished I'd been born twins so that I could enjoy it all even more.

On Highway 74 in the town of Kingston, Route 21 shoots north. Take it—there's hardly a lick of traffic for miles and you receive the benefit of valleys that release you into wide-open plains to give you that pure feeling of riding without concerns or cares. As part of these pastoral scenes, every so often you roll over a creek and into a town where a ramshackle general store reminds you once again that you're on a motorcycle adventure. When you reach Highway 62, head west at Berryville, the final way station before the home stretch into Eureka Springs, one of the most unusual towns you'll have the pleasure to visit.

EUREKA SPRINGS PRIMER

There's something unusual about Eureka Springs, and it's not just knowing that it's in the Boston Mountains of the Ozark Plateau—the only chain that runs east and west. And it's not just realizing that the mountains seem so high only because the valleys are so low, or that the word "Ozarks" comes from *"aux arcs,"* a modification of the French words "of trees" *(aux arbres)*. What's so unusual is that in a town of about 2,300 people, there are more than 30 bed-and-breakfasts, a passion play, a historic railroad, several grand hotels, several dozen massage therapists, a sanctuary for abused big cats and bears, a Native American site, and one of the 20th century's leading examples of architecture.

As it did for Hot Springs, mineral water helped create this town. Visionaries thought they could attract wealthy travelers by hinting that the natural springs could heal the blind. Their efforts paid

Shotgun Weddings

Back in the day, people in the Ozarks were known to get married at the barrel of a shotgun, but things are slightly more refined in today's Eureka Springs. There are several small wedding chapels in the heart of town, but the Marryin' Sam that caught my attention was Jan Ortiz of **All About Love** (470/253-2526 or 888/568-3020, www.eureka-net.com/weddings). She set up shop at the East Mountain Gazebo, with a stunning view of the valley and the historic Crescent Hotel on the opposite hill. When Nance and I showed up, we watched the conclusion of a wedding ceremony and thought it was a fluke—and then looked back at a line of cars carrying an assortment of brides and grooms ready to get hitched. Every 10 minutes, a couple would get out of their car (or pickup), say their vows, sign some papers, pay 40 bucks, and get on their way to a happy, productive, and fruitful life. Get a license, call Jan, and you can do the same.

off in the 1800s and continue today, despite fires that burned down the town three times. It also got a boost from some famous residents, such as Robert Ripley, who featured aspects of the town in several of his *Believe It or Not!* comics, and from Carrie Nation, the impassioned zealot who used a bible as an excuse and a hatchet for efficiency when she smashed up saloons.

Because people aren't sent to Eureka Springs in a corporate transfer, and they don't just stumble across it, arriving here marks the fulfillment of a quest for an unusual assemblage of people from all walks of life: you may encounter hippies, artists, retirees, and punks. In this unusually cosmopolitan community, the National Register of Historic Places has a presence—in fact, the *entire downtown* is on the Register.

There are hundreds of miles of wonderful roads surrounding the town and countless Victorian homes and cottages tucked into the angled hills beside the steep and narrow streets. But one of the more incredible aspects of it all is that, unlike other small towns that have been harmed by their popularity, a local pointed out that Eureka Springs "aggressively fights the Bransonization of the town." To that end, a strong planning commission, historical association, and preservationists have kept things just right.

ON THE ROAD: EUREKA SPRINGS

I guarantee that you'll make time to park your bike and wander around the village, but think about starting your day with a well-balanced breakfast and a sharp little loop that'll get you out into the countryside for a couple of hours. Highway 62 West (Van Buren Ave.) leads out of town, and with only a slight buffer between you and the surrounding countryside you'll

The unusual shape of the Palace Hotel's sign has earned it a fitting nickname: the Phallus Palace.

reach some steep, curving roads right away. Your first destination is **Thorncrown Chapel** (12968 Hwy. 62, 479/253-7401, www.thorncrown.com), which may not mean much to you now, but will soon become unforgettable. About two miles from town, you'll see the entrance hidden in a break in the woods on your right, and you'll see the chapel hidden in the woods themselves. Why is this sanctuary so sacred and revered?

Well, in 2000, members of the American Institute of Architecture ranked Thorncrown Chapel the fourth-best building design of the 20th century—placing it immediately behind Frank Lloyd Wright's Fallingwater and New York's Chrysler and Seagram's buildings. It started when local resident Jim Reed had a vision and recruited architect E. Fay Jones of Fayetteville to create the 48-foot-tall wood and glass chapel. Although it's just a tiny church in the forest in the Ozarks, when you see it camouflaged within the 50-foot-tall trees and enter the chapel and *really* look at the organic design that blends it into the land, you'll understand why it's earned such respect. The subtleties of the design reveal themselves a little at a time. A crown of thorns is created by a lattice work of 2x4 beams, 10 tons of pane glass make the modest chapel seem as large as a cathedral, and at night the interior crosses reflect infinitely into the branches of trees.

Back on Highway 62 West, there's another spiritual center ahead, accessible down a hard-packed dirt road. The **Blue Springs Heritage Center** (479/253-9244, www.bluespringheritage.com, $7.25) was created for peace, reflection, and remembrance at a Native American site where 10,000-year-old artifacts have been discovered and where tribes like the Osage and Cherokees gathered in 1839 when forced from their homes on the Trail of Tears. A natural spring circulating 38 million gallons of water a day creates the White River, which loops around the grounds to create a 250-acre peninsula.

After the town of Busch, turn right on Highway 187, where few things are as pleasing as twisting the throttle and leaping back onto the road, sweeping around corners, and passing log cabins. A few miles ahead you enter Beaver, where the road makes a wide arc and whirls around the perimeter of Beaver Lake. If you were smart enough to read this in advance, you knew to pack a lunch and your trunks so you could enjoy the swimming beach and picnic pavilions. A few hundred yards farther, the **Beaver Dam** (yes, that's right) is impressive and has a pullout midway, where you can park by the No Parking sign, snap some pictures, and peer over the side. After the dam, the road commences to twist and turn until it merges again with Highway 62 to meet the same crooked and steep hills you rode up earlier. You'll recognize Thorncrown Chapel, now on your left, and ride the last few miles to town, where you can count on a good rubdown from a local masseuse.

PULL IT OVER: EUREKA SPRINGS HIGHLIGHTS
Attractions and Adventures
Built into the side of the hill, downtown seems to flow off the mountain which makes it neat to photograph, but tricky to park. Once you're settled, you'll see that for such a compact place there's a hell of a lot to see. More than in Manhattan, I'd claim. There are only two real streets downtown, Main and Spring, with Center splitting up and off Main to create another street of cool shops frequented by thousands of riders and shoppers who will find at least one thing they like.

While you may be tempted to ride your bike everywhere, one option that'll save a little gas and your parking space is spending five bucks on a day pass ($8 for two days) and exploring the surrounding area via the **Eureka Springs Transit System** (479/253-9572, www.eurekatrolley.com). There are several routes around town, and you can board at stops in town and on the outskirts to expand your range. For information on town history, a special tour leaves the visitors center on Highway 62. The hour-long, $10 tour feeds you the intelligence you need to understand the history and diversity of Eureka Springs.

Since 1968, travelers have been attending the **Great Passion Play** (935 Passion Play Rd., 800/882-7529, www. greatpassionplay.com), which features a cast of hundreds recreating the trial, execution, resurrection, and ascension of Christ. Believers may want to make a day of it on a Holy Land tour to watch actors

An Overnight with Cat Class, Cat Style

If the **Turpentine Creek Big Cat Refuge** (479/253-5841, www.turpentine-creek.org, $15) doesn't inspire you, nothing will. Located seven miles south of town on Route 23, the refuge was founded by Tanya Smith, her parents, and her late brother Robert. You'll be amazed at the strength of the powerful tigers and lions and bears they've rescued. Given a new lease on life, Tanya suggests the animals "share the same spirit as a motorcycle rider. They're independent. You can't tame them."

While donations, corporate sponsors, celebrity endorsements, or an Extreme Home Makeover would mark a major change, for now Smith is satisfied with the new habitats she's built for her big cats. Most of all, you'll be satisfied with the human habitats built by artists Lisa and D. Arthur Wilson. The two created five spectacular and impeccable Safari Lodges that are a masterpiece perfectly suited for riders. You'll feel as if you're on the African veldt when you check into dressed-out huts that encircle a fire pit. Starting at $125, they're a bargain for solo or group riders who will get a charge out of waking up to the nearby roar of the big cats.

© NANCY HOWELL

Taking a cat nap at Turpentine Creek, a refuge for abused large cats outside Eureka Springs.

'Nuff said. An essential truth posted in Eureka Springs.

recreate biblical stories and personalities, visit a bible museum containing more than 6,000 bibles in 625 languages, and stare at the massive 67-foot-tall Christ of the Ozarks. This is the largest Christ statue in America, one that theologians believe is far taller than was the actual son of God.

Shopping

Pretty much everything you can shop for—cats, quilts, dulcimers, pipes, hats, loads of leather, and a few thousand other items—are all on sale in the 170-plus stores here. For riders, **Emerald Forest** (31 Spring St., 479/253-6959, www.emeraldforestclothing.com) carries travel and adventure clothing, some cool Indian-beaded leather jackets, and other high-quality clothes. The competition is the **Nelson Leather Company** (34 Spring St., 479/253-7162, www.nelsonleathercompany.com), which carries an impressive lineup of fringed jackets with Indian beading, as well as watches, canes, bullwhips,

and local crafts like hardwood cutting boards, knives, hats, masks, togs, and cowhide purses. The **White River Tobacco Company** (99 Spring St., 479/253-5350) is a "work-free smoke place" that carries the sort of tobacco items you once hid in a cigar box under your dorm room bed. There are a variety of tobacco blends, ashtrays, pipes, hookahs, and novelties, like the cell phone flask to sneak into a game.

Blue-Plate Specials

Main Street Café (9 S. Main St., 479/253-7374) will load you up with basic breakfast items like omelettes, hash browns, grits, and toast that'll hold you until lunchtime. Speaking of lunchtime, seeing as it's attached to a chain hotel, I was astounded to find damn good Southern vittles at **Myrtie Mae's** (207 W. Van Buren/Hwy. 62), 479/253-9768). Fried chicken and the rest of the home-cooked stuff—muffins, desserts, soups, mashed potatoes—were just right. It's real food in the real South.

Musical Motorcyclists

On my last ride through Eureka Springs, I was contacted by a reader who informed me that Ponytail, P. Nutt, and Granny wanted to take me to some back roads and possibly "hit the Pig Trails" on our "motorsickels." I was curiously intrigued.

Ponytail, P. Nutt, and Granny, it turned out, are the stage names for DaWayne George, his brother Randall, and their partner Ted Snow who are avid motorcyclists, amazingly gifted musicians, and the stars of Eureka Springs's **Ozark Mountain Hoe-Down** (3140 E. Van Buren, 479/253-7725 or 800/468-2113, www.hoedown.net). The reader playing matchmaker, Leslie Wright, also plays a girl called Girl. Don't ask.

The hoe-down was down-home, silly, fun and filled with corny jokes like the one about the man caught skinny dipping who was released for lack of evidence. Rivaling the comedy was the musical talent of Granny and P. Nutt who both play sizzling country guitar. The encore performance was a repeated invitation to join them on a ride. Not just me. *You.* Riders arriving from across America often find themselves out on the road with their new Ozark friends who lead them to some of the best roads in the region. Why do they do it? Why do these folks spend time with complete strangers? According to Ted, "When someone calls us and asks us to take 'em out, it doesn't cost us anything and we're glad to do it. Besides, we're one big family and riding is something we love to do."

So, first, see the show. Next, spend some riding time with some of the nicest folks in Arkansas.

The **Cottage Inn** (450 W. Van Buren/Hwy. 62, 479/253-5282, www.cottageinneurekaspgs.com) is different in a good way. It's a motor court, as well as a cozy Mediterranean restaurant created in an old home. Linda Hager studied and traveled throughout Europe, and she brought back dishes, recipes, and wines from Greece, Spain, France, and Italy. If you're a casual gourmet, you'll find the service and setting here fine and relaxing. If you'd like to stay the night, cool cabins are a modest $65–85.

One of the area's best steakhouses is **Gaskins Cabin** (2883 Hwy. 23 North, 479/253-5466, www.gaskinscabin.com), which is the latest occupant of an actual log cabin built in 1864. Not your average roadside restaurant, this is more refined with great service, great steaks like the 21-day aged Omaha Angus, and a friendly neighborhood bar that attracts locals.

Watering Holes

In addition to having mostly everything, Eureka Springs has even more in the way of cool pubs and clubs in the center of town. **Eureka Live** (35 1/2 N. Main St., 479/253-7020, www.eurekalive.net) is a local fave basement bar and destination for riders, where you can get your groove on to rock 'n' roll and order up well drinks and draft specials.

© NANCY HOWELL

Cruising through downtown Eureka Springs: The Gilded Age town of resort hotels and mineral baths is a favorite destination for riders.

Chelsea's Corner Café and Bar (10 Mountain St., 479/253-6723, www.chelseascornercafe.com) is kind of tricky to find. It's a stripped-down bar that has four imports on tap, plus domestic bottle beers, and live music inside or on the enclosed deck.

One of the biggest and most popular games in town is the **Pied Piper Pub** (82 Armstrong St., 479/363-9976), where the motto is The Bikes Stop Here. The pub features fab food and good entertainment seven days a week, "from mid-day to mid-nite." There's a full bar (whiskey, bourbon, scotch) and big beer list with selections from Mexico, Holland, Ireland, Britain, Australia, and Arkansas. Hang out on the deck and take in the town.

Shut-Eye
Motels and Motor Courts
Yet another thing to love about Eureka Springs is the variety of lodging, which includes old-fashioned mom-and-pop motels. Here are a few to consider.

Spotting an old motel, Bob and Ann McCool converted it into a motorcycles-only resort called **Riders Rest** (4092 E. Van Buren, 479/253-9815, www.ridersrestmotel.com, $45–65). A best bet for riders, it's designed specifically for people like you. Ten motorcycle-themed rooms (Brando, Elvis, Andy & Barney) are clean, neat, and provide everything a rider needs and the McCools include free maps that outline the area's best rides. Out back there's covered parking, a fire pit, and a low-key beer garden that's a welcome sanctuary at the end of the day.

A short walk from downtown is the retro-style **Joy Motel** (216 W. Van Buren, 479/253-9568 or 877/569-7667, www.thejoymotel.com). Rates are modest ($43 base rate, $125 high season) and new owners have spiffed things up; even adding a fire pit and an interesting offer: "Discounts? Give it your best shot. We'll deal." The motel features the town's largest swimming pool, serves a continental breakfast with homemade pancakes and Tang ("Yes, Tang!"), provides two queen or full beds, and some cabins as well. Top that, Ritz-Carlton!

The **Cottage Inn** (450 W. Van Buren/ Hwy. 62 W, 479/253-5282, www.cottageinneurekaspgs.com, $65–85) was built in 1937 as a tourist court and restored as comfortable individual cabins with modern conveniences, including whirlpool tubs, to create a quiet and private retreat close to town.

Four miles east of the village at **Bluebird Lodge & Cottages** (5830 Hwy. 62 W, 479/253-6028 or 800/286-4469, www.bluebirdlodgeandcottages.com, $45–65, $125 for cottages), the rooms are large (if basic), with a queen or king bed, whirlpool tub, and private balcony. Their cottages are down a country lane and come with a king bed, double whirlpool tub, fireplace, kitchen, and private balcony.

Opened in 1892 and on the National Register, the **New Orleans Hotel** (63 Spring St., 479/253-8630 or 800/243-8630, www.neworleanshotelandspa.com, $84 and up) is a large, old-fashioned place where the clean rooms have a classic N'awlins look, queen and king beds, and double whirlpool tubs. It's right in the heart of town, with balconies overlooking the village.

There are several chain hotels in Eureka Springs, but I can personally recommend the **Best Western** (479/253-9551, $49–150) at the junction of Highway 62 and Route 23. Rooms are larger than usual, there's plenty of parking, it's clean as a whistle, and the breakfast will increase your body's mass each morning. Nice, nice, nice.

Inn-dependence

If you favor grand hotels, you're also in luck. The **Crescent Hotel and Spa** (75 Prospect Ave., 479/253-9766 or 800/342-9766, www.crescent-hotel.com, $119 and up off-season, $149 and up high season) is a fantastically ornate place, one that every visitor wants to see. You can sense the history when you enter the lobby of the "Grand Old Lady of the Ozarks," here since 1886. Closer to the center of town—actually it *is* the center of town—is the 1905 **Basin Park Hotel** (12 Spring St., 479/253-7837 or 800/643-4972, www.basinpark.com, $93–132 premium room, $229–239 specialty suite), owned by the same folks as the Crescent. Rooms here are not overly elaborate but should satisfy. The 1883 **Grand Central Hotel** (37 North Main St., 479/253-6756 or 800/344-6050, www.grandcentralresort.com, parlor suites $125 and up) was originally an

1800s railroad hotel that now features 14 wonderfully themed rooms that would look at home in the upscale Old West. A spa and fine dining restaurant add to the experience.

Chain Drive

These chain hotels are in town, or within 10 miles of the city center: **Comfort Inn, Days Inn, Howard Johnson, Motel 6, Quality Inn, Rodeway, Super 8, Travelodge** For more information, including phone numbers and websites, see page 439.

SIDE TRIP: BRANSON

Based on its reputation, Branson was one of the last places I would have wanted to visit. Based on experience, I can't wait to go back.

After I heard that sex kitten Ann-Margret was to appear on stage with Andy Williams, I got on the bike and rolled like thunder toward Branson. It's a perfect 50-mile, one-hour road trip away from Eureka Springs. Keep in mind that if you plan to catch an evening show, you may be better off staying the night in Branson rather than riding the pitch-black roads after dark. Don't sweat it—rooms can be found for around $30.

When you leave Eureka Springs on Route 23, the two-lane highway is alternately slow and bending and pitched and dropping, although nothing is too severe. After the town of Oak Hill, the speed drops to a slow 25 mph, and then slow, lazy curves take you through the hills toward Missouri. There's something nice about this countryside; it's very remote and very gentle. When you ride between hills, you drop out of view and get a few moments of privacy. Watch for Highway 86 and head east, after which there's a small town every so often, and the land starts to change into some Tyrolean setting full of pastures and grazing cattle. Sometimes there'll be an uncommonly long straight, and then, to make up for it, you'll be slapped into a series of curves that'll bounce you around like a pinball machine.

Where Highway 86 meets Highway 13, hang a long, loping right toward the town of Blue Eye; and where the road Ts above it, hang a left to follow Highway 86 the rest of the way toward U.S. 65. Along the way, it's a thoroughly enjoyable ride through the countryside, and after you cross the Long Creek Arm of Table Rock Lake, it's only a few more country-perfect miles until Highway 86 dead-ends at U.S. 65, 10 miles south of Branson. The shows I saw there—Andy Williams and Ann-Margret, the Sons of the Pioneers, Jim Stafford, the Roy Rogers Museum, Silver Dollar City—were absolutely dynamite. Although it's been branded as a countrified Las Vegas, if you can deal with the traffic and adjust your attitude, the payoff is a town where working-class folks can spend a little cash and have a hell of a lot of fun.

To see what's shaking in Branson, call 417/334-4084 or 800/214-3661 or visit www.explorebranson.com.

Resources for Riders

Ozark Mountain Run

Arkansas Travel Information
Arkansas Department of Parks—www.arkansasparks.com
Arkansas Game & Fish Commission—501/223-6300 or 800/364-4263,
    www.agfc.com
Arkansas Road Conditions—501/569-2374 or 800/245-1672,
    www.arkansashighways.com
Arkansas State Parks—888/287-2757, www.arkansasstateparks.com
Arkansas Travel and Tourism—501/682-7777 or 800/628-8725,
    www.arkansas.com
Bed and Breakfast Association of Arkansas—www.bedandbreakfastarkansas.com

Local and Regional Information
Eureka Springs Chamber of Commerce—479/253-8737 or 800/638-7352,
    www.eurekaspringschamber.com
Hot Springs Convention and Visitors Bureau—501/321-2277 or 800/543-2284,
    www.hotsprings.org
Ouchita National Forest—501/321-5202, www.fs.fed.us/oonf

Arkansas Motorcycle Shops
Big Boar Powersports—2407 W. Hudson Rd, Rogers, 479/636-7133,
    www.bigboarpowersports.com
Bill Eddy's Motorsports—1205 N. Futrall Dr., Fayetteville, 479/521-7133,
    www.billeddysmotorsports.com
D & D Cycle—2525 W. Hudson Rd., Rogers, 479/621-1024, www.dndcycle.com
Freedom Power Sports—2741 W. Hudson Rd., Rogers, 479/621-6006,
    www.freedompowersportsnwa.com
Greeson's—2219 Albert Pike, Hot Springs, 501/767-2771, www.gogreeson.com
Honda of Russellville—220 Lake Front Dr., 479/968-2233 or 866/466-3219,
    www.hondaofrussellville.com
John's Honda—111 Carl Dr., Hot Springs, 501/623-1495, www.johnshonda.com
Landers Harley-Davidson—205 Garrison, Hot Springs, 501/525-7468,
    www.landersharley.com
Lanny's Cycle World—501 Airport Rd., Hot Springs, 501/623-2483,
    www.lannyscycleworld.com
Pig Trail Harley Davidson—2409 W. Hudson Rd., Rogers, 479/636-9797,
    www.pigtrailhd.com
Yamaha-Suzuki of Hot Springs—111 Buena Vista Rd., Hot Springs,
    501/525-7110, www.suzukiofhotsprings.com

The Magical Michigan Tour

Ludington, Michigan to Mackinaw City, Michigan

As different as they are, Michigan and New York have something in common: Most outsiders assume the entirety of each state is defined by the faults of their most populous cities. It's wrong in New York and, after a ride up its western coast, I can attest that it's one thousand percent wrong in Michigan.

You'll realize this as you follow a path taken by travelers who blazed a new trail more than a century ago. Starting in 1904, much of this route was part of the West Michigan Pike, the "Northern Link of the Dixie Highway," a simple, two-lane road that started in Florida and snaked up the Lake Michigan shoreline from Chicago to Mackinaw City.

Ride here and you'll enjoy some of the most pristine scenery in America. Ride here and you'll be dazzled by lakes, orchards, and natural beauty. Ride here and you'll sense the power of Lake Michigan. It will stay with you for hundreds of miles...

Then for the rest of your life.

LUDINGTON PRIMER

History books show that Father Jacques Marquette landed near here in the mid-

1600s, then died and was buried here in 1675. In the mid-19th century, natural resources were the force behind the creation of Ludington and Mason Counties. Lumber barons harvested the region's tall pines until their greed overcame the resources and the boom went bust. While lumber lasted, railroads made Ludington the western terminus to ship goods across Lake Michigan to and from Wisconsin. In 1914, Ludington created the "million dollar harbor" and the town became a major Great Lakes port. By the 1950s, it was also the world's largest carferry port.

Today, the most familiar sights along this stretch of Lake Michigan are small motels and second homes visited annually by successive generations of families who double the town's population between May and mid-October. The number spikes again when motorists and riders arrive for the annual "Color Tour," a sightseeing excursion focused on seeing the changing leaves. After that, most folks head home and leave Ludington to the people who know how to handle sub-zero

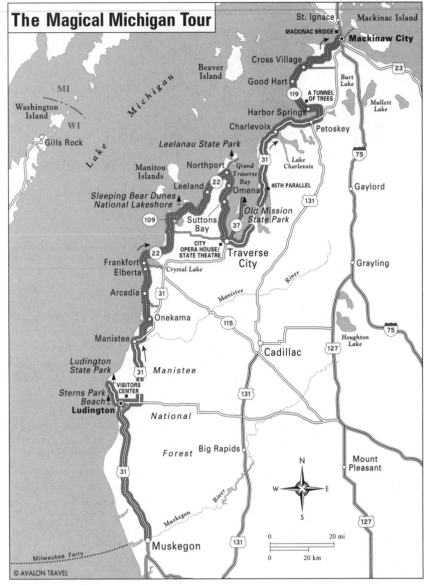

The Magical Michigan Tour

Route: Ludington to Mackinaw City via Manistee, Glen Arbor, Leland, Suttons Bay, Traverse City, Charlevoix, Petoskey, Cross Village

Distance: Approximately 265 miles

First Leg: Ludington to Traverse City (145 miles)

Second Leg: Traverse City to Mackinaw City (120 miles)

Helmet Laws: Helmets are required in Michigan.

temperatures, freezing lake winds, and the ice that forms five miles offshore.

See you next May.

ON THE ROAD: LUDINGTON

If you begin your ride in Ludington, you'll get your first indication that Michigan's coastal communities are incredibly picturesque. I was captivated by downtown, which is intersected by Ludington Avenue (aka U.S. 10) and lined with independent stores, small motels, ice cream parlors, nightspots, and a park. Ride a little further west for an incredible view of Lake Michigan.

To gather more intelligence, stop by the **Visitors Center** (226 W. Ludington Ave.) and then head out to explore the town's 11 marinas, 5 public beaches, 16 parks, 2 lighthouses, 36 miles of hiking trails, 60 inland lakes, and nearly 70 charter boats.

Ludington capitalizes on its most valuable asset with an excellent beachfront. There's plenty of parking, lots of soft sand, a lighthouse at the end of a jetty, and perhaps the cleanest fish cleaning station I've ever seen. Follow the shoreline, and the ride takes you to the picture-perfect Ludington Marina, past some nice public sculptures, and then towards the moored SS *Spartan,* the 410-foot sister ship of the SS *Badger.* No longer seaworthy, the *Spartan* is still useful, providing the *Badger* with spare parts when needed.

You can easily spend a day—or a season—hanging around this cool community, which is easy to navigate and a pleasure to visit.

PULL IT OVER: LUDINGTON HIGHLIGHTS
Attractions and Adventures

Ludington fronts Lake Michigan, and does it nowhere better than at **Stearns Park Beach** (at the end of Ludington

A lighthouse at the end of the jetty at Ludington is a guiding light—and a place for anglers and tourists bidding bon voyage to the iconic SS *Badger.*

© NANCY HOWELL

Ave.), where the half-mile stretch of beach is groomed overnight to be ready for sunbathers and sightseers each morning. Take a swim in Lake Michigan, provided you can handle its peak water temperature of 72 degrees—which is like a mineral bath for the locals.

There are more than eight miles of waterfront walkways. In season, folks gather at the 1924 North Breakwater Lighthouse Pier and wave hello and goodbye to the SS *Badger.* Why is this ship so deserving of the affection? It's the last coal-fired, steam-powered carferry in the Western Hemisphere.

With 60 inland lakes, Lake Michigan, and the Pere Marquette River in the neighborhood, members of **Ludington Area Charterboat Association** (231/843-3474 or 800/927-3470, www.ludington-charterboats.org) are eager to take you out in search of salmon, king salmon, steelhead, trout, perch, pike, and bluegill. If the thought of being outdoors appeals to you, head a few miles north of town to **Ludington State Park** (8800 W. M-116, 231/843-2423, www.visitludington-statepark.com). Back in the 1930s, FDR was busy putting the nation back to work, and got CCC employees busy working on the park's 5,300 acres. Its 347 campsites book up as much as six months in advance in season. Other park features include the Big Sable Lighthouse (circa 1867), a marked canoe pathway, eight marked trails, and the Hamlin Lake Dam.

Shopping

Downtown's shops are well worth seeing. Deciding where to drop in depends on your interests. Wander up one side of Ludington Avenue and down the other, checking out the sporting good stores, antiques shops, markets, and galleries. One standout is **Cole's Antiques Villa** (322 W. Ludington Ave., 231/845-7414, www.cole-santiquesvilla.com), which packs about 5,000 square feet with old advertising, sporting, decoys, linens, coins, postcards, books, jewelry, and local memorabilia; including ephemera on the cool carferry.

Blue-Plate Specials

You'll be impressed by the number of dining choices in town, which far exceed this short list.

Now that you're an adult, you can have dessert before dinner. Do not miss enjoying that privilege at the **House of Flavors** (402 W. Ludington Ave., 231/845-5785, www.houseofflavors.com), a local favorite with a retro-cool 1950s look, a diner menu, and more flavors of freshly made ice cream than you can imagine. It's a top choice.

A few blocks away, the **Blu Moon** (125 S. James St., 231/843-2001, www.theblu-moon.net) is a small bistro with an eclectic

decor and a menu to match. Expect large portions of ribs, pork, perch, salmon, pastas, and comfort foods like meatloaf, pot roast, catfish, and hush puppies.

Le Serving Spoon Restaurant (130 W. Ludington Ave., 231/843-6555) has signature sandwiches including BLTs, Cobb clubs, melts, wraps, paninis, and a variety of salads including Michigan cherry, almond chicken, and Southwest.

With a great view overlooking the harbor, **PM Steamers** (302 W. Loomis St., 231/843-9555, www.pmsteamers.com) is perfect when the weather's nice. As the name suggests, seafood's a specialty.

Here since 1942, the **Old Hamlin** (122 W. Ludington Ave., 231/843-4251, www.oldhamlin.com) is a family restaurant with an expanded menu of American, Greek, Italian, and Mexican entrees, as well as full breakfasts, homemade breads, and pies. The food is average, but it's a local institution.

Watering Holes

Ludington's not exactly upscale or blue collar, and its nightspots also fit somewhere in between. Most bars are also restaurants, places like the **Jamesport Brewing Company** (402 W. Ludington Ave., 231/845-2522, www.jamesport-brewingco.com), which serves lake perch, grilled salmon, sirloin steaks, chicken, and shepherds pie. It's also a brewpub with a dozen handcrafted microbrew beers served in pint and twelve-ounce glasses. Sports bar **Michael's** (129 W. Ludington Ave., 231/845-7411) won my heart with its Beatles and Elvis pictures. It also offers two pool tables, widescreen TVs, a stand-alone full liquor bar, and private booths. Down the street, the **Sportsman** (111 W. Ludington Ave., 231/843-2138) is a traditional Irish bar, adorned with European football banners and American flags. It's dark and busy, the kind of rustic bar you would envision in a town like this.

Shut-Eye

Ludington takes its obligation to welcome summer travelers seriously. The town has the greatest concentration of B&Bs in the state, many of them members of the **Ludington Historic B&B Association** (www.ludingtonbedandbreakfast.com).

Motels and Motor Courts

There are also some neat old-fashioned motels and motor courts, including the **Viking Arms** (930 E. Ludington Ave., 231/843-3441 or 800/299-9214, www.vikingarmsinn.com, from $75 in season) where you can park in front of your ground-level room. Some suites have whirlpool baths and gas log fireplaces, all have Wi-fi, and it's clean. The basic eight-unit **Avenue Motel** (414 E. Ludington Ave., 231/843-8060) is also affordable, with a cute, cottage-style look. The

Stearns Motor Inn (212 E. Ludington Ave., 231/843-3407 or 800/365-1904, www.stearnsmotorinn.com, from $95) is a big motel with king- and queen-size bed as well as fireplace suites, efficiencies, and the Tiki nightclub.

For a quiet retreat, try **Country Haven Resort Motel** (3263 N. Lakeshore Dr., 231/845-5882 or 888/845-5187, www.countryhavenresort.com). It's peaceful with a nice location, four miles north of town on Hamlin Lake. They offer free use of bicycles, kayaks, paddleboats, and bass boats with electric trolling motors, and rent ATVs and Jet Skis. For a more substantial list of Hamlin Lake cottages and motels, check www.hamlinlake.com.

Chain Drive

These chain hotels are in town, or within 10 miles of the city center: **Best Western, Holiday Inn, Ramada** For more information, including phone numbers and websites, see page 439.

© NANCY HOWELL

Lake Michigan, as seen from Stearns Park, is tranquil yet foreboding.

Ferry Land

If you've found yourself in Wisconsin and want to reach Michigan (or vice versa) check out two highly recommended ferry services:

Departing from a port south of downtown Milwaukee, **Lake Express** (2330 S. Lincoln Memorial Dr., 866/914-1010, www.lake-express.com) is a high-speed service that will get you to Muskegon (60 miles south of Ludington) in about 2.5 hours. You may spend about $80 for yourself and $60 for your motorcycle, but you'll save your sanity, gas, 277 miles, and more than five hours of riding through the dense interstate traffic in cities along Lake Michigan. Just ride on board. Tie down your bike with the free straps, and then head upstairs to rest in the lounge—read, watch TV, or sleep—while other riders are caught in the gridlock of Chicago traffic.

In some respects, the better option is the **Lake Michigan Carferry Service** (888/227-7447, www.ssbadger.com) between Ludington, Michigan, and Manitowoc, Wisconsin. This cruise stars the SS *Badger,* the only steam-powered, coal-fired carferry in the Western Hemisphere. Slower than the Lake Express, the crossing aboard the historic ship takes four hours (although you gain an hour when heading west to Manitowoc). Plus, you'll save more than eight hours and 400-plus miles of riding a laborious route through major cities. You'll need to bring your own tie-down straps, but aboard you can reserve a stateroom (not what you imagine, but the two small beds are a relief after a long ride), watch TV and movies, dine at a small café, play in the game room, visit the gift shop, or sun yourself on deck. Casual, cool, and priceless.

ON THE ROAD: LUDINGTON TO TRAVERSE CITY

Although there's a back route to Manistee, the first major town north of Ludington, the trick is some tricky turns that can get you lost out in farmland. The alternative is recognizing that there will be plenty of scenic roads to come, and the simplest route is finding U.S. 31 a few miles east of downtown, and taking it north. It's a long, straight, and lonely two-lane road that'll take you past some remote fields for about 30 miles until you reach Manistee which, although nice, is a little more crowded and a little less picturesque than Ludington.

This vibe continues several miles northeast of town as you follow U.S. 31 to reach the junction of M-22. You'll know you've arrived because on your left you'll see the humongous **Little River Casino Resort** (231/723-1535 or 888/568-2244, www.lrcr.com). If you feel lucky, they feature 1,300 slot machines, three restaurants, a 292-room hotel, and live entertainment. I'd wager, though, that you'll favor the sure bet that comes when you start riding north on M-22.

Gradually the ride begins to improve as you lose the last traces of stop-and-go traffic and enter soft and rolling hills that lead to the village of Onekama, "The Town on Two Lakes" (Lake Portage and Lake Michigan). It's like a time warp, almost, as you pass the quiet old businesses

The Lake Michigan Book Club meeting on the shore at sunset. Lake Michigan is a perfect riding companion, and the roads often lead you to beautiful overlooks such as these.

and taverns and then the road spins past apple orchards and willow and birch trees. Every so often Lake Michigan appears between the hills or through the trees, and it all starts to look like the vintage postcards from your grandparents' Michigan vacation.

The road is low and level and a few miles past Arcadia it rises a few hundred feet. At this point, stop at the pullout and elevated observation deck on your left. Now your gamble pays off with a view of Lake Michigan that is so astounding I had to order an extra box of exclamation points. It's hard to fathom what you're looking at because while it's just a lake, it's so much more. From the highest deck, beachcombers are mere specks, and you can't even begin to see clear to the other side—that's about 70 miles west. The southern shore is about 260 miles south, and about 150 miles north these waters flow into Lake Huron.

Riding north again with Lake Michigan by your side, you're on the Midwest equivalent of the Pacific Coast Highway. Although you may not see Lake Michigan as much as you'd like, other small lakes appear. After you cross a lonely country bridge in Elberta the road twists around to lead to a T at M-115 and M-22. Here, turn left into Frankfort, navigating a few more jogs to stay on M-22. Stick with it because as it shoots north you'll glide around the western shores of Crystal Lake, which is so massive it may be Great Lake, Jr. More lakes provide additional waterfront riding—Long Lake, Platte Lake, and Little Platte Lake—and soon you enter the southern edge of **Sleeping Bear Dunes National Lakeshore** (888/334-8499, www.sleepingbeardunes.com) whose 70,000 acres encompass 35 miles of sandy beaches and the world's largest moving dunes. Throughout this preserve, M-22 does what it does best: skirting along the shoreline or hiding beneath canopy roads and then sweeping along the contour of the state.

© NANCY HOWELL

Hidden in the glare of sunset is 22,400-square mile Lake Michigan.

It's been a full day and from Leland trusty M-22 scoots around Lake Leelanau as it winds its way up to Northport. If there's time before sunset, a string of small roads snake up to the very tip of the peninsula and into **Leelanau State Park** (231/386-5422, http://leelanaustatepark. com) where you'll find the 1858 Grand Traverse Lighthouse that guided sailors and their ships safely into the Manitou Passage and Grand Traverse Bay for well over a century. From Northport, M-22 boomerangs back to the south and when you reach the village of Omena you're in for a treat. The road latches itself to the bay and delivers a nice waterfront view all the way down to the second casino of the day (the Leelanau Sands in Peshawbestown) before reaching the resort town of Suttons Bay, which is filled with shops, restaurants, and galleries and is well worth more time. But I had none. At dusk I could feel the chill and I followed the road hugging the shoreline of Grand Traverse

Bay. The water was clean and glacier-crisp and the road low and level and perfect. Unlike the coastline of my beloved Florida, I had seen no massive developments since leaving Ludington, only small and well-kept villages protected by generations of vacationers.

Sixteen miles past Suttons Bay I was in the heart of Traverse City.

TRAVERSE CITY PRIMER

If you visualize Michigan history, images will likely include Indians, French trappers, lumberjacks, anglers, and priests.

Those are the images you'll call up when you learn about Traverse City.

The first explorers to arrive were Indian hunters and French traders who, after paddling the long crossing across the mouth of the bay, exclaimed *"sacre bleu!"* and dubbed the area *La Grande Traverse.* But neither they, nor the Ottawa and Chippewa, stuck around. It wasn't until 1839 that Peter Dougherty, a young

Presbyterian minister, was sent by the church's Board of Missions to establish a church, school, and settlement near the tip of the Old Mission Peninsula. A decade later and further south came the creation of a remote sawmill town.

Dubbed Traverse City in 1852, new roads opened up new opportunities for additional sawmills and over the next half century the town's lumber barons used their profits to build elaborate mansions and their product to create ornate Queen Anne–style homes. Several blocks away, mill workers carved out their own community, creating an area known at times as Baghdad or Little Bohemia or Slabtown. Yet all enjoyed the economic boom that came in 1885 with the arrival of the Northern Michigan Asylum. Given the belief at the time that healthy food, exercise, and a nice setting could cure mental illnesses, the population of the state institution eventually surpassed that of the town itself.

As you may have guessed, over time the lumber was depleted and new methods of psychology made the institution obsolete. So the town had to look for a renewable economic engine. In time, they came to rely on peaches, apples, grapes, and especially cherries.

For quite a while now, cherries have outperformed lumber by a long shot. In the Grand Traverse region, trees are producing an estimated *360 million pounds* of cherries annually; enough to make one honking big pie and to earn Traverse City bragging rights as home of July's National Cherry Festival. Today the city is in a comfortable place as a destination for boating, sailing, kayaking, wine tasting, and tourism.

ON THE ROAD: TRAVERSE CITY

One of the best parts of Traverse City is its waterfront. A casual ride can take you

on a gentle tour along Grand Traverse Bay which you first saw riding down the eastern edge of the Leelanau Peninsula after leaving Suttons Bay. In Traverse City you'll see that Grand Traverse Bay is separated into east and west bays by the **Old Mission Peninsula** (www.oldmission.com). This is a great place to kayak, ride, and explore.

Highway 37 is an easy two-lane that leads up to the peninsula's tip, often running through the woods or past orchards and vineyards and often skimming along the shoreline. When you reach the end of Highway 37 at the very northern edge, you'll roll right into **Lighthouse Park,** which spotlights the Old Mission Lighthouse, built in 1870 as a safeguard to keep ships away from Old Mission Point.

About three miles south is the village of Old Mission, which was built on the idyllic spot first selected in 1839 by missionary Peter Dougherty. Many of the original mission structures are still standing and in use, including the general store and the **Old Mission Inn** (18599 Mission Rd., 231/223-7770, www.oldmissioninn.com).

Feeling the warmth of the sun on the shores of frigid Lake Michigan, with the Arcadian Peninsula in the background.

If you have time, invest it here because there's so much more to see. Explore the back roads on your own and you'll find more bed-and-breakfasts, restaurants, antique shops, markets, and wineries. By the time you're ready to return to TC, about midway down Highway 37, watch for Peninsula Drive on your right. Veering off of the main road will give you a final gift: a nice waterfront tour along the western side of Grand Traverse Bay.

PULL IT OVER: TRAVERSE CITY HIGHLIGHTS
Attractions and Adventures

If the weather's right, there are six public beaches available to you, three on each bay. You can get off the shore and on the water aboard the schooner *Manitou* (S. West Bay Shore Dr., 231/941-2000 or 800/678-0383, www.tallshipsailing.com) which sets sail on several two-hour cruises daily during the summer. They offer specialty cruises as well.

To understand the history of the town, the **Grand Traverse Heritage Center** (322 Sixth St., 231/995-0313, www.gtheritagecenter.org) is an historical and cultural museum within the city's 1903 Carnegie Library building. From here, volunteers lead 90-minute walking tours ($10) that will help you understand the impressive history of the city while visiting historical sights and homes. Call ahead for tour times.

Remember that TC was once home to the Northern Michigan Asylum which, after decades of sitting vacant, became the focus of one of the nation's largest historic re-use projects. The nearly 500-acre site is now the **Grand Traverse Commons** (www.thevillagetc.com), an urban village of shops, restaurants, apartments, and galleries. In addition to preserving the castle-like Italianate 19th-century buildings, the wooded campus is popular with hikers and cyclists.

Thanks to its boom years a century ago, in addition to the asylum TC had an abundance of historic buildings to recycle. One reborn with the help of an exquisite $8.5 million restoration is the **City Opera House** (106 E. Front St., 231/941-8082, www.cityoperahouse.org). If there's a comedian, play, or special event here...go. It's incredible.

Downtown, the **State Theatre** (233 E. Front St., 231/947-3446) is a restored Art Deco movie house that features first-run art films and is the main venue for July's Traverse City Film Festival.

Finally, if Napa Valley's too far a reach, this region of Michigan features sandy soil with good drainage which has fostered more than 50 wineries with vintners producing award-winning Reislings and Pinot Grigios. For a complete list of wineries and contact information on tours and times, visit www.visittraversecity.com.

Shopping

Just a few blocks from the bay in downtown Traverse City is Front Street, the main shopping district with about 150 boutiques, galleries, and shops, as well as a number of downtown events held throughout the year. For hep fashions, check out **Ella's Vintage Clothing** (157 E. Front Street, 231/947-9401, www.ellasvintage-clothing.com), which stocks retro threads for cool cats and chicks. Outdoor enthusiasts should head to **Streamside Orvis** (223 E. Front St., 231/933-9300, www.streamsideorvis.com), which carries fly fishing tackle, upland hunting gear, sporting gifts, and outdoor clothing. For a comprehensive list of merchants, dining, services, festivals, and attractions, check www.downtowntc.com or call 231/922-2050.

For practical shopping, head over to

the **Grand Traverse Mall** (3200 South Airport Rd. W., 231/922-0077, www.grandtraversemall.com), with more than 100 stores, anchored by Target, JCPenney, and T.J. Maxx.

Blue-Plate Specials

It's a long way around the bay, and there are restaurants nearly everywhere you ride. Assuming you'll be based near downtown, try **Lil Bo** (540 W. Front St., 231/946-6925, www.lilbo.com), established in 1932 and these days known as the "Cheers" of TC. Live music can be Irish or Latin or whatever, and menu items cover burgers, pastas, salads, and gnocchis.

Handcrafted brews are served in a renovated candy factory at the **North Peak Brewing Company** (400 W. Front St., 231/941-7325, www.northpeak.net), along with hearth-baked pizzas, big specialty sandwiches, steaks, seafood, and ribs.

Bubba's (428 E. Front St., 231/995-0570, www.tcfood.com) mixes things up with a menu focused on breakfasts, burgers, wraps, and Mexican food.

Located downtown on the banks of the Boardman River, **Fire Fly** (310 Cass St., 231/932-1310, www.tcfood.com) is a little more upscale casual. The popular hangout for locals specializes in steaks, sushi, and happy hour specials from brews to martinis.

Watering Holes

In addition to the brewpub and bar-enhanced restaurants included in the preceding section, check out **Sleder's Family Tavern** (717 Randolph St., 231/947-9213, www.sleders.com). Built in 1882 as a social club for Bohemian woodworkers, it's still a favorite watering hole in TC's Slabtown Neighborhood. You'll love the original carved mahogany bar and Randolph, the unfortunate moose who's become the bar's mascot. **Union Street Station** (117 S. Union St., 231/941-1930) loves riders. There's always live music (rock or jazz or blues and sometimes even Kid Rock himself) and drink specials everyone can afford. Over at **The Loading Dock** (205 Lake Ave., 231/941-4422) patrons order $1 drafts on Wednesday's Pint Night, listen to local musicians live, and tap into one of their sixteen draft beers.

Shut-Eye

There are more than 4,000 guest rooms in the area, some in cabins and cottages. The town also has mom and pop motels and the most comprehensive and up to date list can be found at www.visittraversecity.com, with links to each.

Chain Drive

These chain hotels are in town, or within 10 miles of the city center:

Best Western, Comfort Inn, Courtyard by Marriott, Days Inn, Econo Lodge, Fairfield Inn, Hampton Inn, Holiday Inn, Howard Johnson, Knights Inn, Motel 6, Quality Inn, Sleep Inn, Super 8, Travelodge

For more information, including phone numbers and websites, see page 439.

ON THE ROAD: TRAVERSE CITY TO MACKINAW CITY

Congratulations, you're about to enjoy one of the most amazing roads in the Midwest. Truly.

When you leave Traverse City, the road rolls in tandem with Grand Traverse Bay, on top of the water almost. It's a clean and decent waterfront four-lane for about five miles before it scoots away from the water and swaps that scenery for quintessential images of Michigan: evergreen, cherry, peach, apricot, and pear trees. There are produce stands and signs promoting items like Farmer White's Fresh Baked Pies. About 20 miles north of town you cross the 45th parallel (which you may have done en route to Northport); this means you're at the exact midpoint between the equator and the North Pole.

For now, the road is low and flat. Ubiquitous firewood is sold for $3 a stack or armload or bundle, but there are still plenty of trees to go around—what's left helps create Michigan's color season, when the leaves turn and riders and motorists hit the road. For many, it's the last chance for adventure before winter. Cruising up these coastal two-lane roads reveals some of the most spectacular autumn landscapes anywhere.

Even without the changing leaves, the sights are enough to satisfy at any time of the year. At some old farms, barns have been recycled as gift shops or produce stands. I'm pretty certain Playskool artists studied in Michigan: Nearly all of the farms have that comforting cartoonish image, with wide green valleys, lush meadows, and cattle, goats, and sheep all grazing before large red barns accented by crisp white latticework.

It's a pleasing country ride for about an hour before reaching one of America's most beautiful towns. This is Charlevoix; you'll know you've arrived because traffic is backed up as travelers creep through town (especially on weekends). To your right, a terraced city park sweeps down a hill before an open bandshell, while on the gleaming bay the marina is speckled with sailboats, motor yachts, and cabin cruisers. A nostalgic Rexall Drugs joins block after block of gift shops and lofts and restaurants and fudge shops. If time permits, stay for lunch or some window-shopping and explore the lakefront neighborhoods, especially the one near Park Avenue and Grant Street. In the 1930s, Earl A. Young

created extraordinary non-linear fairytale homes built out of boulders and cedar shake roofs. If these Brothers Grimm–style homes impress you, a few blocks north is Boulder Manor and even more examples of his work.

The beauty of the town travels beyond the town limits, marked by a row of flowers running along the curbside for nearly a mile, before returning you to the steady pace of U.S. 31. Five miles on, a roadside park awaits you on a perch above Lake Michigan. The view from here shows off a string of islands about a dozen miles offshore. As you slip into Petoskey, you've arrived in yet another charming town that has a thriving downtown where shoppers cover several blocks of independent stores and restaurants. Having used up my allotment of spare time in Charlevoix, I rode on and left town under the watch of a row of Victorian homes on a bluff, each gifted with a commanding view of the bay.

What they see, though, scarcely approaches what awaits you on M-119. While you could take U.S. 31 clear to Mackinaw City, just past Bay Harbor coastal road M-119 opens up on your left and points you towards Cross Village about 30 miles north. The first town you hit along M-119, Harbor Springs, is just as nice as all the other communities you've seen. As you leave town the road elevates you onto a bluff where a sign marks the entrance to "A Tunnel of Trees," a near-perfect arboreal cave that places this stretch near the top of my list of favorite roads. It's an amazingly fun and compact two-lane that scribbles through the countryside and along the shoreline. There are twists and then open fields; there are sharp drops and then revelations of broad Lake Michigan. As you ride deeper into rural Michigan you are traveling through pristine farmland and on a long road that's absolutely perfect for

Mighty Mac

Anyone who's reached Mackinaw City will tell you all about the Mackinac Bridge (myself included). Excuse them because it really is an amazing feat of engineering. Envisioned in the late 1800s, this was known for decades as "The Bridge Which Couldn't Be Built." Before it arrived, at the start of hunting season locals anxious to reach the Upper Peninsula would line up a day in advance for the car ferries, the 16-mile traffic jam flowing down to Cheboygan.

When the $100 million bridge finally got started in 1954, workers sank the double-walled cylinders that form the bases of the two main tower piers into the bedrock of the lake floor 300 feet below the surface. After

A view of "Mighty Mac"—the Mackinac Bridge that spans the Straits of Mackinac—as seen from the shores of Mackinaw City.

that, iron workers strung more than 42,000 miles of wire in the creation of the two main bridge cables. When the bridge was completed in 1957, the finished product was even more impressive. Its total length, from anchor to anchor, is five miles (26,372 feet): the suspension bridge stretches 8,614 feet; the main span rolls for 3,800 feet; and clearance beneath the midspan is an impressive 155 feet. Helping hold it all together are 4.85 million steel rivets. Each year, four million vehicles pay $1.50 per axle to cross the 55-story bridge. When you ride across it, the towers climb 300 feet above your head, you have a commanding view of the deep blue waters of lakes Michigan and Huron, and you can feel your tires wobble on the steel grating. Just past the north toll plaza, look for a turnout into Bridge View Park for a picture perfect shot of you, your bike, and the Bridge Which *Could* Be Built.

This is not a Christmas tree farm, just a typical scene along one of Michigan's wonderful two-lane roads.

your choice of a slow and easy pleasure ride or exciting Le Mans rally. The road envelops you and your bike in the woods and even outside of color season it is phenomenally cool. Even better, since most motorists opt for a direct shot on U.S. 31, this weaving road is nearly deserted as it climbs higher and higher onto the bluffs and to a speck of a place called Good Hart where the road again narrows and enters a winding seven-mile stretch through the woods, breaking into open fields peppered with bales of hay.

Much too soon, M-119 ends in Cross Village and puts you at the doorstep of **Legs Inn** (6425 Lake Shore Dr., 231/526-2281, www.legsinn.com), a "monument to nature" that's part restaurant, bar, pool room, and botanical garden, built in the 1920s from stone, fallen trees, driftwood, and found materials gathered and re-assembled by Polish immigrant Stanley Smolak. It's popular with travelers, who stop to enjoy a Polish meal. Afterward,

look for two signs outside the inn: One points east to C66, the other suggests the "Scenic Road to Mackinaw City" via Lake Shore Drive. Which would you choose? *Correct.*

A few minutes later you're four miles down Lake Shore Drive, where you've conquered a series of twists and are seeing a landscape that packs a lot of voltage all the way to a "T" where, if you hang a left, the road drags you further along Lake Shore Drive to high dunes and pullouts that open views to Lake Michigan. Then there are several miles where the ice and snow and water and weather have roughed up the road, but never so much that you won't enjoy the changing scenery of rural fields and marshes filled with cattails and an almost complete lack of towns and traffic.

When Lake Shore Drive has had enough, it nudges you to the east to hook up with C81. Now you are on a long, straight shot north that'll deliver one more

© NANCY HOWELL

With motorized vehicles banned on Mackinac Island, we traded in the motorcycle for a tandem. Perfect for the location, bicycles can take you to the farthest reaches of the small island.

brush with lakefront riding before placing you right in the heart of Mackinaw City and at the northernmost tip of Michigan's Lower Peninsula.

MACKINAW CITY PRIMER

You know who was vacationing here a few years back? American Indians. Living in the area from about 1000 B.C. to 1650 A.D., they paddled to the "Place of the Great Turtle" (now Mackinac Island) each summer to fish for trout, pike, sturgeon, herring and whitefish. It was a great summer getaway until about 1671, when Europeans showed up and Father Jacques Marquette helped create some missions to suggest to the Huron Indians that everything they knew about the universe was wrong.

About a century later, French soldiers established Fort Michilimackinac as a strategic depot for the Great Lakes fur trade, after which the British acquired it at the end of the Seven Years' War. To safeguard the fort during the American Revolution,

the Brits dismantled it and moved it over to the limestone bluffs of Mackinac Island. Like a game of checkers, it went to the Americans after the Revolution, back to the Brits after the War of 1812, and then back to the Americans again.

After folks had had their fill of wars and furs, fishing took the lead and set a more placid pace for what the town would become: a tourist destination. Today fudge is the main commodity, while the focal point is the impressive Mackinac Bridge. Oddly, those are reasons enough to keep you here.

ON THE ROAD: MACKINAW CITY

Hitting the road in Mackinaw City will have to take a backseat to a modified road trip on Mackinac Island. Three ferry services run across the Straits of Mackinac, the waters that separate Lake Michigan and Lake Huron. The oldest is **Shepler's** (www.sheplersferry.com). This is the one

Weird and slightly eerie, the massive Cherry Bowl drive-in possesses the power to pull you over for a closer look.

I took and I was impressed by how clean, professional, efficient, and fast it is.

Start as early as you can. In about 15 minutes, you'll have crossed the waters, seen the bridge from a new angle, and docked inside Haldimand Bay which, if you've ever landed at a Caribbean port and were immediately assaulted by hustlers and the sound of traffic, is a pleasant surprise. Stepping ashore, the only sounds are the clip-clop of horse-drawn carriages and views that reveal this anachronistic paradise.

Since 1898 motorized traffic has been banned from the island so saddle up on a bicycle. It's a good investment. Rental operations are within a few feet of the dock and if you pedal the entire island you'll travel just over eight miles on the only state highway were cars are banned. On a bicycle you'll clear the fudge shops and boutiques and pass vacation homes, restaurants, and a church en route to Arch Rock (visible from the road, 782 steps will get you to the top). Then you'll ride some waterfront paths along the Straits of Mackinac. A single speed is fine for level riding, but opt for the ten-speeds if you plan to scale the 150-foot bluffs to reach de-commissioned **Fort Mackinac** (231 436-4100 or 906/847-3328, www.mackinacparks. com, $11) which, like the mainland fort, has more than a dozen original buildings filled with exhibits, interactive displays, and special presentations on island history. You can pick up facts on military medicine and soldier life of the era, watch rifle and cannon demonstrations, see re-enactments of courts martial, and tour historic buildings. A film presentation is shown in the commissary, a museum store occupies the soldiers' barracks, and there are demonstrations at the Benjamin Blacksmith Shop. Give him some time and maybe he can pound out a new bike. Or visit the legendary **Grand Hotel** (906/847-3331 or 800/334-7263, www.grandhotel.com), perhaps best known for its supporting role in the Christopher Reeve film *Somewhere In Time*. You can tour the inside of the hotel for $10 and the view from the promenade is worth the price of admission. A glance is all I could afford, and its eclectic decor and the coachman who wears a top hat, knee-high boots, and a red riding jacket helps explain why it's been around since 1887 and why its guests pay about $600 a night. If you're persuaded to spend the night but can't swing the Grand, there are other inns and hotels on the island.

But you'll probably have just as much fun back in Mackinaw City. And they have fudge.

PULL IT OVER: MACKINAW CITY HIGHLIGHTS
Attractions and Adventures

For a town of less than 1,000, Mackinaw City has a bunch of stuff to do. Drawing you towards the shore is the Mackinac Bridge, which changes appearance between dawn and dusk and with every season. One of the best views is by the **Old Mackinaw Point Lighthouse** which was completed in 1889 and kept the coast clear until it was de-commissioned in 1957. Only a few hundred yards east of the bridge, it's been restored to its 1910 appearance. Go inside the old keeper's quarters, where costumed interpreters will show you original fresnel lenses, some hands-on displays, and offer a guided tour to the top. The large lighthouse is just a small part of the 625-acre **Colonial Michilimackinac** (102 W. Straits Ave., 231/436-4100, www. mackinacparks.com, $11) a reconstructed 1715 French fur-trading village and military outpost. It starts with an orientation movie and museum. Inside are more than a dozen reconstructed buildings with exhibits, displays, and period furnishings. They also feature living history re-enactments and musket and cannon firings from the

Brits' 1770 occupation, as well as scenes from the Revolutionary era.

Believe it or not, even the Great Lakes can freeze up, which is why there are icebreakers like the *Mackinaw*. De-commissioned in 2006, it's now the centerpiece of the **Icebreaker Mackinaw Maritime Museum** (131 S. Huron, 231/436-9825, www. themackinaw.org, $10) which opens up the ship for a self-guided tour of the bridge, captain's quarters, engine room, and more. Docents are there to answer questions.

Most folks gravitate north of Central Avenue, drawn by the sight of the Mackinac Bridge, but a few blocks south is a beach reserved for guests at adjacent hotels, as well as a 1,200-foot long fishing pier. Lastly, if you plan to cross over to Mackinac Island, you'll likely take one of three ferry services. They are each high speed, each take about 18 minutes to make the crossing, each offer free parking, and each charge about $25 round-trip. I can vouch for **Shepler's Ferry** (556 E. Central, 906/643-9440 or 800/828-6157, www.sheplersferry.com), and there's the **Star Line** (711 S. Huron St., 231/436-5045, www.mackinacferry. com), as well as the **Arnold Mackinac Island Ferry** (801 S. Huron, 231/436-5542 or 800/542-8528, www.arnoldline.com).

Shopping

The future of Mackinaw City is dependent on consumption of fudge, so do your part and visit one of a dozen fudge shops found on Central Avenue alone. Most stores are along this wide boulevard, and inventory centers around gifts, candy, T-shirts, and souvenirs. Aside from the **Island Bookstore** (215 E. Central Ave., 231/436-2665, www.islandbookstore.com) most fade into a sameness; although a few blocks away is **Mackinaw Outfitters** (220 South Huron Ave., 231/436-4066, www.mackinawoutfittersstore.com), a 30,000 square foot superstore that probably has everything you'd need for fishing, camping, archery, hunting, and boating.

Blue-Plate Specials

Here since 1958, **Darrow's** (301 Louvigny, 231/436-5514, www.darrowsrestaurant. com) remains a popular family restaurant for locals and visitors. It's slightly removed from the center of town, but close enough to detour a few blocks for good food, fair prices, and large portions. Come for the fresh baked bread, soups made daily, brewed coffee, and homemade pie. Also popular with tourists is **Mama Mia's Pizza** (231 E. Central Ave., 231/436-5534), which packs 'em in the brightly lit corner eatery. Upstairs is a free museum that features pictures, stories, and artifacts from the creation of the Mackinac Bridge.

Most restaurants serve fish (whitefish mostly) and one place you can buy it without breaking the bank is **Scalawags** (226 E. Central Ave., 231/436-7777, www.scalawagswhitefish.com), a link in a small chain. It sells affordable baskets of fried whitefish, shrimp, perch, and walleye, along with fries, chicken fingers, and chowder. Opened in 1972, **Cunninghams** (312 Central Ave., 231/436-8821, www. cunninghamsrestaurant.com) is a family restaurant that prides itself on its homemade pasties, soups, chilis, sandwiches, strip steak, fried chicken, liver and onions, pork chops, and whitefish. For hefty appetites, **Anna's Country Buffet** (416 S. Huron Ave., 231/436-5195, www.mackinawdining.com) is an all-you-can-eat experience with chicken, sausage, meatballs, vegetables, salad bar, and soft serve ice cream, as well as hand-carved ham and prime rib for dinner. For breakfast try the **Pancake Chef** (337 E. Central Ave., 231/436-5579, www.pancakechef.com). Their strength is a variety of pancakes:

buttermilk, blueberry, applejack, strawberry, and banana. They are also open for lunch and dinner with a menu that includes salads, wraps, burgers, meatloaf, and whitefish.

Watering Holes

After dropping in a few nightspots, I gathered I was just visiting smoking lounges that happened to serve drinks. The case is proven at **O'Reilly's Irish Pub** (401 W. Central Ave., 231/436-5509, www.oreillysmackinawpub.com) with its beers on taps, a cooler full of bottled beers, a full liquor bar, and classy high-back booths that give you a nice sense of privacy. Smoke also drifts through the **Keyhole Bar and Grill** (323 W. Central Ave., 231/436-7911), which seems quite popular with locals—as it's been since it first opened as a bar in 1893. In addition to beers in cans, on tap, and in bottles, a pool table and bar food adds to the appeal.

Relatively smoke-free and quite stylish is the wilderness lodge–looking **Dixie Saloon** (401 W. Central, 231/436-5449, www.dixiesaloon.com). It's been here since the late 1800s when the Old Dixie Highway ran from Florida all the way to here. The highway has long been overshadowed by I-75, but the Saloon is still here, showing off its cool cathedral ceiling lodge look, saddle seats, and menu of steaks, ribs, burgers and drinks. First rate.

Shut-Eye

As a resort town, there are numerous hotels and motels as well as inns, weekly rentals, and cottages. Check with the visitors bureau for a complete list.

Motels and Motor Courts

If you need room to spread out, the **Baymont Inn & Suites** (109 S. Nicolet St., 231/436-7737, www.baymontinns.

com, $69 and up) is a few blocks from downtown and throws in a nice breakfast and a range of amenities. If you don't mind the drive, you'll likely find lower rates and a rekindled sense of nostalgia at motels a few miles from town. Check out the **Chief Motel** (10470 U.S. 23, 231/436-7981 or 800/968-1511, www.chiefmotel.info, $69 and up); the **Flamingo Motel** (13959 Mackinaw Hwy., 231/436-8751 or 866/436-8751, www.mackinaw-city-motel.com, $50 and up); and the **Mackinac Motor Lodge &** **Resort** (10346 U.S. 23, 231/436-5741, www.mackinacmotorlodge.com, $65, add $20 for kitchenette).

Chain Drive

These chain hotels are in town, or within 10 miles of the city center: **Best Western, Clarion, Comfort Inn, Courtyard by Marriott, Days Inn, Econo Lodge, Hampton Inn, Holiday Inn, Quality Inn, Ramada, Super 8** For more information, including phone numbers and websites, see page 439.

Resources for Riders

Magical Michigan Tour

Michigan Travel Information
Michigan Beachtowns—www.beachtowns.org
Michigan Department of Natural Resources—www.michigan.gov/dnr
Michigan Division of Tourism—888/784-7328, www.michigan.org
Michigan Road Conditions—www.ohsp.state.mi.us
M-22 (Autumn) Color Tour—www.m22colortour.com
West Michigan Lighthouses—www.westmichiganlighthouses.com

Local and Regional Information
Charlevoix Chamber of Commerce—231/547-2101 or 800/951-2101,
    www.charlevoix.org
Ludington Area Convention and Visitors Bureau—800/542-4600 or
    877/420-6618, www.ludingtoncvb.com
Mackinaw City Chamber—800/577-3113, www.mackinawchamber.com
Mackinac Island Tourism Bureau—906/847-6418 or 800/454-5227,
    www.mackinacisland.org
Mackinaw Area Visitors Bureau—231/436-5664 or 800/666-0160,
    www.mackinawcity.com
Sleeping Bear Dunes Visitors Bureau—888/334-8499,
    www.sleepingbeardunes.com
Traverse City Convention and Visitors Bureau—231/947-1120 or 800/940-1120,
    www.visittraversecity.com
West Michigan Tourist Association—616/245-2217 or 800/442-2084,
    www.wmta.org

Michigan Motorcycle Shops
Classic Motor Sports—3939 S. Blue Star Dr., Traverse City, 231/943-9344,
    www.classictc.com
Great Escapes Motorsports—136 N. U.S. 31, Traverse City, 231/943-9800
U-Win Motorsports—2284 W. U.S. 10, Ludington, 231/757-8946,
    www.uwinmotorsports.com
White Road Motorcycle Repair—1051 W. White Rd., Free Soil (Ludington),
    231/464-5038

Wisconsin Thumb Run

Milwaukee, Wisconsin to Door County, Wisconsin

Large cities are so tightly packed that it can be tough to map out a casual ride. But if you're astride a Harley and avoid Milwaukee, you'll have hell to pay at your next poker run since this is where Harley-Davidson was born...and reborn. After experiencing the H-D factory and its magnificent museum, the curve of Lake Michigan will help you escape into a Scandinavian slice of America.

MILWAUKEE PRIMER

Bratwurst. Beer. Baseball. Blue-collar workers. Most Americans have a pretty good idea of what makes Milwaukee tick. We learned about it by watching beer commercials, Fonzie, and face-painting cheeseheads.

But the 600,000-plus citizens here don't see themselves as beer-guzzling Norwegian-, German-, and Polish-Americans (who share the city with a tight contingent of Italians and Irish). They see their city as a smaller, friendlier version of Chicago, and their museums, galleries, and ethnic

festivals offer proof that they are, in fact, patrons of the arts and proud of their cultural diversity.

This may all be true, but chances are you won't appreciate any of it. You'll be here just long enough to see a brewery, catch a ball game, eat some bratwurst, and learn the story of America's most successful motorcycle.

Dat's a purdy good day dere den, eh?

ON THE ROAD: MILWAUKEE

It's hard to find a great ride inside a metropolitan area, but in exotic cities like Miami and Las Vegas, you just have to go for it. Milwaukee certainly isn't exotic, but an act of Congress mandates it as a stop for Harley riders.

Despite the interstates and some less-than-attractive neighborhoods, it's fairly easy to get around on your bike and see a few sights. And the sight you need to see here is the **Harley-Davidson Museum** (400 Canal St., 877/436-8738, $16). The $30 million, 130,000 square foot museum opened on 20

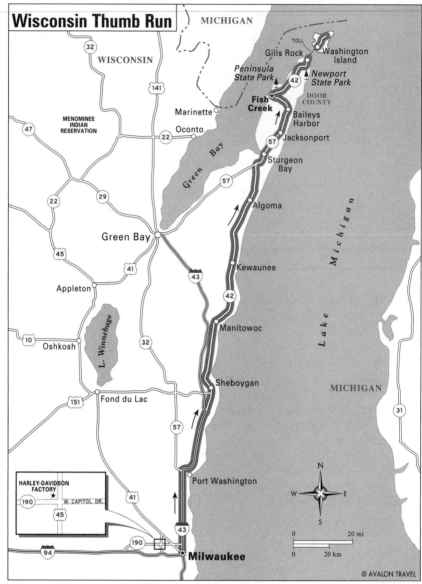

Wisconsin Thumb Run

MICHIGAN

WISCONSIN

32

141

47

MENOMINEE
INDIAN
RESERVATION

Marinette

Oconto

22

22

29

Green Bay

45

41

Appleton

10

Oshkosh

L. Winnebago

32

151

Fond du Lac

57

41

43

HARLEY-DAVIDSON
FACTORY ★
190   W. CAPITOL DR.
45

94   190

Milwaukee

Peninsula State Park

Gills Rock   TOLL   Washington Island

42   *Newport State Park*

Fish Creek

DOOR COUNTY

Baileys Harbor

Jacksonport

57

Sturgeon Bay

57

Algoma

Kewaunee

42

Manitowoc

Sheboygan   MICHIGAN

Port Washington

31

Green Bay

Lake Michigan

N
W   E
S

0   20 mi
0   20 km

© AVALON TRAVEL

Route: Milwaukee to Door County via Port Washington, Sheboygan, Manitowoc, Two Rivers

Distance: Approximately 175 miles

First Leg: Milwaukee to Fish Creek (175 miles)

Helmet Laws: Wisconsin does not require helmets.

© NANCY HOWELL

An iconic image outside Harley-Davidson's Juneau Avenue headquarters. The world-renowned motorcycle manufacturer began operations here in 1903.

acres along the Menemonee River in downtown Milwaukee in July 2008. While the outdoors are impressive (catch the sculpture of the Harley-riding hill climber) it's what's on the inside that counts.

Of today's motorcycle manufacturers, H-D probably has the best story to tell—and so they do. A timeline of the company's history tells you about its entrepreneurial start in 1903 and the challenges it faced during the Great Depression. After World War II came years of prosperity but then the company took a dive in the 1970s. After buying itself back from AMF, H-D had the good fortune to hook up with a fortunate generation that had the luxury to buy motorcycles and hit the road.

An audio tour leads you through the museum where the Archives contains rare H-D documents, historical photographs, cool videos that'll get you worked up, and retro motorcycling apparel that may persuade you to do a wardrobe makeover. There are special exhibits, such as Elvis and the 1956 KH that he purchased two weeks before the release of "Heartbreak Hotel." That bike is here and since I'm as much an Elvis fan as a motorcycle fan, I'm still trying to figure out how to pull off a heist.

In the Engine Room, you'll see how science and engineering has created a machine that transports middle-aged riders back a few decades. There are free and for a fee tours that appeal to history buffs and hard-core Harley fans, and during warmer weather Bike Nights are held once a week. Don't miss the museum's two restaurants that serve hearty American dishes: **Café Racer** for quick food, **Motor** for more upscale entrées.

While I once would have directed you to the suburb of Wauwatosa for a free tour of Harley's powertrain factory, that facility was consolidated into another location in 2009. Instead, before or after you see the museum think about taking an urban ride that motorcyclists love. For this, start in the heart of town and ride north past the beaches on Lincoln Memorial Drive. Slowly the road leads to a slow and steady run along Lake Michigan and onto Lake Drive, a spectacular avenue lined with the unique scenery of historic mansions. When Lake Drive loses its luster miles ahead, many riders simply make a U-turn at Brown Deer Road and repeat this incredible ride in reverse.

Afterward, do what the locals do: Dig into a bratwurst, sit in the stands at a game, hang out in a tavern in the historic Third Ward or on Water Street, or dance a polka at an ethnic fest.

PULL IT OVER: MILWAUKEE HIGHLIGHTS
Attractions and Adventures

You may be inspired to see what else

Milwaukee's known for: Breweries. About 80 of them were here in the 1880s, but most have faded away. For a visit to a stupendous macrobrewery, ride over to the **MillerCoors Brewing Company** (4251 W. State St., 414/931-2337, www.millerbrewing.com). The free one-hour tour (hours vary; call ahead) includes a walk through the packaging line and shipping center, brew house, museum, and historic caves. Memories should come flooding back of your college party days, if you and your buddies ever ponied up enough cash for a half million cases of beer, that is. Yes, a *half million cases* are stacked in the shipping center. There are also giant brew kettles, high-speed bottling lines, and best of all, free frosty samples served in the cozy saloon at the Miller Inn.

Milwaukee hasn't forgotten its brewing roots, and microbrewery tours are equally popular. Opened in 1985, **Sprecher Brewery** (701 W. Glendale Ave., 414/964-2739, www.sprecherbrewery.com, $4) has one of the more popular tours. Five miles north of downtown, it brews traditional beers and gourmet sodas and wraps up its tours with samples of any 14 beers (Black Bavarian, Pub Brown Ale, Irish Stout, Russian Imperial Stout...) served amid oompah music in an indoor Oktoberfest-style beer garden tent. Tour times vary, so call in advance for reservations.

Opened in 1987 with a total output of 60 barrels, the **Lakefront Brewery** (1872 N. Commerce St., 414/372-8800, www.lakefrontbrewery.com, $6) now cranks out handcrafted beer in traditional and innovative styles. Depending on the season, it brews up pilsners, stein beer, cherry beer, pumpkin beer, ales, coffee stout, and root beer. Tours are frequent (check online or call for schedules) and your admission includes a free pint glass and two 8-ounce shots of beer.

Milwaukee is a fascinatingly diverse city and if you visit nearly any time between June and September, you're sure to hit one of the several massive ethnic festivals that take place at the lakefront Henry W. Maier Park. Each fest revels in the music, games, and foods of a foreign land: Asia, Mexico, Germany, Ireland, Africa, Poland, Italy, and so on. The biggest blowout of all is **Summerfest** (414/273-3378 or 800/273-3378, www.summerfest.com), the largest music festival in the world, with national acts appearing on a dozen stages.

In this town, the most popular outdoor activity is watching one of several professional teams. If you ride in on game day, you may want to join the fans of the **Milwaukee Brewers** baseball team (414/902-4000 or 800/933-7890, www.milwaukeebrewers.com). Tickets range from roughly $8–48. The **Milwaukee Bucks** basketball team (414/227-0500, www.bucks.com) are also in town, or you can go puck yourself at a **Milwaukee Admirals** AHL hockey game (414/227-0550, www.milwaukeeadmirals.com).

Blue-Plate Specials

Harley isn't the only Milwaukee institution. According to Glenn Fieber, stepson of the original Solly, "people from all over, everywhere" check into **Solly's Coffee Shop** (4629 N. Port Washington Rd., 414/332-8808) before checking into their hotels. Since 1936, locals and savvy travelers have been traveling a few minutes from downtown and settling in at Solly's twin horseshoe counters, where Milwaukee waitresses serve up hearty breakfasts, buttery sirloin burgers, and hand-scooped malts served in a steel can.

The oldest lunch counter in Milwaukee is at **Real Chili** (1625 W. Wells St., 414/342-6955). This independent purveyor of chili has been here since 1931,

The Motorcycle Museum

Although I list the Harley-Davidson Museum within the chapter, the company's influence on the pastime of motorcycling and the way it conveys an incredible story begun by two young tinkerers warrants this special section. There are no dinosaur bones or Van Goghs here, only motorcycles and a celebration of the culture.

Although it's a large complex, the story is easy to follow because the history of the company is told upstairs on the right side—the side with wooden floors—while the left side presents themed rooms (engines, Gypsy Rallies, Hill Climbers, etc.). Back on the main level, the story continues in 1948 and shows motorcycles in pop culture and as art and icons, and also takes you through the AMF years and how Harley rescued itself.

What's incredible is that of the fleet of motorcycles you see (and there are many), *97 percent* of them are in running condition and every model after 1926 has their original tires. Atop a 10x15 foot outline on the floor that reveals the dimension of the garage that William Harley and Arthur Davidson first worked in, a special case presents the oldest Harley in existence: A 1906 Model 2 Atmospheric Valve Single. A chronological line-up of motorcycles in the main hall reveals the quantum leap that came in the mid-1920s when a new frame and teardrop tank made them look like bikes we'd recognize today.

You'll also see the very first H-D catalogue from 1905; colorful ads from the earliest days of motorcycling; police bikes, military bikes, and sidecars; an exhibit on boardtrack racers; rallies; clubs and clothing; and a spotlight on pioneering women, like the amazing Vivian Bales who first rode across America in 1929, preceding the journeys in this book by more than *70 years*. What a gal. What a story. Don't miss it.

serving celebrities, pro ball players, politicians, and on-the-road travelers. Subs, tacos, chilidogs, and chili served over spaghetti and beans come in mild, medium, and hot. If you need a beer to take the sting out, head to its second location at 419 East Wells Street.

In the heart of downtown on the revitalized Riverwalk, **Rock Bottom** (740 N. Plankinton Ave., 414/276-3030) is a hoppin' spot, especially with its waterside patio on the Milwaukee River. Open for lunch and dinner, it's a good place to hang out, and its five microbrews, brick-oven pizzas, prime top sirloin, pork chops, and short ribs put it over the top—although the setting edges out the food. In the Historic Third Ward, the **Milwaukee Ale House** (233 N. Water St., 414/226-2337, www.ale-house.com) is another waterfront brewpub that is also a local favorite for its neighborhood feel, wide-ranging menu, twin decks that overlook the river, and music and dancing.

Watering Holes

Milwaukee's too large a city to ride around looking for a place to party, so you might want to settle down near the greatest concentration of nightspots. Along Water Street between State and Knapp, you'll find a number of worthy choices. This is the short list.

Water Street Brewery (1101 N. Water St., 414/272-1195, www.waterstreetbrewery.com) is a pub-style micro that serves 10 varieties of its own brews, plus an assortment of other micros. In addition to beer, it offers an extensive menu of fish, steaks, ribs, pizza, nachos, and other bar food. A big-screen TV comes out for big sports events.

McGillycuddy's (1135 N. Water St., 414/278-8888, www.mcgillycuddysmilwaukee.com) is the largest pub on the block. It combines the best elements of an Irish pub with an American sports bar, serving Guinness on tap, other Brit ales, and Irish stew. Order a mug and settle down on the huge patio.

Flannery's Bar (425 E. Wells St., 414/278-8586, www.flannerysmilwaukee.com) has live jazz and blues and makes it all sound better by serving draft pints of Guinness, Harp, and Stella Artois as well as other bottled domestics, imports, and wines.

Shut-Eye

There are a number of chains to choose from in the city, and among two independent options in town is the **Iron Horse Hotel** (500 West Florida St., 888/543-4766, www.theironhorsehotel.com, $149–399). Located across the bridge from the Harley museum, this motorcycle-themed luxury boutique hotel is upscale and designed specifically for riders, catering to motorcyclists by providing covered parking with rag bins and special packages that include check-in bags complete with the Iron Horse Hotel skull cap, sun screen, lip balm, packed lunches for your saddlebag, ride routes, and

suggestions for local bike-friendly spots throughout the area. On Thursdays (unless it's winter), Bike Night brings riders to The Yard for themed rallies. As far as the rooms go—they're urban chic.

In historic old cities like Milwaukee, Gilded Age hotels are plentiful. If your life has been leading to a Harley tour and you really want to live it up, the **Pfister Hotel** (424 E. Wisconsin Ave., 414/273-8222 or 800/558-8222, www.thepfisterhotel.com, $189 and up high season) has been a local legend since it opened in 1893. The lobby is elegant, and the rooms follow suit—celebs and sports stars stay here when they're in town.

Chain Drive

These chain hotels are in town, or within 10 miles of the city center: **Best Western, Clarion, Comfort Inn, Courtyard by Marriott, Days Inn, Doubletree, Econo Lodge, Hampton Inn, Hilton, Holiday Inn, Howard Johnson, Hyatt, La Quinta, Motel 6, Radisson, Ramada, Red Roof Inn, Residence Inn, Sleep Inn, Super 8** For more information, including phone numbers and websites, see page 439.

ON THE ROAD: MILWAUKEE TO DOOR COUNTY

Considering from whence you came, you'll be amazed that a single tank of gas can deliver you to such a bucolic setting. Leaving on I-43 North, it takes several miles to shake Milwaukee and there's not much between the city and Exit 89, which you should take east onto County Road C for a more rural run to lakefront Port Washington.

Located 30 miles from Milwaukee, this small town has the greatest concentration of pre-Civil War homes, and also the advantage of being nestled among seven hills and beside a picture-perfect harbor. There's no compelling reason to stay very long, but Franklin Street features blocks of interesting stores on the shores of Lake Michigan. It'll take about an hour to whisk through the town, slightly longer if you drop in at **Harry's Restaurant** (128 N. Franklin St., 262/284-2861), which serves breakfast, lunch, and dinner. Here since the 1950s, this is where most travelers stop for home-cooked hot beef sandwiches, mashed potatoes, chicken and rice soup, pork chop sandwiches, and lake perch. Up the street, **Port Antiques** (314 N. Franklin St., 262/284-5520), open 10 A.M.–5 P.M. daily, carries a strong collection of nautical antiques, hunting and fishing pieces, and 19th-century matted maps.

When you leave Port Washington, follow the lakeshore north and either return to I-43 for an uneventful ride to Exit 120 for County Road OK (yes, it's actually "OK"), or opt for a rural stretch of riding on Highway LL/32 that'll take you just south of Sheboygan Falls. Whichever route you take, it's a little hard to navigate through here so you may have to ask for directions through Sheboygan until it places you on 15th Avenue (aka Lakeshore Road) which grows up to become Highway LS. This is the uninterrupted lakeshore run that'll take you north all the way into Wisconsin farm country and then into Manitowoc where Highway LS breathes its last and Highway 42 takes over to lead to the quirky town of Two Rivers. You may not have heard of the town, but you're familiar with the dish that was invented here. It was here in 1881 that Ed Berners, my nominee for a Nobel Prize in desserts, put chocolate sauce on a young girl's ice cream, and the ice cream sundae was born.

The original site where the sundae was invented is long gone, but the historical society compensates with the **Washington House** (1622 Jefferson St., just a block off Hwy. 42, 920/793-2490). The restored saloon now houses Berners' Ice Cream Parlor, the town visitors center, and a museum. Docents claim the rare murals in the upstairs ballroom make it the "Sistine Chapel of Two Rivers." It's still early, but the pope has yet to proclaim the Sistine Chapel the "Washington House of the Vatican."

This is the last gasp of city living you'll be subjected to since the road ahead becomes even more placid as you ride through small villages like Kewaunee and Algoma and past longer and more luxurious expanses of Lake Michigan shoreline.

Following Algoma, Highway S takes you into dairy country for a gentle, easy ride straight to Sturgeon Bay, the portal to Door County. The combination of the fresh country air, reliable views of Lake Michigan, and the unhurried pace of it all is extremely satisfying. You'll bypass Sturgeon Bay as you enter Door County, crossing a canal and then veering off to follow Highway 57 North near the eastern shoreline. It's a quieting ride as you pass through Jacksonport and work your way up to Baileys Harbor, where there are a few restaurants and inns.

I'd suggest pushing on to the more active community of Fish Creek, which, judging from the proliferation of flowers, picket fences, and cottage shops, must have been charm school valedictorian. From Baileys Harbor, turn west on Highway F and follow it past pristine farmland, cherry trees, and apple orchards until you roll into one of the most beautiful towns in Door County.

DOOR COUNTY PRIMER

Here's a part of Wisconsin that combines Cape Cod with the Berkshires. It's not only beautiful, it's a pleasure to ride. The "thumb" of the state is about 75 miles long and only between about 2 and 18 miles wide, and it's all criss-crossed by some wonderful country roads. For locals, the appeal is that with its limestone base it makes for fertile farmland. Door County produces 95 percent of Wisconsin's cherries and about 40 percent of its apple crop, giving the roads a pink and white hue when the blossoms spring to life each May.

Fish Creek, which is arguably the most popular destination on the peninsula, began with Asa Thorp, a settler who arrived in 1854 to make his fortune. Building the first pier north of Green Bay, he began selling cordwood to fuel the steamers that plied Lake Michigan. As his fortune increased, Thorp increased his land holdings and then built a lodge for steamship passengers, charging $7.50 a week. When the Wisconsin legislature bought the land to create Peninsula State Park, the sawmills stopped, the small farms reverted to forests again, and tourism took the lead.

Which is why you're here.

ON THE ROAD: DOOR COUNTY

The best part about basing yourself in Fish Creek is that you have easy access to most things worth seeing. Provided you were smart enough not to ride in peak tourist season when the roads and rates reach critical mass, you're just a few minutes from peaceful country settings.

Point your bike in any direction, and as you lose yourself in the ride, a trace of your lost idealism will return. Venture out in the countryside where you'll find that people here actually *live* on farms and actually *make* fresh foods. You'll see this as you pass signs tempting you with fresh fruit jams and jellies, cherries, applesauce, fish, fudge, cheese, milk, custard, and cakes.

It's easy to take a roughly circular ride around the county, but before leaving Fish Creek, wander around the village for a few hours. At the western tip of Main Street lies a small park offering an unobstructed view of Green Bay and its islands. Doubling back via Cottage Row and Spruce Street, you'll circle the block to arrive at a small marina. After that, drop in at any number of shops, many of which were converted from old motor courts.

When you do leave town via Highway 42 North, the first detour is at 3,776-acre **Peninsula State Park** (920/868-3258, www.wiparks.net). After being cooped up for the winter, golfers tee up, couples kayak, and families bike and hike over every trail. Daily admission to the park costs $10, a few bucks less if your bike has Wisconsin tags. Shore Road is fantastic for motorcycles, with small breaks in the tree line to expose the wide waters of Green Bay and provide you a place to pull over. Shore Road rolls by the 1868 Eagle Bluff Lighthouse and then Eagle Tower, a 75-foot observation platform that's easier to climb than Everest and offers a superb view of the park, bay, and neighboring villages.

The road exits onto Highway 42 three miles north of Fish Creek, and simply by turning left, you'll be riding toward Door County's most picturesque town. Ephraim was founded in 1853 as a Moravian religious community and today the steeples of Moravian and Lutheran churches reveal the town's spiritual values and love of natural beauty. Slow down to take in all you see: handsome clapboard inns, sailboats at anchor, horse-drawn carriages, and white sand beaches.

Though Ephraim has no true commercial district, everyone stops at **Wilson's Restaurant and Ice Cream Parlor** (9990 Water St., 920/854-2041, www.wilsonsicecream.com). Here since 1906, this authentic family-owned diner serves fantastic hamburgers, soups, sandwiches, milkshakes, and sundaes (thanks, Ed Berners!). Don't miss this preserved look at Americana, and consider investing in the boat rental concessions across the street.

From Ephraim, follow Highway 42 to its northernmost point. The road is serene, traipsing through the villages of Sister Bay, then Ellison Bay (check out the Pioneer Store, 920/854-2805) and past meadows and marshes to reach Gills Rock and its passenger ferry landing. You've reached the top of the thumb now, but if you continue riding east, Highway 42 leads to one of the most incredible mile-long stretches of road I've found. If you're riding in a group, get ready for some picture-taking as you hit a winding, canopied road with some great moguls.

Alas, you've reached the end of the world. Here in Northport, the vehicle ferry is waiting if you'd like to leave the peninsula and sail north to **Washington Island** (920/847-2546 or 800/223-2094, www. wisferry.com). On a motorcycle, you'll pay about $26 for the round-trip (about $12 for an extra passenger) which gives you access to the largest of Door County's 34 named islands and, as I'm sure you're aware, the oldest Icelandic community in America. As you float across, keep in mind that this route was once known as crossing the "Straits of Death's Door," a reference to the treacherous currents and unpredictable waves. I trust maritime safety has improved over the years. When you reach the island, you'll find a pastoral setting, restaurants, shops, and more than 100 miles of paved country roads. With suspiciously little development, you'll discover a playground for you and your bike.

Back in Door County, you'll have to backtrack on Highway 42 to head south, detouring onto Highway NP if you want

to see the **Newport State Park U.S. Bird Refuge** (920/854-2500), and continue on to Ellison Bay. There, Mink River Road descends toward Rowley's Bay and Highway ZZ drops farther south until it connects with Highway 57 and then Highway Q back down to Bailey's Harbor.

In other words, explore. When you're riding through Door County, the surrounding bays ensure that you can never get lost...

And you'll discover that there's so much to find.

PULL IT OVER:
DOOR COUNTY HIGHLIGHTS
Attractions and Adventures

In Door County, you're surrounded by water on three sides, making water sports the natural pastime. **Stiletto Catamaran Sailing Cruises** (South Shore Pier, Ephraim, 920/854-7245, www.stilettosailingcruises.com) offers seven sailings daily, with shorter daytime cruises (85 minutes, $28) and longer sunset cruises (two hours, $40). On a clear day, go for the sunset cruise—it's incredible.

If you don't see any ice floes drifting past, consider hitting the water. Boat rental rates at **South Shore Pier Boat Rentals** (9993 Water St., Ephraim, 920/854-4324, www.southshorepier.com) range from $74 for two hours on a 21-foot deluxe pontoon boat to $261 for an all-day excursion on a 25-foot pontoon boat (gas is extra). Split the cost with fellow riders, and you've got your own sunset cruise. Traveling solo? Adrenaline-inducing wave runners cost $65 per hour (gas included).

Hubbard Brothers Charters (10929 Bay Shore Dr., Sister Bay, 920/854-2113) began as a family business in the 1920s and remains one of the more reasonably priced fishing charters I've found. The $50 cost of the six-passenger charter includes a captain, poles, and tackle for a half-day excursion; you'll need to spring for the bait, refreshments, and fishing license ($14 for two days). They accept cash only, no cards. It's important to wear warm clothes and shoes, and know that these tough bastards don't cancel for rough seas, rains, or high winds. Say, you ever listened to "The Wreck of the *Edmund Fitzgerald*"?

Like the Hubbards, **Capt. Paul's Charter Fishing** (919 Cottage Rd., Gills Rock, 920/854-4614, www.captainpaulsfish. com) claims to be the longest-running charter in the state and offers four-hour trips in search of salmon and brown trout. The novelty here is that you are *always* fishing. Whenever someone snags a fish, you rotate to the next rod. The 33-foot *Lucky Lady III* has a six-passenger capacity, and bait and tackle are included in the $58 fee; the fishing license is not.

Shake out your sea legs and head to the **American Folklore Theatre** (Hwy. 42, 920/854-6117, www.folkloretheatre. com) for an $18 evening performance held in Peninsula State Park's outdoor amphitheater. If you can endure the mosquitoes, you'll enjoy watching professional actors and musicians perform original musical comedies in a folksy setting—although the novelty can wear off before the last bow.

Shopping

Siobhan's (9431 Spruce St., Fish Creek, 920/868-3353) is a small shop with some epicurean pleasures: a nice selection of California and European wines, as well as champagnes, liquors, cheeses, cognacs, and single malt scotches. A few cigars round out this shop's inventory.

Blue-Plate Specials

As long as you're in Door County, you may want to invest your appetite in a fish boil. Several lodges, resorts, and restaurants host them, including: **Square Rigger Galley** (6332 Hwy. 57, Jacksonport, 920/823-2404), **Viking Grille** (12029 Hwy. 42, Ellison Bay, 920/854-2998), **Wagon Trail Resort** (1041 Hwy. ZZ, Ellison Bay, 920/854-2385), and **White Gull Inn** (4225 Main St., Fish Creek, 920/868-3517). Call ahead, since some require reservations or can arrange a private cookout for your group.

For food that doesn't bubble up from a boiling cauldron of water, try lunch or dinner at **The Cookery** (4135 Main St., Fish Creek, 920/868-3634, www.cookeryfishcreek.com), serving everything you want, done just right. They can load you up on baked chicken, roast pork loin, stuffed pork chops, perch platters, and meat loaf.

Watering Holes

Here since the 1930s, the **Bayside Tavern** (4160 Main St., Fish Creek, 920/868-3441) is a favorite local hangout. It features a large curved bar, small tables, and the world-famous Bayside Coffee—a potent, flaming, liquor-filled concoction. For grub, sample Smilin' Bob's Bar Room Chili. Bob whips up the spices at home, and they're such a secret that even the cooks don't know the recipe—and that's why Bob's smilin'.

Shut-Eye

If you travel in season, you would be foolish—yes, damn foolish—not to reserve a room at one of Door County's many motels, hotels, condos, resorts, cabins, or campgrounds. For help finding one that fits your needs, call 800/527-3529 or www.doorcounty.com.

Motels and Motor Courts

Fish Creek Motel & Cottages (9479

What the Bejeezus is a Fish Boil?

When I heard about the outbreak of fish boils in Door County, I placed a call to the surgeon general. Then someone put me wise. Fish boils are a staple of the Door County diet. Here's what happens, although I'm still not sure why.

Basically, it's a cookout. The process dates back to the days of Scandinavian settlers and lumberjacks who tossed fresh whitefish into a pot of salted water, then added onions and potatoes, stacked flaming boards around the pot, and let the whole thing cook over a boiling fire. The same thing happens today at restaurants throughout Door County.

When everything is cooked to what people deem perfection, the chef completes the ritual. The pièce de résistance, the "boil over," comes when they toss kerosene over the flaming boards to spark a conflagration. This accomplishes multiple objectives: It boils the oils off the fish meat; it indicates that dinner is ready; and it singes the eyebrows off anyone who stands too close to the pot.

Spruce St., Fish Creek, 920/868-3448, www.fishcreekmotel.com) is a combination of modern motel rooms and original rooms with soothing woodland views. Clean and neat, it promises "free bikes," but I'm certain that doesn't mean motorcycles.

The **Edgewater Cottages** (4144 Main St., Fish Creek, 920/868-3551) don't have much going for it by way of furnishings, but the log cabins and clapboard cottages are Bonnie-and-Clyde-hideout cool and provide a nice view of the cove. The rooms are quiet and comfortable, and some have kitchenettes.

Cedar Court (9429 Cedar St., Fish Creek, 920/868-3361, www.cedarcourt.com, $69 and up off-season, $95 and up high season, specialty rooms $119–128) gives you larger lodgings since this is really a compound with guesthouses and a pool

in back. One block from the bay and the shopping area, Cedar Court offers standard amenities in each room and whirlpool tubs in the choice ones.

A few miles away in Ephraim, the **Eagle Harbor Inn** (9914 Water St., Ephraim, 920/854-2121 or 800/324-5427, www.eagleharborinn.com, rooms $98 and up high season, suites $159 and up) rests on five peaceful acres across from the bay. This quiet resort offers breakfast and nice landscaping. Suites, which sleep up to six, have a whirlpool tub, fireplace, kitchen, CD/TV/VCR, and private deck.

In the heart of the village, most rooms at the summers-only **Ephraim Inn** (9994 Pioneer Ln., Ephraim, 920/854-4515, www.theephraiminn.com, $135–195) afford great views of the harbor and tiered green bluffs. A continental breakfast is included.

Resources for Riders

Wisconsin Thumb Run

Wisconsin Travel Information

Wisconsin Association of Campground Owners—608/582-2092 or
 800/843-1821, www.wisconsincampgrounds.com

Wisconsin Department of Tourism—608/266-2161 or 800/432-8747,
 www.travelwisconsin.com

Wisconsin Lodging—www.wisconsinlodging.info

Wisconsin Road Conditions—866/511-9472, www.511wi.gov

Wisconsin State Parks—608/266-2181 or 888/936-7463, www.wiparks.net

Wisconsin State Parks Reservations—888/947-2757, www.reserveamerica.com

Local and Regional Information

Door County Chamber of Commerce—920/743-4456 or 800/527-3529,
 www.doorcounty.com

Ephraim Information Center—920/854-4989, www.ephraim-doorcounty.com

Fish Creek Information Center—920/868-2316 or 800/577-1880,
 www.fishcreekinfo.com

Greater Milwaukee Convention & Visitors Bureau—414/273-7222 or
 800/554-1448, www.milwaukee.org

Milwaukee Weather Information—414/744-8000 or 414/936-1212

Washington Island Chamber of Commerce—920/847-2179,
 www.washingtonislandchamber.com

Wisconsin Motorcycle Shops

Corse's Superbikes—700 E. Milan, Saukville, 262/284-2725,
 www.corsesuperbikes.com

Hal's Harley-Davidson-Buell—1925 S. Mooreland Rd., New Berlin,
 262/860-2060 or 800/966-4443, www.halshd.com

House of Harley-Davidson—6221 W. Layton Ave., Milwaukee, 414/282-2211,
 www.houseofharley.com

Milwaukee Harley-Davidson/Buell—11310 Silver Spring Dr., Milwaukee,
 414/461-4444, www.milwaukeeharley.com

Route 43 Harley-Davidson—3736 S. Taylor Dr., Sheboygan, 920/458-0777,
 www.route43hd.com

Sheboygan Yamaha—N7402 Hwy. 42, Sheboygan Falls, 920/565-2213,
 www.sheboyganyamaha.com

Southeast Sales (BMW, Triumph, Honda, Kawasaki)—6930 N. 76th St.,
 Milwaukee, 414/463-2540, www.southeastsales.com

Stock's Harley-Davidson Motorcycles—2433 Hecker Rd., Manitowoc,
 920/684-0237, www.stockshd.com

Suburban Harley-Davidson/Buell—139 N. Main St., Thiensville, 262/242-2464,
 www.suburbanharley.com

Black Hills Run

Deadwood, South Dakota to Custer State Park, South Dakota

Thanks to the Sturgis Rally, South Dakota attracts its share of motorcycle travelers—but there's far more to the state than a single week in August. In the Black Hills you will see things that reveal the West isn't just a location, but a lifestyle. There are towering structures and wide-open spaces, caves and fossil beds, natural beauty and a desire to preserve it. Almost anywhere you travel, the roads are wide open and free.

DEADWOOD PRIMER

Gold was the key. In the 1870s when word got out that there was gold in Deadwood, tent cities were erected, and the boom was on.

For nearly a century, folks here continued searching for gold but faced the hard fact of diminishing returns. By 1989 the town was in tough straits, with downtown's buildings dilapidated, the water pressure falling too low to fight fires, and Deadwood facing the risk of becoming a 20th century ghost town. Looking forward into the past, a statewide vote gave Deadwood the go-ahead to bring gambling back to the Black Hills and a flood of low-stakes casinos gave Deadwood a new lease on life.

Since then, Deadwood has been placed on the National Historic Register and, in 2004, received a boost that may have helped even more than gambling. That's when HBO premiered *Deadwood,* a gritty drama that focused on the town's more explosive days when you took a gamble just by walking into one of the frontier saloons. The popularity of the series—which showcased the violent power struggle between camp settlers and new arrivals—created another surge in Deadwood's history.

ON THE ROAD: DEADWOOD

There are things to see in Deadwood, but the roads are more appealing. Then again, if you're a Kevin Costner fan, you may never want to leave.

While in the area filming *Dances with Wolves,* Costner fell for Deadwood and opened the Midnight Star casino where

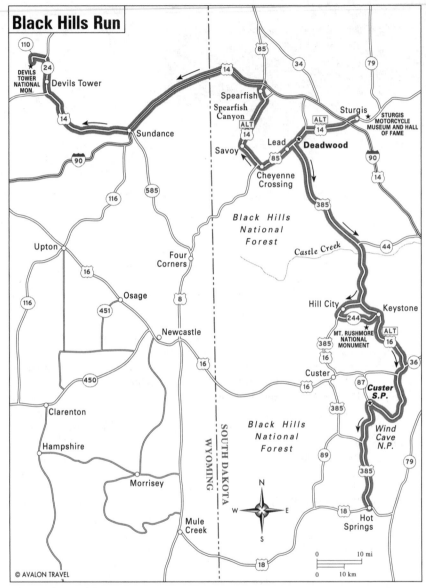

Black Hills Run

Route: Deadwood to Custer State Park via Devils Tower, Sturgis, Hot Springs, Mount Rushmore, Iron Mountain Road

Distance: Approximately 160 miles

First Leg: Deadwood to Custer State Park (160 miles)

Helmet Laws: South Dakota does not require helmets. No helmet is required in Wyoming if you're over 18.

Sturgis Rally and Races

Why in the world do riders head to the barren landscape of South Dakota? Because of a rally started in August 1938 by motorcycle dealer J. C. "Pappy" Hoel. Back then, nine riders raced on a half-mile dirt track for a $500 purse, followed by crowd-pleasing stunts such as head-on collisions with cars, board wall crashes, and ramp-jumping. From this, the Jackpine Gypsies Motorcycle Club was born, and the rally was proclaimed the Black Hills Motorcycle Classic.

After World War II, the rally and race drew up to 5,000 people and 150 competitors. By the 1960s, the Sturgis Chamber of Commerce had begun to take part by hosting barbecues in the park and awarding prizes to the rally queen, oldest rider, best-dressed couple, and the longest-distance traveler. During the rally's 45th anniversary, the governor proclaimed "Pappy Hoel Week" to honor its founder, and attendance peaked at 30,000.

The big leap came during the 50th anniversary rally, when as many as 400,000 riders flocked to Sturgis. In 1991, the event was renamed the **Sturgis Rally and Races** (605/720-0800, www.sturgismotorcyclerally.com) and became (promoters wished) a "family event." In reality, it is a wild drinking, riding, racing party where inhibitions are checked at the door. What started as a down-home event now attracts an estimated half a million riders each year, making it the biggest outdoor event in America.

nearly every costume, prop, and script he ever touched is on display. Much more intriguing than seeing Costner memorabilia is riding out to Devil's Tower via the twisting roads of Spearfish Canyon. All you need to do is look for U.S. 85 and follow it toward the town of Lead (pronounced "leed"). Although the road isn't too attractive, stick with it—it gradually improves.

Just about eight miles from Lead at the junction of U.S. 85 and U.S. 14A, take a right and take a break at the **Cheyenne Crossing Store** (605/584-3510, www.cheyennecrossing.org). Open until 8 P.M. summer weekends, until 4 P.M. midweek, this is a favorite destination for riders and one of those old-fashioned combination café/lodge/souvenir stand/beer stop/bait shop/filling stations. In a perfect world, they'd take my advice and expand their inventory to include plutonium, beetle larvae, and chimpanzees.

Although Spearfish Canyon is ranked as a national scenic byway, I didn't find the scenery to be that fantastic. On the other hand, it does let you explore some intriguing backcountry as Spearfish Creek runs along a curving road that at times gets progressively more narrow and therefore more interesting. By the time you reach the town of Savoy where there's a restaurant, cultural center, and resort, you'll be motivated to keep heading north through the canyon as the road frequently ascends and descends as is evidenced by approaching riders springing up in the oncoming lanes.

When you've completed the canyon, U.S. 14A takes you through the clean streets of Spearfish and onto I-90 West. Although, for a more remote route ride north on U.S. 85 to catch Highway 24 west through Aladdin and Alva to Hulett, before dropping down to Devils Tower in Wyoming. Otherwise, take I-90 past Sundance to hook up with U.S. 14, a nice road surrounded by a landscape that alternates between lush pine forests and open plains. It's an easy ride to reach Highway 24 which you'll take north to reach **Devils Tower** (307/467-5283, www.nps.gov/deto, $5), the icon that haunted Richard Dreyfuss in *Close Encounters*. The only thing that'll haunt you may be the need to yield to RV drivers who started out a little earlier than you did.

From the road, you'll see the 1,267-foot Devils Tower monument thrusting into the sky, and to get closer to it just watch for the entrance to Highway 110 that'll lead you into the park. Numerous pullouts afford views from a distance, but when you enter you gain access to a steeply inclined three-mile road that leads to a museum, bookstore, and 1.3-mile paved trail that surrounds the tower.

What formed this monolith? A Kiowa Indian legend tells it like this: Eight children were playing when suddenly, the lone boy among them turned into a bear. The girls climbed onto a talking tree stump and, as the bear tried to kill them, the stump rose so high that the girls turned into the stars of the Big Dipper. The long gashes on the tower are claw marks from the homicidal boy/bear. Geologists have yet to confirm that this is what happened.

After circling the tower, backtrack to Spearfish Canyon, then to Deadwood for a night at the casinos—and another loving look at the Kevin Costner collection.

PULL IT OVER: DEADWOOD HIGHLIGHTS
Attractions and Adventures

A short ride from Main Street, atop Mount Moriah, are three cemetery plots that should gain your attention. This is where Wild Bill Hickok, Calamity Jane, and local character Potato Creek Johnny are buried. My guess is that if Hickok's head wound hadn't killed him, the procession up this steep grade would've. It's easy to spot Wild Bill's final resting place: it's marked by packs of "aces and eights" left by his fans. Admission is $2.

If you're planning a heist, target some of the displays at **Nelson's Garage Car and Motorcycle Museum** (629 Main St., 605/578-1909, www.celebritycasinos. com, free) at the Celebrity Hotel. Stashed here are Evel Knievel's helmet and jumpsuit (and X-rays from his failed Wembeley Stadium jump), James Bond's suit from

© NANCY HOWELL

Devils Tower, Wyoming has attracted travelers from the Plains Indians to riders today.

Diamonds Are Forever, Sylvester Stallone's Ducati Paso 750 Limited, Steve McQueen's '66 Triumph 650, Harleys owned by Peter Fonda and Ann-Margret, Clint Eastwood's Trans Am, and Paul McCartney's '73 Honda 125. Ship them to me care of my publisher.

I know there are a lot of vintage photo places, but there are actually nice photographs at **Woody's Wild West Portrait Emporium** (641 Main St., 605/578-3807, www.woodyswildwest.com). What's the difference? This large studio features 25 settings and nearly 1,000 costume combinations that allow women to dress in their bordello finest and men to become cardsharps and gunslingers. Another advantage is that riders can bring in their bikes for a Western-style shot.

Blue-Plate Specials

It's hard to find a normal restaurant in Deadwood since you have to navigate a casino to do it. Work your way past the slots and tables and you'll run across a buffet somewhere. If you have a large appetite and a thin wallet, the buffet served at the **Silverado Franklin Hotel** (700 Main St., 605/578-3670 or 800/584-7005, www.silveradofranklin.com) is $7.95 for lunch and $12.95 for dinner and includes chef-carved prime rib and ham, broasted chicken, roasted red potatoes, fresh veggies, and many other entrées and sides. They add unlimited snow crab on Friday and on weekdays their breakfast is reasonable. More than reasonable. Fifty cents for two eggs, potatoes, and toast.

On the second floor of the Midnight Star, **Jake's** (677 Main St., 605/578-3656. www.themidnightstar.com) serves lunch and dinner. Expect fine dining in a nice atmosphere, with entrées like rack of lamb, steaks, and Cajun seafood. High rollers (a relative term in Deadwood) dine here. The third-floor sports bar is less fancy and less expensive.

Watering Holes

Casinos have cornered the market, but for imbibing there are a few joints to check out. Friendly barkeeps at **Oyster Bay** (628 Main St., 605/578-3136) may persuade you to sample the $2.50 "oyster shooter" concoction, created with an oyster, beer, Worcestershire sauce, Tabasco sauce, cocktail sauce, salt and pepper, and other stuff I'm running tests on. If that grabs you, try Walk the Plank: seven oyster shooters increasing in potency until you're over the edge. The beer and oyster bar attracts riders and regular folks from around the world.

Not the saloon where Wild Bill was blown away (that was across the street at #622), the **Old Style Saloon #10** (657 Main St., 605/578-3346, www.saloon10. com) does have his "death chair" (look over the door after you enter). The place feels authentic, with sawdust on the floor (used by saloonkeepers to camouflage dropped gold dust), an 1870s atmosphere, and a full liquor bar. There's often live entertainment and in high season they won't close until 2 A.M. If you draw Hickok's hand (aces and eights) in the casino next door, don't worry, be happy: You've just won $250. But watch your back.

Shut-Eye

An organization called **Black Hills Central Reservations** (800/529-0105 or 866/601-5103, www.blackhillsvacations. com) can arrange rooms, adventures, and activities—and also takes a 5 percent fee. Most hotels in Deadwood are along Main Street, and all have a casino attached.

You can't miss the **Silverado Franklin Hotel** (700 Main St., 605/578-3670 or 800/584-7005, www.silveradofranklin.

com, $89–119), the grande dame of Deadwood. The Franklin has large rooms that make up for the lack of fine furniture, although the owner's celebrity friends (Tom Brokaw, Mary Hart, Jann Wenner, et al.) don't seem to mind. Rates are reasonable, except during rallies, when you won't find a room. There's a motor court across the street, but try to stay in the main hotel, which has a dining room and Durty Nelly's Irish Pub.

Down the street, the **Bullock Hotel** (633 Main St., 605/578-1745 or 800/336-1876, www.historicbullock.com, $120–185) boasts the nicest rooms. Well decorated, they are separated from the noise of the casino and include king or queen beds, shower baths, and some whirlpools. A restaurant, casino, and full liquor bar downstairs mean that you can stay in for the night.

The **Celebrity Hotel** (629 Main St., 605/578-1909 or 888/399-1886, www.celebritycasinos.com, $109–159) is where you'll find the free motorcycle museum as well as clean, functional rooms with a fridge, a TV, and a patio deck that lets you enjoy the weather if it's nice.

Chain Drive

These chain hotels are in town, or within 10 miles of the city center:
Best Western, Clarion, Comfort Inn, Holiday Inn, Super 8
For more information, including phone numbers and websites, see page 439.

ON THE ROAD: DEADWOOD TO CUSTER STATE PARK

This next leg is like taking four rides in one. You could take a few days to do this, but here's one way to do it all at once if you wish.

From Deadwood, it's a short 14 miles down U.S. 14A to Sturgis. Yes, Sturgis.

Although a legend for riders, when the rally's not here there's actually very little to see. Check with the **Sturgis Chamber of Commerce** (605/347-2556, www.sturgis-sd.org) for up to date information on sites and shops. For you, the biggest draw in town is the **Sturgis Motorcycle Museum and Hall of Fame** (999 Main St., 605/347-2001, www.sturgismuseum.com, $5, weekdays 9 A.M.–5 P.M., Saturdays 9 A.M.–4 P.M., Sundays 10 A.M.–4 P.M.).

The museum showcases a jaw-dropping fleet of American and imported bikes in a chronological collection including an '09 Exelsior Auto Cycle, '10 Flying Merkel, '15 Harley-Davidson Boardtrack Racer, '28 Calthorpe 350, '34 Crocker Racer, '48 Royal Enfield Flying Flea, a '52 Vincent Black Shadow, and dozens of others. If you have a museum quality motorcycle you wouldn't mind having displayed for a year, give them a call.

When you leave Sturgis, you'll double-back on U.S. 14A and ride past Deadwood to follow U.S. 385 South. Along the way, odds are you'll see far too many signs that read "X marks the spot. Think." These signs are posted where careless riders lost their challenge with tight turns. So...*think*. Still, it's easy to understand the temptation to accelerate into this steeplechase for bikes. The road spins up, then down, then around every terrain ever invented as the landscape alternates between boondocks, fields, and meadows, with an occasional general store popping up on the roadside.

At Highway 44 there's a turnoff to Rapid City which you'll likely ignore because the road continues with its unpredictable layout, taking you down hills and whipping around corners and just past the Pactola Reservoir to a picturesque spot with pullouts for photos and a National Forest information center on the opposite side.

Before Hill City, a left turn puts you

© NANCY HOWELL

Signs like this are posted where a rider has tempted fate… and lost. So think.

on U.S 16 which you'll follow for about six miles toward Keystone. After you've tracked U.S. 16A for a bit, you'll be in the heart of cluttered Keystone, which rivals Gatlinburg as one of the most touristy places you'll ever see. Depending on whether or not you need a rubber tomahawk, you can hang out in Keystone or follow SR 244 toward the majestic **Mount Rushmore National Memorial** (605/574-2523, www.nps.gov/moru), open 8 A.M.–10 P.M. daily. You'll get an undeniable thrill when that first face peeks through the trees and that uniquely American image you know from calendars and plates and postcards is now larger than life and right before you. It costs $10 to park in the main lot, but if money's tight there's a "no-fee parking area" to your right, just beneath the summit. This lot happens to be the entrance to Gutzon Borglum's studio (the man behind the monument) and steps from here lead to a nice view of the monument.

If you opt to go through the main entrance, you'll arrive in a magnificent center that includes a restaurant, a massive gift shop, and an amphitheater created through a renovation funded by $56 million in donations. The new look is perfect, as evidenced by the floor to ceiling windows that reveal the four faces as a gigantic 3-D testament to our experiment with democracy and to the leadership of four great men.

There's a broad plaza where you can stand and watch the faces, but odds are there'll be a few hundred others here as well. With plenty of room to get lost and forest trails that offer privacy, I'd suggest that you separate yourself from the crowds and find a quiet spot to sit and reflect on this massive undertaking—I'm referring to America as well as the monument.

Back inside, there's a theater and an exhibit hall that features original models and sketches, as well as firsthand accounts of the construction. You'll also read an inspiring explanation of why these presidents were chosen for the honor (respectively, they symbolize the founding, development, growth, and preservation of the country).

Only if you feel comfortable riding supernaturally dark roads, make plans to return here at dusk (usually around 8 P.M. in the summertime) for a first-class presentation. At around 8:30 P.M., patriotic music plays in the amphitheater, and at 9 P.M., a ranger takes the stage to answer questions and explain the lighting ceremony. A short documentary is shown and there's a salute to the armed forces. When the national anthem plays and the audience sings along as the faces are illuminated, there's hardly anyone here who's not choked up.

When you can pull yourself away from Mount Rushmore, get ready for one incredible road. Peter Norbeck, the South

Dakota governor—and later senator—who was instrumental in the creation of Mount Rushmore, the Needles Highway, and the preservation of Custer State Park, rode on horseback to map out Iron Mountain Road. What he created is a magnificent motorcycle run.

Turn south onto U.S. 16A, and the test-track tight turns soon add alternating stretches of canopy roads, great countryside, 15-mph switchbacks, and the occasional "pigtail bridge," an ingenious invention that spans steep climbs within a short stretch.

This road is not for sissies. The turns throw you around like Nature Boy Rick Flair and pumps up your left leg to maximum density with all the shifting. This is a red-hot, helluva fun road. Occasionally, it settles down to a nice ride through the forest, and then it rocks and rolls you over the countryside and into nearly vertical ascensions to give you an upper-body workout while tackling these turns. Since the landscape hasn't been violated, even as you're being tossed around like a rag doll, your spirits will lift.

It's a long ride to Custer State Park, but when you turn right and follow U.S. 16A to the park entrance (where there's an entrance fee), you'll enter the park equivalent of Iron Mountain Road, a place filled with adventure, excitement, and natural beauty.

CUSTER STATE PARK PRIMER

It was doomed General George A. Custer who led a scientific army expedition into the Black Hills in 1874. Although his team found gold, Custer seemed more interested in the area's natural beauty. Fortune seekers weren't so magnanimous. They arrived in droves, and their presence took a toll on the area's wildlife.

By 1913, the South Dakota legislature planned to replenish the wildlife population with bison, pronghorn, elk, bighorn sheep, and mountain goats and a few years later Governor Peter Norbeck helped guide the creation of a 71,000-acre parcel of land where the wildlife and the landscape would be protected. By 1919 the reserve became Custer State Park that, to this day, fulfills the vision of those who planned it. It has all the appeal of Yellowstone and Yosemite, yet on a manageable level. It's as close to a perfect park as you'll ever find.

ON THE ROAD: CUSTER STATE PARK

I'll start with a warning: You may be tempted to sign on for the Buffalo Jeep Safari—but based on experience, I say you'll see just as much, if not more, by riding your bike south on the Highway 87 section of the 18-mile Wildlife Loop Road.

From the State Game Lodge, turn left and follow U.S. 16A west past meadows and creeks until you reach Highway 87, and then head south toward Hot Springs. Get your camera ready: Chances are that while riding a road that twists like a knot you'll spy enough wildlife to fill an ark. Provided you're not impaled by a buffalo, this is one of the best rides you can make. Really. If someone charged you with the task to build a road, this would be it.

As you pass the Blue Bell Lodge and general store and cross French Creek, you couldn't ask for a better ride, complete with picturesque peaks and valleys. At times the road may even place you right in the midst of a buffalo herd. While it'd be safer to be in a car when these powerful 2,000-pound beasts are around, you don't have that option. If you see them blocking the road, wait patiently. Do not try to approach them. Although they appear to be as slow and stupid as paint-sniffing monkeys, they can hit you at 30 mph and pierce you like a pincushion. God, these buffalo are fascinating.

Farther on, you'll hear a high-pitched chirping. A glimpse of a single prairie dog will suddenly reveal thousands of these creatures standing sentinel atop their holes or scattering like rats in front of traffic. If you're lucky and your vision is good, you may also see bighorn sheep, mountain goats, elk, deer, burros, coyotes, falcons, mountain lions, and bobcats—they all roam throughout the park.

When you reach the end of Highway 87, follow U.S. 385 South and detour to the loop road that takes you to **Wind Cave National Park** (605/745-4600, www.nps.gov/wica) where, beneath one square mile of earth, lies 83 miles of tunnels. A one-hour tour is $7, and longer tours (including a two-hour candlelight tour) are $9. If you're an adventurous psychopath, the Wild Cave Tour is a strenuous four-hour caving class that costs $23. If you've never been in a cave before, it's frightening at first, then you think you'll die, then you think about earthquakes, then you're fine, and then the passages get narrow and the ranger turns out the lights and you're frightened again.

Although there are no grand stalactites or stalagmites or waterfalls, the cave is interesting and cool (a constant 53°F). The fact that the ranger carries barf and waste bags tells you this tour isn't for everyone. Avoid it if you're claustrophobic.

When you're back on the road, ride south on U.S. 385 to Hot Springs, an ordinary old town with one interesting site about a mile out of town. The **Mammoth Site** (605/745-6017, www.mammothsite.com, $8) seems as if it would be a tourist trap, but once you're inside, it's like walking into an archaeological dig. About 26,000 years ago, a spring-fed sinkhole formed, and dozens of mammoths that

had dropped by for a drink dropped in and couldn't get out. In the 1970s, when a developer started to clear the land, diggers found bones, and a tourist attraction was born. Archaeologists dig only in July, but it's fascinating to see this bone orchard. Outside of a Beverly Hills plastic surgeon's office, it's the only display of fossilized mammoths in America. The site is open 8 A.M.–7 P.M. daily.

When you're ready to roll, return via the same roads. When you reach Custer State Park again, watch for the eastern side of the Wildlife Loop Road and take that back to the State Game Lodge (or wherever you're staying) to complete the circle. And watch out for them prairie dogs.

PULL IT OVER: CUSTER STATE PARK HIGHLIGHTS
Attractions and Adventures

To explore the park from the vantage point of a saddle, rent a mount from **Blue Bell Stables** (605/255-4700). Horseback rides last for one hour ($30), two hours ($42), half a day ($115), or a full day ($195). Do this in South Dakota, and you'll be a cowboy, my friend.

The Needles, also known as Highway 87 North, comes fully equipped with narrow granite tunnels and hairpin turns. The name comes from the long, slender granite spires that border the road. The 14-mile thrill leads through rugged Black Hills to Sylvan Lake.

Although it's outside the park, it's worth seeing what will become the largest sculpture ever created. **Crazy Horse** (on U.S. 385, 605/673-4681, www.crazyhorse.org, $5) is open daybreak–dusk. Right now, only the face is complete because, out of respect for the subject, sculptor Korczak Ziolkowski turned down federal funds that likely would have helped him complete the project years ago. Why Crazy

Horse? Ziolkowski admired the martyr (he was stabbed in the back under a flag of truce by a U.S. soldier), and he sympathized with Crazy Horse and his people, who endured a string of broken treaties. Ziolkowski died in 1982; his family continues his work.

Shopping

Each lodge at Custer has a general store nearby, but the oversized **Coolidge General Store** near the State Game Lodge gets my vote for best store in a state park. Minnesota shipbuilders built it in 1927 to accommodate the tourists and reporters who accompanied President Coolidge on his visit. Check out the ceiling and you'll recognize that it's the hull of a ship turned upside down. Of course, the smaller general stores are perfect places to stop while you're out for a pleasure ride.

Blue-Plate Specials

As in Yellowstone, you can grab snacks and quick meals at snack bars and general stores in the park. For sit-down meals, there are also dining rooms where you can order breakfast, lunch, and dinner: Enjoy a variety of meals from buffalo, to salmon, trout, steaks, pheasant and other local specialties at **Blue Bell Lodge** (25453 Hwy. 87, 605/255-4531), **Legion Lake Lodge** (12967 U.S. 16A, 605/255-4521), or the **Sylvan Lake Lodge** (24572 Hwy. 87, 605/574-2561). The nicest location may be the **Pheasant Dining Room** (13389 U.S. 16A, 605/255-4541) at the State Game Lodge. Comfortable and rustic, the restaurant serves buffalo, salmon, trout, steak, chicken, and pheasant, and

the service is excellent. Reservations are a smart idea at any park restaurant.

Shut-Eye

The park makes a great day trip, but staying here is even better. For reservations at any lodge, call 888/875-0001. Rates vary widely according to season and type of accommodation (cabin, hotel, or lodge).

It's easy to see why Calvin Coolidge extended his stay at **State Game Lodge and Resort** ($110–135) from three weeks to three months. The idyllic front porch overlooks a sweeping lawn; there's an artist in residence; and, like the park, it is not so large as to be overpowering. The lodge features cool creekside cabins, along with hotel rooms, a small wooden church, and the Coolidge General Store nearby. In 2008 the new 30-unit **Creekside Lodge** was opened adjacent to the State Game Lodge. Open year-round, it features a Great Room, fireplace, meeting rooms, and oversized lodge rooms.

At an elevation of 6,250 feet, **Sylvan Lake Resort** ($135 and up) overlooks a picturesque mountain lake and offers cabins, lodge rooms, and a lounge. You'll need to run the Needles Highway to reach your room (not a bad deal). **Blue Bell Lodge** ($140 and up) is a cowboy resort with cabins, a general store, gas station, campground, and laundry. Trail rides and cookouts leave from here. The least flashy of the lodges, **Legion Lake Resort** ($130 and up) rents cabins that are complemented by a restaurant, gift shop, grocery store, and sport-boat rentals on the lake. For campsite reservations, call 888/875-0001.

Resources for Riders

Black Hills Run

South Dakota Travel Information
South Dakota Department of Tourism—800/732-5682, www.travelsd.com
South Dakota Road Conditions—605/773-3571, www.safetravelusa.com
South Dakota State Parks—800/710-2267, www.campsd.com

Local and Regional Information
Black Hills, Badlands & Lakes Association—605/355-3600,
    www.blackhillsbadlands.com
Custer State Park—605/255-4515, 605/644-7054 (ranger office), or
    888/875-0001 (reservations), www.custerresorts.com
Deadwood Chamber of Commerce—605/578-1876 or 800/999-1876,
    www.deadwood.org

South Dakota Motorcycle Shops
Black Hills Harley-Davidson—1040 Junction Ave. (I-90 Exit 55), Rapid City,
    605/347-2056 or 800/458-1485, www.sturgishd.com
Black Hills Powersports—3005 Beale St., Rapid City, 605/342-5500 or
    888/642-5505, www.blackhillspowersports.com
Petersen Motors—422 S. Fort St., Pierre, 605/224-4242,
    www.petersenmotorcycles.com
Rice Honda Suzuki—301 Campbell St., Rapid City, 605/342-2242,
    www.ricehondasuzuki.com
Sturgis Yamaha-BMW-Suzuki—2879 Vanoker Rd., Sturgis, 605/347-2636,
    www.sturgisyamaha.com

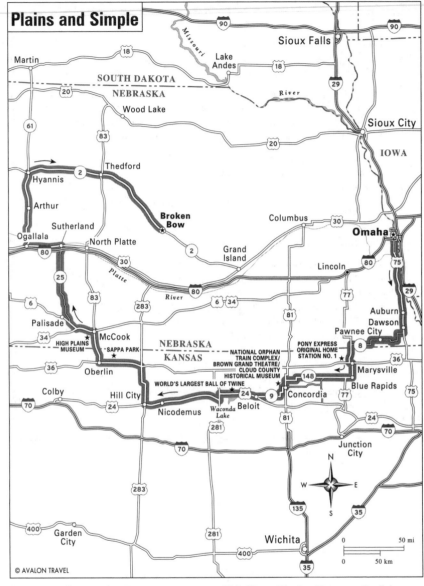

Plains and Simple

Route: Omaha to Broken Bow via Concordia, Oberlin, and Ogallala

Distance: Approximately 725 miles

First Leg: Omaha, Nebraska to Concordia, Kansas (220 miles)

Second Leg: Concordia to Oberlin, Kansas (212 miles)

Third Leg: Oberlin, Kansas to Ogallala, Nebraska (140 miles)

Fourth Leg: Ogallala to Broken Bow, Nebraska (155 miles)

Helmet Laws: Helmets are required in Nebraska. No helmet is required in Kansas if you're over 18.

Plains and Simple

Omaha, Nebraska to Broken Bow, Nebraska

Ask most motorcyclists what they want to find in a road, and most will tell you about a place with twists and switchbacks and steep drops. Maybe they'll mention a road that follows the winding course of a meandering river or the rough shoreline of the sea.

This is a ride that offers none of that. There are no switchbacks, no rivers, no seas. Instead, this is an epic ride across some of the most desolate land in the Midwest. It will take you to some small Kansas towns and across the Nebraska prairie. It's a tour that, I think, symbolizes the mindset of an independent rider—a solo traveler crossing a landscape as remote as any you can imagine.

When he stepped onto the moon, astronaut Buzz Aldrin described what was before him with the memorable term "magnificent desolation."

He could have been talking about Kansas and Nebraska.

ON THE ROAD: OMAHA TO CONCORDIA

Thanks to its size and services, Omaha was a good place to begin what would become a circle tour across the prairie, but it wasn't enough to keep me in town. Just as on my tour across Washington where Seattle was better as a starting point than as a base, I felt the same was true in Omaha. I knew that the real discoveries were waiting beyond the city limits.

From Omaha, head due south towards the Missouri River on U.S. 75. For many miles the city's urban sprawl will cling to the landscape until you reach the rural community of Auburn, where the last signs of city living disappear. If you've ridden for a while, you'll detect that refreshing feeling that comes when you've escaped the clutches of a city and the anxiety that comes with navigating a metropolitan area. In Auburn the scenery changes as well as the smells and the feel of the air. This is where I flipped up the visor and sucked in the sweet aroma of country and looked ahead at an endless straightaway framed by rusting windmills and weather-beaten barns that shared the landscape with… nothing. There was no longer any trace of civilization. Everything had *just stopped*.

On U.S. 75, you'll ride past the town of Dawson and even though you're only a few minutes from the Kansas border, you may now be unwilling to say goodbye to Nebraska. Hooked by the new landscape, I clipped the corner at Highway 8 and headed west, a-ridin' towards Pawnee City. The road itself was as straight as an arrow all the way to the horizon, yet it rolled up and down like a wave across the soft hills. Telltale signs of dust are seen in the distance and the force of the wind reminds you that out here little interrupts the land but you.

Curves in these parts are almost non-existent, so when you have to change direction it's usually handled by a sharp right angle turn. Highway 8 tosses in a few of these and after a jog left followed by a jog right you'll be on the straight and narrow to U.S. 77 where you should head south. The odd thing is that even though maps display U.S. 77 as a major road, it seems more remote than the one you just left. Another pleasant discovery was finding that it sends you on fantastically long stretches across rural America, across the Kansas border, and all the way into the town of Marysville which was once the base for the **Pony Express Original Home Station No. 1** (106 South 8th St., 785/562-3825). The Pony Express only operated for a year and a half, but the museum here shares the tale of the men and boys who pushed it to the limit to get the mail through. If you don't have time for the museum, look for the Pony Express statue that'll make a great backdrop for a shot of your bike.

Stay on U.S. 77 through Marysville which continues falling south all the way down to Blue Rapids, where a sharp right leads you into Waterville where you say so long to U.S. 77 and cast your lot with Highway 9. I had assumed that after a few twists and turns Highway 9 would eventually get me to the first overnight in Concordia. It very well could have, but the lack of any distractions caused me to daydream and miss the turn where Highway 9 dropped south. Unknowingly, I was now riding due west on Highway 148 and for about thirty miles nothing I passed had any real bearing on where I actually was.

Believing I had died and was riding in limbo was tempered as Highway 148 gave me the gift of an incredibly fast and fun roller coaster run on a loose, licorice whip of a road. This is one of the best country runs from here all the way to the sleepy community of Agenda and beyond that to Wayne. Having fought Omaha's urban density, opening the throttle on this wide-open road is like opening your favorite Christmas present. The thrill lasts for miles as each click of the odometer reminds you why you love to ride. After another right angle jog past Wayne, you'll work your way to U.S. 81 and then drop

Riding that ribbon of highway in stark and spare northern Kansas: an unexpected surprise in a state that offers riders miles of solitude and peaceful motorcycling.

south, down through the empty Kansas countryside all the way to Concordia.

CONCORDIA PRIMER

How big is Concordia? Well, city hall is located in what was once Boogaart's grocery store. This town, like others you'll reach along this ride, is small and lonely and lacks the activities you'll find in major areas. This doesn't mean it lacks history.

Sitting in the Republican River Valley 150 miles north of Wichita and 175 miles west of Topeka, Concordia was established in 1872—a few years after it had become one of the stops for an incredible operation called the Orphan Train Movement which relocated an estimated 200,000 orphaned, abandoned, and homeless children out of crowded east coast cities and into new homes across rural America.

Good enough for orphans, the town was later good enough for German prisoners of war who found a temporary home north of town at Camp Concordia. More than a half century later, it became home to "California" Phil Sudduth, who owns Concordia's only H-D parts and service shop. Sudduth doesn't regret his decision to leave Los Angeles for the heartland.

"It's beautiful here," he says. "I'm still discovering all these cool two-lane country roads, and at night you'll see millions of stars, and when the wheat is ripe you can ride and literally see the wind blowing over the amber waves of grain. I just turn off my bike and watch."

ON THE ROAD: CONCORDIA

As in the other towns you'll visit on this run, Concordia doesn't have an overwhelming amount of activities, and the roads around town are similar to the ones you'll see riding west. So today, as in the days ahead, just settle back and see how folks live in rural Kansas.

PULL IT OVER:
CONCORDIA HIGHLIGHTS
Attractions and Adventures

Before arriving in Concordia I had never heard of the Orphan Train Movement. Since then I have never forgotten it. In brief, between 1854 and 1929 trains loaded with orphaned, abandoned, and homeless children left New York City and, as they rolled across America, chuffed to a halt at small depots where rural families arrived to pick out a new kid. Many of these children's descendants are still here, nearly a century after their ancestors rolled in. Learn about these incredible journeys at the **National Orphan Train Complex** (300 Washington St., 785/243-4471, www.orphantraindepot.com). Located in the restored Union Pacific station, there are artifacts as well as tales of the children who rode the trains, some having to leave a brother or sister behind when adopted by a family who wanted only one.

Once considered the finest theater between Kansas City and Denver, the **Brown Grand Theatre** (310 W. 6th St., 785/243-2553, www.browngrand.org) faced ruin before being restored by the town. Today it hosts movies and live performances, but even if the stage is empty you can drop in and take a self-guided tour for a buck or have a docent lead you around for five. Considering where it sits, the Brown Grand may be one of the prairie's most puzzling pieces of grandeur.

I was impressed that I was impressed by the annex of the **Cloud County Historical Museum** (130 E. 6th St., 785/243-4303). It had plenty to keep me intrigued, like art woven from wheat, a stage coach, an old Dodge, an antique soda fountain, and Minnie Cool Blake's 1882 floral wreath made of human hair, which looked similar to the one I keep in my tub drain. The main museum (635 Broadway,

785/243-2866) has more displays, including trucks, tractors, farm machinery, and a biplane.

Blue-Plate Specials

Most dining options in Concordia will either be in someone's kitchen or at a chain restaurant. One place that serves the kind of home cooking you'd hope to find is **Kristy's Family Restaurant** (101 W. 6th St., 785/243-4653), where they serve comfort foods in a diner that's not old-fashioned, it's just plain old. Locals looking for Italian food hang out at **Gambino's Pizza** (202 S. Main St., 660/463-2192) and for barbeque head over to **Heavy's BBQ** (103 W. 7th St., 785/262-4132, www.heavysbbqnck.com) for ribs, prime rib, steaks, salads, and soups.

Watering Holes

Not surprisingly, Concordia's not a place where you'll find wild nightlife. You can grab a brew at a local restaurant—there's a full bar over at **Heavy's BBQ** (103 W. 7th St., 785/262-4132, www.heavysbqnck.com). Or you can pick up something to take to your room after stopping at the **Corner Liquor Store** (237 W. 5th St., 785/243-4246) or the **Liquor Outlet** (1250 Lincoln St., 785/243-1852).

Shut-Eye
Inn-dependence

Aside from some chain hotels, there's a bed-and-breakfast out in the country; far enough out where the night sky looks white with stars, but not so far you feel stranded. That's the **Kansas Creek Inn** (1330 Union Rd. 785/243-9988, $65 and up), a nice retreat with large rooms, a big breakfast, and plenty of space around.

Chance encounters like these are what touring's all about: swapping yarns with the wonderful Mary Esther Holbert, a Kansas farmer, outside Concordia.

Silos like these are all that breaks the loneliness of Kansas roads.

© NANCY HOWELL

Chain Drive

These chain hotels are in town, or within 10 miles of the city center:

Econo Lodge, Holiday Inn, Super 8

For more information, including phone numbers and websites, see page 439.

ON THE ROAD: CONCORDIA TO OBERLIN

I can't emphasize enough how cool it is to wake up in a town like Concordia, get on your bike, and then start the day on a road that doesn't assault you with strip malls, stop lights, or traffic. Here, from horizon to horizon, the prairie is your great escape.

Riding Highway 9 west, the road is familiarly flat and level as it reaches out to hook up with rural U.S. 24 near the town of Beloit. From here, U.S. 24 will be the only road you'll need for the next hundred miles. When I rode in late summer, the sunflowers aimed their periscope tops towards the sky, long trains rolled alongside the highway, and combines were working the ground. There were unusual sights like the one after mile marker 153 where, in the middle of a farmer's field, was a bathtub, shower, and a toilet elevated about ten feet. A sign read, "Shower—5 cents. No checks." When there's not much else to notice, you notice things like that.

I also noticed folks getting up and going to work, although not in a car or taxi or subway. They were on tractors and they were heading out to wrestle with dozens of square miles of farmland. Aside from that, there seemed to be hardly any traffic, which puzzled me because each time I'd park to take a picture, somehow a driver always appeared, passed by, then slowed to make a U-turn and return to ask if I was OK. All of the Kansans I met are decent people.

It was a good feeling and one that lasted as U.S. 24 cleared the region past lonely Waconda Lake and slid into Cawker City where you'll see one of America's most curious curiosities. In 1953, a feller name Frank Stroeber had two things: A little bit of twine, and a whole lot of time. He began making a ball out of that sisal twine and he kept at it, reverting to his personal maxim "Patience + Thrift = Success" whenever his spirits flagged. With that credo and a lot of twine, Stroeber created the **World's Largest Ball of Twine,** which today is more than 40 feet in circumference, weighs more than 18,000 pounds, and would stretch nearly 1,500 miles if unraveled.

Following Cawker City, the landscape loses its Kansas cornfield look and becomes grazing land for cattle. At a ridge past Osborne you'll see another reminder in dimension as the highway punches its way to the horizon. If you recall Westerns showing families crossing the land in their prairie schooners, the scene is familiar. Many hoped to reach the far edges of the Western Frontier but some only made it as far as Kansas, stopping and creating small towns that, more than a century later, are in their golden years. In many of these future ghost towns, entire blocks of buildings are empty and there is no gas, no lodging, no food. In some places, though, stubborn residents aren't ready to give up the ghost.

Nowhere is this sense of determination more evident than in Nicodemus. Founded in 1877, it's America's longest-existing all-black community where about 30 descendents of the town's founders still live in the middle of nowhere. Amidst a handful of single-story homes and a playground, there is a National Park Service office where a lonely ranger patiently awaits guests. Stop in and read the account of a little girl from the Deep South who thought she was moving into the Emerald City. Imagine her reaction when she saw Nicodemus, circa 1880: a vast plain where the lonely residents lived in subterranean sod houses.

Just a few miles ahead, Hill City is an oasis of restaurants and service stations. When I stopped for lunch, a local suggested backtracking to Damar, a settlement founded by French Canadians in 1888. I took him up on it, backtracking on U.S. 24 and then dropping down on Highway 18. The 30-minute side trip took me further out into the countryside and

Surveying bales of hay and fields of corn in Damar, outside Hill City, Kansas.

© NANCY HOWELL

into a neat European-style village lorded over by the towering St. Joseph Church.

Whether you take the detour or not, from Hill City U.S. 283 heads north into one of the nation's largest sensory deprivation chambers. An eerie silence and emptiness surrounds you since, aside from a few fences and telephone poles, there's not a trace of human civilization. I parked at a slight rise in the road and looked around. From horizon to horizon I calculated I was the only one viewing 900 squares miles of emptiness. This alone assured me that I was on the right path.

I let the image affix in my mind and then broke the quiet by starting the bike. It had been quite a day. I headed up U.S. 283 to U.S. 36 and cruised in silence all the way west to Oberlin.

OBERLIN PRIMER

Back in 1873, David Fherrad and J. A. Rodehaver proved they were ahead of their time by receiving the first deeds for land here. By the following spring, immigrants headed up from the southeast part of the county and settled along Prairie Dog Creek.

Although buffalo and wild horses were roaming the ranges here, new residents from the East were bringing herds of cattle to the area, which meant that buffalo and wild horses had to find a new home. But it wasn't long before the cattle would have to cut out. In early 1880, county commissioners passed the "Herd Law" that prohibited meat cattle, horses, swine, sheep, mules, and asses from running at large. With that, cattle ranchers had to give way to agriculturists and today folks in Oberlin are tending to the land that takes care of them.

ON THE ROAD: OBERLIN

As in Concordia, there's not a whole lotta shakin' going on, but since you've already

Beware of oncoming traffic: It arrives once a month on remote Nebraska highways.

seen the road coming in and will certainly see the road going out, some time in town should keep you occupied.

What I like about downtown Oberlin is that it looks like a town from the 1960s. On the wide brick avenue in the center of town, cars park diagonally in front of the town's independent hardware stores, florists, and drugstores. Mosey around, check out some of the shops, and enjoy the serenity of a truly nice Kansas community.

PULL IT OVER: OBERLIN HIGHLIGHTS
Attractions and Adventures

After settlers settled on Indian land, many had to pay the price. A portion of the **Last Indian Raid Museum** (258 S. Penn Ave., 785/475-2712) focuses on the last Indian raid in Kansas, when a small band of Indians escaped their reservation to take revenge on white settlers who'd acquired their land and ended their way of life. Several buildings are filled with artifacts, including a re-creation of a pioneer sod house, a one-room schoolhouse, and a railroad depot.

Two miles east of town is **Sappa Park,** where there are more than five miles of walking and riding trails, camping areas, a golf course, pavilions, and special events such as antique engine and thresher shows, barbeque cook-offs, car shows, and the county fair.

Shopping

Downtown, which is Oberlin's commercial core, isn't so large that you can't cover it. Just wander Penn Avenue and drop in on the interesting collection of antiques shops, gift shops, restaurants, and mercantiles. Owned and operated by the gentleman who runs the Landmark Inn, **Oberlin Mercantile** (189 S. Penn Ave., 785/475-2340) is an old-fashioned gift shop showcasing Kansas books and food, Victorian collectibles, antiques, collectible toys, and jewelry.

Blue-Plate Specials

Perhaps the town's finest dining is at the LandMark Inn's **Teller Restaurant** (189 S. Penn Ave., 785/475-2340 or 888/639-0003, www.landmarkinn.com), a spacious dining room and lounge on the ground floor of the nicest inn in town. Wood ceilings and reproduction gaslights give it a turn-of-the-century feel, and menu items change daily and feature gourmet entrées and specialty desserts.

Watering Holes

In the tradition of dining choices, recommendations for nighttime activities are equally spare. A local suggested the lounge at the **LandMark Inn** (189 S. Penn Ave., 785/475-2340, www.landmarkinn.com) or perhaps, most plausibly, sipping a drink at the **ReLoad** (133 S. Penn Ave., 785/475-2421) which is part diner–part bar, with bar food, a pool table, pinball, cold beer, and wine coolers.

Shut-Eye

Lodging is hard to come by in town, and chain hotels are nowhere to be found. Still, there are some great finds. The highly recommended **LandMark Inn** (189 S. Penn Ave., 785/475-2340 or 888/639-0003, www.landmarkinn.com, $70–110) has been a land office, bank, courthouse, and telephone office. Today it's a seven-room bed-and-breakfast decorated in Victorian style. Rooms are spacious, and downstairs is the very convenient and very tasty Teller Room restaurant.

With its location a little off the highway, the **Frontier Motel** (207 E. Frontier Pkwy., 785/475-2203, $49–60) is a little quieter and perhaps more practical. Dine at the motel's Frontier Restaurant or live it up by hanging out poolside.

ON THE ROAD: OBERLIN TO OGALLALA

To reach Nebraska you only need to find U.S. 83 and shoot north towards McCook. The state border is less than 15 miles away and the road there is much the same as what you recall from the day before, with huge skies above and horizons that open to the ends of the earth.

Depending on your interests, you may decide to stop in McCook to see the **High Plains Museum** (421 Norris Ave., 308/345-3661) which displays authentic pioneer artifacts from the 1870s, archival photographs highlighting Nebraska history, a collection of fossils, and wall paintings from a POW camp. McCook is where you can also take advantage of restaurants and big box stores, although it pleased me to find that, in the 450 miles since Omaha, I had no desire or use for them. So I rode on toward Imperial, first by taking U.S. 6/34, then veering north onto Highway 25 when my original path turned out to be a dud. I was glad to make the switch because Highway 25 put me right back where I wanted to be, and that was riding in the solitude of the high plains. It would be 100 miles before I'd reach Sutherland, but out here distances like this don't seem as distant. Riding through rural communities where maybe 34 or 57 or 62 people lived was akin to riding without a lifeline, freed from all the things that bind you to an office.

After crossing beneath I-80, I reached Sutherland at the junction of U.S. 30, and headed west. Now I was riding the tail end of the Platte River Scenic Trail that was originally built as part of the Lincoln Highway, America's first transcontinental highway. While more populated than where I had been, considering where I had come from it was still quite spare. I had nothing to distract me as the bike found the next stop.

Ogallala.

OGALLALA PRIMER

If you recall the classic mini-series *Lonesome Dove*, you may recall that Ogallala ("the Gomorrah of the Cattle Trail") was a popular conjugal retreat. You may have even heard that in real life a trail boss refused to let his cowhands enter Ogallala because of its wild reputation, an action that marked the settlement as "the town too tough for Texans."

With Texans driving cattle across the Great Plains, between 1870 and 1885 Ogallala gained fame as the "Gateway of the Northern Plains," the end of the line for cattle being shipped out to Wyoming and Montana via the town's Union Pacific railhead. The town was also the end of the line for some unlucky cardsharps and cowboys whose tempers led to deadly duels at the bars and saloons that ran down the Platte River. Sadly, Ogallala was also the end of the line for local Sioux who were crushed by military campaigns before they were shoved onto reservations in 1876.

At least the Sioux had karma on their side. In 1884 an epidemic of "Texas fever" affected cattle and led to massive losses for local ranchers and the violent town's promising fortunes evaporated and it turned into a placid prairie community.

Those Wild West heydays, though, are still celebrated in Ogallala today.

Open road, clear skies, and cattle grazing north of Arthur in wide open Nebraska... and miles to go before I sleep.

ON THE ROAD: OGALLALA

In a town of fewer than 5,000, there's not much shaking. And since the road north is one you'll take to reach the Sandhills, perhaps the best thing you can do is see a few sites, hang out at a saloon, and bunk down for an overnight.

PULL IT OVER: OGALLALA HIGHLIGHTS
Attractions and Adventures

The town's focal point is **Front Street** (519 E. 1st St., 308/284-6000, www.megavision.net/frontstreet), a sanitized recreation of the hangout favored by Texas drovers, tin-horn gamblers, and dance hall gals. Behind a block-long Wild West facade of a jail, undertaker's parlor, tonsorial palace (barbershop), and livery barn is the "world-famous" Crystal Palace Revue that features comics, singers, can-can girls, and a nightly shoot-out throughout the summer.

Another bow to the Old West is Ogallala's **Boot Hill Cemetery** (West 10th St. and Parkhill Dr.), one of about 25 in the U.S. It is named for the days when men were "buried with their boots on." Located on a rise northwest of Ogallala, it was created in the days when the final word was the sharp report of a gun. More than 100 victims of violence are buried here; a high percentage considering the early settlement never exceeded 130 permanent residents. Few of the wooden grave markers weathered the years, so who knows who's underfoot—or the stories they could have shared?

Shopping

Located in the shops of Front Street, the **Petrified Wood Gallery** (525 E. 1st St., 308/284-9996, www.petrifiedwoodgallery.com) reveals the passion of brothers Howard and Harvey Kenfield. They spent half a century gathering ancient woods

Checking out—but not into—the Graybar Hotel at Front Street in Ogallala.

and fossils from around the world and combing the surrounding countryside for Native American arrowheads and artifacts. They donated their collection to the city and opened up this gallery that reveals the beauty of nature and the dedication of two brothers.

Blue-Plate Specials

As well as being an attraction, **Front Street** (519 E. 1st St., 308/284-6000, www.megavision.net/frontstreet) features a restaurant that serves up fare such as buffalo burgers, fried chicken, and mountain oysters (kids love 'em!), prime rib, and seafood.

Equally hearty meals can be found at the **Golden Spur Steakhouse** (203 Stagecoach Tr., 308/284-2300) which, naturally, features NY strip, T-bones, filet mignon, Texas-style country steaks, chopped steak, and burgers, as well as pastas, seafood, soups, and salads. There's also a full liquor bar.

Watering Holes

Ladies and gentlemen, once again...**Front Street** (519 E. 1st St., 308/284-6000, www.megavision.net/frontstreet). Even when the Revue has stopped for the season, the big bar and live entertainment still go on. Likewise, there's also a full bar at the **Golden Spur Steakhouse** (203 Stagecoach Tr., 308/284-2300). Downtown, you'll also find two basic bars at **Champions Bar & Grill** (111 W. 2nd St., 308/284-0804) and the **Underpass** (112 E. 1st St., 308/284-6361).

Shut-Eye

There are several chain hotels in town, as well as the **Grey Goose Lodge** (201 Chuckwagon Rd., 308/284-3623 or 800/573-7148, www.thegreygooselodge.com, $72), a 151-room hotel with an outdoor heated pool and two on-site restaurants.

Chain Drive

These chain hotels are in town, or within 10 miles of the city center:
Best Western, Comfort Inn, Days Inn, Holiday Inn, Rodeway, Super 8
For more information, including phone numbers and websites, see page 439.

ON THE ROAD: OGALLALA TO BROKEN BOW

If you began this run in Omaha, you've already traveled about 600 miles—and this next leg will add another 200 across the fabled Sandhills of Nebraska until you arrive in Broken Bow. Leaving town on Highway 61/92 north, just a few miles out of town the elevation perks up near Lake McConaughy, an artificial lake formed by a dam project in the 1930s. Odds are the first sight of it will have you locking up the brakes and taking a look. On the west side, a pullout gives you a glimpse of "Big Mac's" 35,000 acres and 100 miles of shoreline. If you double back to the east shore there's a park on the peninsula, where the small islands on this side seem to mirror northern Wisconsin wilderness.

With the lake in your mirrors, you'll soon enter grasslands and high plains. The cornfields and sunflowers of northern Kansas are gone now and cattle and horses have free rein over the land here. The roads are low and level and steady and lead to the county seat at Arthur. I've seen a lot of county seats—New York is a county seat, and so are San Francisco and Miami. But here the Arthur County Courthouse is just about the size of a '77 Dodge van.

There are some shops here and an old honky-tonk, but then Arthur disappears. You'll return to the clear country and slowly curving roads where there's little expected of you except to listen to the steady throb of your bike and spend some of your life taking in the sight of the surrounding hills. If you live in a place where there are too many people or too many things, this is where you can stop and watch the cattle graze, see the big sky streaked with clouds, and feel the brute force of the wind as it blows hard across the grasslands. You've reached a part of your ride where nothing is everything.

For about an hour you'll enjoy the luxury of wide open hills and plains before reaching the junction of Highway 2 near Hyannis. While it certainly doesn't look like a place where the Kennedys would live, a conveniently placed service station is here which gives you a place to fill up your bike and yourself before heading east on the next leg of the journey: a 63-mile run to Thedford.

This stretch takes you across Nebraska's fabled Sandhills. At 20,000 square miles, this is the largest sand dune formation in the Western Hemisphere and creates what's considered to be one of the Top 10 scenic routes in the nation. I wouldn't rank it so high, but at least it gives you the same free-range riding you've gotten used to. I was impressed that the structure of the dunes reminded me of being at the beach, although the nearest shorelines from here are 1,500 miles away.

Roughly an hour later (sooner if you take advantage of the absence of law enforcement), you'll have ridden 63 miles and passed Thedford. You'll see that the Nebraska National Forest has taken up position on the southern edge of the byway. Not a forest in a Pacific Northwest sense, trees break up the landscape and mark the last 70-some miles to Broken Bow.

I found I didn't mind these long stretches that presented nothing except a highway. Along the way I'd pass hundred-yard sprinklers and huge silos and travel beside locomotives hauling more than a mile of freight behind them. I would take on the wind and the rain and savor every minute as I rode east through small towns that may not live to see another decade. Later, I'd re-enter the urban atmosphere in Grand Island, Lincoln, and Omaha.

I knew I'd be back. I'd taken a fancy to the Plains.

BROKEN BOW PRIMER

OK, you want to know how the town got such a cool name. The story is that folks starting the post office rejected a few proposed names before a local resident recalled that a broken bow had been found at an old Indian burial ground.

There you go. I can't vouch for the accuracy of that tale, but I'm fairly certain that Broken Bow hasn't changed much since its founding in the 1880s or when an anonymous writer observed in a 1939 Federal Writer's Project Guide that "Broken Bow...is a shipping center for livestock, hay, and grain. It has factories making cigars and brooms, two hotels, and an airport."

The cigar and broom factory have moved on, their commercial impact supplanted by Adams Land and Cattle, the state's largest feed operation. Also gone are the livery stables mills, brickyards, blacksmiths, bottling plants, and Chinese laundry of the 1930s. But as you can deduce from the scenes you see today, progress has been slow and steady around this town, population 3,700.

ON THE ROAD: BROKEN BOW

As in Hill City, Kansas, it feels right to use the word "oasis" to describe Broken Bow. Surrounded by endless miles of prairie, the city has more than 2,000 acres of parks, an Olympic-size swimming pool, softball and baseball diamonds, tennis facilities, a fishing pond, picnic and camping facilities, and playgrounds.

When you wander around downtown, there doesn't seem to be much to do aside from dropping in at some shops, sipping a treat at the old-fashioned soda fountain, and noticing things like the century-old Tom Butler Memorial Bandstand in the middle of town square.

But having traveled for several days across the Great Plains, in Broken Bow the pace feels just right.

PULL IT OVER: BROKEN BOW HIGHLIGHTS
Attractions and Adventures

On the west side of the square, the **Custer County Museum** (445 S. 9th St., 308/872-2203) gives you a glimpse into life as it was in 19th-century Custer County through photos, artifacts, and a recreation of an 1886 general store with original display cases and merchandise. With many more miles of Sandhills lying east of Broken Bow, you may want to drop in at the **Sandhills Journey Scenic Byway Visitor Center** (Hwy. 2, 308/872-8331, www.sandhillsjourney.com) which has a significant amount of information on sights and services along the entire length of the byway.

Shopping

The greatest concentration of stores surround the town square. For lady riders, one stands out: **Way Out West** (424 South 8th Ave., 308/872-5352, www.mywayoutwest.com). A lifelong love of horses and infatuation with the western lifestyle found Cindy Duncan creating Hollywood-accented designs of western jewelry, tack, gifts, home decor, boots, jeans, and unique clothing done with an artistic eye and flair.

Blue-Plate Specials

Ready to take you back a few decades is **Emily's Soda Fountain** (845 South D St., 308/872-5200). After owners Rod and Barb Pracht found an antique soda fountain, they found an 1893 building to put it in. Located right on the town square, it's the type of place you recall you've seen on the movie screen...or after high school.

Located in the Historic Arrow Hotel, **Bonfire Grill** (509 South 9th Ave., 308/872-3363, www.bonfire-grill.com) has a warm and rich look, matched by the quality of the meals, with steaks being (naturally) a specialty. The booths add a sense of privacy, and if you look closely you'll notice they're created from old hotel room doors—just look for the number. I highly recommend the Bonfire Grill.

Watering Holes

Once again, the Arrow Hotel comes

through with the **Bonfire Pub** (509 South 9th Ave.), a welcoming place for quiet contemplation or engaging conversation. It's first rate. **Sylvester's** (723 E. South E St., 308/872-6204) is an energized roadhouse that features live bands playing country and rock.

Shut-Eye

There's a nice selection of lodging around town. The **Gateway Motel** (628 E. South E St./Hwy. 2, 308/872-2478, $40 and up) has queen beds, refrigerators, and microwaves in the rooms. Another favorite with riders is the **Big 12 Motel** (853 E. South E St., 308/872-2412, $50 and up), and the chain hotel, **America's Best Value Inn** (215 E. South E St., 308/872-6428, $70 and up).

If you lean toward inns, the **Rocking Chair Inn Bed & Breakfast** (511 North 10th Ave., 308/872-6580, www.rocking-chairbandb.com, $60 and up) is in an historic Queen Anne–style home, and features two rooms; one with a shared bath and the other with an attached kitchenette. Overnight stays come complete with a full breakfast.

Winning my vote for best looks and lodging is the top notch **Arrow Hotel** (509 South 9th Ave., 308/872-6662 or 866/972-6662, www.arrowhotel.com, $70–146). Quite a surprise in a town the size of Broken Bow, it has an elegant Old West look, a dining room that's tops, a Gilded Age cigar room with swivel leather chairs, stained glass windows, and western-themed art, as well as a seductive pub that'll lure you in for hours. From the circa 1928 front desk to 23 clean rooms and suites, this may be the best option in town.

Resources for Riders

Plains and Simple

Kansas Travel Information
Kansas Camping Information—www.ksrvparks.com or
    www.ks-camping-review.com
Kansas Department of Wildlife and Parks—620/672-5911,
    www.kdwp.state.ks.us
Kansas Road Conditions—http://511.ksdot.org
Kansas Travel & Tourism—800/252-6727, www.travelks.com

Nebraska Travel Information
Nebraska Camping Reservations—402/471-1414,
    www.nebraskastateparks.reserveamerica.com
Nebraska Game and Parks Commission—402/471-0641,
    www.ngpc.state.ne.us
Nebraska Road Conditions—www.511nebraska.org
Nebraska Tourism—877/632-7275, www.visitnebraska.org

Local and Regional Information
Broken Bow Chamber of Commerce—308/872-5691, www.brokenbow-ne.com
Cloud County Tourism (Concordia)—785/243-4303, www.tourcloudcounty.com
Decatur County Chamber of Commerce (Oberlin)—785/475-3441,
    www.oberlinkansas.org
Ogallala Chamber of Commerce—308/284-4066, www.visitogallala.com
Sandhills Byway—www.sandhillsjourney.com

Kansas Motorcycle Shops
California Phil's—902 Lincoln Ave., Concordia, 785/243-9991,
    www.harleypartscheap.com

Nebraska Motorcycle Shops

BMW Motorcycles Of Omaha—6775 S. 118th St., Omaha, 402/861-8488,
www.bmwomaha.com

Breeze Cycle—4961 Center St., Omaha, 402/991-5500, www.breezecycle.com

Clifford Cycles—6132 Military Ave., Omaha, 402/558-8006,
www.cliffordcycles.com

D & J Motorsports—3333 S. 61st Ave., Omaha, 402/891-9821,
www.dandjmotor-sports.com

Dillon Brothers Harley-Davidson—174th and Maple Sts., Omaha,
402/289-5556, www.dillonharley.com

Dillon Brothers MotorSports—3848 N. Cleveland Blvd., Omaha, 402/505-4228
or 800/964-1882, www.powersportspro.com

Frontier Harley-Davidson—205 NW 40th St., Lincoln, 402/466-9100,
www.frontierhd.com

Grand Island Kart & Cycle—3630 S. Locust St., Grand Island, 308/382-3181

Harley Davidson Central—2719 S. Locust St., Grand Island, 308/382-7020,
www.h-dcentral.com

Holstein's Harley-Davidson—4940 S. 72nd St., Omaha, 402/331-0022,
www.holsteinsharley.com

Leisure Life Sports—9004 S. 145th St., Omaha, 402/333-0655,
www.leisurelifesports.com

Lincoln Cycle & ATV—3320 Cornhusker Hwy., Lincoln, 402/464-5551

Motorsports Sales & Service—721 Claude Rd., Grand Island, 308/398-8008,
www.motorsportsgi.com

Star City Motor Sports—6600 N. 27th St., Lincoln, 402/476-7768,
www.starcitymotorsports.com

Tri-City Cycle Works—3234 W. Schimmer Dr., Grand Island, 308/395-8800,
www.tricitycycleworks.com

Werner Cycle Works—14410 Frontier Rd., Omaha, 402/894-3050,
www.wernercycleworks.com

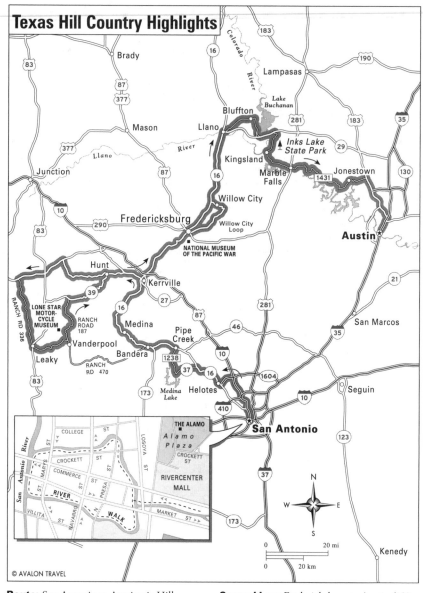

Texas Hill Country Highlights

Route: San Antonio to Austin via Hill Country and Fredericksburg

Distance: Approximately 365 miles

First Leg: San Antonio to Fredericksburg (105 miles)

Second Leg: Fredericksburg to Austin (150 miles)

Optional: Texas Hill Country Loop (110 miles)

Helmet Laws: Texas requires helmets.

© AVALON TRAVEL

Texas Hill Country Highlights

San Antonio, Texas to Austin, Texas

Even if they've told you a million times, Texans will still want to impress upon you a few million more that they live in a very large state. But only one of these messages really drove that point home. In lonely Luckenbach, Virgil the Store Guy pointed out that if you head west to the California line, *half* of your ride will be in Texas...and in Luckenbach you're already halfway across the state.

The breadth of the state made the decision to concentrate this ride within just a portion of expansive Hill Country seem wise since most Texans agree this is the state's most scenic region. Spreading west of Austin and San Antonio, with those cities as an anchor and Fredericksburg as a destination, I found that Hill Country attracts the spiritual heirs of Old West cowboys: riders who savor the joy that comes with reaching open country and freeing their spirits on open roads.

SAN ANTONIO PRIMER

You'll pick up a lot of history on San Antonio when you visit The Alamo and cruise the canals. But before you arrive you need to understand that your image of the city and The Alamo are probably wrong. It's not in the desert, and John Wayne isn't on the parapet wearing a coonskin cap and firing a flintlock. San Antonio's grown up a lot in the last 175 years...and even more since 1691 when Spanish explorers and missionaries reached the riverfront Indian settlement of Yanaguana on June 13, the feast day of Saint Anthony of Padova, Italy. Did the Indians have a say in the name change? Of course not. A few decades later a riverfront fort was established which became the nucleus of a community that would include five missions and an increasing number of soldiers and their families. This eventually led to the largest settlement in Texas.

Historically, the most significant event came in 1836. Antonio López de Santa Anna had rescinded the Mexican constitution of 1824 and the Texians, Tejanos (Texans of Hispanic descent), and newly arriving European immigrants had lost the rights to a representative government. They reacted by taking control of San Antonio and in February 1836 Santa Anna brought his troops up through Mexico and into San Antonio to rout the soldiers at The Alamo. As you'll see, several weeks later Santa Anna paid for the massacre and Texas became a free republic. After that, the town endured minor wars and skirmishes, developed the cowboy culture, and adopted even more citizens from Europe. Today its incredible story and determination to succeed has created an economy based primarily on tourism with support from research facilities and four local military installations.

Plus, it's one of the prettiest major cities around.

ON THE ROAD: SAN ANTONIO

If you find a place to stay downtown chances are you may not have to move your bike. Most things visitors want to see are right here...and they are legion. Most of what you'll want to see is centered downtown (and described below). Commerce and Market Streets are filled with local business people as well as tourists, who frequently descend the steps to stroll along the banks of the tranquil River Walk. There. You'll find hundreds of shops, hotels, restaurants, and photo ops. First-time visitors should head east toward Alamo Plaza, an interesting, old-fashioned thoroughfare where there are some neat clubs, cool shops, a visitors center, and...The Alamo.

PULL IT OVER: SAN ANTONIO HIGHLIGHTS
Attractions and Adventures

Nearly every ad you see for San Antonio includes one of two things: The Alamo and the River Walk. Each is well worth seeing, but I'd suggest starting with the River Walk.

Once threatened with eradication after serious floods, some folks wanted to infill the city's historic canals and create sewers. That was before the San Antonio Conservation Society stepped in. Their protests, which began in 1926, helped keep the idea of a scenic riverwalk alive. Designer Robert Hugman joined the fight, coming up with an eye-catching design in 1929. His vision was to create a cross between Venice and New Orleans. Today considered the Father of the River Walk, Hugman kept the idea alive for seven years until funding came through. The Depression-era WPA saved the canals and set the stage for today's tourism. By starting here, you'll get a good sense of River Walk's serpentine layout and see the sites to revisit. Best of all, you'll be able to explore the town with a better understanding of its history.

Rio San Antonio Cruises (210/244-5700 or 800/417-4139, www.riosanantonio.com, $8) operates a fleet of boats that

River Walk is the centerpiece of San Antonio's social, culinary, artistic, and tourist community.

take easygoing 40-minute tours that reveal waterfalls and cypress trees, a statue of St. Antonio, historic buildings, plenty of restaurants, and an open-air stage marked by five bells symbolizing the city's five missions.

After the River Walk, walk over to Alamo Plaza and in an instant you'll recognize **The Alamo** (210/225-1391, www.thealamo.org, free). Rangers who are passionate about what happened here are vital sources of information, so ask them for the details. In brief, what occurred here culminated in the events of 1836. An assortment of nearly 200 farmers, lawyers, surveyors, and frontiersmen (including Jim Bowie and Davy Crockett) hoped to protect what they believed was the provisional capital of the Republic of Texas. On the final morning of a 13-day siege, the group was barricaded inside The Alamo as thousands of Mexican soldiers breached the walls. Having flown the "flag of no quarter," Santa Anna's men killed all of the defenders who had sought shelter inside the shrine and the Long Barrack. Santa Anna then had the bodies burned. He spared a handful of women, children, and slaves and instructed them to spread the word about what happened.

The following month at San Jacinto, Santa Anna and his 1,400 troops were paid back for what happened at The Alamo when Sam Houston and about 900 volunteers attacked at dawn and routed the Mexican army in 18 minutes. To avoid detection, Santa Anna ditched his ornate uniform. But when Santa Anna's men saluted him, Houston gathered he had bagged his prize. Santa Anna surrendered and the Republic of Texas was freed from Mexican control.

Start at the shrine with a self-guided tour, invest in a 45-minute audio tour, or meet in the oak-shaded courtyard to listen to presentations by rangers. Afterward, take some time to explore the park created as a WPA project in the 1930s, and do not miss the museum within the Long Barrack that details, through videos and artifacts, events leading up to the Texas Revolution.

It's possible, though not likely, you'll visit some of San Antonio's other major attractions, including **Sea World** (10500 SeaWorld Dr., 800/700-7786, www.seaworld.com) and **Six Flags Fiesta Texas** (17000 IH-10 West, 210/697-5050, www.sixflags.com).

Shopping

Most enterprises along the River Walk are restaurants, although **Rivercenter** (849 E. Commerce St., 210/225-0000, www.shoprivercenter.com) is a massive complex that'll grab your attention. The waterfront mall has about 60 stores and a few dozens restaurants to keep you occupied.

For local souvenirs, don't miss the **Buckhorn Museum Curio Store** (318 E. Houston St., 210/247-4000, www.buckhornmuseum.com), which proudly bills itself as "The Oddest Store in the World." Silver belt buckle sets, Indian-made beaded gloves, T-shirts, mugs, film and batteries, and plenty of Texas-centric gifts and souvenirs are for sale. When you're sick of shopping, grab a drink in the saloon.

Just north of the Alamo, **The History Shop** (713 E. Houston St., 210/229-9855, www.thehistoryshop.com) features artifacts found in excavations at the Alamo. It also buys, sells, and displays an intriguing museum-grade collection of original antique maps, antique books, militaria, and antique weapons. The emphasis is on the role of Texas in the Spanish Colonial era, the Texas Revolution, the Republic era, and the Civil War. It's the next best thing to being there.

If you're looking for a cheap place to find more apparel (or nearly anything else you may need for the road), head well south of town toward Lackland AFB. **Flea Mart** (12280 Hwy 16 S., 210/624-2666) has the usual merchandise (including wallets, T-shirts, and leather moto-clothing) as well as live bands and fresh Mexican food.

Blue-Plate Specials

It'd be impossible to pinpoint the few top choice restaurants in a city that has so many, but there are places that have stood the test of time. In 1946, **Casa Rio** (430 E. Commerce St., 210/225-6718, www. casa-rio.com) opened on the banks of the River Walk and sparked the boat tours (created for guests who were waiting hours for tables). It's still here, with tables in a picture perfect setting along the canal and under the bridge. The **Mi Tierra Cafe & Bakery** (218 Produce Row, 210/225-1262, www.mitierracafe.com) opened in 1941 as a three-table café and is now a popular 24-hour destination with a bar, bakery, and strolling musicians. **Boudro's** (421 E. Commerce St., 210/224-8484, www. boudros.com) has an impressive menu of Texas and Southwest dishes, and tables are right on the River Walk. I should also add the downtown **Denny's** (903 E. Commerce St., 210/223-4321) as a low-cost alternative to downtown hotel dining. According to the manager, it's the fourth busiest Denny's in the U.S.

Watering Holes

More than likely, you'll end up settling down with a drink along the River Walk, at a festive restaurant or bar that's filled with lots of people. A little ways south of the Alamo is **Bar America** (723 S. Alamo St., 210/223-7462), which could be classified as a joint. Students, workers, and other cash-conscious locals work on cheap beer (just over a buck) and games of pool (only two bits). Nearby, the **Acapulco Drive In** (609 S. Alamo St., 210/224-2452) serves cold beer with hot Tex-Mex food. Locals refer to it as an "ice house" (a callback to the pre-refrigerator days, when beers was packed on ice). There's more than ice here—add good food and a festive atmosphere. Also ice-cold and dirt-cheap, the **Sanchez Ice House** (819 S. San Saba, 210/223-0588) attracts riders who want to beat the heat with a chilled brew and spicy food. Just a hop, skip, and a stagger from the Blue Star Art Complex is the funky and cool **La Tuna** (100 Probandt St., 210/212-5727, www.latunagrill.com), a tin-clad Tex-Mex eatery and watering hole that's popular with artists and locals.

The **Buckhorn Saloon** (318 E. Houston St., 210/247-4000, www.buckhorn-museum.com) is part of a complex that includes five museums and a curio store. They say this is also where Teddy Roosevelt recruited Rough Riders and Pancho Villa planned the Mexican Revolution.

Shut-Eye

As in most major cities, the best choices for lodging will be chain hotels. Of course, location affects prices and staying near the core of the city will cost more than on the outskirts of town. Then again, you'll be within walking distance of things worth seeing. If you can swing it, the contemporary **Hotel Contessa** (306 W. Market St., 210/229-9222 or 866/435-0900, www. thehotelcontessa.com) is right on the river and has a nice vibe to it: perfect views through the atrium lobby, the cool Cork bar, and a spa.

Inn-dependence

The **Yellow Rose Bed and Breakfast** (229 Madison, 210/229-9903 or

800/950-9903, www.ayellowrose.com, $89–200) is an 1880s Victorian in downtown's historic King William District. If you're not sold on the whole B&B concept, this may be a good place to try it out, since you don't have to eat with other guests. A full breakfast is delivered to your room—or you can skip it altogether and pay a lower rate.

Chain Drive

These chain hotels are in town, or within 10 miles of the city center:

Best Western, Clarion, Comfort Inn, Courtyard by Marriott, Doubletree, Econo Lodge, Embassy Suites, Fairfield Inn, Hampton Inn, Hilton, Holiday Inn, Howard Johnson, Hyatt, Knights Inn, La Quinta, Motel 6, Omni Hotels, Quality Inn, Radisson, Residence Inn, Rodeway, Scottish Inns, Super 8, Travelodge

For more information, including phone numbers and websites, see page 439.

ON THE ROAD: SAN ANTONIO TO FREDERICKSBURG

The ride to Fredericksburg isn't far, but in those short miles you'll be immersed in the feel of Hill Country and the essence of Texas. Before you leave though, heed the advice of a local who noted that the state's four seasons are drought, flood, blizzard, and twister. Check the weather and dress for it.

It'll take you way too long to escape the pull of city traffic, and the fastest way to do it is to take I-10 west and then hook up with the 1604 Loop that drops south toward the town of Helotes on Highway 16. Even after Helotes, though, the road remains sluggish. A few miles ahead watch for Highway P37 on your left. Even though this route takes you out of your way, the *P* stands for *park* and reaching a

remote back road after city traffic is nice. There are low, shallow hills and the two-lane skims over the first of several hundred dry creek beds you'll see over the next few days.

There are only a few straightaways as the pavement bounces around like a mattress, winding through the country before hooking up with County Road 1283. While this road isn't as nice as the one you just left, it's good enough to head north and bring you back to Highway 16 and a place known as Pipe City. A short stretch ahead on your left is **Hole in the Wall,** a biker's bar; but, if you're riding without a bicycle chain in your pocket, keep going. Just ahead on your right is an abandoned filling station with some Good Gulf gas pumps that make a dynamite backdrop for a photo.

Right now you're about 30 miles outside of San Antonio and fast approaching the quirky motorcycle-friendly town of Bandera, the "Cowboy Capital of the World."

Taking a break by the good Gulf gas pumps near Pipe City, Texas.

A real biker bar can be found in Pipe City, midway between San Antonio and Bandera.

You'll agree they've earned the title when you turn right to follow Highway 16 and find a downtown that'd be right at home in the Old West. Arriving on a holiday weekend, I parked it for a while to watch cowboys and cowgirls riding horses down Main Street and a stagecoach rolling past. Outside the rider-friendly **11th Street Cowboy Bar** (307 11th St., 830/796-4849, www.11thstreetcowboybar.com), I struck up a conversation with two very friendly *Lonesome Dove*–style cowboys. With their horses tied to the hitching post, they explained how they raise a good horse and they accepted my compliments for preserving the cowboy lifestyle. They also asked me to share with you their admiration for motorcyclists. Good men, them cowboys.

If you can carve out some time in Bandera, there are neat stores that sell cool silver and turquoise jewelry and restaurants that cook up barbeque and home cooking. And then there's the old general store with an old-fashioned soda fountain and a floor that made me nervous by trembling beneath my feet. I stepped outside to investigate and through a non-descript red door headed down a dark flight of stairs and into one of the coolest honky-tonks I'd ever seen. It was **Arkey's Blues Silver Dollar Saloon** (308 Main St., 830/796-8826) and if you time it right (usually evenings and weekends) you may think you've walked into the 1930s. Cowboys and cowgirls in their finest Stetsons, blue jeans, boots, and denim shirts pack the floor and twirl to the red-hot rhythms of a Western swing band. The faces, fashion, and music were straight from the *Grapes of Wrath* and, God almighty, I wanted to stay and be part of it since I could've sworn I saw Hank Williams. But time interfered and I was back on the road, riding Highway 16 towards Medina where the road really cuts loose to release you into the Hill Country.

The road slips and slides across the countryside, giving you some nice patches of greenery and more dry creeks. The ride is long and lonesome for miles and miles as you ride into rural townships one second and ride out seconds later. There's not much to note but much emptiness to satisfy you as you round slow curves and glide beneath a few canopy roads. Soon you'll arrive at **Koyote Ranch** (23233 Hwy. 16, Medina, 830/589-4695 or 800/225-0991, www.koyoteranch.com), whose owners deserve special credit for creating a clean, well-placed, and completely unexpected sanctuary for Hill Country riders. The complex features cabins and camping for overnight travelers, maps of local rides, food, services, supplies, and a good vibe generated by motorcyclists who use Koyote as a base or rendezvous and the site of November's Three Sisters Rally.

With lodging waiting about an hour north, I got back on the road and found the blacktop springing open like a steel coil. Now I was given some great twists as the road started to scale sharper ascents and pack in a tighter series of turns. The energy of it all lasted until I reached the outskirts of Kerrville. It's a nice place; but it has all of the stores and services that dominate your everyday life. Hoping to clear it quickly, I reached the northern edge of town and rode beneath I-10. A few hundred yards later the town and its coast-to-coast highway disappeared behind me and the Texas countryside once again took control. The final 24 miles offered free range country cruising. Hardly demanding, the curves would arc like a rainbow as the road unraveled slowly all the way to one of the more unusual towns in Texas.

FREDERICKSBURG PRIMER

As you may have gathered from its name, Fredericksburg is steeped in German tradition. It was founded in 1846 when a group of German immigrants worked their way

Just follow these signs and you're on the right path.

up through Texas and came here. Among them was the elaborately titled nobleman Baron Otfried Hans von Meusebach. The baron had a similarly elaborate professional title: Commissioner General of the Society for the Protection of German Immigrants in Texas. By the time the Civil War kicked off 15 years later, the baron had renounced his title, changed his name to John O. Meusebach, and welcomed other liberal and educated Germans who helped Gillespie County resist talks of secession. Although they decided to stick with the fate of the Union (unusual in a state that sided with the Confederacy), they also decided to preserve their language, which became known as Texas German. Meusebach helped broker a peace treaty with local Commanches. Even though the Commanches could've held a grudge against Europeans for stealing their land, it was one of the few treaties the Indians could count on and it's still observed to this day.

The Legend of Luckenbach

U. S. POST-OFFICE
1850 LUCKENBACH, TX. 1971

Virgil the Store Guy keeps watch at the general store and post office in Luckenbach, Texas (pop. 0).

© NANCY HOWELL

Of all the places in America that've hit the jackpot of unwarranted popularity, the leader is about 10 miles outside Fredericksburg in lonely Luckenbach, Texas (pop. 0), www.luckenbachtexas.com.

After Willie Nelson and Waylon Jennings released their hit single in 1977, folks from around the world started making their way here…and they're still coming. Many arrive out of curiosity, others arrive in the evening to listen to a band and shuffle around the broad dance hall.

It was curiosity that brought me here and it was good fortune that I met Virgil Oldham ("Virgil the Store Guy"). He explained that in 1970, Hondo Crouch, a local rancher who wanted a place to drink and dance, joined in a partnership to purchase the town. The selling price? $30,000. Since then, music, mythology, and word of mouth have made this expanse of nearly nothing a global legend.

While sitting on the porch of the general store—which sells an amazing inventory of souvenirs and includes a quite inviting bar in back—I overheard Virgil sharing a story with a friend. Read this with a Texas drawl, for this is how I heard it:

…A guy comes in last Sunday and tells me his buddy's on his fourth tour in Iraq…and his son's about to be born in Twenty-nine Palms, California. Well, that didn't settle well with his buddy knowing that his boy's first steps were gonna be on California dirt and not on Texas dirt. So he comes out here and I help him scoop up some Luckenbach dirt out of the creek bed there and he's gonna drive it out to California for him so his daddy'll know that his li'l boy's first steps will be in Texas dirt.

You can't make this stuff up.

© NANCY HOWELL

Keeping sentinel over a parched Texas field, a lonely windmill is ready for action.

Skip ahead a century and you'll start to recognize today's Fredericksburg. First, Lyndon Johnson lived just a few miles away and during the late 1960s, while he was president, he hosted meetings at the LBJ Ranch (known as the Texas White House). This brought Hill Country to the attention of the world. Another step forward came in the late 1970s when city officials realized that a town based on agriculture was dependent on the weather. They began playing up their town as a tourist destination and, with its German heritage, wineries, and preserved downtown, it became just that. *Das ist wünderbar.*

ON THE ROAD: FREDERICKSBURG

Right now you're as far west as this tour goes—unless you leave town. So go. It'll be a long ride, but one that'll take you on a loop tour that'll get you on 1.5 legs of the legendary Three Sisters (Ranch Roads 335, 336, and 337), with complete freedom to take on the other half if time allows.

Before heading out, pick up a Hill Country map. The one that I found useful and easy to read was a free one I picked up earlier in Medina at Koyote Ranch, but it's also found at local hotels, restaurants, and businesses advertised on the map borders. With that in hand, I retraced the ride south on Highway 16 to Kerrville. I then headed west on Highway 27 where about five miles later the texture of the road and land changes and you need to watch for where Highway 39 veers to the left to follow the Texas Hill Country Trail.

Ahead the land gradually turns more verdant as a tributary of the Guadalupe River starts to follow the road. The road in turn becomes springy and bouncy and adds twists and dips as it splits off to follow County Road 1340 near the town of Hunt. Ahead came interesting surprises like folks leaping into the river from rope swings, cowboys on horseback, and then, around the corner, Stonehenge and Easter Island. Well, it's really just two massive Easter Island faces and a two-thirds scale model of Stonehenge; but hey, discoveries like this can make your day and justify why you ride. So why is this quirky goof in the middle of nowhere? Come to Texas and find out for yourself.

From here, the highway is aquiver with arrow straight lanes mixed in with short turns and then it passes ranches, traces of desert, short waterfalls, and a clear shallow river that's often framed within the border of towering limestone bluffs. When you lose the river, the land becomes broken and brittle and ready to snap. Most stunted scrub oaks are alive, yet others seem to have died of fright. The Hill Country seems to be not quite forest, not quite prairie, not quite desert. Instead, it's all of these and none of these.

In the middle of Hill Country comes an unexpected sight: An Easter Island head and a two-thirds replica of Stonehenge. Why? Beats me.

No matter the land's appearance, level CR 1340 lets you pour on the speed until it finally winds down and loses its zip as it T's at Highway 41. Heading southwest, the next 17 miles are mostly rocket-straight shots where the road starts buckin' like a bronco up and down and across the sand hills where little lies ahead of you except the horizon. A junction signals U.S. 83, but pass that to reach curious Ranch Road 336, the first of the Three Sisters. While you may have thought the highways you just tackled were lonely, this is a road that lives in exile.

Only a small sign announces the entrance south on Ranch Road 336, where the road starts to dash and scribble across the roughhewn land and you're now about as far removed from civilization as you can be on the 26-mile ride to Leakey. But here the blacktop is smooth, the shoulders absent, and all of your images of Hill Country appear before you as you rock and roll on steep grades and sharp curves that slide across the hills. The terrain compensates for the lack of scenery as the black ribbon screams into narrow stretches and keeps you alert with a variety of warning signs for loose livestock, standing water, falling rocks, and flash floods...enough to make you think you should have stayed in bed.

Sheltered by high rocks and safety rails, though, it's becomes much like a ride in the Alps as Ranch Road 336 hauls you around, then puts you on some rises so steep you can't see the road ahead. From higher elevations there are overlooks above a valley and as you drop out of the hills the land turns greener as you approach Leakey, which is a town...almost. There are a few stores, a bar, and a service station; but I suspect that primarily its location is what brings riders here.

Heading east out of Leakey on Ranch Road 337 (the eastern half of the second of the Three Sisters) begins a 16-mile run towards Vanderpool, starting slow then leading to a stretch where the road is tied like a string to the mountains. You'll soar and swoop around Hill Country for a good 10 miles until you reach a peak and get the nicest views of your journey so far. You'll stay with Ranch Road 337 until it Ts at County Road 187 north. Aside from concentrating on this long easy stretch, focus on finding the **Lone Star Motorcycle Museum** (36517 CR 187 North, 830/966-6103, www.lonestarmotorcyclemuseum.com, $5). Open Friday–Sunday, there are dozens of well-preserved and restored classic bikes as well as the Ace Café. Don't miss it.

This glimpse of civilization appears and disappears quickly as you continue on this really solid road, one that rarely changes the entire way to Highway 39.

© NANCY HOWELL

Rejoining Highway 39 starts to close the loop as you ride north, once again getting some bumps and drops with the Guadalupe River flowing in and out of sight. It's a nice view that improves with buttes and bluffs and canopy roads, followed by even better river views and large homes of stone and timber. A general store appears at the junction of Highway 39 and County Road 1340, as does an unusual roadside eatery where folks dine alfresco at picnic tables beside the river. A few miles ahead comes Ingram Dam where folks splash in Lake New Ingram and kids slide down the algae-coated concrete into the Guadalupe River.

From Ingram, Highway 27 continues back to Kerrville. For a different route back to Fredericksburg, just past Wal-Mart turn left at Highway 783 where, once again, it doesn't take long to get back into the country and beside ranchlands and open range. Ride Highway 783 all the way to U.S. 290 where you can rack up 20-odd average miles back to Fredericksburg. Long ride, big memories.

PULL IT OVER: FREDERICKSBURG HIGHLIGHTS
Attractions and Adventures

The town is justifiably proud of its favorite son Admiral Chester Nimitz, the local boy who made good by becoming Commander-in-Chief of the U.S. Pacific Forces in World War II. These credentials helped establish the **National Museum of the Pacific War** (340 E. Main St., 830/997-8600, www.nimitz-museum.org, $7), a multi-venue complex that covers several blocks. It begins in a museum focused on Nimitz's upbringing and subsequent career and continues with a one-hour guided tour at the Pacific Combat Zone, which includes a hangar with an ATBM Avenger,

a PT boat, a scale version of a beachhead and Japanese defenses, a Quonset hut, field hospital, and a mock cemetery. Reopened in December 2009, the museum's 40,000-square foot George H.W. Bush Gallery presents a midget Japanese sub that tried to reach Pearl Harbor, the casing for a Fat Man atomic bomb that was never dropped, a dive bomber, and anti-tank weaponry. There's also a Japanese Peace Garden, Veterans Walk of Honor, Memorial Wall, and bookstore. Admission is valid for two days—although docents suggest about three hours may do it, six if you take your time. The museum is open daily (except Thanksgiving and Christmas), 9 A.M.–5 P.M.

Shopping

In many small towns, stores sell a similar line up of identical stuff. Fredericksburg's different, with several standouts in the commercial district. If you recall old stores with hardwood floors, suspended fluorescent lights, broomstick ponies, Beemans gum, coonskin caps, rubber band guns, wind-up alarm clocks, and Mexican jumping beans, then **Dooley's 5-10-25** (131 E. Main St., 830/997-3458) will appeal to you. The all-purpose store also sells a diverse selection of shotgun shells, belt buckles, camping plates, plastic flowers, and Radio Flyer wagons, and a whole bunch more.

The cool western wear of **Remember Me Too** (109 E. Main St., 830/997-6444) is mixed in with western paintings and artwork, dude ranch pictures, Texas cuisine cookbooks, and a broad spectrum of quality stuff. Pushing the Western look a little more is **Headquarters** (122 E. Main St., 830/990-8510, www.headquartershats. com). That's a small store jam-packed with hats, belts, and, especially, boots that are either practical or extravagantly stitched

Black boots may be alright for a motorcycle ride, but for dimestore cowboys and cowgirls, super-jazzed boots come with cool stitching and designs.

with patterns, logos, and designs from longhorn cattle to the Virgin Mary.

You can find items for camping, hunting, and exploring scenic back roads at **Hill Country Outfitters** (115 E. Main St., 830/997-3761). Sample over 400 gourmet items at **Rustlin' Rob's** (121 E. Main St., 830/990-4750, www.rustlinrobs.com) that sells a huge range of sauces, rubs, chow chow, grilling sauces, ciders, and salsas. If you've got a notion to be a singing cowboy, head over to **Hill Country Music** (151 E. Main St., 830/997-0900, www.hill-country-music.com) that carries git-boxes, along with mandolins, fiddles, blues harps, real harps, accordions and kazoos.

Blue-Plate Specials

If you're new to Fredericksburg, you may find it unusual that Texas steaks and ribs may share a menu with German bratwurst and wienerschnitzel. For some reason, immigrants from Deutschland settled in large numbers in the Lone Star State and here in particular. At **Wheeler's** (204 E. Main St., 830/990-8180) they pay tribute to the town's heritage with a multi-national lineup of chicken-fried steak, English fish and chips, German sandwiches, smoked bratwurst, and catfish filets. At **Winslow's** (106 E. Main St., 830/990-0168, www.winslows-restaurant.com) it's almost the same: chicken and dumplings, Reuben sandwiches, breakfast tacos and pancakes, and what they claim are the best burgers in town. You'll find a retro soda fountain at super neat **Clear River** (138 E. Main St., 830/997-8490, www.icecreamandfun.com), along with sandwiches, soups, coffee, and homemade ice cream you can enjoy in a booth or at the counter. Eat here and you'll think you're on *Ozzie and Harriett*. For a menu with no trace of Teutonic influence, head over to **Mamacita's** (506 E. Main St., 830/997-9546, www.mamacitas.com), a colorful and friendly Mexican restaurant with an expansive menu and nice lounge.

Watering Holes

Once again, Fredericksburg comes through with a number of choices for a cold drink and conversation. The **Fredericksburg Brewing Company** (245 E. Main St., 830/997-1646, www.yourbrewery.com) has a cool beer hall look with international flags flying above the long hall, six huge kettles filled with micros like Pedernales Pilsener and Admirals Amber Ale, and a decidedly festive atmosphere. Open later, the **Auslander** (323 E. Main St., 830/997-7714, www.theauslander.com) plays German tunes on the sidewalk outside; inside, there's blues playing and there's the area's widest and most diverse selection of beers. Dine out back or settle inside where the windows open onto the outdoors. Occupying an old house is the comfortable **Silver Creek** (310 E. Main St., 830/990-4949, www.silvercreekfbg.com), where folks gather beneath umbrellas on what was once the front yard, watch bands on what was once the front porch, and hang out in the bar and biergarten in back to nurse brews and sample the Creek's "Texclectic cuisine."

Shut-Eye

Chain hotels have a presence in this tourist town. Although if you're OK riding about 10 miles out of town, you'll find the **Full Moon Inn** (3234 Luckenbach Rd., 830/997-1124, www.fullmooninn.com), a place that's extremely popular with riders and a short hop to the dance hall at Luckenbach. Why do riders love it? Credit the peace and quiet, log cabins, cottages, large rooms, steakhouse and BBQ restaurant, lounge, and covered parking. Elsewhere in town and across Gillespie County are motor courts, motels, hotels, campgrounds and RV parks. An in-depth source of information includes all of them at www.fredtexlodging.com.

Chain Drive

These chain hotels are in town, or within 10 miles of the city center:

Best Western, Comfort Inn, Days Inn, Econo Lodge, Hampton Inn, Holiday Inn, La Quinta, Motel 6, Quality Inn, Super 8

For more information, including phone numbers and websites, see page 439.

ON THE ROAD: FREDERICKSBURG TO AUSTIN

The ride to Austin is otherworldly, taking you way out into the wilderness and giving you some cool scenes en route. You could jump on Highway 16 for a steady ride to Llano; but for variety you can start a roundabout ride by heading east out of town and looking for Olive Street, which is also County Road 1631. In an instant you're back in the farmlands and it's all plain and simple, just a place where you can ride and not have to think about much

Taking a much-needed break near Inks Lake State Park, in the heart (and heat) of Hill Country.

The LBJ Ranch

Depending on how you feel about LBJ, when you leave Fredericksburg for Austin, you may want to detour about 15 miles east on U.S. 290 to the **Lyndon B. Johnson State Park and Historic Site** (199 State Park Rd. 52, Stonewall, 830/644-2252, www.nps.gov/lyjo). His entire ranch is open. When you stop at the Visitors Center, they'll give you a loaner CD (or printed brochure if you don't have a sound system) that guides you around the roads across his former ranch. The tour explains the history of the place and leads you to an old log cabin; the one-room schoolhouse Johnson attended; a nature trail; a Hill Country botanical exhibit; wildlife enclosures stocked with bison, white-tailed deer, wild turkey, and longhorn cattle; and the Johnson family cemetery where the former president is buried. If you have an extra half hour, "The Texas White House" where Johnson held court and conducted business when he was home from Washington is open for guided tours.

except the barren country. The highway splits up towards the northeast and you're now riding towards County Road 1323; you'll reach it where the road Ts. Turn left here and you'll be riding towards Willow City, the namesake of the 20-some mile Willow City Loop. Near the town, you'll have to peel off to the right to follow the road signs that read "Willow City Loop." Riders love it most in spring when the bluebonnets are in bloom. Even when they're not in bloom, it's still a good run on a narrow road that feels similar to the Three Sisters' Ranch Road 336 with cattle guards, water level markers, and some springy riding.

When it reconnects with Highway 16, the road north is as straight and steady as the landscape and presents an unrelenting string of cactus, sagebrush, and sawed-off oaks all the way to Llano, the town that bills itself as "The Way Texas Used To Be." I think they're right. Around the town square, you'll find a general mercantile, Colonel Crow's Trading Post, the local newspaper, the Lan-Tex theatre, and

Acme Café. Could be the 1950s. Across the bridge are more commercial enterprises and some popular restaurants including **Cooper's BBQ** (604 W. Young, 325/247-5713, www.coopersbbq.com) and (what a name!) **Mom's Café** (910 W. Young St., 325/248-0750), where you can get good home cooking and good service.

Leaving Llano on Highway 29, a few miles east, County Road 2241 angles northeast to once again put you in the country and once again deliver remote riding that lets you clear your head. About 10 miles later Bluffton appears. There's a service station and then the road stays straight as it becomes Ranch Road 261 and starts to spin south around what's left of Lake Buchanan. A punishing drought seems to have punished the communities here as well, and you may sense a depressing vibe as you pass waterfront homes that are now high and dry and businesses, that once catered to anglers, are now shuttered. Even the sight of withered Buchanan Lake and the Buchanan Dam are stark and sobering.

Relief comes a few miles past the dam where Park Road 4, part of the Hill Country Heritage Trail, appears on your right and right away it takes you past a golf course and sinuous lake and then lifts you into the hills and to a promontory overlooking a canyon at the Devil's Waterhole. A few miles ahead you pass Inks Lake State Park. The road unwinds for several more miles before it reaches the turn off onto County Road 2342 on your right. The first portion of this is steady and pleasant, but after you reach a T at Highway 1431 in Kingsland you think the whole ride will peter out—stick with it. Even though the road is swallowed by dense city traffic in the dozen miles between here and Marble Falls to the east, when it leaps past U.S. 281 things start looking up. From here to near Austin, Highway 1431 is going to become your best friend.

Now you're in wide open country and pouring it on as you slam down a wide two-lane that takes off like a rocket. Open and nearly endless, a series of curves repeat themselves mile after mile after mile and often the blacktop banks you from side to side, moving you around just the way pilots twist their hands to simulate flying. Best of all, there's hardly any traffic. While I'm not sure why this is, it's a blast being one of a handful of people smart enough to take advantage of this very impressive 30-mile stretch. The experience starts to slow as you approach Lago Vista and even though you'll sense the fringes of Austin's urban core here, the road has one more treat. It gives you a final burst of great riding as you pass Jonestown on your way to U.S. 183, a traffic-filled road that heads to Austin. I'd suggest opting for U.S. 183A, the toll road that's a little less trafficked en route to I-35. The break will give you time to think about where you've been and what adventures await you in Austin.

AUSTIN PRIMER

Austin has two distinct eras: one historical and one musical. The historic part first involved nomadic tribes (Comanches, Apaches, Tonkawa). Then, after the Republic of Texas was established in 1836, Texians, Tejanos, and European immigrants (Germans, mostly) began settling down in a Central Texas village then called Waterloo.

The new capital was to be moved here from Houston, platted on land that fronted the Colorado River and sat between two creeks. Waterloo would be renamed Austin and at the summit of the grid would sit the new Texas State Capitol. It made sense to a lot of people, but not to Sam Houston. The president of the Republic of Texas and the man who defeated Santa Anna tried to leverage some Mexican incursions into San Antonio as a reason to relocate the capital to his choice: Houston. To push the point home, in December 1842 he sent men to sneak into Austin and steal the state archives and bring them closer to Houston at Washington-on-the-Brazos. The plan was foiled when Angelina Eberly, an innkeeper who was part of the town's vigilance committee, fired a cannon to rouse the residents. Citizens caught up with the archive-stealing thieves the next day. After Texas became part of the United States in 1845, Austin earned its title and Eberly earned a spot in Texas history.

Then there's music. Building on the success of Armadillo World Headquarters, an unusually successful and eclectic music venue created within an abandoned National Guard Armory, Clifford Antone arrived and Austin's reputation as a music capital took off. With a passion for the blues and a lack of interest in college, in the early '70s he began bringing in old blues artists to town, giving them a venue and introducing them to a new generation of fans. It worked. He helped revive languishing careers; they helped revive languishing nightclubs along East 6th Street. They also inspired hopeful young musicians like Stevie Ray Vaughn whose career was directly affected by what he'd seen and heard in Austin. And even though Antone passed away in 2006, his legacy is still rocking the streets.

ON THE ROAD: AUSTIN

You've already covered a lot of ground, so today just stick around town. There are five must-sees in Austin. To better understand those sites and the city, invest in **Austin Overtures** (209 E. 6th St., 512/659-9478, www.austinovertures.com), a 90-minute tour that explains the geology of Hill Country, the history of Austin and Texas, and expands your perspective of Austin as it travels to the outskirts, surrounding hills, and through the core of the downtown historic and entertainment districts and onto the campus of the University of Texas.

PULL IT OVER: AUSTIN HIGHLIGHTS
Attractions and Adventures

You could spend several weeks or several years in Austin and always find something new; but if you're here for a day or two focus on a couple of the places locals suggest as must-sees. Each are downtown and most are free.

First, the **Texas State Capitol** (1100 Congress Ave., 512/305-8400, www.tspb. state.tx.us): You can explore alone or join a free guided tour that departs every 15 minutes on weekdays, every half hour on weekends. It's well worth the time to get the lowdown on the history of the state and explore one of the most beautiful public buildings in America. And it's big, too. From the floor of the rotunda, it's 218 feet

to the top of the ceiling, which makes the eight-foot star there look like a Christmas ornament. The tour will take you into the Senate and House chambers and you can even go into the Governor's Reception Office if he's away. Below the building are offices and a cafeteria open to the public. Between January and May it's probably packed with field-trippin' school kids, so time it accordingly.

You can increase your knowledge of Texas history at the **Bob Bullock Texas State History Museum** (1800 N. Congress Ave., 512/936-8746, www.thestoryoftexas.com, $7, films extra), named for the late lieutenant governor who advanced a series of civic improvements in the 1990s. There are three floors of interactive exhibits that add an historical perspective to the land, identity, and opportunities that created the Texas character. The film *Star of Destiny* tells the story of the state's founding, and an IMAX Theatre features the epic *Texas: The Big Picture.*

The next three prime destinations are at or affiliated with the University of Texas, and the first is the most visited presidential library in the nation (maybe because it's free). That's the **LBJ Library and Museum** (512/721-0200, www.lbjlib.utexas.edu), which contains personal items, White House furniture, and about 45 million pages of historical documents (although none adequately explain why he picked up his beagles by the ears). Must-see number four is the **Jack Blanton Museum of Art** (512/471-7324, www. blantonmuseum.org, $7, closed Mondays, free on Thursdays), the second largest art museum on any college campus (Harvard edges them out). It has the distinction of having a nice mix of contemporary and classic art.

Rounding out the Top Five is the

Harry H. Ransom Research Center for the Humanities (512/471-8944, www. hrc.utexas.edu, free) which has a collection even larger than its name. There are 36 million literary manuscripts, a million rare books, five million photographs, and more than 100,000 works of art. The treasure trove also includes scripts, screen tests, costumes, rare comic books, Woodward and Bernstein's Watergate notes, a Guttenberg Bible, and, what thrilled me, the oldest photo ever taken: an image of a scene from a French window, circa 1826.

If you can carve out additional time don't miss these runners-up. The **Texas State Cemetery** (909 Navasota St., www. cemetery.state.tx.us) is the final resting place for Stephen Austin, Ann Richards, John Connelly, Barbara Jordan, and other Texas notables. For a refresher course in refreshing, each day a natural wonder called **Barton Springs** (2101 Barton Pkwy., 512/476-9044, $3) pumps out 27 million gallons of crystal clear and very cold (a constant 68 degrees) water. It's a blessing for locals who use the three-acre pool to temper summer temperatures that can hover above 100.

Finally, around dusk, line up along the **Congress Avenue Bridge.** As the sun goes down, an estimated 1.5 million bats roosting beneath the bridge fly out, some getting started on a flight all the way to Mexico. When locals discovered the bat colony living here, they were appalled. But after experts explained that they eat tons of mosquitoes each night and those that reach Mexico help fertilize the guava trees with their poop—guava that's essential in blending the margaritas Texans love so very much—the bats were welcome.

Shopping
Way too many stores to peruse. But in a

musical town, **Wild About Music** (115 E. 6th St., 512/708-1700, www.wildaboutmusic.com) is most excellent. Even if you don't play music or are completely tone deaf, you'll want to see the original paintings, musical merchandise, prints, sculptures, photography and assorted artwork that would look great in a music room.

On another note, **Waterloo Records** (600A N. Lamar, 512/474-2500, www. waterloorecords.com) is one of the nation's best and most popular independent record shops. Along with an incredible collection of LPs and CDs reflecting every musical genre, there's plenty of musical swag. Waterloo is also one of the founders of the "Keep Austin Weird" movement.

Even if you're pleased with your riding boots, you'll be even more pleased with a pair from **Heritage Boots** (117 W. 8th St., 512/326-8577, www.heritageboot. com). The super cool vintage boot shop isn't a box store at all—it's the creation of Irishman Jerry Ryan, who has a knack for creating super-cool artistic boots. Although they start at around $400, it's a sure bet that no one else will have a pair like yours.

Blue-Plate Specials
As with shopping and entertainment, Austin runs the board when it comes to dining. Again consider this the short list and visit the tourism website for a more extensive list. That said, Texas competes with other states for barbeque, but other states don't have **County Line** (Bee Cave Rd. past 360, 512/327-1742, www.countyline. com). A bit removed from downtown, this eatery was created in an old lodge back in 1934 and since then it's been the favorite for students, politicians, celebs, families, and anyone else who likes big food and good service. Traveling in a group? Order the Cadillac, a massive platter of

(pick five) sausage, chicken, turkey breast, pulled pork, brisket, beef ribs, or pork ribs plus potato salad, coleslaw, beans, bread, and ice cream. There'll be enough here to feed everyone. Not just at your table. Across Texas.

For high quality Tex-Mex at a mid-range price, head downtown to **El Chile** (918 Congress Ave., 512/326-8577, www.elchilecafe.com). It's known for great enchiladas, smoky salsas, icy margaritas, and an endless range of appetizers and entrees.

Although you may know it as a super-market, Austin's **Whole Foods** (512/477-4455, 601 N. Lamar Blvd., www.wholefoods.com) is a culinary amusement park. This, the flagship store, opened in Austin in 1980 and has become one of the city's leading tourist attractions with more than a dozen eatery counters that serve pizza, BBQ, roasters, seafood, a raw bar, cheese, wine, and handmade candies. Drop in and fill up.

Ride down South Congress Avenue and soon you'll spy a collection of Airstream trailers that have set up on an empty lot. Inside, independent restaurateurs are selling a variety of dishes, from cones filled with high-end regional game to cupcakes, tamales, and popcorn.

Watering Holes

Austin has more live bands playing here than in any other city. When you wander around you'll pick up country, blues, rock, Tejano, and alternative tunes drifting down from rooftops, pounding from warehouses, and blasting out of honky-tonks. There are distinct districts in town—Red River, University of Texas, South Austin, East Austin, and Market among them—but the one that gets the most attention is 6th Street. It's loud and crowded and your interest in it will depend on your age since it attracts primarily college-age fans who appreciate the wide mix of music.

One of the granddaddies of the Austin music scene is the **Continental Club** (1315 S. Congress Ave., 512/441-2444, www.continentalclub.com). Here since 1957, it was a juke joint and burlesque house before a renovation made it home to local legends like Jerry Jeff Walker and Stevie Ray Vaughan. Named one of the nation's best bars by *Playboy* magazine a few years back, the Continental still presents a good mix of folk, rock, and rockabilly bands.

In the Warehouse & Downtown District, the bands are playing for older (25 and up) audiences. Aside from **Antone's** (213 W. 5th St., 512/320-8424, www.antones.net), which earns credit as the original blues club, it's impossible to tell you which will appeal to you. The best advice, then, is either walking around and tuning into the sounds of the clubs, or picking up a copy of the free *Austin Chronicle* (www.austinchronicle.com), an alternative weekly that covers local news and politics as well as listing nearly every performer at every club in town. That's how I found The Gunhands, an Allman Brothers-Johnny Cash-ZZ Top hybrid rocking atop a club roof beneath the midnight moon. Perfect way to end the ride.

Shut-Eye

Built in 1939 as a modern motor court, the **Hotel San Jose** (1316 S. Congress Ave., 512/852-2350 or 800/574-8897, www.sanjosehotel.com, $95—165) has evolved to become a hip boutique hotel. Cool music's always playing and the rooms are kind of Miami cool. If you can stand to share a bath, rooms start at $95; add about $70 more for a standard room with a private bath. The location, right near the Continental Club, is a big plus.

Keep in mind that you'll pay more for a room near the entertainment districts, but you can walk back when the evening's over. If you're looking for a bargain, your best bet for lodging is going to be one of the chains. Otherwise, head to the outskirts of town.

Chain Drive

These chain hotels are in town, or within 10 miles of the city center:

Best Western, Clarion, Comfort Inn, Courtyard by Marriott, Days Inn, Doubletree, Econo Lodge, Embassy Suites, Fairfield Inn, Hampton Inns, Hilton, Holiday Inn, Howard Johnson, La Quinta, Omni Hotels, Radisson, Ramada, Residence Inn, Rodeway, Sheraton, Super 8, Travelodge

For more information, including phone numbers and websites, see page 439.

Resources for Riders

Texas Hill Country Highlights

Texas Travel Information
Ride Texas Magazine—866/418-5552, www.ridetexas.com
Texas Bed & Breakfast Association—512/371-9884 or 800/428-0368,
    www.texasbb.org
Texas Hill Country Trail—www.txhillcountrytrail.com
Texas Outside (links to golf, hunting, fishing, festivals, camping, lodging, etc.)—
    www.texasoutside.com
Texas Parks and Wildlife—512/389-4800 or 800/792-1112 (park reservations
    512/389-8900), www.tpwd.state.tx.us
Texas Road Conditions—800/452-9292, www.dot.state.tx.us
Texas Tourism—800/888-8839, www.traveltex.com

Local and Regional Information
Austin Convention & Visitors Bureau—512/474-5171 or 800/926-2282,
    www.austintexas.org
Austin Visitors Center—512/478-0098 or 866/462-7846
Bandera Convention & Visitors Bureau—830/798-3045 or 800/364-3833,
    www.banderacowboycapital.com
Fredericksburg Convention & Visitors Bureau—830/997-6523 or 888/997-3600,
    www.fredericksburg-texas.com
Hill Country Cruising—www.hillcountrycruising.com
Llano Tourism—www.llanotexas.com
San Antonio Convention & Visitors Bureau—210/207-6708 or 800/447-3372,
    www.visitsanantonio.com

Texas Motorcycle Shops
Alamo City Harley Davidson—11005 N. I-35, San Antonio, 210/646-0499,
    www.alamocityharley.com

Alamo Cycle Plex—11900 IH-10 West, San Antonio, 210/696-2000, www.alamocycleplex.com

Bill Kasson Yamaha—2603 S. Congress Ave., Austin, 512/444-7482 or 800252-7004, www.kassonmotorcycles.com

Caliente Harley-Davidson—7230 NW Loop 410, San Antonio, 210/681-2254, www.calienteharley.com

Central Texas Harley-Davidson—2801 N. IH-35, Round Rock, 512/652-1200, www.centraltexasharley.com

Cowboy Harley-Davidson of Austin—10917 S. IH-35, Austin, 512/448-4294 or 866/500-4294, www.cowboyharleyaustin.com

Cycle Rider—202 Braniff Dr., San Antonio, 210/349-9534

Ducati Austin—812 E. Braker Ln., Austin, 512/236-8822, www.motoaustin.com

Harleys and More—8711 Broadway St., San Antonio, 210/832-8558, www.harleysandmore.com

Joe Harrison Motor Sports—9710 N. I-35, San Antonio, 210/656-9400, www.jhms.com

KC International Motor Sports—23011 1H I-10 West, San Antonio, 210/764-9990, www.kc-international.com

Lone Star BMW Triumph—10600 N. Lamar Blvd., Austin, 512/451-7979 or 800/729-3807, www.lonestarcycle.com

Napalm Motorsports—12112 N. 620, Austin, 512/345-7433 or 877/263-8689, www.napalmmotorsports.com

Texas Powersports Kawasaki—13220 W. U.S. 290, Austin, 512/301-7433, www.texaspowersports.com

T Js Cycle Sales—6208 N. Lamar Blvd., Austin, 512/453-6255 or 800/570-4079, www.tjs-cycle.com

Woods Fun Center—11405 N. IH-35, Austin, 512/459-3311, www.woodsfuncenter.com

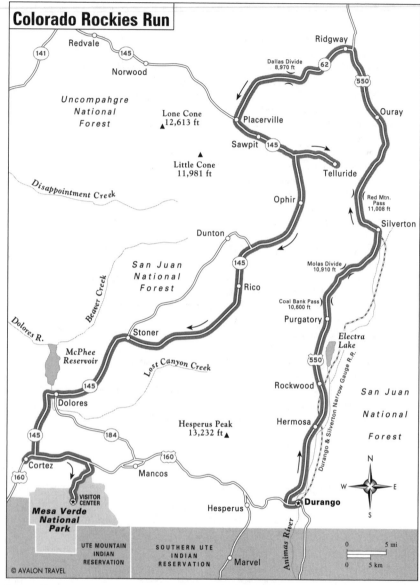

Colorado Rockies Run

Route: Durango to Mesa Verde via Silverton, Million Dollar Highway, Ouray, Telluride

Distance: Approximately 200 miles

First Leg: Durango to Telluride (120 miles)

Second Leg: Telluride to Mesa Verde (80 miles)

Helmet Laws: Colorado does not require helmets.

Colorado Rockies Run

Durango, Colorado to Mesa Verde National Park, Colorado

This ride won't take very long, but the memories it generates could last a lifetime. Every image of a standard Colorado beer commercial is evoked here. There are repeated images of waterfalls, mountain switchbacks with sheer drops, frontier towns in no hurry to leave the 19th century, and a mysterious village frozen in time. You'll ride across mountain passes at 11,000 feet, and have the option of renting a Jeep to climb beyond 13,000 feet...if you don't mind a collapsed lung.

DURANGO PRIMER

After the Ancestral Puebloans had vanished from the land and the Utes, Navajo, and Spanish had come and gone, what is today's Durango was born by way of the rails.

With the San Juan Mountains overflowing with gold and silver, the folks at the Denver and Rio Grande Railroad had a brainstorm. In 1880, they established the town of Durango as the base point for their railway. By 1882 the tracks had been completed and by the time the line stopped in the 1960s, miners had removed about $300 million worth of gold and silver from the hills.

Durango was a wealthy town at the turn of the 20th century and, judging by the architecture, it still looks well-off today. But it's not just money that makes this town rich. Its natural setting on the free-flowing Animas River and the town's proximity to cool, lush forests and broad, powerful mountains both play a role. And its greatest asset is arguably its people, whose hospitality and lack of pretense would make Tibetan monks look like schoolyard bullies.

ON THE ROAD: DURANGO

Trust me that the upcoming ride north will more than satisfy your thirst for adventure, so while you're here you might as well just hang out in downtown Durango. And if you have an extra day to invest, consider boarding a steam train for a real cliffhanger of a ride.

The epicenter of downtown activity is along Main Avenue, stretching between 5th and 12th streets. On most days, there's a showroom's worth of motorcycles angled along the curb, and they're all here because this happens to be an Old West walking town that hasn't lost its flavor. When mall developers were flashing their cash and looking for tenants, the independent merchants, local saloons, and historic buildings here gave the folks in Durango every reason to stay put and stick with downtown.

Along Main Avenue and spreading out on the cross streets, you'll find leather and saddle shops, newsstands, old photo shops, and a one-of-a-kind hatmaker. After strolling Main Avenue, don't leave town by bike. Not yet. Seriously consider a run on the **Durango-Silverton Narrow Gauge Railway** (479 Main Ave., 970/247-2733 or 888/872-4607, www.durangotrain. com). Back in the 1880s, about the same time the Rolling Stones released their first wax cylinder, mining up in Silverton was going full steam and the best way to get the goods back down to Durango was via this narrow gauge railway.

If you think the San Juan Skyway is gonna be tricky on a four-cylinder bike, surrender the job to the engineer of a 50-ton, circa 1923 coal-fired steam train as he creeps it along the cliffs of the Animas River Gorge. When you enter the mountainous terrain and peer 400 feet straight down, you'll understand why cruising at 10 mph makes sense.

The locomotive chuffs along the canyon for more than three hours, rising from 6,512 feet in Durango to 9,288 feet in Silverton (a town you'll see later on your bike, even if you don't take the rail). The round trip lasts about nine hours, with the layover in Silverton lasting only two hours—just enough time to eat, down a

beer, and buy some cheap souvenirs. If you get a kick out of historic modes of transportation and have never ridden a steam train, then it could be worth the price (about $80, and closer to $150 to reserve a parlor car). Reservations are recommended for the ride. If you skip the trip, you can still tour the museum and railyard for five bucks.

Back in Durango, rest up and get ready for an old-fashioned evening listening to a honky-tonk pianist at the Diamond Belle Saloon or watching live entertainment at the Henry Strater Theatre. When you're in Durango, this sure as shootin' beats a night at a sports bar.

PULL IT OVER: DURANGO HIGHLIGHTS
Attractions and Adventures

With a river like the mighty Animas sitting in your backyard, you'd be a dope not to use it. Outfitters here wring maximum use out of the Animas with river runs that range from serene to extreme. **Outlaw Rivers and Jeep Tours** (690 Main Ave., 970/259-1800, www.outlawtours.com) offers excursions on the rapids lasting from two hours ($25) to a full day ($65), as well as Jeep rentals ($135 daily) and Jeep and Hummer tours that travel to ghost towns and mining districts. **Durango Rivertrippers** (720 Main Ave., 970/259-0289 or 800/292-2885, www.durangorivertrippers.com) provides whitewater rafting from $25 for two hours to $39 for a half day plus lunch. You can also do it yourself in an inflatable kayak.

Trimble Hot Springs (6475 CR 203, 970/247-0111, www.trimblehotsprings. com) doesn't exactly qualify as a water adventure, since whitewater only appears when someone does a cannonball. You can ease your saddle-sore muscles at this natural spa that features Olympic pools, massages, herbal wraps, and mineral-rich waters ranging from a tepid 85°F to a muscle-melting 108°F. The springs are open 8 A.M.–11 P.M. daily.

When you see the sublime setting of the airstrip at the **Durango Soaring Club** (27290 U.S. 550, three miles north of Durango, 970/247-9037, www.soardurango.com), you may never want to leave. But the lure of the sky is undeniable and when you soar from ground level (which is already at 6,500 feet) you'll be towed to as high as 10,000 feet before popping off from the tow plane and soaking up tremendous views of the San Juan Mountains, as far away as 100 miles, and seeing the Animas River snake through the valley. If you're in a pack, your friends will be nearly as content sunning themselves on the observation deck. The weight limit is 300 pounds and reservations are suggested. Flights start at $100 for 15 minutes in the air.

Shopping

Long before trendsetters beatified cigars, **Hall's Brothers Smoke Shop** (113 W. College Dr., 970/247-9115 or 800/742-7606, www.durangosmokeshop.com) was smoking. Claiming to be the "tobacconist to the Four Corners," Hall's stocks many cigars, Zippo lighters, Indian peace pipes, and risqué postcards.

Thomas and Melissa Barnes are experts at making custom hats and saddles, which they do with great skill and care at the accurately named **Durango Custom Hats and Saddles** (723 E. 2nd Ave., 970/385-8486). After you've had your head examined, it'll take Thomas a few months to create a hat that you'll own for a lifetime. Motorcycle seats, too, are a specialty and for about $650, he'll measure your seat, get your input, and go to work to create a custom saddle displaying anything that

can be carved, tooled, or stamped on it. Avoid unicorns and rainbows.

Blue-Plate Specials

Francisco's Restaurante y Cantina (619 Main Ave., 970/247-4098) is a local favorite for its homemade soups, great Mexican food, impressive wine list, and full bar, where margaritas are a specialty and locals gather to watch the big game. Expect a long wait if you travel in peak season. It's open for lunch and dinner.

The **Ore House** (147 E. College Dr., 970/247-5707, www.orehouserestaurant.com) looks like it's placed in a rustic miner's shed, which sets the stage for a great evening retreat. The chefs start with pan-fried steaks and work their way up to chateaubriand; in between, they whip up center-cut bacon-wrapped filets stuffed with king crabmeat, steak ranchero, and the Ore House grub steak. Eat dinner here and annoy a vegetarian.

Inside a renovated Ford tractor showroom, the **Steamworks Brewing Company** (801 E. 2nd Ave., 970/259-9200, www.steamworksbrewing.com) draws local college students and a smattering of tourists for lunch and dinner and for five regular and three seasonal microbrews. The style is basic, with corrugated tin walls, copper vats, and smooth concrete floors. Oh yeah, the food: Mexican, chicken, pastas, sandwiches, and pizza. The patio deck is great for all of this plus a cold one and conversation.

The **Durango Diner** (957 Main Ave., 970/247-9889, www.durangodiner.com) is a local landmark, and it keeps going thanks to its no-frills meals. Beyond serving breakfast all day, it spices up the menu with its trademark green chili, Southwest salsa, and enchilada sauces—sold here and across the country. If you're afraid you'll run out of gas on the San Juan Skyway, stop here first.

Watering Holes

You cannot *not* have a good time at the **Diamond Belle Saloon** (in the Strater Hotel, 699 Main Ave., 970/247-4431 or 800/247-4431, www.strater.com). This corner bar, locked in the 1880s, boasts a full line of drinks, from beer to bourbon. From the flocked wallpaper to the honky-tonk piano player to the nude painting to the sign that suggests "work is the curse of the drinking classes," this is one of the best bets for bikers I've seen. Chances are you'll meet people from around the world. The only thing missing here is Festus. It's open 11 A.M.–midnight daily.

If you're driven by thirst, check out **Lady Falconburgs** (640 Main Ave., 970/382-9664), open 11 A.M.–2 A.M. daily. The rathskeller-style interior isn't that impressive (the basement of a shopping mall), but the establishment pours 100 types of bottled beer, 38 beers on tap, and serves a five buck sampler. There are two dollar pints all day on Mondays and Thursdays. Bottoms up.

If your nights aren't fueled by beer, the **Henry Strater Theatre** (at the Strater Hotel, 699 Main Ave., 970/375-7160, www.henrystratertheatre.com) is a venue where live performances include comedians, bluegrass, blues, Western swing, and stage shows.

Shut-Eye

The city operates a central reservations line (800/525-8855, www.durango.org) for lodging, activities, and the Durango-Silverton train. Most chain hotels are north of downtown on Main Avenue.

Inn-dependence

A block off the main drag, Kirk Komick and his mom, Diane Wildfang(!), run both the **Leland House** and **Rochester Hotel** (721 E. 2nd Ave., 970/385-1920 or 800/664-1920, www.rochesterhotel.com, $169 and up high season). Both offer superb rooms. I liked the Rochester for its Western film–themed rooms (some with kitchens), the mighty rugged decor, huge breakfast, fresh coffee and tea, and the fact that it used to be a bordello. Yowsah! Then again, both give you the comfort of an inn with the conveniences of a hotel.

The magnificent **Strater Hotel** (699 Main Ave., 970/247-4431 or 800/247-4431, www.strater.com, $169 and up in summer) was built in 1887 and is one of the nicest restored hotels you'll have the pleasure of finding. The antiques are real, the restoration flawless, and the saloon will add flavor to your tour. Not only are the 93 rooms large and quiet, the elegant Gilded Age accoutrements throughout the lobby will turn you into a frontier high roller. Western novelist Louis L'Amour loved room 222—he said the ragtime music from the bar below gave him inspiration for the plots and characters of his Sackett Series novels.

Chain Drive

These chain hotels are in town, or within 10 miles of the city center:
Best Western, Comfort Inn, Days Inn, Doubletree, Econo Lodge, Hampton Inn, Holiday Inn, Quality Inn, Ramada, Residence Inn, Super 8, Travelodge
For more information, including phone numbers and websites, see page 439.

ON THE ROAD: DURANGO TO TELLURIDE

Before you saddle up for the San Juan Skyway, heed the advice offered by local riders: Plan to stay longer than you expect; be aware that at night, it gets supernaturally dark; be careful of gravel on mountain corners; and watch for wildlife that includes bighorn sheep, elk, mountain goats,

Riding at High Elevations

If you're not accustomed to riding in the high mountains, the first few nights may find you experiencing symptoms that accompany reduced amounts of oxygen: insomnia and headaches. If you're in good physical condition, you'll have better reserves to cope with the change in altitude, but it's smart to gradually adapt to physical activities over several days—especially if you'll be residing or riding at elevations over 6,000 feet.

black bears, and mule deer. Although I suggest Telluride as the first overnight, you'll ride through other intriguing towns where you can stay the night without disappointment.

You're going to love what's coming. The 236-mile-long loop road known as San Juan Skyway is designated as an All-American Road, a National Forest Scenic Byway, and a Colorado Scenic & Historical Byway. It's recognized as one of the most beautiful drives in America and noted as the place "where the road touches the sky."

When you leave via U.S. 550 North, the road rises slightly as you enter the San Juan National Forest. Soon you are surrounded by nothing but Colorado, where the purple mountains' majesty will elicit enough *Oh, my God!*s to start a new religion. After Cascade Creek, it gets trickier, but you will fear no mountain, even as you ride over 10,000 feet into thin air. If you parked your bike and trotted 50 feet, you'd be panting like a dog.

When you reach the Coalbank Pass Summit at 10,640 feet, you may think you've hit the highest height—but you haven't. There's much more to come, but for now observe the waterfalls, great timber, Alpine meadows, and switchbacks that open the trapdoor into valleys below and then rise again to 10,910 feet at Molas

Pass. If you wanted to go underground, you wouldn't need the FBI's help. You'd just camp out here.

Ride with caution: What follows are miles of steep grade, yet only a two-foot-high guardrail stands between you and eternity. When you reach the overlook outside of Silverton, make sure your seatback's in its upright position for the final approach.

Silverton (elevation 9,318 feet), the terminus for the narrow gauge steam train, is a Victorian mining town that dates to 1874. As you cruise into town, the information center lies on the right (open 9 A.M.–5 P.M. daily), followed by a small village of gift shops, bakeries, small hotels, and markets. The same is found on notorious Blair Street, where bordellos once thrived. If you never rode the Durango train, listen for its cacophonous grand arrival, and then roam around town. If you're an early riser as well as an early rider, the **Brown Bear Cafe** (1129 Greene St., 970/387-5630) has the best breakfast in town with thick cut bacon and great hash browns to power you over the pass. The owner, Fred, is a rider. If it's later, drop by **Handlebars** (117 13th St., 970/387-5395, www.handlebarsco.com), a combination bar and paraphernalia-cluttered restaurant, where you can order up big food for lunch or dinner, or a big brew.

Succeeding Silverton is a fantastic ride on Russian immigrant Otto Mears's Million-Dollar Highway, where roadside creeks flow outside rainbow-wide curves. Be careful here, since both the air and the road are thin and there's no margin for error in the mountains, especially when you approach Red Mountain Pass, which, at 11,075 feet, is the highest pass on your journey.

From here, it's back to Monaco riding, with more twists than a Hitchcock film. Some of the sharpest banked curves are right here, and the road becomes confused, not knowing which way it's supposed to turn. The repetitive corners give way to high canyon walls and valley overlooks that will remain with you for years, especially as you approach the town of Ouray (elevation 7,706), an optional overnight. For lodging information, check with the **Ouray Chamber of Commerce** (970/325-4746 or 800/228-1876, www.ouraycolorado.com).

Like Silverton, Ouray (you-RAY) made and lost its fortunes through mining. It recovered and remade itself as the "Switzerland of America." Jah, they did. Whether you stay overnight or not, don't miss **Box Canyon Falls** (970/325-7080). If you venture across the steel grating ($3 fee) to get close to the falls within this narrow gorge, the spring runoff thunders and throws the full weight of its freezing waters on you.

If your body's aching after the long ride, head to Ouray's main attraction, the **Hot Springs Pool** (970/325-7073), right on Main Street. You'll pay $10 to soak in waters ranging from pleasantly warm to a muscle-melting 106°F.

Ouray also has Jeep tours and rentals that peel you off your bike and thrust you into the country and up to the stratosphere, with trails climbing past 13,000 feet. **Colorado West Jeep Rentals** (701 Main St., 970/325-4014 or 800/648-5337, www.coloradowestjeeps.com) and **Switzerland of America Jeep Rentals** (226 7th Ave., 970/325-4484 or 866/990-5337, www.soajeep.com) rent Wranglers and Cherokees for half- and full-day excursions. Most riders, though, seem to prefer to leave the driving to guides who know area history and the right roads to reach fields of wildflowers, mining districts, waterfalls, and Alpine meadows. Either way, with a Jeep, you can explore ghost towns, old mining camps, and gold mines in and around Ouray. Bring warm clothes, food, a camera, and around $60 per person (for tours) to $149 (on your own).

One must-see is the **Bachelor-Syracuse Mine Tour** (970/325-0220, www.bachelorsyracusemine.com). Take U.S. 550 North to County Road 14, and then turn right and follow a gravel road to the mine entrance. Save room for food since the cowboys here cook killer breakfasts and lunches. After boarding a rickety mine car ($17), you'll head 3,350 feet through a cool (55°F), CAT scan–style tunnel eight feet wide by eight feet tall. It's eerie as hell riding along the veins of gold and silver, and it's even worse when the guide turns out the lights. Guides will provide a historical perspective to give you an in-depth and painless education on the hazards faced by Western miners. Don't miss it.

The second leg down to Telluride is easier than the first, starting atop a plateau that gives way to a valley floor. When you reach Ridgway, before you turn left at Highway 62 you may want to take a lunch break at the rustic, rider-preferred **True Grit Café** (123 N Lena St., 970/626-5739). Located on the west side of the park in town, it pays tribute to the classic John Wayne film that was shot around here.

The landscape grows larger and more impressive, and the consistently nice road affords several photo ops. This is not a road to be hurried through. This is slow-paced cowboy country and chances are you'll be tempted to unscrew the footpegs and string up some stirrups instead. The curves, neither dangerous nor demanding, lead easily to Route 145, which turns south on the western side of the San Juan Skyway.

The road rides through Placerville, into a canyon, and then beside red rock cliffs and into the Uncompahgre National Forest. Sixteen miles after you reach Route 145, Telluride comes into view and you'll stare in awe at staggering Bear Mountain Pass, a zigzag, motorcycle-destroying road that scales the mountainside beside a gushing river.

A great introduction, and the follow-up will not disappoint.

TELLURIDE PRIMER

Telluride has a mighty strange history, friend. The nomadic Utes arrived in the Telluride Valley searching for elk, deer, and mountain sheep, and then they split. The Spanish arrived in the 1700s searching for an overland route to the Pacific Coast, but they didn't stay either. The settler who decided to stick it out was a man who had a reason to stay: prospector John Fallon.

Fallon staked his claim above the town in 1875, registered the Sheridan Mine, and then struck it rich with zinc, lead, copper, iron, silver, and gold. This was the Silicon Valley of the 1870s, drawing fortune-seekers from around the world: Finns, Swedes, Irish, French, Italians, Germans, and Chinese. But unlike today's California technogeeks, the boys here had gambling halls, saloons, brothels, and friends like Butch Cassidy, who arrived to plan his first heist at the San Miguel Valley Bank in June 1889.

When the mining boom collapsed, the town suffered a slow decline until the 1960s when it approached ghost-town status. That's when a few resolute citizens realized that "white gold" (aka snow) could save their town. With a few shakes of entrepreneurial spirit, they transformed Telluride into a ski resort.

The result will keep you satisfied. There are hippies trying to re-create the halcyon days of Haight-Ashbury; there are art galleries; there's a surplus of natural beauty; and attractive young ski bums (who make life worth living for some middle-aged women and comparably depressing for some middle-aged men). And then there is money, lots of it, imported by recent transplants and celebrity residents.

Beneath it all, however, this is an ordinary mountain town. There are small markets, a hardware store, the Free Box with donations for the needy, and a calendar of events from Telluride Blues & Brews to the Bluegrass Festival to the legendary Telluride Film Festival.

It's a great little town. Have fun.

ON THE ROAD: TELLURIDE

You entered through the valley's one-way entrance when you arrived in Telluride, so a pleasure ride isn't worth the effort—at least, not on a bike. There are ways to get around and experience the town, most of which you can do fairly easily.

I'd suggest starting before 9 A.M., when the morning light bathes the mountains in a rich gold and the streets are perfectly deserted for photos. After grabbing a breakfast with the locals at **Maggie's Cafe** (110 E. Colorado Ave., 970/728-4882), walk over to the gondola on the south end of Oak Street. When it's not hauling skiers in winter, it hauls sightseers and mountain bikes in summer. And it's free.

Wait for an empty car and start your

13-minute trip to the summit. From this vantage point, the aerial views of the town and mountains grow increasingly more majestic—but hold off on photos until the return trip so ski or bike racks won't block your view. There are two stops along the way, the first at Sophia Station (just under 11,000 feet) and the second at Mountain Village (9,545 feet), a picturesque and affluent—yet oddly artificial—neighborhood. Return for a nighttime ride and you can soak in equally magical views.

When you return to town, it's small enough to do on foot. Don't pressure yourself. Just savor the mountain air and views and the fact that you're not in an office.

PULL IT OVER: TELLURIDE HIGHLIGHTS
Attractions and Adventures

You can wander around searching for individual outfitters and rental companies, or you can save some shoe leather by stopping at **Telluride Sports** (150 W. Colorado Ave., 970/728-4477 or 800/828-7547, www.telluridesports. com). Since 1972, it's been a one-stop shop for all things outdoors: fly-fishing, whitewater rafting, horseback riding, and kayaking. Prices range from $26–51 for a mountain bike day rental, although prices for guided excursions and adventures are much higher.

It'd be a shame to be way out West without saddling up at least once. A professional wrangler and full-time character named Roudy offers "gentle horses for gentle people, fast horses for fast people, and for people who don't like to ride, horses that don't like to be rode." Choices at **Riding with Roudy** (off Hwy. 145—call for directions, 970/728-9611, www.ridewith-roudy.com) include a variety of trail rides starting at roughly $30 an hour, as well as dinner rides ($60) and custom pack trips.

If you ride, ride with Roudy—he's good company.

Telluride Outside (121 W. Colorado Ave., 970/728-3895 or 800/831-6230, www.tellurideoutside.com) is a full-service provider of fly-fishing and float trips, whitewater rafting, ballooning, and Jeep tours.

Shopping

If you haven't already invested in a custom hat from Thomas Barnes in Durango, I'm sure Ann McClelland, proprietor of the **Bounty Hunter** (226 Colorado St., 970/728-0256, www.shopbountyhunter. com), would like to take a crack at your skull. She and her family of hatmakers have created custom hats for Ted Nugent, Madeleine Albright, and the Clintons and can easily make a classic customized beaver-skin hat for you in a variety of styles (Rodeo, Rio Grande, Explorer, Rancher, etc.). They also craft custom-made python or alligator boots, belts, straps, and Western art.

A cool little neighborhood spirits shop, **Telluride Liquors & Wine Shop** (123 E. Colorado Ave., 970/728-3380) features about 450 wines—100 in the wine cellar—and 250 bottled beers, as well as a small humidor with a good selection of cee-gars. Its counterpart and competition is **Telluride Bottle Works** (129 W. San Juan Ave., 970/728-5553, www.telluridebottleworks.com), which has delivery service, a wider selection, and lower prices.

Now that most antiques shops claim that *Flintstones* jars are collectibles, it's great to find a place like **Telluride Antique Market** (324 W. Colorado Ave., 970/728-4323), which sells quality antiques, such as silver-plated Indian prints, cheesecake calendars, art deco items, and old travel posters and prints.

Blue-Plate Specials

Perhaps the best place to grab an early breakfast, **Maggie's Cafe** (110 E. Colorado Ave., 970/728-4882) is the hometown gathering spot. A favorite with locals, they gather for mean breakfast burritos, French toast, and fresh baked goods. Also on the menu are a variety of sandwiches and salads.

Noticing a dearth of affordable dining options, **Smugglers Brewpub and Grille** (225 S. Pine St., 970/728-0919, www.smugglersbrew.com) opened in 1998 and gained an instant following for its 10 onsite microbrews, ribs steeped in barbecue sauce, drunken chicken breasts, Philly cheesesteak sandwiches, and an interior created from an old miner's warehouse. Open for lunch and dinner, this casual, laid-back joint is a great place to grab a brew on the patio.

If you're on a writer's budget, you'll be pleased with **Baked in Telluride** (127 S. Fir St., 970/728-4775), serving breakfast, lunch, and dinner. You can grab a baked breakfast, slice of pizza, deli sandwich, soda pop, or big salad. Nothing fancy, but the food's real groovy.

Watering Holes

There are two authentic hangouts in Telluride. And the **Last Dollar Saloon** (100 E. Colorado Ave., 970/728-4800, www.lastdollarsaloon.com) is one of them. "The Buck" (as locals call it) comes complete with hardwood floors, brick walls, tin ceiling, jukebox, full liquor bar, bottled beers, and a few on tap. Can't do much better when you want a main-street view and a place to meet real people.

O'Bannon's Irish Pub (121 S. Fir St., 970/728-6139) is the other authentic hangout. This one's a small and loud basement bar with $4.50 pints of Harp, Bass, and Guinness; a pool table; a jukebox; a well-worn bar; and a ceiling draped with flags of Ireland.

One of the town's original drinking establishments, **Sheridan Bar** (231 W. Colorado Ave., 970/728-3911) is open 3 P.M.–2 A.M. daily. The oldest bar in town is topped out by a tin ceiling and features an old upright piano, long bar, and mighty cool pool hall in back. You'll feel like a cowboy.

Shut-Eye

There are no chain hotels in town, but lodging options abound in Telluride. Rates peak during winter and are higher in summer than in spring and fall. The town offers a booking service: **Telluride Central Reservations** (970/728-3041 or 888/355-8743, www.visittelluride.com) handles lodging as well as air service, performance tickets, and activities. Keep in mind that some accommodations require two-night minimum weekend stays, and prices rise during special event weekends like the film and Bluegrass festivals.

Inn-dependence

The **New Sheridan Hotel** (231 W. Colorado Ave., 970/728-4351 or 800/200-1891, www.newsheridan.com, $169–289 high season) is one of the town's best bets. It was built in 1891 and has since gotten itself gussied up with 26 spacious, tasteful rooms and suites with nice furniture and spa tubs. There are also a few condo-style suites. The full breakfast, library, and fitness room are impressive, but what puts it over the top are the two rooftop hot tubs with spectacular mountain views.

ON THE ROAD: TELLURIDE TO MESA VERDE

The overwhelming beauty of this run will either inspire you or cause cardiac arrhythmia. Leave Telluride via West Colorado and turn left after the service station on Route 145. You're back on the San Juan Skyway now, gearing up for scenery you cannot imagine.

Within minutes, you're riding into the mountains for a view of wildflowers, lakes, cliffs, and valleys slung between jagged mountain peaks. The road curves, drops, dives, and twists, taking your bike down into portions of these valleys like an elevator falling down a shaft. This section of highway is where all your Colorado visions come together. The curves are not difficult, but the overwhelming combination of colors and textures is hard to fathom. Drink in multiple shades of green from the rail-straight pines, fields of brilliant wildflowers, black-and-white mountains, and surreal blue skies.

The road is reluctant to become routine, and the surge of energy it triggers may spark you to goose it—but watch your speed, since some curves can be deceptively tight. You'll cross the 10,000-foot plateau once again and see tundra and meadows before descending to 8,827 feet into the little town of Rico.

After Rico, the road transforms into an ordinary ride through the country. It may not be as inspiring as the earlier run, but when you consider the alternative—bending paperclips in an office or sitting in city traffic—you should have no complaints.

Ride past red rocks and, before you know it, you've reached the Colorado Plateau between the San Juan Mountains and Sonoran Desert. When you reach the end of Route 145, turn left onto U.S. 160 East toward Durango. As you ride toward Mesa Verde, look to your left; about 40 miles away, you'll see the mountains you conquered a few hours earlier.

From here, it's only seven miles to **Mesa Verde National Park** (970/529-4465 or 970/529-4465, www.nps.gov/meve).

Although if you opt to stay the night at Far View Lodge (the park's only indoor lodging option), you'll have another 15 miles to go as you head deep into the park.

Whether or not you stay inside the park or in nearby Cortez, get ready for the grand finale of your nearly circular run. After springing for the $5 fee (free if you carry an annual $80 America the Beautiful Pass), you'll ride a road that rises like a phoenix, with fantastically sharp ascents that open up to endless views of the desert plains.

Four miles later, the Morefield Campground has a launderette and café, as well as the park's only option for gas. The road continues with curves similar to those of the Pacific Coast Highway, with each corner opening up to an ocean of earth. Once you've risen to the top of the mesa, take everything you recognize—and then erase it from your databank. That is what you'll see—absolutely nothing. The emptiness lasts for mile after mile, with the only constant being the shifting, braking, and cornering you'll undertake to reach the visitors center.

Now the mystery begins.

MESA VERDE PRIMER

Mesa Verde is a strange and mysterious place. Take the tales of ghost ships and the Lost Colony, multiply them by a hundred, and you still won't even begin to understand Mesa Verde.

The Ancestral Puebloans (the term now preferred over the previously common Anasazi) settled here, carving homes into the cliffs. They were hunters, traders, artisans, and farmers, and this area was the heart of their civilization for nearly 800 years.

They built stone villages on mesa tops and cliff dwellings within canyon walls, and they created elaborate stoneworks,

The Mesa Verde Mystery

You'll soon recognize Mesa Verde as one of the most mysterious places you'll visit. Someone else who was intrigued by this abandoned region was novelist Willa Cather who, in 1925, wrote:

I saw a little city of stone asleep…that village sat looking down into the canyon with the calmness of eternity, preserved with the dry air and almost perpetual sunlight, like a fly in amber, guarded by the cliffs and the river and the desert.

ceremonial kivas, intricately designed pottery, and four-story housing structures. Then, around 1300 A.D., the inhabitants of Mesa Verde packed it up. No one knows what they left with, but they left behind crops and personal belongings. Since they had no written records, to this day no one knows for sure why they left. Some archaeologists believe they moved to New Mexico and Arizona where their descendants still live today.

Their very existence remained a mystery until 1888, when ranchers Richard Wetherill and Charles Mason rode through the area to round up stray cattle. That's when Wetherill saw Cliff Palace hidden within the canyon. A few years later, amateur archaeologist Gustaf Nordenskiold arrived from Sweden to document the dwellings and sites.

What's intriguing is that there are mysteries that remain to this day. Even though the park and services aren't on the level of Yellowstone or Yosemite, Mesa Verde was still selected the world's number one historic monument by readers of *Condé Nast Traveler*—even ranking ahead of the Vatican. In 1978, UNESCO, a United Nations organization, named the park a World Heritage Cultural Site, and Mesa Verde was also the first park dedicated

to the preservation of cultural resources. While it doesn't feature the multitude of services you can find in Durango and Telluride, it's a logical and fascinating archaeological find that'll wrap up your San Juan Skyway run.

ON THE ROAD: MESA VERDE

Unless you're an anthropologist or Indiana Jones, there's a smart way to see—and really understand—Mesa Verde: Take one of the half-day tours departing from the Far View Lodge. I admit that the ride around the park's juniper- and piñon-dotted landscape is fantastic, but I'd argue that it's just not worth traveling solo—at least not yet. You can always ride later, but for now borrow some insights from trained guides and let them share what happened here or you'll simply be looking at your free map and at structures and struggling to comprehend close to 5,000 identified sites. By the way, according to the modern Pueblo people, these are *sites* and not ruins since they believe their ancestors spirits still inhabit the place, and after time the structures will return to nature.

So start deep in the park at the **Far View Visitor Center** (15 miles from park entrance, open mid-April–mid-October, 8 A.M.–5 P.M.) and arrange a special ranger-led tour ($3) to either Cliff Palace, Balcony House, or Long House, since demand restricts guests to one site per day. Hold off on touring the park's museum—it will make more sense once you've taken the tour.

On just the half-day bus/walking excursion, I learned more in three hours than I did in three years of high school. The first sites you see are ordinary, but the stories and structures become increasingly more fascinating as you move on. Starting with a simple kiva (a ceremonial room), you'll eventually reach Spruce Tree House, an elaborate structure of 130 rooms and eight kivas that you can walk to and, in some sections, through. Keep in mind that with ingenious hand and toe-holds carved directly into the cliffs, many of these structures were accessible only by scaling cliff walls. You also have to walk a half-mile down to reach it, although it seems like two miles coming back up. Wear comfortable shoes and carry your own drinking water—none is available at any site.

I can't even begin to explain what you'll see and learn here so, as I've stressed, just swing by the Far View Visitor Center, sign up for a tour, and talk to the rangers who are more than ready to share what they know. When you're done, plan to return to some of the places you missed, such as the visitor center and **Chapin Mesa Archaeological Museum** (20 miles from park entrance, open 8 A.M.–6:30 P.M. daily), where dioramas and exhibits on pottery, jewelry, tools, weapons, and beadwork will fill in some of the blanks. The park also has well-stocked bookstores as well as inexpensive and informative pamphlets on specific sites. And now that you're armed with a history of the place, it's time to hit the road and see it on your own.

Hard to explain how cool this is. You have to see it for yourself.

PULL IT OVER: MESA VERDE HIGHLIGHTS
Attractions and Adventures

The entire park is a historic site, with guided bus tours departing from **Far View Lodge** (800/449-2288). Half-day tours ($42) leave at 8 A.M. and 1 P.M. from early April to late October. Make reservations, especially in peak season.

Adjacent to the Chapin Mesa Archaeological Museum, **Spruce Tree Terrace** sells silver jewelry, etched and painted pottery, and sand paintings and there's also a shop at the Far View Terrace.

Blue-Plate Specials

There are few places to eat at Mesa Verde. Snack bars and cafeteria-style restaurants at Far View and Spruce Tree are adequate if you're not agile enough to kill and skin a rabbit with an *atlatl*. If you can swing it, the **Metate Room** at Far View Motor Lodge is the park's signature restaurant. No corn dogs here—load up on dishes such as Rocky Mountain Elk Tenderloin, Mesquite Smoked Buffalo, Blue Corn and Pine Nut-Dusted Trout, and Foxfire Farms Lamb Shank. The Southwestern-style dining room has a huge wall of windows that reveals the mesas and finger canyons, so the views are as good as the cuisine.

Shut-Eye

If you don't stay in the park, the town of Cortez, 10 miles west, has loads of chain hotels. Durango is 36 miles east of the park entrance station on U.S. 160. The park offers two options. The exterior of the top-of-the-line **Far View Lodge** ($118–132) is 1970s ugly, and the interior is generic hotel, but you get a balcony with stunning views from a 2,000-foot plateau.

The **Morefield Campground** ($20 tent, $30 full hookups), a popular spot if you don't mind roughing it, has 435 campsites with picnic tables, grills, and benches, as well as a grocery store, showers, and a laundry. Reservations for either can be made by calling 800/449-2288 or 888/896-3831 or visiting www.visitmesaverde.com.

Chain Drive

These chain hotels are in the nearby town of Cortez:

Days Inn, Econo Lodge, Holiday Inn, Rodeway, Super 8, Travelodge

For more information, including phone numbers and websites, see page 439.

Resources for Riders

Colorado Rockies Run

Colorado Travel Information
Bed & Breakfast Innkeepers of Colorado—800/265-7696,
   www.innsofcolorado.org
Colorado Division of Wildlife—303/297-1192 or 303/291-7534,
   www.wildlife.state.co.us
Colorado Road and Weather Conditions—303/639-1111 or instate 877/315-7623,
   www.cotrip.org
Colorado State Parks Reservations—303/470-1144 or 800/678-2267,
   www.parks.state.co.us
Colorado Travel and Tourism—800/265-6723, www.colorado.com

Local and Regional Information
Durango Area Chamber Resort Association—970/247-0312 or 800/525-8855,
   www.durango.org
Mesa Verde National Park—970/529-4465, www.nps.gov/meve
Mesa Verde National Park Reservations—602/331-5210 or 800/449-2288,
   www.visitmesaverde.com
Silverton Chamber of Commerce—970/387-5654 or 800/752-4494,
   www.silvertoncolorado.com
Telluride Chamber of Commerce—970/728-3041 or 888/605-2578,
   www.visittelluride.com
Telluride Visitor Services—888/353-5473, www.telluride.com

Colorado Motorcycle Shops
Basin Motorcycle Works—200 U.S. 160 Frontage Road, 970/259-9489,
   www.basinmotorcycleworks.biz
Durango Harley-Davidson—750 S Camino Del Rio, Durango, 970/259-0778,
   www.durangoharley.com
Fun Center Suzuki-Kawasaki—29603 U.S. 160 East, Durango, 970/259-1070,
   www.funcentercycles.com
Handlebar Motorsports—346 S. Camino Del Rio, Durango, 970/247-0845,
   www.handlebarmotorsports.com
Mesa Verde Motorsports—2120 S. Broadway, Cortez, 970/565-9322
Ridgway Motorsports—566 Hwy. 62, Ridgway, 970/626-5112

Red Rocks Run

Sedona, Arizona to Zion National Park, Utah

Over the next several days, you'll find that just as the Calistoga–Sausalito–Carmel run is a perfect showcase for California towns and roads, Sedona–Grand Canyon–Zion is the right blend for Arizona and Utah. With the exception of the wild landscape and canyons around Sedona, the roads are not very challenging. Still, you may not mind too much. The vast openness of this part of the country is intriguing in its own way.

SEDONA PRIMER

Sedona. It's a beautiful name for a beautiful place. But would you feel the same way if you were riding into Schnebly Station? That was the first name proposed by settler T. Carl Schnebly when he wanted to establish a post office here in the early 1900s. When the postmaster decided the name was too long for a cancellation stamp, the honor went to Schnebly's Pennsylvania Dutch wife, Sedona.

Turn back the clock a little further, and you'll see that it's taken nature about 350 million years to make Sedona what it is today. No standard-issue brown and gray rocks here. Sedona's fire-red buttes and mesas, spires, and pinnacles are the result of a prehistoric sea washing over and receding from the area several times. The cyclic sea coverings left behind a patina of iron oxide that colors these hills.

First settled around A.D. 700, the area was home to the Sinaguans, who stuck around until 1066, when a volcano blew. They left, and the Ancestral Puebloans (also known as the Anasazi) arrived to take advantage of the recently fertilized soil and introduce modern amenities like multistoried pueblos and burglar-proof homes. Low doorways forced intruders to crouch upon entering, so the vigilant homeowner could bash their brains out.

No one knows why the Ancestral Puebloans left in the 1300s. Spanish explorers came looking for gold in the 1500s, but when they didn't find any they left, too. Prospectors, pioneers, and trappers began to arrive in the early 1800s and got

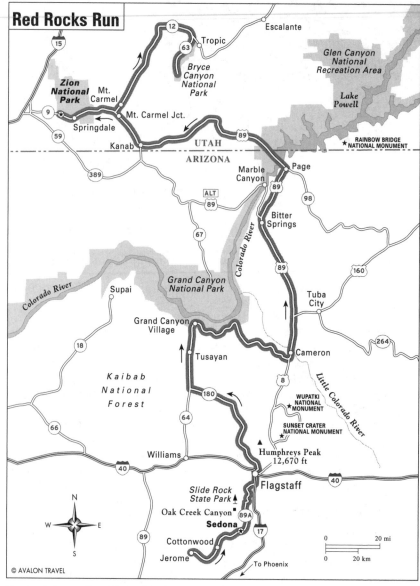

Red Rocks Run

Route: Sedona to Zion National Park via Oak Creek Canyon, Tusayan, Grand Canyon, Page, Lake Powell, Bryce Canyon

Distance: Approximately 365 miles

First Leg: Sedona to Grand Canyon, Arizona (110 miles)

Second Leg: Grand Canyon to Page, Arizona (143 miles)

Third Leg: Page, Arizona to Zion, Utah (112 miles)

Helmet Laws: Arizona and Utah do not require helmets.

along fine with the new tribes who were living here until the white man began fencing off the hunting grounds of Native Americans who rightfully argued that the land was theirs. The U.S. Army didn't want to argue, so in 1872 they shoved the Native Americans off their land.

Despite the injustice, Native Americans are well represented throughout Sedona. Today, this is a major cultural center with dozens of artists, actors, writers, and musicians gaining their inspiration from the beauty outside their doors. New Age disciples also congregate here, claiming Cathedral Rock is Sedona's most powerful female "vortex"—an electromagnetic energy force rising from within the earth. If you believe, you may find balance in health, relationships, work, and money.

Chances are you'll spend the majority of your time in Uptown Sedona, the older commercial district, or take a quick run down Oak Creek Canyon, the path that'll later lead you towards the Grand Canyon. There's nearly nothing you'd want to do indoors except sleep and eat, which makes this a natural for motorcycle travelers.

Wherever you ride, the roads will be right.

ON THE ROAD: SEDONA

It's been said that God created the Grand Canyon, but he resides in Sedona.

Sedona *is* divine. When you arrive, you'll see that the physical beauty combines the mountains of Vermont, the rocks of California, and the clay of Georgia's back roads. If it looks at all familiar, you may recall seeing a similar landscape from Pathfinder's mission to Mars.

There's a lot to see on surrounding roads, and perhaps the most popular stop for motorcycle travelers is about 30 miles away in Jerome, an old mining town that's become a strangely popular destination.

The ride's not that spectacular, but if you didn't go there your friends might beat you with sticks.

From Uptown Sedona, South Highway/West Highway 89A is a wide four-lane road that passes franchise restaurants and rides away from the red rocks which look outstanding in your mirrors. The road remains the same until you near Cottonwood, where you turn left at the gas station in Clarkdale and begin your steep ascent. It's another four miles up the mountain, where it seems that the landscape was left behind from a Saturday-morning cowboy matinee.

Next to Taos, it seems that the town of Jerome has done the best job of creating something out of nothing. In its heyday as a copper mining community, it was the third-largest city in Arizona. After copper bottomed out, residents headed out and today the town can't even rustle up a gas station, grocery, doctor, or pharmacy. None of this will matter after you park your bike with all the others outside the **Spirit Room** (144 Main St., 928/634-8809, www.spiritroom.com) and consider yourself at home.

This joint has become the base for local riders making their way across high mountain country, low desert, red rocks, and canyons in easy one-day rides. No fighting, no country music, no pointy boots here, just a watering hole for riders who appreciate the lack of a cover, live music, cold brews, and Bloody Marys that can hurt you. You can add to the bar's collection of graffiti or donate a bra (if you wear one).

Farther down on Main Street, **Paul and Jerry's** (206 Main St., 928/634-2603) has been a saloon since 1887. Today, it serves beer and has a full bar and three pool tables in back. **Mile High Grill & Inn** (309 Main St., 928/634-5094, www.jeromemilehighinn.com), built in 1899, is one of a few restaurants here, with an upscale appearance that runs counter to a fairly basic menu of hamburgers, enchiladas, soups, and appetizers.

Unless you've got a mighty deep hankering for a drink, Jerome should take only a few hours. When you return to Sedona, you'll be tempted to examine the red rock monoliths that contrast beautifully with the green of piñon, juniper, and cypress trees. Pick up a Sedona map that identifies the monoliths, which are named for their appearance: Cathedral, Courthouse, Snoopy, Elephant...You'll have to find the local off-color favorite on your own.

Since you'll be running down Oak Creek Canyon on your way north, head down Highway 179 to Chapel Road and turn left to reach the **Chapel of the Holy Cross** (780 Chapel Rd., 928/282-4069, www.chapeloftheholycross.com). A labor of love, the chapel was purposely designed to appear like part of the rock formation, with a magnificent cross seeming to project from the mountainside. From its summit, you have an unobstructed view of Courthouse Butte, Bell Rock, and the Two Nuns. Time this for late afternoon and you'll be here to witness one of the most spectacular sunsets in the country.

Afterward, the town is yours to explore. Wander around uptown or go deeper into the desert on a Jeep tour. Sedona is a great town—you shouldn't cheat yourself.

PULL IT OVER:
SEDONA HIGHLIGHTS
Attractions and Adventures

The term "great outdoors" doesn't do justice to Sedona. It's actually much greater than that here, but largely inaccessible to touring bikes. Other modes of transportation—rental Jeeps, guided tours, and hot air balloons—can be almost as much fun if you can afford it. Most ground-based tours take you on rugged and historic trails leading to off-the-beaten-path canyons and mountains.

Ride with a guide on **Sedona Red Rock Jeep Tours** (270 N. Hwy. 89A, 520/282-6826 or 800/848-7728, www.redrockjeep.com). Choose from an introductory vortex tour to a horseback ride. Everyone needs a gimmick, and **Pink Jeep Tours** (204 N. Hwy./W. Hwy. 89A, 928/282-5000 or 800/873-3662, www.pinkjeep.com) has chosen color. These folks offer tours ranging from a $45 90-minute Coyote Canyons ride to the $72 Ancient Ruin ride. The 2.5-hour trip heads to a Sinaguan Indian cliff dwelling, where a guide points out and explains the rock art. Roughriders can try the Broken Arrow run, which offers two hours of heavy-duty 4x4-ing.

A Day in the West (252 N. Hwy. 89A, 928/282-4320 or 800/973-3662, www.adayinthewest.com) has an array of tours. Photo tours, Jeep tours, horseback rides, and chuckwagon trips are planned by guides "who've been riding these trails so long, there's red dust in their veins." Prices range from $45 for the pioneer trail ride to $170 for a Jeep/horseback/Western dinner.

Although it's mighty 'spensive and you won't see the rocks up close, **Northern Light Balloon Expeditions** (928/282-2274 or 800/230-6222, www.northernlightballoon.com) offers the most peaceful way to see the hills—provided you can shake yourself awake for the sunrise flight. These folks will pick you up at your place and get you worked up for an hour flight (nearing $200), but the entire experience lasts up to four hours when you consider there's the inflation and post-flight champagne picnic. The payoff for the early day is that you'll feast on a brilliant palette of colors found only in nature. And Sedona.

If you're looking for a concentration of Southwestern art, you'll find it in Uptown or at **Tlaquepaque** (tah-lah-ca-POK-ee, Hwy. 179, 928/282-4838, www.tlaq.com) at the bridge, open 10 A.M.–5 P.M. daily. Modeled after a Mexican village, the shopping district spreads out and rambles through shaded courtyards and ivy-covered walls.

Blue-Plate Specials

It looks like a hole in the wall, but at **Cowboy Club Grille & Spirits** (241 N. Hwy. 89A, 928/282-4200, www.cowboyclub. com), "high desert cuisine" goes hand in hand with Old West tradition and hospitality. Try the rattlesnake(!), pistachio-crusted halibut, buttermilk fried chicken, or buffalo(!) sirloin, low in fat, high in protein. There are other dining choices here, too—Redstone Cabin and the Silver Saddle Room—and the bar is great, too, with legendary margaritas. The prices seem fair and the service excellent. Cowboy is open for lunch and dinner. Oh, and the Cowboy Artists of America was founded here.

I usually wake up before breakfast, so it was a boon to find the **Coffee Pot Restaurant** (2050 W. Hwy. 89A, 928/282-6626), which can create—upon request and with no help from confederates—101 types of omelettes. I ordered one with pencil shavings, string, and gravel and got the bejeezus beat out of me. Here since the 1950s, the Coffee Pot is the place for locals, celebs, and any traveler who wants a hearty breakfast or lunch.

Shut-Eye

For a complete listing of nearly 20 bed-and-breakfast inns that are inspected and approved by the Sedona Bed & Breakfast Guild, check 800/915-4442 or www. bbsedona.net. The **Sedona Chamber of Commerce** (928/282-7722, www.sedonachamber.com) is a good source of information on the many cabins of Oak Creek Canyon.

Motels and Motor Courts

The **Sedona Motel** (218 Hwy. 179, 928/282-7187, www.thesedonamotel. com, $90–100) is an old-fashioned motel just over a half mile from the town center. Clean and neat, it offers 16 ground level rooms with microwaves, coffee makers, and mini fridges.

La Vista Motel (500 N. Hwy. 89A, 928/282-7301 or 800/896-7301, www. lavistamotel.com, $69 and up) is one of the most economical choices. Don't expect luxury from this family-owned motel, but for a clean room close to everything, it's a fine place to bunk down.

Inn-dependence

The highly ranked **Creekside Inn** (99 Copper Cliffs Dr., 928/282-4992 or 800/390-8621, www.creeksideinn.net, $199 and up) rests—coincidentally—right beside Oak Creek. Although the setting is wild, the inn is not—it's Victorian, with swank guestrooms featuring jetted tubs and a furnished garden patio. This is the place for grown-ups who've paid off the mortgage.

If you're traveling in a pack or need room to spread out, **Junipine** (8351 N. Hwy. 89A, 928/282-3375 or 800/742-7463, www.junipine.com, $190–320) features one-bedroom, two-bedroom, and creekside cottages—all in the heart of Oak Creek Canyon. The cottages (ranging from 900 to 1,400 square feet) contain a fully equipped kitchen, private deck, living room, and two fireplaces. The secluded, wooded setting may make it hard to break away.

Chain Drive

These chain hotels are in town, or within 10 miles of the city center: **Best Western, Comfort Inn, Days Inn, Fairfield Inn, Hampton Inn, Hilton, Hyatt, Radisson, Super 8**

For more information, including phone numbers and websites, see page 439.

ON THE ROAD: SEDONA TO THE GRAND CANYON

If you weren't able to resist temptation, you may have already ridden up this road. Not a bad idea, because this route is definitely worth a second look.

The beginning of this run is a perfect goodbye to Sedona since it is just as beautiful, albeit in a lush, more verdant way. You'll notice the topography changing as North Highway 89A slides into Oak Creek Canyon and from the seat of your bike, you command a vantage point not enjoyed by motorists. The canyon appears on your right, clinging so close to the guardrail that it seems much deeper than it actually is.

For several miles this gentle ride doesn't demand a lot, except that you pay attention to nature and the guardrail barely high enough to keep you out of the canyon. Just when you didn't think it could get better, it does, with red rocks on one side and a canopy road on the other. You're descending into the canyon now and approaching **Slide Rock State Park** (6871 N. Hwy. 89A, 928/282-3034, http://azstateparks.com/parks/slro), a slippery run down the rocks that's worth a stop if you have a bathing suit in your bags. Admission is $10 per vehicle in the summer, $8 off-season, with visitors crowding the park and parking lots in summer.

Continuing north, you'll pass small motels and creekside cabins before, gradually, the red rocks give way to white granite formations that look like El Capitan in miniature. Soon you begin your ascent into hearty pine forests, riding up to 6,000 feet and facing some exciting 20-mph twisties. As the ride continues it gets even more thrilling when you look straight up and see the Babel-esque–road winding overhead. While it can be tricky riding, it's quite a bit safer thanks to a sprawling chain-link fence that keeps the mountain from falling on top of you.

At 7,000 feet, pull off at Oak Creek Vista, often where a contingent of Native American merchants are selling silver and turquoise jewelry and other handcrafted artwork. This is a great place for a break and a picture—look over the side and see Oak Creek rushing past 1,500 feet below you.

Just about the time you've gotten used to the curves, the road levels out in a pine forest before Oak Creek Canyon Road surrenders to I-17. A few miles ahead is I-40, but bypass it and veer to the west of Flagstaff to find U.S. 180, a two-lane that forks to the left and takes you on a roughly 30-mile tour of pine forests and mountains. You are riding in proximity to Humphrey's Peak which, at 12,633 feet, is the highest point in Arizona. As the road skims along its base, you have the privilege of continuing the same pine forest run that's become a part of your life. You won't face the challenge of switchbacks, nor will you suffer from the hypnotizing effects of straights either. Instead, the road is marked by slow, meandering curves that glide across a fairly level landscape. As soon as you've grown accustomed to the richness and verdant green of the forest, nature decides to change the scene. You start dropping slowly and imperceptibly as you cruise into the high desert. As you ride steadily along U.S. 180, you'll cross another 20 miles of desert and sagebrush before reaching the junction of Highway 64, with U.S. 180 taking a sharp turn to the north.

Even though the road is flat, you may have the same gut feeling I did, namely that you're riding atop the crest of an abnormally massive mountain. In reality, you are. This is the Kaibab Plateau and you're cruising across the wide, flat peak of a low, rounded mountain. While you still have about 30 miles to ride before hitting Grand Canyon, the ease and solitude of the landscape around you grant abundant time to just relax and think, especially near mile marker 196 when the land rises slightly and an incredible vista of the plains spreads out before you. It's moments like this that enhance a ride—creating memories that'll follow you back home and find you planning future road trips. On a clear day, look to the horizon and you can see the Grand Canyon, just a black streak from here.

There's little to note between here and there, just straight riding until you reach the growing village of Tusayan—and your destination.

GRAND CANYON PRIMER

Each time a magazine or TV program does a "Best of America" piece, you can bet you'll see an image of the Grand Canyon—and for good reason. It's large, it's beautiful in an empty sort of way, and, as a national park, it belongs to you.

Back in 1530, though, it belonged to Don Lopez de Cardenas, a captain in Coronado's expedition. It was de Cardenas who discovered the Grand Canyon—which was news to the Indians who were already here.

Fast forward to the 20th century. The Grand Canyon was named a national monument in 1908 and a national park in 1919 and it was obvious why it deserved the honor. If you've never seen it, every image you can picture in your mind pales in comparison to the real thing because it is far larger than anything you can imagine. Even when you're actually there and standing at the rim, you're seeing only a fraction of the entire canyon. Measured by river course, the dimensions are staggering. The chasm is 277 miles long and up to 18 miles wide, and has an average depth of one mile. It took six million years (give or take a few hours) to cut the Grand Canyon, and nature is not finished yet. Rain, snow, heat, frost, and wind are constantly sculpting new shapes, bluffs, and buttes. The reed-thin creek at the bottom is the Colorado River, which averages 300 feet wide and up to 100 feet deep. It is this relative sliver of water that is the erosive force that carved the canyon.

If your schedule permits, try to avoid a summer tour. Naturally, when the kids are out of school they're all here with their parents and the Grand Canyon Village is packed. Summer's also the season when vehicles—even your faithful mount—are restricted from riding Hermit Road to clear the way for a fleet of more practical shuttle buses. Overall, the combined crowds and dense traffic can detract from the experience. Whenever you arrive the colors of the canyon seem to change throughout the year, from the crisp frosts in winter to the cool autumn hues. Try to arrive in the morning before the high sun washes out its colors. If you have the wherewithal, see it via mule train, helicopter, or raft.

ON THE ROAD: THE GRAND CANYON

You'll pay $12 to enter the park (free with the $80 America the Beautiful Pass) and unless you've already invested in an aerial tour or have some sense of the canyon's history, your first stop should be the park's visitors center. Here you can get a map of the park that shows the best overlooks, watch an introductory film, and see a very large-scale model of the canyon that, in proportion, would make you as thin as a paper match.

When you reach the canyon rim what you'll see is Sedona in reverse. Every red rock is sucked down into the earth until the heroic hole loses all sense of dimension. Whether you look at the canyon from a helicopter, airplane, mule, or just standing at its edge, it looks as if the Colorado River far below is just a squirt-gun stream, and an 8,000-square-foot boulder on its banks appears no larger than a pebble. I've said it before: The canyon's architecture is far larger than anything you can comprehend. You can take pictures until you pass out, but unless you blow them up to actual size they won't begin to reflect the breadth, width, depth, and grandeur of this place.

What you *can* appreciate is that the view is different from each overlook, although one thing that remains the same is the sight of tourists who seem to flock to the same point at each protective barricade. Be bold. Walk about 30 feet to either side and you'll likely find a secluded spot where the view is just as nice and you can find a secluded promontory to call your own, a place where you can relax uninterrupted and contemplate the scene before you. If you have time—and you should allow some—arrive near dusk and head down Hermit Road to watch the canyon moon rise and the shadows fall like the sweep of a watch's second hand.

Perhaps the most spectacular view is several miles east in Desert View. Climbing the 70-foot Watch Tower, built in 1932 as an observation station, places you a total of 7,522 feet above sea level. Of all the vista points at the Grand Canyon, this is definitely worth a stop, and the pictures are priceless.

PULL IT OVER: GRAND CANYON HIGHLIGHTS
Attractions and Adventures
Grand Canyon: The Hidden Secrets

is a must-see. Catch it at the National Geographic Visitor Center's **IMAX Theater** (Hwy. 64, Tusayan, 928/638-2203, www.explorethecanyon.com, about $13). The film captures great views of the canyon, offers a historical perspective, and earns your undying respect for the one-armed stuntman who portrays explorer William Powell shooting the rapids on the Colorado. How he didn't paddle in circles, I'll never know. Some scenes in this film are so scary, you'd swear you're in the raft yourself. Outside, the tourist information center and gift shops are a convenient stop.

There are abundant fun and freakishly expensive opportunities to kick up your adrenaline. Helicopter and airplane tours are the most popular, but if you can swing it (because it *is* pricey), invest in a helicopter tour. Flying lower and slower than an airplane (although no one can fly beneath the rim), you'll cross the 18-mile-wide canyon twice at about 100 mph and receive the benefit of the pilot's narrative along the way. Among the stories guides tell is the tale of Louis Boucher, a man who obviously didn't like company. When a settler encroached on Boucher by establishing a homestead two miles away, the silver miner retreated into the Grand Canyon for a little privacy.

The easiest way to make reservations for area helicopter, airplane tours, and Jeep tours is to contact the **Grand Canyon CVB** (928/638-2901, www.grandcanyonchamber.com) and let them do it for you. They can also explain the advantages of each tour and steer you in the direction you need. If you'd prefer to make arrangements yourself, here are a few helicopter services to contact, each are open from about 8 A.M.–6 P.M. daily during summer, 9 A.M.–5 P.M. in the winter, and charge approximately $130 for 30 minutes, and about $200 for a 50-minute tour. Choose from **Grand Canyon Helicopters** (928/638-2764 or 800/541-4537, www.grandcanyonhelicoptersaz.com); **Papillon Grand Canyon Helicopters** (928/638-2419 or 800/528-2418, www.papillon.com); or **Maverick Helicopters** (702/261-0007 or 888/261-4414, www.maverickhelicopters.com).

If you don't trust helicopters, opt for an airplane tour, which starts at around $75 for a 30-minute flight, and around $95 for 50 minutes. **Grand Canyon Airlines** (928/638-2359 or 866/235-9422, www.grandcanyonairlines.com) takes you up in a twin-engine Otter for one of the longest (45–50 minutes) and most complete air routes permitted over the canyon. Operating since 1927, the Otters fly more slowly than other planes, and their high wings and panoramic windows are designed for aerial sightseeing. Flights cost around $95. **Air Grand Canyon** (928/638-2686 or 800/247-4726, www.airgrandcanyon.com) offers flights from 30 minutes long, with extended trips flying over the western canyon so you can see waterfalls and the Native American village.

If you'd rather be on the river than up in the air, choose from nearly 20 Colorado River outfitters, who take either gentle cruises down the river or hair-raising, coronary-busting, life-threatening (or life-affirming) races through the rapids. Some are one-day affairs, most go overnight or longer. The best source for information on these companies is the **Grand Canyon River Trip Information Center** (928/638-7843 or 800/959-9164, www.nps.gov/grca). The center also provides updates on which launch dates have been cancelled. Rafting is popular enough to recommend reservations up to six months in advance.

Less thrilling than a raft ride, **Grand Canyon Mule Trips** (303/297-2757, www.xanterra.com) nevertheless can be fun and save your feet. On one-day trips to Plateau Point (around $160), you'll spend about six hours in the saddle. Another pricier proposition is taking an overnight to Phantom Ranch, located at the bottom of the canyon. Although the ranch is not luxurious, you get a sack lunch on the way down, a stew or steak dinner that evening, and breakfast the following morning. Cabins include bunk beds and showers, and prices vary based on the number of people in your party. The more you bring, the less you'll pay. As a guideline, this'll cost about $430 each for two people. Both are physically rigorous trips and there's a weight limit of 200 pounds.

Outside the park, the center of Grand Canyon commerce lies in the **Tusayan General Store** (Hwy. 64, Tusayan, 928/638-2854). This grocery store serves double duty as a post office and gift shop. While it's certainly not an adventure, the general store is a convenience place to gather supplies.

Blue-Plate Specials

Choices inside the park are limited, but you can find meals at the Maswic Cafeteria, Yavapai Cafeteria, the Arizona Room, the Bright Angel Restaurant, and at other park service hotels. The only one that requires reservations is the fine dining restaurant **El Tovar Dining Room** (inside El Tovar Hotel, www.grandcanyonlodges.com). You can get the full rundown on this and other Grand Canyon choices by calling 928/638-2631. In Tusayan, the **Canyon Star** (inside Grand Hotel, 928/638-3333, www.grandcanyongrandhotel.com) serves big food, such as hand-carved steaks and turkey, and features a large salad bar. The entertainment (folk singers or Native American dancers) doesn't cost you a dime.

Shut-Eye

For general information on lodging within the park itself, call the park at 928/638-7888 and they can detail some of your options. Bear in mind that if you do stay inside the park, prices are pretty steep (illustrating the lesson of supply and demand).

All told, more than 2,000 rooms are available in adjacent Tusayan and the Grand Canyon Village, and the park has several campgrounds including **Mather Campground** (800/365-2267, www. recreation.gov, $18) which features full amenities, a store, and showers, and takes reservations. Sites at **Desert View** (928/638-7851, $12), are available on a first-come, first-served basis, but organized groups of 9–40 people may make reservations ($2 per person, plus $2.50 per campsite). Facilities include restrooms and picnic tables, but no showers.

Grand Canyon National Park Lodges (303/297-2757 or 888/297-2757, www. grandcanyonlodges.com or www.xanterra. com) features the most prized lodging options, and reservations can be made up to two years in advance; same-day reservations are taken at 928/638-2631. The 78-room **El Tovar Hotel** ($174–250) is the most expensive and most beautiful lodge, although only four suites have a view of the canyon. Opened in 1905, the precursor to Yosemite's Ahwahnee features a stone-and-timber design, concierge and room service, and fine dining at the on-site restaurant. Less than 40 steps from the rim, it also includes a gift shop and small general store. Other less attractive options include **Maswik Lodge,** which is a quarter mile from the canyon's edge and features cabins as well as motel-style rooms with

two queen beds and a full bath ($90–170). Other choices that lack the traditional Western look the park calls for include the **Bright Angel** ($79 and up for a basic room with a shared bath, $90 with a private bath; around $140 for a rim cabin). The ugly-ass **Thunderbird and Kachina Lodges** range from $170–180.

Less expensive options are the chain hotels and suites that line Highway 64 in Tusayan. The **Grand Hotel** (928/638-3333 or 888/634-7263, www.grandcanyongrandhotel.com, $85 and up) styles itself after an Old West national park resort, but is housed in an attractive and relatively new building. The rooms are large and comfortable, and at night they feature Western entertainment and Native American dancers.

Chain Drive

These chain hotels are in town, or within 10 miles of the city center:
Best Western, Holiday Inn, Quality Inn
For more information, including phone numbers and websites, see page 439.

ON THE ROAD: GRAND CANYON TO PAGE

When you head east on Highway 64 cruising along the South Rim, you'll start to see a little more of the Grand Canyon. The ride starts out gently, with pine forests on both sides and, occasionally, a turnout where you can pull over for one last, less crowded look. After Navajo Point, you'll pass the Watch Tower, which is definitely worth a stop, and then depart the park by the East Rim.

The road is nice and wide, and the way it's laid out you can cruise into curves low and slow. The landscape can be deceptive: When you leave the Grand Canyon, you assume the views are behind you, but now you are granted just enough elevation to afford glimpses into the canyon's tributaries. Unfortunately, the near seamless natural beauty is often interrupted by the self-derogating signs of roadside Navajo trinket stands: "Nice Indian behind you! Chief sez turn back now! Chief love you!" Kind of sad, really.

Like the highway through Death Valley, Highway 64 is breathtaking in its desolation and that emptiness is only broken when you reach U.S. 89 at Cameron. Turn left (north) and ride a few hundred yards to a good fuel and food stop. The **Cameron Trading Post** (928/679-2231 or 800/338-7385, www.camerontradingpost.com) is a mini-empire with a motel, artwork, fudge, gas, moccasins, cowboy hats, ponchos, rugs, replica weapons, jackets, and Indian headdresses priced at hundreds of bucks. Other than that economic anomaly, prices are fair here and the merchandise is of surprisingly good quality. Get gas here—the next leg across the Navajo reservation is relatively empty. Speaking of empties, if you need evidence of the alcohol problem on reservations, just look at the roadside, where beer bottles bloom like sagebrush.

There's scant scenery as it's typically defined, but you may be satisfied that you can observe a different way of life here. No suburbs or neighborhood beautification programs, just a scattered collection of old trailers that come complete with horse and truck.

Things pick up about 34 miles south of Page, where great red cliffs rise on the horizon. About 10 miles later, near Bitter Springs, you'll start to ride right into those red cliffs. They are majestic and overpowering, and as you ride directly down the throat of one of these giants, the road turns and you ascend to one of the most amazing vistas on the trip. Stop here and take a long look. A gorgeous gorge opens up far below and the plains spread out for hundreds of miles. I stopped here for quite awhile, pleased to be away from phones, desks, and computers and focused on nothing but the pleasure of riding a motorcycle and making chance discoveries like this. Nature's not finished yet. After you saddle up, around the corner is yet another fantastic sight: You're riding through a red cavern created where a road was laid between a mountain. Although the sensation only lasts for a few hundred yards, when the walls dwarf you it creates another memorable moment.

After twisting your bike through canyon walls, you'll encounter mile after mile of nothing but plains at 6,000 feet with nearby cliffs rising higher. The desert floor is red and white and brown and yellow and speckled with sagebrush. At sunset the light reaches out to the farthest points on the horizon and over the wonderful buttes that dwarf actual smokestacks. It sounds strange, but seeing this endless vista makes you feel as if you're part of infinity.

Let this scene fix itself in your mind. After that, you can turn to Page.

PAGE PRIMER

Back before Page was Page, the Navajos thought that this barren land was a bewitched place where the trees had died of fear. They didn't care too much after 1956, when they swapped about 20 square miles of this land with the government for a larger tract in Utah.

Back then, Page was just a construction camp for workers building the nearby Glen Canyon Dam. When they weren't busy, workers applied their engineering skills to the sand and rock and turned this into a frontier town of metal structures.

Page was incorporated in 1975, and in the last quarter century or so, this slow-paced town of about 8,000 has become a base for water sports on Lake Powell, which now fingers its way up into Utah. There's not much to see here unless you plan on fishing, skiing, or sitting on a houseboat. Page is the hub of the "Grand Circle," though, and from here you can opt to continue the final 115 miles to Zion or 133 miles to Bryce Canyon, or go off script and ride the 235 miles to Mesa Verde National Park.

ON THE ROAD: PAGE

Page still feels a little too new to be of too much interest, but the people are nice and if you stay over, just ride down to the visitors center at the **Glen Canyon Dam** (928/608-6404 for visitors, 928/608-6072 for tour information) for a look at the dam and displays on geology, water, turbines, and dams. By any measure, this is a damn big dam. At 1,560 feet across, 710 feet high, and 300 feet thick at the bottom, it holds back the force of a 186-mile-long lake. Bear in mind that the dam only scratches the surface of the 1.25 million-acre **Glen Canyon National Recreation Area** (928/608-6200, www.nps.gov/glca).

Since the roads here are relatively ordinary, you may be better off cruising on Lake Powell. With its sinuous stretch across the desert, to see every nook and inlet on the lake you'd sail nearly 2,000 miles—nearly the width of America—to see blue waters lapping at cliffs, buttes, and gentle sands where the color of the canyon changes as evening shadows fall. The easiest way to get on the water is through the **Lake Powell Resorts & Marinas** (928/645-2433 or 800/528-6154, www.lakepowell.com), which has cornered the market on water sports. The recreation area's largest marina and lodging facility, five miles north of Glen Canyon Dam on U.S. 89, has gift shops, campgrounds, RV park, laundry, showers, and a service station. From here, you can rent houseboats,

powerboats, personal watercraft, and assorted water toys, or arrange a fishing excursion for bass, catfish, bluegill, crappie, trout, and walleye. Float down below the dam, where the cold waters are a favorite spot for trophy trout.

Remember: Dam. Good fishing.

PULL IT OVER:
PAGE HIGHLIGHTS
Attractions and Adventures

Page is at the front door to the Navajo Nation and if you want an introduction to the Navajo culture and their way of life, visit the **Navajo Village Heritage Center** (Coppermine Rd. and Hwy. 98, 928/660-0304, www.navajovillage.com). They offer an evening tour ($50, 2.5 hours) that touches on the Navajo Creation Story and progression through its four worlds. You learn about silversmithing, rug weaving, living on Mother Earth, and appreciating all things under Father Sky. The tour includes a traditional dinner and entertainment by the Red Moccasin dancers. Reservations are required.

Although early settlers did their best to crush the Indian culture, the Navajos retained some of the nation's most amazing landscapes. Near Page it is **Antelope Canyon** (928/698-2808, www.navajonationparks.org), a fantastically deep, narrow, and extraordinarily colorful slot canyon carved into the layers of sandstone by water and wind. The Navajo Nation parks system operates the upper and lower canyons. Check the website for a list of guides who can lead you to one of the most beautiful places on earth.

It's not an adventure per se, but **Stix Bait and Tackle** (5 Lake Powell Blvd., 928/645-2891, www.stixbaitandtackle.com) is Page's favorite fishing spot. Locals congregate here before dawn to swap fish stories and plan their fishing strategies.

The store has everything: licenses, tackle, sporting goods, rod and reel rental, guide referral, groceries, snacks, pop, beer, liquor, coolers, ice, bait (live, plastic, or frozen), fresh anchovies, coffee, and doughnuts.

Colorado River Discovery (130 6th Ave., 928/645-9175 or 888/522-6644, www.raftthecanyon.com) offers a calming half-day cruise ($75) into historical canyons first navigated by Major John Wesley Powell. Guides are part pilot, part historian as they explain ancient petroglyphs left by Ancestral Puebloans. Bring a wide-brimmed hat, tennis shoes, a bathing suit, and a camera. A bus will drive you to the base of Glen Canyon Dam for the cruise, and then pick you up at Lee's Ferry for the one-hour trip back to Page. Water and soft drinks are provided on the rafts, and box lunches are available from the River's End Café at the outfitter's.

For a full list of activities or to make reservations for water sports on Lake Powell, call the **Wahweap Reservations Service** (800/528-6154, www.lakepowell.com).

Blue-Plate Specials

Serving big food for lunch and dinner, **Ken's Old West** (718 Vista, 928/645-5160) is appropriately accented with miner's lamps, sturdy wooden beams, and an old upright piano. Entrées include thick meat—steaks and barbecue ribs. The backroom bar and dance floor make it one of Page's few nightspots.

Finding an authentic, unpretentious '50s diner is a rarity, so don't miss **R. D.'s Drive-In** (143 Lake Powell Blvd., 928/645-2791). Settle in a booth and pretend you're Fonzie. Open for breakfast, lunch, and dinner, R. D.'s serves all the good and occasionally greasy foods your parents fed you on road trips (before you heard about cholesterol), including flavor-burst cones, chili, burritos, shakes, fries, and the "famous" R. D. burger. Good food, cheap.

Whiners, crybabies, penny pinchers, and complainers are barred from the **Dam Bar & Grille** (644 N. Navajo Dr., 928/645-2161, www.damplaza.com), a restaurant/saloon serving dinner and the self-proclaimed "best bar by a dam site." The huge dining room serves all the basic food groups, including porterhouse steak, king crab, ribs, dirty Sonoran chicken, and pastas.

Also part of the Dam Bar is the **Blue Buddha Sushi Lounge** (644 N. Navajo Dr.). Exotic dishes include hip presentations of traditional sushi created with southwest flair, like the Lake Powell Roll created with salmon, mango, jalapeno, avocado, and a sweet chili sauce topping. Save room for the deep-fried Oreos.

Watering Holes

Next door to the Dam Bar, the **Gunsmoke Saloon** (644 N. Navajo Dr., 928/645-2161, www.damplaza.com) features a large rectangular bar, numerous widescreen TVs, several beers on tap, a fireplace, dance floor, billiards, and darts. **Slackers** (635 Elm St., 928/645-5267) serves beer and "burgers that will change your life," all in a casual setting with flat screen televisions tuned to sports. Another joint for billiards and dancing is the **Windy Mesa** (800 N. Navajo Dr., 928/645-2186), a popular local hangout with live entertainment and a variety of beer and stronger beverages.

Shut-Eye

Page has several chain hotels, so take your pick. The **Lake Powell Resort** (100 Lake Shore Dr., 928/645-2433 or 888/896-3829, www.visitlakepowell.com, $165–225) features 250 hotel-like rooms—some that overlook the lake—a restaurant, a convenience store, and a gift shop, along with boat rentals, boat tours, and marina services.

Chain Drive

These chain hotels are in town, or within 10 miles of the city center:

Best Western, Courtyard by Marriott, Days Inn, Holiday Inn, Motel 6, Quality Inn, Rodeway, Super 8

For more information, including phone numbers and websites, see page 439.

ON THE ROAD: PAGE TO ZION

As you rode north from the Grand Canyon you may have noticed colorful examples of geological rioting. That trend continues as you leave Page. During the last 10 million years innumerable rock compressions, deformations, and uplifts created Grand, Zion, and Bryce canyons as well as cliffs that change color from chocolate to vermilion, white, gray, and pink.

You'll be cruising through the Vermilion Cliffs on your ride to Zion, which begins with views of scattered sagebrush and grazing cattle. Less than 10 miles out of Page you arrive in Utah where the rocks begin to take on new shapes with the forces of wind, water, and erosion applying a whitish finish to these cliffs.

After awhile the scenery dissipates and the long, straight roads change little in elevation until about 18 miles into Utah when you reach a section of the Grande Escalante (Grand Staircase). Arches striped red, brown, and white monitor the landscape, and you'll spot numerous caves that'll tempt you to park your bike and go look for Injun Joe.

After that, the lull in scenery returns and the ensuing lack of visual activity can tend to make you less alert, but the roadside monuments for dead motorists who suffered the same malady may rouse you. After covering about 50 miles, you'll see a town in the distance. This is Kanab. Although folks in Page speak of Kanab with a reverence usually reserved for the Holy Trinity, I didn't find much here.

Now you're not so far from Zion National Park, and U.S. 89 continues winding across the plains. Foreshadowing what's to come, as if created from a watercolor painting, the cliffs add more swirls and colors to their composition. Embedded in the coral pink rocks are designs suggesting knotted rope, tire marks, and the fluid pattern of whipped cake batter.

When you reach Mount Carmel Junction, where U.S. 89 veers sharply north, you'll likely be tempted to detour 60 miles to Bryce Canyon. If so, you'll find an ordinary road, a few valleys, and a town called Orderville, where there's a rock shop, then another rock shop, and across the street— a rock shop. A little farther along on the left, there's a rock shop. The road and the riding is easy. When you reach Bryce itself, by following Highway 12 East toward Tropic, at first glance you'll know it was worth the ride. The landscape is not so much red as orange, and it beckons you with short rock tunnels and arches followed by a ride on a wide-open plain with mesas.

At Highway 12, turn right and you'll see **Ruby's Inn** (435/834-5341 or 866/866-6616, www.rubysinn.com), a small town disguised as a gas station/hotel/restaurant/rodeo arena/store. Here since 1916, this may not be a bad place to bunk down if you're tired of riding and you'd like to rest up and appreciate what's ahead. It's only a few miles more until you've arrived at **Bryce Canyon National Park** (435/834-5322, www.nps.gov/brca). Twelve bucks takes you and your bike to overlooks where you'll see the fabled "hoodoos," pillars of red rock created about 60 million years ago in a prehistoric lake. If time is short, the first five pullouts should give you a sense of the park fairly quickly.

If you forsake Bryce, stick with Highway 9 into Zion National Park. For roughly four miles, you get a few twists and curves, and the speed limit drops to 30 mph—slowing not for curves, but for cows. A few miles later, you'll reach the east gate of Zion National Park. Although you may have booked a room at Zion Lodge in the park, more likely your night's rest awaits in the town of Springdale, a few miles beyond the southern exit. Either way, right now you'll get a small taste of Zion—enough to inspire you to feast on the park once you've settled down.

ZION PRIMER

It's no small praise that, even when compared to Yosemite and the Grand Canyon, Zion exudes a stronger sense of nature. Zion National Park contains less than one-tenth of 1 percent of Utah's land area, but it contains more than 70 percent of the state's native plant species. Within its 229 square miles are plateaus, canyons, waterfalls, creeks, and narrows. Differences in elevation, sunlight, water, and temperature have created microenvironments that nurture hanging gardens, forested side canyons, and isolated mesas. It is altogether a beautiful place.

If you're wondering where "Zion" came from, credit the Mormons, who borrowed the Hebrew word for "a place of safety or refuge" to name the area in the 1860s. Today, Zion is a refuge for 2.7 million visitors a year, a figure that suggests that you should ride well before or after the summer peak. Another reason is that from Easter weekend to October, shuttles—and not cars or motorcycles—are the only transportation for park guests traveling from Springdale to the Temple of Sinawava at the far reaches of the park. Only hikers, bicyclists, shuttle vehicles, and overnight lodge guests are allowed on the Zion Canyon Scenic Drive, although the rest of the park is open for riding.

With that in mind, accept this advice: Cash in your 401(k), build a log cabin, live here, and be happy.

ON THE ROAD: ZION

What can I say about the perfect blend of road and land? Once you enter Zion ($12), you have nearly free rein to ride and gorge yourself on the impressive and endless views. From the east gate, the Checkerboard Mesa appears just as its name implies. Unlike at other national parks, you have the freedom to park your bike and stride up rippled, textured rocks.

Around each copper-colored curve are rocks with fantastic shapes and variegated swirls ranging from dark red to light orange to pink and white. This wonderful ride connects 15-mph switchbacks with the magnificent motorcycle-friendly Zion-Mount Carmel Tunnel. Too small for large motor homes, this tunnel offers one of the best biking experiences you'll ever have. As if a cosmic drill punched through the mile-long mountain, the passage loses daylight on both ends before you're halfway through. The adrenaline rush continues when you exit and see another mile or two of switchbacks ahead, the first of which propels you into the presence of a natural amphitheater created inside a cliff at least a quarter mile wide. On these curves, beware the low retaining wall that's just high enough to snag a footpeg and toss you over the side.

You can't help but gun it past the 35-mph limit when you realize that the best Le Mans roads aren't in Monte Carlo, but right here. Again, the seven-mile Zion Park Scenic Drive is great if you can ride through, but, again, it's open only to shuttle buses Easter weekend–October. Whether on a shuttle or on your cycle, when you head north on this road you'll pass the Zion Lodge. Keep going and eventually you'll reach beautiful sites like Angels Landing, Weeping Rock, and the Temple of Sinawava.

Plan to pull over frequently—around each bend, another perfect photo beckons. To really give you a sense of the park, rangers offer programs and lead guided hikes from May through September, which will get you beyond the implied barriers and into places like The Narrows, rock passages that are 60–100 million years old and tower 1,500 feet overhead. You've come this far. Don't blow it.

PULL IT OVER: ZION HIGHLIGHTS
Attractions and Adventures

For a basic understanding of what you'll see, there's a free orientation film shown in the park's **Zion Human History Museum** auditorium on the hour and half hour throughout the day. It's located a half-mile north of the park's south entrance on the main park road. Another option is watching the film *Zion Canyon: Treasure of the Gods,* an impressive—although often fictionalized—introduction to the park. The 40-minute shows are daily on the hour between 11 A.M.–7 P.M. at the **Zion Canyon Theatre** (145 Zion Park Blvd., 435/772-2400, www.zioncanyontheatre.com, $10). Few things can do justice to the beauty of this park, but this large-format film comes close. You'll travel back to meet the Ancestral Puebloans (or ancient Anasazi) and in some stunning footage experience what it's like to be a high altitude rock climber.

I learned a good lesson here from a local: The average tourist heads down the scenic drive, walks down a sidewalk, sees some steps, and turns around. Zion boasts the best canyons in the world, most of which are hidden behind the hills. If you get off your bike, carve out some time to see what everyone else is missing.

The first stop you should consider making before wandering into the wilderness on your own is the **Zion Adventure Company** (36 Lion Blvd., Springdale, 435/772-1001, www.zionadventures. com), which (for $19) provides the maps and gear you'll need to hike through the Narrows. Donning a drysuit and carrying provisions and a walking stick, you'll trudge through thigh- to waist-deep water and enter silent, sublime passages. This is the signature Zion experience; it may whet your appetite for its Jeep tours and rock climbing classes. Guided Narrows tours are also available, although the price leaps. If you'd rather let a horse do the walking, **Canyon Trail Rides** (Zion Lodge, 435/679-8665, www.canyonrides.com) offers one-hour ($40) and half-day ($75) tours through the park.

Shopping

Since it's nearly impossible to capture nature's intricate beauty with a disposable camera, Michael Fatali has done the work for you. Lugging his camera to canyons and mountains you don't even know exist, he has spent years looking for the perfect shot. His efforts show in the colorful, passionate photographs on display at **Fatali Gallery** (145 S. Zion Park Blvd., 435/772-2422, www.fatali.com). Using just the right light (no filters or digital enhancement) he captures exquisite shadows and surreal natural colors to give ordinary objects a different and far more interesting visage.

Blue-Plate Specials

The **Bit and Spur Restaurant and Saloon** (1212 Zion Park Blvd., 435/772-3498, www.bitandspur.com) claims to be one of the best Mexican restaurants in Utah, but it's hard to judge since it's so packed it's hard to get inside to eat the food. Serving dinner daily and breakfasts on weekends, the eatery uses locally grown produce in traditional Mexican favorites, and it pours a great selection of Utah microbrews like Provo Girl Pilsner, Squatters Hefeweizen, and the Mormon favorite, Polygamy Porter—why have just one? To top it off, the restaurant features a garden patio, billiards, and sports TV.

Zion Pizza and Noodle Company (868 Zion Park Blvd., 435/772-3815, www. zionpizzanoodle.com), in an old church, serves lunch and dinner. Along with creative pasta dishes, salads, and Utah microbrews (Wasatch and Squatters), the menu features specialties like Thai chicken pizza and hot and spicy Southwestern burrito pizza. A back porch patio and front porch deck are perfect when the weather is right, and it usually is.

Shut-Eye

The only place to stay inside the park, **Zion Lodge** (435/772-3213 for same-day booking, 303/297-2757 or 888/297-2757 for advance booking, www.zionlodge. com, $159 and up) was designed in the 1920s, destroyed in 1966 by a fire, and rebuilt without the classic rustic design and historic appearance. The oversight was corrected in 1990, and now it looks as it should—an outdoors lodge in the heart of beautiful country. With only 120 rooms and a restaurant, the lodge often fills up, so don't be disappointed if you can't get in.

In the town of Springdale, your choices of lodging are surprisingly diverse. The **Zion Park Inn** (1215 Zion Park Blvd., 435/772-3200, www.zionparkinn.com, $110 and up) is a link in the Best Western chain, but in a small town where conveniences are hard to come by, it's a nice option. The inn features a pool, hot tub, gift shop, guest laundry, state liquor store, large and comfortable rooms, and a terrific restaurant—the Switchback Grille. Slightly more upscale, yet surprisingly reasonable, is the **Desert Pearl Inn** (707 Zion Park Blvd., 435/772-8888 or 888/828-0898, $148 and up). Swank, cathedral-ceiling rooms come with a TV, fridge, and microwave; outside are a waterfall and sparkling blue pool. The rooms are not quite suites, but with growth hormones, they would be. Old-fashioned describes the **Pioneer Lodge** (838 Zion Park Blvd., 435/772-3233 or 888/772-3233, www.pioneerlodge.com, $129 and up high season, $69 and up off-season). It gives you what you want, if you just want a bed, a pool, and a neat old motel diner that claims to be the "home of home-cooked cooking."

Resources for Riders

Red Rocks Run

Arizona Travel Information

Arizona Association of Bed & Breakfast Inns—www.arizona-bed-breakfast.com
Arizona Road Conditions—888/411-7623, www.az511.com
Arizona State Parks—602/542-4174, www.pr.state.az.us
Arizona Travel Center—866/275-5816, www.arizonaguide.com

Utah Travel Information

Bed & Breakfast Inns of Utah—www.bbiu.org
Utah Road Conditions—800/492-2400
Utah State Parks—801/538-7220 or 877/887-2757, www.stateparks.utah.gov
Utah Travel Council—801/538-1030 or 800/200-1160, www.utah.com

Local and Regional Information

Grand Canyon Chamber of Commerce—928/638-2901 or 888/472-2696,
    www.grandcanyonchamber.com
Grand Canyon Road and Weather Conditions—888/411-7623
Grand Canyon Switchboard—928/638-7888, www.nps.gov/grca
Grand Canyon Visitors Center—928/638-7644
Page/Lake Powell Chamber of Commerce—928/645-2741 or 888/261-7243,
    www.pagelakepowelltourism.org
Sedona–Oak Creek Canyon Chamber of Commerce—928/282-7722 or
    800/288-7336, www.sedonachamber.com
Zion Canyon Information—435/772-3256, www.nps.gov/zion
Zion Canyon Visitors Bureau—888/518-7070, www.zionpark.com

Arizona Motorcycle Shops

Grand Canyon Harley-Davidson—I-40 at Exit 185, Bellemont, 928/774-3896,
    www.grandcanyonhd.com
Northland Motorsports—4308 E. Rte. 66, Flagstaff, 928/526-7959,
    www.northlandmotorsports.com
Outdoor Sports Lake Powell—910-B Coppermine Rd. Vista Ave., Page,
    928/645-8141, www.outdoorsportsaz.com
Sedona Motorcycles—6560 SR 17, Sedona, 928/284-3983

Wild West Run

Livingston, Montana to Jackson, Wyoming

It's hard to find a tour as good as this. It begins in an authentic Western town before traversing a kaleidoscope of natural wonders and coming to a close in another Western town— one with a nice twist. Although the roads are not exactly challenging, the ride is unforgettable since it gives you access to some of the most magnificent scenery and wildlife in America.

LIVINGSTON PRIMER

Everything was going fine in Clark City until the Northern Pacific Railroad decided to relocate its line. That's when 500 people, six general stores, two hotels, and 30 saloons packed up and headed to nearby Livingston. In 1872, when Congress established Yellowstone, the completion of the park branch of the Northern Pacific brought Livingston new business.

The town profited from the railroad and mining and in the 1880s, cattle, sheep, and grain became the major economic forces. Livingston hasn't grown a whole lot since then, although there's a distinct difference today. The town's year-round population of about 7,500 swells when part-time residents arrive to take advantage of the spells of good weather. Folks who call Livingston home at least part of the year include celebs like Jeff Bridges, Tom Brokaw, Dennis Quaid, and Margot Kidder. Sure, the veneer here may be Old West, but Livingson has a sophisticated soul.

ON THE ROAD: LIVINGSTON

Start by swinging by the well-stocked **Visitor Center** (303 East Park St., 406/222-0850, www.livingston-chamber.com), where there's a surplus of local maps and guidebooks and folks to point out numerous great loop roads outside of town. Considering there's a ride ahead, though, you may want to spend some time around the anachronism that is Livingston. Because the town seems tied to a time warp of Eisenhower-era America, your senses won't be assaulted by the familiar and redundant sight of franchises and chain stores. It's their absence, I think, that makes

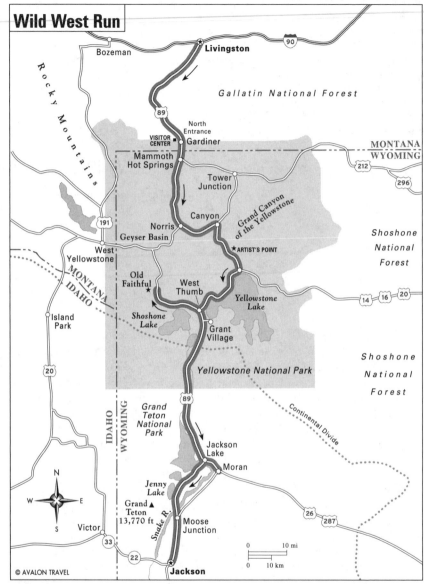

Wild West Run

Route: Livingston to Jackson via Yellowstone National Park, Grand Teton National Park

Distance: Approximately 210 miles

First Leg: Livingston, Montana to South Yellowstone, Wyoming (125 miles)

Second Leg: Yellowstone to Jackson, Wyoming (82 miles)

Helmet Laws: Montana and Wyoming do not require helmets.

wandering around downtown as satisfying as any ride.

On the surface, Livingston may seem to be an ordinary Western town. But when you dig a little deeper, you'll detect a level of sophistication that's revealed in more than a dozen art galleries, eclectic restaurants, and encounters with ranchers who probably carry more money than the Federal Reserve.

So, for now, park your bike and look around. The road will be waiting for you.

PULL IT OVER: LIVINGSTON HIGHLIGHTS
Attractions and Adventures

The great outdoors is big around Livingston, and several outfitters can take you to it. While it certainly doesn't sound like a name that would pump up the testosterone, the objective of **Rubber Ducky River Rentals** (15 Mount Baldy Dr., 406/222-3746, www.riverservices.com) is to get you out on the Yellowstone River for hair-raising whitewater rafting trips as well as scenic floats, fishing excursions, rowing instruction, overnight kayak tours, canoe floats, fishing, and raft and gear rentals.

The Zen experience of fly-fishing is one of Livingston's greatest attractions, and to help novices and professionals experience the serenity and challenge of the sport is **Dan Bailey's Fly Shop** (209 W. Park St., 406/222-1673 or 800/356-4052, www.dan-bailey.com). One of the most famous names in the sport, Dan Bailey's has been a town presence since 1938, and the store is packed to the gills with everything you need and hundreds of things you don't. How many hours of sleep have you lost wondering where you could find strung schlappen, hackle capes, and bumblebee popper foam? You'll rest easy after a visit here, open 7:30 A.M.–6 P.M. Monday–Saturday, and 7:30 A.M.–3 P.M. on Sunday. A word of warning: It'll cost. Bailey's organizes daylong fishing excursions that start at $425 per person (three bucks bought me a four-minute session); but if you can swing it, this may be the best place to get hooked on the sport.

In town, the **Livingston Depot** (200 W. Park St., 406/222-2300, www.livingstondepot.org, $3) is a museum built within a beautiful restoration of the Northern Pacific passenger depot. Open May–September, it features exhibits on Western life and art, and hosts annual events such as railroad swap meets. Check out the building's ornate brickwork and lion's-head accents, and in the basement of the baggage room there's a model railroad exhibit. Call for hours.

Just down the road is Yellowstone, but right here in town is where you can learn about its incredible history. The **Yellowstone Gateway Museum** (118 W. Chinook St., 406/222-4184) has an extensive collection of artifacts, exhibits, photos, and oral histories that cover the area's natural history and geology as well as the stories of pioneers, prospectors, lawmen, the railroad, the park itself, and the Old West. If your ancestors came from these parts, the museum maintains birth, death, and cemetery records and the staff can help you conduct genealogical searches.

Shopping

Gil's Got It (207 W. Park St., 406/222-0112), open 9 A.M.–5 P.M. daily, carries everything you used to crave when your parents were lugging you around the country in the backseat of the Buick. Here since 1914, it's approaching the century mark by giving the people what they want: things like straw cowboy hats, popguns, and wallets with cowboys on them.

Pardner, if you collect Old West memorabilia, then mosey on by the

Cowboy Connection (110 1/2 N. Main St., 406/222-0272, www.thecowboyconnection.com). Stocked items include gambling mementoes, antique Colts and Winchesters, saddles, chaps, spurs and bits, Stetsons, artwork, bronzes, boots, frock coats, knives, and shotguns.

Blue-Plate Specials

At the corner of 8th and Park streets, **Mark's In and Out** is a drive-in where you can fuel up on the four food groups: burgers, hot dogs, onion rings, and milkshakes. Clean as a whistle, Mark's service and prices are straight out of the 1950s—fitting, considering it opened in 1954. Burgers and cheeseburgers are easily affordable and if you don't mind bypass surgery, order a mess of Cadillac fries with gravy, chili, or cheese sauce.

Filled with local characters who hang out at the bar (open 'til 2 A.M.), **The Stockman** (118 N. Main St., 406/222-8455) also serves lunch and dinner to folks who believe that this small restaurant's got the best steaks in town. Weekends are packed, so try to go on a weeknight for a hand-cut top sirloin, New York strip, or rib eye. Bring cash—credit cards aren't accepted.

The best thing about **The Sport and Spaghetti Western** (114 S. Main St., 406/222-3800) is that it's not a sports restaurant. The original opened in 1909, when the popular sports were hunting and fishing; women weren't allowed in until the late 1940s. This must-see restaurant has an authentic Old West atmosphere with mounted heads, worn wooden floors, and tin ceilings. While the menu continues the Western flavor with steaks, the accent is now Italian.

Northern Pacific Beanery (108 W. Park St., 406/222-7288, www.thenpbeanery.com) was once filled with ranchers, cowboys, and working folks sitting at well-worn countertops. Located at the old railroad depot, the century-old eatery has been jazzed up to cater to a new clientele, although they bow to tradition by serving old favorites like chicken fried steaks and homemade corned beef hash. The Beanery serves breakfast and lunch 'til 2 P.M., and dinners Thursday through Saturday 'til 9 P.M.

For the big Western food you'd expect in these parts, drop by **Montana's Rib & Chop House** (305 E. Park St., 406/222-9200), which serves lunch and dinner in a bustling atmosphere. Featured on the menu are half-pound burgers, cedar plank salmon, coconut shrimp, pulled pork sandwiches, rack of ribs, baseball cut sirloin, and lamb ribs.

Not much to argue with at the **49er Diner** (404 E. Park St., 406/222-4414), where you can settle in for good home-cooked breakfasts and lunches. Nothing fancy, but simple, hearty, and affordable.

Watering Holes

I only drink to excess, so I had a hard time staying out of Livingston's bars. Each has the feel of a Western roadhouse, bartenders who can be sassy or sympathetic, and enough smoke to trigger the oxygen masks. They're all over downtown Livingston, but there are a few standouts. The bar at the Murray Hotel is the logically-named **Murray Bar** (201 W. Park St., 406/222-9816), which features two pool tables, seven beers on tap, a full liquor bar, live bands, and lots of energy. If you stepped into a time machine and were transported back to the '40s, you'd see just what you missed at **The Mint** (102 N. Main St., 406/222-0361). Break out the booze and have a ball.

There used to be a brothel upstairs at the **Whiskey Creek Saloon and Casino** (110 N. Main St., 406/222-0665), but no more—if there were, the ladies on call would be pushing 100. The bar still attracts locals who come early and stay late. **The Office Lounge** (128 S. Main St., 406/222-7480) has drinks and eats and has won local polls for being the best bar, having the best happy hour and staff, and being the best place to play pool and watch sports. Why the "Office?" It offers free Wi-fi and complimentary computers, copies, and faxing.

Shut-Eye

Not a motel, but a legend, **The Murray Hotel** (201 W. Park St., 406/222-1350, www.murrayhotel.com, rooms $89 and up, suites $119 and up) premiered in 1904 and has since greatly enlarged its pleasant rooms while retaining the touches of an old-fashioned hotel. Check out the washbasins in the rooms, rocking chairs in hallway alcoves, and desk clerks who double as elevator operators. But be prepared—noise from the bar and nearby trains may keep you up at night.

Chain Drive

These chain hotels are in town, or within 10 miles of the city center:
Best Western, Comfort Inn, Econo Lodge, Quality Inn, Rodeway, Travelodge
For more information, including phone numbers and websites, see page 439.

ON THE ROAD: LIVINGSTON TO YELLOWSTONE

The interesting thing about the 55-mile straight shot to Yellowstone National Park is that even though the ride doesn't compare to the park itself, south of Livingston the landscape of Paradise Valley starts to look larger and actually becomes a portent of things to come. The country ride introduces mountains on your left and hills to your right, but it takes a while to

notice that there *is nothing out here.* You are so swept up with the emptiness that you forget to notice the absence of homes, stores, and billboards. At some point the Yellowstone River shows up and brushes against the road and then retreats toward the mountains. As for you, you have only to enjoy the sun and the mountains, pausing if you wish at a roadside chapel and rest stop about 30 miles south of Livingston. Later, as the river starts picking up steam, rolling and boiling and churning as it flows north, the road tries to match its energy by adding some curves and descents. This all builds up to your farewell to mighty Montana—a state that God must have designed for motorcycling.

The town of Gardiner is just north of the Wyoming state line and it's where you'll find restaurants, motels, and service stations. If you don't need them, just roll around the corner and you'll find a perfect photo op for you and your machine. The Roosevelt Arch says more than the words inscribed on it: "Yellowstone National Park. For the Benefit and Enjoyment of the People. Created by Act of Congress March 1, 1872." Well, you are the people, and you're about to enjoy something spectacular.

Unless you have an America the Beautiful Pass (available from the National Park Service, it's an $80 investment that gets you into every national park for one year), motorcyclists pay $20 to enter Yellowstone (www.nps.gov/yell). The Yellowstone pass is valid for the Grand Tetons as well. Even though you may have seen the park in elementary school filmstrips, you've never seen anything like the real thing.

YELLOWSTONE PRIMER

Instead of its history, consider what makes up Yellowstone National Park: steaming geysers, crystalline lakes, thundering

Animal Sense

Riding a bike through Yellowstone poses an element of danger. Seriously. People in cars can shield themselves from bears and bison, but you can't. Here are some tips that may save your life:

- Give animals plenty of space when they are crossing the road.
- If one animal crosses the road, wait to see if another is following before proceeding.
- Don't try to entice any animal with food.
- If you see an animal and wish to stop, try to park in an established turnout, not in the middle of the road.
- If you're shooting photographs, don't try to get closer to the animals. For a good shot, use a telephoto lens.

waterfalls, and panoramic vistas sprawled across two million acres of volcanic plateaus. This was the world's first national park and accounts for 60 percent of the world's active geysers. The Lower Falls on the Yellowstone River are nearly twice as high as Niagara's. The land rises in elevation from 5,282 feet at Reese Creek to 11,358 feet at Eagle Peaks Summit. Yellowstone is home to 10 tree species, more than 80 types of wildflowers, 67 mammal species, and 322 species of birds.

Yellowstone contains five "countries." Mammoth Country, a thermal area in the northwest, is home to elk, bison, hot springs, and limestone terraces. Geyser Country, in the southwest, encompasses Old Faithful, fumaroles, mud pots, and hot pools. Lake Country, in the southeast, is habitat to native cutthroat trout, osprey, and bald eagles, as well as moose, bison, and bears, which wander the 140-mile shoreline of Yellowstone Lake. Roosevelt Country, in the northeast, recaptures the Old West. And Canyon Country comprises the Lower Falls, Hayden Valley, and the Grand Canyon of the Yellowstone. Free ranger-led programs, sightseeing tours, fishing, boating, horseback riding, and more than 1,210 miles of marked hiking trails all conspire to help you explore the park.

Believe it or not, all of this takes up less than 4 percent of the park itself. The rest is wilderness.

ON THE ROAD: YELLOWSTONE

Why do I love Yellowstone? Let me count the ways...Commercial trucks are prohibited; it has more wildlife than a hundred zoos; it fulfills every image I had formed about it; and it delivers what the government intended when it protected these lands in 1872.

The road from Tower Junction to Canyon Junction over Dunraven Pass in the northeast corner is the first to close and last to open when snow hits, so there's a good chance you won't be able to ride it. If it's open, terrific; if not, start at the park's north entrance section at Gardiner and head south, soaking in the views as you climb a quick 1,000 feet to blow past a mile as you ascend to 6,200 feet. Dealing with the campers who clog the road is discouraging at first, but within about two miles you'll have the satisfaction of crossing the 45th parallel—the midway point between the equator and the North Pole.

Your first stop should be the **Albright Visitors Center** at Mammoth Hot Springs to talk to a park ranger, get maps, and check on programs. You'll see it as you arrive through the main entrance on the north. From 1896 to 1916, this was the site of Fort Yellowstone, where the U.S. Army protected the park from poachers, vandals, robbers, and anyone or anything that threatened the preserve and its early tourists. Today a ranger's job is much easier. They can help you decide how and where to allot your time, and you'll find that time is precious since there's much to see and you'll be moving slow. Even though the speed limit's usually 45 mph, chances are you'll be riding closer to 30. Be selective on what you see if you're on a schedule.

Follow the road south to the Mammoth Terraces, which constantly builds tier upon tier of cascading terraced stone. These are interesting not only for their beauty but also because, despite clearly visible warning signs, some idiots have scalded or burned themselves to death by stepping out on them before falling through the fragile layer of minerals.

Soon you'll smell a familiar aroma. This is no kitchen cleanser, though—it's just the trees emanating the original pine-fresh scent. Around you the geological wreckage of mountains is omnipresent, and when you approach Swan Lake Flat it feels like you're on top of the world. If you ride in the late spring, you may share my good fortune and see a grizzly and her cubs—an experience that made me appreciate nature and wish my bike had automatic door locks. Moments like this remind you that, despite the string of roads here, this is actually wilderness and it doesn't belong to you, it belongs to the animals. Respect them.

Riding on, you'll spot the glacial green waters of North Twin Lakes, and past the Gibbon River there could be buffaloes grazing. It should go without saying that you should steer clear of these brutes. They're big enough to wreck a Humvee and could easily demolish a bike.

Near the Norris to Canyon road (in the middle of the figure 8 formed by roads), the Norris and Firehole River Geyser Basins feature the largest display of geysers. Steamboat Geyser, at Norris, is the world's tallest, with infrequent, unpredictable eruptions that reach an astounding 400 feet. Next, head east on the middle road toward Canyon Village. The landscape isn't quite as impressive here, but if you head straight until you reach the Grand Canyon of Yellowstone you won't mind the break. The 24-mile-long canyon sneaks up on you, and, once in full view, is majestic. At 800–1,200 feet deep and 1,500–4,000 feet wide, it is marked by rainbow-hued cliffs of orange, yellow, pink, white, and tan. It is also marked by another natural wonder.

At first, you can only hear the steady roar of the 308-foot-high Lower Falls, and then when it appears through the trees it'll take your breath away. You've reached a geological crossroads, where hot springs have weakened the rock and spout into the river to create an unusual confluence of waterfalls, cliffs, canyon, and geysers.

Down the road, a bridge crosses to Artist's Point on the opposite side of the canyon. When you get back on the road, the ride improves as the road follows the river's winding course. While the frostbite on your fingers tells you you're reaching higher elevations, there's something else in the air...bubbling, churning, sulfurous mud boils that smell worse than the awards ceremony at a baked bean festival.

Depending on where you're staying, you could wrap up a long day by resting at the Lake Lodge or the Lake Yellowstone Hotel or by continuing the journey to Old Faithful. Either way, monumental Yellowstone Lake opens up on your left. Big enough to create its own weather, the lake is actually a large crater formed by a volcano and then filled in by glaciers about 12,000 years ago. It'll follow you for miles and miles and while you would swear this lake should come to a close, it has a lot of stamina. Even after miles of lush forests block the view, you round the corner... and the lake's still there. Eventually, you'll adopt the lake as your riding buddy and hope it continues.

After about 45 minutes, less than half of its 140 miles of shoreline finally come to a close and you're alone again as you ride to the West Thumb Geyser Basin. This is where you'll find the quirky Fishing Cone, so named because anglers catching trout from the frigid lake cooked them still on the hook in the cone's boiling waters.

Between here and Old Faithful, a long but enjoyable 17 miles away, the thrill of the road may depend on the weather. When the snow is packed up high on the sides, it's like being in a bobsled race as the road rises and falls like the Roman Empire. Even though there's not a lot to see, the flow of the road may make this the best stretch for motorcycle travelers.

If you've timed it right, when you reach the exit to Old Faithful you shouldn't have long to wait before the geyser blows. Approximately every 92 minutes, thousands of gallons of thundering, hissing, steaming water blast into the sky. An American icon, it's worth seeing and the benches close to the Old Faithful Inn may afford the best view.

From here, you can double back and commence your trip south, or check into whichever lodge you were smart enough to book in advance.

PULL IT OVER: YELLOWSTONE HIGHLIGHTS
Attractions and Adventures

Yellowstone is less like a park and more like a nation. Seven full-service gas stations and four auto repair shops function within the park. *Yellowstone Today,* a free newspaper available at visitors centers and at the entrance, carries seasonal news and current information about park facilities and programs. The powers that be have also developed a complete retinue of tours and adventures that, depending on your budget, will be a natural or an extravagance. Check the park's website (www.nps.gov/yell) for non-fee activities; although the places and excursions you'll have to pay for can be found through a concessionaire at 307/344-7311 or 866/439-7375, and at www.travelyellowstone.com. Check with them for complete details and to reserve choices such as a horseback ride to the **Roosevelt Cookout** ($66–80); the **Stagecoach Adventure** ($10); various guided tours ($9–52); horseback trail rides (one hour, $37; two hours, $56); guided fishing trips (from $152 for two hours, with longer excursions available); power-boat rental ($47 per hour); and photo safaris ($15–81, offered June–September). There are also several all-day bus tours (about $65) that roam across the park and deliver information on the park's history, geology, and botany. If you'd like to do things on the cheap, rely on the NPS rangers who can tell you what's worthwhile and who also lead free tours that can help you understand this most incredible park.

Blue-Plate Specials

With the number of snack bars, delis,

cafeterias, fast food joints, and grocery stores you'll find, sometimes you'd suspect you were in New York and not Yellowstone. Since roads are supernaturally dark after sunset, for dinner try to stick around the **Mammoth Hot Springs Hotel, Old Faithful Inn, Grant Village, Canyon Lodge,** or **Lake Yellowstone Hotel**—each of which features dining rooms (which also serve breakfast and lunch). Dinner menus include prime ribs, steak, seafood, and chicken; reservations are strongly recommended at all restaurants, and required at the Lake Yellowstone Hotel and Old Faithful Inn. Grant Village and Roosevelt Lodge feature family-style restaurants. If you've got a hankering for cowboy cuisine, an Old West Dinner Cookout leaves from Roosevelt Lodge. You won't need your bike, instead you ride on horseback through Pleasant Valley to reach a clearing where there's a hearty dinner of steak, corn, coleslaw, cornbread muffins, homemade Roosevelt beans, watermelon, and apple crisp. For dining or cookout reservations, call 307/344-7311 or contact any lodging front desk, dining room, or activities desk.

Shut-Eye

I have to underscore that the best riding will be just before or after the peak summer tourist season. But if you do ride when the park is packed and the roads filled, definitely make reservations well in advance by calling **Xanterra** (307/344-7311 or 866/439-7375, www.travelyellowstone.com) the concessionaire that takes reservations for this and other national parks. Lodging options range from rustic cabins to fine hotels, but because of the park's remoteness, few rooms have phones, and none have televisions. Request a private bath if that's important to you and also be aware that prices tend to rise each year.

An iconic classic, the **Old Faithful Inn** ($98 shared bath, $213 upscale room) is your best bet. Built in the winter of 1903–1904 with local logs and stones, it features a towering lobby with a 500-ton stone fireplace and a handcrafted clock made of copper, wood, and wrought iron. This stunningly beautiful hotel offers a nice dining room, fast food restaurant, gift shop, and the Bear Pit Lounge. The inn shares a general store and service station with the **Old Faithful Snow Lodge and Cabins,** which opened in 1998 and charges around $99–201, while the **Old Faithful Lodge Cabins** fetch from $69–113. Completed in the 1930s, **Mammoth Hot Springs Hotel and Cabins** ($79–121) offers hotel rooms and cabins with and without private baths.

A classic historic hotel, **Lake Yellowstone Hotel and Cabins** opened in 1891 and has been restored to the grandeur it enjoyed during the 1920s. Even the original wicker furniture has been returned to service. The sun room, a sitting area designed for relaxation and conversation, affords wonderful views of the lake and is also a good place to relax with a cocktail and listen to piano-playing or chamber music in the evening. Choices range from deluxe historically renovated hotel rooms to more moderately priced annex rooms. Rooms are the most luxurious (and expensive) at $216–227; annex rooms are more affordable at $151; and cabins even more so at around $135. The motel-like **Grant Village** ($145) sits at the west thumb of Yellowstone.

You'll also find lodges and cabins (with and without baths) at the **Lake Lodge** ($70–157), **Canyon Lodge** ($74–173), and **Roosevelt Lodge** ($68–113), as well as more than 2,100 campsites (about $18 per night), and you'll need to call for reservations (advance reservations 307/344-7311 or 866/439-7375, same-day reservations 307/344-7901).

ON THE ROAD: YELLOWSTONE TO JACKSON

After you slip out of Yellowstone via U.S. 89 heading south, you'll notice little to distinguish Yellowstone from the neighboring **Grand Teton National Park** (307/739-3399 or 307/739-3300, www.nps.gov/grte). Between the pristine wilderness of Yellowstone and the Grand Tetons you'll enjoy what's a very quiet ride, interrupted only by the **Flagg Ranch Resort** (307/543-2861 or 800/443-2311, www.flaggranch.com). If you do stop here, it's likely because you want to savor every minute of the overpowering scenery or it could be because this gives you a chance to get some food and fuel. You can also rest easy here with Flagg's camping and lodges.

Just past Flagg Ranch, the vistas have received a booster shot of spectacular scenery thanks to efforts made in 1929 when more than 500 square miles were set aside to preserve and protect the land around the Teton Range. In 1950, that area was expanded when John D. Rockefeller Jr. donated adjacent lands. You can also thank the Rockefellers (I'm sure they'd enjoy a lovely bundt cake) for purchasing the land needed for Acadia National Park as well the area around Woodstock, Vermont.

One fantastic way to experience this park on your bike is by checking out the Jenny Lake Loop. Actually, the first body of water you'll see is Jackson Lake, which deserves a few hundred photos and its own miniseries. The water of the broad lake mirrors the mountains beyond and the result is a surreal, colorful blend of green waters, white mountain peaks, and blue sky. Even as the mountain chain recedes in the distance, the peaks appear uniform in height and shape, which offers a clue to why French trappers called them Les Trois Tetons (The Three Breasts).

Four miles later, the road has risen in elevation to place you midway between the lake and the towering peaks. At Colter Village there is a museum, store, and gas station. But by now you may be so inspired by the visuals that you'll just stick with the road. Not a bad choice since the mountain chain stays with you as you rocket toward Grand Teton, which, at 13,770 feet, is the largest mountain in the chain.

In addition to seeing these most incredible peaks, you get to ride Alpine runs, then pine-bordered roads and quick drops when the valley floor opens and the road dives right into it. Seemingly custom-designed for bikes, after riding it I felt like I needed a cigarette—and I don't even smoke.

At some point well south of here, the road Ts and you turn right to head into another stretch of vast emptiness. You are in Jackson Hole, the 48-mile-long valley that actually began just south of the Yellowstone entrance. Although it all seems like a lonely, deserted land, just wait, cowboy. A few miles later and you'll reach one of the nicest towns in the West.

JACKSON PRIMER

Trailblazers were the ones who made their mark on this town. The territory was named Jackson's Hole (later Jackson Hole) after trapper David E. Jackson. Prior to Jackson's arrival, however, there were summer residents: the Shoshone, Crow, Blackfoot, and Gros Ventre tribes.

What made this town stick was that with six trapping trails converging at Jackson Hole, it became a popular fur trading area. Around 1845, the trade—not to mention the animals—was in decline and for about the next 30 years, the isolated area lay dormant until the Hayden

Expeditions of 1871 and 1878 introduced the region to the rest of the country. After Yellowstone was formed, big game hunters, foreign royalty, and East Coast "dudes" started showing up.

The town itself was founded in 1921 and soon after cattle ranching took hold. Nearly a century later, this mix of hard-working locals and affluent outsiders still typifies the town, though tourism and skiing have long since supplanted ranching. One thing that'll likely remain the same is the landscape: Only about 3 percent of Teton County is privately owned, with the rest contained within Grand Teton National Park, the Bridger-Teton National Forest, and the National Elk Refuge.

It's hard to imagine a more perfect town.

ON THE ROAD: JACKSON

You can't disguise it. Jackson is a cowboy Carmel. There's lots of money here, generated by tourism and movie executives who invest part of their time and much of their fortunes here.

As in Montana, great rides await you on the outskirts of town, but wandering around Jackson is damned fun. Everything here centers around the Town Square which is marked by the famed Antler Arches. Each year, Boy Scouts have exclusive permission to scour the nearby National Elk Refuge and collect the horns that had been shed. The horns that aren't used to create arches in the park are auctioned off, purchased by western export houses, regional craftspeople, and Asian druggists who believe that powdered elk horn works faster than Viagra. It doesn't. *Trust me.*

Around the square, wooden sidewalks lead you through numerous shops, bars, restaurants, and art galleries. Take an afternoon, find some places on your own,

check out a few listed here, and enjoy a pocket of civility in an otherwise harsh world.

PULL IT OVER: JACKSON HIGHLIGHTS
Attractions and Adventures

Whitewater rafting is the warm-weather equivalent of Jackson's winter ski season. Most excursions run the same rapids and charge about the same rate (from around the mid-$50s). Some trips combine whitewater and scenic float trips with the majestic Grand Tetons as a backdrop. Ask if trips include breakfast and/or lunch. If you have time, for around $150 or so, you may be able to find ones that offer overnight rafting/camping trips.

I can't attest to all of these, so you'll have to make the call on selecting the best whitewater rafting outfitters. I would recommend avoiding those that advertise high casualty rates. Try **Charlie Sands Wild Water River Trips** (307/733-4410 or 800/358-8184, www.sandswhitewater.com); **Dave Hansen Whitewater** (307/733-6295 or 800/732-6295, www.davehansenwhitewater.com); **Jackson Hole Whitewater** (307/733-1007 or 800/700-7238, www.jhww.com); **Lewis & Clark Expeditions** (307/733-4022 or 800/824-5375, www.lewisandclarkexpeds.com); and **Mad River Boat Trips** (307/733-6203 or 800/458-7238, www.mad-river.com).

The beauty you'll see in the American West is so inspiring that you may be motivated to ride a few miles north of Jackson on U.S. 89 to the **National Museum of Wildlife Art** (307/733-5771 or 800/313-9553, www.wildlifeart.org, $10). This is the premier collection of wildlife art in America, from prehistoric carvings to art created by mound dwellers to the sculptures and paintings of historic and contemporary Western American artists like W. R. Leigh, C. M. Russell, Robert Bateman, and Andy Warhol. In all, the museum showcases more than 2,000 paintings, sculptures, photographs, and works on paper by more than 100 wildlife artists. No unicorns and rainbows here—this is fine art that could turn a condo into a lodge.

Shopping

Sure, you can buy a hat off the rack, but you'd end up looking like a dude. For a custom-made beaver felt hat, walk over to the nationally-known **Jackson Hole Hat Company** (245 N. Glenwood Ave., 307/733-7687, www.jhhatco.com). I agree that a custom hat may not be cheap, but just think: *You will own an American original.* If you like leather (and I imagine you do), **Hideout Leather** (40 Center St., 307/733-2422) has a dynamite collection of hand-painted custom clothing, moccasins, boots, chaps, Native American headdresses, flying helmets, and leather jackets with fringe and studs and buckles and zip-out linings and body armor.... Having a nicotine fit? Head to **Tobacco Row** (120 N. Cache Dr., 307/733-4385) and check out the cigars, pipe tobacco, and hand-carved pipes.

Blue-Plate Specials

Whether they're cowboys or corporate execs, locals fuel up on breakfast and lunch at **Jedediah's House of Sourdough** (135 E. Broadway, 307/733-5671). Breakfasts are big, with inexpensive sourjack pancakes, Teton taters, eggs, waffles, and bacon. You may have to waddle out, but you'll have no regrets.

Bubba's BBQ Restaurant (515 W. Broadway, 307/733-2288) serves breakfast, lunch, and dinner for folks that love meat. It's basic and inexpensive grub that includes ribs, chicken, pork, sandwiches, baked beans, coleslaw, and corn on the cob. On the high end of the spectrum, **Snake River Grill** (84 E. Broadway, 307/733-0557, www.snakerivergrill.com) was named Jackson's best restaurant by *Wine Spectator*. That said, don't expect the place to be diner cheap. For some, though, the premium has a payoff. The Grill serves only fresh fish and free-range veal and chicken, as well as more than 200 wines, plus ports and single-malt scotches. In this casual Western setting, you can order Chilean sea bass, venison chops, double-center-cut pork chops, and a bunch of other stuff I love to eat when somebody else is buying.

Watering Holes

Images of the **Million Dollar Cowboy Bar** (25 N. Cache Dr., 307/733-2207, www.milliondollarcowboybar.com) still stick with me. This is one of the absolute coolest bars you'll ever see, from the cutout stagecoach in the chandelier diorama to the saddle seats at the bar, from the chiseled faces of the patrons to the Western swing bands who lure the wallflowers out on the dance floor, this place has got it all. And the patrons aren't just drugstore cowboys. On weekends, ranchers who sowed their wild oats here 50 years ago return, their faces filled with more character than you'd find in a dozen Louis L'Amour novels.

Attached to one of the nation's Top 10 historic hotels, the Wort Hotel, is the **Silverdollar Saloon** (50 N. Glenwood Ave., 307/733-2190 or 800/322-2727, www.worthotel.com). Although it doesn't have the character of the Million Dollar, it's accented with saws, saddles, antlers, and a few thousands dollars worth of silver dollars embedded in the bar. The saloon serves wines, microbrews, and bar food. It's open 11:30 A.M.–11 P.M. daily.

Sidewinders American Grill (945 W.

Broadway, 307/734-5766, www.sidewind-erstavern.com) has a classic Western look which is a perfect backdrop for their full slate of regional microbrews, wines, and whiskeys; all of which tend to overshadow the fact that it's a restaurant.

Shut-Eye

For such a small town, Jackson offers many options for bunking down. A central number for the **Town Square Inns** (800/483-8667, www.townsquareinns.com) puts you in touch with four reasonably priced, generic, and clean motels.

Motels and Motor Courts

The **Cowboy Village Log Cabin Resort** (120 S. Flat Creek Dr., 307/733-3121 or 800/483-8667, www.townsquareinns.com, $122 and up) rents great little air-conditioned cabins equipped with combinations of queen beds, sofa sleepers, kitchenettes, TVs, tub/showers, covered decks, and barbecue grills. It also throws in a continental breakfast.

Inn-dependence

The **Parkway Inn & Spa** (125 N. Jackson St., 307/733-3143 or 800/247-8390, www.parkwayinn.com) borders on a motel, but the rooms are large and clean; it sits a few blocks outside the rush of Town Square; it feeds you a good breakfast; and the pool and hot tub are just right after a day on the road. If you arrive preseason (April–May), you'll pay around $109—in the summer, it'll more than double. Ka-ching!

Chain Drive

These chain hotels are in town, or within 10 miles of the city center:
Best Western, Holiday Inn, Motel 6
For more information, including phone numbers and websites, see page 439.

Saddle Up

Read this only if you think you may want to park your bike for a week and rough it on the saddle of a real horse. Within 20 miles of here, dude ranches and trail rides are a cottage industry (actually, a bunkhouse industry). While I can't attest to any of these, check 'em out if you'd like to live the life of Hoss.

Among them are **Triangle X Guest Ranch** (307/733-2183 or 800/860-0005 www.trianglex.com); **Gros Ventre River Ranch** (307/733-4138, www.grosventreriverranch.com); **Lost Creek Ranch** (307/733-3435, www.lostcreek.com); and the **Red Rock Ranch** (307/733-6288, www.theredrockranch.com). Most dude ranches include one or a variety of activities, including trail rides, fly-fishing, swimming, horseback riding, float trips, pack trips, cookouts, hunting, square dancing, hiking, scenic tours, photography, breaking stock, and shoeing horses. Lodging will usually be in log cabins. Prices aren't inexpensive, but they may be a bargain for what you get and how many people you can crowd into a group rate. Plus, at most ranches, you get your own horse and a chance to ride like the Lone Ranger. Hi-yo!

Resources for Riders

Wild West Run

Montana Travel Information
Montana Bed & Breakfast Association—www.mtbba.com
Montana Camping Reservations—877/444-6777, www.recreation.gov
Montana Fish, Wildlife, and Parks—404/444-2535, www.fwp.mt.gov
Montana Road Conditions—800/226-7623, www.mdt.mt.gov/travinfo
Travel Montana—800/847-4868, www.visitmt.com

Wyoming Travel Information
Wyoming Game and Fish—307/777-4600, gf.state.wy.us
Wyoming Inn and Ranch Adventures—307/359-1289,
   www.wyomingbnb-ranchrec.com
Wyoming Road Conditions—888/996-7623, www.wyoroad.info
Wyoming State Parks and Historic Sites—307/777-6323,
   www.artsparkshistory.com
Wyoming State Parks Camping Reservations—877/996-7275,
   wyoparks.state.wy.us
Wyoming Tourism—307/777-7777 or 800/225-5996, www.wyomingtourism.org
Wyoming Weather—307/635-9901 or 307/857-3827

Local and Regional Information
Jackson Hole Area Chamber of Commerce—307/733-3316,
   www.jacksonholechamber.com
Jackson Hole Central Reservations—888/838-6606, www.jacksonholewy.com
Livingston Chamber of Commerce—406/222-0850,
   www.livingston-chamber.com
Yellowstone Activities and Reservations—307/344-7311, or 866/439-7375,
   www.travelyellowstone.com
Yellowstone National Park Visitors Services—307/344-2107 or 307/344-7381,
   www.nps.gov/yell

Montana Motorcycle Shops
Alpine Yamaha—301 N. Main St., Livingston, 406/222-1211
Yellowstone Harley-Davidson—540 Alaska Frontage Rd., Belgrade,
   406/388-7684, www.yellowstoneharley.com

Wyoming Motorcycle Shops
Jackson Hole Harley Davidson—40 S. Millward St., Jackson, 307/739-1500,
   www.tetonharley.com

Mighty Montana Run
Missoula, Montana to Bozeman, Montana

Montana shines with mountains, rivers, ghost towns, and saloons, while its residents project a refreshing self-reliance and strength of character. The essence of the state is palpable on this journey since this is a grand ride: large in scope, large in scenery, and large in memories.

MISSOULA PRIMER

Geographically, this is the perfect setting for a town. The Flathead Indians called the area Nemissodatakoo, meaning "by or near the cold, chilling waters." It's an apt moniker, considering that four trout-rich rivers—Rock Creek, Blackfoot, Lower Clark Fork, and Bitterroot—converge here. Lewis and Clark passed through this way in the early 1800s. But the first permanent settlement, Hellgate Village, wasn't established until 1860. Four miles from Missoula's current location, the town limits encompassed the flour and sawmills; but when the railroad came to town, folks painted over the Hellgate sign and changed the name to the more welcoming Missoula.

Missoula offers a great starting point and a great way to get used to Montana. The third-largest city in Montana, Missoula is easy to tour. It also reveals reasons to love this state: there's no sales tax; saloons and roadhouses still have character; and the citizenry is comprised of a pleasing mix of university students, artists, and regular folks.

ON THE ROAD: MISSOULA

Don't expect to ride into Missoula and stay indoors. The town is surrounded by some of the most pristine country and abundant waters in America, which is why fly-fishing is as popular here as jai alai is in Miami and purse-snatching is in Central Park.

The road south is a fine ride—and you'll see it soon—but first spend a few hours wandering around downtown through the heart of the city where independent merchants, junk shops, and watering holes haven't changed much in half a century. Reserve Street is one of the

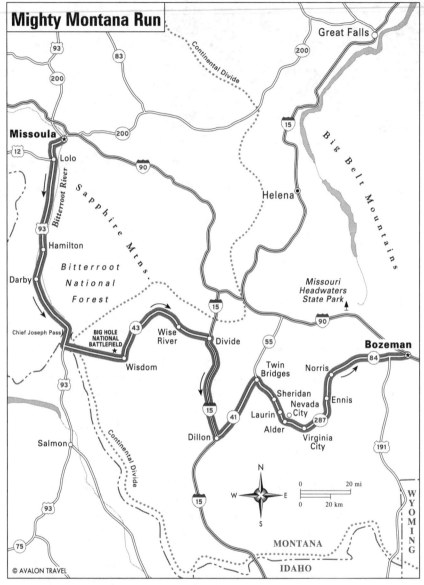

Mighty Montana Run

Route: Missoula to Bozeman via Lolo, Hamilton, Big Hole National Battlefield, Divide, Dillon, Sheridan, Nevada City, Virginia City, Ennis, Norris

Distance: Approximately 335 miles

First Leg: Missoula to Dillon (210 miles)

Second Leg: Dillon to Bozeman (123 miles)

Helmet Laws: Montana does not require helmets.

busiest thoroughfares, and the arrival of box stores has made it a hassle. That said, look for Higgins Avenue, a great road for reminiscing and tripping into a 1950s time warp. On Saturday morning, local farmers and craftspeople set up shop on side streets to sell their plants, handcrafted rugs, jewelry, and weavings. The University of Montana is also near downtown, as are bookstores, cool, dark saloons, and the historic and eye-popping art deco **Wilma Theatre** (131 S. Higgins Ave., 406/728-2521, www.thewilma.com), which hosts concerts and shows current and classic flicks.

PULL IT OVER: MISSOULA HIGHLIGHTS
Attractions and Adventures

At the **Smokejumpers Center** (5765 W. Broadway/U.S. 10, 406/329-4934, www.smokejumpers.com) trainees learn how to skydive behind fire lines in the remote wilderness and fight forest fires. It's open 8:30 A.M.–5 P.M. daily in season. The center features free tours, videos, a lookout tower, and exhibits showing the history and training requirements for these brave bastards. If riding across the country isn't exciting enough for you, they're always looking to recruit new members…

Montana rivers and streams teem with trout: rainbows, cutthroats, browns, and brook. Guides can take you to where the fish are; most head out about 60 miles to find a favorite fishing spot. Some gear can be rented, licenses and other items must be purchased, and a tip is never included in prices. This is admittedly an expensive proposition, since an angling adventure can start at around $400 for a day's outing for you and a buddy. Fishing trips are offered by **Missoulian Angler** (401 S. Orange St., 406/728-7766 or 800/824-2450, www.missoulianangler.com) and **Grizzly**

Hackle (215 W. Front St., 406/721-8996 or 800/297-8996, www.grizzlyhackle.com).

To those of us who live in towns and cities, Montana's stretches of wilderness are so vast it looks like a foreign world. In addition to exploring this relatively pristine frontier on your bike, you may want to see it from other angles by walking in the footsteps of America's greatest explorers. **Lewis and Clark Trail Adventures** (912 E. Broadway, 406/728-7609 or 800/366-6246, www.trailadventures.com) offers biking, hiking, and whitewater trips, including overnights, where all meals, tents, camping, and rafting gear are provided and where there are no roads, no cities, no phones…Paradise.

If you'd rather climb every mountain, **The Trailhead** (221 E. Front St., 406/543-6966, www.trailheadmontana.net) rents gear for camping, climbing, kayak, and canoe excursions. Not a bad start for novices.

The fastest-growing wildlife conservation center in the country, **Rocky Mountain Elk Foundation** (5705 Grant Creek, 406/523-4500 or 800/225-5355, www.rmef.org) works to preserve more than 2.4 million acres of elk country (depleting by an estimated 5,000 acres a day, they claim) by hosting exhibits, talks, and displaying stuffed dead elk. This is an inspirational stop for outdoors enthusiasts. Summer hours are 8 A.M.–6 P.M. Monday–Friday, 9 A.M.–6 P.M. weekends.

Blue-Plate Specials

A Northwestern-style downtown restaurant, **Iron Horse** (501 N. Higgins Ave., 406/728-8866, www.ironhorsebrewpub.com) has a good vibe with college students and mature people. Lunch and dinner fare includes steaks, quesadillas, hamburgers, and pub food. A pitcher of cold beer here is particularly enjoyable at the sidewalk café. It's a good place to hang out, with nightly drink specials and a bar that's open 'til 2 A.M.

It was at the **Double Front Cafe** (122 W. Alder St., 406/543-6264) where I ordered a chicken and an egg just to see which would come first. It sold its first chicken in the 1930s, and the current owners have been plucking and frying here since 1961. You can order burgers and seafood in the restaurant, but the big deal is the $8 chicken dinner, chased by a glass of pop. Check out the full bar in the basement, and then go back upstairs and get some more chicken. A Missoula legend.

Absolutely appetizing is **Doc's Gourmet Sandwich Shop** (214 N. Higgins Ave., 406/542-7414, www.docsgourmet.com). This nice retro diner in the heart of town serves an impressive range of big sandwiches and homemade soups. The menu also features a concoction known as "hangover stew," a potato corn chowder with an active ingredient of green chiles.

Watering Holes

Drop in at any bar along Higgins Avenue, and you'll find a hole in the wall filled with cowboys and mountain folk and a distinct personality. Here are a few to try.

Enter the **Oxford** (337 N. Higgins Ave., 406/549-0117), and you fall into a Steinbeck novel. It's been here since the 1880s and in its present location since the 1940s. It's open 24 hours a day. Step inside to a full liquor bar, an interior unchanged since World War II, gun displays, a card room in back, pool tables, and a revolving lineup of local characters. **Charlie B's** (428 N. Higgins Ave., 406/549-3589) stays open 'til 2 A.M. As you enter, notice the wall of photos of regular patrons and, when your eyes get accustomed to the dark, check out the elk heads, pool tables, and mountain folk. Charlie B's is regularly a leading contender in *Esquire's* "Best Bars" poll in which a voter suggests that it's "Without question the best place in the country to find a beautiful woman who can gut her own trout."

The Rhino (158 Ryman St., 406/721-6061) has a slightly less impressive lineage (it's been around only since 1988), but it compensates by having 50 beers on tap. What's more, the beer flows through a beer engine, which uses air instead of $CO2$ to make the cask-kegged beer smoother and creamier—exactly the way they poured it in the Old West (before cowboys would go in the street and kill each other).

Shut-Eye

Most of Missoula's best lodging choices are chain hotels.

Chain Drive

These chain hotels are in town, or within 10 miles of the city center:
Best Western, Clarion, Comfort Inn, Courtyard by Marriott, Days Inn, Doubletree, Econo Lodge, Hampton Inn, Hilton, Holiday Inn, La Quinta, Motel 6, Quality Inn, Sleep Inn, Super 8, Travelodge

For more information, including phone numbers and websites, see page 439.

ON THE ROAD: MISSOULA TO DILLON

As you leave Missoula, Montana doesn't assault your senses. It just grows on you until you realize there is no other state quite so attractive and no great outdoors quite so great. As Missoula recedes in your mirrors, the sky ahead opens up and draws you forward.

U.S. 93, a wide four-lane road, sweeps you up and over Missoula toward Lolo, then south through the Bitterroot Valley toward Hamilton. The road opens into a straightaway and, spotting mountains far on the horizon, you get your first inkling of how large this trip will be. Ahead, the stretches of emptiness are long. When they are interrupted, it's usually by Montana businesses, such as **Gulli Totem Poles** (964 U.S. 93, 406/961-4853, www.gullitotempoles.com) in Victor. The wood carver here can carve you a nice made-to-order totem pole of any size, with any configurations of totems. I ordered one that includes the entire Brady Bunch.

Hamilton appears after you cross the Bitterroot River, offering several opportunities for gas and food, like at the **Coffee Cup Cafe** (500 S. 1st St./U.S. 93, 406/363-3822). Try to make this your lunch stop since there's great home cooking, homemade soups, and mighty tasty pies and cakes that'll push you back into husky pants.

After Hamilton, the road is effortless. The slow curves don't ask much, and thus begins a perfect combination of scenery and landscape. Fires in 2000 took out thousands of acres of forest, but nature has done what it can to replace the loss. The road widens and does something special— it gives you room to simply breathe and to think and enjoy the ride. Sheep graze in the fields, and as you roll past small towns like Darby, you're witness to the American West without the pretense. Only about 970,000 people live in America's fourth-largest state, which is an average of six people per square mile. All around you the land reflects this pioneering spirit.

About 25 miles south of Hamilton, the road narrows and the riding becomes more challenging. As you enter the backcountry and head toward the Bitterroot River, the road leads through the valley and to the **Sula Country Store** (7060 U.S. 93 S., 406/821-3364, www.bitterroot-montana.com), which, according to the owners, is "one of the cleanest and friendliest stops

you'll make." Although I suggest riding miles ahead, if you'd like to stay awhile and explore the expansive backcountry of the **Bitterroot National Forest** (Sula Ranger District, 7338 U.S. 93 S., 406/821-3201, www.fs.fed.us/r1/bitterroot), they offer lodging here as well. There are cabins, cottages, a campground, gas, a diner, fishing licenses, and a nice front porch to kick back on, and every reason to stop and do absolutely nothing.

Civilization lies behind you and for the next 13 miles, you'll see every vision the name Montana brings to mind. The road wraps around mountains, swings into 25-mph curves, and propels you into snow-capped elevations. Keep one eye on the gravel and the other on the vistas that appear as you top this mountain chain. Pine trees puncture the snow cover, and when you reach the Lost Trail Pass at 7,014 feet, you're on top of the world.

This is only the beginning. On Highway 43 at the Montana/Idaho border, turn left to reach Chief Joseph Pass (7,241 feet) and cross the Continental Divide. Great descents, pristine woodlands, and the first of hundreds of miles of split-rail fencing follow. You're not riding through some puny East Coast farm country now. You're into something far greater. This is big.

Although the entrance to **Big Hole National Battlefield** (17 miles from the turnoff at U.S. 93 on Hwy. 43, 406/689-3155, www.nps.gov/biho, free) isn't well marked, it's the only detour for miles, so you should be able to spot it on your left. It's as sad a place as I've seen, and here's why: In the summer of 1877, five bands of Nez Perce had fled Oregon and Idaho to escape the U.S. Army and General Oliver Howard, who were trying to round them up and put them on a reservation. They outmaneuvered the army in nearly a dozen battles across 1,200 miles as they tried to reach safety in Canada. But when they made it here, Colonel John Gibbon's Seventh U.S. Infantry attacked their sleeping camp on August 9 and 10, 1877, killing men, women, and children. Despite the surprise attack, the Nez Perce managed to kill or wound nearly 70 soldiers and drive them back.

The Nez Perce beat the army again at Canyon Creek but surrendered in October 1877, at Bear Paw Battlefield, just 40 miles from Canada. Nez Perce civil leader Chief Joseph had had enough. He told Colonel Nelson Miles, "Hear me, chiefs. I am tired; my heart is sick and sad. From where the sun now stands, I will fight no more forever."

In my opinion, this reflects the very worst of American history. And while I shouldn't feel personally responsible for what happened here, I sure felt bad.

When you leave the center, the breadth of the land you see becomes phenomenal. There is enough earth here to build new planets. You're in the Big Hole Valley, riding at an average elevation of 1.2 miles. Even though the horizons are empty, the view is more inspiring and far more beautiful than you can comprehend.

A few miles later, when you ride into Wisdom (pop. 100-plus), you'll encounter something else to file in your growing collection of "on the road" stories. Pull into the **Big Hole Crossing Restaurant** (105 Park St., 406/689-3800, www.bigholecrossing.com) and you've entered an anomaly. The restaurant is no Montana greasy spoon. They serve up damn good food here (breakfast, lunch, and dinner) and have as a backdrop a toasty fireplace, an art gallery, and a clothing store where handcrafted dresses sell for as much as $250 and cool leather jackets for $1,000. If you're on a liquid diet, next door is **Antlers Saloon** (100 Main St., 406/689-

9393), where cowboys shoot stick and locals work out with 16-ounce weights. The decorative touches, antlers, and guns recall an early roadhouse. I expect that by now the sights have tempted you to become a part-time Montanan. Don't. A local told me that if you're not ready to "earn your spurs," leave the state to the people who belong here, those who endure its hardships and deserve its rewards.

If your mind can handle it, the road and landscape following Wisdom improve exponentially. The Great Plains lay themselves out beneath your wheels, sunlight falls in large shafts on the valleys below, and the landscape grows so large that even grazing horses look as insignificant as Shetland ponies. You're in the "Land of 10,000 Haystacks." By the time you're through riding, only reconstructive surgery will be able to erase the smile from your face.

Amid the straights and curves and low sloping hills, something is missing: This great land is uncluttered by houses, billboards, factories, gas stations, and strip malls. There is nothing but land and the road, which, when you get down to it, is really all you need.

The ride's grandeur sustains itself as you cruise alongside the Wise River, taking 40-mph turns as the water churns and boils on your left. In the town of Wise River you'll be seduced by the Wise River–Polaris Road (NF-73), a scenic byway that slices south through the 3.3-million acre Beaverhead Deerlodge National Forest. The bad news is that the road's seldom open because of impassable snows and even when it is it's not all paved and you'll have to contend with sections of gravel. That said, if it *is* open and you have time and a taste for adventure, go off on a tear and enjoy what one local says is the most beautiful scenery in the region, filled with coniferous forests of lodgepole pine and Douglas fir.

Odds are, though, that you'll keep plowing along on Highway 43 toward Divide, where you'll find **Blue Moon** (406/267-3339), a mile off I-15 in Divide. The gas station and saloon are filled with friendly locals, and odds are you'll want to stop and have one for the road. From here it's tempting to jump on the lonesome interstate and head south, which is not as bad as urban highways since you can ride without hardly seeing any other car, truck, or bike. Odds are that for the last 40-some miles you'll want to continue that lonely country riding you've enjoyed. Old Highway 10 (aka SR 361) leads you south, eventually switching identities and becoming Highway 91 as it rolls into Dillon.

I can't claim that there's a lot to do here, but in lonely Montana, lonely Dillon's a fine place to rest up and prepare for the next day's ride.

DILLON PRIMER

Dillon had an impressive start. It was born when the Utah and Northern Railroad headed toward Butte in 1880, but the railroad stopped when it reached rancher Richard Deacon's spread. He wouldn't let the line continue until a group of businessmen promised to raise enough cash to buy him out. While the railroad stalled here during the winter of 1880–1881, the site where they stopped was named after railroad president Sidney Dillon.

That's really about all you need to know. Dillon also enjoyed a gold boom that went bust, and today the town relies on agriculture. There's not much else shaking here. Not much at all.

ON THE ROAD: DILLON

Thumb through this book, and you won't find another town like Dillon. Usually even if there's nothing to see in a town, there's something to talk about. Not so much here. I won't belabor the point. There are a few chain motels, a grain silo, a quiet downtown, the University of Montana-Western, and, most important, a Dairy Queen. There's a popular rodeo here each Labor Day, but overall it's a pretty remote town in a pretty remote area.

About 25 miles southwest of Dillon is the ghost town of Bannack, which was Montana's first territorial capital and where the first major gold strike struck. It was also here in the self-proclaimed "Toughest Town in the West" that a renegade sheriff, Henry Plummer, created a terrorist network credited for killing and robbing more than 102 victims, which was about 102 too many for the town's law-abiding citizens. Forming a vigilante squad, the good guys tracked down the sheriff and 28 of his gang, and gave them a serious going away party by letting them hang on the same gallows Plummer had built. Today the town is the site of **Bannack State Park** (Bannack Bench Rd., 406/834-3413, www.bannack.org), which, if you have time for a ride, is a nice and nearby destination.

If you want to know more about local history and nearby sites that include mountain lakes and reservoirs and forests, mountains and kilns, stop by **Dillon Visitors Information Services** (10 W. Reeder St., 406/683-5511) and the folks on duty will tell you why they're here and why you should stick around.

Shut-Eye
Chain Drive

These chain hotels are in town, or within 10 miles of the city center:

Best Western, Comfort Inn, Super 8
For more information, including phone numbers and websites, see page 439.

ON THE ROAD: DILLON TO BOZEMAN

Leaving Dillon on Route 41 North takes you right back to the prairie and photo ops with a Rocky Mountain backdrop. The landscape varies little, so just let your mind wander until you've gone about 25 miles to Twin Bridges which is as close to not being a town as any town I've seen. The road forks here; turn onto Highway 287 toward Virginia City.

About now, you'll notice a few things: The fierce wind smacks your body as it pours over the plains; every pickup you've passed since Missoula has a dog in back (I believe they come standard with Montana trucks); and there is so much of nothing around you that it's really something.

Sheridan will come and go, too, fizzling to a close and merging with the prairie as you head out of town. About five miles later, you'll pass Robber's Roost on your right, the place where desperadoes, rustlers, and Wall Street execs came to plan their heists. Beyond that, random towns crop up when nothing else is around, such as Laurin, Ruby Valley, and Alder, each of which grows progressively dirtier and more lonesome.

The landscape beside the road is rapidly changing into mining country. The ground is gritty with sagebrush and the mean brown creeks that penetrate the deadwood. This is the perfect setting for **Nevada City** (Hwy. 287, www.virginiacitymt.com), a strange shambles of a place that's half ghost town, half museum. Restored by the Bovey family between 1945 and 1978, there's a hotel here worthy of *Gunsmoke*, a saloon where you can bring your own drinks, and a complete town hidden beyond the streetfront buildings. Check out the darkened music hall and find nickelodeons, fortune telling machines, and the "famous and obnoxious horn machine" stashed inside. In the village, they've saved everything from a two-story outhouse (lookout below!) to stores stocked with unopened merchandise.

Your decision to ride will be repaid in full on the wide-open roads of Montana.

© NANCY HOWELL

A hundred years ago and a few miles southeast of Nevada City, six discouraged prospectors stopped to pan for enough gold to buy tobacco. Within three years, the Alder Gulch gave up $30 million in gold and **Virginia City** (Hwy. 287, 406/843-5555 or 800/829-2969, www.virginiacity.com) was born. It's a more modern town than Nevada City, but the term is relative since Virginia City is still a frontier town as well—although it does have a few great shops, saloons, and restaurants.

Without embellishing, I can say the road from here to Ennis is about as magnificent a road as you'll ever ride. As you climb into the hills, the glorious country is at your feet, and soon you'll reach an overlook hundreds of feet above the Madison Valley. *This* is a sight that will dazzle and humble you with mountains, rounded hills, broad beams of sunlight, and far more beauty than your mind can take in. Now's a good time to thank whatever gods you believe in for their handiwork.

Descending from the promontory is a kick. If you're traveling with others, take time to stage a few photographs on this wide open road. I did, and it's the one I treasure most. When you reach Ennis, turn left on Highway 287 toward Norris. Ride toward the brink of a cliff and look down the shaft of a long, empty valley where shadows of clouds smudge the ground. When you reach Norris and the junction of Highway 84, turn right, and the terrain takes you back into hill country where the low, flat road gives you instant twists beside the fantastic Madison River.

Anglers wade in the waters here, and the canyon turnouts are perfect for resting your bike, peeling off your boots, and cooling yourself with a walk into the river. Try this, and when you shut off your bike

and listen to the silence, I defy you to imagine a more beautiful country.

As you continue into Bozeman, the land turns into farmland. Hear the wind pouring over your helmet and the engine's low-pitched, pulsing hum.

Combined with Montana, it is a symphony.

BOZEMAN PRIMER

Others arrived here before Lewis and Clark, but in 1805 and 1806 those two were the first to generate a written description of the valley. Decades later when gold was discovered, Bozeman Trail became the chosen path west—and then east, when the prospectors returned here to create the town in 1864.

By 1883, the Northern Pacific Railroad had completed its line through the town, and Montana Agricultural College held its first classes in 1893. With settlers arriving from around the country, Bozeman developed a unique local heritage. Today, the town has eight historical districts, more than 40 properties listed on the National Register of Historic Sites, and is the home to Montana State University (which explains the abundance of students you'll see in the saloons).

While the outskirts of town look suspiciously like everyplace else, the heart of downtown still has a 1940s flavor, with 10-gallon hats, pointy-toed boots, drugstore cowboys, and antiquated signage at stores like Western Drug at 44 East Main Street.

Mosey on down and check it out.

ON THE ROAD: BOZEMAN

As in Missoula, the road has been so generous that it's satisfying to stay in town and see what's shakin'. Main Street is the main part of town, more compact than Missoula's. Just a few hours up and down the street will acquaint you with the more interesting shops. Beyond that, see some local attractions, head out into the wilderness on a fly-fishing excursion, or just savor the opportunity to take it easy in the Old West.

PULL IT OVER: BOZEMAN HIGHLIGHTS
Attractions and Adventures

If you've never been fly-fishing, there's no better place to start than right here. What does it take to take up this sport? Money, mostly. Guides charge $300–450 for a half to a full day of fishing, but as you learned in Missoula, that doesn't include gratuities, a license, or equipment. In most shops, you can rent a rod, reel, and waders, but you have to buy gear and flies—unless you've got some plastered on your visor. Most excursions depart at 8:30 A.M. and return about nine hours later. Bear in mind that this is catch and release—you're fishing for the fun of it (if you think spending 450 bucks is fun). The shops below also arrange trips and guides.

Opened in 1944, **Powder Horn** (35 E. Main St., 406/587-7373) is sacred ground for sports enthusiasts, featuring books, rods, reels, clothing, boots, rifles, shotguns, shells, and cooking supplies. It also represents 20–30 local guides—not college students—who know where to go. Working with novice to serious fly fishers, **Bozeman Angler** (23 E. Main St., 406/587-9111 or 800/886-9111, www.bozemanangler.com) offers walk/wade or float trips on the Yellowstone, Beaverhead, Gallatin, Madison, and Missouri rivers. A few miles outside of Bozeman in the town of Belgrade, Dave Warwood at **Bridger Outfitters** (15100 Rocky Mountain Rd., Belgrade, 406/388-4463, www.bridgeroutfitters.com) can arrange a half-day horseback ride, a full day with sack lunch, or a full-on adventure that

lasts four days and three nights and features overnight camps, cattle drives, horseback rides, and fishing in backcountry lakes and streams. Does he know his stuff? He grew up in the business his great-granddad started almost 100 years ago.

The biggest draw in Bozeman, the **Museum of the Rockies** (600 W. Kagy Blvd., 406/994-3466, www.museumoftherockies.org, $10 museum and planetarium) is a great source of intelligence that centers around dinosaur fossils unearthed by local legend Jack Horner. I'm glad I came here. I was investing my money in coprolite until I learned that it's just fossilized dinosaur crap. You'll get a kick out of knowing that when you're riding in Montana, you're riding atop what was once the stomping grounds of the stegosaurus and T-Rex. On display are fake dinosaurs, CAT-scanned dinosaur eggs that reveal embryos, skulls of a triceratops and tyrannosaurus, and thoughtful exhibits on Native Americans and Lewis and Clark. It presents a massive amount of information in intriguing displays, so pace yourself and concentrate only on the exhibits that catch your interest. The museum is open daily 8 A.M.–8 P.M. in the summer; 9 A.M.–5 P.M. in fall and winter.

The free **Gallatin County Pioneer Museum** (317 W. Main St., 406/522-8122, www.pioneermuseum.org) pays tribute to the history of Bozeman and the pioneers who settled in the Gallatin Valley. Take a look at the travels of your spiritual ancestors, Lewis and Clark, who are honored in this old jail at the L&C library. Other exhibits include an 1870s log cabin, American Indian exhibits, a sheriff's room with a hanging gallows, a whiskey still, and more than 11,000 archival photos from the early days of the town.

Blue-Plate Specials

A downtown explosion in 2009 destroyed

three of Bozeman's finest restaurants and one of its legendary bars. Until they're resurrected, try the **Western Cafe** (443 E. Main St., 406/587-0436) which opens at 5 A.M.—just in time to serve early rising regulars tins of fresh-baked cinnamon rolls and pies. When lunch rolls around, it rolls out the T-bone steaks, chicken-fried steaks, homemade soups and stews, and dinner rolls. The only drawback? There's just not enough time to eat it all—closing time's 2 P.M.

Even if you've never been to Bozeman, you probably know the proprietor of **Ted's Montana Grill** (105 W. Main St., 406/587-6000, www.tedsmontanagrill.com): media magnate and philanthropist Ted Turner. The first Montana link in a nationwide chain, this destination is where you can dine inside or on an outdoor patio, relaxed by its turn-of-the-century Arts and Crafts design and the architectural touches of the 1929 hotel in which it resides. The classic American grill focuses on affordable made-from-scratch comfort foods, fresh vegetables, and hand-cut premium beef or bison steaks, chicken and seafood.

Watering Holes

If you wear boots even when you aren't riding, you may feel at home at **Crystal Bar** (123 E. Main St., 406/587-2888), open 8 A.M.–2 A.M. daily. This country cowboy bar attracts its fair share of college students, and it opens a second-floor rooftop beer garden in the summertime. Year-round, you'll find a few pool tables and lots of beer.

The clientele changes throughout the day at **The Cannery** (43 W. Main St., 406/586-0270), from doctors and lawyers after work, to college students after class, to regular folks later at night. Open 11 A.M.–2 A.M. daily, this joint features sassy bartenders and a pool table attached to the ceiling.

A bit removed from downtown is a collection of three taverns which comprise the "Bar-muda Triangle." Beer, mixed drinks, live music and more can be found at **The Haufbrau** (22 S. 8th Ave., 406/587-4931), **Scoops** (712 W. Main St., 406/522-9141), and **The Molly Brown** (703 West Babcock, www.mollybrownbozeman.com).

Shut-Eye
Motels and Motor Courts
The **Lewis and Clark** (824 W. Main St., 406/586-3341 or 800/332-7666, www.lewisandclarkmotel.net, $79 and up) is a best bet for riders, with sheltered parking or a space in front of your room, rags to clean your machine, and fresh coffee and banana bread when you return from the ride. Its retro look goes along with its dining room, coffee shop, and lounge as well as 50 clean and large rooms with a king or two queen beds. Plus, it all comes with a heated indoor pool, fitness room, and three taverns right next door.

Chain Drive
These chain hotels are in town, or within 10 miles of the city center: **Best Western, Comfort Inn, Days Inn, Fairfield Inn, Hampton Inn, Hilton, Holiday Inn, Ramada, Residence Inn, Rodeway, Super 8**
For more information, including phone numbers and websites, see page 439.

Resources for Riders

Mighty Montana Run

Montana Travel Information
Montana Bed & Breakfast Association—www.mtbba.com
Montana Camping Reservations—877/444-6777, www.reserveusa.com
Montana Fish, Wildlife, and Parks—404/444-2535, www.fwp.m.t.gov
Montana Road Conditions—800/226-7623, www.mdt.mt.gov/travinfo
Travel Montana—800/847-4868, www.visitmt.com

Local and Regional Information
Beaverhead Chamber (Dillon)—406/683-5511,
    www.beaverheadchamber.org
Bozeman Chamber of Commerce—406/586-5421, www.bozemanchamber.com
Bozeman Visitors Bureau—406/586-5421 or 800/228-4224,
    www.bozemancvb.com
Missoula Chamber of Commerce—406/543-6623, www.missoulachamber.com
Missoula Convention and Visitors Bureau—800/526-3465,
    www.missoulacvb.org
Missoula Weather—406/329-4840

Montana Motorcycle Shops
Adventure Cycle—201 E. Helena St., Dillon, 406/683-2205,
    www.adventurecycleandsled.com
Al's Cycle—619 U.S 93 S., Hamilton, 406/363-3433, www.alscycleyamaha.com
Big Sky BMW Kawasaki—2315 South Ave. W., Missoula, 406/728-5341,
    www.bigskybmwkawasaki.com
Five Valley Honda-Yamaha—5900 U.S. Hwy. 93 S., Missoula, 406/251-5900,
    www.fivevalleyhondayamaha.com
Mike Tingley Suzuki Yamaha—2150 South Ave., Missoula, 406/549-4260
Mountain Motorsports and Marine—620 U.S. 93 S., Hamilton, 406/363-4493,
    www.mms-motorsports.com
Team Bozeman Polaris/Kawasaki/Yamaha—2595 Simmental Way, Bozeman,
    406/587-4671, www.team-bozeman.com
Yellowstone Harley-Davidson—18 W. Main St., Bozeman, 406/586-3139; and
    540 Alaska Frontage Rd., Belgrade, 406/388-7684 or 877/388-7684,
    www.yellowstoneharley.com

Sawtooth Range Run
Boise, Idaho to McCall, Idaho

Remote and expansive plains usher you into sometimes intricate yet always scenic low-mountain riding. Start with a wide-open ride custom-designed to relieve stress and cleanse your mind, and then cruise across the charcoal-black cinders of an ancient lava bed. After rolling into a valley retreat favored by cowboys, skiers, and America's most powerful people, ride out on a final run combining the majesty of wild rivers and scenic byways.

ON THE ROAD: BOISE TO KETCHUM/SUN VALLEY

If you're heading to Idaho specifically for this ride, odds are a major road will lead you toward Boise. It's a nice city, but doubtful one that you'd explore on a motorcycle, so look at your map and consider following a roundabout counterclockwise route from here and then into the heart of Idaho.

There's not a scenic way to exit Boise, but in a state of only 1.4 million residents, even the interstates are relatively empty. It's much faster to reach the junction of U.S. 20 at Mountain Home by taking I-84 East, but a better alternative is enduring a little bit of congestion to reach some more good stuff on the horizon.

Set your coordinates and depart Boise via I-84 West, riding toward the suburb of Nampa, where Route 45 drops due south. After about 30 minutes into the ride the last residue of urban traffic dissolves and you are in farm country, where the hills and valleys are the Gem State's finest welcoming committee.

If you were watching television on September 8, 1974, the sight of Snake River should ring some bells. This is the river Evel Kneivel planned to clear aboard a rocket-powered motorcycle called the X-2 Skycycle. Although Evel had trouble crossing the river from his launch pad near Twin Falls, thanks to a well-placed bridge, you'll have no difficulty whatsoever.

More impressive than memories of Kneivel's jump is the terrain Snake River helped create. Where Route 45 joins Route 78, the landscape is slowly washed clear

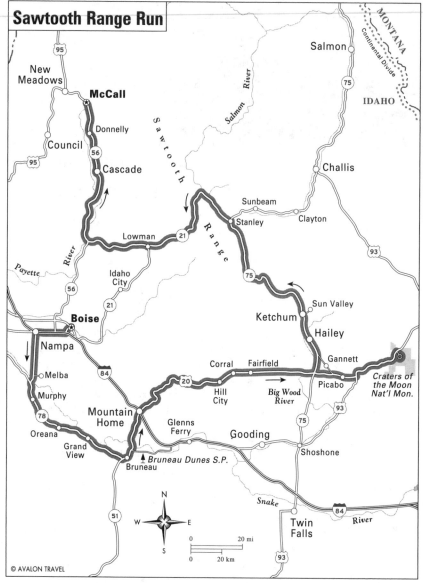

Sawtooth Range Run

Route: Boise to McCall via Nampa, Bruneau, Mountain Home, Ketchum, Sun Valley, Stanley, Banks, Cascade

Distance: Approximately 450 miles

First Leg: Boise to Ketchum (235 miles)

Second Leg: Ketchum to McCall (215 miles)

Helmet Laws: In Idaho, helmets are optional if over 18.

of everything, including the constricting sights of strip malls, stores, and city traffic. Free of all this, you can gun it and pour yourself into the wind, taking advantage of the highway where speed limit signs should include the promise of "100 percent satisfaction guaranteed."

The town of Murphy is here…and gone, memorable if only for a nice dip that hugs both the summit and plummet of a hill. By the time I reached Oreana, the land had worked its magic on me. I looked at the road leading to the horizon and, for the first time in my life, I had a new appreciation for an old song. As I watched the world through the windscreen, Woody Guthrie's endless skyway and ribbon of highway were no longer just lines from "This Land Is Your Land"—they were a very real part of this ride.

Ahead there was a sparse desert region that led me into one of my favorite environments. As a solo rider, I find that deserts invariably match my mood and desire for privacy. While this stretch gave me enough curves to keep me alert, at times I rode upon straights that pierced the land for as much as six arrow-true miles. And when the road turned and decided to sneak up on Snake River, it revealed the nice high walls of the canyon. Between Grand View and Bruneau, the 20 or so miles that divide the towns give you a perfect mixture of riding as you reach a weird confluence of mountains and desert and fertile farmlands irrigated by 300-yard long sprinklers poised above the fields.

In addition to the scenery (or lack of it), what also impressed me about Route 78 was its speed. There were few towns and no switchbacks, and since I couldn't recall passing any troopers, Route 78 became a very fast road. If you've ever thought about setting a land speed record, forget the Salt Flats and consider Idaho.

Near Bruneau, Route 78 swings to the north, where it wants you to cross Snake River and roll onto Highway 51. Don't go yet. Stay on Route 78 for two more miles for a stop at **Bruneau Dunes State Park** (27608 Sand Dunes Rd., 208/366-7919). When you enter the park, a winding road leads to the park office, which has information on what's ahead. Until you get there, here's the skinny: It's a five-mile run to the end of the trail, and along the way are 12,000-year-old soot-colored dunes, one of which—at 470 feet—is the largest single-structured sand dune in North America. Unlike the dunes of Florence, Oregon, though, there are no dune buggies here—but there are lake, marsh, desert, prairie, and dune habitats to explore. If you decide to bunk down at the campground or cabins here and stay the night, the popular Bruneau Dunes Observatory has a collection of telescopes that'll help you see into the clear country skies.

Returning to Highway 51, the road spans Snake River (take that, Evel) and points you north toward Mountain Home. Here the highway is marked with periodic "open range" signs that I'm sure refer to livestock, but you'll get the sense that it also means free-range motorcycling.

On this open road, the lure of the landscape will find you twisting the throttle to rocket down the road. The intensity of the ride may be tempered if you're lapped by one of the jets screaming back to the neighboring Mountain Home Air Force Base. Aside from the random jet, there is nothing—nothing—here except the flat, endless prairie and the strip of asphalt that divides it. The emptiness continues until you hit a touch of density in and around Mountain Home, after which you squeeze under I-84 and work your way toward U.S. 20 East, at which point you're bound for glory. For an alternative route, swing southeast on I-84 toward Twin Falls, near the center of the Great Rift. This 635-square mile geological phenomenon spreads across the Snake River Plain to create one of the earth's most impressive plumbing systems; it's a series of fissures, spatter cones, and lava tubes from 60 lava flows and 25 volcanic events.

When you're back on U.S. 20 once again, the road ahead is clean and spare. You may spy a home every 10 miles or so, and when a curve does appear, its arc is so long and slow that you may think you're still on a straight. Rolling on toward an area called Tollgate, you can look around and realize this desert was once the floor of an ancient ocean, as shifting sands and the trails of long-evaporated streams lead off to the horizon. You can you see all of this as the road slowly elevates you above the landscape and presents wonderful aerial views of the ride ahead.

There's not much shaking in Hill City or Corral or Fairfield, save for the random gypsy wagon parked in the middle of a field. The hills are snug, low, and packed tightly together to create repetitive, easy corners. Creeks and ravines intersect the land, and wonderful scenes that were new to me appeared, like the random woodchucks that crept toward the road before dashing away from the growl of my bike.

U.S. 20 becomes increasingly more alluring, no thanks to any magnificent formations but really to the lack of them. This lasts for about 20 miles until you reach the junction of Highway 75 and well beyond it. Trust me—after the months you've spent planning and then waiting for the office clock to tick down to the zero hour, wonderful emptiness like this is what you need.

Depending on your schedule, you may want to invest time to ride over to yet another unusual parcel of real estate. To see it, pass the junction of Highway 75 for now and stick with U.S. 20 toward Picabo. Along the way, there is almost omnipresent desolation. To your right, the southern horizon is flat and endless. From horizon to horizon, you will not see a living soul; and clouds probably 50 miles away look quite strange and surreal, since there is nothing at all to break the view. Gradually, scrub brush and desert sand are replaced by black lava rock, and off in the distance at about 2 o'clock, there's an ancient volcano that looks as if it coughed up this very ground.

The artificially-made views here are limited to a few service stations, homes, and ranching supply stores. But nature delivers towering formations lacerated by rocks piercing through the grass, and more beds of crisp black lava tell you you've reached the entrance of the mysterious **Craters of the Moon National Monument** (U.S. 20/26/93, 208/527-1300, www.nps.gov/crmo, $4). Before heading down the loop road, stop at the visitor center where you can get a basic education on what happened here. In short: Several times during the past several thousand years, a parallel line of fissures in the area erupted through volcanic buttes and cones to spread a flow of lava that cooled into either pahoehoe (pa-HOY-hoy), a ropelike lava, or Aa (AH-ah), a rough, jagged rock. No one was here to see the last eruption 2,000 years ago, but you can check out old volcanoes and see where lava beds created caves that you can explore.

So unusual is this area that Apollo XIV astronauts came here to study geology when training for their moon mission, to get a sense of what the moon's surface would look like. So, in a sense, for the next few hours, your bike will become a lunar rover.

There are several stops on the seven-mile loop, such as Big Craters, Devils Orchard, and an extinct 6,181-foot tall volcano called Inferno Cone. Since you're already just a few hundred feet from the summit, you can hike to the top of the cone fairly quickly and easily, although the pebblelike consistency of the black gravel contrasts with the steep 14-degree grade of the hill. And when you reach what you thought was the summit, you'll see another plateau ahead. To a chorus of crunching rocks, swift winds, and your own chuffing breath, you pass several peaks before reaching the final one to find that the reward is a view well worth the effort. There is no crater left here, just a few flat boulders and a lone tree that draws your eyes to the east, where another extinct volcano rests far, far, far away. On a quiet day, you may be the only fool on the hill. Alone in private, you can scan the entire world. If you've ever considered meditation, there's no better place where you can reflect on your ride and your life.

Back down the hill, the loop road leads to other overlooks and then to the enticing "lava tubes"—caves hidden beneath a crust of lava. It may be tempting, but if you're alone or lack the right gear, such as a hardhat and lantern, heed the warning signs that remind you help may be a long time coming. And if you're wondering if you'll be able to leave the park with a few lumps of lava—the answer is no. Every year a few truckloads of rock are collectively pilfered from the park, and some even chip souvenir chunks off delicate formations. Keep in mind that what erupts in Idaho should stay in Idaho. So take pictures, and file away mental images, but leave the lava alone if you want to avoid a $250 fine.

Now you have the pleasure of backtracking to Highway 75, one of the nicest roads in Idaho, which takes you to Ketchum and beyond. Rather than riding U.S. 20 all the way, watch for a spur road to the right just past Picabo that'll take you northwest on Gannett Road (Route 23) toward Bellevue and Hailey. At Highway 75, head north toward Hailey, where today's downtown bears little resemblance to the Hailey of yesteryear. What changed? Bruce Willis. He and Demi Moore moved here to raise their kids, and even though they split, their presence helped put a little Hollywood hep into the Wild West.

From here, it's just another 10 prairie-rich miles to Ketchum and Sun Valley, one of the leading "lucky break" stories of the 20th century.

KETCHUM/ SUN VALLEY PRIMER

Ketchum has always had a penchant for wealth. Originally known as Leadville, back in 1879 prospectors came here to rip gold, silver, and lead ore out of the mines—but only after they had ripped the Tukudeka Indians from the land. After the tribes were gone and the mines were spent, Basque sheepherders from Spain showed up and began guiding their flocks through the crossroads of Wood Valley.

Aside from silver and sheep and a stab at creating a spa from local hot springs, Ketchum didn't really catch on until 1936. That's when Averell Harriman, the chairman of the Union Pacific Railroad (and later Secretary of Commerce under Harry Truman), sent Austrian Count Felix Schaffgotsch on a mission to find one place in America that could rival European ski resorts such as St. Moritz. After several months of scouting, the Count was getting ready to wire Harriman that he had failed when an Idaho rep of the railroad directed him to the old mining town. Fewer than 100 people lived in Ketchum then, but the site was perfect.

Backed by his fortune and connections,

The Dawn of Sun Valley

So what's the appeal of Sun Valley, the place that's accepted as "America's First Destination Resort?" You can find out for yourself by taking a short walk east of downtown Ketchum.

Sun Valley (208/622-2001 or 800/786-8259, www.sunvalley.com) is centered around the main hotel that was built in 1936, and at the lodge are a few restaurants, a sports lounge, and a circular heated pool that looks hedonistic when it's steaming up in the cool months. There's a vintage six-lane bowling alley in the basement, and behind the lodge is an ice-skating rink where Olympic skaters practice during the day and appear in a popular, free ice show each Saturday in the summer. On the second floor, Room 206 was Ernest Hemingway's favorite and where he wrote *For Whom The Bell Tolls.*

Down a winding sidewalk, a mock Alpine village features more of the resort's dozen stores, 13 restaurants, and five bars, as well as a theater where, each afternoon at 5 P.M., you can watch *Sun Valley Serenade,* filmed here in 1941. Elsewhere, you'll find a shooting club, trail rides, ski lifts, and golf.

It's a neat little operation, and the best part of it all is that it's not always so expensive. Travel between seasons and you can get one of its 500 rooms for less than a hundred bucks.

Harriman bought the 4,300-acre Brass Ranch and, just 11 months and five days after the count hit town, millionaire socialites from the east and stars from Hollywood hit Sun Valley. The blend of money and celebrity worked and today's Ketchum was born. Called the "American Shangri-La," in 1941 Glenn Miller came here to film *Sun Valley Serenade* with Sonja Henie. Clark Gable, Robert Kennedy, Ginger Rogers, and Lucille Ball were frequent guests and even he-man Gary Cooper came by to go duck hunting with pal Ernest Hemingway who liked shooting ducks and, apparently, himself. After his 1961 suicide he was buried in the last row of the Ketchum Cemetery on Highway 75.

The popularity of this hole-in-the-wall resort has seldom abated. Power players from Washington and Hollywood have made this a favored retreat, and the power surges each summer when CEOs and CFOs from leading entertainment, technology, communications, and computing companies arrive for a summit at a Sun Valley retreat.

After the business leaders jet out, long-term residents and annual visitors stick around so there's always a chance you may run across a generous share of celebrities that call this home. Despite the panache of the town, prices on basic goods and lodging are still reasonable—just don't plan on buying a home and settling down. Why not? Here in Ketchum, revealed a local, "The billionaires are pushing out the millionaires."

ON THE ROAD: KETCHUM/SUN VALLEY

The surrounding area has more than enough to keep you occupied for a day—perhaps even a few years if you happen to bump into Oprah and she wants to marry and support you. If you're here for one day, though, half the day will keep you grounded, and the other half should have you heading for the hills.

If I were in your boots, I'd start at the **Visitors Center** (491 Sun Valley Rd., 800/634-3347, www.visitsunvalley.com), which has a library's worth of brochures and information on the local area, as well as maps and guides for sites on the outskirts of town and across Idaho. Then take your pick. There are mountains all around you and even in the summertime the ski lift still clips along to the top of Bald Mountain. What does that mean to you? While you can't get your bike to the top of the peak, you can get a *bicycle* there.

There are several rental shops in Ketchum, and one of the largest and oldest (since 1948) is **Sturtevants** (340 N. Main St., 208/726-4501 or 800/252-9534, www.sturtos.com). Provided you're not the size of Billy or Benny McCrary (the world's fattest twins), for about $35 a day you can rent a sturdy cross-country mountain bike and ride the high-speed quad lift to the top of Bald Mountain. During the summer, the lift station at River Run lets you slap your bicycle on a rack, take a 10-minute ride to the peak, and then hop off at Lookout Lodge where you can grab a light lunch at the grill and settle back with some outstanding views of the surrounding Pioneer and Sawtooth ranges. After living in the moment for a moment, spend the next hour riding down from 9,000 feet, burning off lunch as you navigate foot-wide trails carved out by animals and motocross riders.

If the idea of riding a bicycle down a steep hill strikes fear into your heart, here's an alternative: Jump off the mountain. *Oui, monsieur, c'est ci bon.* Sure, it's expensive (about 200 bucks) but you'll never forget it. When the weather's right, you can sign up for a tandem paragliding leap with **Fly Sun Valley** (160 W. 4th St., 208/726-3332, www.flysunvalley.com). Strapped to your guide, you literally step straight ahead as the winds lift you off the side of Bald Mountain. You'll swirl through the air for up to an hour before swooping in for an approach at a nearby parking lot or soccer field. What about your friends on the bicycles? Those poor bastards are still pedaling.

PULL IT OVER: KETCHUM/ SUN VALLEY HIGHLIGHTS
Attractions and Adventures

If you're active, there are enough outdoor adventures to keep you occupied for well over a week. Within a five-mile radius of Ketchum there are more than 100 miles of hiking trails: Fox Creek, Adams Gulch, Trail Creek, and others at Sun Valley. They're all free and maps are available at the **Ketchum Ranger Station** (206 Sun Valley Rd., 208/622-5371).

There are a host of organized options available at **Sun Valley** (www.sunvalley.com). A few that may do it for you are **guided trail rides** (208/622-2387) on horseback up to Dollar Mountain and skeet shooting at its **Gun Club** (1.5 miles east of Sun Valley Lodge, 208/622-2111). Rent one of the Beretta shotguns and try trap, double trap, wobbletrap, and duck tower shooting. Smack a few clay pigeons, and you've got yourself a dinner. Good eatin'.

Shopping

With about 20 square blocks of stores, galleries, thrift stores, and restaurants to see, shopping is a significant part of life in Ketchum. I didn't hit all of them, but the few that I did visit seemed pretty all right.

For a comprehensive listing of galleries in town, pick up a *Sun Valley Gallery Association* guide (208/726-5512, www.svgalleries.org) at any of the galleries the chamber of commerce, or a grocery store.

At heart, this is a tourist destination which means that someone *has* to sell T-shirts. Here, the store is **T's & Temptations** (Giacobbi Square, 4th and Leadville Sts., 208/726-9543). Along with T-shirts and sweats, it also sells baseball caps, stickers, and other Ketchum and Sun Valley souvenirs.

A jim-dandy bookstore (and a bookstore *can* be jim-dandy, dammit) is **Iconoclast Books** (671 Sun Valley Rd., 208/726-1654, www.iconoclastbooks.com). If you fall ass-over-teakettle for Idaho, odds are you'll want to peruse the new and used volumes here. They provide great historical and photographic references of the state and, most important, the areas you'll explore. It's not just regional guides, either—there are volumes on philosophy, art, history, and literature, as well as collectible first editions.

If you're staying in a cabin or efficiency or plan a picnic out in the wilderness, **Atkinson's Market** (4th and Leadville Sts., 208/726-5668), is a large market that has aisles of groceries, coolers of beer, a full-service deli, and drugstore.

Blue-Plate Specials

Ketchum is an important part of a well-balanced diet. There are some great restaurants here, and despite the deep pockets of many locals, prices at most places felt pretty fair to me.

Looking upscale is the affordable **Sawtooth Club** (231 N. Main St., 208/726-5233, www.thesawtoothclub.com), which opens into a cool bar, with the dining area on the second floor. It puts a creative spin on basic dishes to create super

good chicken Senegalese, mesquite-grilled steaks, chops, ribs, and wood-grilled duck and lamb. Often voted the Valley's best overall restaurant, the food's so nice I ate here twice.

Completely starving, I dined at **The Kneadery** (260 Leadville Ave., 208/726-9462) and fully expected to finish just a single sandwich. I couldn't. It was way big, as were the massive home-style breakfasts that were defeating other diners. The portions are large and the prices medium, and the Rocky Mountain lodge look went a long way to please this rider.

For a fresh and inexpensive Mexican meal, try **Desperado's** (211 4th St., 208/726-3068, www.despossv.com). Founder and owner Jim Funk believes in fresh ingredients and fresh salsas, a recipe that's worked for him—and has pleased a fan base of locals and visitors—since the mid-1980s. There are plenty of beers on tap (including Tecate and Dos Equis) and a patio for dining out when the weather's right.

Watering Holes

You've probably realized that Ketchum has just about everything you need. At night, it has even more. Every bar and saloon in sight is built for locals, and they all have at least two things in common: a real good vibe and a moose head on the wall. Even if you don't imbibe, these are some good places to hang out with locals—and each saloon complements its drinks with an impressive menu.

As mentioned, the **Sawtooth Club** (231 N. Main St., 208/726-5233) is a wonderful restaurant, but there's an even better bar and lounge downstairs. Fat, padded armchairs and couches around a fireplace make it seem like a combination dorm room/gentlemen's club.

Stumble across the street to **The Roosevelt Grille** (280 N. Main St., 208/726-0051, www.therooseveltgrille.

com), another restaurant whose twin is a lounge (Roosevelt Tavern). A Western theme is the obvious choice, accented by a sign asking what is now so very clear: "24 hours in a day, 24 beers in a case. Coincidence? I think not." Count on at least 10 beers on tap, 15 brands in bottles, and specialty martinis. In good weather, head on upstairs—way up—to the roof to drink a brew under clear Ketchum skies.

The Casino (351 Main St., 208/726-3200) isn't a place where you'd really gamble, but you can bet on it. Here since 1936, it's had decades to become what it is: a place with three pool tables, a long, long bar, $2 Pabst on tap, and some micros. Down the street you'll discover that The Pioneer Saloon (308 N. Main St., 208/726-3139) is just that. Once a place where mountain folks and people of the frontier hung out and conducted business over a drink and a handshake, it still has an authentic saloon-style atmosphere. The restaurant's fancy, although the lounge and bar are where you'd want to relax at the end of the day.

Shut-Eye

You shouldn't have any trouble finding a place to bunk down. Even if everything's full in Ketchum, you have two options: Lodging's available and less expensive 10 miles south in Hailey and 15 miles south in Bellevue. In addition to motels, in Ketchum you're surrounded by the Sawtooth National Recreational Area—which is government-owned land, so camping's free in the wilderness (although there's a charge at serviced campsites).

Here and throughout Idaho, a *free* service that'll save you the trouble of finding the right lodging is the McCall-based **www.inidaho.com.** One call or email will provide rates and references to hotels, cabins, condos, and inns, call 800/844-3246 or

check online. The service also creates packages that combine lodging with outdoor adventures such as rafting and trail rides.

Chain Drive

These chain hotels are in town, or within 10 miles of the city center:

Best Western, Clarion

For more information, including phone numbers and websites, see page 439.

ON THE ROAD: KETCHUM/ SUN VALLEY TO McCALL

Somewhat challenging and almost always picturesque, the trip north will put you in the midst of some tricky riding and the beauty of four scenic routes.

As you get started on the Sawtooth Scenic Byway (aka Highway 75), the often elaborate homes and condos of Ketchum will fill the roadside. Some are delicately and expertly constructed for CEOs and CFOs, while other older shacks look like shop-class projects after the kids got hold of a case of wood glue. The residences gradually taper off and disappear and are replaced by wooden structures known locally as spruce, aspen, fir, ponderosa, and lodgepole pine.

If you plan on camping or spending more time in the region, about eight miles north of Ketchum, just past the Big Wood River, is the headquarters of the **Sawtooth National Recreational Area** (208/727-5013 or 208/727-5000, www.fs.fed.us/r4/sawtooth), a great stop for information. There's a steady incline to the road, and while it's not a dramatic ascent, what it delivers for the next 20 miles is the money shot. As you ride, the breadth and width of land are sensational, with straights stretched taut across the plains. As this rekindles memories of the road from Boise, you'll run into steeper drives that haul you into the heart of the Sawtooth Mountains.

If viewed from space, the road ahead

would appear to be scribbling back and forth like a seismograph needle during an earthquake. Now you get to take full advantage of it. For several miles, your attention will switch from the road to the drops to the curves, and as you navigate these jigsaw ridges and twisted corners, you may be looking at high-elevation pine trees still sugar-coated with snow. Eventually, you'll reach the road to the **Galena Lodge** (Hwy. 75, 24 miles north of Ketchum, 208/726-4010, www.galenalodge.com), an old resort that's managed to survive and become a landmark destination.

Racing another five miles and several hundred feet higher into the atmosphere, you'll tackle six-degree grades to reach the 8,701-foot summit at Galena Pass. Two miles ahead, your reward is reaching one of the nation's finest overlooks. More than a mile below and shooting clear to the northern horizon is Sawtooth Valley. I'd argue that scenes like this have appeared on too many postcards, calendars, and inspirational bookmarks, but the real-life sight of this hallowed ground drives home the absolute beauty we're blessed with in America. Quite a while passed as I contemplated this vision, and even though the miniscule images I collected on camera will never do it justice, I hope they add something to my new calendar of postcard-sized inspirational bookmarks.

After meditating, you and your bike fall down the mountain, rolling swiftly around corners that lead to Smiley Creek, an out-of-place place marked by the **Smiley Creek Lodge** (16546 Hwy. 75, 208/774-3547, www.smileycreeklodge.com), a store, restaurant, and lodge that offers cabins and teepees. Now there's nothing between you and the town of Stanley. Really, *there's nothing*. Around you, it's a Cinemascope view of the world, with nothing for more than 20 miles except flat-open land

stretched across the earth, tacked down by mountains on the horizon. Just south of Stanley, though, on the laserbeam straight near mile marker 174, look for the pullout where you can park and look around. Do this and shut off the bike. With pure silence as a soundtrack, tune into the sound of the wind and birds you can hear, but which may seem lost in the emptiness. Around you is an almost complete circle of the mountains, which pulls your view from side to side to see the sharp peaks of the Sawtooth Range and then to the Salmon River that leaps into view, kept at a distance behind a crisscrossed timber fence.

Only a mile ahead at the junction of Highways 75 and 21 is the town of Stanley. Stanley gets an unusual amount of attention, roughly as much as Chicago, but when you ride in, you may wonder why. It's quite desolate and quite strange, and even though it's as small as a residential subdivision, there are tens of thousands of travelers who join Stanley's 100 residents for backcountry hiking, rock climbing, whitewater rafting, and all the things outdoor adventurers do outdoors. If this style of solitude appeals to you, the **Mountain Village Resort** (junction of Hwys. 75 and 21, 208/774-3661 or 800/843-5475, www.mountainvillage.com) anchors a combination market, service station, motel, and restaurant, all run by the same family. Make use of the gas pumps—there won't be any for quite a while.

By now you've completed the fantastic Sawtooth Scenic Byway, and the next stage takes you west on Highway 21 to put you on the Ponderosa Pine Scenic Route, the habitat of eagles, osprey, heron, elk, deer, bear, and fox. For several miles, though, scenic is just a rumor. Routine views and mile after mile of straight riding through a low-key forest sets the tone as you enter what should be grazing land but where nothing's grazing. As on the ride out of

Ketchum, though, things are happening behind the scenes. You are in the Salmon-Challis National Forest on a plateau that's slowly and surely increasing in elevation. The lack of traffic may trigger the part of your brain that says "ride faster," and if you do, you'll quicken your arrival to Banner Summit, at an elevation of 7,200 feet.

Although there are no open views from the summit, what did draw my attention were the snow drifts that, I learned, had shut the road down only a few days earlier. Keep in mind this was in late May. The weather here can get squirrelly, and had the gates been down to block my path, I'd have been forced to double back to Ketchum. To be safe, contact the **Idaho Transportation Department's Road Reports** (888/432-7623, http://511.idaho.gov) to check on road conditions and closures.

As you ride, on your left is the Sawtooth Wilderness Area and its 217,000 acres of ponderosa pine and steelhead fishing. On the right is the Challis National Forest, gateway to the 2.3-million-acre Frank Church River of No Return Wilderness Area, where there are fewer roads than anywhere else in the Lower 48. Nearly 40 miles out of Stanley, the mountains become steeper and more angular, and the South Fork of the Payette River introduces itself and decides to stay with you for the next 50 miles to Banks. It's a great riding partner, sticking with you when it narrows to a mere stream just a few feet from the road, and still hanging around when it switches to furious rapids in a chasm far below.

The cliffs and low mountains, jackstraw pines, and loneliness of the ride continue for 20 more miles to Lowman, which is a town like Stanley's a town. You've ridden 120 miles now, and although Highway 21 makes a slow curve to the south at Lowman to head back towards Boise, take a quick jog to follow a new part of the route, the Wildlife Canyon Scenic Byway. For quite a stretch, this is a paved pep pill, with 25-mph curves and fast ascents that bring to mind the Scottish Highlands as the lanes reach higher and the canyons plummet deeper. Signs warn you to watch for hikers and falling rocks, and with the pitch of the terrain, you'd expect to see falling hikers. Seriously, what you need to watch for are not huge boulders that'll knock you off of your bike, but the hundreds of small chunks of gravel that'll knock your bike off of you.

Curves start shaking fast and furious here because—as you've probably learned—the roads that always seem right are the ones that follow the free-form flow of a wild river. It's true in the Smoky Mountains, in Arizona, and right here. The Payette River leads through remote country, even more remote than what you challenged south of Stanley.

The land changes again, with green swaths created where the Payette meets another creek, and civilization comes back near Garden Valley, with its churches and sporadic log cabins. After 10 miles of this high-test scenery, the byway spits you out at Highway 55 and the town of Banks. Although you'll be heading north, just a few hundred yards south is the kind of diner that you've frequented from Acadia to San Simeon. The **Banks Country Store and Café** (208/793-2617) has been here since 1915, serving its first guests slightly more than a decade after the invention of Ford's motorcar. With nearly a century of experience, it's learned its lessons well. When you stop for lunch (no gas), you can recall the beauty of the ride so far and enjoy the freedom of feasting on a Big Bubba burger at a table by the river.

Turning true north once again, you've reached the fourth of the day's scenic runs: the Payette River National Scenic Byway. Like Cash's ring of fire, you're going down, down, down, swallowed by

© NANCY HOWELL

When there's not much to look at, you notice things like this: an old hotel with a retro sign.

the gravity of the river in the heart of a gorge. There's not much to look at, but there's so much to see, like the old swinging bridge and the pullout where you can stop and listen to the crushing sounds of the river. The pine forest layered through here creates a nice wooded ride within the Boise National Forest, and the river and a railroad track on the far bank follows you around curves and across bridges and into the backcountry.

This joy continues for miles and slowly gives way to flatlands near Smiths Ferry, where the **Cougar Mountain Lodge** (9738 Hwy. 55, 208/382-4464) is a convenient market and bar that appears out of thin air. Surrounding you is the Round Valley, an area that takes on a Swiss, rather than Scottish, visage—which is important because it gives me the rare opportunity to use the word "visage." The thin river that you recall from earlier is now the wide North Fork of the Payette, seen across the pastures far to your left. The ground is coated with sandbars, driftwood, and rocks. A waterfall appears as you close in on the start of a four-

mile stretch of S-curves and vertical mountain slopes that make you feel somewhat vulnerable until you reach a safe pocket of civilization in Cascade. I'm sure there are things here besides the retro Chief Hotel sign, but that's all I remember about it.

North of town, the swift and sharp road darts through the center of hills and beside a lake. Horses graze and trot on the plains, but they're enjoying the outdoors only half as much as you. The wide-ranging range is split by the Gold Fork River, where you'll see the entirety of Donnelly and its little red schoolhouse before graduating, 13 miles later, to the second-most popular tourist destination in Idaho.

Last call for McCall.

McCALL PRIMER

Like nearly every area in the nation, the Long Valley region of Idaho was populated by Native Americans; in this case, the Shoshone, Bannock, and Nez Perce tribes. Eventually, as Chief Joseph of the Nez Perce was pursued into submission, there was a void to fill. So, in 1891, on the shores of Payette Lake, homesteader Tom McCall arrived in the area that would become his namesake. Thanks to help from more than 30,000 Chinese workers, the Warren and Marshall Mountain Mining District fueled the area's economy, with McCall's Brown Tie and Lumber Company hiring the bulk of the town's citizens. Naturally, the twin industries sparked a loose and open society highlighted by lakeside whorehouses, dance halls, and casinos. Sadly, they are gone now, but their effects lasted for decades. Guns were finally banned from local bars only in the early 1980s.

Relatively recently the arrival of the Tamarack Resort, about 15 miles south, helped elevate McCall's profile—but the relationship wasn't reciprocal and after a rough run the resort declared bankruptcy in 2008. Regardless of Tamarack's fate, McCall remains the second-most popular resort destination in the state, which begs the question: Why is it so small? I cannot tell you.

ON THE ROAD: McCALL

As I hinted, the center of town is about the size of a walnut, and there may not be much to hold your interest—but after a great ride up here, you may be satisfied with just walking around town. Another option is cruising up the west shore of Payette Lake on Warren Wagon Road, en route for a circle tour up and around the lake. Pick up a map at the visitors center, and you'll see that, near the terminus of the loop, a scenic overlook on a peninsula is accessible via Scenic Drive.

If you do walk around town, you'll be surprised to find you can cover the whole thing on foot in a few hours, tops. In the center of town, you're at the south end of the lake. A few blocks west is the **Manchester Ice and Event Centre** (200 E. Lake St., 208/634-3570, www.manchester-icecentre. com), an impressive facility that occupies a good chunk of prime real estate and is open for ice hockey, curling, and skating.

From here on out, the day is yours.

PULL IT OVER: McCALL HIGHLIGHTS
Attractions and Adventures

McCall is within the **Payette National Forest** (208/634-0700), a massive parcel of land that contains more than 2,100 miles of trails, 2,500 miles of roads, 15,000 miles of streams and rivers, and 30 campgrounds. Within the national forest on the eastern and northern shores of the lake is the **Ponderosa State Park** (208/634-2164), the peninsula that leads to the scenic overlook.

The park is on the shores of Payette

Lake, a 5,377-acre playground that's nearly two miles wide, more than six miles long, and as much as 300 feet deep. With that in mind, you'd be missing a lot if you didn't check in with **Cheap Thrills Rentals** (303 N. 3rd/Hwy. 55, 208/634-7472 or 800/831-1025, www.cheapthrillsrentals.com) which rents boats, wave runners, and water tow-toys that'll get you cooled off while heating things up in the middle of the lake.

Shopping

With so little ground to cover, there are just a few places to hit. One, in my opinion, was a pretty cool shop called the **Granite Mountain Nature Gallery** (317 E. Lake St., 208/634-1111), in the small McCall Mall. Dennis DeLaet turned his passion for collecting one-of-a-kind fossils of starfish, trilobytes, and plants into a profession. What's so cool about all of this is the age of his inventory: between 40 million and 500 million years old. He also peddles shadowboxes of butterflies and butterfly wings (made in Mexico—illegal here), as well as displays of some of the creepiest-ass insects I've ever seen, including the cave spider, a grossly overgrown arachnid nearly 10 inches in diameter.

Aside from the standard gift shops in town, **McCall Drug** (1001 2nd St., 208/634-2433) may look suspiciously familiar if you can recall drugstores from the 1950s. This place encompasses everything, including a pharmacy, toy department, a record store, office supplies, a bookshop, a candy counter, and a soda fountain that serves huckleberry milkshakes. Dig the nostalgic Johnson's Toasted Nut display case with a rotating pan.

Blue-Plate Specials

A few miles from town on the west side of the lake is **Lardo's** (600 W. Lake St., 208/634-8191), a big, barnlike restaurant and saloon where locals hang out. The name, by the way, stems from the tale of an overturned wagon that dumped out a shipment of fat here. The entrées, though, are more appetizing, with the menu listing "old-time spaghetti" (whatever that means), as well as assorted configurations of the "famous" Lardo Burger and fries. After dinner, you may find yourself hanging out at the bar.

The Mill (326 N. 3rd St./Hwy. 55, 208/634-7683, www.themillmccallidaho. com) seems to be at the center of McCall's social circle. It's usually the first place locals recommend, although after looking at the prices on the menu, you may want to check on your credit limit. Of course, you'll get what you pay for—a quality dining experience. You enter what feels like an old mine and arrive at a circular fireplace where chairs, some made from old ski lifts, provide a comfortable place to hang out and go to work on a drink. The low-ceiling dining room's down another mine shaft, where you sit down to a big dinner of Western beef: strip steak, ribeye, tenderloin, porterhouse, and prime rib. Connected to the restaurant, Beside the Mill is a sports bar with seven televisions, cocktails, specialty drinks, pool, and darts.

Watering Holes

In addition to hunkering down at the warm bars of Lardo's and The Mill, the local brewpub is the self-explanatory McCall Brewing Company (807 N. 3rd St., 208/634-3309), where cowboys, blue collars, and mountain folks hang out and watch sports to the accompaniment of the pub's eight brewed beers. To temper the effects of the alcohol, the kitchen whips up burgers, sandwiches, prime rib, and sirloin. Dine inside or grab some basic grub on the rooftop beer garden.

Shut-Eye

As in Ketchum, when in McCall consider checking with www.inidaho.com (800/844-3246), which is a free service that can give you rates and references to hotels, cabins, condos, and inns here in McCall and throughout the state.

Motels and Motor Courts

One of the smartest-looking motor courts I've seen is the Brundage Bungalows (1005 W. Lake St., 208/634-2344 or 800/643-2009, www.brundagevacations. com, $79 and up high season). The rooms are across the street from Payette Lake and have that cool old-fashioned knotty pine or log interior. Some have fireplaces and some have a kitchen or kitchenette—but all are really cool. The same folks also rent rooms at the Brundage Inn and Brundage Motel. The larger cabins sleep as many as six.

Inn-dependence

Opened in 1904, the Hotel McCall (1101 N. 3rd St., 208/634-8105 or 866/800-1183, www.hotelmccall.com, $135–150) is close to an inn—it's the largest hotel in town and sits within a few feet of Payette Lake. In addition to a clean, old-fashioned feel in its 34 rooms, there's a library; lounge; and the Epicurean, the in-house restaurant that serves award-winning beef Wellington, chicken and crawfish crepes, rack of lamb, and New York strip.

Chain Drive

These chain hotels are in town, or within 10 miles of the city center:
Holiday Inn, Super 8
For more information, including phone numbers and websites, see page 439.

Resources for Riders

Sawtooth Range Run

Idaho Travel Information
Idaho Outfitters and Guides Association—208/342-1438 or 800/494-3246,
 www.ioga.org
Idaho Parks and Recreation—208/334-4199 or 888/922-6743,
 www.idahoparks.org
Idaho Road Conditions—888/432-7623, http://511.idaho.gov
Idaho Tourism—208/334-2470 or 800/494-3246, www.visitidaho.org
Idaho Vacation and Travel Assistance—800/844-3246, www.inidaho.com

Local and Regional Information
Boise Convention and Visitors Bureau—208/344-7777 or 800/635-5240,
 www.boise.org
McCall Chamber of Commerce—208/634-7631 or 800/260-5130,
 www.mccallchamber.org
Payette National Forest—208/634-0700
Sawtooth National Recreation Area—208/727-5013, www.fs.fed.us/r4/sawtooth
Stanley Ranger Station—208/774-3000
Stanley-Sawtooth Chamber of Commerce—208/774-3411 or 800/878-7950,
 www.stanleycc.org
Sun Valley/Ketchum Visitors Bureau—866/305-0408, www.visitsunvalley.com

Idaho Motorcycle Shops
Adventure Motorsports—2469 Kimberly Rd., Twin Falls, 208/733-5072,
 www.ams-twinfalls.com
Big Twin Cycle Center—2816 S. Orchard St., Boise, 208/336-0367,
 www.bigtwincycles.com
Boise Cycle—9621 Ustick Rd., Boise, 208/375-9431, www.boisecycle.com
Carl's Cycle Sales—5550 W. State St., Boise, 208/853-5550, www.carlscycle.com
High Desert Harley-Davidson—2310 E. Cinema Dr., Meridian, 208/338-5599,
 www.highdeserthd.com
Hinson Power Sports—13924 Hwy. 55, McCall, 208/634-7007,
 www.hinsonpowersports.com
KTM MotoSports—6481 Overland Rd., Boise, 208/375-5660 or 800/203-2353,
 www.ktm-motosports.com
Snake Harley-Davidson—2404 Addison Ave. E., Twin Falls, 208/734-8400 or
 888/788-9809, www.snakehd.com
Woodside Motorsports—4040 Glenbrook Dr., Hailey. 208/788-4005,
 www.woodsidemotorsports.net

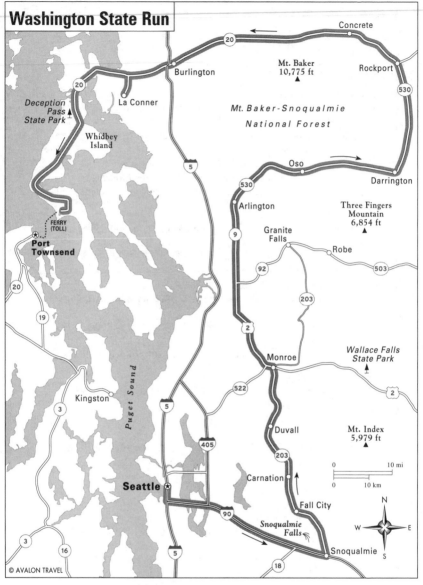

Washington State Run

Concrete

20 ← (arrow)

Mt. Baker
10,775 ft
▲

Rockport

Burlington

530

20

La Conner

Deception
Pass
State Park

*Mt. Baker-Snoqualmie
National Forest*

Whidbey
Island

5

Oso

530

Darrington

→ (arrow)

Arlington

Three Fingers
Mountain
6,854 ft
▲

FERRY
(TOLL)

⊛
**Port
Townsend**

9

Granite
Falls

Robe

503

20

92

19

203

2

3

Kingston

5

Monroe

*Wallace Falls
State Park*

Puget Sound

522

2

405

Duvall

Mt. Index
5,979 ft
▲

203

0   10 mi

0   10 km

Seattle ⊛

Carnation

3

16

90

Fall City

→ (arrow)

*Snoqualmie
Falls* ⟸

N

W   E

S

5

Snoqualmie

© AVALON TRAVEL

18

Route: Seattle to Port Townsend via
Snoqualmie, Fall City, Carnation, Duvall,
Monroe, Arlington, Darrington, Whidbey
Island

Distance: Approximately 245 miles

First Leg: Seattle to La Conner (196 miles)

Second Leg: La Conner to Port Townsend
(46 miles)

Helmet Laws: Washington requires helmets.

Washington State Run

Seattle, Washington to Port Townsend, Washington

Washington is a big state with more than its share of natural beauty. The mountains are snowcapped even in summer, and the bays, islands, and glacier lake are more striking than any postcard you've seen.

There are a few downsides to this tour. There was no perfect starting point, although Seattle's legend is so large I started there. In the countryside, I learned that many back roads are either poorly marked, clogged with logging trucks or, off-season, blocked by snow. But trying to stick with tradition, I created this to get you to some neat towns and onto some back roads.

I gave it my best shot.

Now it's your turn.

ON THE ROAD: SEATTLE TO LA CONNER

From Seattle, you can point your bike in any direction and find great destinations: Mount Rainier, Mount St. Helens, or the Olympic National Forest. The challenge is getting there via a combination of cool roads and decent walking towns. Regardless, there are some options.

When you leave Seattle via I-90 you'll understand why this state is so popular—even the federal highway is scenic. By the time the road has extricated you from city traffic, suddenly you're riding on a wide road that flows past lakes and mountains. About 30 minutes later when you reach the turn off for Snoqualmie at Exit 25, you're entering even more desolate countryside. The country road winds around to reach the speck of a town known as Snoqualmie and its main attraction: Snoqualmie Falls. If you ever watched the cult favorite program *Twin Peaks,* you'll recognize this water feature. At 270 feet, Snoqualmie is 100 feet higher than Niagara and the spray kicks out for hundreds of yards. If you've stowed some food, settle down at a picnic table by the gazebo. If you have time and a healthy heart, hike the half-mile trail that winds down to the riverbanks. Add the fragrance and brilliance of the flowers and the sounds of nature and this is a must-see and a nice marker for the real start of your ride.

When you're ready to move on, the road runs briefly through a dynamite combination of woods, rivers, and hills. Canopy roads give way to country roads, and soon you reach the junction of Route 203 at Fall City. Turn right onto Route 203 and head north on the low and level two-lane road that winds ever so slightly toward the towns of Carnation and Monroe. Carnation is a nice little town, but I was more impressed by what I saw as I was riding out of town—open fields and wide valleys that reminded me of Vermont's classic Route 100.

There's not much to note between here and Duvall aside from noticing that you're actually in the country and on your motorcycle and miles away from the pressure and politics of work. So settle back and roll through Monroe which features a few restaurants and pubs and brings you to U.S. 2, where the ride northwest will have you navigating some dense growth before freeing you into mile after mile of farmland to reach Highway 9 North. This isn't a great road, but the Mountain Loop Road to Darrington usually is not an option, since long sections of gravel (or late snows) often make it impassable. Option B (Highway 9) takes you up to Arlington, where the ride gets nice in a hurry.

At Arlington look for Route 530, which will guide you straight toward Darrington, a short 25 miles away. While there had been some spells of good roads, this is more consistent and what you've been waiting for. Instantly, the road gets better and wider, and you're riding between majestic Washington mountains. The smells are hearty; the grass is plump. Tufts of clouds stuffed between the summits slowly tug at their granite moorings, break free, and drift away. Even in early summer,

slivers of snow from the peaks pierce into the woods below.

Past the town of Oso, pull off alongside the creek, and everything is perfect—with the glaring exception of clear-cut forests that have scarred the mountaintops. Why this makes any sense to anyone is beyond me.

Then comes Darrington where there's a quick jog north on Route 530 that puts you in the Sauk Valley of the Mount Baker-Snoqualmie National Forest. This is a fun road, delivering another boost of good riding as every slow corner leads into a magnificent run through a tunnel of 50-foot straight-as-nails pines. This wonderful road runs beside and over the Sauk River; it's a brilliant forest run. Regardless of the dense urban traffic surrounding nearby Seattle, here there is nothing but woods on both sides and fresh air all around you. At mile marker 60, the river, woods, and mountains converge and the twisty road drops you past meadows, moss, and an almost fluorescent green landscape.

When you reach Highway 20 at Rockport turn left. Around here, natural beauty takes a backseat to small towns like Concrete and larger ones like Sedro Woolley. So you'll enjoy only a decent, not breathtaking, ride. But once you cross beneath I-5, the mood of the road switches instantly from commercial to agricultural.

Farmland stretches from horizon to horizon and when you reach the community of Whitney, you'll see the turnoff south to La Conner. From here it's a quiet country ride down to tulip town.

LA CONNER PRIMER

It was a town built on a trading post and then evolved to focus on the shipping industry, canneries, and farms. Ultimately, La Conner became a retreat for artists and writers. It was a great place for a retreat since it occupied a point of land inaccessible by rail and folks had to make an effort to reach it.

Not much has changed since those early days. Commercial development hit Skagit County, but distance has preserved La Conner. It remains a waterfront community relatively unaffected by the explosion of technology and music a few hours south in Seattle. Victorian-era buildings are still in use more than a hundred years later; pleasure boats are moored in the Swinomish Channel; and countless acres of fields burst into a rainbow each April when the tulips are in bloom.

ON THE ROAD: LA CONNER

At first glance, it doesn't seem as if La Conner would be intriguing or popular. But it is, and there are reasons why.

In addition to presenting springtime's kaleidoscope of tulips, the town has re-invented itself as an artists' colony. There are more than 20 galleries, pubs, antique shops, and restaurants packed into one condensed area, so you can park your bike and easily explore everything on foot. Another advantage of La Conner's is its location. Equidistant from Seattle and Vancouver, nearly every Friday it's one of the most popular destinations for week-enders arriving from both cities.

This is the kind of town I prefer on a ride—not so large you think you've missed something, and not so small you go stir-crazy. La Conner can easily fill an afternoon and give you a place to relax at night. You can ride past the flower fields on the way out of town, but first just park your bike and walk down Morris and 1st Streets. Notice the street window artwork displays, most of which are based on the nature of Washington state, with wood carvings, glassware, and paintings featuring grizzly bears, eagles, wolves, or a combination of the three.

For details on walking tours, trails, and whale-watching excursions, stop by the **Visitor Information Center** (606 Morris St.). Sometimes, though, you may have other priorities. In La Conner, you can just enjoy the town at a leisurely pace, give yourself time to relax, ride across the Rainbow Bridge once or twice, and then just kick back and watch the flowers grow.

PULL IT OVER: LA CONNER HIGHLIGHTS
Shopping

There's a whole grab bag of shops and galleries around town, and you'll probably just park your bike and wander around until you find something that catches your attention. There were a few I found interesting, like the shop owned by Jon Peterson. He's got a limited market, but if you collect antique fishing tackle, pay a visit to **Plug Ugly** (313 E. Morris St., 360/466-1212). Open 11 A.M.–5 P.M. Thursday–Sunday, this place sells duck decoys and marine gear as well.

Good thing La Conner has a well-stocked grocery store like **Pioneer Market** (416 Morris St., 360/466-0188). This way, you can stock up on road food and supplies before you go. Even better, it's open 'til 10 P.M. every night.

Blue-Plate Specials

On the outskirts of town just off Highway 20, **The Farmhouse Restaurant** (13724 La Conner-Whitney Rd., 360/466-4411, www.thefarmhouserestaurant.net) serves old-fashioned big road food for breakfast, lunch, and dinner. Within this cavernous restaurant, you can get platters filled with steak, ham, chicken 'n' dumplings, grilled pork chops, hot turkey sandwiches, pies, and cakes. After dinner here, I puffed up to 438 pounds.

Not only is **La Conner Brewing**

Company (117 S. 1st St., 360/466-1415, ww.insidelaconner.com/LaBrew.html) a warm and intimate family restaurant serving wood-fired pizzas, soups, wings, quesadillas, and salads for lunch and dinner, it also has a great and active bar serving wines, ales, lagers, porters, stouts, pilsners, and dopple bocks. Can you believe it? Dopple bocks!

La Conner Seafood and Prime Rib House (614 1st St., 360/466-4014, www.laconnerseafood.com) is a traditional waterfront hangout open for lunch and dinner. Using only two base ingredients—fish and meat—this restaurant has created about 100 different dishes, including firecracker prawns, shrimp-smothered red snapper, Cajun prime rib, and more. If you have a hearty appetite, sample the buffet.

Watering Holes

If the Brewing Company's too tidy, **La Conner Pub** (702 S. 1st St., 360/466-9932) is the alternative. This blue-collar bar has two pool tables, some old folks, a few young'uns, bottled and tap beers, and a full bar open until at least 1 A.M. Try to ignore the family restaurant in the next room.

Shut-Eye

La Conner has relatively few lodging choices, with most options being inns. For a chain motel or hotel you'd need to travel more than 10 miles out of town. Contact the **La Conner Chamber of Commerce** (360/466-4778 or 888/642-9284, www.laconnerchamber.com) for assistance in finding a room.

Inn-dependence

The **Wild Iris Inn** (117–121 Maple Ave., 360/466-1400, www.wildiris.com, $109–189) has 18 large rooms—12 with hot tubs—and provides a full breakfast. More basic, the **La Conner Country Inn** (107 S. 2nd St., 360/466-3101, www.laconner-lodging.com, $159 and up high season) provides generic, motel-like rooms (some with king beds) and then adds a continental breakfast.

ON THE ROAD: LA CONNER TO PORT TOWNSEND

When you're ready to leave La Conner behind, look for Morris Street, which bypasses Highway 20. This short detour will take you to a patch of beautiful farmland, which, in the spring, will likely provide you with a fantastic photo op of your bike poised before a spectacular field of flowers. Less than a half-mile from town, Morris Street zigzags and turns into Chilberg Road; once you've ridden past Best Road, start looking for Beaver Marsh Road. I suggest this little detour because when you turn left here, you'll be able to see why La Conner's earned the reputation for its proliferation of tulips.

It's a few miles to reach **Roozengaarde** (15867 Beaver Marsh Rd., 360/424-8531), where even in the off-season a small garden of multicolored tulips will give you an idea of what the fields look like when they're in full bloom. It's open 9 A.M.–5 P.M. Monday–Saturday. Admission is free.

When you leave, follow Beaver Marsh Road north and watch for McLean Road and make a right onto it. If you need some last-minute supplies, you can stop in at the old-fashioned **Evergreen Grocery Store** (16016 McLean Rd., 360/424-4377). After stocking up, head out a few blocks more to Avon-Allen Road where you hang a left to wind up on CR 536 en route to Highway 20—which is the last number you'll have to think about for the next several days.

With the Washington breeze in your face, you'll pass sporadic mountains and a few commercial enterprises before turning left to follow Highway 20 west toward Whidbey Island. The island's just about a dozen miles away and marks the entrance to the Olympic Peninsula. Near Sharpes Corner there'll be a sharp corner as Highway 20 drops south where, almost immediately, images from rides of motorcycling past will flash into mind since this stretch looks comparable to the Berkshires, Yosemite, and the Blue Ridge Parkway.

On your right, you'll see a glacier lake that looks frigid even at the height of summer. Several miles ahead near mile marker 43, watch for Pass Lake and a pullout where, if you're riding in a group, you can grab a wonderful shot that uses the lake and mountain as a backdrop.

This level of scenery continues for several miles and it all brings to mind the look of a 1940s *Field and Stream* magazine. Ahead, the Straits of Juan De Fuca can be seen to the right, but one of the most impressive sights of the trip arrives as you round the corner and approach Deception Pass. At the spot where the Canoe Pass and Deception Pass bridges span a huge gorge, the vista is breathtaking. At the bottom, blue-green water floods back to the sea and the shores are packed with massive trees washed ashore like twigs. It's all a larger-than-life scene and there's another convenient pullout if you want to park your bike and grab a shot with the bridge in the background.

When you ride across the span it seems more thrilling than running the Golden Gate. At the opposite side of the 976-foot bridge are restrooms, a parking area, and a trail that you should walk down even if you have a heart condition, gout, and a wooden leg. The views around each bend in the trail are fantastic, and the pine forest scents are reminiscent of a Christmas tree farm.

Less than a mile later, consider pulling into the 4,128-acre **Deception Pass State Park** (360/675-2417 or 360/675-7277, www.parks.wa.gov, free). Built primarily by the Civilian Conservation Corps in the 1930s, this marine and camping park boasts 30 miles of hiking trails, 19 miles of saltwater shoreline, three freshwater lakes, 246 campsites, freshwater swimming, fishing, and canoeing. The old-growth forest is sprinkled with cedar, spruce, yew, apple, and cherry trees, as well as fields of foxglove, lupines, rhododendron, and roses. Due to the temperate climate here, wildlife thrives and there's a strong chance you'll spy bald eagles in flight.

Now I hate to have to break this to you, but following this spectacular introduction to Whidbey Island, the scenery fizzles. From here to Port Townsend, the landscape is pockmarked by random development, so even after you get your mojo going on a good run, it withers out when you encounter trailer parks and hideous commercial sprawl.

From south of Coupeville, all you need to do is watch for the turnoff to the **Port Townsend Ferry** (206/464-6400). For about $5, you and your machine can take a 30-minute sea cruise to one of the nicest towns on the peninsula.

PORT TOWNSEND PRIMER

Before Port Townsend was infected with quaintness, it was a real town—a real get-drunk-in-the-bar-get-laid-upstairs kind of town. A century ago, Port Townsend was home to 40 saloons and 17 brothels (the most prosperous of which was adjacent to City Hall). A writer visiting town remarked that the "stench of whiskey permeates Port Townsend to a depth of nine feet"—although no one knows how he measured it. I lost the scent at four feet.

It was an affluent town that

accommodated a thriving maritime port and the consulates of 17 countries. As in other resurrected cities, a period of decline was eased by the arrival of hippies in the 1970s. From the luxury of their smoke-filled VW buses, artists and writers emerged and fueled a creative spark that sustains itself today. The hippies grew up and learned the rules of business and restored old homes and then rich Californians came in and bought the homes and turned them into inns. And the town was turned around.

One unusual quirk you may notice is that citizens seem to take obsessive pride in the movie *An Officer and a Gentleman,* which was filmed around here in the early 1980s. If a cardinal from Port Townsend were ever elected pope, you can bet the new pontiff would recall Richard Gere's character and adopt the name Pope Zack Mayo.

Aside from that devotion to a long-ago film, what you'll see today is a tight-knit community that combines new money, young hippies, established businesses, and trendy shops in Woodstock-era ambience.

Far out.

ON THE ROAD: PORT TOWNSEND

Like much of Washington, riding in the vicinity of Port Townsend poses a dilemma. If you check the map, **Olympic National Park** (360/565-3130, www.nps.gov/olym) seems so close, and a ferry trip to Victoria, British Columbia, looks so tempting. In the end, I chose to hang out in town for several reasons. A trip to Victoria makes for a very long day—the ferry trip lasts several hours, and reaching the boat takes about as long. Olympic National Park didn't pan out either. After riding halfway there via Highway 20 and U.S. 101, I realized that the road was

beating me into submission with its slow-moving traffic and a disturbing lack of scenery. Port Townsend calmed me down and kept me entertained. I was content. But if your schedule affords you more time, give them both a try.

Port Townsend is a great walking town, and the people are friendly. If you hang around town, definitely stop at **Bergstrom's Antique and Classic Autos** (809 Washington St., 360/385-5061). Based on the building's exterior, you wouldn't expect to find much, but inside you'll usually find a collection of old motorcycles, scooters, and classic cars as well as garage memorabilia, hubcaps, lighters, and technical manuals representing a fleet of antique vehicles.

A short ride away lies **Fort Worden State Park** (360/344-4431 or 360/344-4400, www.parks.wa.gov/fortworden), which is where they filmed...*An Officer and a Gentleman!* The 19th century base is closed now, which makes it look like Fort Knox after Goldfinger's ladies sprayed the soldiers with knockout gas. There are still parade grounds, officers' quarters, gun batteries, an artillery museum, a natural history museum, a theater, and a performing arts center, as well as nice shoreline beside the frigid waters of the straits. If you're traveling with a large group, you can reserve lodging space in some of the seriously cool renovated barracks and officers' quarters.

With a decent map, you'll likely find some nearby back roads to satisfy your desire to explore, and you shouldn't miss the stretch of restaurants and stores in the section of town known as uptown Port Townsend, which is higher up the bluff. Aside from that, just appreciate the broad waters of the Straits of Juan De Fuca and the magnificence of Port Townsend Bay.

PULL IT OVER: PORT TOWNSEND HIGHLIGHTS
Attractions and Adventures

If you don't mind devoting some touring time to a movie, you may as well do it at the restored **Rose Theatre** (235 Taylor St., 360/385-1089, www.rosetheatre.com). Buy some licorice and Necco wafers at the counter, and then sit back in the classic theatre for the moving picture show.

A center for maritime education, the **Wooden Boat Foundation** (Cupola House, Port Hudson, 360/385-3628, www. woodenboat.org) offers several courses—each of which will get you on the water. You can learn to sail a large wooden ship, sail a small wooden boat, or rent a rowboat and explore on your own. If you appreciate fine craftsmanship and tales of the sea, hang out at the chandlery and talk boats.

You cannot avoid fly-fishing in the Northwest. Do not even try. The folks at **Port Townsend Angler** (940 Water St., 360/379-3763, www.ptangler.com) have all the gear and arrange guides for fishing in streams and on the Sound. They claim this as the best spot for wild steelhead fishing in the Lower 48. But it's an expensive hobby: A full day of fly-fishing for two will cost around $250 and up, and then you have to add the gear. If you can swing it, it'll be a memorable wilderness experience. Too much? A McFish sandwich costs two bucks.

Shopping

Joe Euro runs **Wine Seller** (940 Water St., 360/385-7673 or 888/629-9463, www.ptwineseller.com), the oldest wine shop on the peninsula. Open around 10:30 A.M.–6 P.M. daily, the small shop features an array of wines (including generic "cheap white" and "cheap red" wines), plus cigars, gourmet cheese, smoked salmon, and free back issues of *Wine Spectator*.

Blue-Plate Specials

Silverwater Cafe (237 Taylor St., 360/385-6448, www.silverwatercafe.com), serving lunch and dinner, features creative spins on fresh seafood, meat, and vegetarian entrées that are often prepared with ingredients purchased from local farms and anglers. The meals are upscale, but the clientele casual—an unusual mix, but it works here. In its quiet corner location, you can dine in peace.

Also open for lunch and dinner, **Waterfront Pizza** (951 Water St., 360/385-6629) sells takeout by the slice downstairs, and the upstairs dining room serves pizza that keeps the locals coming back.

Watering Holes

Waterstreet Brewing and Ale House (639 Water St., 360/379-6438, www.waterstreetbrewing.com) sits on the site of the old Town Tavern and features an 1800s bar, three pool tables, two fireplaces, and a dozen beers on tap (six of them brewed right here).

With a broad deck that overlooks Puget Sound, **Sirens** (823 Water St., 360/379-1100, www.sirensbar.com) is a real great spot to work on a pitcher of beer. There are 11 micros, hot pizza, live music, and a Wednesday open mic night that turns this into a hipster's hootenanny with local musicians playing jazz, blues, or rock to a packed bar full of locals.

More coffeehouse than bar, **Upstage** (923 Washington St., 360/385-2216, www.upstagerestaurant.com) pours wine and draft microbrews. An eclectic entertainment calendar changes nightly, featuring everything from open mic to blues to swing.

Shut-Eye

Surprisingly remote, Port Townsend does not have any chain hotels. It does, however, have plenty of inns. Check with the **Port Townsend Visitors Center** (360/385-2722 or 888/365-6978, www.ptguide.com) for the full slate, and consider this list just the tip of the iceberg.

Inn-dependence

The **Quimper Inn** (1306 Franklin St., 360/385-1060 or 800/557-1060, www.quimperinn.com, $98–165 year-round), a large 1888 home, rests on a hill overlooking Port Townsend. It's elegant without the clutter. Kick back on the second-story terrace or relax in the living room and talk to innkeeper Ron Ramage about his Porsche collection and rebuilt Triumphs.

The **Palace Hotel** (1004 Water St., 360/385-0773 or 800/962-0741, www.palacehotelpt.com, $59–109) is a nicely restored 1889 hotel on the town's main drag. Large rooms and suites (ask for a private bath) sport an Old West look.

Resources for Riders

Washington State Run

Washington Travel Information
Washington State Ferries—206/464-6400, www.wsdot.wa.gov/ferries
Washington State Parks—360/902-8844 or 888/226-7688, www.parks.wa.gov
Washington State Road Conditions—800/695-7623, www.wsdot.wa.gov/traffic
Washington State Tourism—800/544-1800, www.experiencewa.com

Local and Regional Information
La Conner Chamber of Commerce—360/466-4778 or 888/642-9284,
    www.laconnerchamber.com
Mt. Baker-Snoqualmie National Forest—425/783-6000 or 800/627-0062,
    www.fs.fed.us/r6/mbs
Olympic Peninsula—360/437-0120, www.olympicpeninsula.org
Port Townsend Visitors Center—360/385-2722 or 888/365-6978,
    www.ptguide.com
Whidbey Island Information—www.visitwhidbey.com

Washington Motorcycle Shops
Bellevue Kawasaki—14004 N.E. 20th St., Bellevue, 425/641-5040,
    www.bellevuekawasakiwa.com
Downtown Harley-Davidson—3715 E. Valley Rd., 425/988-2100 or
    800/474-4647, www.dowtownhd.com
Eastside Harley Davidson—14408 NE 20th St., Bellevue, 425/747-0322,
    www.eastsideharley.com
Eastside Motorsports—13029 NE 20th St., Bellevue, 425/882-4300,
    www.eastsidemotosports.com
Everett Powersports—215 SW Everett Mall Way, Everett, 423/437-4545,
    www.everettpowersports.com
I-90 Motorsports—200 NE Gilman Blvd., Issaquah, 425/391-4490,
    www.I-90motorsports.com
Lake City Powersports—12048 Lake City Way NE, Seattle, 206/364-1372,
    www.lakecitypowersports.com
Port Townsend Honda—3059 Sims Way W., Port Townsend, 360/385-4559
Renton Motorcycle Co.—3701 E. Valley Rd., Renton, 425/226-4320 or
    800/460-6451, www.rmcmotorsports.com
Seattle Cycle Center—10201 Aurora Ave. N., Seattle, 206/524-0044,
    www.seattlecycle.com
Skagit Harley-Davidson—1337 Goldenrod Rd., Burlington, 360/757-1515,
    www.skagitharley.com
South Sound BMW—3605 20th St. E., Fife, 253/922-2004,
    www.southsoundbmw.com

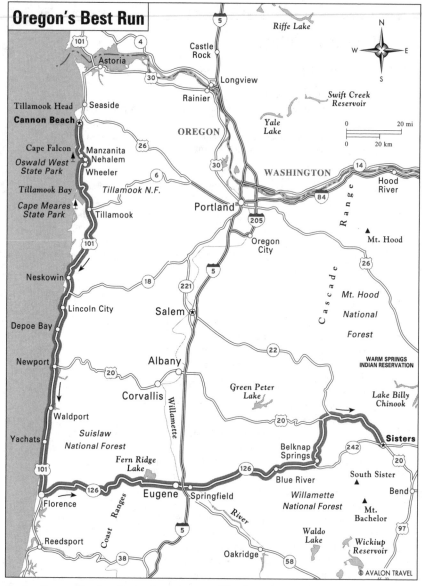

Oregon's Best Run

Route: Cannon Beach to Sisters via Manzanita, Tillamook, Lincoln City, Newport, Florence, Eugene, Vida, Santiam Pass

Distance: Approximately 325 miles

First Leg: Cannon Beach to Florence (160 miles)

Second Leg: Florence to Sisters (165 miles)

Helmet Laws: Oregon requires helmets.

Oregon's Best Run
Cannon Beach, Oregon to Sisters, Oregon

Incredible coastal scenery preserved a century ago by a visionary governor creates a ceaselessly awe-inspiring tour. Begin in a beachside community that could serve as the model for future coastal towns, and then enjoy the finest 160-mile stretch of two-lane you may ever ride. Stop in a character-filled old town enveloped within a larger town lacking the same; hang around for an adrenaline-pumping, mind-blowing dune buggy attack on the sand; then head east where the forests, falls, and mountains herald your arrival in a new Old West village.

CANNON BEACH PRIMER

There are several dozen communities along Oregon's coast, and whether it was a river, a ravine, or a forest, each needed something to root the town as it grew. In Cannon Beach, it was a rock. Granted, it is not your ordinary rock. First of all, Haystack Rock really looks like a stack of hay. Second, it happens to be 235 feet tall, which makes it the third-largest coastal monolith in the world.

In addition to this icon, which you may have already seen on countless postcards and calendars, consider the origin of the town's name. In 1846, the U.S. Navy schooner *Shark* was pulling out of the Columbia River into the Pacific Ocean. After waves tore the ship to shreds, a section of the deck with a cannon and capstan on it floated down the coast and came to rest on a stretch of shore that would become known as Cannon Beach. Thank god it wasn't the poop deck.

Also ranking high in the town's history is the Lewis and Clark Expedition. Cannon Beach was the farthest south the explorers traveled, venturing here for an overnight in 1806 when they heard they could carve some blubber off a dead whale. And that's it. A shipwreck, a rock, and a rotting whale anchored the town long enough for it to evolve into a natural preserve that some folks consider a mini-Carmel. It has art galleries, bistros, bookstores, kites, sandcastle contests, tide pools, hiking trails, natural sanctuaries,

Oregon's coastline is visually dynamic; and nowhere more than at Cannon Beach. At 235 feet tall, Haystack Rock is the third largest coastal monolith in the world.

© NANCY HOWELL

and a migration of tufted puffins that flock to Haystack Rock each year to lay their eggs.

That's been enough to see Cannon Beach through its sesquicentennial—and it should keep you satisfied for a few days.

ON THE ROAD: CANNON BEACH

Cannon Beach is a place where you go to avoid having to go to your room. Each minute you're here, outdoors is where you want to be. To get outdoors, Hemlock is the street you'll need to know, since it's the main coastal route that leads to and through the center of town. With it, you can ride north to Ecola State Park or south to the beach, or stop in the middle and see the town. And it's worth seeing. After I get done cleaning out my gutters, I'm going to get started on building a beachside community of 1,600 people, and I'll use Cannon Beach as a blueprint. It's not so large as to be impersonal, or too small to be dull.

Another bonus is that no building here is more than three stories tall, a far different architectural principle than you'll find on coastlines in Florida and California. In Oregon, the ocean is for everyone.

That said, the best way to see the best of Cannon Beach is to check out the attractions and adventures that follow.

PULL IT OVER: CANNON BEACH HIGHLIGHTS
Attractions and Adventures

When I asked at the visitors center how someone would spend a perfect couple of days in Cannon Beach, I was sure they were wrong telling me to just head to **Ecola State Park** (503/436-2844 or 800/551-6949) and see the tide pools at Haystack Rock. Then I went.

From the center of town, the road north connects with a fork that leads right onto Ecola Park Road and into the woods. Accustomed to Florida scrub pines, I had never seen anything like what was ahead:

an old-growth rainforest where the trees were a near-luminescent green, which, when mixed with the fog and mist and the moisture, seemed strangely prehistoric. Riding this land of the lost in the midst of a stalled storm when the midday sun was hidden by rolling clouds was an exciting and, to be honest, eerie experience. The warped road passes massive trees and a forest bed of ferns before it reaches the ranger station, where you'll pay $3 for the day. What you'll see in a few minutes is worth that and far more.

From the parking area, a walkway leads to a lookout point, where you'll savor a vision that will last a lifetime, especially if you've never had the privilege of seeing the Pacific Ocean. The ocean is massive and awe-inspiring, with views seeming to last for billions of miles. To the south, several miles of arched shoreline are swept by an infinite series of waves. To the west, a column of curving rocks slips into the ocean like a dragon's tail. To the north, an inlet

What's so special about riding in Oregon? Take a look at this road and you'll know.

© NANCY HOWELL

dips into shore and springs out again, directing your view to the Tillamook Rock Lighthouse, perched on a rock 12 miles offshore. Construction of the lighthouse began in 1879 and took two years and the lives of a few workers before it went into service. Decommissioned in 1957, in 1980 it became—can you believe this—*a columbarium.* Twice a year, cremated ashes are flown out and deposited for an eternity at sea.

Sublime and weird things like this aren't all Ecola gives you. From the parking area, the Tillamook Head trail is an eight-mile walk to Seaside, while the Clatsop Loop Trail is a short, two-mile hiking path that connects Ecola Point to Indian Beach, following a path blazed by members of the Lewis and Clark Expedition. Elk graze in the meadows, eagles and falcons catch the currents, and in winter and summer, more than 20,000 gray whales pass by in the midst of a 12,000-mile migration. The spiritual effect of it all is ceaseless, magical, and a miracle. You'll be pleased to hear that you can look forward to 160 miles more of this on your journey south.

Descending from the hill, ride south again to the second stop: **Haystack Rock.** There are parking areas along Hemlock Street, although if you're staying at a beachside lodge, you'll just walk along the shore to reach it. What will you see when you're there? Tufted puffins, possibly. The chunky, pelagic seabird lives on land only when it's time to nest, hanging out here from the end of April to late July. Bring binoculars to spot the squat black body, white face, bright orange bill, and tufts of feathers above the eyes of the bird sailors call the "sea parrot." Sharing a piece of the rock with the puffins are pigeons, guillemots, cormorants, and seagulls, whose leisure time is occasionally interrupted by eagles that swoop to the ground, isolate a gull—like fighter pilots peel off bombers—and take it down.

It's unusual to admit there's pleasure in looking at a rock, but there is, although you may need the assistance of a ranger to understand what you're looking at. During the summer, volunteers are on the beach to host **Haystack Rock Awareness Programs** (503/436-1581) and explain the intricate ecosystem that supports dozens of creatures living in tide pools left by the receding ocean. Look closely, and in the shallows you'll see limpets, barnacles, starfish, hermit crabs, sea sculpins, and anemones. Be careful where you walk, and leave the creatures where they are.

If you have a hard time leaving the beach, plan to come back later. The oldest business in town is **Sea Ranch Resort** (415 Fir St., 503/436-2815, www.searanchrv.com). Here since 1927, it rents horses for daytime group rides between mid-May and Labor Day that follow the Ecola Creek to Chapman Point and south to Haystack Rock. When there's a low tide, moonlight rides are offered.

Shopping

Remember this while you visit Oregon: There's no sales tax. Keep this in mind when you buy food or souvenirs or a new bike. While you're in Cannon Beach, your best investment is walking around Hemlock Street. Granted, this delivers all the things a tourist town should (taffy kitchens, T-shirt shops), but there are also places like **Mariner Market** (139 N. Hemlock, 503/436-2442). Sidewalk benches are reserved for Democrats or Republicans, and aisles are inventoried with beer, deli meals, tide charts, videos, groceries, readymade and ready-to-be-prepared foods, and everything you'd need for a beachside cookout.

As you'll discover, the history and images of Oregon's coast, roads, and lighthouses are fascinating, and you can find good regional research materials at the library or at the **Cannon Beach Book Company** (130 N. Hemlock St., 503/436-1301, www.cannonbeachbooks.com).

Cannon Beach has earned a reputation as an artists' colony and, judging by many of the galleries here, I'd tend to agree. Not knowing your taste in art, I'd suggest you pay a pre-ride virtual visit to see some of the extraordinary paintings, ceramics, oils, acrylics, and woodcarvings online via the **Cannon Beach Gallery Group** (www.cb-gallerygroup.com).

When it's bleak and drizzly and Oregon gray, I doubt that anyone's shouting "Surf's up!" But think how cool it'd be to tell your friends that you did…Whether you're a Gidget or a Grommet, you can shred a tube on a tri-skeg stick rented from **Cannon Beach Surf** (1088 S. Hemlock St., 503/436-0475, www.cannonbeach-surf.com). It offers lessons and rents wetsuits, skim boards, and boogie boards.

Blue-Plate Specials

Even though Cannon Beach features several great restaurants, think about dining at an open-air café: the beach. Bonfires are allowed, and at the **Mariner Market** (139 N. Hemlock, 503/436-2442) you can stock up on hot dogs, marshmallows, corn, and everything else you'd need for a cookout. So live it up at your personal makeshift oceanside restaurant. You don't even need a permit—all you need are matches. Just keep your fire at least 25 feet from wooden seawalls, beach grass, or driftwood, and don't wait for the tide to extinguish the flames when you're done. Do it yourself.

If the weather craps out and you're locked in your room, **Fultano's Pizza**

(220 N. Hemlock, 503/436-9717, www. cbfultanos.com) delivers traditional and gourmet pizza hot—steam lines drawn on the boxes attest to this. Its dining room, too, is an option.

The Lumberyard (264 3rd St., 503/436-0285, www.thelumberyardgrill. com) is a big Pacific Northwest–style restaurant where locals gather around the bar to draw on about a few dozen beers (some brewed here) served in bottles or on tap in pint glasses. Diners settle into natural wood booths and dine on rotisserie-grilled chicken, pork loin, pot pies, turkey meat loaf, barbecue pork, oven-roasted pizzas, and plank salmon made in the open kitchen. It's also a great place to drop in for a nightcap. The Lumberyard is big and clean and neat.

Fuel up for the day at the **Pig 'N Pancake** (223 S. Hemlock St., 503/436-2851, www.pignpancake.com). There are 35 varieties of breakfast here, which is something Einstein hypothesized in 1905. The kind of diner you look for when touring,

it also offers homemade soups, chowders, and desserts, including some made from family recipes.

Watering Holes

For a small town, Cannon Beach has more than enough places to relax and map out future rides or take a break at the end of the day. Again, you'll find homemade micros at **The Lumberyard** (264 3rd St., 503/436-0285, www.thelumberyardgrill. com) or two other local hangouts that have a good vibe. The grandpappy of them all is **Bill's Tavern and Brewhouse** (188 Hemlock St., 503/436-2202), which opened as a café in 1923. The local gathering spot is in the heart of town, where you and your buddies can grab a booth and feast on hamburgers, fried oyster burgers, albacore, cod, and seafood stew. Along with beers made right here, there are about a dozen beers on tap in the warm, inviting bar.

The **Warren House** (3301 S. Hemlock St., 503/436-1130) is a smokehouse that serves burgers and steaks, which you can

© NANCY HOWELL

Crossing through—not over—one of the magnificent mountains of Oregon.

wash down with beers brewed here. The beer garden has an ocean view.

Shut-Eye

Although there are no chain hotels in Cannon Beach, there's something better: old-fashioned motor courts.

Motels and Motor Courts

Like most things, Cannon Beach does lodging well as well—although rates can double from winter to summer, so get ready to dig deep. There are condos, inns, and places like the triplex of **The Waves, Argonauta Inn,** and **White Heron Lodge** (503/436-2205 or 800/822-2468, www. thewavesmotel.com, $119 and up high season). Under one owner, they occupy several sites and present a combination of choices that range from motel rooms to suites to home-style accommodations that have kitchens, fireplaces, and hot tubs. Rates can double for the homes and they may require a two-night minimum.

Back in the old days, folks would take motoring trips down the coast and find a place like **McBee Motel Cottages** (888 S. Hemlock St., 503/436-1392 or 800/238-4107, www.mcbeecottages.com). Even through the McBee opened in 1941, it's been gussied up a bit since which is why basic rooms that go for $65 off-season sell for as much as $140 in high season. On the plus side, they're just steps from the beach, they're cozy, some units feature fireplaces and kitchens, and all have old-fashioned touches to complete the effect.

Chain Drive

Chain hotels are eight miles north of Cannon Beach in Seaside:

Best Western, Comfort Inn, Holiday Inn

For more information, including phone numbers and websites, see page 439.

ON THE ROAD: CANNON BEACH TO FLORENCE

…And we have a winner! Of all the rides I've taken since 1974, this day's tour down Oregon's coast really did it for me. With no frame of reference to go on, nearly every turn delivered more than I thought was possible. I owe this to Oswald West and U.S. 101. When planning most rides, I'd research alternate byways and look for other routes just in case the road fizzled out. This was different. The combination of Oregon's coast and U.S. 101 delivered mile after mile. In hindsight, though, I did err. I thought the first five miles were the finest "first five" I'd ever seen. It turned out that the first 20 miles (followed by the remaining 140) were truly great. Here's how your day will unfold.

Hemlock Street rolls out of Cannon

© NANCY HOWELL

Riding in the Pacific Northwest comes with one near certainty: perpetual rains. If you can deal with that, you'll savor the times when the weather clears and you're given exquisite country riding.

Oswald West

It's a shame that politicians these days have little interest or desire in creating something for the people. For inspiration, they should ride the Oregon Coast and think of Oswald West, described by one writer as "by all odds the most brilliant governor Oregon ever had." I learned about West at the magnificent lookout point south of Cannon Beach, where a plaque offered a glimpse of his life and a reminder of what public service makes possible. He was described as a charismatic and intelligent man, with "a keen sense of humanity and an open mind." Tired of corruption in government but undaunted by a lack of funds and influential friends, he rode on horseback to campaign in small communities across the state. He ran to make a difference, and he won.

As you ride, you're experiencing one of the greatest achievements of "Governor Oz," as another plaque here attests: "If sight of sand and sky and sea has given respite from your daily cares, then pause to thank Oswald West, former governor of Oregon, 1911–1915. By his foresight, nearly 400 miles of the ocean shore were set aside for public use, from the Columbia River on the north to the California border on the south."

All hail the great and powerful Oz.

Beach and slides into U.S. 101 about three miles south of town. Immediately the friendly scent of the pines joins you on a journey that adds close-up views of ravines, rainforests, and the Pacific on a winding stretch of two-lane traffic. The road has an old-fashioned feel to it—diners and motor courts would be right at home here. Although they were absent, what did appear before me was a magnificent tunnel punched directly through the center of a mountain; the kind Wile E. Coyote would have painted on the side of a hill. It doesn't seem real, but it is, and it is overwhelming.

Even at 45 mph, you won't ever feel rushed, because here and for the rest of the ride, there are frequent pullouts giving speeding cars the option to pass you. In these initial 10 miles, you set a pattern for the entire trek: You ride beside the ocean until the road weaves to the east, and that's when you enter the rainforests where the trees and trunks and ferns are the same iridescent green that you found at Ecola. Past Necarney Creek, you'll enter the **Oswald West State Park,** and a few miles farther south, you can roll off to a pullout to see one of America's most marvelous overlooks. I'd like to say this panorama is picture-perfect, but a thousand pictures wouldn't even begin to convey how wonderful this is.

As a flatland Floridian, I've always had a sea-level view of the sea. Now I was hundreds of feet above a shoreline that opened up majestic views of the coast to the north and south, the endless waves flying past rocks and onto the curving beach. I stayed awhile to enjoy the free show, gave a silent thank-you, and then resumed the ride south. At 1,661 feet, upcoming Neahkahnie Mountain is one of the highest points along the coast and as the road's seven-degree grade wraps around its base, the pleasure of the path increases as you ride. Things change slightly when you pass Manzanita and then enter Nehalem, where you'll wonder when things changed. Suddenly you're aware it's not the coast any more; you're in a valley surrounded by forests, rivers, and farmlands. If magically changing views like these don't do it for you, just stop your bike right now and take a bus home.

You'll cross the Nehalem River to enter Wheeler (pop. 400), where there's a visitors center and some antiques shops and not much more than that. Afterward, as you ride to and through Rockaway Beach and Farview, the scenery suffers slightly, but you stick with it because you have no choice, and your gut tells you that soon you'll clear it to the coast. Personally, I admire the tenacity of residents in these small towns who stuck with it through financial hardships and are building communities to be proud of.

One subtle yet intriguing feature that'll hold your attention is that each of these ordinary towns has a certain presence and personality. Towns like Garibaldi where, in the middle of extraordinary emptiness, is a monumental smokestack still standing long after the lumber mill it served vanished into history. The smokestack still towers over estuaries that rise and fall with the tide, so during the day you'll ride beside a sea of mud as you cruise into the town of Tillamook, the "Land of Cheese, Trees, and Ocean Breeze." Since this was yet another place I knew nothing about, my gut instinct was to race through it and stay on my self-imposed schedule. But at the town's visitors center I was instructed to go next door to **Tillamook Cheese** (4175 U.S. 101, 503/815-1300 or 800/542-7290, www.tillamookcheese.com). Even though I really didn't want to see a cheese factory, I went, and I was honestly glad I did.

Inside, a self-guided tour leads to an observation platform where you watch a platoon of Oompa-Loompa-ish cheesemakers at belts and slicers and rollers turning single 40-pound blocks of cheese into forty symmetrically sliced one-pound units. Across the hall, workers are whipping up and packaging ice cream. I watched all of this for far longer than my doctor would have advised before heading downstairs to a restaurant for a grilled cheese sandwich and double scoop of some of the freshest, most pure ice cream I've ever tasted. A weirdly intriguing stop, I look back and see this was a reminder to lose my self-inflicted schedule and allow the day to reveal itself.

From Tillamook, there are three ways to go. The first is staying on U.S. 101 and continuing the ride south. Or you can take the Three Capes Loop Road detour to the coast, which will present a bag full of scenery while adding only an additional 10 miles before reconnecting with U.S. 101 further south. The third is mixing up the two with half a loop that'll take you to the coast and the Cape Meares Lighthouse and back to Tillamook. That was my choice.

Turning right on 3rd Avenue, which is also the Netarts Highway, I rode west where, I'm reluctant to say, the aroma of cow crap was a pleasant reminder I was back in the country. Dairy country, no less—hence all the cheese. A few miles down, Bay Ocean Road shoots off a subtle fork to the right, over a river, and into a road slipped into place beside Tillamook Bay. The fact I was now riding north on my journey south was at first disconcerting and then comforting, a fresh reminder that motorcycling is designed for the journey and not the destination.

At low tide the view of moist, soot-colored mud lasted for several miles until I reached a junction at Crab Harbor, where the road led to the left and a sign warned "rough roads for the next five miles." How true. The rough gravel road on this Alpine pitch managed to rattle my shocks and shock my rattles before a short, narrow bridge opened up a view of the coast and compelled me to ride on toward the lighthouse.

The opening to **Cape Meares State Park** (503/842-3182) is on your right, and the road to the summit, with its pitch, gravel, and twists, creates a hat trick of good riding. From the parking area, it's a short walk to Oregon's shortest lighthouse. Built in 1890, the 38-foot beacon sits 232 feet above the waves. The other attraction here, the Octopus Tree, is a multi-trunked Sitka spruce that's an equal distance through the woods in the opposite direction. Better than both, I thought, were the overlooks above inlets carved into the cliffs over the course of millions of years. Waves continued to flood in with the tides and small waterfalls poured over the ledges and added to the sea.

Back on the loop toward Netarts with the Pacific Ocean still in sight, the high-pitched roads were again perfect for riding. Netarts itself offered a gas station and then it was back to the two-lane forest run that brought back memories from a few hours earlier. At a junction immediately south of town, you can turn left and follow the Netarts Highway back to Tillamook. If you take the right fork, you'll whip into Whiskey Creek Road, which zips past Cape Lookout and eventually Cape Kiwanda before merging again with U.S. 101 just past Pacific City. If I'm lucky enough to be reincarnated as myself, I'll take that route next time around.

I made the loop back to Tillamook to catch the **Tillamook Air Museum** (6030 Hangar Rd., 503/842-1130, www. tillamookair.com). Even a blind person couldn't miss this place. On the east side of U.S. 101, this is the largest clear-span wooden structure in the world: a massive hangar built in 1943 to house U.S. Navy blimps searching for Japanese submarines. Nearly 200 feet tall and 1,072 feet long, it encloses enough space for six football fields. Today, it's a museum housing more than 30 historic aircraft, including a great assortment of World War II warbirds. Nearly as large is **Munson Falls,** which you'll find about six miles south. Tucked out of sight nearly two miles off the main road, it's worth the effort to reach it. The 319-foot waterfall springs out of a mossy cliff and is the highest in the coast range. Amazingly, everything you've seen today has been within 50 miles of Cannon Beach, and there's another hundred ahead.

Even though you're on Oregon's main coastal highway, there is little clutter to distract you from enjoying the tour, only mountains and pines spiked on the hills and rhododendrons that may be in bloom. You'll pass homes of people you'll never meet on a road you'll never forget, and you'll witness scenes that are new to you but destined to become part of this memorable experience. You'll go deep in the woods now, then south of Neskowin, where the ocean appears again, completely undisturbed—it's perhaps the longest stretch of coastline I've seen that hadn't been destroyed by development. When you enter Siuslaw National Forest, the scenery isn't thrown at you. Instead, the well-placed pullouts, small towns, farms, valleys, hills, beaches, and bays appear for you at perfectly timed intervals.

Civilization returns in Lincoln City, where you cross the 45th parallel. Back at home, tell your friends you rode across the midway point between the equator and the North Pole, and they should be impressed. Past the city, there's not much privacy until Depoe Bay, after which you'll be dipping into the woods and the water.

Pullouts sewn onto the shores of the ocean allow you to park your bike and spy lighthouses, such as Oregon's tallest, a 93-foot-tall model flashing out at Yaquina Head, followed four miles south by the Yaquina Bay lighthouse by the bridge. As you ride through Alsea and Waldport and contemplate the end of the line in Florence, you'll reflect on the ride and may agree that it's been most excellent. For a grand finale, it's about to get even better.

After Yachats (ya-HOTS) comes one of the coolest views I've ever seen: the road spinning around a curve, shooting up an incline, and hugging the side of a cliff into extreme elevations. It spun and snapped and popped across the land, and that good riding lasted for a dozen miles and beyond, all the way past the **Heceta Head**

Lighthouse (541/997-3851 or 866/547-3696, www.hecetalighthouse.com), the most photographed on the Pacific Coast. Built in 1894, this light sends out a glow that can be seen 20 miles away. If you can swing it, a bed-and-breakfast is in the old lighthouse keeper's cottage.

I couldn't swing it, so I pressed on another mile to **Sea Lion Caves** (U.S. 101, 541/547-3111, www.sealioncaves.com, $11). This is the way old tourist attractions were created: Someone would find a natural phenomenon, buy the land, and sell tickets. That's what happened in 1932, 40 years after William Cox discovered sea lions in the world's largest sea cave. From the gift shop, walk down to an overlook, where, a hundred yards below, approximately a hundred Steller sea lions are sunbathing on a flat rock, their chorus of yawps and aarps sounding like a frat house after a kegger. From here, an elevator within the mountain lowers you 180 feet into a massive hollow where sea lions

© NANCY HOWELL

The satisfaction of completing my favorite one-day ride ever—from Cannon Beach to Florence—is seen in my expression at Heceta Head.

The Siuslaw Bridge as seen from the Old Town district of Florence.

surge in with the sea and doze atop the basalt rock formations. The sound of the water adds to the impressive sight of the two-acre, 125-foot-tall domed cavern.

After passing the seals, the road swoops down from the cliffs to the dunes for the final 10 miles into Florence. A most memorable ride has come to a close.

FLORENCE PRIMER

Several hundred years before I got the idea to explore Oregon's coastline, the Spanish were doing it from the sea, creating maps as they cruised along the coast. English explorer Captain James Cook, who was used to driving on the left side of the road, headed over in 1778 to make some maps that he could read. Watching this from shore were the Siuslaws who, like nearly every tribe in America, were destined to be displaced when white settlers showed up.

By 1900, 300 residents were making a living in this remote community either by logging, fishing, or working in a sawmill, saloon, newspaper, cannery, or general store. One enterprising resident who was making a killing by opening a ferry service across the Siuslaw River was likely quite furious when the picturesque Siuslaw River Bridge opened in 1936.

By accident or design, the original village—today called Old Town—was preserved on a bend in the river and has been revitalized with shops, restaurants, galleries, and gift shops. Without this important asset, odds are you'd see Florence as just another generic village. But it's here, as is another vital attraction, the **Oregon Dunes National Recreation Area.** There are 38,000 acres of sand mountains here, and if that doesn't sound like much...then just you wait.

ON THE ROAD: FLORENCE

The previous day's ride may still have you buzzing, and it's tempting to consider zipping 11 miles north back up the coast around Heceta Head or, perhaps riding south along the Pacific for an enjoyable thousand-mile run down to San Diego.

If you just want to experience Florence, though, you can fill up the better part of the day with just two activities: shopping and sand dunes. The former is pedestrian but satisfying, a low-key, laid-back approach that won't take much out of you. The latter is one of the most outlandish adventures you'll ever experience, kind of like plunging a syringe of adrenaline into the middle of your heart.

Have a nice day.

PULL IT OVER: FLORENCE HIGHLIGHTS
Attractions and Adventures

I've had the good fortune to do a lot of cool stuff (motorcycling across America included), but rarely, if ever, have I done anything quite as cool as heading to the Oregon Dunes National Recreational Area and hitting the sands with Darin of **Sand Dunes Frontier** (83690 U.S. 101, 541/997-3544, www.sanddunesfrontier. com). I thought a dune buggy ride would include going to a clambake with Frankie and Annette, and I also thought I'd drive the dune buggy myself. Thankfully, I've never been so wrong.

Arriving early (and off-season), I was the only passenger and I was quickly in the passenger seat and neatly trussed up in a net of harnesses. Darin rode slowly through the woods, and since I thought *that* was the ride, I was creating excuses to bail. But when we reached the edge of the forest, I saw Oregon's most unusual landscape. It wasn't simply a patch of shoreline between us and the ocean, it was immense towers of sand as high as 300 feet that stretched about 40 miles north and south. He gunned the engine and the huge tires bit into the sand and sent us on a 50-degree ascent to the peak of a dune that I knew would propel us into the unknown or on a collision course with another driver racing up the opposite side. My death grip threatened to crush the metal cage around me, but at the peak, in a split second he triggered a small handbrake that slapped the tail parallel with the seam at the top of the dune. We raced on, the dune buggy slipping over the side but clinging like a knife in the sand. For the next 30 minutes, I was driven like a maniac to peaks and then down dangerous hills and, at one monumental moment, around the 60-degree basin of a Daytona 500-style bowl called the NASCAR berm. This is where I am certain I achieved a higher level of consciousness.

Perhaps a large part of my fascination was being here when no one else was on the dunes, which made the experience seem like we were driving on the moon. In peak season, as many as 3,000 dune buggies and ATVs clog the sands each weekend, so try to get there early, invest $22, tie yourself down, and experience the motorized equivalent of a heart paddle.

A sedative about three miles south of the bridge is **Jessie M. Honeyman Memorial State Park** (800/452-5687). Created by the CCC in the 1930s, this 500-acre park has three freshwater lakes, with swimming and canoeing on 85-acre Lake Woahink. There are picnic pavilions, guided kayak tours, and a campground with 191 tent sites available for around $25 a night.

Shopping

As you ride into town, a buffer zone of new development surrounds the real and unique shopping village of Old Town which is tucked beneath the bridge on the banks of the Siuslaw River; after you park your bike you can see several blocks of stores, gadget and gift shops, and restaurants. Part of the town's appeal is its layout, with numerous old buildings recycled for today. The drawback is that after a national magazine ranked Florence as one of the best places to retire, too many merchants hoping to capitalize on the momentum rushed in and ended up selling an identical inventory of... *junque.*

One exception is the **Sticks & Stone Gallery** (1368 Bay St., 541/997-3196, www.sticksandstonesgallery.com). If you've avoided wildlife art galleries because you've seen too many paintings of mustangs galloping across the plain, this place offers a cure. There are twigs made into lamps, metallic trout leaping in a metal stream, schools of wooden salmon, driftwood eagles, and tigers painted on bird's-eye maple, as well as fish, frogs, and pheasants etched, carved, and painted in a variety of mediums.

Blue-Plate Specials

Oregon often amazed me, and it did it yet again with the **Waterfront Depot** (1252 Bay St., 541/902-9100). Roughly the size of a small home, the old train depot is now the setting for an Irish bar (which explains the Peter O'Toole/Richard Burton poster), as well as a fantastic restaurant based on an international tapas menu. For less than 10 bucks, you can mix and match entrées like crab-encrusted halibut, jambalaya pasta, and wild coho salmon. For a great experience, wait for a window seat overlooking the river.

Basic but popular meals are served at **Mo's** (1436 Bay St., 541/997-2185). Right on the river, the interior has the look and feel of a Howard Johnson's, circa 1950. That's a compliment, too, since it's packed with regular folks ordering seafood basics like clam strips, popcorn scallops, albacore tuna melts, and chowders. In addition to

adding beer to the batter, Mo's also pours it into frosted mugs.

If you're craving home-away-from-home cooking, ride about two miles south of the bridge to **Morgan's Country Kitchen** (85020 U.S. 101, 541/997-6991, www.morganscountrykitchen.com). Serving down-home cooking since the 1950s, Morgan's is still at it with breakfast and lunch dishes like biscuits and sausage gravy, pecan waffles, roast beef, and chicken-fried steak.

In the heart of Old Town is the popular **Firehouse Restaurant** (1263 Bay St., 541/997-2800). Ribs, steaks, sirloin, "Code 3" burgers, salmon, halibut, sandwiches, and pasta cover most of the bases—and sidewalk dining and a lounge will take you the rest of the way home.

Watering Holes

The local favorite, **Beachcomber Tavern** (1355 Bay St., 541/997-6357) seriously exemplifies its name. A tavern since 1936, this really looks and feels like one of those places where people who like to drink, drink. It helps the cause by opening at 9 A.M., serving pub food and dishes like deep-fried prawns and Cajun-grilled oysters, and running a full bar.

Shut-Eye
Motels and Motor Courts

There's abundant quality lodging in Florence, and three great old-fashioned choices—two of which are within easy walking distance of Old Town. The **River House Motel** (1202 Bay St., 541/997-3933 or 888/824-2454, www.riverhouseflorence.com, $99 and up off-river, $125 on-river) is the best-placed place of all—less than a hundred yards from Old Town. Rooms have two queens or a king, and some have terraces to watch the drawbridge and fishing boats.

South of the Siuslaw is the **Ocean Breeze Motel** (85165 U.S. 101, 541/997-2642 or 888/226-9611, www.oceanbreezemotel.com, $80 and up high season). Although its appearance harkens back several decades, it seems quite modern, thanks to its meticulously clean rooms, each with a queen or two.

A block from the river and a short walk to Old Town, the **Lighthouse Inn** (155 U.S. 101, 541/997-3221, www.lighthouseinnflorence.com, $84 and up) has that cool old knotty pine look working for it. Queen and king beds are offered, some rooms include sleeper sofas to add another couple to the mix, and family suites sleep five.

The **Old Town Inn** (170 U.S. 101, 541/997-7131 or 800/570-8738, www.old-town-inn.com, $79–99) is a large complex a few blocks north of Old Town. Rooms are clean and basic, and include free Wi-Fi, microwave, fridge, coffee, cable, and local calls.

Chain Drive

These chain hotels are in town, or within 10 miles of the city center:

Best Western, Comfort Inn

For more information, including phone numbers and websites, see page 439.

ON THE ROAD: FLORENCE TO SISTERS

It's hard to leave Florence behind, because this also means saying so long to the Pacific Ocean and U.S. 101. On the north end of town, Highway 126 shoots straight toward the heart of Oregon, and as the waves wave goodbye, you ride into an area of river and grass. A railroad trestle spans the river and heads into the woods for God knows where, and when that passes you look around and see a living life-insurance calendar of rivers, hills, forests, and wide-open landscape.

Within 15 miles, you'll pass the Siuslaw River and reach the low hills and a canopy road that could pass for the Berkshires of Massachusetts. Ahead there's nothing but green and the road and a tunnel to draw you farther into the ride. There's something cool about tunnels like this, and it's not just the temperature—it's the echo that makes your bike sound 10 times more powerful and muscular. Two lanes lead into more hills, and when you reach Mapleton, the road splits off to the right for a stretch of dips and nice riding. After the Siuslaw National Forest eases up, there are 40 miles of wide country riding ahead. Wide lanes and slow traffic announce the metropolis of Eugene and, as you can guess, the town doesn't offer a speck of the enjoyment you've received from the casual cruise. It's sluggish riding from about 10 miles before Eugene to about six miles past it. So now's a good time to enjoy intermission....

And we're back. I hope you enjoyed your visit to Eugene, and after you pass Springfield and enter the McKenzie State River Recreation Area, you can start to look forward to 100 miles of overwhelming Oregon riding. With the return of two-lane roads and the absence of city traffic, you'll notice a distinct change in mood that improves when you enter pristine country accented by Christmas tree farms and groves of hazelnut trees (locals call them "filberts"). There are also abundant signs of rural living, namely comparably small homes that occupy comparably vast acres of land.

The McKenzie Valley is really great and the road, of course, is just as nice. Meandering and lazy, it's bordered with ivy and wildflowers as it follows the course of the McKenzie River all the way to a neat dam that powers the town of Leaburg. Just past the town, an old wooden bridge named after racing legend Barney Oldfield crosses the Leaburg canal, but I don't know why. Vignettes like this—finding a nice little river and a walking path on its banks—are still nice discoveries.

A short distance east, the same flowing creek leads to one of the nicest covered bridges I've seen. Lane County's **Goodpasture Bridge** was built in 1938 and is one of the most photographed covered bridges in Oregon. It seems to convey the spiritual vibe of this ride with its Gothic-style louvered windows and master carpentry. From here, you may notice an unusual sensation as you ride and I think it must be that the road mimics the river, curving sharply where there are rapids and smoothing out when the river rolls out of view. All you have to do to enjoy it is hold the throttle and drift into a glide track. It's effortless riding mile after mile.

You ride past Nimrod, Finn Rock, and Blue River, and the road never fails. Before Belknap Springs, watch for **Harbick's Country Store** (541/822-3575), a well-stocked service station, restaurant, and motel that's worth a stop since there's precious little ahead in terms of conveniences. A few miles east, if weather permits, follow Highway 242—the McKenzie Pass Scenic Byway—for the final 38 miles to Sisters. Aside from summer months, though, the road is usually impassable due to heavy snows that clog the Cascades. If you can take it here, you'll be able to cross the McKenzie Pass that runs through one of the state's most recent lava flows. How recent? About 3,000 years ago. At the top of the 5,325-foot pass, the Dee Wright Memorial is a CCC-built lava rock observatory with trails to follow, and Proxy Falls is an ethereal wonder; a pair of horsetail falls just a short walk from the road.

What's more likely, however, is that between November and June you'll be sticking with the road ahead which is not a bad consolation prize. Not at all. It's a scenic arc north through the Willamette National Forest and guiding the way are enormous Douglas firs that stand like an honor guard as you roll down the blacktop. It's a magnificent experience to be heralded into the woods this way. About a dozen miles up the road is the entrance for Koosah Falls, and a half-mile later is the entrance and parking area for Sahalie Falls. Park at Sahalie and get ready for a magnificent spectacle. Just down a short wooded path you'll hear thundering waters that draw your eyes ahead to the Sahalie (Chinook for "heaven"), and when you reach the falls, you'll marvel at a torrent of water rocketing over a short cliff. It all seems more incredible and more gorgeous when combined with the mossy green rocks and trees surrounding you in the canyon. Take the time to walk the loop trail beside the frothing, tumbling whitewater cascades and you'll discover Koosah ("sky") Falls about a 15-minute nature walk away. There are few things you'll see in your life that rival finding a nice waterfall while on a forest run like this.

Back on the road, you may want to make another stop a mile or so on at Clear Lake, the headwaters of the McKenzie River. The "lake born of fire" got its start 3,000 years ago when lava from Sand Mountain reached the river and backed up water to form the lake. The water's cold as hell, and you can't swim in it, but canoeing, fishing and boating are available, and the absence of motorized boats helps keep things clear. How clear? Look into the water, and about 100 feet below the surface you'll see the remainder of tall trees submerged when the lake was formed.

Three miles north, Highway 126 laces itself up with U.S. 20 before the tandem road hooks to the right and then starts falling southeast. Highway 126 attacks the Cascades, taking you up and over Santiam Pass at 4,817 feet. The higher elevations inject clean air into your lungs and carburetors and deliver soothing views of firs and mountain hemlock, lodgepole and ponderosa pines as you ride into the high desert. It's soothing because, unlike on most mountain roads, nothing is dangerous or drastic. In fact, it's quite quiet and peaceful and calming as you snatch glimpses of the horizon across the Mount Washington Wilderness, with snowcapped mountains and miles of forests.

Take it easy, and when the road falls away to the south, you can look forward to spending the night with Sisters.

SISTERS PRIMER

I wouldn't call Sisters's theme Wild West. Maybe more like Mild West. I'll explain why in a minute. First, though, I can tell you its history includes visits by Indians and fur traders and soldiers who established soon-to-be-abandoned Camp Polk in the 1860s. In the 1880s, Sisters became a supply center for sheep shipments passing through, and after that, lumber took the lead until the 1960s, when the last mill closed.

That's when some folks in Sisters decided to create a new look for the town. But it wasn't the city council that requested the facelift. It was the owners of the Black Butte Ranch, a new local resort. It offered merchants a generous sum if they'd slap up an Old West facade over their storefronts, and everyone looked at the languishing town and agreed to go along with the scheme. The plan was implemented and in the early 1970s, the city passed a resolution dictating that future construction would exhibit an 1880s frontier theme. And whatd'ya know…it all works. When you mosey around town, you aren't wondering why Sisters looks the way it does because *it just does*. As to why it's named this way, look to the three mountain peaks visible from town. From north to south, the "sisters" are Faith, Hope, and Charity.

Footnote: After I came home, I recalled the energy of the town. The citizens there generated such an unusual and active vibe, I assumed there were at least 20,000 residents making it all work. On the contrary. Fewer than 2,000 people are driving Sisters's mojo. And they're doing it all for you.

You go, Sisters.

ON THE ROAD: SISTERS

Although there's an all right ride out of town that will take you north to Mount Hood, in comparison to what you've already experienced, much of it's fairly routine. If you eventually have to ride north, however, within the 145-mile ride to Mount Hood and up to the Columbia River Gorge, you'll ride through the Deschutes and Mount Hood national forests to reach the communities of Hood River and The Dalles. Of this, I'd estimate that around 65 percent of it is decent riding in hills, on promontories, in canyons, and by rivers.

Since Sisters is the end of the line for this chapter, however, I'll suggest a day wandering around downtown. It may not take a full day, but from cowboy boots to fine art, the stores here can occupy a good part of the day. If you get done early, the city of Bend is only 20 miles south.

PULL IT OVER: SISTERS HIGHLIGHTS
Attractions and Adventures

In addition to the annual **Sisters Rodeo** (541/549-0121 or 800/827-7522, www.sistersrodeo.com), held in June, there's a wad of adrenaline pumping in the great outdoors. **Destination Wilderness** (541/585-2904 or 800/423-8868, www.

wildernesstrips.com) in nearby Bend plans adventures on the McKenzie, Clackamas, Umpqua, and Salmon rivers—and all over Oregon, for that matter. The streams here are filled with rainfall and melting snow from above 10,000 feet, so the waters are crystal-clear. You'll run Class II and III rapids on trips that last from half a day ($75) to two full days ($295), and include all your gear, food, and transportation. If you'd rather fish, Destination Wilderness can gear you up for fly- and spin-casting excursions. Avoid the rapids and angle for trout with the **Flyfisher's Place** (151 W. Main Ave., 541/549-3474, www.flyfishersplace. com), who can take you out on the McKenzie and Metolius rivers. This is a hugely popular sport, but the biggest catch of the day may be the day rate: from around $330 to $440 per person. Riders love to get away and **Wanderlust Tours** (143 SW Cleveland Ave., Bend, 541/389-8359 or 800/962-2862, www.wanderlusttours.com) helps you scratch that itch with a full slate of tours that take participants off trail, away from other people, and into the heart of the Cascade Mountains and Deschutes National Forest. Choices include canoe, kayak, hiking, caving, volcano exploration, GPS eco-challenge, and starlight float trips.

Shopping

Wandering around Sisters is an all right experience since, in addition to the standard retinue of ordinary inventory, there's some pretty cool stuff as well. As always, you'll be hard-pressed to find junk small enough to put on your bike, but if there's something you really dig, consider shipping it home. Some of the big stuff's at **Sisters Log Furniture** (140 W. Cascade Ave., 541/549-8191, www.sisterslogfurniture.com), where chainsaw-carved cowboys and bears and big wooden beds are sold alongside Western-themed metal and horseshoe art, paintings, rugs, and jewelry.

McKenzie Creek Trading Company (290 W. Cascade Ave., 541/549-8424, www.mckenziecreeksisters.com) carries the kind of outdoor wear you'd expect to find in the Pacific Northwest: hiking boots, Minnetonka moccasins, cowboy hats and belts. Women riders get a kick out of **Outwest Designs** (103 B Hood St., 541/549-1140, www.outwestdesigns.com) which carries crystals, trade beads, stone, glass, eclectic beads, copper, silver, and turquoise for creating your own jewelry designs.

Compared to California, New York and Florida, Oregon is such an overlooked state that it's good to find a place like the **Oregon Store** (271 W. Cascade Ave., 541/549-6700, www.theoregonstore.com) that sell goods that have style and exude a sense of place. Across Oregon craftspeople, artists, and manufacturers are creating the merchandise you'll find here—cool stuff like knives, saddle blankets, myrtlewood bowls, Oregon jams, syrups, stoneground flour, Native American robes, and Immigrant American T-shirts.

When an artist really makes it, that's really something. One who's done very well, thank you, is Lorenzo Ghiglieri. You may not know his works, but look who has: Ronald Reagan, Pope John Paul II, Tiger Woods, Al Gore, Mikhail Gorbachev, and Queen Elizabeth; they've all received his commissioned pieces. Like Remington, he's a sketch artist, oil painter, and sculptor who has a fascination with the West, as seen in pieces that focus on buffalo, cattle, elk, horses, explorers, bears, and Indians. His impressive statue *Victorious Flight* is an eagle carrying an American flag, and it would make a great gift to me. You may run across Lorenzo working at the **Lorenzo Ghiglieri Gallery** (411 E. Cascade Ave., 541/549-8751 or 877/551-4441, www.art-lorenzo.com).

For mostly everything else, there's

Sisters Drug Co. (211 Cascade Ave., 541/549-6221). The corner drugstore carries household goods, specialty foods, wine, gifts, and T-shirts, and has a pharmacy.

Blue-Plate Specials

When in Sisters, you must order up some big food at a big restaurant. **The Gallery** (171 W. Cascade Ave., 541/549-2631), a favorite with locals and tourists, serves old-fashioned family-style food like pork chops and meat loaf and soups, soft rolls, homemade pies, and cinnamon rolls. If you're riding early, it opens at 6 A.M. It's friendly and filling. A full bar and lounge are in back.

Another place with an Old West theme is **Bronco Billy's Ranch Grill & Saloon** (190 E. Cascade Ave., 541/549-7427, www.broncobillysranchgrill.com). It specializes in ribs, but it's not a rib joint—there are burgers, sirloin, tacos, pork bowls, chicken, and more. Housed in an old hotel, former rooms upstairs can be reserved for private dining. As at The Gallery, there's a jumping bar here.

Watering Holes

As I've mentioned, you may do best by looking for nightlife at The Gallery or Bronco Billy's Saloon. They're already a hit with locals, and you're bound to fit right in at these joints where the clientele seem pretty loose and friendly. Popular with local riding clubs is **Scoot's Bar and Grill** (175 Larch St., 541/549-1588, www.scootsbarandgrill.com), which encourages their dedication by adding a motorcycle theme. In addition to several dozen varieties of brews (draft, bottled, and microbrews) and half-pound burgers, Scoot's has live entertainment, pool tables, flat-screen TVs, an open patio, and afternoon happy hour.

Shut-Eye
Motels and Motor Courts

One of the friendliest motor courts I've run across is the **Sisters Motor Lodge** (511 W. Cascade Ave., 541/549-2551, www.sistersmotorlodge.com, $89 and up for rooms, $195 for extended-stay suites). Built in 1942, it's become a national historic landmark and each room has handmade quilts, cable TV, and fully stocked kitchenettes. The in-town location is conveniently close, yet perfectly secluded.

Inn-dependence

One of the best built and well-run B&Bs I've stayed at is the **Blue Spruce Bed & Breakfast** (444 S. Spruce St., 541/549-9644 or 888/328-9644, www.bluespruce-bandb.com, $169–189). About four blocks from downtown, the house was built as an inn, so rooms are large, with fireplaces. The beds are soft, the bathrooms have hot tubs and towel warmers, the den is massive, and your breakfast is as large as a water tower.

Chain Drive

These chain hotels are in town, or within 10 miles of the city center:
Best Western
For more information, including phone numbers and websites, see page 439.

Saddle Up

If the artificial Old West theme of the town seems real to you, then you may be inclined to wander over to **Long Hollow Ranch** (71105 Holmes Rd., 541/923-1901 or 877/923-1901, www.lhranch.com). This is a real cattle ranch where you'll work with wranglers, explore the ranch on horseback, dine on home-cooked meals, fish in the reservoirs, practice roping, or hang around the yard pitching horseshoes—just as they did in the Wild West.

Resources for Riders

Oregon's Best Run

Oregon Travel Information
Central Oregon Visitors Association—800/800-8334,
   www.visitcentraloregon.com
Oregon Dunes NRA—877/444-6777, www.recreation.gov
Oregon Parks and Recreation—800/551-6949, www.oregon.gov/OPRD
Oregon Road Conditions—800/977-6368, www.tripcheck.com
Willamette Forest Headquarters—541/225-6300

Local and Regional Information
Cannon Beach Chamber of Commerce—503/436-2623, www.cannonbeach.org
Cannon Beach Weather Information—503/861-2722
Florence Chamber of Commerce—541/997-3128 or 800/524-4864,
   www.florencechamber.com or www.oldtownflorence.com
Lane County (Eugene)—541/484-5307 or 800/547-5445,
   www.travellanecounty.org
Sisters Chamber of Commerce—541/549-0251 or 866/549-0252,
   www.sisterschamber.com

Oregon Motorcycle Shops
Bandit Motorsports—195-C Cap Ct., Eugene, 541/343-7433,
   www.bandit-motorsports.com
Bend Euro Moto—1064 SE Paiute Way St., Bend, 541/617-9155,
   www.bendeuromoto.com
BMW of Western Oregon—2891 W. 11th Ave., Eugene, 541/338-0269,
   www.bmwor.com
Cascade Harley Davidson—63028 Sherman Rd., Bend, 541/330-6228,
   www.cascadeharley.com
Cascade Motorsports—20445 Cady Way, Bend, 541/389-0088,
   www.cascademotorsports.net
Cascade Motorcycle—4065 W. 11th Ave., Eugene, 541/344-5177,
   www.cascademotorcycle.tripod.com
Cycle Sports—555 River Rd., Eugene, 541/607-9000, www.cyclesports.net
Doyle's Harley-Davidson—86441 College View Rd., Eugene, 541/747-1033,
   www.doyleshd.com
Florence Yamaha—2130 Hwy. 126, Florence, 541/997-1157
Motorcycles Of Bend—63056 Lower Meadow Dr., Bend, 541/617-0444,
   www.motorcyclesofbend.com
The Moto Shop—61445 S. Hwy. 97, Bend, 541/383-0828

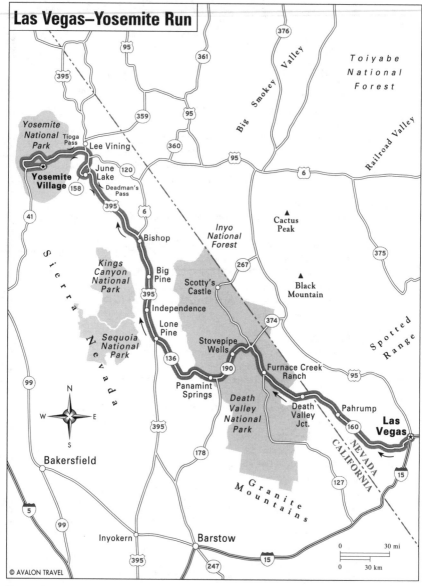

Route: Las Vegas to Yosemite via Death Valley, Lone Pine, Bishop, Lee Vining

Distance: Approximately 640 miles

First Leg: Las Vegas, Nevada to Lone Pine, California (240 miles)

Second Leg: Lone Pine to Yosemite, California (200 miles)

Optional Third Leg: Yosemite to Lake Tahoe, California (200 miles)

Helmet Laws: Both Nevada and California require helmets.

Las Vegas–Yosemite Run

Las Vegas, Nevada to Yosemite National Park, California

Of all the runs profiled in this book, my gut feeling is that this is the most exciting, frightening, grueling, exhilarating, fascinating, inspiring, and humbling.

From the materialistic and surreal city of Las Vegas, the mood descends to the stark landscape of Death Valley. What follows are arguably the grandest vistas in America at Yosemite and, if you desire, the clear and clean waters of Lake Tahoe. It's a ride that'll test your mettle and reward your efforts.

LAS VEGAS PRIMER

Las Vegas is a town steeped in excess. From multibillion-dollar themed hotels to less-than-discreet prostitution, Las Vegas is where the circus came to town—and never left.

A little more than half a century ago, it was a way station in the middle of nowhere—until the Mafia saw an untapped oasis of cash. You know the rest: Sammy and Frankie and Dean begat Elvis and Engelbert and Wayne. When the stakes were raised, old hotels were blown up and corporations muscled in to build casinos disguised as hotels. In the late 1990s, when the local convention bureau needed to fill more beds, it decided to position Las Vegas as a great family getaway, but no one was buying it. That's when they retooled the party line and admitted it's a place where you can do all the kinds of things that you would never dare tell your wife, husband, children, employer, co-workers, priest, minister, rabbi, carwash attendant, caddy, convenience store clerk, produce manager, or a complete stranger.

So just accept that Vegas is busy, pricy, noisy, borderline profane, and no place for kids (unless you're teaching them about escort services and loan sharking). But if you're an adult who's prepared for a juiced-up, high-tension, all-night bacchanal, however, it can be the fuel for a long and winding journey.

Just don't blow your gas money.

ON THE ROAD: LAS VEGAS

It's impossible to condense and define Las Vegas, especially for motorcycle travelers.

Gettin' Hitched

Tying the knot in Vegas is either a romantic or pathetic blend of hormones, love, and kitsch. More than 70 wedding chapels (including ones themed for *Star Trek* and Graceland) operate in town, and if you want to get married (please, not to someone you just met through an escort service), the only requirement is a $50 license (exact change required), which you can get at the seven-day-a-week **Clark County Courthouse** (200 S. 3rd St., 702/671-0600).

You can ride your bike anywhere in the country and be content with yourself, your thoughts, and a few possessions stuffed in the saddlebags. Seconds after you ride into Vegas, you may be swept up in an orgy of greed and desire. Pray that the feeling vanishes when you leave town or you'll be the most miserable sumbitch on the road.

This concludes the warning. From here, it's a pleasant surprise to find that most employees are hospitable and the roads easy to navigate. The city is laid out roughly like a grid, with Las Vegas Boulevard as the main north–south artery. A section of this street is "The Strip," where you're most likely to spend your time and money. The magnet for tourists and conventioneers, it is where old hotels are destroyed and then rebuilt, phoenixlike, as billion-dollar resorts.

The farther north you go, the less impressed you'll be unless you're searching for vintage pre-resort Vegas. Fremont Street has been retooled as an enclosed pedestrian mall where chain-smoking seniors on gambling junkets try to score mediocre food at cheap buffets. I'm not a gambler, and it struck me that too many marathon slot-machine players press buttons in a sad choreography, looking like research monkeys awaiting the dispensation of banana-flavored pellets.

The stakes are raised as you ride south and pass the Sahara, Stratosphere, Flamingo, Aladdin, and Circus Circus casinos and when you reach the core of the Strip, you'll enter a universe of world-class hotels and high rollers. But whether you've reached Fremont Street or a deluxe resort, there seems to be a certain sameness to every venue: the ringing bells of an electronic arcade, the absence of windows and clocks, and VIP status applied based on your value as a loser.

Clearly I have mixed feelings about the town. The futile quest for quick fortune bugs me, but overall I'm impressed by the sheer magnitude of Las Vegas and its legend. Because, frankly, it's not all gambling. This is a playground for adults where you can feel the same kind of freedom you experience on your bike. Experience it for yourself.

PULL IT OVER: LAS VEGAS HIGHLIGHTS
Casinos

Larger and louder than life, the most impressive casinos are found along the Strip. Each is a community unto itself, with a distinct theme, headlining acts, guestrooms, nightclubs, restaurants, pools, and abundant services. Rates vary wildly—often daily—especially if there's a major convention in town, and suites naturally cost more. Rather than listing rates, then, I recommend you call in advance or check online for discounted prices on

© NANCY HOWELL

It takes a little while to clear Las Vegas, but along the way the congestion clears and the road travels through beautiful country… all the way to Hoover Dam.

Vegas rooms. Sunday through Thursday is a better time to look for discounts (unless a convention's in town). Even if you don't stay at a hotel, ask about the hotel's headliner—a very big draw here.

Luxor (3900 Las Vegas Blvd., 702/262-4000 or 800/288-1000 for room reservations, or 800/557-7428 for show reservations, www.luxor.com) sports an Egyptian theme and a pyramid out front. You'll see its spotlight at night.

Clean up NYC, multiply it by 10, and you have **New York New York** (3790 Las Vegas Blvd., 702/740-6969 or 800/693-6763 for room and show reservations, www.nynyhotelcasino.com).

A subtle Hollywood theme sifts through the **MGM Grand** (3799 Las Vegas Blvd., 702/891-1111 or 800/929-1111 for room and show reservations, www.mgmgrand.com), just a very large hotel with big shows and special events.

The Mirage (3400 Las Vegas Blvd., 702/791-7111 or 800/627-6667 for room reservations, or 800/963-9634 for show reservations, www.mirage.com) features the Cirque du Soleil extravaganza *LOVE*, based on the music of the Beatles. I love the Beatles, couldn't stand the show.

At **Treasure Island** (3300 Las Vegas Blvd., 702/894-7111 or 800/944-7444 for room reservations, or 800/392-1999 for show reservations, www.treasureisland.com) the big show is Cirque du Soleil's *Mystère.*

An old favorite that attracts families and fans of old Vegas, **Circus Circus** (2880 Las Vegas Blvd., 702/734-0410 or 800/634-3450 for room reservations, www.circuscircus.com) has a Big Top theme. Not real clean, not exactly dirty, it's an option.

Theoretically, there's a French Riviera theme at the **Monte Carlo** (3770 Las Vegas Blvd., 702/730-7777 or 800/311-8999 for room and show reservations, www.monte-carlo.com), which is home to popular Vegas headliner Lance Burton, Master Magician!

Caesars Palace (3570 Las Vegas Blvd., 702/731-7110 or 634-6661 for room reservations, or 800/634-6001 for show reservations, www.caesars.com) is one of the city's traditional favorites and the place where you can enjoy high-caliber performers like Elton John, Celine Dion, and Bette Midler. I'd give the waitresses here my vote for best costumes.

Excalibur (3850 Las Vegas Blvd., 702/597-7777 or 800/937-7777 for room reservations, or 800/933-1334 for show reservations, www.excaliburcasino.com) has a medieval castle theme. Why not?

A mixture of the tropical, mystical, and upscale chic, **Mandalay Bay** (3950 Las Vegas Blvd., 702/632-7777 or 877/632-7000 for room and show reservations, www.mandalaybay.com) features a House of Blues, stage shows, and off-off-off-Broadway productions.

The mighty large **Venetian** (3355 Las Vegas Blvd., 702/414-1000 or 888/283-6423, www.venetian.com) materialized where the Sands once stood. The Italian-themed resort of more than 4,000 suites gets raves on the swank-o-meter and credit for once hosting "Art of the Motorcycle."

Attractions and Adventures

If you'd like to experience skydiving and live to tell about it, **Vegas Indoor Skydiving** (200 Convention Center Dr., 702/731-4768, www.vegasindoorskydiving.com) offers a one-hour program for $75 where you don skydiving clothes and step out and float above what looks like a monstrous bathroom blow dryer. No parachute, no worries. No experience necessary.

I'm not sure if this next recommendation will fly with most riders, but you gotta give Liberace credit. In the flamboyant tradition of Gorgeous George and '70s Elvis, Liberace epitomized the vanity of

Vegas and at the **Liberace Museum** (1775 E. Tropicana Ave., 702/798-5595, www.liberace.org, $15) you'll see some surprising exhibits that cannot help but impress: an Excalibur car covered with rhinestones, a customized Bradley GT, a red, white, and blue Rolls, a Rolls-Royce Phantom V Landau limousine (one of only seven, this one dons the license tag "88 Keys"), as well as a custom rhinestone-covered Stutz Bearcat with a matching rhinestone-covered toolkit. The museum is open 10 A.M.–5 P.M. Monday–Saturday, noon–4 P.M. Sunday.

The accessory branch of Las Vegas H-D/Buell, the **Harley-Davidson Shop** (4th and Fremont Sts., 702/383-1010, www.lvhd.com) carries the requisite overdone clothing, parts, and souvenirs. A bulletin board announces motorcycle-related products and services.

Blue-Plate Specials

Hundreds of restaurants line the Strip, both inside and outside the resort casinos. Surprisingly, the quality indoors is actually pretty good, and choices range from quick snacks to very elaborate meals. In fact, Vegas is gaining a reputation as a fine-dining capital, with dozens of celebrity chefs showing up to open high-end restaurants. For your purposes, however, there are lower-end choices such as the buffets offered at most major resorts. Most range between $20 and $30 and can keep you full and fueled for an entire day. Or week.

If you think that no one understands your passion for bikes, you'll find a sympathetic ear at **Harley-Davidson Cafe** (3725 Las Vegas Blvd., 702/740-4555, www.harley-davidsoncafe.com). The café boasts plenty of parking out back, while the inside looks like an assembly line. Gleaming Harleys ride up and around the room, passing before a large map of Route

66 and a giant American flag created from red, white, and blue chains. What else? Oh, yeah. Food.

Shut-Eye

In good economic times when Las Vegas turns into a convention clearinghouse, many of the 135,000 rooms are booked months in advance. That's when you should make reservations as early as you can—perhaps as part of a gambling package which will knock the rates down considerably. If not, you'll probably pay a premium to stay in a substandard hotel. Keep in mind that staying at a casino hotel can be soul-rattling after a peaceful desert ride. The local convention bureau has opened a hotel hotline and a website: 877/847-4858, www.visitlasvegas.com. Another nationwide reservation service that covers Las Vegas may help find you a room and save you some money: 800/964-6835, www.hotels.com.

Motels and Motor Courts

OK, so they're not really motels, but here are a few places I really like. For peace and quiet without a premium, **La Quinta** (3970 S. Paradise Rd., 702/796-9000, $65 and up) is a bargain and includes a continental breakfast. Just a few blocks from the action, it also has a pool. Even cheaper is the **Golden Gate Hotel and Casino** (1 Fremont St., 702/385-1906 or 800/426-1906, www.goldengatecasino.net, $39 and up). It offers cable, a free newspaper, and not much else besides a restaurant that's served 30 million giant shrimp cocktails since 1959. The **Hard Rock Hotel** (4455 Paradise Rd., 702/693-5000 or 800/473-7625, www.hardrockhotel.com, $89 and up) hits the jackpot with great accents like Flying V door handles, a Beatles display case, and an H-D Hardtail Springer owned by Motley Crüe's Nikki Sixx. It's

more inviting than the darkened casinos, but rates here leap around like Pete Townshend, so call ahead. The on-site restaurant is another reason to stay here—it displays one of Elvis's jumpsuits and Roy Orbison's Electra-Glide.

Chain Drive

These chain hotels are in town, or within 10 miles of the city center: **Best Western, Clarion, Comfort Inn, Courtyard by Marriott, Days Inn, Doubletree, Econo Lodge, Embassy Suites, Fairfield Inn, Hampton Inn, Hilton, Holiday Inn, Howard Johnson, Hyatt, La Quinta, Motel 6, Residence Inn, Rodeway, Super 8, Travelodge**

For more information, including phone numbers and websites, see page 439.

ON THE ROAD: LAS VEGAS TO LONE PINE

Of all the rides in this book, this one will require the greatest degree of guts. It demands that your bike be in peak condition, that your nerves be sure, and that you are ready to face the challenge of fierce, twisting curves in the Inyo Mountains and the barren loneliness of Death Valley.

Leaving Las Vegas on Highway 159 West, it'll take a half hour to shake the Vegas glitter off your bike and reach Red Rock Canyon. This is a magnificent sight and, if you ride the scenic loop road that rolls across the conservation area, one that affords possible views of bighorn sheep, gray foxes, and wild burros. Otherwise, head south toward Blue Diamond and Highway 160, and then west towards Pahrump. Immediately, the road is a lonely stretch. There are no twists, no turns, just rolling desert. The road wakes up near Spring Mountain Ranch State Park, giving you curves to compensate.

When you reach Pahrump, it's just

a lump of a town—an embryonic L.A. that spreads across the sands. There's a well-stocked gas station at the junction of Highways 160 and 372, but mostly it seems fairly empty and akin to that classic scene in *2001: A Space Odyssey* where the caveman tosses a bone into the sky. Head a few miles north of Pahrump and watch for Bell Vista Avenue that cuts west towards Death Valley Junction. Take it.

After 4 miles of twisties and 15 miles of straightaway, the big, empty desert starts to look like the Grand Canyon (minus the canyon). It's wide, open, and empty for about 30 miles until you reach the intersection of Highways 190 and 127 where you'll find the strange and fascinating **Amargosa Opera House and Hotel** (760/852-4441, www.amargosa-opera-house.com, $60–75). Built by the Pacific Coast Borax Company in the 1920s, the combination office space and hotel had fallen into disrepair by 1967. Then New York dancer Marta Becket drove through, had a flat tire, and fell in love with its desolation. She bought the forlorn complex and now rents rooms. As if that's not enough, on Mondays and Saturdays from October to May, Marta and friend Tom Willett still perform a ballet and mime revue in the adjacent opera house. Now that's entertainment! No phones, no television, no food (a restaurant's seven miles away), but a place for some well-deserved rest before the upcoming ride.

From where you stand, you are poised for your ride across Death Valley. Now things get mighty strange here, sheriff. If you've ever judged times to reach distant points, don't expect to do it here. The land is so flat and barren, it'll take 20 minutes to ride to an object that you can see halfway to the horizon. This lasts for mile after mile after mile as you ride across the Amargosa Range and pass 20 Mule Team Canyon. If you have the time and curiosity, just before Zabriskie Point a one-way, 2.7-mile dirt loop road detours south again through the canyon until it decides to bring you back to the highway. Then in the middle of all of this nothing is really something: a four-star resort, in fact. In a desolate land where a snack machine could win an award for fine dining, **Furnace Creek Resort** (Hwy. 190, 760/786-2345, www.furnacecreekresort.com) is a mystery. You can stay the night in below-sea-level luxury, go horseback riding, or take a break on the verandah and view the upcoming 104-mile challenge. If you want to play golf on the lowest golf course in the world, the one here is 214 feet *below sea level*. Despite its existence in exile, the resort is popular and the rates prove it: from $265 at the inn and $128 at the ranch. Reserve in advance if you think you'll stay. If not, get ready for a most incredible ride.

A few miles down the road, there's a gas station that will gouge you on gas, but fill 'er up again. You're about to start a heart-stopping ride.

As you start your descent into the valley, you'll see into the future. Car headlights can be seen from 10 miles away, and when you're about 20 miles outside of Furnace Creek you'll feel the absence of life echoing around you. You may share my experience and feel a most humbling and spiritual moment here. After running a satisfying series of mountain curves, you take a wide, sweeping left and then 3, 2, 1…you've fallen hundreds of feet below sea level and are riding in the basin of Death Valley.

Picture yourself, a black speck alone in a place as flat and desolate as any on earth. Solo riders especially will feel the emotional deprivation of this silent world. If your bike is finely tuned, stop and experience the mystical solitude. It is as memorable as any experience you will have on the road.

When you turn your attention back to riding, the quiet continues until you reach **Stovepipe Wells** (Hwy. 190, 760/786-2387, www.stovepipewells.com). It has an elevation of five feet, but don't let anyone sell you lift tickets. If you're tired of riding, Stovepipe offers an Einstein-smart option. It has 83 motel rooms, an RV park, gas, a general store, swimming pool, and saloon. It's a welcome sight and rooms here go for an affordable $80–120.

Between here and the next oasis, you'll ride through the anti-valley as you face some of the most harrowing and dangerous dips and twists you'll encounter. Six-degree grades and serious shifts in terrain roll on for miles at a time. Minus any guardrails, a moment's distraction can easily turn your bike into scrap metal, but if you stay focused, this ride is rich in adventure. Accelerating drops let you click into neutral and speed through twists at 60 mph, propelling you into valleys where the emptiness is sublime in its beauty. Realize that this is the same desert you may have flown over countless times, but here and now it is a new planet that you've tamed beneath your tires.

When you reach **Panamint Springs Resort** (775/482-7680, www.deathvalley.com, rooms $79 and up, tent sites $15 and up), you have another excuse to stay the night in a 15-room motel and reminisce about the ride. You may have doubted your resolve or the belief you could find beauty in this wasteland, but by now the desert has spoken to you. Chances are you'll be keyed up for the last 48-mile leg to Lone Pine—and this will be frickin' fantastic.

From Panamint Springs, you'll ride to the backbone of a mountain range, with sheer drops on your side and no barriers to break your fall. The pavement is hyperactive as it wraps and twists around the jagged peaks like barbed wire. The road will challenge you for dozens of miles and then reward you with countless reasons to stop and shoot photos. Father Crowley Vista Point (elev. 4,000 feet) is a good bet, and when you park your bike in the middle of the road I doubt you'll be hassled by oncoming traffic largely because there is probably no traffic oncoming.

By the time you reach the intersection of Highway 136 North, take it to reach U.S. 395, and turn north for a long final leg and a well-deserved rest in the historic Hollywood cowboy town of Lone Pine.

Yippeeiyay.

LONE PINE PRIMER

Lone Pine (elev. 3,700 ft., pop. 2,060), the first town of any size west of Death Valley, flares up for a few blocks and then disappears back into the sand. Lexicographers believe the phrase "blink and you'll miss it" was coined here.

But there's more to Lone Pine than meets the eye. If you're old enough to recall matinee cowboys falling off cliffs only to return the following week, you'll have already seen Lone Pine. If you frequent antique shows, looking for a Hopalong Cassidy lunch box or Roy Rogers guitar, you'll have Lone Pine to thank.

More than 300 Westerns were filmed here, from serial episodes to full-length features. Capitalizing on this unique history, each October the Lone Pine Film Festival draws a few surviving stars of Hollywood's Old West movies.

Even if you were born too late to recall Lash LaRue and the Cisco Kid, being in Lone Pine and at the gateway to Mount Whitney is a purely American experience. After Death Valley, you deserve it.

ON THE ROAD: LONE PINE

One stoplight, three blocks, and years of history. It's enough for an interesting ride, primarily because of the Whitney Portal, a long and winding road to the majestic mountain. After defeating Death Valley, you may want to take a break from mountain roads, but if not, you can take a curvaceous 12-mile run to the base of Mount Whitney, California's highest peak (elev. 14,495). There are no mountain roads here, but a slew of hiking trails if you want to go it by foot.

Otherwise, stay a while in Lone Pine. After all, stopping in small towns offers some of the most enjoyable moments of a ride. If you're ready to rest, you can see downtown in about 25 minutes—a half hour if you take your time. One must-see is at the lone stoplight. The **Indian Trading Post** (137 S. Main St., 760/876-4726) was a favorite stop for stars such as Edward G. Robinson, Jack Palance, Errol Flynn, Chuck Connors, Maureen O'Hara, Gary Cooper, and Barbara Stanwyck, who scribbled their names on the walls and window frames while shooting in town. Today, the walls are a priceless piece of Americana.

After the mountain and the town, there's not much else to do but settle back at the diner, grab a beer at the saloon (yes!), do your laundry, and, if you share my good fortune, see a real live prospector walking down the street with his pickaxe and shovel.

PULL IT OVER:
LONE PINE HIGHLIGHTS
Attractions and Adventures

You're surrounded by natural beauty, and there are two places to visit to take full advantage of this. **Mount Whitney Ranger Station** (640 S. Main St., 760/876-6200, www.fs.fed.us/r5/inyo) has maps and also issues the wilderness permits you'll need to enter the Whitney Portal area. There's no charge to enter, but if you want to camp here ($6–14), you'll need to make arrangements well in advance. A mile south of Lone Pine, at the junction of U.S. 395 and Highway 136, the **Interagency Office** (760/876-6222) stocks information about Death Valley, Mount Whitney, the Inyo National Forest, and other natural parks and sights.

Blue-Plate Specials

Besides a few pizza places and Mexican diners, eateries in Lone Pine are few, but it's easy to find some good USDA-approved road food if you know where to look. The largest joint in town is the **Mt. Whitney Restaurant** (227 S. Main St., 760/876-5751). Here since the 1930s, the family-owned diner offers—dig this—venison, buffalo, ostrich, and veggie burgers. Ask politely, and maybe they'll make you a real one with beef. Open from morning to evening, it's popular with riders thanks to the pool tables, pinball, beer and wine, and football on a 50-inch TV. Open 24 hours for breakfast, lunch, and dinner, the **High Sierra Café** (446 S. Main St., 760/876-5796) is another family-owned restaurant that serves breakfast anytime, beer and wine later on, and entrées include American favorites like chicken-fried steak and chopped sirloin with mushrooms and grilled onions.

Open for dinner only, the **Merry-Go-Round** (212 S. Main St., 760/876-4115) is a quirky, cozy hole-in-the-wall place that specializes in steaks and seafood and gets marks for good service.

Watering Holes

One of the most enjoyable bars you'll find in America, **Jake's Saloon** (119 N. Main St., 760/876-5765) is open daily 'til midnight. The bar is a perfect place to settle down after your Death Valley run and crack your thirst with a cold beer.

Shut-Eye
Motels and Motor Courts

For a small town, Lone Pine offers more than adequate lodging choices. In the middle of town, the 50's-era **Dow Villa Motel** (310 S. Main St., 760/876-5521 or 800/824-9317, www.dowvillamotel.com, $95–145) features clean rooms, a pool, outdoor spa, and rooms with TVs, VCRs, king and queen beds, and mini-fridges. Be sure to check out the John Wayne exhibit in the den that includes a poker table from a movie he shot here (he'd stay in Room 20). They also run the historic Dow Hotel where rooms without a shared bath start at $50. At the south end of town, the **Comfort Inn** (1920 S. Main St. at the junction of U.S. 395 and Hwy. 136, 760/876-8700, www.comfortinn.com, off-season $80 and up) is as clean as can be, with larger than normal rooms and a nice view of Mount Whitney (in back) and the Alabama Hills (in front). Rooms feature two queen beds, bathtubs, mini-fridges, and microwaves. Note that in high season rates can double.

Chain Drive

These chain hotels are in town, or within 10 miles of the city center:

Best Western, Comfort Inn

For more information, including phone numbers and websites, see page 439.

ON THE ROAD: LONE PINE TO YOSEMITE

Aside from facing a monumental wall of wind due to the absence of anything to stop it, the ride north is easy—at least until you turn onto Highway 120 to reach Yosemite. That's when you may want to call your stunt double.

For now, the road out of Lone Pine stays true to form: impressive mountains and straight runs. Fourteen miles later, bypass Independence, and then slow down through well-patrolled Big Pine. Forty miles from here, Bishop's oasis of green lawns, trees, golf courses, and restaurants may entice you to stop.

Taking a left on U.S. 395 you'll continue north with the ride becoming fairly comfortable as you blaze down the road: the Sierra Nevada on your left and the Inyo Mountains on your right. You'll be thankful you've been freed from the confines of a car as the spicy fragrance of the desert is just as bracing as the chill of the mountain air. You're in the groove now, and can look forward to another 120 miles of motorcycle-friendly roads ahead. Forget the canopy lanes of New England; here in the American west the wide-open road has placed you in God's country.

After passing sprawling Lake Crowley on your right, the road rises forever, ascending to 7,000 feet at Sherwin Summit, and then, miles later, Deadman's Pass at 8,036 feet. The change has been so gradual that you may not have noticed that the desert has been replaced by rich, green California forest. If you have time to prolong your ride and acquire other indelible images, watch for Highway 158, which introduces you to the June Lake Loop. Most motorists bypass it, but it's worth the detour for motorcycle travelers. If you follow this road, a small creek running on your right soon spills into one of the most beautiful mountain lakes you'll encounter, and the combination of road, forest, lake, and sky is as picturesque as Switzerland's Lake Lausanne. The road skirts through a ski resort town, so the off-season traffic is lighter and makes it easy to stop for coffee in the small lakefront village. You'll continue the ride for several more miles, rolling quietly past snowcapped mountains, log cabins, and waterfalls until, suddenly, you'll notice an eerie silence. There is a striking absence of movement and people and the landscape has an unusual science fiction look. It's a weird feeling, a remote feeling.

I look back at Highway 158 like taking an extra helping of dessert. With all of the fantastic riding you've done so far you don't really need it, but it's good to have a little more. When the loop connects back with U.S. 395, turn left and ride to Lee Vining, a nice town with a few motels and restaurants. If you're scared of heights or aren't prepared for the demanding two-hour, 74-mile push to Yosemite Village, you should stop here and look for a room. Seriously. Since there's an abundance of incredible sights on the road ahead, racing the sun just to get a room inside Yosemite isn't worth it. You may also be stopped in Lee Vining when Highway 120 closes following the first big snowstorm after November 1.

But if the sun is high and the roads are clear, turn left onto Highway 120 and, after about a quarter mile, you'll see on your left the **Tioga Gas Mart** (22 Vista Point Dr., 760/647-1088). The supermarket-size station gives you a place to stock up on food and supplies for Yosemite. If the weather's nippy, now's the time to get comfortable in a survival suit before heading for the mountains.

Already at 8,000 feet, you'll head up a steep grade on your way to the even higher Tioga Pass (elevation 9,941 feet). Muscle-flexing turns are rampant for the first several miles, and the road demands attention. At the ranger station, pay $10 per motorcycle ($20 for other vehicles) and $10 per passenger (unless you've purchased the $80 America the Beautiful Pass) and enter the mother of the mother

of all national parks. The simple and helpful park pamphlet will be tempting to look at, but chances are you'll be focused on wilderness scenery that'll drop your jaw onto your gas tank.

The two-lane road is fairly wide, and a collection of slow curves and pine forests soon gives way to boulders and cliffs. Guardrails are few and drops precipitous, so be on your best biking behavior. You'll be sucked into several tunnels and spat out to glimpse coming attractions in the distance, and unusually noticeable are the textures you can distinguish. Wood, rock, water, or light, everything appears—if this makes any sense—to be better than nature.

Speeds can reach 60 mph on straights and drop to 20 mph on tight curves, and even though you could make the trip from Lee Vining in two hours, allow an extra hour just to stop at turnouts, shoot pictures, or savor the visual feast of twisting roads and the golden glow of nature.

About 55 miles into this leg, you'll reach Highway 41. Turn left and follow the signs to Yosemite Village. It is bigger and better than anything you can imagine.

YOSEMITE PRIMER

Yosemite conjures thousands of images and raises expectations to dizzying heights. You'd think it would fail to deliver, but it doesn't. It is just as beautiful, wild, tame, rich, and sublime as you'd expect.

While it's tempting to think the rest of America would look like this if we hadn't beat Mother Nature into submission, there is only one Yosemite. Initially set aside by President Lincoln in 1864, Yosemite Valley and the Mariposa Grove of giant sequoias were to be "held for public use, resort, and recreation…inalienable for all time."

In 1890, an act of Congress preserved 1,170 square miles of forests, fields, valleys, and streams equal in size to Rhode

The Bear Facts

Although lead poisoning killed off California grizzlies in the 1920s (they were shot), other bears are still sniffing out food in Yosemite Village. They can easily tear a car to shreds when searching out uncovered food, so when you leave your bike, take anything perishable with you. Better yet, leave items in your room. If you're camping, invest in bear-proof containers. Maybe buy one large enough to sleep in.

Island. Today, it is traversed by nearly 200 miles of paved road, about 70 miles of graded road, and 800 miles of hiking trails. Yosemite is home to 150 species of birds, 85 species of mammals, and close to 1,500 species of flowering plants.

The park is as bold and as beautiful as America. Enjoy it.

ON THE ROAD: YOSEMITE

While you could take your bike and explore the park on your own, you may be better off by putting yourself in the hands of Yosemite's park rangers. They are knowledgeable and courteous and will likely be able to answer every question you have.

Although it sounds like high cheese, the tram tour (or bus tour in cold weather) is the best way to see Yosemite Valley, the most visited section of the park. The tour also stops at Bridalveil Fall and offers great views of Half Dome, and monumental El Capitan. If you've only seen it in a book, wait until you see it here.

Although the size of the high granite edifice may not impress you at first, take a few moments and look at it closely. When you spot a pinpoint dabbed on the mountain you'll get an instant education in proportion. *That* is a mountain climber. And those parsley sprigs tucked in slivers of rock? Those are pine trees you are looking at, and they are at least 80 feet tall. Soak

this in, and respect for those pin-headed climbers increases.

The tour takes you by lush meadows that make up only 20 percent of the park but support 80 percent of its flowers. How do I know this? Because just about every guide thinks they're at a *Jeopardy!* audition and freely fling out data on botany, geology, and forestry throughout the two-hour tour. When it's over, you'll be armed with plenty of information, a good sense of direction, and an understanding of what you'd like to revisit.

After a tour, exploring on your own may be the most rewarding experience of Yosemite. At Curry Village and Yosemite Village, you can fill up a backpack with water, snacks, camera, and film, and the park is yours. Hiking trails, which range from easy to very strenuous, deliver you to impressive sights, such as giant boulders and trees as wide as Cadillacs. The woods are welcoming in their solitude and open your senses to every movement, sound, and fragrance. Rustling leaves recall a rushing stream, flaked bark peels off the gnarled trunks of cedar trees, acorns drop, and pine cones fall with a soft splat.

Stopping to feel the environment is akin to slowing down on a great ride and at times it feels far more satisfying. When you take time to rest when you want and where you want, there's immense pleasure in knowing that the "real world" is hundreds of miles away and your office even farther. If you absolutely have to do something, check the lodges for listings of daily events, such as fishing, photography classes, and nature talks.

When night falls, the sky looks more white than black, since stars can be counted by the millions. It's been only two days since leaving Las Vegas. There, the city demanded you stay up late. Here, the rewards of Yosemite are offered when you rise early and take advantage of another day in paradise.

PULL IT OVER: YOSEMITE HIGHLIGHTS
Attractions and Adventures

As mentioned, sightseeing tours are a good way to get acquainted with the park and several different types are available; call 209/372-1240 for details on each. Led by park rangers or tour guides, the most popular is the introductory **Valley Floor Tour** ($25), which lasts two hours and travels 26 miles through the heart of Yosemite. A full day's adventure, the **Grand Tour** ($82) winds through Glacier Point and Mariposa Grove, site of the famous giant sequoias. The **Glacier Point Tour** costs $41 round-trip, $25 one way.

When you're not in a bus or on your bike, you may be in Yosemite Village in the heart of Yosemite Valley. Like a small downtown, it's complete with post office, groceteria, pizza parlor, deli, auditorium, museum, cemetery, and the Ansel Adams Gallery that features works for sale by Adams and other wildlife photographers. At the visitor center, you can sign up for photo courses or ranger-led activities, check road conditions, or buy some books. Over at Curry Village, there are gift shops, a tour center, bike rentals, and snack shops.

If you plan to fish at Yosemite, you need

a fishing license, available at the Sport Shop in Yosemite Valley, the Wawona Store, and the Tuolumne Meadows Store. But if your thirst for adventure is higher and you were inspired by the climbers you saw earlier, take the first step toward tackling El Capitan and sign up for climbing lessons by calling the **Mountaineering School** (209/372-8344).

Blue-Plate Specials

After a day of grazing on picnic grub or at concession stands, experience lunch or dinner at the **Ahwahnee** hotel (209/372-1489, www.yosemitepark.com). At this four-star hotel the setting is extraordinary, the meals perfect, and the service flawless. The entire experience is enhanced by the architectural style called National Park Service Rustic that characterizes this massive room. Call me, and I'll join you.

Shut-Eye

Yosemite used to reach peak popularity between Memorial Day and Labor Day; today, stretch that from April to the end of November. Make reservations as far in advance as possible. For **hotel reservations** within the park, call 801/559-5000 or visit www.yosemitepark.com. For **campground reservations,** call 877/444-6777 or visit www.recreation.gov.

The park boasts a range of facilities, from dirt-cheap rustic to over-the-top indulgent. In the heart of the park, Yosemite's fabled **Ahwahnee** (209/372-1407, $439 and up) tops the price list. One of the most beautiful inns in America, it was built in 1927 and is breathtaking in design, superb in service. You'll find character and tradition in the grand fireplace, massive timbers, Great Room, and baronial dining room. Reserve one of 123 rooms, at eyebrow-arching prices, as far in advance as possible. Other choices offer greater variety at a wider price range, the difference depending on whether they are actual buildings, cabins, canvas tents, or have private baths. Choose from the motel-style **Yosemite Lodge** ($153–185), **Wawona Hotel** ($128–199), or **Curry Village tents and cabins** ($85–152).

SIDE TRIP: YOSEMITE TO LAKE TAHOE

The road so far has been rich in both kindness and treachery. If you think it's been more of the latter, leave Yosemite Village on Highway 120 West and head for home. Otherwise, get ready for another adventurous 200-mile run, returning via Highway 120 East to U.S. 395 and on to Lake Tahoe. Warning: Make this a daytime ride, since the tight curves can be dangerous after dark.

Even if you never ride another mile, you'll have experienced the most complicated blend of riding in terms of terrain, scenery, sociology, psychology, and climate. And there's more to come.

About three miles north of Lee Vining, Mono Lake reveals itself from a highway vista. Now drying out like a Miami retiree as folks in Los Angeles drain the lake for their lawns and bathwater, the exposed white sands are a curiously surreal landscape.

Six miles later, you're at 7,000 feet and climbing, with the vast Mono Basin in the distance on your right. This run soon places you back in a desert landscape, a curious fact when you cruise past 7,700 feet and look back to see Yosemite's Tioga Pass. The rise in altitude also introduces winds that can kick your tires out from under you. Keep a low profile.

It's difficult to fathom that these changes are occurring during one incredible journey. And to prove its power, nature will once again change environments on you. After you cross the Conway Summit at 8,138 feet, the desert leaves the stage and you enter California ranch country where small cow towns come into view. Scan the horizons and you may spy snow falling in one section, clear blue skies in another, rain in a third. It is altogether impossible to absorb the varying expressions of nature that surround you, but you don't really need to. Just file this information away under Memorable Motorcycle Run.

Past Bridgeport, the slow winding roads get their act straightened out and whisk you into Devil Gate's Summit at 7,500 feet, sharpening your senses for the impending pinball run. But for now, the hills are low and rolling and fun.

Although you've already defeated the toughest terrain, you now face Walker Creek Canyon. After 10 miles of tranquility, the winding roads snatch you back into the challenge of rushing water, boulders, pine needles, and fallen trees. As you catch fleeting glimpses of red rocks and black rocks and sand, you'll be making mental notes to thank the highway engineers and sign up for the Sierra Club.

When the canyon breathes its last, you'll enter the tiny town of Walker, where nothing seems to be living, and then Coleville (pop. 43), which makes Walker look like Chicago. The next town, Topaz, is your cue to look for Highway 89; if it's open, it will be on your left.

For a minor road, Highway 89 is amazingly beautiful. Three miles into it, you climb to 6,000 feet and enter a fertile valley rich with fields of pines and sagebrush. You have no choice but to keep riding, and you won't be disappointed. The higher you ride—and you will—the more spectacular the view. As your attorney, I advise you to stop at the peak and look back over the valley. It is an image that will stay with you for a long, long time. You can look for miles down the valley's breadth, and with keen eyesight you may make out stacks of logs that are, in fact, remote cabins locked within the breeches of behemoth mountain walls. I don't know what type of people live out in this wilderness, but I admire the fact that they do.

No picture can do justice to this image; only your memory will capture the scope of this incredible vista. Desert, snow, mountains, valleys...It's a view that is as inspiring as it is humbling.

You are nearing Monitor Pass at a mighty 8,300 feet which guarantees that the imminent descent will be a gift to enjoy. Drop it into neutral and rest your engine for several miles as you glide your bike into easy curves and experience the decline of western mountain ranges.

Continue on Highway 89 toward Markleeville, 32 miles south of Lake Tahoe. You may decide to stop here for several reasons. If the sun is setting, the mountains you just crossed will look like a Maxfield Parrish landscape painted with pinks, violets, blues, and crimson, and you should certainly avoid the upcoming roads at night. Another good reason is the **Cutthroat Saloon** (14830 Hwy. 89, 530/694-2150). It's quite popular with riders because of the Western Victorian decor, the adjoining Wolf Creek restaurant, and the ladies'

underwear pinned on the ceiling. Maybe you'll find something in your size. With 11 units, the **Creekside Lodge** (530/694-2511) is the lodging option here.

From here, the road is pleasing and predictable and leads to South Lake Tahoe. Although you'll find motels, hotels, and cabins here, the city's large population is why you may prefer to ride to the less populated northern shore.

To wrap up the ride with a final burst of excitement is Highway 28 along the west shore. Unlike most lakefront roads that blend into the shoreline, this one has dangerously high cliffs, skin-tight switchbacks, and eye-popping glimpses of Lake Tahoe from inlets and Alpine vistas. In a way, this heart-throbbing run is the natural counterpoint to the artificial fun of Las Vegas.

Shut-Eye
Chain Drive
These chain hotels are in South Lake Tahoe, or within 10 miles of the city center:

Best Western, Days Inn, Embassy Suites, Holiday Inn, Howard Johnson, Motel 6, Quality Inn, Rodeway, Super 8, Travelodge

For more information, including phone numbers and websites, see page 439.

Resources for Riders

Las Vegas–Yosemite Run

Nevada Travel Information
Nevada Road Conditions—877/687-6237, www.safetravelusa.com/nv
Nevada State Parks—775/684-2770, www.parks.nv.gov/
Nevada Tourism—800/638-2328, www.travelnevada.com

California Travel Information
California Association of Bed & Breakfast Inns—800/373-9251, www.cabbi.com
California Division of Tourism—916/444-4429 or 800/862-2543,
    www.visitcalifornia.com
California Road Conditions—800/427-7623
California State Parks—916/653-6995, www.parks.ca.gov
California Weather Information—916/979-3051

Local and Regional Information
Lake Tahoe Forecast and Road Conditions—530/542-4636, ext. 3
Las Vegas Chamber of Commerce—702/641-5822 or 702/735-1616 (info center),
    www.lvchamber.com
Las Vegas Visitors Information Center—702/892-7575 or 877/847-4858,
    www.visitlasvegas.com
Lone Pine Chamber of Commerce—760/876-4444 or 877/253-8981,
    www.lonepinechamber.org
North Lake Tahoe Resort Association—530/583-3494 or 888/434-1262,
    www.gotahoenorth.com
Yosemite Information—209/372-0200, www.yosemite.com or www.nps.gov/yose
Yosemite Road Service—209/372-0200, ext. 1

Nevada Motorcycle Shops
Carter Powersports—6275 S. Decatur Blvd., Las Vegas, 702/727-6365,
    www.carterpowersports.com
Las Vegas Harley-Davidson—2605 S. Eastern Ave., Las Vegas, 702/302-4936 or
    888/218-0744, www.lasvegasharleydavidson.com
Motorcycles 702—2010 Western Ave., Las Vegas, 702/645-1500,
    www.motorcycles702.com
Red Rock Harley-Davidson—2260 S. Rainbow Rd., Las Vegas, 702/876-2884 or
    866/965-8224, www.redrockharley.com

California Motorcycle Shop
Golden State Cycle—174 S. Main St., Bishop, 760/872-1570,
    www.goldenstatecycle.com

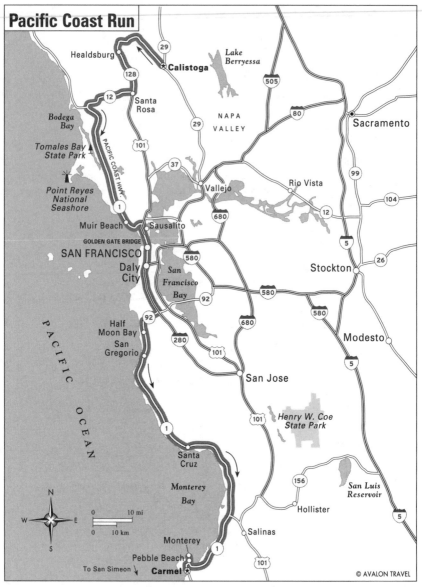

Pacific Coast Run

Route: Calistoga to Carmel via Sausalito, Monterey, Big Sur, Pacific Coast Highway

Distance: Approximately 310 miles

First Leg: Calistoga to Sausalito (80 miles)

Second Leg: Sausalito to Carmel (120 miles)

Optional Third Leg: Carmel to San Simeon (112 miles)

Helmet Laws: California requires helmets.

© AVALON TRAVEL

Pacific Coast Run

Calistoga, California to Carmel, California

As evidenced by the ride through Death Valley, Lone Pine, and Yosemite, eastern California was designed by God specifically for motorcyclists. Apparently that must have given God a lot of confidence since he managed to repeat his success on the West Coast as well. Get to Napa Valley and it's the closest you'll come to riding along Mediterranean roads, unless you ship your bike to Athens. And although the region is marked by affluence, you don't need deep pockets since the roads are free.

From the luxury of Calistoga's spas to the pure beauty of the San Francisco skyline, from Carmel's fantasy architecture to the dream world of Hearst Castle, this run features short rides on roads that are just right. What's more, the journey from valley to hill to coastal highway creates a satisfying blend of environments.

CALISTOGA PRIMER

Some motorcycle travelers make an unfortunate error when visiting Napa Valley—and that's deciding to stay in the valley's namesake, Napa. Far more appealing is the town of Calistoga. As your advance team, let me tell you why you need to stay here.

Several thousand years ago, a volcano named Mt. Konocti erupted 20 miles away and plopped about five feet of ash on the valley floor. Around the 1500s, the Wappo Indians realized the ash had mixed with the naturally heated mineral water and started bathing in the mud and water. They finished up with a sweat wrap, and they felt good. Damn good. The Wappos called the valley Tu-la-ha-lu-si ("Oven Place").

When Sam Brannan, California's first Gold Rush millionaire, arrived here in the 1860s, he saw the potential for a resort spa town. At a promotional supper, he proclaimed that this would be the "Calistoga of Sarafornia!" The slip became a marketing ploy, and Calistoga was born. Farewell, Wappos. Riding the wealth of the mines and the natural hot springs, Brannan's

What's in a Mud Bath?

You know how you can get achy after too many hours in the saddle? A mud bath will loosen you up faster than an Ex-Lax smoothie. How does it work? A mud bath is a mixture of heated mineral water and volcanic ash and/or peat moss. After you settle into this gloop, the thick mixture heats up to penetrate your body, relax your muscles, and alleviate stress, tensions, aches, and pains. Ten–twelve minutes should be enough, or stay muddy longer if you're really keyed up.

community became the central point for a railroad serving the upper valley, and it sustained itself through the turn of century, past World War II, and into a new millennium and never lost its appeal.

As in Brannan's day, Calistoga appears to be riding the crest of a prosperous wave. Spas and businesses are thriving now and the film *Sideways* impressed an already intense subculture of San Francisco wine sippers, who continue to flock to town for vineyard runs and body wraps. But if you see 'em, don't even mention merlot. The most telling sign that this is a good place for a base are the motorcycles parked up and down Lincoln Avenue, their riders frequenting small saloons and planning sorties into the surrounding mountain roads. One of the state's more pleasing towns, it is the perfect starting point for this journey.

ON THE ROAD: CALISTOGA

I've come to believe that the best towns to visit are those where you can ride in, park for free, and check out the town on foot. Calistoga is just such a place and one of the best motorcycle towns you'll ever find—especially if you like drinking wine and having someone upgrade the condition of your muscles to happy. From Dr. Wilkinson's Hot Springs and Mud Baths to the fine restaurants, this is the Old

West with a 21st-century facelift. Unfortunately, you'll have to wait to see all that it offers, because the roads of this region are so damn tempting you'll be hard-pressed to sit still.

Open a map and you'll see that the number of riding options rivals that of vineyards. Even better, these are not ordinary roads; they seem to offer the same sort of riding that you'd find in the Greek Peloponnese, Swiss Alps, and Italian Dolomites. Within minutes, you can take comfort in roads as curvaceous as Marilyn Monroe, traverse hills that are soft and low, ride over green creeks and past drooping brown trees and pumpkin patches and groves bursting with almonds, avocadoes, and black walnuts. Not only will your ride be visually exciting, it will be redolent with the fresh, fragrant aroma of nut trees, strawberries, grapes, and flowering plants.

It is a thrilling experience to be here, where the outdoors are treasured, not tamed. You should see all of this and travel beyond the hills, but also consider a manageable trip to the region north of Napa Valley.

Although the larger wineries are in the southern Napa Valley, head north on Highway 29 (aka Silverado Trail), on the east side of the valley. Turn left on Tubbs Lane, and then right at Highway 128. Soon you're on twisting canopy roads that offer some of the finest motorcycle riding in the country. Motorcycles springing up and over the hills look like ants on a mound; but be careful when the afternoon sun and shadows play tricks on the pavement.

Head north, and you'll ride into Alexander Valley. Although there are no major towns, you must stop in Healdsburg at the strangely well-stocked **Jimtown General Store** (6706 Hwy. 128, 707/433-1212, www.jimtown.com). Think back a few decades and then discover that they've recovered part of your childhood with Mary Jane candies, bubble-gum cigars, Chinese finger traps, whoopee cushions, old toys from the '40s and '50s, a convenient deli, and, if your name is Jim, a chance at immortality by signing the autograph hound.

From here, you can head farther north, south, east, or west to explore other valley back roads. Like those around New Hope, Pennsylvania, all roads lead to a great ride.

PULL IT OVER: CALISTOGA HIGHLIGHTS
Attractions and Adventures

If you want a spa treatment without feeling obligated to stay at a resort, you have two options and each of these have stood the test of time. Established by town founder Sam Brannan in 1871, **Indian Springs** (1712 Lincoln Ave., 707/942-4913, www.indianspringscalistoga.com) is the oldest continuously operating thermal pool and spa in California. Mud baths, thermal geysers, massages, and a mineral pool are spread across 16 acres of volcanic ash. **Dr. Wilkinson's Hot Springs** (1507 Lincoln Ave., 707/942-4102, www.drwilkinson.com) was founded in 1951 by Doc Wilkinson. Aside from a great name and continuous family ownership, the spa

features mud baths, mineral whirlpools, steam rooms, facials, and an indoor mineral pool.

Of course one of the main reasons you're here is because of the more than 150 wineries in this region. You can get information and directions to all of them by making a few calls, doing a little pre-trip online research, or stopping at the **Chamber of Commerce and Visitors Center** (1133 Washington St., 707/942-6333, www.calistogavisitors.com) for maps and discount coupons to wineries and spas. The hunt is well worth it since the roads to the vineyards are unusually seductive. For more information contact the **Napa Valley Vintners Association** (707/963-3388, www.napavintners.com), the **Sonoma County Wineries Association** (707/522-5840, www.sonomawine.com), or **Alexander Valley Wine Growers** (888/289-4637, www.alexandervalley.org).

As you may have gathered, the terrain throughout these valleys is beautiful and found nowhere else in America. It's great to ride it, but there's also a way to soar above it with **Napa Valley Balloons** (707/944-0228 or 800/253-2224, www. napavalleyballoons.com). The experience is as extraordinary as the price ($220); although the steep fee includes breakfast before the launch from the Domaine Chandon Winery and flights of up to two hours. Another choice is right in Calistoga: the appropriately named **Calistoga Balloons** (707/942-5758 or 888/995-7700, www.calistogaballons.com). Their sailings also include breakfast and a flight lasting around an hour. Check online for discounts that drop the price just south of $200. The **Bonaventura Balloon Company** (133 Wall Rd., Napa, 707/944-2822 or 800/359-6272, www.bonaventura-balloons.com) is another option with similar rates (around $235). Each operation includes add-ons for breakfasts, picnics, or champagne brunches. Before deciding on any flight, ask how many passengers share your basket, whether or not you'll be able to help (if you'd like) as part of the crew, and if you can suck in some helium to change your voice.

For a visual representation of Calistoga's history, see how it was portrayed by a gifted artist. Ben Sharpsteen made good by becoming an Academy Award–winning animator, producer, and director for Walt Disney. His love for his adopted hometown led to the creation of the surprisingly fascinating **Sharpsteen Museum** (1311 Washington St., 707/942-5911, www.sharpsteen-museum.org). The downtown museum provides a great introduction to Calistoga and the history of upper Napa Valley. With careful detail, its 32-foot diorama depicts 1860s life at the opulent resort. Sam Brannan's cottage is connected to the main museum, which is open 11 A.M.–4 P.M. year-round. Admission is free—but they'd appreciate it if you slipped 'em a few bucks.

Who knows if you'll take advantage of this next one? But the type of spa treatment here is so unusual you'll remember it for years. West of Calistoga is **Osmosis** (209 Bohemian Hwy., Freestone, 707/823-8231, www.osmosis.com), where, after a Japanese tea ceremony, you strip down until you're absolutely bare naked and recline within a wooden tub filled with antiseptic cedar fiber, rice bran, and 600 active enzymes. An attendant takes a shovel and covers you up with the sawdust and then you spend the next 20 minutes in this compost heap throwing off more sweat than Secretariat. After you're dug up, you're hosed down and then invited upstairs for the pièce de résistance—a massage. Surreal, relaxing, and it'll do a number on your muscles. The enzyme bath is $85; add the tea ceremony and a massage and the 2.5-hour experience costs $180.

Blue-Plate Specials

Locals agree that one of the best breakfast spots is the **Café Sarafornia** (1413 Lincoln Ave., 707/942-0555), the "last old-fashioned diner in the Valley." A casual start to an extraordinary day's ride, the breakfasts—scrambles, omelettes, blintzes, crepes, and oat bran pancakes—range between a modest $4–12. There are also hamburgers, sandwiches, and salads for lunch.

Perhaps the nicest restaurant in town, **Brannan's Grill** (1374 Lincoln Ave., 707/942-2233, www.brannansgrill.com), serves lunches and dinners that are elegant, simple, and creative. The wide-open dining room and fireplace are settling, and the pace never seems rushed, even when it's packed. The menu changes seasonally, so check its website for current appetizers and entrées.

A low-key local favorite, **Pacifico Restaurante Mexicano** (1237 Lincoln Ave., 707/942-4400, www.pacificorestaurante-mexicano.com) uses only fresh ingredients ("no cans, no way") to create traditional Mexican food for lunch and dinner. It wins high marks for its chips, salsa, guacamole, and hand-shaken margaritas. The full bar is a rarity in Napa Valley.

Watering Holes

Open daily 'til 2 A.M., **Susie's** (1365 Lincoln Ave., 707/942-6710) is literally a hole in the wall. Head down a narrow hallway and you end up here, at a cool, dark refuge in the netherworld between "dive" and "joint." Regulars are quick to befriend strangers, and you'll soon settle in at the only pool tables in town. You're also welcome to try your hand at the piano (provided you can play). Happy hour? All day long. The Redwood Empire HOG Chapter dubbed Susie's a biker-friendly bar.

You'll find a microbrewery and full bar at the **Calistoga Inn** (1250 Lincoln Ave., 707/942-4101); the type of Napa wine bar you visualize at **Bar Vino** (1457 Lincoln Ave., 707/942-9900, www.bar-vino.com) inside the Mount View Hotel; and a full bar all by its lonesome at the **Hydro Bar and Grill** (1403 Lincoln Ave., 707/942-9777), where there's live music and 20 microbrews on tap.

Shut-Eye

Calistoga is so perfect, you may want to extend your stay by a year or two. Most lodging options include a spa, so plan on at least one massage to complement your visit. You can search for these yourself or save yourself some time by contacting the **Calistoga Visitors Center** (707/942-6333, www.calistogavisitors.com) for recommendations and reservations for lodging, spas, winery tours, etc.

Motels and Motor Courts

The **Roman Spa** (1300 Washington St., 707/942-4441, www.romanspahotsprings. com, $135 and up) has ordinary rooms but lush landscaping and a laid-back atmosphere. After a ride, you can rest outside in a mineral pool, jet spa pool, or sauna. Its spa services include the standard lineup of mud baths, mineral baths, and massages. Rates here run about 20 percent less off-season.

Inn-dependence

One of the most pleasing places you can stay is the **Cottage Grove Inn** (1711 Lincoln Ave., 707/942-8400 or 800/799-2284, www.cottagegrove.com, $250 and up). These luxurious Napa Valley cottages are shaded by towering trees and feature whirlpool tubs, fireplaces, private porches, and distinct themes (fly-fishing, equestrian, Audubon, musical, etc.). The price may induce panic in most riders, but the cottages sleep three and they *do* include breakfast.... Check them out; you may think it's worth it just to be able to park your bike out front and walk downtown. No loud pipes, please.

Chain Drive

These chain hotels are in town, or within 10 miles of the city center:

Best Western, Clarion, Comfort Inn, Motel 6

For more information, including phone numbers and websites, see page 439.

ON THE ROAD: CALISTOGA TO SAUSALITO

There are several ways to get out of Calistoga, two of which are quite different. For a fast, ordinary, straight shot, ride west to U.S. 101 and then drive south until you reach Sausalito. But there's an alternative for experienced riders ready for a challenge.

Route 12 South (also called Calistoga Rd.) heads about 30 miles due west to the coast, passing through the congestion in Santa Rosa and then past some less than spectacular scenery. A slight detour on the Bodega Highway will introduce you to Highway 1 and take you north towards Bodega Bay, the setting for Alfred Hitchcock's *The Birds*. If you like the movie or cool harbor towns, stop over and take a look. From here, fabled Highway 1 (aka the Pacific Coast Highway, or PCH) is about to prove to you why it's a legend. The wild stretch from Bodega Bay south to Sausalito can be pretty spooky, unless you've replaced your tires with mountain goats. Seriously. Curves are very sharp and safety rails nonexistent, the twists can be hypnotic, and sometimes the road's lay-out can range from impassable to impossible. But if you're ready, here's what you'll experience.

After you get on Highway 1 near Bodega Bay, the road sweeps east and far beyond the view of the coast. To compensate, there are great straightaways, and your path follows the rise and fall of the mountains. You'll ride toward Tomales Bay, which is a long drink of water that'll ride with you for about 15 miles. It's a lonely stretch where the rustic cabins of anglers crop up every few miles.

The scenery remains a constant quiet; there are simple villages that appear, the road sometimes leads into a forest, and then there are a brief but enjoyable series of 20-mph turns and shady, slow twists. Miles later, you're still rumbling along the mighty low road beside this smooth and graceful inlet.

When you reach Point Reyes Station, glance at the map and then at your watch and see if you have time to follow the path blazed by other bikers and head out to the Point Reyes Lighthouse. If you pass it by, the next really big show is waiting for you south of Stinson Beach.

The ability to ride from here for about 12 miles past Muir Beach and Tamalpais Valley to reach U.S. 101 is what separates humans from animals. Throw back a few Maalox tablets and get ready to meet a road that's a paved funhouse of gravel, dangerously sharp turns, and very steep drops. Maybe it was because I was riding a monster bike, but I often tapped it into first to navigate turns at a speed exceeded only by tree sloths. While you may get an adrenaline rush out of this, as I was working it out my mood alternated between excitement and sheer panic. Just about the time I was wondering how I got mixed up with a mess of blacktop like this, I was dumped out into level-headed Tamalpais Valley which gave my nerves time to settle as I rolled onto U.S. 101 for a short, citified ride in Sausalito.

About time.

SAUSALITO PRIMER

It's almost a cliché to find that a quaint seaside town was once a hotspot for drunken sailors, bawdy saloons, and come one, come all bordellos—but I still get a kick knowing that all this happened in Sausalito. It has the essence of the Cote d'Azur in France, and this European style is no accident. The town was discovered by Juan Manual de Ayala in 1575 and later became a favored shelter for full-rigged sailing ships from around the world. Today, those ships have been replaced by private yachts.

During World War II, Sausalito was a major shipbuilding site, with Liberty ships, landing craft, and tankers taking shape here. Afterward, the area became a haven for writers and artists—as evidenced by the galleries along Bridgeway Street. It's an uncommonly exotic town, and I guarantee you'll enjoy it.

ON THE ROAD: SAUSALITO

You've already enjoyed a ride from the northeast, and later you'll embark on a great ride south. For now, just park your bike and enjoy the town. You'll never tire of the view, which is even more impressive than that of Camden, Maine, where the Appalachians dissolve into the Atlantic.

Sausalito also has plenty of restaurants and galleries and pubs, and if you need even more, simply head over to San Francisco via ferry or the mighty Golden Gate Bridge.

I chose to continue the low-key theme I'd grown accustomed to in Calistoga and decided to stay in town. Not a bad choice. The heart of Sausalito is as foreign as any village along the Mediterranean and evokes the loveliness of the Riviera.

Besides, the views from here rival any in the world, from the San Francisco skyline to the fogbanks rolling over the bay. The only thing missing is the Golden Gate Bridge, hidden from view behind some ill-placed hills.

In town, the Plaza de Vina Del Mar Park has a visitors center and, more prominently, two 14-foot-tall elephant statues created for the Panama-Pacific Exposition of 1915. The architecture defies generic business district, instead blending Victorian, French, Spanish, and Irish accents. Not only are the people friendly and the setting perfect, you'll find the town to be as cosmopolitan and as relaxed as any you'll find as you explore the central district.

This is clearly a town of affluence. I deduced this from the forest of yachts I saw at the marina, which is just a short and pleasant walk from the park. As you roam the town, a few shops are worth exploring in greater detail. The **Venice Gourmet Delicatessen** (625 Bridgeway St., 415/332-3544, www.venicegourmet.com) has been here since 1969 and continues to be the local favorite. The shop is cluttered with copper kettles, baklava, dried sausage, soft drinks, and premium wines.

If you finish making the rounds early, you may opt to visit San Francisco, or head north on Bridgeway to reach Caledonia Street, which is an authentic Sausalito neighborhood.

Then, in the evening, as ferryboats start knocking across the waters to shuttle workers back from San Francisco, you can relax on the promenade or inside a waterfront restaurant and watch the most spectacular city skyline in America come to light.

PULL IT OVER: SAUSALITO HIGHLIGHTS
Attractions and Adventures

While an inmate on Alcatraz, I was only able to cruise the bay on my inner tube. Now released, I can cruise to SF cheaply aboard the **Blue and Gold Ferry** (415/773-1188, www.blueandgoldfleet.com). The ships depart Sausalito several times daily ($9.50 one way, $19 round-trip) for Fisherman's Wharf. From the Wharf, **Alcatraz Cruises** (415/981-7625, www.alcatrazcruises.com, $26) has boats that'll take you to and from the shuttered prison, which includes a cell house audio tour. Make reservations in advance, tours can sell out. **Golden Gate Ferry** (415/923-2000, www.goldengate-ferry.org) avoids Fisherman's Wharf and goes to the foot of Market Street; fares are $7.85 one way. Sorry, no room for motorcycles.

Mark Reuben Vintage Gallery (34 Princess St., 415/332-8815 or 877/444-3767, www.markreubengallery.com) displays thousands of vintage photographs, many taken from the original negatives. Matted and framed original pictures include those of Harley and Davidson, the Beatles, and Marlon Brando in *The Wild One*. You could spend days in here. Topics cover sports, history, entertainers, political figures, and other photos perfect for the office and home. Shipping's available.

Blue-Plate Specials

Neighboring San Francisco has more restaurants and variety than you could experience in a lifetime, but if you prefer to dine in Sausalito, here are two choices that may satisfy. A great way to start the day is at the **Bridgeway Cafe** (633 Bridgeway St., 415/332-3426). With a great view of the city and the bay, this friendly little diner serves all-day breakfasts, lunches, and dinners, and the waitstaff is kind and considerate.

When the evening falls, consider **Horizons** (558 Bridgeway St., 415/331-3232, www.horizonssausalito.com). In addition to its rich woods and high ceilings, the wide bay windows and patio dining reveal a breathtaking view of San Francisco. Serving lunch and dinner, the waterfront restaurant features fettuccini jambalaya, five-cheese spinach cannelloni, and lobster tails.

Watering Holes

At the **No-Name Bar** (757 Bridgeway St., 415/332-1392), there's character in abundance, a fireplace inside, and a garden patio outside. Owner Al Stanfield rides and often makes the 2,000-mile jaunt to Sturgis. His place delivers live jazz on weekends, blues on weekdays, and pub food in the afternoon. Beers and spirits abound in this mighty beautiful bar. **Smitty's** (214 Caledonia St., 415/332-2637, www.smittysbar.com) is a "friendly neighborhood bar" that's been around since 1938. To this day, it remains a favorite of locals who appreciate the casual feel, the easy camaraderie, and the truth in advertising of "damn fine drinks."

Shut-Eye

I'd suggest making every effort to stay the night in Sausalito, but across the bridge in San Francisco exists every chain hotel known to man.

Inn-dependence

There are three unique and (thankfully) non-generic hotels in Sausalito and, for what they offer, they seem affordable. The **Casa Madrona Hotel** (801 Bridgeway St., 415/332-0502 or 800/288-0502, www.casamadrona.com, $149 and up high season) opened in 1885. It features single

cottages and elevated rooms with perfect bay views. The staff is friendly; the rooms are plush; the gardenlike atmosphere is soothing; and it's all within sight of one of America's largest and loudest cities. Room 315 lets you soak in the tub while watching the city lights. Included in the rate is an evening social hour that affords the opportunity to get looped on some free wine.

On the park, **Hotel Sausalito** (16 El Portal, 415/332-0700 or 888/442-0700, www.hotelsausalito.com, $155 and up) is the most European of them all. The rich, warm, gold tones of this hotel perfectly mirror the sunrise over the bay. The hotel offers 16 1920s-style rooms and suites with modern amenities and views of the park or harbor.

The priciest option is the **Inn Above Tide** (30 El Portal, 415/332-9535 or 800/893-8433, www.innabovetide.com, $325 and up) which, as the name implies, is on the waterfront. All 30 rooms face the hillside city, although they are more modern than I prefer. You may be lured by the free breakfast and sunset wine and cheese receptions.

Chain Drive

These chain hotels are in town, or within 10 miles of the city center: **Best Western, Clarion, Comfort Inn, Courtyard by Marriott, Days Inn, Econo Lodge, Hilton, Holiday Inn, Howard Johnson, Hyatt, Motel 6, Omni Hotels, Quality Inn, Radisson, Ramada, Rodeway, Sheraton, Super 8, Travelodge**

For more information, including phone numbers and websites, see page 439.

ON THE ROAD: SAUSALITO TO CARMEL

The next leg of the journey revs you up for some spectacular scenery and also offers the unforgettable experience of riding across the Pacific Ocean in less than five minutes.

When you leave Sausalito, take Bridgeway Street and follow it south. Three minutes from the center of town, you'll round the bend and see the twin towers of the Golden Gate Bridge straight ahead. Before you cross the bridge, get in the right lane and watch for a lightly trafficked access loop road that leads to Point Bonita at the Marin Highlands. Taking this road will afford one of the best souvenir photos you'll ever take. Turn right, and a few hundred yards ahead, pull off and pose with your bike. With the Golden Gate Bridge, the bay, and city behind you, you've got a photo suitable for framing. To your left, on the northeast corner of the bridge, there's another pullout called Vista Point.

When you get back on the road, you'll pay five bucks to cross the bridge and even though you'd think it would be paid off by now, it's worth it. To your left is the bay and to your right is the Pacific Ocean, which will be your traveling companion for the next 100-plus miles.

Navigating through town to reach PCH is a little tricky and trying to explain how to do it can drive a man to drink. The abridged version is this: After crossing the bridge, veer to the right to reach 14th Avenue—which is also Highway 1—which soon jogs further to the west over to 19th Avenue to take you through residential neighborhoods toward Daly City. At some point Highway 1 joins up with I-280 until, just beyond Exit 48, the road splits again to give you the opportunity to follow Highway 1 over to the coast for a waterside ride.

But after suffering through slow city traffic I wanted to blow out the cobwebs, so I stuck with I-280 and rode farther south to reach Route 92 which leads west toward Half Moon Bay. Surprisingly, it wasn't bad. The farther from the city you get, the greater the pleasure as you see buildings and urban sprawl wither away into the natural landscape. Another surprise was Route 92 West itself, which took me back to the land of curvy roads and nice lakes. There were also miles and miles of flower farms which emitted a far sweeter aroma than what I sniffed in Amish country.

The road ends at PCH, and from here, it's 100 miles south to the Monterey Peninsula. Unlike Highway 1 north of San Francisco, the road here is fairly flat, straight, and ordinary. It is less mountainous and more fertile, which explained the wealth of roadside produce stands. I deduced from the handmade signs that the farmers of this fertile region raise artichokes, pumpkins, carrots, hot dogs, and soft drinks.

It's impossible to explain how easy this road is. Flat and smooth, the pleasure is in the tranquility of the environment that lasts for about 60 coastal miles until you reach the Santa Cruz county line. Then, almost in an instant, the scenic ride ends.

Unfortunately, you have to run a gauntlet of urban ugliness to reach your final destination. For more than 10 miles comes a crappy highway with fast food joints, gas stations, and bike shops. It's also a shame that the ocean remains hidden behind miles of land and there's not a thing you can do about it. The one remedy is to look forward to reaching one of the most enchanting towns in California. After passing Monterey, look for Ocean Avenue, turn right, and head straight into a dreamscape called Carmel.

Most extraordinary Carmel.

CARMEL PRIMER

Carmel may be the crown jewel in the Monterey Peninsula, one of California's more naturally beautiful regions. The

Esselen Indians knew it when they made it their home in A.D. 3,000–500. Next the Ohlone Indians showed up, and they were doing just fine until their time started running out in 1542, when Spanish explorer Juan Rodriguez Cabrillo sighted the white sand beach and pine forest. Even though Cabrillo couldn't land because of rough waters, he decided he could claim it for Spain anyway.

Yes, he did. And I've decided that I own the Bahamas.

Several explorers later, in June 1770, Father Junipero Serra, a Spanish governor and a Franciscan priest, proclaimed the area the military and ecclesiastical capital of Alta, California.

With natural beauty and easy access to the ocean, it was obvious why people have coveted the Monterey Peninsula. Mexico owned it but later surrendered it to the U.S. Navy without a fight. In 1906, refugees from the San Francisco earthquake headed south and made it their new home. And in 1916, bohemian artists with no architectural training showed up and formed the village of Carmel on Halloween. Maybe it was their lack of training and artistic gifts that made it what it is.

From the town's earliest days, art was in the forefront. When Hugh Comstock's wife asked him to build a separate house for her doll collection, he did and then got busy building 20 more whimsical cottages that are still highly prized (and livable) today. While best known as Clint Eastwood's domain (he served as mayor from 1986 to 1988), the town of 4,500 remains true to the original vision of its founding artists and preserves an oasis of art and extraordinary beauty.

ON THE ROAD: CARMEL

Before you start wandering around the village, you may want to stock up on a few dozen digital cameras and memory cards, since you could easily use them up shooting every picturesque building, alcove, courtyard, and garden in town.

On one street, you may photograph a Swiss village, turn the corner and enter a Spanish *mercado,* and then spy the rounded archways and thatched roof of an English cottage. It has the feel of a village and it will always be that way since restrictions prohibit neon signs, street numbers, parking meters, high-rises, plastic plants, and high heels. Really.

One other thing to love about Carmel is that it embodies the freedom you seek on a motorcycle tour. You can walk a few blocks to the beach, take it easy at a sidewalk café, or just hang out. A great way to understand the essence of the village and appreciate its history is with **Carmel Walks** (831/642-2700, www.carmelwalks. com), which offers two-hour guided tours through secret pathways, courtyards, and side streets and is filled with some insider information. Tours ($25) are given at 10 A.M. and 2 P.M. on Saturday, 10 A.M. Tuesday–Friday. Alternatively, you can take a free walking tour with a map provided by the visitors center, which is upstairs on San Carlos between 5th and 6th.

Touring downtown is only the beginning. Off Ocean Drive, for $9.25 you can gain access to the Carmel Gate of legendary 17-Mile Drive, which rolls out and around Pebble Beach. But there's a catch: motorcycles aren't allowed. If you're determined (and you should be, since this is a hyperfun run), maybe it's worth renting a car—a convertible perhaps? With the top down and sea winds blowing, it's the next best thing to being on a bike.

If you can swing it, after paying the toll you'll get a map listing points of interest along 17-Mile Drive, and you can drive in and out from various gates around the loop. Theoretically, road signs should direct you on the tour, but they're often hard to follow. Just follow the map's red dashed line that signifies the route. Soon it'll take you close to the coastline where you should have your camera ready.

Several points jut into the Pacific, each with turnouts that reveal the sheer beauty of this rugged coastline. At Pescadero Point, white foam wraps around rocks, and at Cypress Point, a lone tree estimated at 250 years old sits alone on a rocky point, the inspiration for one of California's signature icons. A little farther, at Bird Rock, the seals and birds bark and caw without pause.

Although you may not have your favorite clubs with you, it'd be a shame to miss **Pebble Beach** (800/654-9300, www.pebblebeach.com). Golfers consider this America's St. Andrews and are charged accordingly: Non-residents pay a whopping $495(!) for 18 holes. Personally, I'd invest that kind of cash in an income-producing troupe of skating monkeys. Even if you don't golf, it's worth driving through just to see the dynamic shoreline.

You can exit at the gate at Pacific Grove, a wonderfully cool village that's home to rows of bungalows, Victorian homes, and a neat main street. There's something else about this village: Each October, swarms of monarch butterflies return here, just as sure as vultures return to roost in Washington, D.C.

Eventually, the roads and advice of well-intentioned friends will guide you to Monterey and Cannery Row. According to brilliant American writer and native son John Steinbeck, Cannery Row was "a poem, a stink, a grating noise, a quality of light, a tone, a habit, a nostalgia, a dream." Now it's all this, plus some tacky tourist shops. Fisherman's Wharf is part carnival midway, where merchants seem to believe that the world's problems could be solved if everyone ate "chowder in a bun," a concoction that looks suspiciously like a bread bowl full of vomit. To be fair, the vibe is changing as new luxury hotels and spas move in, and if you're in town during July's Red Bull U.S. Grand Prix at the Mazda Raceway Laguna Seca, the entire street is closed for all but motorcycles who get front and center parking at all Cannery Row locations.

Above all, the definitive attraction is the **Monterey Bay Aquarium** (886 Cannery Row, 831/648-4888, www.montereybayaquarium.org, $29.95). More than 100 galleries and exhibits highlight the diverse habitats of the bay, and most are larger than life. In addition to the million-gallon outer bay exhibit, there are whale skeletons, a stingray petting pool, and an otter exhibit (did you know otters have pockets?). If you don't scuba dive, the aquarium is a good substitute, and the outdoor promenade puts you on the 50-yard line of the pounding waves.

From here, you can return to Carmel via 17-Mile Drive or work your way over to PCH and take the Ocean Avenue exit back.

PULL IT OVER:
CARMEL AREA HIGHLIGHTS
Attractions and Adventures

John Steinbeck was one of our greatest writers, and his favorite topic, America, places his works among the best road-reading material you'll find. The **Steinbeck Center** (1 Main St., Salinas, 831/796-3833, www.steinbeck.org, $11) celebrates his life and work. Open 10 A.M.–5 P.M. daily, the center exhibits items taken from the pages of his books, but the focal point is his GMC camper, Rocinante, from *Travels with Charley*—the inspiring cross-country journey he made with his poodle. If you love Steinbeck, you'll love the 30,000-piece archives that include original manuscripts, oral histories, first editions, photographs, and gifts in the museum store

Hey, Nanook! Wanna see a seal up close? Kayaks are big in this area, and you can rent them from **Adventures by the Sea** (299 Cannery Row, 831/372-1807, www.adventuresbythesea.com) as well as **Monterey Bay Kayaks** (693 Del Monte Ave., 831/373-5357 or 800/649-5357, www.montereybaykayaks.com). Each charges $30 per day, $50 for a docent-led guided tour that explains the bay's natural history as you paddle among the harbor seals, kelp forests, sea lions, otters, snowy egrets, and tourists. The bay is protected from large swells, so it should be smooth sailing.

Besides the sea, there are ranch lands inland to explore. You can ride trails in Carmel Valley at **Molera Horseback Tours** (831/625-5486 or 800/942-5486, www.molerahorsebacktours.com), which depart from and ride through a 4,800-acre state park and onto the adjacent beach. Rates range from $50-70 for 1.5-2.5-hour rides that wind through groves of sycamore and ancient redwood trees, beds of clover and fern, across the Big Sur River, and along the sandy Pacific shore. Rides depart at various times, with a special sunset ride that's magical.

Okey-doke, Icarus, here are a few aerial adventures for you. Forty-five minutes away in Hollister (where a biker's bacchanal inspired *The Wild One),* **Bay Area Glider Rides** (Hollister Airport, 831/636-3799 or 888/467-6276, www.bayareagliderrides.com) features introductory sailplane rides and lessons from $139, thrill-seeker rides from $299, and a pricy but unforgettable one-hour $400 soaring adventure that will glide back to Monterey and out over the Pacific. If you've never

flown in a sailplane before, it's akin to riding a bike in the sky.

People who call you crazy for riding a motorcycle would bust a vessel if they saw you cavorting with the folks at **Skydive Monterey Bay** (721 Neeson Rd., Marina, 888/229-5867, www.skydivemontereybay.com). After just 15-20 minutes of training, you can take the world's highest tandem fall—from 18,000 feet! If you're motivated, it offers accelerated free-fall and static-line training programs. Reservations are suggested for the $159 first jump. Naturally you'll pay in advance.

The draw at Laguna Seca, an unusual county park and campground hybrid about 20 minutes northeast of Carmel, is the **Mazda Raceway Laguna Seca** (Hwy. 68, 831/242-8201 or 800/327-7322, www.mazdaraceway.com). Only one motorcycle race is held here each year, but that may be enough to make it worth a visit. In July, the Red Bull US Grand Prix Moto GP World Championship draws SBK and AMA riders to a super showdown.

Shopping

Even though there are stores upon stores upon stores in Carmel, you can have a good time just window-shopping and then dropping into at least two must-sees. **Wings America** (Dolores St. and 7th Ave., 831/626-9464, www.wingsamerica.com) presents aviation accent pieces, flight jackets, signed pictures, tropical shirts, aviation scarves, nearly full-size models, and aerodynamically dynamic accessories designed with an aviation theme. A revolving line of unique memorabilia has included a prop from a DC-6 and a tile from space shuttle *Columbia.* Buy several thousand and build your own spacecraft. The same person owns **Boatworks** (Ocean Ave. at Lincoln St., 831/626-1870, www.boatworkscarmel.com), which is nautical and nice. Like its high-flying counterpart, this shop sells cool clothes, nautical instruments, great steamship posters, ship models, and unusual items like a WWII Japanese sextant. If you made the mistake of ordering the optional boat rack from your bike dealer, you can put it to use with a sleek $28,000 wooden canoe. Both are open 9:30 A.M.–6 P.M. daily.

Blue-Plate Specials

Katy's Place (Mission St. between 5th and 6th Aves., 831/624-0199, www.katysplace-carmel.com) has one of the largest breakfast and lunch menus in Californi-yi-yay, even offering 10 varieties of eggs Benedict alone. Joining the lineup: blintzes, pancakes, hash, burritos, omelettes, French toast, buckwheat cakes, bacon, sausage, steak, eggs, cereal, bagels, and muffins.

In a cozy cottage with a fireplace, **Em Le's** (Pantiles Court Delores between 5th and 6th Aves., 831/625-6780) is hot at breakfast with French toast, omelettes, pancakes, and fresh orange juice. At lunch, the menu switches to burgers, sandwiches, soups, and salads. In addition to having a soda fountain, it serves beer and wine.

There's a fine Italian restaurant at **Il Fornaio** (Ocean Ave. at Monte Verde St., 831/622-5115), but I recommend trying its adjacent bakery for a casual breakfast. This is where the locals go for conversation, coffee, and quiet. It's not fancy, but it smells great and the rounded, draped room features a fireplace and newspapers.

You'll look like a local if you drop in for breakfast or lunch at the **Tuck Box** (Dolores St. between Ocean and 7th Aves., 831/624-6365, www.tuckbox.com), a nonlinear fairytale cottage/breakfast nook. Even if you don't eat breakfast, you need to see this place. One of Comstock's original cottages, it seems it's somewhere beyond the looking glass. Here since 1940, it opens at 7 A.M.

Watering Holes

It's hard, but not impossible, while in Carmel to find a place to have a quiet brew and talk with friends. If there's a designated rider, nightspots on Monterey's Cannery Row have replaced sardines as the main source of commerce.

A local tradition for food and drink since the 1970s, the setting at **Jack London's Bar & Grill** (Dolores St. between 5th and 6th Aves., 831/624-2336, www.jacklondons.com) will seduce you. Tucked inside Su Vecino Courtyard, it's a quiet and secluded place to relax. The menu here offers burgers, calamari, steaks, and Mexican dishes that are all just precursors to a pint in the outdoor setting. Kick back for a while and take advantage of the full bar, seven TVs, and 10 beers on tap.

Forge in the Forest (5th Ave. and Junipero St., 831/624-2233, www.forgeinthe-forest.com) also has a cool outdoor dining area and an even cooler saloon. If you travel in a pack (like the animal you are), set up your summit meeting at the brick-thick 15-foot table. The place is cluttered with antlers, skates, maps, and dozens of restroom signs, which you'll give thanks for after polishing off a Bass or Spaten Pils.

Shut-Eye

About 50 bed-and-breakfasts and hotels dot the peninsula. And even though Carmel reeks of wealth, rates are remarkably reasonable. If everything's booked in town, numerous chain hotels can be found in nearby Monterey.

Inn-dependence

Tops in my book (and it *is* my book) is **La Playa** (Camino Real and 8th Ave., 831/624-6476 or 800/582-8900, www.laplayahotel.com, $190 and up), a large and gorgeous Mediterranean hotel a few blocks from the ocean. The building's design, character, gardens, pool, and flowers all combine to make this a spectacular choice. A second-floor terrace restaurant and five cottages make it even nicer. Much more affordable, in the heart of the village is the **Normandy Inn** (Ocean Ave. and Monte Verde St., 831/624-3825 or 800/343-3825, www.normandyinncarmel.com, $98 and up). This is an excellent choice, with a collection of buildings and cottages connected by shaded courtyards. Large rooms that feature featherbeds and mini-fridges are pricier; some have fireplaces, and all include a continental breakfast. There's also a pool. Carmel offers more than enough choices, but the **Seven Gables Inn** (555 Ocean View Blvd., 831/372-4341, www.pginns.com, $175–385), in appealing Pacific Grove, is another option. The classic Victorian may seem a far cry from what motorcycle travelers are looking for, but the view from the bay window may be enough to compensate. A full breakfast, four o'clock tea, and a park across the street round out the amenities.

Chain Drive

These chain hotels are in town, or within 10 miles of the city center:

Best Western, Clarion, Comfort Inn, Days Inn, Doubletree, Econo Lodge, Embassy Suites, Hilton, Holiday Inn, Howard Johnson, Hyatt, Knights Inn, La Quinta, Motel 6, Quality Inn, Ramada, Rodeway, Super 8, Travelodge For more information, including phone numbers and websites, see page 439.

SIDE TRIP: CARMEL TO SAN SIMEON

If you have a fear of heights, consider this ride a pleasant form of aversion therapy. As natural forces continue to pound boulders into pebbles on the shoreline, you'll rise above it all on this 112-mile route that scribbles along the Pacific Ocean. There's a reason why this is one of motorcycle travelers' most favored rides. It combines slow curves, sharp turns, and elevations magnified by the view of mountains and sea.

Watch for the sign south of Carmel: Curves ahead next 74 miles. But unlike the psychologically brutal Stinson Beach/Muir Beach/Tamalpais Valley ride, you can experience these slow curves and broad vistas without fear of death. In other words, this ride doesn't challenge your mortality; it affirms your vitality.

As you ride south, get used to miles of weaving curves that foreshadow upcoming jolts of adrenaline. You'll want to keep an eye open for loose gravel and unpaved shoulders that mark these roads. You'll also want to make sure your brakes are in working order, because you'll stop often to photograph the handsome cliffs and endless ocean. This is a sustained pleasure that spikes about 30 miles into the run, when you take your bike across the fabled Bixby Creek Bridge. Get those cameras ready, folks.

Construction on the "Rainbow" started in 1919 and took until 1937 to complete, but it was worth the wait. Thanks to some anonymous engineers and the fact that you wanted to get out of the house, you're riding 260 feet above sea level on a 718-foot race to the other side of the mountain.

After this jolt, the road is like a Chesterfield—it satisfies for the next 20 miles. When you arrive in Big Sur, you may start looking for the commercial district but you won't find it here. Big Sur is a decentralized region where residents enjoy the solitude and don't feel compelled to build city halls and shopping malls. That's the reason why writers and artists come here, and where Henry Miller rediscovered his creative spark while living in an abandoned convict labor camp.

Hearst Castle

Hearst Castle (Hwy. 1, 805/927-2020 for recorded information or 800/444-4445 for reservations, www.hearstcastle.org, $24) reminds me of my first apartment—except this place has 165 rooms, 30 fireplaces, and 127 acres of gardens. If not for Hearst Castle, San Simeon (pop. 18) would be nothing surrounded by nothing else. But after losing three runs for political office, William Randolph Hearst decided that his bid for immortality would come not through ballots, but through building.

Everything begins at the visitors center, where you buy a ticket for the mansion that includes the National Geographic IMAX movie *Hearst Castle, Building the Dream*, which describes how the castle was designed, built, and decorated. Then you'll board a bus for a long and winding ride to the mansion.

The scale here is off the scale: Guesthouses are the size of overwhelming mansions; the gardens are Edenic; the dining room is royal. A seductive and sensual outdoor pool holds 345,000 gallons of spring water, and a smaller indoor Roman pool contains a paltry 205,000 gallons. Furnishings are equally dazzling, and it's worth noting that Hearst had so much extra stuff stashed in a warehouse that he could have built five more castles. At least, that's what Bob the Tour Guide said.

The home is now owned by the citizens of California. Don't be jealous. They also own San Quentin.

The most active address on this stretch of road is **Nepenthe** (48510 Hwy. 1, 831/667-2345, www.nepenthebigsur.com), a stop as necessary for motorcyclists as breathing. Constructed around land and a log cabin once owned by Orson Welles and Rita Hayworth, Nepenthe (Greek for "sorrow banisher") was purchased by Lolly and Bill Fassett and expanded by Rowan Maiden, a disciple of Frank Lloyd Wright. Today, it is a restaurant/overlook where lunch includes such fare as broiled swordfish sandwiches and the famous Ambrosia Burger; sunset dinners focus on steaks and fresh fish. Even if you're not hungry, stop here and feast on the view from the terrace, 800 feet above the shoreline. From this height, the surf below sounds like muffled cannons and adds another memorable experience to your journey.

A quarter mile south of Nepenthe, the **Henry Miller Library** (Hwy. 1, 831/667-2574, www.henrymiller.org) is more of an artists' village than a library, but people still stop. It's open Wednesday–Monday (closed Tuesday) 11 A.M.–6 P.M. Beyond this, PCH gets back into the rugged and exhilarating coastline you've come to love. Within miles, you'll be riding past different environments—ocean, desert, pine forests—each constantly interchanging. One other thing you should be on the lookout for are riders and drivers who've granted Highway 1 status as a test track. It's tempting to race, but it's better to live.

There are few places in the nation more

suited to your purpose. Take advantage of turnouts, where you can just park it and watch the water swallowing rocks the size of mountains and pounding the hell out of monoliths. In some spots, the water seems as clear as the Caribbean, and a few miles later, the coastline disappears into fog.

As you ride south, you'll experience the satisfaction that comes with knowing you're six feet closer to the ocean than those poor bastards in the oncoming lane. When you reach the small town of Gorda there's a convenient service station and general store. From here, the rises are subtle and surprises appear, like views of the ocean that open up and show you 200-foot cliffs that reach down to the sea.

The final miles to **Hearst Castle** (Hwy. 1, 805/927-2020 for recorded information or 800/444-4445 for reservations, www. hearstcastle.org, $24) lose their scenic punch, but I promise that you will look back on this run and agree that this—like your ride across America—was everything you expected it to be. It was dangerous within limits, vast beyond measure, and beautiful beyond description.

Resources for Riders

Pacific Coast Run

California Travel Information
California Association of Bed & Breakfast Inns—800/373-9251, www.cabbi.com
California Division of Tourism—916/444-4429 or 800/862-2543,
    www.visitcalifornia.com
California Road Conditions—800/427-7623
California State Parks—916/653-6995, www.parks.ca.gov
California Weather Information—916/979-3051

Local and Regional Information
Calistoga Chamber of Commerce—707/942-6333 or 866/306-5588,
    www.calistogachamber.com
Carmel Visitors Center—831/624-2522 or 800/550-4333, www.carmelcalifornia.org
Monterey Peninsula Visitors Bureau—888/221-1010 or 877/666-8373,
    www.montereyinfo.org
Napa Valley Visitors Bureau—707/226-5813, www.legendarynapavalley.org
Pacific Grove Chamber of Commerce—831/373-3304 or 800/656-6650,
    www.pacificgrove.org
Sausalito Chamber of Commerce—415/331-7262, www.sausalito.org
Sonoma County Visitors Bureau—707/522-5800 or 800/576-6662,
    www.sonomacounty.com

California Motorcycle Shops
BMW Motorcycles of San Francisco—790 Bryant St., San Francisco,
    415/503-9988, www.bmwmotorcycle.com
California Choppers—1490 Howard St., San Francisco, 415/431-8181,
    www.californiachoppers.com
Dudley Perkins Harley-Davidson—333 Corey Way, So. South Francisco,
    650/737-5467, www.dpchd.com
Golden Gate Cycles—1540 Pine St., San Francisco, 415/771-4535,
    www.goldengatecycles.com
Golden Gate Harley-Davidson/Buell—7077 Redwood Blvd., Novato,
    415/878-4988, www.gghd.com
Monterey County Harley-Davidson—333 N. Main St., Salinas, 831/424-1909,
    www.montereycountyhd.com
Monterey Peninsula Powersports—1020 Auto Center Pkwy., Seaside,
    831/899-7433, www.sports-center.com
North Bay Motorsports—2875 Santa Rosa Ave., Santa Rosa, 707/542-5355,
    www.northbaymotorsport.com
Salinas Motorcycle Center—1286 N. Main St., Salinas, 831/442-3511 or
    800/750-2953, www.salinasmc.com
Santa Rosa BMW—800 American Way, Windsor, 707/838-9100,
    www.santarosabmw.com
Santa Rosa Powersports—910 Santa Rosa Ave., Santa Rosa, 707/545-1672,
    www.santarosapowersports.com
Santa Rosa Vee Twin—1240 Petaluma Hill Rd., Santa Rosa, 707/523-9696,
    www.santarosaveetwin.com

Resources

MOTORCYCLE WEBSITES

Great American Motorcycle Tours
www.motorcycleamerica.com
Partner site for this book, with abridged ride descriptions, photographs, and links.

Moto-Directory
www.moto-directory.com
Perhaps the best bike site, with roughly 10,000 links to events, rallies, magazines, videos, tours, stolen bike reports, riding clubs, rental operators, dealers, and salvage yards.

Motorcycle Roads—1
www.motorcycleroads.us
Super site with recommendations from riders on popular and seldom traveled roads across America, viewable state-by-state. Links for submitting your favorites and finding travel resources.

Motorcycle Roads—2
www.motorcycleroads.com
Nationwide guide with recommended rides and tours listed state-by-state, graded by scenery, road quality, and roadside amenities, activities, and attractions.

Motorcycle-USA
www.motorcycle-usa.com
News, product reviews, bike tests, photo galleries, classifieds, message boards, and ride ratings.

Trader Online
www.cycletrader.com
The online version of the popular *Trader* magazines. Search by model, size, year, price, location, etc.

Harley-Davidson Links
www.hdlinks.com
Connections to H-D and other American motorcycle related sites.

Motorcycle Accessories Warehouse
800/241-2222
www.accwhse.com
Parts, supplies, and thousands of links to clothes and closeouts, from goggles to tank covers.

Motorcycle Online
www.motorcycle.com
Digital motorcycle magazine with bikes, products, reviews, videos, clubs, events, how-tos, rides, classifieds, financing, and chats.

Rider Magazine
www.ridermagazine.com
Links to *Rider* and *American Rider* magazines, archives, and ride maps.

Sport-Touring
www.sport-touring.net
Extensive discussion forum for tour, tech, and sales information.

SELECTED MANUFACTURERS

Most manufacturers' sites will lead to showrooms, accessories, clothing, riders clubs, FAQs, dealers, and riding products.

BMW
800/831-1117
www.bmwmotorcycles.com

Buell
www.buell.com

Ducati
www.ducati.com

Harley-Davidson
800/258-2464
www.harley-davidson.com

Honda
310/532-9811 or 866/784-1870
www.hondamotorcycle.com

Kawasaki
800/661-7433
www.kawasaki.com

Moto Guzzi
www.motoguzzi.it

Suzuki
www.suzukicycles.com

Triumph
678/854-2010
www.triumph.co.uk

Victory
www.victory-usa.com

Yamaha
800/889-2624
www.yamaha-motor.com

SELECTED MOTORCYCLE ORGANIZATIONS

American Motorcyclist Association
800/262-5646
www.ama-cycle.org
If you belong to one motorcycling organization, make it the AMA. The association sponsors thousands of sanctioned events and provides a monthly magazine, trip routing, hotel discounts, and club information for approximately 250,000 members.

Motorcycle Events Association
727/343-1049 or 866/203-4485
www.motorcycleevents.com
Provides information on Daytona, Sturgis, Laconia, and other major rallies as well as charity rides and motorcycle shows across America.

Motorcycle Product News
800/722-8764
www.mpnmag.com
Lists products, distributors, manufacturers, parts, and accessories; primarily used by dealers and rental operators.

Motorcycle Riders Foundation
202/546-0983 or
800/673-5646
www.mrf.org
Lobbying group for riders' rights, with links.

Motorcycle Safety Foundation
800/446-9227
www.msf-usa.org
Offers safe riding courses throughout the United States; participation can lower your insurance rates. Also features information on rider training and industry contacts.

SELECTED RIDING CLUBS
American Gold Wing Association
www.agwa.com

Blue Knights
207/947-4600 or 877/254-5362
www.blueknights.org

BMW Motorcycle Owners of America
636/394-7277
www.bmwmoa.org

Christian Motorcyclists Association
870/389-6196
www.cmausa.org

Gold Wing Road Riders Association
623/581-2500 or 800/843-9460
www.gwrra.org

Harley Owners Group
800/258-2464
www.hog.com

Honda Riders Club of America
800/847-4722
www.hrca.honda.com

Motorcycle Clubs & Associations
www.moto-directory.com/clubs.asp

Riders of Kawasaki
877/765-2582
www.kawasaki.com/rok

Women on Wheels
800/322-1969
www.womenonwheels.org

SELECTED RALLIES
Each year across the country, there are thousands of rallies of all shapes and sizes. Here are links to some of the largest—visit their websites for upcoming dates. Most rally sites include information on registration, rides, vendors, lodging, histories, and entertainment.

Americade Motorcycle Rally
518/798-7888
www.tourexpo.com
Lake George, New York

Bikes, Blues & BBQ Motorcycle Rally
479/527-9993
www.bikesbluesandbbq.org
Fayetteville, Arkansas

Bike Week and Biketoberfest
386/255-0981 (Bike Week)
www.officialbikeweek.com
386/255-0415 or 800/854-1234
(Biketoberfest)
www.biketoberfest.org
Daytona Beach, Florida

Laconia Rally
603/366-2000
www.laconiamcweek.com
Laconia, New Hampshire

Sturgis Rally and Races
605/720-0800
www.sturgismotorcyclerally.com
Sturgis, South Dakota

SELECTED MOTORCYCLE RENTAL COMPANIES
California Motorcycle Rentals
858/456-9577
www.calif-motorcyclerental.com

EagleRider Motorcycle Rental
310/536-6777 or 888/900-9901
www.eaglerider.com
Nationwide service, renting fully equipped Road Kings, Softails, Fat Boys, and Electra Glides. Locations in America, Mexico, and Europe. Also conducts tours.

Harley Motorcycle Rental
415/456-9910 or 888/812-9253
www.motohaven.net
Novato, California

Motorcycle Rental Resource Page
www.harleys.com/mrrp.html
Rental operators listed by state.

Route 66 Riders Motorcycle Rentals
310/578-0112 or 888/434-4473
www.route66riders.com
Marina Del Ray, California

GENERAL TRAVEL INFORMATION
Historic Hotels of America
800/678-8946
www.historichotels.org
Affiliated with the National Trust for Historic Preservation, HHA is a diverse collection of uniquely American lodgings, from rustic inns to elegant hotels. Rates at these member properties may be on the high end, but if you split the costs, you may do all right.

Kampgrounds of America (KOA)
www.koa.com
Information on more than 500 campgrounds nationwide.

Mad Maps
www.madmaps.com
Superb, informative motorcycle maps custom-designed to highlight scenic roads and popular routes across the country.

MapQuest
www.mapquest.com
Trip planning, route, and mileage information.

National Forest Service
www.fs.fed.us
Links to national forests and campgrounds.

National Parks Camping Reservations
800/436-7275 or 877/444-6777
www.recreation.gov
A one-call-books-all national company that handles reservations for 45,000 campsites at 1,700 national forest campgrounds across America. Books for most national parks, but does not include state parks.

National Park Foundation
202/354-6460 or 888/467-2757
www.nationalparks.org
Partner site of America's national parks, designed to introduce you to the parks and assist in trip-planning.

National Park Service

www.nps.gov

Central point for links to parks and recreation, history and culture, nature, science, interpretation, and education.

Road Conditions

www.usroadconditions.com

Links to information on road conditions in every state.

Road Trip USA

www.roadtripusa.com

Eleven cross-country riding routes to get you off the beaten path and onto pre-interstate roads.

Scenic Byways

www.byways.org

An excellent site detailing thousands of miles of scenic byways and back roads across the nation. Also offers links for trip-planning and personal journals.

State Motorcycle and Helmet Laws

www.amadirectlink.com/legisltn/laws.asp

State and National Park Links

www.llbean.com/parksearch

State Parks

www.stateparks.com

Comprehensive state-by-state listing with contact information, links, and information on hundreds of state parks.

State Park Reservations

www.reserveamerica.com

Facilitates campsite reservations for many state and private parks and campgrounds in North America.

Weather Channel

www.weather.com

ROAD TIPS

America the Beautiful Pass

Each year, America's National Parks are visited more than 265 million times, a figure totaling more fans and guests than visit NFL games, Disney parks, and Universal Studios attractions combined. If you plan to visit more than one national park, invest in the National Parks pass. For $80, the pass will provide admission to any national park for a full year. You're 62 or older? Even better—the cost drops to $10! How far will your money go? As far as 80.7 million acres of park land at 379 national parks, from Acadia in Maine to Zion in Utah, all cared for and explained by more than 20,000 rangers, archaeologists, historians, biologists, architects, laborers, and gardeners.

Food Faves

One of my favorite vocations while riding is finding great roadside diners along the highway or in a village. Two of my favorite American writers are Jane and Michael Stern, who, in addition to writing the classic *Elvis World*, wrote *Eat Your Way Across the USA: 500 Diners, Lobster Shacks, Buffets, Pie Palaces, and Other All-American Eateries.* While my book can lead you to a handful of restaurants, their book is a buffet of great American greasy spoons, hash houses, doughnut shops, cafeterias, and small-town cafés.

Offbeat USA

If your motivation to ride is partially fueled by the chance discovery of kitsch Americana, check out www.roadsideamerica.com. This site is the online guide to offbeat tourist attractions, and it may provide you with some side-trip ideas when you're in the vicinity of places like the Zippo Lighter Visitors Center in Bradford, PA, or the giant advertising statues that still plug businesses across the United States.

Selecting an Organized Tour

As the popularity of motorcycles grows, so does the proliferation of motorcycle tour operators. If you decide to ride on a prearranged trip, there are two constants you'll encounter: You will need a major credit card and a motorcycle endorsement on your license. There are also several variables. For instance, you may or may not need to bring your own bike, helmet, or rain gear.

With these variances, play it smart by asking the "stupid" questions. Ask who covers specific expenses: lodging, meals, tolls, fuel, laundry, tips, insurance. What type of lodging can you expect? Is it a flophouse, campground, or inn? Private bath? Shared rooms? Carrying a passenger will cost extra—how much? As you sift through these questions, also ask if you'll be allowed to break away from the group and meet them later. Is there a guide? A support vehicle? A trained mechanic? Does the ride include overnights, or do you return to the same city each evening?

Make sure that if your ride is cancelled because of inclement weather, your deposit will be refunded (you may want to safeguard your investment by taking out traveler's cancellation insurance).

CHAIN HOTEL GUIDE

Best Western
800/528-1234
www.bestwestern.com

Clarion
800/252-7466
www.choicehotels.com

Comfort Inn
800/221-2222
www.choicehotels.com

Courtyard by Marriott
800/321-2211
www.marriott.com

Days Inn
800/329-7466
www.daysinn.com

Doubletree
800/222-8733
www.doubletree.com

Econo Lodge
800/553-2666
www.choicehotels.com

Embassy Suites
800/362-2779
www.embassy-suites.com

Fairfield Inn
800/228-2800
www.fairfieldinn.com

Hampton Inn
800/426-7866
www.hampton-inn.com

Hilton
800/445-8667
www.hilton.com

Holiday Inn
800/465-4329
www.holiday-inn.com

Howard Johnson
800/446-4656
www.hojo.com

Hyatt
800/233-1234
www.hyatt.com

Knights Inn
800/843-5644
www.knightsinn.com

La Quinta
800/687-6667
www.laquinta.com

Motel 6
800/466-8356
www.motel6.com

Omni Hotels
800/843-6664
www.omnihotels.com

Quality Inn
800/228-5151
www.qualityinn.com

Radisson
800/333-3333
www.radisson.com

Ramada
800/272-6232
www.ramada.com

Red Carpet Inn
800/251-1962
www.reservahost.com

Red Roof Inn
800/843-7663
www.redroof.com

Residence Inn
800/331-3131
www.mariott.com

Rodeway
800/228-2000
www.rodewayinn.com

Scottish Inns
800/251-1962
www.reservahost.com

Sheraton
800/325-3535
www.sheraton.com

Sleep Inn
800/627-5337
www.sleepinn.com

Super 8
800/800-8000
www.super8.com

Travelodge
800/578-7878
www.travelodge.com

Index

XYZ

Acknowledgments

It's never far from my mind that an ongoing project like this requires assistance from others—and I've had it. There are hundreds of people across the nation who've pitched in to make this possible. As always, they're listed in order of their favorite Beatle.

John Lennon: John McKechnie, Bud McKechnie, Ian McKechnie, all McKechnies everywhere, Peter Fonda, Kevin McLain, Darren Alessi, Donna Galassi, Peg Goldstein, Cassandra Conyers, Dianna Delling, Robyn McPeters, Mike Zimmerman, Jennifer Gruber, Amanda Lee, Ty van Hooydonk, Michelle Greco, Joel Cliff, Walter Yeldell, Carrie Saldo, Beth Krauss, Ron Dusek, Jennifer Williams, Mary Ann McClain, Matthew Carinhas, Evelynn Bailey, David Lorenz, Amy Seng, Mike Norton, Andy Moon, Mike Houck, Dana Alley, George Milo, Ken Thompson, Jessica Icenhour, Fred Good, Jana Greenbaum, Chuck Haralson, Ken Grimsley, Lisa Richardson, Tracy Brown, Alissa Clark, Bill Seratt, Mary Beth Romig, Carl Whitehill, Anne Barney, Tessy Shirakawa, Bronwyn Patterson, Marci Penner, Kathy Giffin, Cindy Andrus, Chad Sterns, Dan Bookham, Valerie Ryan, Jimmy Sample, Jeff Feldman, Eden Umble, Celeste White, Heather Hermen, Walter Yeldell, Barbara Golden, Jennifer Haz, Erik Skindrud, Lou Ann Nelson, Heather Falk, David Fantle, Jon Jarosh, Jeri Riggs, Lynn Berry, Nick Noyes, Jo Sabel Courtney, John Formichella, Anne Marie Basher, Nancy Arena, Ruth Parsons, Stacey Fox, Philip Magaldi, Charles Hardin, Melody Heltman, Erika Backus, Rich Wittish, Chris Nobles, Melina Martinez, Michelle Revuelta, Josie Gulliksen, Emy Bullard Wilkinson, Beverly Gianna, Jon Jarosh, George Milos, Jezal McNeil, Phil Lampert, Kelly Barbello, Kim Latrielle, Judy Siring, Jay Humphries, Anne Barney, Sandy Smith, Kim Cobb....

Paul McCartney: Jean James, Lin Lee, Susan Albrecht, Patricia Kiderlen, Lynn Dyer, Judith Swain, Suzanne Elder, Phyllis Reller, Karen Baker, Gwen Peterson, Tony Fortier, Ken McNenny, Susan Sullivan, Pepper Massey-Swan, Karen Connelly, Liz Porter, Steve Lewis, Shelly Clark, Susie Haver, Jenny Stacy, Susan Belanski, Jack Dunlavy, Phillip Magdali Jr., Paula Tirrito, Steven Skavroneck, Valerie Parker, Joel Frey, Lenore Barkley, Jan Osterman, Howard

Gray, Christine DeCuir, Sandy Tucker, Don Sparks, DeRoy Jenson, Ed and Minna Williams, Rennie Ross, Didi Bushnell, Jim Pelletier, Stan Corneil, Chris Mackey, Amy Ballenger, Jeff Ehoodin, Jeff Webster, Nina Kelly, Todd Morgan, Dave Blanford, Nancy Borino, Tom Lyons, Krista Elias, Shannon Mackie-Albert, Carolyn Hackney, Rachel Keating, Maureen Oltrogge, Mike Finney, Julia Scott, Sue Bland, Natasha Johnston, Janie McCullough, Laura Simoes, Tessie Shirwakawa, Aimee Grove, Melanie Ryan, Steve Lewis, Jan Mellor, Jennifer Wess, Kathy Lambert, Dwayne Cassidy, Ron Terry, Erika Yowell, Kathleen New, Wyndham Lewis, Dennis Cianci, Marjie Wright, Karen Hamill, Sue Ellen Peck, Tom Hash, Rick Gunn....

George Harrison: Rick Wilder, Ken Crouse, Donna Bonnefin, Pettit Gilwee, Keith Walklet, Amy Herzog, Susan Carvalho, Kathy Langley, Kirk Komick, Jennifer Franklin, Mike Pitel, Jody Bernard, Sarah Pitcher, Nancy Brockman, Paul Schreiner, Bev Owens, Billy Dodd, Heather Deville, Sarah Baker, Joel Howard, Annie Kuehls, Bob and Paula Glass, Troy Duvall, Matt Bolas, Carrie Clark, Trey Hines, Tony Hayden, Chris Jones, Haley Gingles, Greg Lasiewski, Jan Plessner, Tim Buche, Cheryl Smith, Trish Taylor, Hal Williams, Emily Raabe, Cara O'Donnell, Alan Rosenzweig, Barbara Ashley, Janet Dutson, Mary Bennoch, Jeff Lupo, John and Diane Sheiry, Croft Long, Mel Moore, Mark Kayser, Lisa Umiker, Rich Gates, Ray Towells, Julie Smith, Scott Gediman, Mike Dorn, Wendy Haase, Jan Dorfler, Mary Cochran, Traci Varner, Dirk Oldenburg, Mark Reese, Scott Heath, Linda Adams....

Ringo Starr: Trevor and Regina Aldhurst, Rosemary and Fabrizio Chiarello, Frank and Mary Newton, Mary Beth Hutchinson, Anna Maria Dalton, Karen Hedelt, Emily Case, Pauli Galin, Carol Jones, Sue Mauro, Beth Culbertson, Ron Gardner, Ellen Gillespie, Timothy James Trifeletti, Carrie Wilkinson-Tuma, Elmer Thomas, Nancy and Tom Blackford, Karen Suffredini, Mike McGuinn, Susan Williams, Virginia Mure, Ron and Sue Ramage, Leslie Prevish and Joe Hice....

Pete Best: Every engineer, surveyor, road crew, and chain gang that helped build America's beautiful back roads.

Great American Motorcycle Tours

Avalon Travel
a member of the Perseus Books Group
1700 Fourth Street
Berkeley, CA 94710, USA

Editor: Kevin McLain
Copy Editor: Naomi Adler Dancis
Graphics and Production Coordinator:
  Darren Alessi
Cover and Interior Designer:
  Darren Alessi
Map Editor: Mike Morgenfeld
Cartographers: Kat Bennett, Brice Ticen
Indexer: Rachel Kuhn

ISBN: 978-1-59880-364-8
ISSN: 1540-8965

Printing History
1st Edition — 2000
4th Edition — May 2010
5 4 3 2 1

Text © 2010 by Gary McKechnie.
Maps © 2010 by Avalon Travel.
All rights reserved.

Printed in Canada by Friesens